EUROPE AND THE MIDDLE AGES

Third Edition

Edward Peters
University of Pennsylvania

Prentice Hall, Upper Saddle River, New Jersey 07458

Library of Congress Cataloging-in-Publication Data

PETERS, EDWARD
    Europe and the Middle Ages / Edward Peters. — 3rd ed.
      p. cm.
    Includes bibliographical references and index.
    ISBN 0-13-105982-3
    1. Middle Ages—History.   I. Title.
  D118.P452   1997
  940.1—dc20

                                                       97-7267
                                                       CIP

To my brother Jack,
and to Ann, Heather, and John,
in memory of
EDWARD LOUIS PETERS (1964–1981)

Acquisitions editor: *Sally Constable*
Editorial assistant: *Justin Belinski*
Production editor: *Jean Lapidus*
Copy editor: *Maria Caruso*
Manufacturing buyer: *Lynn Pearlman*
Cover design: *Bruce Kenselaar*

This book was set in 10.5/12.5 Baskerville by BookMasters, Inc.
and was printed and bound by RR Donnelley & Sons Company.
The cover was printed by Phoenix Color Corp.

 © 1997, 1989, 1983 by Prentice-Hall, Inc.
Simon & Schuster/A Viacom Company
Upper Saddle River, New Jersey 07458

Printed in the United States of America
10 9 8 7 6 5 4 3

ISBN 0-13-105982-3

PRENTICE-HALL INTERNATIONAL (UK) LIMITED, *London*
PRENTICE-HALL OF AUSTRALIA PTY. LIMITED, *Sydney*
PRENTICE-HALL CANADA INC., *Toronto*
PRENTICE-HALL HISPANOAMERICANA, S.A., *Mexico*
PRENTICE-HALL OF INDIA PRIVATE LIMITED, *New Delhi*
PRENTICE-HALL OF JAPAN, INC., *Tokyo*
SIMON & SCHUSTER ASIA PTE. LTD., *Singapore*
EDITORA PRENTICE-HALL DO BRASIL, LTDA., *Rio de Janeiro*

CONTENTS

Preface: x

PART I: EUROPE AND MEDITERRANEAN ANTIQUITY   1

1   The Beginning and End of the Roman Peace   1

The Roman Empire in the Mediterranean and
  European Worlds   1
The Roman Empire and Roman Society   6
Hadrian's Travels   8
Germania   11
The Third-Century Crisis   16
Diocletian and Constantine: Reform and
  Recovery   20
Further Reading   23

2   Religion and Society in Antiquity   25

Gods of the House, Communities, and
  Individuals   25

Judaism in Palestine and the Diaspora   29

The Emergence of Christianity   32

Spirit and Flesh, Body and Gender   36

Conversion and Opposition   37

Orthodoxy and Heterodoxy: Normative
  Christianity   39

Christians Abandoning the World: Hermits
  and Monks   43

Christians Ordering the World: Emperors and
  Churchmen   46

Further Reading   51

3   The Transformations of the Roman World   54

New Rome and Old Rome   54

Migrants and Invaders   56

The World of Galla Placidia   59

The Age of Theoderic: Ostrogoths, Franks, and
  Visigoths   62

Boethius and Cassiodorus   66

Unity and Diversity in Late Mediterranean
  Antiquity   70

Further Reading   73

PART   II: TWO HEIRS OF THE ANCIENT WORLD   75

4   The Making of Byzantine Civilization   75

The East Roman Empire, 450–527   75

The Emperor Who Never Sleeps   78

The City   83

The Age of Heraclius   87

Byzantium   89

Further Reading   92

5   The Rise of Islam   93

The Arab Peoples Before Muhammad   93

The Prophet   94

The Faith   95

The Protectors of the Faith and the Spread
  of Islam   97

The Umayyad Dynasty at Damascus   100
The Abbasid Dynasty at Baghdad   101
Islamic Civilization   102
Further Reading   104

PART   III: THE EARLY MIDDLE AGES   **105**

6   Christian Rome and the New Europeans   **105**

Italy in the Sixth and Seventh Centuries   105
God's Consul   107
The Desert in the West: Monks, Missionaries,
     and Culture   110
The Conversion of Ireland   112
Angles and Angels   115
Further Reading   118

7   The Environment of North Temperate Europe   **119**

The Physical Geography of Transalpine Europe   119
Landscape and Folkscape   122
Families, *Gentes,* and Kingdoms   125
Gender in Early Medieval Europe   129
Religion and Culture   132
Further Reading   134

8   The Book and the Sword   **135**

The Long-Haired Kings   135
An Island Set Beyond the World   136
The Last of the Long-Haired Kings   139
The Expansion of Frankish Power   143
The Carolingian Renewal   148
The "Kingdom of Europe" and the Empire of
     the Romans   151
Further Reading   157

9   Europe Emerges   **159**

Empire, Kingdoms, and the Last Invaders   159
The Vikings   162
Kings and Warlords   165
The Emergence of "Englaland"   166

The Puzzle of "National" Origins   167
Sailing to Byzantium   171
The Garden of Islam and the House of War   175
Further Reading   178

PART   IV: CHRISTENDOM: AUTHORITY AND ENTERPRISE,
950–1150   **180**

10   Material Civilization   **180**

The Population Growth of Medieval Europe   180
The Agricultural Revolution   183
Manor and Village   186
Servitude and Freedom   188
Town and City   189
The Adventure of Trade   192
Further Reading   195

11   Power and Society   **196**

Lordship and Kingship   196
East *Francia,* Germany, and the Imperial Title   199
From West *Francia* to France   201
Anglo-Norman England   204
The Iberian Peninsula: Conquest or
   Reconquest?   206
From Lordship to Kingship in South Italy
   and Sicily   210
Further Reading   211

12   Christendom East and West   **213**

The Idea of Reform   213
Popes, Emperors, and Christian Society   217
New Monks in a New Desert   221
The Expedition to Jerusalem   225
Further Reading   229

PART   V: CULTURE AND SOCIETY IN THE HIGH MIDDLE AGES,
1150–1325   **231**

13   New Art and New Learning   **231**

A White Robe of Churches   231

Schools and Scholars   235
Anselm of Bec/Canterbury   236
Peter Abelard and Heloise   236
Law and Learning in the Twelfth Century   240
Canon Law and Theology   243
The Universities   245
Further Reading   248

14   Religion and Society   **250**

The Rise of Papal Authority   250
The Fourth Lateran Council and the
   Community of the Faithful   252
Dissent and Heresy   256
The Athletes of God   260
Heresy, Crusade, and the Inquisitorial Office   261
Christian Attitudes toward Non-Christians   263
Jews in Christian Europe   264
Further Reading   269

15   The Political Culture of Christian Europe   **271**

The Political Community   271
The Old Order: Papacy and Empire   273
England: From Angevin Empire to
   Island Kingdom   282
The Iberian Peninsula   288
The Most Christian Kings of France, 1108–1328   290
A New Order: The Conflict between the Papacy
   and the Territorial Monarchy   298
Further Reading   301

16   Reason and Imagination in the Gothic World   **302**

The Triumph of Aristotle   302
Thomas Aquinas and Bonaventure   307
Gothic Architecture and Engineering   308
The Knight between the World and God   314
The World of Dante   321
Medieval Women in City and Convent   324
Further Reading   327

PART VI: THE LATER MIDDLE AGES, 1325–1519   329

17 Material Civilization: Crisis and Recovery   329

Apocalypse Then: The Four Horsemen   329
The Pale Horseman: Plague in Medieval Europe   332
The Red Horseman: War and Society   335
The Black Horseman: Financial Collapse and
    Recovery   337
Further Reading   343

18 The Church and the World   345

Christendom and Europe   345
The Revolt against Aristotle and Aquinas   349
The Popes at Avignon   351
The Great Schism and the Council of
    Constance   352
Varieties of Devotion on the Eve of the
    Reformation   354
Further Reading   357

19 Power and Order   360

Thinking about Politics   360
Kings, Princes, and Cities in Germany, 1250–1519   362
The Hundred Years' War: England and France   364
Patterns of Recovery: France   369
"I, a Woman, Dare . . ."   370
Patterns of Recovery: England   372
The Great Duchy of the West: The Burgundian Netherlands   372
Further Reading   377

20 Frontiers and Horizons   380

The World on the Last Day   380
The Third Rome   383
The First Rome   384
Ancients and Moderns   388
"Here There Bee Tygres"   392
The Ambassadors   399
Further Reading   403

General Bibliography **405**

Index **427**

MAP LIST

Expansion of Roman territorial holdings under
  the Republic   12
Roman territorial holdings under the Empire   13
Germanic invasions of the Roman Empire   58
Germanic kingdoms about 526   63
The Byzantine Empire   83
Constantinople   85
The expanding Muslim zone   98
Medieval Christianity   115
Physical map of Europe, Western Asia and
  Northern Africa   121
Carolingian Empire and Anglo-Saxon England   154
Invasions of Europe, seventh through eleventh
  centuries   162
Spread of the Slavs and the Kievan Rus   174
Medieval cities and trade routes   193
The Crusades   229
Medieval Germany and Italy   278
Medieval France and England   293
Thirteenth-century Paris   296
Spread of Black Death   334
The Hundred Years' War and English rule
  in France   365
Mongol and Ottoman Turkish invasions of
  eastern Europe   382
Europe encounters the world: voyages from
  1487 to 1610   394

PREFACE

MARKING TIME

The term "Middle Ages" is an instance of the historian's habit of dividing the past into distinct periods in order to focus more clearly on the problem of continuity and change in collective human experience.

When other disciplines use historical periodization, they usually possess reasonably limited and generally undisputed criteria for defining change. Measurable physical changes in the earth's structure, for example, account readily for geological periodization. Significant differences in the record of material culture account for periodization in archaeology. But because human beings are not merely earth or material objects, the past of human societies offers a much broader and more widely debated spectrum of things to measure, describe, and analyze. Our lives are short and our experience limited, but we have always desired a much greater—and greatly changing—access to the human past than our own personal experience and memory can provide. We have invented the study of history to provide us with that access.

Different methods of historical investigation and explanation came into existence precisely because of the different questions about the past that people asked. In the late fourteenth century, as the last chapter of this book will tell, a number of literary moralists asked why the great power of the Roman Empire seemed to have collapsed around A.D. 500, why the Roman Empire "declined and fell." They also thought that in their own time they had managed to revive, or give rebirth to, many of the cultural values of ancient Rome. They came to call their own age (from the year 1350 or so) the period of rebirth, the "Renaissance" of Roman and later Greek values. With the glories of ancient Rome at one end, and the perceived glories of revived Roman and Greek culture at the other, the period from around 500 to 1350–1450 came to acquire a negative shape. What seemed to be conspicuous about it was its "un-Romanness," between two periods of "Romanness." And so people took to calling it "Middle"—middle between two more admirable periods of human energy, order, and achievement.

Religious reformers in the early sixteenth century added to this picture their accusations that at the end of the Roman Empire an authentic, evangelical Christianity had begun to be perverted and had not been purified until their own time. This view reinforced the first definition of "the Middle Ages." It was itself reinforced in the later sixteenth and seventeenth centuries by thinkers who argued that even if their age had not exactly recreated the glories of ancient Greece and Rome, it had done something even better—it had created a greater civilization, "the Modern Age."

By all these criteria the millennium after 500 A.D. indeed seemed dark, rusty, monkish, leaden, dull, and barbarous, ruled, as the first American medieval historian, Henry Charles Lea (1825–1909), once observed, by "superstition and force."

Both scholarly research and cultural change began to revise this image by the end of the nineteenth century. A series of scholarly disciplines for the study of human society arose in the early nineteenth century—archaeology, sociology, political science, anthropology, comparative religious studies, art history, and others. These approaches raised fundamental questions about the nature of the past that older political, religious, or progressive methods and perspectives could not answer. As a result of these changes, historians began to reshape their culture's past.

Historians and students of history still mark time, but the techniques of marking change. Periodization requires that we identify what changed and what did not, how and where change took place, and how the consequences of that change worked themselves out in human society. We ask sharper and more precise questions partly because we have improved the techniques of historical research and partly because our own cultural experience has compelled us to.

Throughout this process of responding (sometimes very slowly and not always usefully) to changing cultural demand, historical scholars improved their technical skills at handling evidence, from the reading of ancient languages and difficult documents to the realization that what in one period might have been considered "politics," "economics," "social class," "religion," and "masculine and feminine" meant different things in the past and touched different areas of life and thought. The discipline of historical study—and historical criticism based on a professional methodology—slowly came into its own in the late nineteenth and twentieth centuries. History, the artificial memory of a culture, could no longer be turned quite so readily to the interests and service of fashionable ideas, ideology, confessional wrangling, or the reinforcement of various kinds of power.

The history of historical study and method has produced a particular kind of knowledge—historical knowledge—that can be tested rationally and critically and yet still respond to the questions that our culture asks it.

Like other situations in which professionals inform nonprofessionals, the configuration of historical study must range between two poles: the detailed research of the specialist, about which few nonspecialists care to know in detail, and the "living past," the common received opinion of the past that most members of a culture have at any particular time in their own lives. In that part of the human past with which this book deals, the first is represented by a host of complex techniques for dating and authenticating manuscripts, reconstructing population figures, and interpreting many kinds of sources that are no longer produced by modern societies, such as saints' lives and royal and papal documents. The second is represented by the "popular" ideas about knights and ladies, or the predominance of ecclesiastical institutions over many aspects of daily life.

In spite of the entirely new picture of the Middle Ages in Europe that historical study has created in the last century, popular imagination and scholarly convenience have preserved the name "Middle" for a period that witnessed the beginning of a distinctive European civilization, created out of old and new elements by peoples of many different cultures who arrived and settled in Europe in its early stages and whose descendants are still there. Modern Europeans and Americans are *not* the only cultural descendants of ancient Greece and Rome, but we are the *only* descendants of medieval Europe.

We cannot remember that past, but the discipline of historical study permits us to know about it what is possible to know. Human beings live in time, but, as novelists and physicists continually remind us, we perceive our own passage through time in subjective and distorted ways. Perhaps there is no other way to live through time. But historical study has created an intellectual tool that permits us to observe other people living in time without the distortion that prevented them, and often prevents us, from perceiving what living in time means. At one level, perhaps the most important, we are able to experience time and to understand, however incompletely, that our experience of time may be measured in other ways, and that the study of history sharpens that awareness and elaborates our individual and collective self-consciousness. And it makes our lives more interesting.

The study of any period of history will do this, for this is what historical study does best. In this book a particular segment of the intelligible past, isolated from early value judgments based on nonhistorical criteria, as well as from ideology, confessionalism, and the reductionism and blandness of static social science, is described in terms that have been tested, criticized, and required to be intelligible to interested specialists and readers in the last quarter of the twentieth century. The description will constitute a part of artificial memory, cultural memory. Its aim is to bridge the gap between specialized historical research and "the living past" that this culture maintains.

Alexander Murray once observed that, "Without any vision at all history books are waste paper." Vision is not, however, always expected or wanted in survey texts, and yet there is no reason to write them without some vision. The vision behind this one is simply that the Middle Ages constitute the first part of the history of modern European and Atlantic civilization, that the period represents a beginning, not a "middle," and that even a survey text, when it bridges the gap between specialized research and general misinformation, may be a useful literary exercise.

ACKNOWLEDGMENTS

The history of this edition began with an earlier book, *Europe: The World of the Middle Ages,* which Prentice-Hall published in 1977. Many readers of that book—and of the first and second editions of this book (published in 1983 and 1989)—passed suggestions on to me which have been incorporated wherever possible. I remain very grateful to all readers, both those invited by the publisher and those inspired to comment by a sense of collegiality or pure reader's interest. For this edition in particular, I am especially grateful to Ruth Mazo Karras and Ann Matter, as well as to the readers invited by Prentice-Hall.

Edward Peters

FURTHER READING

On the term "medieval" and its (usually erroneous) modern usages, see Fred C. Robinson, "Medieval, the Middle Ages," *Speculum* 59 (1984), 745–756. On its place in contemporary concerns, see Milton McC. Gatch, "The Medievalist and Cultural Literacy," *Speculum* 66 (1991), 591–604. *Speculum,* the journal of the Medieval Academy of America, is an important source of current scholarship and reviews on all aspects of medieval studies.

Some of the great figures in shaping the subject are considered in *Medieval Scholarship: Biographical Studies on the Formation of a Discipline,* Vol. I, *History,* Helen Damico and Joseph Zavadil, eds. (New York: Garland, 1995). There is an excellent collection of studies on the subject *The Past and Future of Medieval Studies,* John Van Engen, ed. (Notre Dame-London: University of Notre Dame Press, 1994).

1

THE BEGINNING AND END
OF THE ROMAN PEACE

THE ROMAN EMPIRE IN THE MEDITERRANEAN
AND EUROPEAN WORLD

The empire ruled by Rome was the first empire in the ancient world that centered on the whole of the Mediterranean basin and provincialized the Mediterranean hinterlands in North Africa, Europe, and Asia. In this respect it differed greatly from the earlier, more eastern-oriented empires of Egypt and Persia and from the predominantly Greek empire of Alexander the Great (356—323 B.C.). It built upon earlier colonizing efforts in the central and western Mediterranean by individual Greek and Phoenician city-states. It brought under a single political and administrative unity both the culturally homogenized ruling classes of the Mediterranean city-states and the inhabitants of the hinterlands that ringed the Mediterranean. Because the Mediterranean is a sea with similar coastal areas but extremely diverse hinterlands, its shores had proved relatively easy for Greek and Phoenician migrants to colonize westward from the eighth century B.C., and travel between seaports was always easier and faster than travel overland.

The colonization movement of Greeks and Phoenicians not only ringed the Mediterranean with cities of a similar culture, but it produced the rise of one Phoenician colony, Carthage, to the role of capital of a prosperous seaborne power. It also allowed the Greeks and Carthaginians to encounter and influence other Mediterranean societies and their neighbors: tribal Celts in southern Gaul and Iberia; Etruscans and Latins in Italy; Egyptians, Numidians, and Berbers in North Africa. This territorial widening of the Greek cultural horizon also affected Greek ideas of human society and the world. For centuries Greek thinkers had conceived of the individual city-state, the *polis*, as the ultimate center of Greek social and cultural life. But after the conquests of Alexander and the colonization movement westward, Greek writers began to speak more frequently of the *oikumene*, the whole world of human cities, as the natural community for humans. Thus, with the spread of Greek colonies there also went the Greek language and Greek literary, philosophical, and religious culture and the idea of a common world defined by the new Greek standards. That world was the entire Mediterranean and Black Sea areas and those hinterlands in which an urban style of life could be lived comfortably by the ruling orders of society. The Mediterranean basin was socially and culturally homogeneous well before it became politically and militarily unified by Rome.

The culture of the Mediterranean world was based largely upon that of the Greek world after the death of Alexander the Great, and it is therefore usually called *Hellenistic* (the Greek word for Greece is *Hellas*). In spite of the imperial ambitions of a number of Alexander's successors during the late fourth and third centuries B.C., political power remained largely regional until the rise of Rome to political prominence after the third century B.C. Located in the west-central coastal region of the Italian peninsula—that is, on the western fringe of the Hellenistic world—the small agricultural city-state of Rome lay originally between two other cultures that were far more developed and influential. In the north of Italy the civilization of the Etruscans long overshadowed and influenced that of Rome. In south Italy and Sicily colonial Greek-founded city-states (modern Naples, Syracuse, and Agrigento) brought Rome into contact with Hellenistic culture and mainland Greece. The hilly location of Rome was easily defended, and the Tiber River was easily forded or bridged. At the mouth of the Tiber was the convenient seaport of Ostia, and a number of trade routes passed through Roman territory. After throwing off the rule of kings in the late sixth century B.C., Rome established a republic, ruled by two elected officials called *consuls* and administered by members of its leading families holding a variety of public offices. Roman military strength, based on an army of tough, well-disciplined peasant soldiers, permitted Roman power to expand in central Italy, and by the third century B.C. brought it into political contact and military rivalry with the Hellenistic and Carthaginian worlds.

Beginning in 265 B.C. Rome fought three wars—generally termed the Punic Wars—to defeat Carthage, accomplishing this in 146 B.C. The defeat of Carthage brought the Romans into North Africa and Iberia. At the same time, Rome was invited to participate on one side or another of local Greek wars, and by 146 B.C. Rome had also come to rule all of Greece. Rome's involvement in Greece brought it into the affairs of a number of Hellenistic kingdoms in Asia, where it created a province in 129 B.C. With the conquest of Egypt in 31 B.C. Rome had assembled its Mediterranean empire.

Because the Roman empire was put together piecemeal over several centuries, its "frontiers" were at first the frontiers of the territories that Rome had conquered. But with the advent of a single power in all these territories, frontiers had to be reconsidered. When the Romans conquered Iberia, for example, they recognized the importance of southern Gaul as a land route between Iberia and Italy. After defeating a confederation of Celtic Gauls in 125 B.C., Romans founded their first city in Gaul, *Aquae Sextiae* (modern Aix-en-Provence— Provence deriving from the Latin word *provincia*) in 123. Between 123 and 118 B.C. southern Gaul became a Roman province, *Gallia Narbonensis*, and two characteristic Roman institutions were introduced: another city (*Narbo Martius*, modern Narbonne), and a road, the *Via Domitia*, connecting Roman Italy with Roman Iberia through what was rapidly becoming Roman Gaul. Other Roman towns in Gaul, such as *Arelate* (modern Arles) and the Greek-founded *Massilia* (modern Marseilles), followed. The settling of southern Gaul brought Romans into direct contact with the world of Celtic Gaul and northern Italy. Thus, Roman colonists and soldiers had to secure the new province in the north, and the needs of defense required the frontier to move northwards to strategically defensible ground.

However, the Roman colonization of Gaul was not exclusively a military operation. Romans assimilated many Celtic Gauls into Roman provincial society, creating a distinctive Gallo-Roman culture that survived even the end of the Roman empire itself. The problem of the northern frontier of Gaul offered considerable opportunities to ambitious Roman politicians and generals. One of these, Julius Caesar (102–44 B.C.), made his public reputation by a series of campaigns that he recorded in his *Gallic Wars*, and Caesar's conquest of northern Gaul laid the foundation for the Roman conquest of Britain, which was accomplished by 43 A.D. Eastward across the English Channel, the Roman European frontier was gradually stabilized along the valleys of the Rhine and Danube rivers, running to the Black Sea.

Elsewhere in the Mediterranean world Rome encountered similar problems. The conquest of Asia Minor and the establishment of the province of Asia brought Rome into direct contact with the peoples around the Black Sea and with the Parthian Empire of Persia, which had been founded in 248 B.C. and lasted until 224 A.D., when it was replaced by the strong and more hostile Sasanid Empire. The conquest of Egypt drew Roman forces far up the Nile River. The conquest of Numidia brought them to the edge of the Sahara Desert. Although the problem of coherent and manageable frontiers was not always or everywhere as urgent as it had been in Gaul, the line of the frontier and the provinces it defined consumed the energies of Roman rulers, administrators, and soldiers for the next several centuries.

Between the third century B.C. and the end of the first century A.D. the Romans had conquered two worlds: that of the Iron-Age Celts and others in transalpine Europe and that of the Hellenized world of the Mediterranean basin. But for several centuries Rome was able to balance these worlds, first, because Rome, developing from the margins of the Hellenistic world, had never become completely Hellenized itself, and second, because Rome offered a relatively easy process of Romanization to its provincial subjects in Europe and extended its influence beyond the Rhine-Danube frontiers through trade, tribute, and later military recruiting.

Finally, Rome itself underwent considerable internal changes with its acquisition of an empire. Latin literature, for example, which had begun (except in legal literature, where Rome showed a particular intellectual independence) as a pale and often awkward imitation of a rich Greek literature, quickly developed a distinctive identity and power of its own and made Latin the language of imperial administration and law as well as the common spoken language of the western parts of the empire. Greek, however, remained the language of philosophy and much literature throughout the Roman world, as well as the common spoken language in most of the eastern part of the empire. At the height of the empire, most of the ruling classes throughout the empire were bilingual in Greek and Latin.

The creation of the empire also transformed Rome's older Republican form of government, which rested on the consuls and other public magistrates as well as the Senate, an advisory body of former holders of public office, into a form of government resembling a monarchy but preserving initially many of the republican elements that Romans had come to venerate. The transition in government had begun with a series of civil wars among contending strongmen, including Julius Caesar, in the first century B.C., but its final form was designed by Caesar's adopted son, Octavian Augustus (63 B.C.–14 A.D.). While preserving the form of republican rule, Augustus assumed personally and for life a number of key magistracies, as well as the direct command of several key provinces and armies. The title emperor (from the Latin *imperium*, the right to command) was joined to Augustus's own name and assumed by his successors, who were his personal heirs wielding his accumulated offices, immense personal wealth, and military authority.

By preserving the republican forms of government, Augustus and his successors preserved at least the fiction of the identity of the emperor and the Senatorial order, which created senatorial support for most emperors of the first two centuries, except for those who autocratically rejected it. Outside Rome itself, Augustus and his successors were regarded as world-kings in the manner of Alexander the Great and other earlier imperial rulers, and by the second century A.D. as gods. Since the emperors governed the empire chiefly with the advantage of Rome and Roman citizens in mind, Rome and central Italy were the original beneficiaries of the Mediterranean conquests; wealth poured into Italy.

In the hinterlands and the remoter provinces, Romanization and Hellenization touched smaller elites, although a provincial form of Romanization developed and influenced both provincials and peoples living beyond the frontiers. Classical towns and country estates (villas) appeared first in Gaul, North Africa, and Syria, later in Britain, the Rhineland, and the valley of the Danube. Leading families in provincial towns imitated those in the great cities, privately donating the attributes of Mediterranean urban civilization—great amphitheaters and public baths, statues, gates, monuments, temples, paved streets, and market-places. Wherever possible, they built Roman-style houses with open interior courtyards and tile roofs.

The cities, especially in the western parts of the empire, were centers of administration rather than production, consumers of revenue and private largesse rather than producers of income. Except for the occasional early waves of wealth that came from new imperial conquests and imperial generosity, the empire depended on private initiative in both local public works and governmental administration. The number of imperial administrators was very small, and most of the empire was administered by a combination of local effort and loose imperial supervision.

For the ruling elites, however, the empire offered a privileged and secure existence, homogeneous throughout a larger world. The historian Peter Brown has characterized this aspect of imperial life.

For a short time an officer's mess modelled on an Italian country villa faced the Grampians in Scotland. A checkerboard town, with amphitheater, library, and statues of classical philosophers, looked out over the Hodna range, at Timgad, in what are now the bleak southern territories of Algeria. At Dura-Europos, on the Euphrates, a garrison-town observed the same calendar of public festivals as at Rome. . . . One of the main problems of the period from 200 to 700 was how to maintain, through a vast empire, a style of life and a culture based originally on a slender coastline studded with classical city-states.[1]

So successful did Rome's internal and external affairs appear in the first and second centuries A.D., and so little were the frontiers troubled—even disastrously inept emperors like Caligula (37–41 A.D.) and Nero (54–68 A.D.) did not destroy or even significantly weaken the government—that this period has often been termed the *Pax Romana*—the Roman Peace. In the midst of imperial aggrandizement, Cicero (106–43 B.C.), who appreciated the spread of Roman power and did much to popularize Greek philosophy in the context of Roman public service, remarked that under Roman rule, *orbis terrarum est civitas*—"the whole world has been turned into a single [Roman] city-state." To Cicero and others, the *orbis terrarum,* literally "the circle of the lands," was the Mediterranean and its shores and hinterlands. Poets, historians, and philosophers praised Rome's rule and recognized that they lived in a political and cultural world unlike any seen before. They even called the Mediterranean simply *Mare nostrum,* "our sea."

---

[1] Peter Brown, *The World of Late Antiquity* (reprint, New York: W.W. Norton & Co., Inc., 1978), p.11.

THE ROMAN EMPIRE AND ROMAN SOCIETY

In the course of creating an empire Roman society and the Roman economy underwent rapid and irreversible change. Rome had begun as a community of prosperous peasant farmers in which the male heads of households held absolute power, including that of life and death, over members of their own households (the original meaning of the Latin word *familia* included not only the domestic household proper, but also all other dependents including slaves). In law, the power of the father was termed *patriapotestas*. The Roman economy was originally agricultural, producing the essential Mediterranean diet crops of grain, olive oil, and grapes. Even urban patricians retained deep rural roots, and the peasant armies of early Rome were recruited from among the holders of small farms. Roman aristocrats long preserved this image of themselves as frugal, morally upright, paternalistic heads of agricultural households, and they preserved much of this image in Roman law.

Because Roman citizens of high rank were responsible for the legal affairs of their households and clients and valued the steps on the way to holding public office, much of their energies and interest turned to the field of law. Roman law developed early and precociously, and much Roman social history is reflected in the law. *Patriapotestas* regulated much of Roman domestic life, initially allowing no independence—and hence no right to hold political office—to women and retained even adult married children in dependence upon their father until he died. Marriage was regulated by male heads of households, and fathers and husbands originally possessed virtually complete legal responsibility for and power over the women, children, and dependents of their households. Tutelage of this kind was originally continued even for adult women who had neither husband nor father. Several religious cults were open only to women, and occasionally women were recognized as possessing prophetic powers. But women's cults were often morally or politically suspect, and the recognition of prophetic powers itself represented rather an aspect of marginalization. To the Romans, masculine identity entailed a primarily active and dominant role in social activities, including sexual relationships. Feminine identity was understood to be passive, domestically confined and family identified. As one Roman (male) argued, opposing a law restricting the personal adornment of Roman women,

No offices, no priesthoods, no triumphs, no decorations, no gifts, no spoils of war can come to them; elegance of appearance, adornment, apparel—these are women's badges of honor.

Such adornment and apparel identified Roman women according to family, social rank, and protected, passive social role. Roman men also frequented socially inferior prostitutes and sexually used female slaves. Throughout Roman history concubinage was recognized, although the social status of the concubine was lower than that of the man, and concubines never received the formal respect paid to Roman married women.

In the course of the second and first centuries B.C. and the first several centuries A.D., however, the early Roman social and economic world was transformed. The immense influx of wealth permitted money to play a dominant part in Roman economy and society. The small farms gave way to larger and larger estates providing a life of rural leisure for their owners and worked by gangs of slaves and increasingly dependent free laborers. The small farmer still thrived in the provinces until the fourth century. The great estates of Italy tended to produce more sheep and cattle, while the production of grain was increasingly transferred to the vast fields of Sicily and North Africa. The greatly extended line of communication between the new major grain-producing regions and Italy became a major problem in later centuries, when interruption of the great grain fleets raised the threat of starvation in the vast cities of the empire. For the empire now began to provide food for much of its urban population. Free bread, and cheap wine and oil came to be regarded as a prerogative of the inhabitants of the cities of Italy. Public provision of food (and entertainment, as the phrase "bread and circuses" indicates) became one more responsibility of urban elites, just as did many public services and the maintainance and decoration of cities.

Although highly skilled craftsmen and artisans worked in Italy, most manufacturing was provincially localized and made for local consumption. In the European provinces, much production was done for the armies, and settlements of soldiers often shaped and gave a distinctive economic and cultural stamp to areas near the frontiers.

The economic transformation also entailed a social transformation. The status of women, initially aristocratic women, gradually improved in both legal and social terms. Because marriages continued to be arranged by families throughout the imperial period (since marriages were arranged usually for political, social, or economic reasons) the institution itself was particularly vulnerable to changes in the political, social, or economic climate. These aspects of marriage turned out to work to the advantage of women. Gradually in law women were able to control their own property, separate property they possessed before marriage from the property of their husbands, and to acquire substantial rights in property, including their dowries, after the end of a marriage. Divorce became more readily available for women as well.

Although upper-class women acquired greater freedom and were generally well protected, women of other classes continued to be particularly subject to violence and insult, and they possessed few resources to counter these assaults, except for appeals to the law and to their own relatives. Often, neither was of much help. The definition of gender roles in the Roman world changed slowly, and not at the same rate for everyone.

Because the imperial government was run on the model of a household, female relatives of emperors probably led the way in acquiring a degree of independence, but political opponents could also mischaracterize their activities as unwomanly and insult their male relatives as men who submitted to the domination of women. Other difficulties also plagued the imperial office, including its dependence upon the vagaries of birth and adoption of imperial successors. A number of Augustus's successors conspicuously lacked his own political skills and temporarily weakened the imperial office. Some of them alienated the senatorial aristocracy, permitted the administration of the empire to slip into the hands of inept favorites, the Praetorian Guard (the military bodyguard of the emperors), the imperial civil servants, or the armies.

HADRIAN'S TRAVELS

From 64 to 96, rival contenders for the imperial office raised armies and fought each other, until the succession of the elderly senator Nerva (96–98) inaugurated a revival of senatorial influence and a series of able and diplomatic emperors, the Flavians and Antonines, who ruled through most of the second century. It is not surprising that the Age of the Antonines (98–180) has long been regarded by historians as the golden age of the Roman empire, when Rome seemed to have resolved the social/economic and political crises attendant upon the creation of the empire. This attitude is reflected in the opening sentence of Edward Gibbon's classic work *The Decline and Fall of the Roman Empire.*

In the second century of the Christian era, the Empire of Rome ruled the fairest part of the earth and the most civilized portion of mankind.

The modern world may criticize Gibbon's categorical standards of judgment, but it will also be sensitive to the ironies of his characterization, and it must remember that many second-century Romans would have agreed wholeheartedly with his sentiments. Thus, the second century was regarded by the wealthy, privileged, and powerful classes of the empire as ruled by conscientious, considerate, socially acceptable, talented rulers who adopted promising protegés and trained them in imperial duties. Trajan (98–117), an Iberian and Nerva's immediate successor, extended the frontiers to their farthest limits. By Trajan's reign the Roman empire extended 1600 miles from north to south, from northern Britain to the edge of the Sahara Desert, and 2800 miles from west to east, from the Atlantic coasts of Spain and Morocco to the Caucasus Mountains and the valleys of the Tigris and Euphrates. The empire held around 50 million inhabitants, unevenly distributed with the heaviest concentrations in the eastern regions, and with nearly a million of them in the city of Rome itself. In area, the empire was about the present size of the United States. Its population was about the size of medieval Europe around the year 1300, and about one third that of the United States today.

   The accidental frontiers had been shaped into a generally well-guarded border. Trajan had pursued a policy of expansion of parts of the empire with his conquest of Dacia north of the Danube to secure Illyria/Pannonia. Trajan and

A Scene from Trajan's Column. This detailed scene showing a battle at a wall is typical of the extraordinary wealth of pictorial display commemorating the triumphs of the emperor.

his advisers had realized the importance of the Pannonian plain north of the Danube as a migration route into Europe, and they secured the Danube frontier and its provinces with eleven legions of troops, nearly double the number that protected Britain and the Rhine valley combined. Trajan's reign also saw Roman trading contacts extended from south Arabia and Upper Egypt to India and Ceylon across the Indian Ocean. Within the frontier the different Roman provinces had attained nearly equal footing with the capital of the empire, and by the early second century A.D. the imperial administration had achieved a certain degree of uniformity throughout the empire, but without destroying all signs of local culture and tradition.

The Roman view of the empire and its military triumphs is illustrated in the great column that Trajan had dedicated in the year 113 to commemorate his victory over the Dacians and the triumph of Rome. In a spiral frieze 3 feet high and 670 feet long climbing a 100-foot-high column, Trajan's artists skillfully illustrated the military victory of the conquering emperor. Under Trajan too, the internal peace of the empire was restored. The reign of Trajan's successor, Hadrian, is an ideal point from which to survey both the extent of the empire in the middle of the second century and some of its most important neighbors.

Hadrian (117–138) was also a Spaniard. By the end of the first century A.D., membership in the senatorial aristocracy had widened to include the elites of the old provinces. Just as Italy no longer exclusively provided senators, the reigns of Trajan and Hadrian proved that it no longer exclusively provided emperors. Indeed, one of the chief results of imperial history was the slow process of transforming Rome from being the head of subordinate territories to becoming the center of an association of provinces, the oldest of which—Spain, Gaul, and North Africa—considered themselves as venerable as Rome itself. By Trajan's reign 40 percent of the senatorial class was made up of provincials, and by the end of the second century, the Senate represented the upper classes of the entire empire. One reason for the success of the Antonine emperors was that they, like the Senate, were cosmopolitans who moved easily throughout the empire. They were traditionally educated and were as comfortable speaking Greek as Latin. More and more, they thought of the empire as a whole, not simply as an appurtenance of the city of Rome.

And they did not remain exclusively in Rome. Trajan was a widely traveled aristocratic general; Hadrian a widely traveled scholar and administrator. Both emperors probably knew the empire from personal experience and inclination better than any of their predecessors had. Hadrian spent nearly twelve years of his twenty-one-year reign moving about the empire, accompanied by a retinue of officials, architects, engineers, and cultural and artistic advisers. Part of Hadrian's purpose was practical: He wanted to know firsthand how his administrators worked, how efficient or oppressive they were, how good the defenses were, what his subjects desired and needed, and also to give immediate impetus to change where he thought it necessary. On the other hand, Hadrian had an insatiable curiosity about the varieties of life and thought and religious beliefs in the empire. He was bilingual in Latin and Greek, well read, and had excellent artistic taste, as his villa at Tivoli and his tomb in Rome, now the Castel Sant'Angelo, illustrate. When he traveled, he inquired about local customs, religious beliefs, and history.

Hadrian's travels informed the emperor about everything, but they informed him most about administration and defense. His legal reforms gave the empire a uniform code of law. Much of his travel resulted in a pulling back and tightening of frontiers. Perhaps its best-known legacy is Hadrian's Wall, which the emperor ordered built on his visit to Britain in 122. From Wallsend on the mouth of the River Tyne to Bowness on the Solway Firth, Hadrian and his architects personally surveyed the seventy-three-mile distance across the width of northern Britain and helped design the long stone wall linking sixteen forts and many small guard posts and watchtowers. Although the wall was not intended primarily to keep the invading northern Picts out, it divided hostile peoples in the north and made an impressive display of Roman might on the far northern edge of the empire. From Bowness and Roman frontier stretched eastward along the wall to the North Sea, and then, in a chain of frontier towns and forts, down the Rhine and Danube rivers to the Black Sea. It then ran south from the Black

Hadrian's Wall. Looking westward across northern Britain, the course and fabric of the wall suggest the achievement of the emperor-engineer after whom it is named. (*Courtesy of the British Tourist Authority*)

Sea coast, down the valleys of the Tigris and Euphrates rivers, and turned west across Palestine, Arabia, Egypt, and North Africa, all the way to Morocco on the North African Atlantic coast.

Hadrian's visits to the provinces increased the sense of community among the provincial ruling classes, as did Hadrian's commissioning statues of the personified provinces for his museum, the Hadrianeum in Rome, and his issue of coinage depicting twenty-five different provinces and cities. All these acts suggest the cosmopolitan character of the emperor and the empire just before the middle of the second century A.D.

GERMANIA

Romans referred to peoples living beyond the imperial frontiers, the *limes,* as *externae gentes,* "the peoples outside." But the choice of the particular Latin term informs us (the singular is *gens*), the Romans had a number of very different words that they used to describe different categories of "people." Romans categorized non-Roman peoples in terms of the approximate similarity of their cultures and forms of social organization to those of Rome itself. A people might be a *populus,* virtually identical to Roman standards; a *gens,* not yet culturally developed or politically organized, or a *natio,* or as we would say, a "horde," a body of individuals supposedly related by common descent, but lacking the technical and intellectual culture or sociopolitical organization of a *gens.*

The Greeks, too, had classified non-Greek peoples, but on a slightly different basis. People who could learn to speak and read Greek were regarded as

Expansion of Roman territorial holdings under the Republic.

potentially respectable members of the *oikumene*; those who could or would not were *barbaroi*, "barbarians," people whose languages (as far as Greeks were concerned) consisted of nothing but incomprehensible sounds. The identification of barbarism with the misuse of a literary language has survived in many modern languages. Romans also applied the term (Latinized as *barbari*) to the *externae gentes* and *nationes* beyond the frontiers. Nineteenth-century anthropologists borrowed some of this terminology in classifying all human societies as "savage"—possessing neither domesticated plants nor animals; "barbarian"— possessing domesticated plants and animals but lacking writing; and "civilized"—possessing a written language. These terms have generally passed out of use, but the term "barbarian" is still sometimes used to designate migrants and invaders of the Roman empire from beyond the frontiers.

Roman literary sources concerning the peoples of northern Europe are not very informative before the first century B.C., but archaeological research has greatly illuminated the societies and cultures of the *externae gentes* north of the Roman European provinces. Archaeology dates late prehistory according to the dominant type of metallic technology and identifies periods in terms of locations at which particularly important discoveries have been made.

Roman territorial holdings under the Empire.

By the end of the Bronze Age (2300–750 B.C.), an accomplished group of peoples inhabited western and central Europe, making distinctive tools, weapons, and ornaments and capable of adapting these to new technologies and designs. Linguistically they were—like Greeks and Romans—speakers of languages in the Indo-European family. They possessed rulers and complex social organization, constructing sophisticated fortifications on hilltops, as well as large and small villages. The Iron Age (750 B.C.–300 A.D.) is generally considered in two broad stages, the first identified with remains discovered at Hallstatt in the salt-producing region of Upper Austria (750–500 B.C.), and the second with remains discovered at La Têne, a town near Neuchâtel in Switzerland (450–100 B.C.) and usually described as "Celtic."

Celtic Europe is distinguished by distinctive and highly complex art forms, iron metallurgy, and the appearance of large and prosperous settlements that Julius Caesar, at least, did not hesitate to designate with the Latin words *oppidum* and *urbs*, "town" and "city." Greek geographers and ethnographers, however, were the first to record the characteristics of the Celts—and to name them. Such broad and general names, which have survived to the present, often misunderstood, actually conceal a rich variety of cultures. Names like "Celts" and

"Germans" are descriptive only from the Roman or Greek perspective and cannot be interpreted in anything resembling a modern ethnic or cultural sense.

Late Iron Age society was based on the kin-group and the somewhat larger "tribe" (even the word "tribe," deriving as it does from an internal designation in Roman society, is technically misleading). As Roman soldiers, settlers, and provincial administrators encountered the Celts in northern Italy, Gaul, and the Danube valley, they readily assimilated many of them, and provincial Roman European culture was a mix of central Italian and Celtic peoples. Vergil (70–19 B.C.), the greatest Roman epic poet and author of the *Aeneid,* was a Celt from northern Italy.

Celtic societies lived from both agriculture (chiefly barley, wheat, and oats) and stock-raising, chiefly cattle and pigs. These provided the northern European diet that contrasts sharply with the Mediterranean bread, oil, and wine: heavier bread, butter, meat, and beer. Much of Celtic agriculture was the domain of women, as was the weaving of fine textiles. Celtic men were reckoned wealthy in terms of the number of cattle they owned and prestigious according to their skill in battle.

Initially, there was little to distinguish Celts from Germans. The earliest Latin usage of the term *Germani* was applied early in the first century B.C. to designate rebellious slaves who had come from east of the Rhine. Later in the century, Julius Caesar's *Gallic Wars* emphasized great distinctions between Celts and Germans, but probably to support Caesar's policy of establishing the Rhine as Rome's ideal eastern frontier in Europe by designating the eastern territory and those living in it as too savage to provincialize. The establishment of a Roman frontier after Caesar probably helped make these distinctions somewhat more substantial, that is, Celts east of the Rhine probably became "Gemanized," while Germans living west of the Rhine became "Celticized." But the difference was the Roman provincial frontier and Roman provincial culture, not inherent ethnic characteristics.

By the reign of Trajan, the central European frontier of the Roman empire had fluctuated considerably. Caesar had indeed established it at the Rhine, but under Augustus it was pushed to the Elbe, from which Roman forces were driven back in 9 A.D. Trajan determined to hold the frontier at the Rhine and to penetrate no further east.

Around the year of Trajan's accession, 98 A.D. the leading Roman historian, Tacitus, produced a description of the peoples in his book, the *Germania,* that is our first literary evidence concerning Germanic life and society. Tacitus's *Germania* is a short, but complex text. Parts of it do indeed contain descriptions of Germanic society, derived from the interrogation of direct observers, but parts also appear to consist of political propaganda and moral criticism of contemporary Roman society by idealizing the Germanic peoples to the disadvantage of the Romans. Tacitus had done something similar in his essay on Britain, which is a commemoration of his father-in-law's provincial governorship of the

Roman province of *Britannia*, and a rich source for Celtic society, but marked by the same political and moral considerations as the *Germania*. It must be checked against modern archaeological literature in order to assess its reliability for the historian. This is but one of many cases in very early European history in which, even for the historian, archaeological science must take precedence over the texts that historians usually work with.

Tacitus begins by emphasizing the unknown character of the inhabitants of *Germania*. They are isolated from other peoples and live in a region of endless swamps and trackless forests (here Tacitus is echoing Caesar's geopolitical point). Some Germans are distinguished from others by noble birth, and after distinguishing themselves in battle they might be admitted to the council that rules the folk. "They choose their kings for their noble birth," says Tacitus, "and their war leaders for their bravery," suggesting two types of kingship, of which the second is a military type. The Germans venerate and often seek advice from their women, who accompany them into battle and encourage them in combat. The council decides ordinary issues and disputes, but actions that involve the whole folk must be debated in an assembly of warriors. In battle, leaders fight alongside their retinues, sworn bodies of young fighters who have taken oaths of personal loyalty to their leaders (the Latin term for this association of young warriors with a leader is *comitatus*, and it has a long later history in European society). Organized routinely for war, the Germanic peoples of Tacitus were fierce and formidable, but Tacitus is contemptuous of their laziness and lack of discipline during peacetime.

Tacitus's description of the Germanic peoples nearest the Roman frontiers is generally accurate. Their fierceness, lack of discipline, and repellent lands are emphasized only in order to dissuade any Romans who might want to absorb them and their lands into the empire, that is, on the Roman scale to imply that they are merely *nationes*, hardly *gentes*, and certainly not *populi*. Tacitus emphasizes his point as he describes peoples further away from even those across the frontier as progressively more exotic, fierce, and barbarous, ending his description with a people known only as the Fenni.

They care for nobody, man or god, and have gained the ultimate release: they have nothing to pray for. What comes after them is the stuff of fables—Hellusii and Oxiones with the faces and features of men, but the bodies and limbs of animals.

Although Tacitus's text was lost to medieval Europeans until the fifteenth century, other sources for his last remarks about the sub- or nonhuman character of peoples distant from the frontier in other parts of the world remained common "knowledge" in the fabulous geography and anthropology of medieval Europeans.

The peoples whom Tacitus describes were already undergoing momentous transformations during the reign of Hadrian, and Tacitus is no longer a reliable source on Germanic society after the mid–second century A.D. Anthropologists and archaeologists have shown that the Germanic, western Asiatic, and

Iranian peoples along the edges of the Roman world were not complete strangers to that world. The very creation of Roman provincial society and Roman frontiers had influenced Germanic culture. Moreover, it was in the Romans' interest partially to assimilate some Germans as immigrant farmers and soldiers, and to destabilize border societies by tribute, bribery, political influence, and trade. The proximity of Germanic peoples had in turn influenced Roman provincial culture. In short, from the second century on, the "barbarians" were not nearly as barbaric and primitive as modern novels, films, and too literal attention to Roman sources often suggest. From the second century on, barbarians served more frequently in Roman military forces and were admitted as agricultural immigrants to depopulated parts of the European provinces. In the third, fourth, and fifth centuries the influence of Romans on barbarians and barbarians upon Romans became reciprocal. During these centuries events along the frontiers and their repercussions in both the central Roman empire and the vast world beyond the Roman frontiers—even beyond the Danube, the Rhine, and the plains of northern Gaul—created a distinctive and enduring European civilization.

The Mediterranean center of the Roman empire had entailed a Roman presence in Europe, at least, that extended far from the Mediterranean coast. Although Romans tried (and for more than three centuries handsomely succeeded) to live a Mediterranean life style in Roman houses and on a Roman diet (the Roman frontier may also be correlated with those areas in which it was possible to produce locally or import easily the fundamental grain, olive oil, and wine on which Romans preferred to live) in much of what is now Britain, France, Belgium, Germany, Switzerland, Austria, Hungary, Romania, and Bulgaria, the proximity of "outside peoples" came more and more to transform both Roman and "barbarian" life. The crisis of the third century greatly accelerated the transformation.

THE THIRD-CENTURY CRISIS

Hadrian's two successors, Antoninus Pius (138–161) and Marcus Aurelius (161–180) continued both Hadrian's administrative concerns and his personal learning. Indeed, Marcus Aurelius has been claimed as the last classical Greek philosopher. But the events of his reign suggest that the golden world of Trajan and Hadrian was already coming to an end.

For the first time in nearly two centuries a Roman emperor, Marcus Aurelius, had to fight three major defensive wars—one against the Parthian Empire of Persia (161–180) and two against large confederations of barbarian armies on the Danube River (167–175 and 177–180). In addition, a great plague struck the empire in 166. Marcus Aurelius completed his book of philosophical reflections, the *Meditations,* in a military camp and died on the Danube near Vienna in 180. His incompetent son and successor Commodus (180–192) ended the Danube wars only by making an excessively generous treaty with the invaders. He displayed utter indifference, however, to both the provinces and armies. His lenient treatment of the barbarians certainly stimulated barbarian interest in making war on Rome again, and his indifferent treatment of the army stimulated revolt. Commodus's assassination in 192 was followed by a period of civil wars.

At the end of the civil wars, the North African general Septimius Severus defeated his rivals and ascended the imperial throne with the backing of the Danube army. Septimius Severus did not come from the provincial senatorial elite that had produced the Antonines, nor did he possess universal interests. He was married to Julia Domna, a wealthy Syrian whose intelligence and wide religious interests mark her as the first consort of a Roman emperor who was intellectually distinguished in her own right. Unlike Commodus, Septimius Severus strove to retain military support. He restored the frontier defenses (including Hadrian's Wall), increased the size of the army to around 400,000 men, increased the army's pay by half, and threw the imperial service open to favorites from all corners of the empire. His greatest concern was to secure the imperial succession within his own family. He eroded the authority of the senatorial aristocracy and began the process of militarization and bureaucratization that quickly influenced government and finance. He died in 211 in a military camp near York, in northern Britain.

But in spite of Septimius Severus's favoring of the army, the frontiers remained troubled. Neither Severus's son Caracalla (211–217) nor Alexander Severus (222–235) was able to guarantee the security of the frontiers. An army revolt led to Alexander Severus's assassination in 235, and from that year on the army created the emperors. Until nearly 270, with most of the empire's frontiers under attack, no emperor ascended the throne without the support of his army; when a stronger candidate, backed by a stronger army, challenged his rule, civil war decided the issue. Thus, after 235 neither the Senate nor an imperial dynasty, the traditional sources of successful emperors, played a significant role in the rule of Rome. Not only did the army make the emperor, but the emperor was usually a soldier himself, sometimes a soldier who had been born in a remote province and been a peasant farmer before joining the military. Working his way up through the ranks, where talent, rather than social status, was rewarded by promotion, a peasant soldier might become a general, and a successful and popular general who made the right promises to his troops had a ready-made faction to support his imperial candidacy. Sometimes generals were virtually forced to revolt because their very success and popularity made them threats to the current regime.

A successful imperial candidate had to reward his troops; to do this and maintain the frontiers he had to raise more and more money from the population of the empire. He also had to spend more and more money on administration—even raising money cost money. Armies, imperial bureaucrats, and heavier and heavier taxes were the chief features of public life inside the empire during the third century. With them went debased coinage, inflation, and heavier and heavier burdens on those citizens who were forced to pay the taxes. Having imposed harsh financial burdens, the new emperor had to be ruthless in enforcing the law. Lacking the social and educational training of earlier emperors, he substituted instead the grim discipline of the army and borrowed the ceremonial trappings of the kings of the Persian East. From the mid–third century on, the figure of the emperor in documents, sculpture, and court ceremonial grew more remote, godlike, forbidding, and capricious. Dressed either in military uniform or elaborate ceremonial robes, the third- and fourth-century Roman emperors were far different figures from Trajan, Hadrian, and Marcus Aurelius. Within a century the core of the empire, the imperial office, had been drastically transformed.

Between 235 and 270, however, emperor after emperor went down to military defeat or assassination. Decius (249–251) was lost with his army fighting on the Danube. Valerian (255–260) was defeated in battle and captured by the great king Shapur II of Persia. Between 260 and 268 most of Gaul was seized by an imperial pretender, Postumus, who claimed to establish a "Gallic Empire." From 267 to 270 the great caravan city of Palmyra, under its queen Zenobia, declared the independence of a vast stretch of the Persian frontier, including Syria, the Levant, and northern Arabia. Even the inner provinces of the empire felt the impact of these disasters, and not only in a financial way. In 271 the emperor Aurelian built a fortified wall around the city of Rome itself—a grim reminder of just how deeply the empire was threatened.

Even the empire's enemies had changed from the second century. In 224 the decaying Parthian monarchy was overthrown by the vigorous dynasty of the Sasanids. The Sasanid kings created a powerful, highly centralized state with a common religion (Zoroastrianism) and developed strong armies. Under the greatest of its kings, Shapur II (241–272), the Roman emperor Valerian was captured in battle, as we have seen, and led in Shapur's triumphal march to his capital at Ctesiphon, where the great victory was commemorated in large and beautifully executed relief sculptures. From Shapur's reign until the end of the Persian Empire in 626, Persia proved the most formidable and threatening of Rome's enemies. No emperor could rule or deal with a crisis elsewhere in the empire without covering the Persian front.

The societies of the Germanic invaders of the Rhine and Danube had also changed. Instead of tribes and small peoples on raiding parties, the Germans beyond the frontier tended from the late second century on to assemble into larger confederations. Armed and trained by fighting either in or against the Roman army, they were geared to a predominantly military way of life. The confederation of the Marcomanni fought Marcus Aurelius. In the third and fourth centuries the confederations of the Alamanni (not an ethnic designation, but a term meaning "all men") and the Franks (a term meaning the "fierce," and later "the free" men) threatened the Danube and Rhine frontiers. Migrating eastern Germanic peoples, such as the Goths, also broke through the Danube frontier in the third century. It is not surprising, with the kinds of pressures on the Danube frontier in the third century, that Roman armies on the Danube, comprised of tough Balkan peasants, provided the core of Rome's defenses. Nor is it surprising that a series of talented generals from those armies succeeded each other on the imperial throne from 260 to 305, reformed the army, and saved the empire.

The size of the Roman army increased to around 600,000 men, a 50 percent increase over the army of Septimius Severus. Barbarians as well as provincials were permitted to serve in the army, and the command of the army was placed in the hands of professional soldiers. After 260 the members of the Senate were excluded from military command. As the old Roman legion disappeared, the army was divided into two new kinds of troops. The *limitanei*, as their name suggests, were stationed permanently on the frontiers and were expected to hold off an invasion, if only for a short time. The *comitatenses*, a mobile field army made up of heavy cavalry, specially trained infantry, and archers, were stationed at the new command bases behind the *limitanei*. The *comitatenses* were elite troops; they could be deployed rapidly, and at their best they were certainly the equals and often the superiors of their enemies.

Changes in the structure of the Roman armies paralleled changes in the structure of Roman society. Beneath the rank of senator Roman society consisted of two broad groups, the *honestiores* and the *humiliores*. The *honestiores* constituted a kind of professional middle class, consisting of city officials, army officers, teachers, physicians, and the civil servants of the imperial administration. They were the salaried managers of society who, when they could afford to, bought land and aimed at achieving senatorial rank. Beneath the *honestiores* were the *humiliores*, the merchants and traders, craftsmen, and small farmers. And beneath these two social groups were the slaves. Slaves, however, were used somewhat less frequently under the empire, partly because the conquest of foreign peoples—the chief source of slaves—ceased once the empire had ceased to expand, and partly because after the second century A.D. mines, fields, and industries tended to use more free labor. Slaves predominated in domestic service, however, down to the level even of the household of *humiliores*. Besides, barbarians had found new careers in the empire after the second century. Instead of becoming slaves, they could enroll in the army of Rome or lease agricultural land in the provinces.

From the third century the senatorial class was localized throughout the empire, performing imperial administrative services, receiving imperial administrative titles, and displaying little of the public-mindedness and public generosity that had characterized its earlier members. The financial burdens of the state fell more and more on the *honestiores* and *humiliores*. The economic decline of the third century, therefore must be regarded chiefly in terms of its effect on the lower ranks of society—the men and women whose ability to lighten the new economic burdens of taxation and inflation was strictly limited.

DIOCLETIAN AND CONSTANTINE: REFORM AND RECOVERY

The military, economic, and administrative crisis of the third century was reversed by the reform of imperial government by the emperor Diocletian (284–305) and his successor Constantine. Although these reforms produced another century of general stability for the empire, in the long run they proved immensely expensive. During the fourth and fifth centuries the eastern part of the empire, with its many prosperous cities, strong commercial economy, productive peasantry, and larger population survived better than the western part of the empire. The west felt the consequences of having fewer people, less productive and fewer cities, a less-developed economy, and more frequently attacked frontiers that were closer to the main centers of government. The cities of the western Roman Empire had developed chiefly as centers of administration of provinces, and they did not have the resilience that eastern cities did, nor the economic base. The western peasantry grew more and more oppressed by powerful large landholders. In short, the response to the crisis of the third century produced a transformed empire in which the eastern parts fared far better than the western.

The 270s and 280s produced a series of military victories that for a time pacified the frontiers and allowed the emperors to turn to the pressing need for internal reforms in finance and governmental organization. One of the military emperors, Diocletian, turned out to be an immensely skillful reformer. Diocletian's reforms touched all levels of society. He regularized the new and heavy taxes. He attempted to "freeze" the structure of society by legislating that laborers and their children remain in key trades and professions. He attempted to set strict price controls on all goods sold in the empire. He increasingly bureaucratized imperial government. His close supervision of the law courts extended imperial governmental institutions and officials deeper and deeper into the daily life of most of the empire's population. The new competence and ruthlessness of imperial officials carried out the emperor's reforms so that, by Diocletian's retirement in 305, the Roman Empire had been subjected to the most complete overhaul of governmental institutions the ancient world had ever seen.

Although not all of Diocletian's reforms took root, many had a quick and enduring influence. Not only did he reform society, but Diocletian even took on the dramatic reform of imperial governance. He created a second Augustus, a partner-emperor for himself, and announced the division of the empire into two halves, the *pars orientalis*, or eastern half, and the *pars occidentalis*, or western half. One Augustus was to rule in each. Each *pars* was in turn broken into two parts: In one the Augustus ruled, and in the other a Caesar, the Augustus's assistant and prospective successor, ruled. The *Tetrarchy*, or rule of four—

The Majesty of Emperors. This colossal head of Constantine the Great, nine times life size, was once part of a gigantic statue of the emperor that stood in the Basilica of Constantine in Rome. The size and imperial facial expression suggest the remoteness and majesty of late imperial portraiture. (*Hirmer Fotoarchiv. Munich*)

two *Augusti* and two *Caesares*—proposed to solve the two perennial problems of Roman imperial rule: the question of succession and the needs of government and defense. Each Augustus was to rule for twenty years, and then retire.

In 305 Diocletian retired to Split (in modern Croatia), having arranged, or so he thought, the appointment of the next four rulers. Diocletian's arrangements, however, foundered upon the equally perennial problem of dynasticism. Maxentius and Constantine, the sons of the first two Caesars, had been passed over in the succession, and their armies revolted and proclaimed them emperors. Constantine eliminated Maxentius in 312, and his other rivals and a large part of his own family over the next twenty years. Diocletian's reforms, which had been partially discontinued during the wars, survived, however, in Constantine's redivision of the empire and in his creation of a new army and civil service.

Constantine also continued the administrative redivision of the empire. Each *pars* was subdivided into prefectures. The four imperial prefectures were those of the East and Illyricum (for the *pars orientalis*) and those of the Gauls (Britain, Gaul, and Spain) and Italy (Italy and Africa) for the *pars occidentalis.* Rome and Constantine's new city of Constantinople each had its own urban prefect. Constantine continued and completed Diocletian's restructuring of Roman society. Members of the class of municipal officials were forbidden to leave the towns and cities for a life in the country or service in the army; free farmers were legally tied to the soil they cultivated; membership in the trade corporations of the towns was also made hereditary.

Constantine also transformed the army high command, creating a master of infantry (*magister peditum*) and a master of cavalry (*magister equitum*). These new ranks commanded a greatly transformed Roman army. For the army, too, had become a hereditary occupation. Moreover, recruits native to the provinces in which they served also entered military service, strengthening the local identity of locally stationed troops, marrying local women, and dominating much of the local economy and governmental offices. When Caracalla granted Roman citizenship to all free subjects of the empire in 216 (not as an example of imperial affection, but as a device to increase the pool of those obliged to pay the new inheritance tax imposed on Roman citizens), citizenship itself enhanced the status of these newly localized and militarized provincial societies.

In addition, increasing numbers of barbarians had long been recruited into the Roman army, originally as *laeti*. These small groups were permitted to settle in underpopulated provinces on the condition that they and their children agree to serve in the army. In the late third and fourth centuries, however, larger groups of barbarians, termed *foederati*, were allowed to settle inside the empire, also in return for military service. The practice of admitting barbarians into the European provinces for military purposes further contributed to the transformation of provincial culture. The increasing sense of localism in the provinces and the increasing numbers of barbarians living closely with Roman provincials created new provincial societies, with barbarians and Roman provincials sharing land, tax revenues, and responsibility for defense. The tendency to homogenize Roman provincial society in this way in areas close to the frontier paralleled the growth of the autonomy of great aristocratic private landholders in the older areas of the provinces. The aristocracy's interests, too, became more localized, and senatorial aristocrats were increasingly willing, when their own interests seemed to demand it, to support imperial pretenders during the periodic revolts of the third and fourth centuries, to serve barbarian rulers when it seemed in their best interests to do so, and to assume high office in the Christian church. The increasing cooperation between provincial aristocrats and barbarian rulers became a marked feature of Gallo-Roman society from the third century on. By the mid–fourth century, barbarian *magistri* routinely commanded Roman armies.

Diocletian's and Constantine's reforms have been called the earliest and most thoroughgoing form of state socialism the West has ever seen. The price paid by Italian and provincial society for protection and government grew heavier and heavier. The most important social consequence of these changes was the instrumentalization of all social orders in order to preserve the apparatus of government and defense. Although these changes pressed most heavily on the poorest orders of society, they did not leave the aristocracy untouched. Its ranks were increased by the "new aristocrats" in imperial service, and its loyalties to the empire were severely challenged and ultimately weakened. As long as the peace of the frontiers and at least the outward form of the life of the inner empire could be maintained, however, the emperors and the aristocracy could avoid a direct conflict of interests. By the third quarter of the fourth century, however, new migrations and military conflicts subjected their relationship to a strain that it could not survive. In spite of the vast efforts of Diocletian and Constantine, the peace that was preserved through much of the late third and fourth centuries bore less and less resemblance to the *Pax Romana* that earlier writers had praised, and increasingly there was very little peace at all.

FURTHER READING

On the expansion of Rome, see Fergus Millar, *The Roman Empire and Its Neighbors* (London: Weidenfeld & Nicholson, 1967), and for the center of Roman power, Fergus Millar, *The Emperor in the Roman World* (Ithaca-London: Cornell University Press, 1977); J. B. Campbell, *The Emperor and the Roman Army* (Oxford: Clarendon Press, 1984); Andrew Lintott, *Imperium Romanum: Politics and Administration* (London: Routledge, 1994). On the frontiers, see C. R. Whittaker, *Frontiers of the Roman Empire* (Baltimore: Johns Hopkins University Press, 1994), and Steven K. Drummond and Lynn H. Nelson, *The Western Frontiers of Imperial Rome* (Armonk, NY: M. E. Sharpe, 1993).

A brilliant, short, and well-illustrated treatment of the material covered in Parts I and II of this book is Peter Brown, *The World of Late Antiquity* (1971; reprint W. W. Norton & Co., 1978). A longer and more systematic treatment is A. H. M. Jones, *The Later Roman Empire*, 2nd ed., 2 vols. (Baltimore: Johns Hopkins University Press, 1986).

On the Roman Mediterranean world, see Peregrine Horden and Nicholas Purcell, *The Mediterranean World: Man and Environment* (Oxford: Basil Blackwell, 1987). On the Roman European provinces, see Edith Mary Wightman, *Gallia Belgica* (London: Batsford, 1985); J. F. Drinkwater, *Roman Gaul: The Three Provinces, 58 B.C.–A.D. 260* (London and Canberra: Croom Helm, 1983); Peter Salway, *Roman Britain* (Oxford: Clarendon Press, 1984); Anthony King, *Roman Gaul and Germany* (Berkeley-Los Angeles-London: University of California Press, 1990); T. W. Potter, *Roman Italy* (Berkeley-Los Angeles-London: University of California Press, 1987); S. J. Seay, *Roman Spain* (Berkeley-Los Angeles-London: University of California Press, 1988). See also A. L. F. Rivet, *Gallia Narbonensis: Southern France in Roman Times* (London: B. T. Batsford, 1988).

For the European world inside and outside the Empire, see Barry Cunliffe, ed., *The Oxford Illustrated Prehistory of Europe* (Oxford-New York: Oxford

University Press, 1994); Cunliffe, *Greeks, Romans and Barbarians* (London: Methuen, 1988); Stuart Piggott, *Ancient Europe* (Chicago: Aldine, 1965); Herbert Schutz, *The Prehistory of Germanic Europe* (New Haven: Yale University Press, 1983); Malcolm Todd, *The Northern Barbarians, 100 B.C.–A.D. 300* (1975; reprint ed. Oxford: Basil Blackwell, 1987); Peter S. Wells, *Farms, Villages, and Cities: Commerce and Urban Origins in Late Prehistoric Europe* (Ithaca-London: Cornell University Press, 1985); Françoise Audouze and Olivier Buchsenschutz, *Towns, Villages and Countryside of Celtic Europe* (Bloomington: Indiana University Press, 1992); Klaus Randsborg, *The Birth of Europe: Archaeology and Social Development in the First Millennium A.D.* (Rome: L'Erma di Bretschneider, 1989); Lotte Hedeager, *Iron-Age Societies: From Tribe to State in Northern Europe, 500 B.C. to A.D. 700* (1992).

For the East, see Fergus Millar, *The Roman Near East, 31 B.C.–A.D. 337* (Cambridge: Harvard University Press, 1994). A popular account of the Roman view of Romans and non-Romans is that of J. P. V. D. Balsdon, *Romans and Aliens* (Chapel Hill: University of North Carolina Press, 1979). On Tacitus, see Ronald Martin, *Tacitus* (London: Batsford, 1981).

On Trajan and Hadrian, see Lino Rossi, *Trajan's Column and the Dacian Wars* (Ithaca-London: Cornell University Press, 1971), and A. D. Divine, *Hadrian's Wall* (Boston: Gambit, 1969). On Hadrian and Rome, see Maria Taliaferro Boatwright, *Hadrian and the City of Rome* (New Haven: Yale University Press, 1988).

Several recent studies in Roman social history and the history of women in the ancient world are outstanding: Susan Treggiari, *Roman Marriage* (New York: Clarendon Press of Oxford University Press, 1991); Philippe Ariès and Georges Duby, eds., *A History of Private Life*, Vol. I, *From Pagan Rome to Byzantium*, Paul Veyne, ed. (Cambridge: Harvard University Press, 1987); Suzanne Dixon, *The Roman Family* (Baltimore: Johns Hopkins University press, 1992); Sarah B. Pomeroy, *Goddesses, Whores, Wives and Slaves: Women in Classical Antiquity* (New York: Schocken, 1975); Jane F. Gardner, *Women in Roman Law and Society* (London: Croom Helm, 1986); Ross Shepard Kraemer, *Maenads, Martyrs, Matrons, Monastics: A Sourcebook on Women's Religions in the Greco-Roman World* (New York: Oxford University Press, 1988), and *Her Share of the Blessings: Women's Religions among Pagans, Jews, and Christians* (New York: Oxford University Press, 1992); Aline Rousselle, *Porneia: On Desire and the Body in Antiquity* (Oxford: Blackwell, 1988).

On the crisis and Rome's response see Ramsay MacMullen, *The Roman Government's Response to Crisis A.D. 235–337* (New Haven: Yale University Press, 1976); Timothy D. Barnes, *The New Empire of Diocletian and Constantine* (Cambridge: Harvard University Press, 1982); Stephen Williams, *Diocletian and the Roman Recovery* (New York: Methuen, 1985), and Ramsay MacMullen, *Constantine* (1969; reprinted. New York: Harper and Row, 1971).

2

RELIGION AND SOCIETY IN ANTIQUITY

GODS OF THE HOUSE, COMMUNITIES, AND INDIVIDUALS

The oldest and most deeply revered deities of the Greco-Roman world were the domestic and local gods who protected the house, the family, the fields, woods, and groves. These "little gods" were the closest that the ancient world came to personal deities, although they paled beside the cult of the Olympian gods—powerful deities of the heroic age of Greece whose worship survived and prospered in the Greek city-states. The family of Olympian gods, headed by Zeus, the Jupiter of the Romans, were very different from the older local gods. They were eternal, but otherwise resembled superhuman beings, immensely wiser and more powerful than even the greatest human heroes and supremely beautiful. The proper human attitude toward them was awe and deference.

Besides their cults and temples, the gods lived on in poems, especially those of Homer and Hesiod, in the ninth and eighth centuries B.C. By the sixth century B.C., the gods' conduct in these literary works had begun to offend religious thinkers, whose sensibilities recoiled at tales of gods' lusts, jealousies, and petty vanity. The culture of the city-states developed strongly in the direction of ethical thought and metaphysics, and the Olympian gods came to seem somewhat old-fashioned and gross to the philosophers. Some of these produced elaborate explanations of the gods' behavior in Homer and Hesiod, arguing that Homer's text was not to be understood literally but figuratively; it concealed higher truths from uninitiated human minds. Although cult worship of the Olympian gods survived in Greece and Rome, most sophisticated religious thinkers after the fourth century B.C. speculated upon the possibility of a transcendent deity, a single god whose actions could account for the complexity of life.

Such speculation, however, was more often the property of philosophers. Most Greeks and Romans had other, to them more pressing, criteria for religious belief and behavior: There were many gods, and humans should revere all of them, particularly those of one's own ancestors and city. To be a monotheist—that is, to argue as Jews and, later, Christians and Muslims did, that there was only one divinity—was regarded as atheism and impiety. There was also a hierarchy of deities: Some lived above earth, some upon it. Gods spoke to their followers through their images, through wonders, oracles, divinations, omens, and dreams. Each deity required a cult, and in this world "religion" has been defined as "the sum of things to be sought openly in sacred precincts [of a temple or shrine]." If one behaved with piety, following the cult of one's ancestors and homeland, and respected the religious practices of others, one's own gods might bestow health, beauty, children, wealth, and many other tangible rewards. Beyond piety lay impiety—improper behavior toward the gods—*superstitio* (paying the wrong kind of attention to a deity), and magic (seeking things it was trivial or improper to pray for in temples, usually with the help of charlatans or real magicians who stood at the borders of religion). These last practices, especially impiety, invoked the wrath of the gods.

These religions had no missionary component, nor did they have a particular system of defined beliefs: One "had" a god rather than "believed" in one. There is little evidence of the prospect of an afterlife in one's own personality. Cults were supported locally, by local resources, as part of that beneficence that characterized the aristocracy of the cities and towns. Although cults of the same deity might exist in many cities, each city performed its own rites in its own way, and there was no central religious authority capable of dictating either belief or behavior across a wide and divergent world.

In the Roman world, religion was also a component of good citizenship. *Philanthropia,* a benevolence toward humans, was thought to be an attribute of the gods, and when cult worship was properly performed and the proper deference paid to the gods, entire communities were thought to benefit. In this sense, the practice of religion conferred corporate benefits on entire communities. Conversely, the improper practice of religion endangered entire communities.

Although particular emperors might favor one god over others, there is little evidence for anything resembling a Roman "state religion." Because Rome's good fortune in assembling an empire indicated divine favor toward the city, *Dea Roma*—"Goddess Rome"—was first worshipped in the conquered provinces, but the cult did not reach Rome itself until the second century A.D. From the end of the first century, Roman emperors themselves were considered divine beings, also initially in the provinces and only later in Rome. Far more than the worship of particular gods, Roman officials insisted on the veneration and worship of all the proper gods.

The Romans permitted many cults, even in Rome itself. Some features of particular cults, however—human sacrifice, ritual prostitution, and ceremonial mutilation—had to be eliminated for Roman approval. Otherwise, the lively religious world of the Mediterranean basin continued unchanged. The domestic gods, the Olympians, the philosophers' gods, and the many regional gods suggest some of the variety—and some of the limitations—of Greco-Roman religion in the early centuries of the empire.

Much of the traditional fabric of Greco-Roman religion survived with little change until the end of the fourth century A.D. Evidence for both its character and survival consists of literary and archaeological remains, however, and both sources must be used with great care to avoid hasty generalizations. The literary sources consist of discussions of the gods' nature and the obligations of humans toward them, and, in a large body of inscriptions, expressions of praise for a god and expressions of supplication or gratitude. Archaeological evidence consists of cult sites, statues, coins, and pottery. The great mass of both kinds of evidence peaks between the early second century A.D. and the early third century, and is thus not as reliable as it might be for the late third and early fourth centuries.

At the two poles of ancient religious sensibility were the philosophical sensitivity and skepticism of a very small, literate elite on the one hand, and the ritual practices of a large mass of people on the other. The appeal of philosophers, however, was limited—to join them required a substantial income and leisure time, a rigorous educational program, and commitment to an entire way of life, which varied according to the school of philosophy one chose to follow. Moreover, philosophical schools often contended with one another, pointing out each other's errors and undercutting each other's dogmata. From the late second century on, philosophy contributed to its own discrediting in religious matters, regardless of how developed and complex its ethical and metaphysical claims became. As an alternative to philosophical training and commitment, the religious sensibility of late antiquity increasingly offered divine revelation, in which all that was necessary to know was communicated to the initiate directly from the god through oracles or from the initiated followers of the god. With the increased importance of revelation, philosophical inquiry concerning religion became less and less popular during the third and fourth centuries, and the oracle became more popular.

In addition, traditional philosophical explanations for evil in the universe failed to deal with the perceptions of evil that characterize the late second and third centuries. Earlier philosophical explanations had focused upon divine wrath at human sin or at human error. With the growing influence of dualistic views of the universe—the idea that evil was an active presence, rivaling the powers of good gods—defense against evil became an active element in religious sensibility. The Persian religion of Zoroastrianism elevated this principle to a major doctrine. Zoroaster, who probably lived in the sixth century B.C., taught that the world was created by a good god, who was always in conflict with an evil god. Humans, caught in this cosmic struggle, will eventually be saved by the good god, some of them after purification following death. This most complex and assertive statement of religious dualism influenced some later Jewish apocryphal scriptures and also affected both paganism and Christianity, particularly in its personification of evil. Such a view also sharpened and changed the character of the Greco-Roman *daemones*, lesser deities who influenced human life and who now became more formidable agents of disaster.

Just as access to religious truth and the presence of evil shaped late antique religious sensibility, so too did the concept of existence after death. Vague and indifferent in classical religious thought, the concept of immortality of at least a part of the self became more and more emphasized from the second century on. In dualist religious schemes, this immortality divided those who were saved from those who were lost, but in most religious cults the problem of the passage of a part of the self through life and a series of ordeals and tests after death took on greater prominence.

Conventional interpretations of late antique religion have often emphasized it as full of anxiety, superstition, and open to the influence of exotic and bizarre religions, usually lumped together as "Orientalism." In fact, what seems to characterize it most strongly is a sense of *urgency* as well as its new emphasis on the role of the gods in human life and after death. With such changes, religious beliefs that offered help and truth were able to rival the traditional local, ancestral, and conventional cults of an earlier period, or at least to join them in pursuing new religious ideals. People in late antiquity could follow many cults, and conversion to a new one did not necessarily oblige the convert to desert the old.

Throughout the third and early fourth centuries even emperors reflect some of these changes. Some emperors enhanced and restored much of the traditional religion of the Olympians; the dynasty of Septimius Severus brought the worship of the Syrian sun god Elgabal to Rome; some third-century emperors also worshipped the sun, but under the title *Sol Invictus*—"The Unconquered Sun"—along with other deities. From Hadrian's curiosity about many different religions it is possible to pass into the third century and see Alexander Severus actively worshipping many different gods, including, it is said, the god of the Christians.

Although some ancient cults, serving mostly an elite, practiced secret rituals in obscure locations or at night, most of the so-called mystery religions relied on spectacles that were open to the public, consisting of recitations, music, and dancing that contained the revelation of a god to believers and potential converts. Most of these religions were ancient in Greece and Rome, and their devotees varied according to economic and social status. Their form was also adopted by some newer cults, notably those of Isis and Mithras, and one of their chief features lies in the fact that they were tied to no place of origin. They could be founded anywhere and did not depend on an original holy location or ethnic or civic sympathy among their converts. In this flexibility, they reflect some of the social characteristics of the later empire.

Mithraism, for example, which had existed since the fourth century B.C. and was made the personal religion of the emperor Commodus (180–192), acquired a certain popularity, perhaps most strongly among the more mobile elements of the imperial population such as the army. Mithras was said to have slain a great bull before he ascended to the heavens, and from the bull emerged all creatures of the world. A series of rituals above-ground and in subterranean chambers introduced initiates and a graded hierarchy of adepts to a message of Mithras's requirement that ritual purification would enable the individual soul to pass through the ordeals immediately after death and to join the saved in a pleasant afterlife. Ritual initiation saved the initiate from the dangers of "this" world and enabled the believer to use this life in order to prepare for the ordeals of the next.

Far from consisting of either pure philosophy or pure credulity, religious sensibility in late antiquity is striking in its wider scope, in its attention to more of human life, and in its concept of the individual self and its place in the cosmos.

JUDAISM IN PALESTINE AND THE DIASPORA

Judaism resembled other ancient Near Eastern religions in its ethnic and regional character, in its possession of a central cult site in Jerusalem, and in its expectations from the divinity. But it differed sharply from all others in its concept of the divinity, its rejection of all images or pictorial representations of the divinity, in its insistence on the divinity's absolute transcendence, and in its use of a book to establish and regulate belief and behavior. The God of the Jews was the creator and only divinity of the universe; he had entered into a series of covenants with the Hebrew people, whom he favored above others, in the persons of Noah, Abraham, and Moses. Just as God had made the world, one day he would end it.

The terms of the convenant were established in the text of Torah—Genesis, Exodus, Leviticus, Numbers, and Deuteronomy—which became the first five books of the Bible. These books contain a history of the creation of the universe and the world, a history of the Hebrew people, the terms of the covenants between the divinity and the Hebrews, and the rules according to which they were required by the divinity to live. Although Torah is often termed a code of law, to Jews it has always been a summation of all wisdom. The full canon of Hebrew scripture—the "books" (*biblia* in Greek) that distinguish Jews from all other peoples—as it was formalized in the first two centuries of the common era, also included two other kinds of text, the Prophets and the Writings.

The covenants were understood to have promised Hebrews an earthly kingdom of their own. The first kingdom was established around the turn of the first millennium B.C. under the kings Saul, David (1000–962 B.C.), and Solomon (961–922 B.C.), divided into the northern and southern kingdoms of Israel and Judah and lasted until 587 B.C., when the Hebrew kingdoms were conquered and many Hebrews themselves deported to Babylon. The term "Jew" derives from the name of Judah.

However, the faith survived the period known as the Babylonian Captivity, and the writings of the prophets, most strikingly those of the great poet known as Second Isaiah, not only helped to preserve the faith, but also deepened, intensified, and universalized it.

When the Babylonian Captivity ended in 537 B.C., many Jews remained in the Near Eastern World outside Palestine. For those who returned, since there was no king or royal dynasty, leadership was found in the temple priesthood and interpreters of the Law, thus actively restoring the centrality of the Temple at Jerusalem and the importance of Torah in regulating private and community life. Those Jews who remained outside Palestine shared the increasing mobility of many other peoples in the ancient Near East and Mediterranean worlds. This dispersal of the Jews, known as the *Diaspora*, located large Jewish communities in Babylon, Alexandria in Egypt, and in other cities that ringed the Mediterranean basin. Both in Palestine and in the Diaspora Jews were subjected more and more to cosmopolitan outside influences from a rapidly changing world. If the texts of the Prophets focused on a dynamic, intensified Judaism, many of the texts in the Writings—especially the books of *Proverbs* and *Wisdom*—strongly resemble contemporary non-Jewish thought and parallel non-Jewish literature. Scripture itself was translated into Greek from the third century B.C. on to serve the needs of Jews who knew no Hebrew. The most influential of these translations, the *Septuagint*, became the basis for later Christian use of Jewish scripture.

In the Jewish state after 537 B.C., priests and teachers urged obedience to the Law and reminded Jews that they were separate from non-Jews (Gentiles) and must remain so. At the same time the community was preserved under the influence alternately of Persia and Egypt until the early second century B.C. Then, the ruler of Syria, Antiochos IV Epiphanes, demanded that his own image be displayed in the Temple at Jerusalem and that Jews pay him divine honors. Jewish outrage led to a revolt that is chronicled in the *First Book of Maccabees*, and to the establishment of a much more independent Jewish state, which took its place among the other states of the region and entered into diplomatic relations with them.

The Hasmonean kings of the new state, however, began to alienate some of their earlier supporters, chiefly because they admitted some gentile social institutions and practices. One group, known as the Pharisees, became generally indifferent to the state, practicing the study of the Law, strictly observing the laws of purity and tithes, and remained indifferent to outside religious and philosophical influences. Another group, the Sadducees, were a priestly party, equally committed to the supremacy of scripture and to the ritual integrity of Judaism, but differing from the Pharisees at some points and more closely tied to the monarchy and the state. Still other groups practiced cults of personal holiness, individual devotion to God, and emphasized the mystical interpretation of the Psalms rather than the strict and literal observance of the ritual laws.

Some Jewish thinkers in Alexandria attempted to combine Greek philosophical speculation and techniques of literary interpretation with their understanding and observance of the Law. Philo Judaeus (25 B.C.–25 A.D.) devised a complex system of interpreting Jewish scripture according to which the literal sense of what scripture said was simply the first of several levels of meaning, each more esoteric than the last. Philo's technique did not immediately exert great influence among Jewish thinkers, but it later exerted enormous influence on Christian biblical scholarship and theology.

Yet another group, the Essenes, withdrew from society completely, retired to the desert, and waited for the act of divine intervention that they expected to occur at any moment. The discovery in 1947 of the Dead Sea Scrolls, the writings of a hitherto little-known Jewish sect at Qumran, has shed considerable light on the beliefs and practices of Essenes and similar groups. Still other groups focused more intensely on the apocalyptic dimension of Judaism—the idea that the end of time is at hand and that preparation for it is the greatest obligation of the believer.

Finally, besides various large groups and smaller sects, there appeared individual visionaries, prophets, and holy men whose teachings attracted groups of followers. The best-known of these to Christians was John the Baptist. Dressed in rough animal skins and living on the simplest of foods, John the Baptist taught that the judgement of God was soon to come upon His people and that repentance was essential. Repentance could be signaled by a symbolic washing in water—baptism.

These varieties of religious sensibility developed within a kingdom that came increasingly under the domination of Rome after 67 B.C. As the Roman Empire grew, Rome intervened at first indirectly, then directly in Jewish affairs, although Rome also recognized a unique status on the part of the Jews: They alone were exempted from the religious obligations that were imposed on other Roman client states. In 37 B.C., Rome installed Herod, an Idumean, as king of Judea, and Herod began to rebuild the Temple of Solomon and to admit outside social and cultural influences into the kingdom. When Judea became a Roman province in A.D. 6, Jerusalem remained its sacred city, but the port city of Caesarea became its Roman capital. Increasingly, resentment toward the successors of Herod and to the Romans on the part of some Jews made the local rulers suspicious of any movement that remotely resembled a political danger, and such repression revived the political dimension of religious sentiment. In the mid–first century A.D., a group was founded that urged the expulsion of the Romans as the only way to preserve authentic Judaism. This group, the Zealots, participated in the great revolt against Roman rule that lasted from A.D. 66 to A.D. 73 and included the destruction of the Temple in the year 70 and the slaughter at Masada in A.D. 73. After a second revolt that lasted from 131 to 135, Palestine remained a conquered Roman province until its conquest by Persia early in the seventh century and by Muslims later in the century. With the destruction of the Temple at Jerusalem, the priestly caste declined, and teachers of the Law emerged as the primary guides to worship and conduct. During the late first and second centuries A.D. the figure of the rabbi (the teacher) emerged as the chief official of each Jewish community, and the rabbinic office and the synagogue came to be characteristic features of Jewish life in Palestine and in the Diaspora.

In the late second century A.D. a revised law code called the *Mishnah* was established by a rabbinical court. Subsequent commentaries on the Mishnah by scholars in Palestine and Mesopotamia produced the Talmud, the great guide to rabbinical Judaism that formed, with Scripture, the backbone of later medieval Judaism. A second great achievement of the early rabbinical period was the final determination of the canon of authentic Scripture, which also took place in the late first and second centuries A.D.

The failure of the kingdom, the destruction of the Temple, and the annihilation of the priests and political leaders by the Romans drastically transformed the Jewish community after the first century. Scattered now throughout the Greco-Roman world, possessing only Scripture and Mishnah, the Jewish communities, led by rabbis, preserved the faith of the Law and prayer in the face of increasing indifference on the part of gentiles and increasing hostility on the part of Christians.

But Jewish history and religious genius were not the sole legacies of Judaism to the ancient and modern worlds. Among the varieties of religious sentiment that existed around the turn of the common era, one set of beliefs took shape and grew in such a way that it transformed the entire Greco-Roman world.

THE EMERGENCE OF CHRISTIANITY

Shortly before the middle of the first century A.D. a group of men and women in Galilee claimed that their master, Jesus of Nazareth, who had been tried and executed by the Romans, had been a messenger of God. They claimed that John the Baptist had so identified Jesus (Mark 1:2). They recorded Jesus' sayings, circulated them among themselves, and taught them to others. They argued that Jesus had fulfilled the central prophecies concerning the Messiah (an Aramaic term with varying interpretations, ranging from a conquering king to a messenger of God: in Greek, *ho Christos,* "the anointed one" [John 1:41]), and they embedded Jesus' sayings in a group of biographical narratives that were written between 64 and 110 A.D. These narratives, which were called *evangelia,* or "good news," were the *Gospels,* and they gave shape, consistency, and definition to Jesus' teachings, as well as inspiring great loyalty among his followers.

The problem of "the historical Jesus" has produced a vast and disputatious literature. From one perspective, Jesus as a historical figure must be understood in terms of the place and time in which he lived. The gospels illustrate much of the context of Jewish society in Judea in Jesus' lifetime. Sadducees, Pharisees, scribes, religious and political Zealots, the repentance and purification demanded by John the Baptist, guarded but sincere respect for the Temple and its priests, the urgent sense of prophecies about to be fulfilled, a filial relationship with God, and a sharp conception of sin and evil—all were current ideas in Judea during and after Jesus' lifetime. In this respect, Jesus may be understood historically as a charismatic Jewish teacher (a *hasid*: Matthew 7:28–8:1), not unlike John the Baptist himself (although Jesus personally baptized no one, his followers later did so in his name). His earliest followers were clearly rooted in the Jewish community: they practiced circumcision, worshiped at the synagogue, paid temple tithes, observed Jewish dietary laws, and worked largely among Jews for the recognition of Jesus as the prophesied Messiah.

From another perspective, however, the life of Jesus represents a sharp break with the conventional role as previously described. The biographies in the gospels of Mark, Matthew, and Luke (the last of these was really the first half of a single literary work, the second half of which is the *Acts of the Apostles*, which follows the gospels in Christian scripture) focus only on parts of Jesus' life: the circumstances of his conception and birth (which placed great emphasis on the person of his mother, Mary, and the cosmological significance of the event represented by the appearance of angels to nearby shepherds and the new celestial phenomena that guided the astrological calculations of the wise men), his confounding the learned teachers of the Temple in preparation for his coming of age, his baptism by John the Baptist and John's proclaiming that Jesus was greater than he, and the final three years of itinerant preaching, working wonders, and attracting followers (initially according to the Gospels, twelve *apostles*—the term means "those who are sent"—and a number of *disciples*). The gospels also recounted the circumstances of Jesus' trial and execution, but they also stated that Jesus had risen from the dead, resumed life among his companions for a short time, commissioned them to continue preaching his message, and rose into Heaven, from which he would soon return to judge the world. The sense of the immediacy of the Second Coming (*Parousia*) was very strong in the years following Jesus' execution, and it has remained a powerful aspect of Christianity ever since.

Although Jesus professed respect for religious institutions and ritual, he also insisted that love—between humans and God and among humans themselves—was the central religious law:

You must love the Lord your God with your whole heart, with your whole soul, and with your whole mind. This is the greatest and the first commandment. The second is like it: you must love your neighbor as yourself. On these two commandments rest the whole law, and the prophets also.

(Matthew 22:34–40)

This message is reiterated in the single commandment that Jesus was said to have added to the original ten: "This commandment I give you: that you love one another" (John 15:16). This command gained authority by the gospels' insistence that Jesus *was* God. Christians also argued that since the Godhead had long been described in terms of divine Power, Wisdom, and Love, and since the Gospel of Matthew (28:19) claimed that Jesus had commanded his followers to "baptize men everywhere in the name of the Father, the Son, and the Holy Spirit," that the divinity was in fact three persons in unity. This doctrine of the Trinity became a centerpiece of Christian theology. The problem of working out both the problem of the human and divine natures in Jesus (Christology) and that of the relation among the three persons of the Trinity (Trinitarianism) were the focus of much of the subsequent formation of Christian theological doctrine and the occasion for the most complex forms of theological disagreement. Thus, to the explicit Jewish assertion that there was only one God and that God had entered into historical covenants with the Jewish people, the followers of Jesus added a second specific historical dimension—the life, death, and resurrection of Jesus—and the assertion that as the supreme act of love God had become human and given a new definition to the obligations of humans toward God.

The beliefs of Jesus' earliest followers spread slowly, first throughout the Jewish world of Palestine and later through the Diaspora. Their enthusiasm and certainty was surely one element contributing to the success of their message, but there were other aspects of Christianity that increased its appeal as well. The doctrine of a single God who had assumed human nature at a specific historical time and in a known individual, insisting upon love as the bond between the divine and human and among humans themselves (the Christians developed the little-used Greek word *agape*, poorly understood in the twentieth-century meanings of "charity," as a designation of this love), offering salvation on the condition of repentance, belief, and a reformed code of conduct, and urging very close social bonds among believers in anticipation of the Second Coming appealed to a broad spectrum of Mediterranean society.

One of the earliest problems that Jesus' followers had to face was the question of the extent to which following Jesus was consistent with Jewish identity. Those followers who had known Jesus personally, especially Peter and James, clearly lived according to Jewish observance and preached chiefly to Jews. Resistance among Jews probably increased as the Christian message was spelled out more clearly and its implications better understood. With the increasing crisis of Jewish identity during the revolts against Rome in 66–73, the resurgence of Pharisaical Judaism limited the possibility of extending the Christian appeal among Jews, although various forms of Jewish Christianity survived in the Mediterranean world for several centuries.

The most dramatic change that came over the followers of Jesus in the decades following his execution was the increasing awareness that Christian (the term was first applied to followers of Jesus at Antioch around 66 A.D.) teachings were not to be limited to a Jewish audience but were meant for all people, gentiles as well as Jews. The central figure in this transformation was Saul, a Pharisee who had once persecuted members of the new sect, but after a vision of Jesus became an inspired interpreter and preacher of Jesus' teachings. Saul, who used the Greco-Latin form of his name, Paul, in dealing with gentiles, claimed that Jesus' teachings were aimed at all humanity, that they had entirely replaced the older covenants, even Torah itself, giving a "new law" for the "new man" that baptism had created. The earliest texts that Christians came to regard as scriptural were a series of letters that Paul sent to the various Christian communities he had visited or known, the *Epistles*. They emphasized both the universality of the Christian message and the necessity of peace and agreement within individual communities. The *Acts of the Apostles* depicts the missionary adventures of Jesus' followers, particularly in the light of Paul's ideas, and the principles of organization of the earliest Christian communities.

The appeal of Paul's message was considerable. Gentiles who became Christians were not obliged to assume a Jewish ritual identity; the command of charity broke traditional—and very strong—social and gender barriers. Jesus' earliest followers had been ordinary people, and the command of communal solidarity offered an alternative community to many gentiles, one based on love and devotion to Jesus rather than to conventional social divisions. Christians considered themselves to be a "new Israel," living under a new covenant, whose members would readily give up life itself for the sake of their beliefs. During the intermittent persecutions of Christians during the first three centuries, the steadfastness and brotherly love displayed by the martyrs ("witnesses" in Greek) attracted many converts and much respect from those who remained pagan. Tending their sick, caring for the poor and orphans, visiting prisons, sharing ritual meals, and providing decent burial for fellow-believers also reflected the attractiveness of the Christian sense of community.

Besides ameliorating some of the most oppressive effects of social barriers—including the astonishing assertion by Paul that in Christianity there was no spiritual distinction between the slave and the free person—Christianity also broke gender barriers. Although Roman law had come to recognize considerable independence on the part of women, Christianity offered women considerably greater dignity and status. Husbands were commanded to treat their wives with respect and love. Even the new Christian asceticism—the rejection of the appeal of this world in order to intensify spiritual life—offered dramatic new opportunities for feminine self-realization. Celibate virginity and widowhood became respected forms of feminine life within organized Christian communities, with particular eminence in liturgical life. Moreover, as benefactors, women who contributed property and patronage to Christian communities held a public place that was entirely new in the Roman world. The dissenting sect of Montanism included women as especially gifted prophets. Women also were notable—and extensively memorialized—victims of persecution of Christians, especially martyrdom. An important text known as *The Martyrdom of Perpetua* is the authentic memoir of the last days in prison before her execution of a young mother executed at Carthage in 202. In the veneration of martyrs, who succeeded the apostles and disciples of Jesus as the most heroic representatives of authentic Christianity, there was indeed no difference between masculine and feminine. Although Paul himself reflected considerable ambiguity about the public role of women in Christian communities, and this new ordering of gender identities and roles was greatly altered in the course of the next several centuries, the role of women in "living" Christianity throughout the Middle Ages constituted an original and immensely creative dimension of the Christian life.

SPIRIT AND FLESH, BODY AND GENDER

One important means by which Christians distinguished themselves from both Jews and pagans was the way they took up a theme that was prominent in late antique thought—the division between material and spiritual reality. A number of influential Christian thinkers applied this division in areas of religious life as different as the proper understanding of scripture (Christians were said to understand scripture "spiritually" while non-Christians, especially Jews, were said to understand it "carnally"), the authenticity of prayer and other forms of devotion (Christians prayed spiritually, others carnally), and sexual relationships. Although normative Christianity did not go to the extreme of utterly rejecting the physical body or human sexuality, it nevertheless insisted that these be lived and used in a spiritual manner. The body used in a spiritual manner could become the locus of holiness. Christians assumed that the earliest followers of Jesus had been holy, and that those Christians who had suffered martyrdom had also used the body in a spiritual way. Thus, the material bodies of these early Christian heroes (women as well as men)—that is, their relics as well as their burial places—retained that holiness, and many writers insisted that the material body as well as the soul would be resurrected after death.

Some Christian writers reinterpreted the Fall of Adam and Eve in the Garden of Eden as the result of carnal sexual activity, and they interpreted the domestic dependence and preoccupations of Roman women in marriage as reducing the spiritual capacity of women. Therefore, many early Christian writers argued for the superior spiritual status of virginity and chastity in order to overcome not only the distractions of living in the world, but the power of the senses as well as of the need to spiritualize the body.

However, not all early Christian writers agreed on these points. Some argued for an extreme rejection of the body and sexuality; others accepted and formulated a doctrine of legitimate Christian marriage. Some retained many of the Roman signs of gender differentiation, even in identifying masculinity as the true life of the spirit and femininity as signifying the flesh and the material world. Men, thus defined as having an active role, possessing power, and signifying the spirit, should rule in the Christian community. Women, passive, pow-erless, signifying the flesh, should be ruled and their spiritual experience guided and protected.

On the other hand, even the range of gender distinctions in ancient Christianity was potentially disruptive of Mediterranean tradition. Virgins could reject those aspects of marriage and domesticity (including personal wealth, clothing, and other elements of personal adornment that had defined Roman women) that critics had argued limited and distracted them from true spiritual life. Freed from those burdens, they might confine themselves to a life of prayer and study—or travel and engage autonomously in all other activities of the new Christian life. Virginity and chastity (among the married, abandoned, or wid-owed) came to be seen as a kind of parallel to martyrdom, and hence holy. Both virgins (male and female) and the chaste were believed to possess a power of prayer that benefited the entire community. Christian marriage, chaste friend-ship, and virginity thus all contributed to the transformation of older gender roles in the late antique Mediterranean world. Many women rejected outright the subordinate role (even as virgins and chaste women) that some men had as-signed to them and took seriously those elements of Christian belief that urged all Christians to dissolve bonds that might be oppressive and "material," whether to family, community, or world in order to become *new* people. Aristocratic women might remain virgins or live in chaste relationships in order to acquire personal—and spiritual—freedom. At the other end of the social scale, prosti-tutes, too, could reject their former lives, styles of dress, appearance, and be-havior, and their stories also became a popular component of early Christian devotional literature. Virgins and chaste men and women produced spiritual children—their fellow Christians whom their own devotion had inspired to lead more spiritual lives. Until the end of ancient Christianity, the debate over the lim-its and freedoms of the married, chaste, and virgin lives constituted a major element of Christian self-definition.

CONVERSION AND OPPOSITION

Christians believed that Jesus' death and resurrection from the dead freed them from the consequences of the Fall of Adam and Eve in the Garden of Eden. The Christian interpretation of the Fall insisted that all later humans carried in them original sin—the guilt incurred by Adam and Eve for disobeying God's com-mand. In this reading of Genesis, as in others, Christians came to differ sharply from Jewish interpretations, which considered the Fall as having only personal consequences for the first humans. Commitment to this doctrine made the Christian, as Paul said, "a new man," one who had literally turned his back (made a *conversio*) upon his old sinful life and nature, "the old Adam." Baptism was thought to remove the stain of original sin. Conversion stories thus came to play an influential role in understanding the Christian life, especially the story of

Paul's own highly dramatic and miraculous conversion. Conversion and the new life of bearing witness to the truth (including suffering persecution and even martyrdom) became the center of Christian conduct.

One sign of the attractiveness of Christianity is the nature of the hostility it generated. As the nature of its beliefs and practices was progressively more precisely spelled out, of course, its increasing distance from Judaism became apparent to Christians and Jews alike. Hostile pagans saw little out of the ordinary in Jesus' miracles, including the raising of the dead, since wonder-workers were routinely thought to do this. Christians not only had to separate themselves from Judaism, then, but also from accusations of being the ignorant and gullible followers of an ordinary lower-class provincial magician. Later Christian definitions of and attitudes toward genuine miracles and magic (even in northern Europe, where non-Christianity was very different from the ancient pagan world) were shaped by these early experiences.

By the second century learned pagans began to take hostile notice of Christianity's popularity. Some pagans considered it a mere eccentric offshoot of Judaism or yet another mystery religion—a "barbarian theosophy," as the philosopher Plotinus called it. One such writer, Celsus (ca. 180), produced a long diatribe against Christianity, suggesting that even intellectuals were compelled to take notice of it. One of the landmarks of early Christian literature is the long refutation of Celsus's work, the *Contra Celsum*, written by Origen (185–254), a priest of Alexandria and the greatest early Christian biblical scholar. Increasingly, other Christian writers also defended their beliefs from what they considered unfair and misrepresentative Roman pagan hostility. By the middle of the second century many of these apologists (the term means "explainers," not apologists in the modern sense) were converts from paganism and intellectuals as well. Besides Origen, the most influential of these were Justin Martyr (100–165) and Tertullian of Carthage (160–220). By the end of the second century, the appearance of Christian intellectuals who challenged pagan opponents on their own ground marks an important stage in the spread of Christianity in the Roman world. It is in the work of Tertullian, for example, that the Christian scriptures were first called the "New" Testament, thus equating them (but on a superior level) with Jewish scriptures (which Tertullian termed the "Old" Testament), and at the same time appropriating Jewish scripture for Christian use.

The first Christian communities were loosely structured societies devoted to the commemoration and expressions of loyalty to Jesus, which included a meal of thanksgiving (the original meaning of the term *eucharist*) as well as acts of charity. As Christian literature increased, communal readings followed, and Christians recognized the necessity of deciding which writings were to be considered authentically inspired, which were acceptable for purposes of increasing piety, and which were to be rejected. Considerable dissension arose over which of the many *Acts* and *Gospels* attributed to various apostles were to be regarded as authentic. By 200, however, the present canon of Christian scripture was widely accepted, and the canon was formally closed at the Council of Carthage in 397.

The fact that Christian scripture was officially accepted by a council—a formal meeting of leaders of Christian communities—suggests the organizational articulation and definition of Christian communities between the mid–first and late fourth centuries. The early Christians organized their communities (which were private clubs—and hence subject to the official licensing of private clubs, one of the justifications for legal persecution) by consciously avoiding the religious terminology of both Judaism and paganism. They termed their group an *ecclesia* (Latin; in Greek *ekklesia*), a religiously neutral term simply meaning "assembly." Both the congregation and the private buildings in which it originally assembled were termed *Kyriakos oikos*, "the lord's house (or household)"—a term that later became simply "church" in a number of modern languages. The first officers of these communities also had religiously neutral titles, including that of "overseer" (*episkopos, episcopus, bishop*), "elder" (*presbyter*, later *priest*), and "servant" (*diaconus*, later *deacon*). These titles originally designated managers of community property and organizers of meetings.

ORTHODOXY AND HETERODOXY: NORMATIVE CHRISTIANITY

Besides legal persecution from the Roman state and intellectual attacks from gentile philosophers, Christians also faced considerable dissension within their own communities. Some of this dissension occurred over the question of the Jewish character of Christianity; other issues soon followed, some of them supported by alternative versions of Scripture, the apocryphal *Acts* and *Gospels* that circulated widely before the canon of Christian scripture was closed at the Council of Carthage in A.D. 397.

The first and second centuries knew other Scriptures as well. In 1945 a discovery was made at Nag Hammadi in Egypt that was as important for the early history of Christianity as that of the Dead Sea Scrolls at Qumran. The fifty-two texts of Nag Hammadi constitute a library of Christian writings, much of it proporting to be scriptural, that reveals the widely held differences that had emerged by the late first and early second centuries among Christians. Although scholars had long known that the earliest writings of churchmen against dissidents within the Christian communities were written against such divergent beliefs, the Nag Hammadi manuscripts revealed the full extent of the variety of those beliefs for the first time.

The religious ideas they describe were called *Gnosticism*. A religious movement that probably predated Christianity, Gnosticism flowered when it was combined with selected texts of the Christian Scriptures and the story of Jesus. Gnosticism, as its name implies, offered *gnosis*, "knowledge," to its initiates, specifically a more important kind of knowledge than the normal Scriptures professed and one that was concealed from the average Christian. The Gnostic initiate, after studying highly selective versions of authentic Scripture and other texts such as those found at Nag Hammadi, discovered that the Christian story was a veil of myth concealing the "true" story of the imprisonment of the spirit in the material world and containing instructions as to how the spirit might free itself and rejoin the divinity. The attraction of Gnosticism was very powerful, and recent studies have shown that the life and beliefs of the earliest Christian communities varied far more than had once been thought.

The brief appeal of Gnosticism and the powerful criticisms of gentile philosophers suggest that the early Christian communities were as strongly influenced by the world in which they grew up as had been some of the schools of Jewish thought out of which they had emerged. But Christians did not all simply reject Gnostic ideas and ignore the criticisms of the philosophers. Slowly, Christianity absorbed some of the features of the learned and semilearned Mediterranean world. For reasons that are still not clear, Christian literature favored the use of the *codex,* a kind of manuscript book that depended on a sequence of folded sheets of papyrus or parchment bound at the edges—the earliest form of the modern book—over the older *biblos,* the scroll, from which the word *Bible* drives. Christians also adopted much of the philosophical terminology of the Greek language and some Greek patterns of thought. The Gospel of John and the sequence Luke-Acts are generally considered the earliest examples of such influence. One of the greatest pagan influences on Christianity was Neoplatonism, a philosophical movement that reached its height in the third century A.D. Its greatest pagan representatives, Plotinus (205–270), Porphyry (232–303), and Iamblichus (250–330), insisted on a rigorous program of disciplined study throughout one's life. They also provided a philosophical approach to the relation between the invisible world of pure spiritual being and the material world. They led the philosopher to perceive the subtle and harmonious links between the spiritual and material worlds, and thus elevated the material world above the sharp condemnations of original Platonic thought, on the one hand, and Gnosticism on the other. Neoplatonism thus helped provide a conceptual vocabulary for some of the controversies of Christianity, particularly in the debates over the relation between the human and divine natures of Christ. The greatest Christian representatives of Neoplatonism, Origen, and Saint Augustine, shaped the earliest philosophical terminology of Christianity.

The last assault of pagan Rome on Christianity occurred during the persecutions of Diocletian and his associates between 298 and 312. When Constantine defeated his rivals in 312, however, he claimed that the Christian God had helped him, and he made Christianity a legal religion. The so-called Edict of Milan issued by Constantine is regarded as the first legal charter of Christianity in the Roman Empire, although it did not make it an official state religion. From the reign of Constantine until the end of the Roman Empire in the West, the emperors retained their character as supreme and awesome rulers, but they also underwent one momentous change. At the end of his life Constantine proclaimed himself a Christian and was baptized. His successors, with the exception of his nephew Julian (361–363), were all Christians. Thus, although the Roman emperor could no longer call himself a god, he could—and did—act as God's representative on earth. The privileges and wealth they bestowed on the Church and the extensive influence that Christian emperors exerted on the Church's structure altered the character of Christianity as well as the nature of the relation between religion and government.

The new imperial favor greatly strengthened structures of authority that had been developing in the Christian communities since the end of the first century. With the passing of the generation which had known Jesus, and the apparent delay of the Second Coming, communities of Christians faced the problem of the location of authority, and the alternative of profound divisions of opinion, belief, and practice within individual communities and between different communities. Since all Christians agreed that the apostles had received Jesus' authentic teaching, in both the "laying on of hands" and the appearance to them of the Holy Spirit at Pentecost, the "practices" of the apostles and the idea of descent of teaching authority through the apostles came to be considered one kind of legitimation of authoritative teaching. By the second century at the latest, the figure of the bishop had come to be considered the local successor to the apostles, and hence the authentic teacher and interpreter of doctrine.

A number of texts also emphasized particular events in the life of Jesus that were interpreted as having universal importance to Christians. Thus, the baptism of Jesus was incorporated as a ritual accepting new members into the Christian community; the Last Supper was identified with the eucharistic meal and understood as a participation in the substance of Jesus; the act of making a bishop (originally locally elected, and later blessed by other bishops) was also regarded as deriving from significant and prophetic events in Jesus' life. These ritual acts came to be called *sacraments*, and the right to administer them restricted to bishops, although some of them might be delegated to presbyters, deacons, and originally at least to virgins and widows. Bishops therefore came to be thought of as possessing sacramental, magisterial (teaching), and governing authority.

On the basis of this process of organization and the emergence of the figure of the bishop, the agreement of the bishops of different communities created what has been called "normative Christianity," or "catholic [universal] Christianity," that is a set of doctrines, sacred texts, and ritual practices that were accepted by legitimate authority and passed on to successive generations of authority as *tradition* ("that which is handed down"). Bishops agreed on short statements of doctrine to which their communities were expected to assent—creeds (from the Latin *credo*, "I believe"). Bishops assembled in occasional meetings, particularly after the legalization of Christianity in 312, that came to be called *synods* and *councils*. Councils produced widespread agreement about common matters, including the official, or "canonical" text of Christian scripture. This process of organization contributed to the homogenization of normative Christianity across the Roman Empire and constituted a framework of doctrinal authority against which dissent and deviance might be measured and defined. Belief and behavior that agreed with the universal consensus was termed *orthodoxy* ("right teaching or opinion"). Increasingly, whatever belief and behavior that did not agree was termed *heterodoxy* ("different teaching or opinion"). Before the legalization of Christianity in 312, these matters were internal to the Christian communities of the Roman Empire. After 312, however, and particularly after the conversion of Constantine and later emperors to Christianity, they became matters of state as well.

By the fourth century religious dissent within Christianity had proliferated and acquired new forms. Although Gnosticism ceased to be a problem by the end of the third century, other sets of belief had arisen to take its place, several of them not, strictly speaking, theological at all.

The first problem of dissension among Christians that came to imperial attention was that of Donatism, a sect originating in a disputed episcopal election in North Africa. Donatists claimed that Christian clergy who had submitted to imperial threats of persecution during the period 298–312 had to be rebaptized before being accepted again into the Christian community. By extension, Donatism posed the larger question of the relation between the moral character of individuals, priests, or lay persons and the indelibility of sacraments. How could a community be absolutely certain of the moral worth of its clergy and members? A secret sin by a priest might wipe away his sacramental power and plunge his entire congregation into damnation. The orthodox response to Donatism became a fundamental ecclesiological doctrine of the Christian community. The efficacy of the sacraments depends only upon the canonical ordination of a cleric, not upon his personal state of grace. With a little help from Roman law, one of the fundamental premises of ecclesiology took shape in the fourth-century Donatist experience.

The Donatist schism was resolved formally by a council of clergy that met under imperial direction at Carthage in 411. The institution of an assembly of churchmen under imperial supervision dealt with many similar crises in the ensuing two centuries, and this first great age of Church councils had a major influence upon the shape of Christian belief and life. Struggles between orthodox and heterodox beliefs, often with "orthodoxy" becoming sharply defined after the fact, also centered on Christology (the problem of the divine and human natures of Christ) and trinitarianism (the character of the three persons in the Trinity).

The most significant heresy in Christological history was that of Arius, a priest of Alexandria, who maintained that Christ had been created by God and hence was inferior to the Father, a doctrine that had wide appeal and wide consequences. Christ-founded institutions, for example, the Church and the sacraments, could be considered inferior to the power of the Father, or the emperor. The ensuing quarrels brought into Christian theology the full force of the Greek philosophical vocabulary, and the quarrel raged for more than two centuries.

The Council of Nicaea in 325 laid down what ultimately became the orthodox dogma, that Christ and the Father were *homoousios,* "of the same essence." Nevertheless, the divisions among the clergy, the contrary opinions of successive emperors, and the philosophical arena that had been opened by the free discussions of learned bishops heralded many of the future difficulties in the definition of theological orthodoxy. The imperial Christianity of the fourth century transformed both the empire and the Church.

Religious dissent and ecclesiastical organization were not the only areas of imperial activity to benefit the Christians. Christian emperors also drifted further away from paganism, even from the purely formal priesthoods and titles that they held as part of the imperial office. By the third quarter of the fourth century, emperors had become actively hostile to paganism. In 382 Gratian withdrew many of the funds that had supported pagan cults and priesthoods, and he removed the Altar of Victory, a venerable pagan symbol, from the Senate House. In spite of moving and articulate appeals from pagans, Saint Ambrose, bishop of Milan (339–397), convinced the emperors to keep such pagan symbols out of public places. The emperor Theodosius (379–395) outlawed all pagan practices in 392. As the aristocracy, the intellectuals, and the emperors themselves became Christians, the intellectual and social prestige they had once brought to paganism was diverted to Christianity. Only the popular culture of the urban lower classes and the rural peasantry of the empire were providing significant resistance to Christianity by the end of the fourth century. These classes provided both the last pagan resistance in the ancient world and some of the most significant new movements within Christianity itself.

CHRISTIANS ABANDONING THE WORLD: HERMITS AND MONKS

The problem of the conflict between the flesh and the spirit that produced such differing views on scriptural interpretation, prayer, conscience, and sexuality in ancient Christianity was not finally resolved by the Christianization of the Roman Empire. In fact, as tensions developed between imperially organized and culturally assimilated Christianity and individuals who feared that Christianity would be swallowed up by too close an identification with the "world," the ascetic element in ancient Christian thought became more and more prominent. To accept the world or to flee it in various ways was a choice that opened a divison in Christian Roman society from the highest to the lowest ranks—both aristocrats and peasants could make the choice to withdraw from the world and its temptations. The development of the ascetic Christian life constituted a second major consequence of the problem of Christianity and the world.

About the year 269, Anthony, a young man from a prosperous peasant family in Egypt, moved by Christ's injunction to "go, sell all you have and give to the poor and follow me," left his family and the narrow agricultural belt of the

Nile Valley and went out into the desert to live a life of devotion. From the time of earliest Egyptian civilization, the desert had symbolized the emptiness of the world and the habitation of demons. To Egyptians the desert represented the annihilation of everything remotely connected with civilization, and Anthony's self-imposed exile was a literal and figurative rejection of both the imperial church and the ancient, deep-rooted Egyptian terror of the waste. The name that Egyptians gave to Anthony and whose who followed him was a Greek word, *anachoresis,* which traditionally described those who had fled from the pressures of civilization into the hostile wilderness. The first anchorites were thus thought of as rejecting both the dangers of a secularized church and the social roots of civilization itself. Anthony attracted a number of followers, although he moved several times further away from civilization. His struggles with the demons of the desert, themselves a combination of Christian belief and traditional Egyptian peasant folklore, attracted much admiration, and by the midfourth century the image of the isolated holy man had developed as a successor to the more dramatic ideal of an earlier Christian age—that of martyrdom and persecution suffered for the faith.

The *Life of Saint Anthony,* written by Athanasius, the pugnacious Alexandrian defender of orthodoxy against Arianism (the heresy of Arius), was translated into Latin before 386 and started a new genre of Christian literature. The lives and passions of the early martyrs had constituted the most popular literature in the third- and early fourth-century Church. In the era of religious persecutions of 298–312 martyrdom came to be considered the highest stage of the life of the spirit, one that brought man and woman to the very threshold of heaven. Anthony and the other hermits of Egypt and Syria offered a new kind of religious ideal, the monk. Here was a "martyr" whose martyrdom consisted of making himself "dead" to the world and achieving in the desert—through rigorous self-discipline, contemplation, combats with demons, and, ultimately, mystical experience—that stage of the spiritual life that the martyrs had reached in so different a way in so different a world.

The spiritual biographies of early monks, inspired by the vast popularity of Athanasius's *Life of Saint Anthony,* became the new literature of piety and the guide to the new spiritual life. Ironically, the spread of monastic popularity attracted the interest of the very world that the monks had rejected so dramatically. Lives of the "desert fathers" were widely read, and Christians thronged into the desert to consult the holy men, just as they had once made pilgrimages to the sites of earlier martyrdoms, some taking up the monastic life themselves and some returning to the corrupting world invigorated by their brief contact with the monastic ideal.

Increasingly, as the historian Peter Brown has shown, holiness in late antiquity began to shift its location from things and places to persons—to holy men. Such figures were thought to possess not only divine favor, but literally some of the power that characterized both divine and high levels of human power in society. Thus, holy men became for a time also intercessors between local communities and the authorities of the larger world. They replaced both the aristocratic patron and the pagan oracle, and their power was thought to manifest itself through miracles, curses, and exorcism—the driving out of demons—as well as through the social and economic benefits that they brought to the communities that venerated them.

Anthony and Athanasius were both men, but the ascetic life was not restricted to men. Just as virginity and chastity offered new roles and a new degree of freedom to women, so did the ascetic movement. Aristocratic women, too, might divest themselves of their wealth and their social and domestic responsibilities in order to pursue a quest for religious freedom in much the same way as men. And although aristocratic women had a better opportunity to do this, women from other social orders could follow a similar renunciation of the world. Two of the most prominent literary motifs in this movement are conversions to the ascetic life of the aristocratic woman and the reformed prostitute, each of whom could become a new person, not by assuming male identity or power, but by changing their former lives in so radical a way as to find in one type of the Christian life an original form of religious expression. Jesus himself had given the example of the two sisters, Mary and Martha, which later Christians interpreted as representing the contemplative and active lives, as they interpreted the biblical figures of Rachel and Leah, showing greater favor to Mary, the contemplative. Alongside the "Desert Fathers" there lived the "Desert Mothers," who asserted that the ascetic life, virginity, chastity, poverty, and world-renunciation were an ungendered neutral ground for both masculine and feminine religious expression. The place of religious women in the movement of hermitism and monasticism was the cause of a long debate in subsequent centuries of Christian Europe.

The variety of forms of monasticism was great during the fourth century. Some men retired to caves in the desert; some, especially the Syrians, took to living atop tall pillars for decades; some subjected themselves to extreme bodily tortures and privations. In the late fourth and early fifth centuries monasticism began to change. Small communities grew up around famous hermits, and these began to become organized. Under the influence of Saint Pachomius (286–346), a former soldier in the army of Constantine, an organized monastic life appeared in Egypt. Later, under the influence of Saint Basil of Caesarea (329–379), monastic organization evolved in the east as well. By constituting a model, or "perfect," Christian society, these communities offered a moral pattern whose elements might be absorbed slowly by the broader society around them. People considered the monastery, untroubled by the upheavals of the world around it, the example of ideal Christian society, a copy of heaven. By the beginning of the fifth century, monasteries were flourishing in Gaul and Italy as well as in North Africa, Egypt, Syria, and Greece. The monks, the new heroes of

Christianity, represented the tradition of rejecting the secularization of Christianity, which the martyrs had originated. The appeal of the monks, like that of the martyrs, transcended the bounds of learning, philosophy, and social class. In monasticism the devotion of the humble man and woman to God was raised to the highest level of Christian life and therefore militated against the increasing secularization of the Church.

Monasticism in a sense balanced the secular success of the Church in the fourth and fifth centuries and thus helped the Church retain its deep roots in the lower orders of society and in its concept of the relation between the individual, however lowly, and God. Henceforth, the Christian adaptations of pagan learning and Christian monasticism were to be the twin supports of the spread of Christianity, both inside Roman imperial society and in the world of the barbarians, a world ultimately more important than the demon-infested deserts or the well-stocked libraries of the urban fathers.

CHRISTIANS ORDERING THE WORLD: EMPERORS AND CHURCHMEN

The new prestige of bishops in the Christianized Roman Empire brought a new kind of adviser into the imperial court. Leaders of Christian communities were the only ones able to advise emperors about ecclesiastical matters; emperors in their turn relied more and more upon bishops as a kind of administrative class for ecclesiastical affairs and for those imperial affairs that touched ecclesiastical interests. Under Constantine, the bishops Hosius of Cordoba and Eusebius of Caesarea served as theological advisers. Eusebius wrote not only Constantine's biography but also the first history of the Church, which ended with his vision of a golden age of Christianity under benevolent Roman emperors. At the same time, the Church itself was strengthened by the appearance of a new, militant type of churchman, whose career, influence, and writings helped shape an administrative kind of ecclesiastical authority that was strong enough to survive the later collapse of Roman imperial government in the West and furnish a prototype of ecclesiastical authority that later influenced medieval and modern ecclesiastical institutions.

An excellent example of this type is Ambrose. He was born into the Roman aristocracy, the son of the praetorian prefect of Gaul, at Trier around 339. Ambrose entered the imperial civil service and became governor of Milan, one of the important centers of imperial administration. When the Arian bishop of Milan died in 374, the orthodox population acclaimed Ambrose as bishop, although Ambrose was only a believer and had not yet been baptized.

Ambrose at first protested his inadequacy, but he then devoted himself for more than twenty years to his flock. Throughout his episcopacy Ambrose stoutly defended orthodox beliefs, maintained the independence of the Church from the imperial government, and created in his writings what has ever since been the standard guide for a Christian bishop. In 390, after the emperor Theodosius ordered the massacre of the Christian population of Thessalonica because it had disobeyed an imperial command, Ambrose forbade Theodosius from participating in Christian liturgical ceremonies and forced the emperor to perform penance for his act. Thus, Ambrose may be regarded as one the strongest early defenders of the superiority of the spiritual authority over the temporal power, especially in matters of belief and ecclesiastical moral discipline. Ambrose's writings not only made him the model of the ideal Christian bishop, but they also reveal in his life and thought the influence of late antique Neoplatonic philosophy and the continuing influence of traditional Roman concepts of public responsibility and civic morality that had been expressed by Cicero.

Ambrose and Theodosius were not the only remarkable ecclesiastical-political figures of the late fourth century. The pontificate of Damasus (366–384) as bishop of Rome helped increase the prestige of that see by renewing the Christian history of Rome, turning the catacombs into shrines, and patronizing the cults of the martyrs in the city. Damasus also cooperated with Theodosius's ecclesiastical pronouncements on orthodoxy, and in return Theodosius recognized formally the preeminence of the bishop of Rome as successor to Peter the Apostle.

Damasus was one of the first of a series of dynamic popes whose efforts to elevate the see of Rome over other churches laid the foundations of the medieval and modern papacy. Angered by Theodosius's elevation of the patriarch of Constantinople, "the new Rome," to a position of personal authority second only to that of Rome, Damasus became the first Pope to use the title "apostolic" in connection with his see and began addressing other bishops as "sons" instead of "brothers" in his correspondence. Damasus's fifth-century successors as bishop of Rome continued the struggle for ecclesiastical primacy. Siricius (384–399) was the first to use the title *papa*, or pope, for the bishop of Rome, and Innocent I (401–417) claimed that important cases should be judged only by the pope. By the time of Pope Leo I (440–461), the greatest of the popes who held office before the end of the sixth century, the bishop of Rome had clearly emerged as the successor of the senatorial guardians of imperial tradition and as the highest-ranking churchman in Christendom.

The prestige of individual bishops such as Saint Ambrose and the slow rise to prominence of the bishop of Rome were two of the forces that contributed to the success of Christianity between 350 and 450. The devotion of Theodosius shaped the structure of imperial Christianity, and the emergence of a series of remarkable theologians between 350 and 450 marked the Christian absorption and transformation of pagan culture. The most articulate and influential spokesman for Christianity during this period, though far from the most politically powerful, was the African Augustine, bishop of Hippo in North Africa. Augustine was one of the "new provincials" whose secular and ecclesiastical career revealed much about Christianity and about Roman society as well.

The Silver Plate of Theodosius. This plate shows a highly formalized scene of the emperor Theodosius investing an official with his rank of office, catching the extreme sense of hierarchy still present at the end of the fourth century. (*Photographie Giraudon*)

The great Cappadocian Fathers of the mid and late fourth century—Basil of Caesarea, Gregory of Nyssa, and Gregory Nazianzus—also represented the intellectual and spiritual vigor of what had hitherto been remote and backward provinces on the fringe of the empire. Their influence extended not only to monasticism and the eastern churches but to the arch-Roman, Ambrose, himself.

Born at Thagaste in North Africa in 354, the son of poor, free peasants, Augustine was reared by his Christian mother, Monica. Augustine's parents were unable to afford more than minimal schooling for their precocious son, but a wealthy fellow citizen undertook the expense of his continuing education at Carthage. From Carthage Augustine's success as a teacher of rhetoric brought him to Rome, and thence, in 384 under the sponsorship of the great pagan noble Symmachus, to the professorship of rhetoric at Milan, then the greatest city in Italy and an imperial capital.

Until Augustine was thirty, his career as a successful intellectual had been a classical illustration of "making it" in an open and receptive social system. From his professorship at Milan, Augustine was eligible for marriage into an aristocratic and wealthy family. With these credentials he could obtain a high administrative post in the empire, possibly a provincial governorship or the position of tutor to a future emperor. A generation earlier, the Bordeaux professor Ausonius had parlayed his own status as tutor of the emperor Gratian into a praetorian prefecture and a position of power behind the throne of Gratian. There was no reason, save one, why Augustine's career should not have followed a similar path. That reason was Augustine's restless spirit.

In the course of his education and social success, Augustine had encountered intellectually the rich spectrum of spiritual experience that the fourth-century Roman world had to offer. He had embraced Neoplatonism and the dualist Manichean heresy, a derivative of Persian Zoroastrianism that had grown up in the third century A.D., and flirted with mystery religions. Two hundred years before, the brilliant North African Apuleius had embraced the mystery religion of Isis and left a remarkable novel, *The Golden Ass,* which paints a vivid picture of imperial life and the attraction of such mystery religions. But Augustine was not to be another Ausonius, or another Apuleius either. The pressures from his mother had followed him to Italy, and the emptiness in his own heart, as he was later to say, made the varieties of spiritualism he had experienced so far only dim and faulty shadows. In Milan, however, Augustine met Ambrose and the influence of the older man began to turn the professor's mind back to the Christianity that he had ignored for so long. After a moving personal religious experience, Augustine returned to Christianity in 386, renounced his professorship, and returned to Africa, there to become the bishop of the coastal city of Hippo Regius.

Augustine left one of the most remarkable documents in literary history, his *Confessions,* written in 397. This work is the first intellectual self-portrait in history; in it Augustine offered not the external events of his life but the "history of a heart," the story of his own religious experience told from the viewpoint of a middle-aged bishop. In his *Confessions* Augustine transformed the traditional conversion story into the scheme of a whole life of individual struggles to come to terms with the traces of God—the *vestigia Dei*—in the human soul. For Augustine, the discovery of the will of God, the conversion, was the climax of human life. But Augustine's work was not one of saccharine spiritualism; the *Confessions* read more like "the account of a great spiritual disease and its convalescence" than like the heroic martyr or conversion stories of old. Augustine keeps constantly before his and the reader's eyes the full complexity of human feeling and habit. Nowhere does he betray that complexity, nowhere does he offer an easy life as a result of his experience. Augustine was perhaps the first writer to reveal his own personality as the only means of describing accurately both the spiritual disorder that pervades the life of the man who ignores God and the continuing burden of the human condition after conversion, even during the episcopate. While bishop of Hippo (395–430), Augustine witnessed the great ecclesiastical reforms of Theodosius and his successors, but his role was not that of imperial adviser of Ambrose. Augustine ruled his city and wrote commentaries on Scripture and treaties on dogma, sermons, and letters—270 of them—on all aspects of Christian belief and thought. More than any other Church Father, Augustine shaped the future intellectual development of Western Christianity.

Augustine's vast literary output made him the foremost Latin theologian of the Christian world, a thinker whose work has influenced churchmen, lay people, and philosophers down to the present. His commentaries on Scripture formed the basis for all later medieval and Reformation biblical interpretation, and his letters and treatises laid down advice and combated heresy throughout his life.

Perhaps his most influential work was his immensely long and intricate treatise *The City of God.* The military disasters of the early fifth century had called forth from many pagans the accusation that Rome's misfortune was the result of the abandonment of her old gods and the taking up of the Christian religion. From 413 to 426 Augustine undertook to refute this argument and to lay down the principles of the ideal relations between earthly society and the spiritual community of Christian believers. His thesis was that there were two "cities," the city of God and the city of the world. Insofar as Christians have to live in the world for a time, they may make use of worldly institutions in order to have peace in fallen nature. But the Christian's ultimate loyalty and concern ought to be directed to the afterlife and salvation, and no earthly society, not even a Christian Roman Empire, is anything more than the unstable creation of mortals. The duty of the rulers of any earthly society, especially Christian rulers, is to curb the baser instincts of fallen human nature and preserve that earthly peace that is necessary for the conduct of the Christian life. Such a ruler is a "godly magistrate," rather than an absolute sovereign, and his duties are regulatory and punitive, rather than constructive and progressive. Augustine further denied that the pagan gods had ever helped Rome. *The City of God* became the first and in many ways still the most impressive expression of a Christian philosophy of both history and government. As such, it has remained one of the most influential works of the late antique world and a challenge to the validity of any purely secular view of history or governmental philosophy.

Ambrose and Augustine came to be considered the first of the Latin Fathers of the Church because of the sanctity of their lives and the subsequent influence of their thought. The third Latin Father was Jerome. Jerome received a good literary education, became influential in aristocratic and learned circles in Christian Rome, and was a protégé of Pope Damasus I. Upon Damasus's death Jerome was considered as his potential successor, but social and literary rivalry prevented his election. Jerome settled in Bethlehem and devoted the rest of his life to doctrinal disputes and to his great translation of and commentaries on Scripture. Jerome's knowledge of historical Greek and Hebrew was pressed into service as he undertook this work, and he finally translated the entire Old and New Testaments into Latin, a monumental work both of scholarship and of cultural achievement. The Latin Vulgate, as his translation is called, provided for the first time the entirety of Scripture in a language available to everyone in the West. Jerome's choice of a middle-style, administrative Latin instead of an elaborate literary Latin made a great impact on both Latin theology and the later development of European thought.

Under the rule of generally cooperative Christian emperors during most of the fourth and fifth centuries, not only did Christianity become the only legal religion—and the official religion—of the Roman Empire, but it developed a strong Latin character it had not originally possessed. The great works of fourth- and fifth-century Latin Christianity distinguished their own period and have exerted organizational and intellectual influences ever since. Even with the final transformation of the Roman world and the disappearance of imperial government in the West, the foundations of Latin Christian culture survived to influence the new rulers and peoples of Europe for many centuries.

FURTHER READING

On gentile Greco-Roman religion, see Ramsay MacMullen, *Paganism in the Roman Empire* (New Haven-London: Yale University Press, 1981); John Ferguson, *Religions of the Roman Empire* (Ithaca-London: Cornell University Press, 1970); J. H. W. G. Liebeschutz, *Continuity and Change in Roman Religion* (Oxford: Clarendon Press, 1979); Luther H. Martin, *Hellenistic Religions* (New York: Oxford University Press, 1987); Arnaldo Momigliano, *The Conflict Between Paganism and Christianity in the Fourth Century* (Oxford: Oxford University Press, 1963); Johannes Geffcken, *The Last Days of Greco-Roman Paganism* (New York-Amsterdam: North Holland, 1978).

On Judaism, see the General Bibliography.

On the "historical" Jesus, see the work of Geza Vermes, most recently, *The Religion of Jesus the Jew* (London: SCM, 1993), and Paula Fredriksen, *From Jesus to Christ* (New Haven-London: Yale University Press, 1988).

On the early communities of Christians, see Howard Clark Kee, *Who Are the People of God? Early Christian Models of Community* (New Haven-London: Yale University Press, 1995), and Wayne A. Meeks, *The First Urban Christians* (New Haven-London: Yale University Press, 1983). On the impact of Christianity, see

Robin Lane Fox, *Pagans and Christians* (New York: Viking, 1986); Robert L. Wilken, *The Christians As the Pagans Saw Them* (New Haven-London: Yale University Press, 1984); Ramsay MacMullen, *Christianizing the Roman Empire* (New Haven-London: Yale University Press, 1984); Stephen Benko, *Pagan Rome and the Early Christians* (Bloomington: Indiana University Press, 1984); R. A. Markus, *Christianity in the Roman World* (London-New York: Thames and Hudson, 1974).

On the history of sacred architecture, see L. Michael White, *Building God's House in the Roman World: Architectural Adaptation among Pagans, Jews, and Christians* (Baltimore: Johns Hopkins University Press, 1990).

For early Christianity in general, see Angelo Di Berardino, ed., *Encyclopedia of the Early Church* (New York: Oxford University Press, 1992), and Everett Ferguson, et al., *Encyclopedia of Early Christianity* (New York-London: Garland, 1990).

On Christian anti-Judaism, see Robert L. Wilken, *John Chrysostom and the Jews* (Berkeley-Los Angeles: University of California Press, 1983), and Arnaldo Momigliano, *On Pagans, Jews, and Christians* (Middletown: Wesleyan University Press, 1987). On the Christian appropriation of Palestine, see P. W. L. Walker, *Holy City, Holy Places? Christian Attitudes to Jerusalem and the Holy Land in the Fourth Century* (Oxford: Clarendon Press, 1990), and E. D. Hunt, *Holy Land Pilgrimage in the Later Roman Empire A.D. 312–460* (Oxford: Clarendon Press, 1982).

On the question of the body and gender, see the work of Ross Shepard Kraemer, cited at the end of Chapter 1, and A. Cameron and A. Kuhrt, eds., *Images of Women in Late Antiquity* (London: Croom Helm, 1983); Gillian Clark, *Women in Late Antiquity: Pagan and Christian Lifestyles* (Oxford: Clarendon Press, 1993); Peter Brown, *The Body and Society: Men, Women and Sexual Renunciation in Early Christianity* (New York: Columbia University Press, 1988); Elizabeth Clark, *Women in the Early Church* (Wilmington: Glazier, 1983); Jo Ann McNamara, *A New Song: Celibate Women in the First Three Christian Centuries* (New York: Haworth, 1983); Joyce E. Salisbury, *Church Fathers, Independent Virgins* (London-New York: Verso, 1991).

On normative Christianity, see Joseph H. Lynch, *The Medieval Church: A Brief History* (London-New York: Longman, 1992). On dissent, see Edward Peters, *Heresy and Authority in Medieval Europe* (Philadelphia: University of Pennsylvania Press, 1980). Useful source collections are those of Karl F. Morrison, *The Church in the Roman Empire*, University of Chicago Readings in Western Civilization, Vol. III (Chicago: University of Chicago Press, 1986), and Brian Croke and Jill Harries, *Religious Conflict in Fourth-Century Rome* (Sydney: Sydney University Press, 1982). On Gnosticism, see Giovanni Filoromo, *A History of Gnosticism* (Oxford: Basil Blackwell, 1988).

On the ascetic life, see Philip Rousseau, *Pachomius: The Making of a Community in Fourth-Century Egypt* (Berkeley-Los Angeles: University of California Press, 1986), and Rousseau, *Ascetics, Authority and the Church in the Age of Jerome and Cassian* (Oxford: Clarendon Press, 1978); C. H. Lawrence, *Medieval Monas-*

ticism, 2nd ed. (London-New York: Longman, 1989); Giles Constable, *Medieval Monasticism: A Select Bibliography* (Toronto: University of Toronto Press, 1976).

On Augustine, see Peter Brown, *Augustine of Hippo* (Berkeley-Los Angeles: University of California Press, 1969); on Jerome, J. N. D. Kelly, *Saint Jerome* (London: Duckworth, 1975).

Much of both pagan and Christian late antiquity has been illuminated by the works of Peter Brown: *The World of Late Antiquity* (cited in Chap. 1); *Religion and Society in the Age of Saint Augustine* (New York: Harper & Row, 1972); *The Making of Late Antiquity* (Cambridge MA: Harvard University Press, 1978); *The Cult of the Saints: Its Rise and Function in Late Antiquity* (Chicago: University of Chicago Press, 1981); *Society and the Holy in Late Antiquity* (Berkeley-Los Angeles: University of California Press, 1982); *The Body and Society* (previously cited); *Power and Persuasion in Late Antiquity: Towards a Christian Empire* (Madison: University of Wisconsin Press, 1992).

3

THE TRANSFORMATIONS
OF THE ROMAN WORLD

NEW ROME AND OLD ROME

The unity of the ancient Mediterranean world, that of "a slender coastline studded with classical city-states," was economic, cultural, and political, but it was felt
most by a small ruling elite and their servants. In the third and fourth centuries
the demands of the vast hinterland empire that protected the coastline put great
strains on both imperial resources and the unity of the Mediterranean world. The
diplomacy of Trajan and the universal curiosity of Hadrian gave way, once the
military and political problems of the third century had been settled, to the heavy-
handed managerial techniques of Diocletian and Constantine. Although their
fourth- and fifth-century successors attempted to restore the civilian and aristocratic character of the empire, the divisions within the Mediterranean core of the
empire became sharper as the fourth and fifth centuries wore on. Besides the increasingly sharp divisions between the eastern and western halves of the empire,
the emergence of Islam in the early seventh century introduced yet a third force
into that world. From the early seventh century on, although some elements of
Mediterranean unity were preserved, the most striking feature of Cicero's *orbis terrarum*—the "circle of the lands"—was its division into three parts, each of which
became the share of one of the three great civilizations that characterized the medieval world: East Roman, West Roman/Northern European, and Islamic.

For six centuries the Roman empire ruled, but never fully absorbed the Mediterranean world. Local languages, cultural forms, and material technology continued to exist under the indifferent surface of imperial government and elite culture. In the late fourth and fifth centuries imperial government made greater demands on all levels of imperial society, but it also eroded some of the structural elements that had for a long time sustained the universal character of the empire. During this period local culture, economy, and technology broke through the surface of imperial civilization and reasserted themselves, often in the face of imperial resentment and impotence.

The network of cities and the communications links among them, the observance of public calendars, and even the villas of aristocrats all changed. The cities, those "checkerboard towns" previously mentioned, had long depended on the private support of both local aristocrats and the decurion order; as private wealth declined within the cities and public responsibilities increased, the maintenance of cities lost its chief support. Aristocrats and decurions alike withdrew to their private estates, and the villa with its private interests and leisure replaced the city and its responsibilities in the attentions of those on whom the support of the cities had long depended. The observance of a common universal imperial calendar tended to disappear. In the eastern part of the empire, where there were 900 cities, most of them productive and possessing strong commercial institutions, this transformation was slow and never complete. In the western part of the empire, where there were only 114 cities, the transformation was drastic. One useful way of indicating the consequences of this long process is to tell a tale of two cities—Rome and Constantinople.

The emperors in the western part of the empire during the fourth century found that Rome was no longer an efficient capital, and they ruled instead from a number of different cities in northern Italy and Gaul: Trier, Milan, and finally, at the end of the century, from Ravenna on the northeastern coast of Italy. Not only was Ravenna easily defensible against invaders and closer to the sphere of the Rhine-Danube frontier, but it was a port city, and from it the imperial court had easy access to the new capital of the eastern part of the empire, Constantinople, the "New Rome."

After his victory at the Milvian Bridge in 312, Constantine turned against the Roman Senate and the praetorian guard that had supported his rival Maxentius, dissolved the guard forever, and several years later departed from Rome for the east. There, on the site of the small fishing town of Byzantium, he founded a new city named after himself: Constantine's *polis*, or Constantinople. Located on a triangular peninsula between the Bosporous and the Sea of Marmara (bodies of water that link the Black Sea with the Aegean) and the point at which Asia and Europe meet, Constantinople benefited from Constantine's generosity and that of his successors. It became a vast new city that rivaled and surpassed old Rome. In 450 Theodosius II expanded the city walls, creating masterpieces of fortification that withstood nearly every invader until they were breached by

Ottoman Turkish cannon in 1453. The location, wealth, and security of Constantinople proved to be extremely effective in ruling the eastern part of the empire, and the eastern part of the empire remained attractive to those in the West, particularly in periods of insecurity and invasion. The sea route between Constantinople and Ravenna was, until the eighth century, the connecting link between the slowly separating cultures of the two halves of the Roman Empire.

The founding of Constantinople was an act of Roman daring—and of Roman genius. Not only was the city strategically located to rule the eastern part of the empire efficiently, well managed to provide a high standard of living for its inhabitants, and securely fortified, but it also constituted a center for using the vast resources of the largely Greek-speaking, urbanized, agriculturally and commercially prosperous, and intellectually developed East Mediterranean world. The cities of Antioch, Alexandria, Beirut, Thessalonica, and Athens were centers of a developed intellectual, educational, commercial, and religious and artistic culture. Agricultural technology permitted small landowners and small towns to prosper. Literary and educational traditions permitted intellectual and religious life to flourish and provided a body of personnel for governmental administration. From the lowest levels of society all the way up to the imperial court, the East Roman Empire was far better prepared to meet the invasions and other crises of the late fourth and fifth centuries than was that of the West.

From the late fourth century on, the strength of Constantinople and the East Roman Empire was demonstrated beyond any doubt, as wave after wave of invading peoples broke through the imperial frontiers, failed to take Constantinople (or, except on a few occasions, before the sixth century, *any* substantial part of the East), and invariably moved west to assault the weaker and less resourceful centers of the western part of the empire. The experience of invasion was one of many elements that sharpened the divisions between East and West Rome and contributed substantially to the creation of new worlds.

MIGRANTS AND INVADERS

The relations between Romans and *externae gentes* had always been more complex even than writers like Julius Caesar and Tacitus wanted to admit. The provincial Romanization of Celts and Germans, the mixed society on either side of the Rhine-Danube frontiers, the existence of *laeti,* and the admission of whole peoples as *federati* of the Roman state and army all blurred any clear line between Romans and "barbarians"—if such a line had ever existed anywhere but in the imagination of Roman writers and politicians. The Roman society that encountered Germanic and other migrants and invaders from the late fourth century on was very different from that which had created the empire in the first place, and its own circumstances must be understood in order to understand the impact of barbarian migrants and invaders in the late fourth, fifth, and sixth centuries.

The rising costs of the armies, the bureaucratic steps taken to meet them—taxation and a larger imperial bureaucracy—and the increasingly barbarian composition of the armies placed great strain on the Roman tradition of voluntary public service upon which much of the empire in the west depended. Those who could afford to do so—and were not prohibited from leaving the cities by imperial decrees—withdrew from civic participation to the leisure of their country estates. They became increasingly indifferent to public matters, even supporting rebellious imperial claimants or local barbarian rulers when it suited them. One manifestation of the transformed concerns of Gallo-Roman aristocrats was their assumption of the role of Christian bishop—perhaps as a substitute for their failed former role as voluntary civic benefactors. The emergence of the aristocratic bishop was one consequence of the transformation of the fourth-century Roman provincial world in Gaul.

Others from lower social orders also fled the network of imperial bureaucrats, tax collectors, and soldiers to the protection of landed aristocrats. Even members of these orders contributed, as did their aristocratic protectors, to the increasingly private character of the Roman west. The new society at the end of the fifth century had two levels—aristocratic lords and protectors, virtually independent of any public authority, and their politically and economically dependent servants. Such a society could accommodate any public authority that did not make excessive demands and permitted it to go its own way, whether that authority was Roman or barbarian.

It is in this context that the problem of the "barbarians" in the late fourth, fifth, and sixth centuries must be understood. From the encounters in the late second century between Marcus Aurelius and the Marcomanni, it is clear that the formation of Germanic peoples beyond the frontiers had changed from its earlier character. Large-scale migrations from the area of the Baltic Sea moved southward, restructuring existing peoples along the frontier into new and larger groups increasingly geared for war. Far to the east of the Roman frontier, still other "barbarian" peoples, Asiatic nomadic pastoralists and warriors, also assembled military empires, this time in Central Asia, either absorbing neighboring peoples or driving them east or west, into China or western Eurasia. These migratory "empires" and the peoples they accumulated lived on tribute and the pillage of conquered lands. Peoples who were not absorbed or destroyed by them or were driven ahead of them looking for safety rather than conquest. Between the second and the sixth centuries, these two quite different transformations of peoples far from the Roman frontiers stirred two continents and moved migrants and invaders both toward the frontiers of the Roman empire.

The history of the "Goths" offers a telling example. In the late second and early third centuries the small people known as the Goths assembled a powerful military force and threatened the Roman-Danube frontier in the mid–third century and was destroyed by the emperors Claudius II and Aurelian. In the early fourth century two new Gothic kingdoms arose, both of which were led by a

Germanic invasions of the Roman Empire.

military king and his warriors, reducing the public role of the old free Germanic warrior to an inferior and subordinate status.

Allied with Rome, one of these new-style Germanic kingdoms (later termed the *Visigoths*) was itself threatened by the appearance of the Huns, a nomadic warrior empire from Central Asia. The Huns possessed new and fearsome weapons, and they excelled in light cavalry warfare. By the beginning of the third century they occupied the steppe north of the Caucasus, and by late in the fourth century they pushed further west and south, where they destroyed the Visigothic kingdom on the Black Sea in 374/5 and sent its remnants fleeing toward the Roman-Danube frontier seeking asylum and protection from their old allies the Romans.

Although the Romans permitted the Visigoths to enter the empire en masse (the first time the Romans had ever admitted an entire people under its own leaders and preserving its own organization), Roman soldiers and officials mistreated them savagely. The Visigoths revolted in 378, destroyed a Roman army and the emperor Valens at the battle of Adrianople, and began their migration through the western empire, periodically concluding short-lived agreements with Roman imperial officials. By the early fifth century, the Visigoths were in Italy itself, briefly capturing and sacking the city of Rome in 410, and then moved north and west into Gaul and Iberia. There they patched up yet another treaty with Rome and settled down to establish an independent Germanic kingdom inside the western part of the Roman empire.

The other Gothic kingdom, more assimilated by the Huns, yet also preserving its own collective identity, survived as part of the Hunnic confederation, took on the name of Ostrogoths, and remained a component of the Hunnic threat to Rome until the destruction of the Huns in the mid–fifth century.

In the winter of 405 and 406 other Germanic peoples pushed across the Rhine and penetrated deeply into Gaul. For two years the invaders—the Vandal, Suevian, and Burgundian peoples—sacked Gaul and settled in parts of it. The Burgundians occupied a large part of eastern Gaul, while the Vandals and Suevians crossed the Pyrenees into Spain. One of the terms of the alliance of the Romans and Visigoths had been the stipulation that the Visigoths would help the Romans to control the Vandals and Suevians. For fifteen years the Visigoths fought the Vandals, until the latter crossed the straits of Gibraltar in 428 and began their occupation of Roman North Africa. Within the next decade, under their king Gaiseric, the Vandals systematically removed Roman North Africa from imperial control and cut off the flow of grain from Africa to Italy, the lifeline of much of the peninsula's food supply. The Suevians remained in central and western Spain under the strong influence of the Visigoths.

THE WORLD OF GALLA PLACIDIA

When the Visigoths revolted and killed the *augustus* of the East, Valens, at the battle of Adrianople in 378, the surviving *augustus,* Gratian, appointed a retired Iberian general, Theodosius, as *augustus* of the East in Valens's place. By 392 Theodosius was the sole emperor. He established the Theodosian dynasty, the last actively to rule both the eastern and western parts of the empire, and, both with Gratian and alone, completed the establishment of Christianity as the only legal religion in the empire. Theodosius's relatively short reign (379–395) is significant both for its success in controlling for a time the problem of barbarian migrants and invaders and for making Christianity the Roman state religion. The reign also reveals several shifts in power within the ruling circles of empire, further localization and privatization of public interests, and the relative impact of barbarian migrations and invasions on the eastern and western parts of the empire.

One of the most striking features of the Theodosian dynasty—and of several other imperial dynasties that had preceded it—was the place of women in the domestic and public affairs of the empire. This place had been shaped by the changing position of women in Roman imperial society, briefly traced earlier.

In imperial dynasties women who were Christian played prominent roles from the fourth century on. Helena, the mother of Constantine, not only was alleged to have discovered the cross on which Jesus was crucified, but she also founded a number of churches, including Santa Croce in Gerusalemme in Rome. As successful military adventurers turned their families into imperial dynasties, the female members of those families also became politically important. Justina, the wife of Valentinian I (ruled 364–375) and mother of Valentinian II (ruled 383–392), played a crucial role in the war policy of the early years of Theodosius I.

At his death in 395, Theodosius left three children: Arcadius, *augustus* of the East; Honorius, *augustus* of the West, and his daughter, Galla Placidia. The world of Galla Placidia was one of both internal and external turmoil for the empire, and in it Galla Placidia proved considerably more able than her brothers, although she held no official title.

Galla Placidia was the daughter of the second marriage of Theodosius, and spent her early life at Constantinople and Rome, where she was probably educated in traditional Greek and Roman literature, trained in Christian morality, and given the stylized domestic education traditionally offered to aristocratic female children. She remained unmarried far longer than was usual among imperial children. After being captured in Rome in 409 by the Goths, who kept her in respectful captivity, she witnessed the sack of Rome in 410 and accompanied the Goths north on their exodus from Italy. In 412 Athaulf temporarily settled the Goths in western Gaul, around Bordeaux and Toulouse, and in 414, the year before he entered into a treaty with the Roman emperor in order to maintain a kind of order in the lands in which he and his people were now settled, he married Galla Placidia.

Athaulf is an ambiguous figure in the early history of Europe. The Spanish historian Paulus Orosius, who had been driven from his home in Spain by the events of 406–413, recounts a story in which Athaulf is alleged to have once planned to replace "Romania" with "Gothia," but found that his disorganized people could best be used for preserving Roman glory and restoring Roman power by Gothic arms. Athaulf's alleged observation concerning the new role of the Goths as the defenders of Roman culture was to have an interesting future and to serve as a rationale for later barbarian masters of provinces of the empire. Together with his marriage to Galla Placidia, his remark has often been interpreted as a rationale for a complete integration of barbarian and Roman in the new world of the early fifth century. In fact, neither of these actions was to have much issue. Athaulf died in 415, having moved his people into northern Spain.

The continued harassment of the Goths by Roman forces, the blockading of the ports on which the Goths depended for the importation of food, and the Goths' lack of success in sailing to Africa forced the successors of Athaulf to come to some sort of terms with the Romans, who, in spite of Athaulf's proclamation of himself as a protector of Roman culture and his obvious affection and respect for Galla Placidia, had never ceased their hostility toward the Goths. Galla Placidia was returned to her brother Honorius in 416, and as a result the Goths received a commission from the Romans to attack other barbarians. In 417, Galla Placidia was married at her brother's order to Constantius, an able general and a Roman nobleman who had emerged as Honorius's most influential adviser. Through Constantius, Honorius managed to restore imperial influence among the barbarian invaders of the western part of the empire.

Although it may appear that Galla Placidia's life was largely one more instance of a valuable woman manipulated into and out of marriage by men, it was, in fact, far more autonomous and influential than it seems. Other women of imperial dynasties had served as consorts for socially insecure emperors and generals, and still others would for centuries in the surviving East Roman Empire. Like her grandmother Justina, Galla Placidia was far more a driving force in imperial policies in the early fifth century than she was their victim. Like her older contemporary Hypatia of Alexandria, she marks perhaps the most distinctive and impressive female presence in the later Roman world.

Galla Placidia was considerably more intelligent and able than her brothers or their successors. In the West, Honorius (395–423) and Valentinian III (425–455) proved incompetent, their courts torn by rivalry among contending factions, incapable of adopting a consistent imperial policy for dealing with the new threats posed by the invasions. This became disastrous with the advent of the Huns into western Europe.

The Huns moved west in 435, attacked a Roman army at Châlons in Gaul in 451, and were checked only by the intervention of the Visigoths on the side of the Romans. The Huns, whose migration out of western Asia in the 370s had begun the vast movement of peoples toward the Roman frontiers, were regarded by both Romans and Goths as unspeakably savage, greedy, and irreligious, respecting nothing in their path. Undaunted by the check at Châlons, the Huns, led by their able and talented King Attila (ruled 434–453), then invaded Italy and marched upon Rome itself.

Hunger and sickness among the Huns weakened the army, however, and a deputation of Roman nobles, which included the bishop of Rome, Leo I (440–461), persuaded Attila to withdraw, probably with the promise of supplies and a military armistice. The Huns moved back to the Danube, where Attila died suddenly in 453. An uprising by a subject people against the remnant of the Huns resulted in the little-documented battle of Nedao in 454, when the Huns were destroyed as a people. Their survivors were either absorbed into the local Balkan population or migrated elsewhere, possibly joining the later Asiatic invaders known as the Avars and the Bulgars.

The invasion of the Visigoths across the Danube, the breaching of the Rhine frontier in 406, and the struggle with the Huns all affected the western Roman Empire far more than the eastern. In 446 a mixed army of Picts, Irish, and Saxons invaded the province of Roman Britain, from which the defending armies had been removed before 410 for service elsewhere. In the century following this invasion, Roman Britain slowly gave way to the Germanic kingdoms of Anglo-Saxon England. In 455 Gaiseric, the Vandal king of North Africa, sacked the city of Rome and threatened to seize all of Italy. By the second half of the fifth century other Germanic peoples had crossed the broken Rhine and Danube frontiers.

Theodosius II (408–450), *augustus* of the east, and Valentinian III (425–455), *augustus* of the west, were the last of the Theodosian dynasty to rule the empire. When Theodosius died, his sister Pulcheria raised her husband, Marcian, to the imperial throne without bothering, as the law required, to consult her cousin Valentinian, the senior *augustus*. This indifference to western imperial recognition suggests further the extent of the division between the eastern and western parts of the empire.

From 445 on, both eastern and western imperial courts were dominated by barbarian masters of soldiers (king-makers and king-removers), beside whom the emperors were for the most part puppets. Because of the structure and resources of the eastern part of the empire, however, the rule of the masters of soldiers was brief. Under the emperors Leo I (457–474) and Zeno (474–491), the control of barbarian generals was finally thrown off and the office of emperor restored to much of its former power. Although Leo, Zeno, and their successors had to fight off other invaders, the eastern Roman Empire proved sufficiently resilient to recover from the fifth-century threat.

In the West, however, the masters of soldiers wielded much greater power, and a series of puppet emperors sat powerless on the throne until 476. Then Odovacar, the master of soldiers in the west and effective ruler of all Italy, deposed the last western emperor, Romulus Augustulus, and sent the imperial regalia back to the emperor Zeno at Constantinople. Odovacar remarked that the empire needed only one emperor, and he appointed himself regent for Zeno in Italy. Zeno was incapable of mounting a military offensive against Odovacar, but he could—and did—use diplomacy against his western "subordinate." His diplomacy introduced the Ostrogoths into Italy.

THE AGE OF THEODERIC: OSTROGOTHS, FRANKS, AND VISIGOTHS

The Ostrogoths were a branch of the old Gothic kingdom that had been destroyed by the Huns in 375. By the mid–fifth century, however, the Ostrogoths had recovered much of their power, and under their young king Theoderic (453–526) they attacked Constantinople itself. Zeno diverted the Ostrogoths from the city by offering Theoderic a commission as master of soldiers and the charge of moving to Italy to destroy Odovacar and restore Italy to the empire. By 493 Theoderic had invaded Italy, killed Odovacar with his own hands, and established himself as ruler of Italy, combining the Roman titles of patrician

Germanic kingdoms about 526.

and master of soldiers with his own title of king of the Ostrogothic people. But although Theoderic's titles were far more legitimate than those of Odovacar, his position was no less insecure. Theoderic's considerable talents as a ruler and his genuine ambition to rule Italy moderately always faced the problem of intrigue from Constantinople. The Age of Theoderic witnessed great possibilities of cooperative rule between Romans and Ostrogoths, but political, religious, and cultural differences between the two peoples prevented his reign from creating a new kind of Roman-Germanic state. Within a decade of Theoderic's death in 526, the armies of Constantinople and of the Ostrogoths clashed in a long series of wars that destroyed the Ostrogothic kingdom and laid waste much of Italy itself.

The Ostrogoths were Christians when they arrived in Italy, having been converted to Arian Christianity by missionaries who arrived among them to minister to Roman prisoners they held. One of these missionaries, Ulfilas, translated parts of the Bible into the Gothic language, the first written work we possess in a Germanic language. But the heterodox Christianity of the Ostrogoths was one cause of friction with the orthodox Christianity of Italians and Byzantines.

Theoderic, however, had spent part of his youth as a hostage in Constantinople and had received a Roman education. Able and intelligent, he set a goal for himself in the west that would have been impossible in the more thickly settled and more closely administered east: the peaceful establishment of his people, their culture and faith intact, in the midst of Roman Italy in a kind of economic and political symbiosis. Theoderic greatly admired many of the Roman social institutions and methods of governance. He employed high-ranking Romans in his administration. And although he was king of his own people, he never claimed a royal or imperial title over Romans. He ruled from Ravenna, not Rome, and his architectural works in Ravenna and elsewhere in Italy represent a significant effort to restore some of the material fabric of Italy.

Within Theoderic's hybrid Roman-Ostrogothic state, the Germanic warriors were the only military force in Italy and were separate from the Roman senatorial class and bureaucrats. The settlement of Goths on Roman land was conducted according to the principle of *hospitium,* the sharing of land between Roman "hosts" and Gothic "guests," and in affairs of law, taxes, coinage, and administrative institutions, Goths and Romans were under separate systems of rule. For the Romans, however, the old imperial institutions remained largely intact. Civil posts were restricted to Romans, the senate continued to sit at Rome, public festivals and entertainments continued, and Theoderic's official proclamations were properly called *edicts*—that is, administrative pronouncements issued by a Roman official subordinate to the emperor. The emperor's image continued to grace the coins struck in Ostrogothic Italy, and his foreign policy was designed to maintain different barbarian peoples in the provinces without permitting any one group to become too strong.

Even with his imperial commission and the strength of his kingdom in Italy, Theoderic had to work hard to influence the political disorder in Gaul and Spain. The Visigothic kingdom extended from southern Gaul into Spain; a Burgundian kingdom bordered it on the northeast in the upper Rhone Valley, and to the east of the Burgundians the Alamanni built a strong kingdom on the upper Rhine. With these there existed in uneasy relations a number of Roman provincial states, and in all of them except the Alamannic kingdom there survived a provincial Roman aristocracy consisting of laity and clergy, in not all cases as cleanly separated from their Germanic neighbors as in Theoderic's own Italy.

The most pressing diplomatic problem in northwest Europe during the late fifth and early sixth centuries, however, was posed by the Franks. The Franks were a group of peoples who migrated south along the North Sea coast in the third and fourth centuries. They originally settled in parts of what are now the Netherlands and Belgium, and they occasionally served with Roman armies as *federati* (allied troops under their own commanders). Later in the fifth century they broke from Roman alliance, harassed Roman cities in the lower Rhineland, and formed small independent kingdoms in northern Gaul. One leader of a group of Franks was Childeric I, son of Merovech (from which the name of his dynasty, the Merovingians, is derived), who died in 482 and was buried at Tournai. In 1653 the tomb was excavated and its contents described. Weapons, jewelry, hoards of coins, and the head of the king's war horse were found, along with an elaborately brocaded and jeweled cloak. Such graves provide considerable archaeological evidence for the period.

The Franks settled and farmed as well as fought, and after Childeric's death the kingdom expanded rapidly under his son, Clovis. In 486 Clovis defeated a Roman ruler, Syagrius, and proceeded to consolidate his power among several divisions of the Franks. At his accession, Clovis had been petitioned by Remigius, bishop of Reims, to respect the church and protect the defenseless. The offer of active support from the aristocratic Gallo-Roman bishops and his marriage to a Catholic Burgundian princess influenced Clovis' decision to convert to orthodox Latin Christianity some time around 500 rather than to the Arian heretical form of Christianity of the Visigoths and Ostrogoths. Clovis's new prestige and support not only permitted him to emerge as the champion of Catholic Gallo-Roman Christianity against the Arianism of other Germanic rulers, but also influenced a new ideal of Christian kingship. The value of Gallo-Roman support for his ventures is revealed in the letter sent to Clovis by Avitus of Vienne after Clovis's baptism:

We saw (with the eyes of the spirit) that great sight, when, a crowd of bishops around you, in the order of their holy ministry, poured over your royal limbs the waters of life; when that head feared by the peoples bowed down before the servants of God; when your royal locks, hidden under a helmet, were steeped in holy oil; when your breast, relieved of its cuirass, shone with the same whiteness as your baptismal robes. Do not doubt, most flourishing of kings, that this soft clothing will give more force to your arms: whatever Fortune has given up to now, this Sanctity will bestow.

The transformation of Clovis's success from fortune to sanctity, indicating as much the unreserved cooperation of the episcopate as spiritual benefits, goes far to account for Clovis's image in the eyes of later generations. Of all the barbarian rulers, only he had met with absolute success. Legends circulated quickly around Clovis's baptism, the most persistent and influential being that the Holy Spirit had descended from heaven with the baptismal oil. This legend was fleshed out by later claims of French kings to be anointed at their coronations with the same oil and to possess alone the title of "Most Christian King."

In 506 Clovis led the Frankish armies against the Alamanni at Tolbiac and destroyed them, taking the defeated enemies as his subjects. In Aquitaine, the Visigoths, now intensely concerned at Clovis's success, fell before his army at the battle of Vouillé in 507. As a result of these triumphs, Clovis was able to consolidate his kingdom in northern Gaul the next year. Clovis died in 511, leaving behind him a new kind of Frankish—and Germanic—kingdom, far enough from the Mediterranean centers of political strife to retain its independence and vigor, and orthodox enough in its faith, or at least in the reputed faith of its ruler, to leave not only a memory but a legend of Clovis as the "new Constantine," a Germanic Christian king.

Although Theoderic actively mediated between the Franks and Visigoths and was partially responsible for the ability of the Visigoths to consolidate themselves in the Iberian part of their old kingdom, he could not prevent the rise of the Franks to control of northern Gaul. Theoderic's diplomacy included the marriage of his daughters to the kings of the Burgundians and Visigoths, of his sister to the king of the Vandals, and of himself to a sister of Clovis. Even with these considerable efforts, Theoderic's diplomacy seems to have been aided more by the death of Clovis and the division of his kingdom among his sons.

Moreover, religious and political frictions in Italy soon turned Theoderic's attention from Gaul and Spain to Italy itself. Friction between Arian Ostrogoths and Romans made Theoderic's rule progressively harsher, however. In 526, the year of his death, Theoderic persecuted Pope John I (523–526) and demanded that all Christian churches be turned over to his Arian Goths. In 524 he executed his Roman master of offices, Boethius, on a charge of treason.

Theoderic was succeeded by his able daughter Amalasuntha, but Gothic internal politics resulted in her assassination. The Gothic kings who succeeded her were unable and unwilling to improve relations with Constantinople, and they ruled their Roman subjects with heavier and heavier hands. By the 530s the Ostrogothic kingdom of Italy was poised for war with the Roman Empire at Constantinople.

BOETHIUS AND CASSIODORUS

The attitude of Theoderic toward Roman culture, and the state of learning during the transformation of the Roman world in general, can best be illustrated by the careers of two remarkable men, Boethius and Cassiodorus. Both were highborn Romans, both were scholars of considerable achievement, and both were "prime ministers" of the Ostrogothic king in Italy.

Anicius Manlius Severinus Boethius was a descendent of the highest senatorial aristocracy. Born about 480, he was raised in the family of another representative of the oldest traditions of the senatorial order, Quintus Aurelius Symmachus. After receiving the still elaborate Roman aristocratic education, Boethius met Theoderic around 505, and from that date until his death in 524 he became an important figure in the royal court. First an adviser on what seem to have been purely technical matters—he designed, among other things, a water clock that Theoderic presented to his brother-in-law Gundobad, king of the Burgundians—Boethius soon acquired a series of public offices, which culminated in the consulship in 510 and the important post of master of offices in 523. Boethius's tasks made him the most important civil official in Italy, a constant companion of Theoderic, and, in another sense, a symbol of the extraordinary wealth of willing Roman talent available to the Ostrogothic king.

The public service of Boethius, important as it was, was not the only side of this remarkable man. Like many of the Italian and Gallic aristocracy, Boethius had considerable learning and certainly worked at scholarship during his public career. His greatest ambition was to translate both Plato and Aristotle into Latin, and with that end in view he produced several works that were to serve for the next seven centuries as the introduction to philosophical and logical thought for all Europeans. One of his first works was a translation of and commentary on Porphyry's *Introduction* to the *Categories* of Aristotle. Later, he translated some of Aristotle's other works on logic, primarily the *De Interpretatione*.

The importance of this body of work is immeasurable. By beginning with broad questions dealing with the art of classifying objects external to the mind and by classifying further all remarks that can be made on any subject, Boethius left one of the greatest legacies of late antiquity. The nature of that legacy is often difficult for modern readers to appreciate. Essentially, it involved devising in Latin a vocabulary capable of discussing the intricate mental processes that had hitherto been written about in Greek. By systematizing a Latin philosophical and logical vocabulary that could be applied effectively to the analysis of mental processes, the classification of valid arguments, the detection of logical errors, and the accurate description of the world around him, Boethius left to the European West the tools for the elaboration of theology, law, logic, and metaphysics. In this sense, Thomas Aquinas and Descartes are his direct heirs, but the entire West used these works of Boethius as its own introduction to logical thought. In the great revival of the study of logic that occurred in the eleventh and twelfth centuries, the work of Boethius played the most important role. There are no more important legacies in terms of vocabulary and critical language than Jerome's translation of the Bible into Latin early in the fifth century and Boethius's translation of Aristotelian logical works into Latin a century later.

Nor was formal philosophical scholarship Boethius's only other contribution to the early sixth century and to history. He never finished—indeed, he hardly began—his vast plan of translation. But he composed other works, works that differed from both public service and philosophy. He wrote a number of treatises on Christianity that constitute one of the first attempts to apply the logic of Aristotle to the theological ideas of Christianity, an attempt that played a crucial role in the shaping of later Christian thought.

Yet Boethius's most famous work really falls into none of these categories. To see it in its proper context, we must turn briefly to the problems of the last years of Theoderic's reign. Continuing eastern resentment of the Ostrogothic domination of Italy was sharpened by the renewal of the persecution of Arian heretics in the east early in the sixth century. Other eastern attempts to undermine Theoderic's rule appear to have occurred at the same time. One such attempt may well have been an appeal to Roman antiquity that was designed to break the loyalty of the Roman senatorial class to its barbarian master. In any case, secret communications between Constantinople and Rome appear to have taken place, and early in 524 both Boethius and his father-in-law Symmachus were accused by Theoderic of treason and imprisoned. Boethius remained in prison for nearly a year and was summarily executed in 524. The executions of Boethius and Symmachus (in 526) suggest how effective eastern imperial opposition to Theoderic had been.

During his year in prison Boethius wrote his most famous work, a dialogue called *On the Consolation of Philosophy*. The setting of the dialogue is Boethius's prison, where he has been seeking means to console himself for the undeserved fate that had befallen him. Philosophy enters, personified as a woman, and the remainder of the work is a dialogue between the two in prose, with moving verse interludes, written in a clear, simple Latin. In the course of the dialogue, Philosophy leads Boethius through various logical steps to a consideration of the nature of true happiness and the highest good, which Philosophy identifies with God, although not with any specifically Christian aspects of God. This apparent avoidance of Christianity has led many scholars to believe that Boethius was only a surface Christian, and that in time of trouble he reverted to an older and deeper-rooted philosophical paganism. It seems, however, that Boethius was attempting to resolve the problems of misfortune and justice, good and evil, within a philosophic framework. The dialogue culminates in a description of the philosopher's obligation to accept the essential justice of the divine plan and to interpret the fragments of experience accordingly. The work became so popular that it was translated in the ninth century by no less a person than King Alfred of England, and in the sixteenth century by no less a scholar than Queen Elizabeth I. Certainly Boethius was the most popular—along with Vergil and Ovid—of all Roman writers in the Middle Ages, even finding a local cult of sainthood and a place in Paradise in Dante's *Divine Comedy*. As late as the eighteenth century Boethius was described by Catholic hagiographers as Saint Severinus. But Boethius's later reputation was not his only revenge. After the conquest of Ostrogothic Italy by the East Roman Empire in the middle of the sixth century, Boethius's widow received imperial permission to destroy many statues of Theoderic as an act of private revenge.

The deaths of Boethius and Symmachus and their implications for the stability of Ostrogothic Italy loom over the unhappy last years of Theoderic and the regime he founded. It is in the career of Boethius's successor at Theoderic's court, Cassiodorus, that these implications were felt most fully. Cassiodorus did not come from the same high aristocratic circles of Symmachus and Boethius.

He was a noble holding extensive lands around Squillace in Calabria. He had studied extensively, and one of his teachers was the great Dionysius Exiguus, one of many Greek-speaking scholars, a translator, and later an influential figure in the development of Western law. Dionysius was also a mathematician and became an expert in correlating the complex dating systems of the ancient world. In the process of calculating tables projecting the dating of Easter (a movable feast, whose date changed every year), Dionysius hit upon the idea of dating history from the Incarnation of Christ. Although his idea was not immediately accepted (his manuscripts passed on to Cassiodorus, who himself wrote on the conversion to A.D. dating), his influence from the eighth century on defined the most common chronology in the modern world.

Cassiodorus's work for Theoderic was a different kind from that of Boethius. The aristocratic philosopher left a body of work that was the legitimate occupation of a learned Roman nobleman of the sixth century—philosophy, translations, poetry, and high theology. Cassiodorus was far more concerned with the historical phenomena that he saw before him in sixth-century Italy—not philosophical verities but the day-to-day problems of explaining Roman culture to the Goths and the Gothic character to the Romans. Boethius's major works required no knowledge of the Goths in order to be understood, but Cassiodorus's major work is wholly inexplicable without an acquaintance with the Gothic kingdom.

When he succeeded Boethius as master of offices in late 524 he undertook, in the official correspondence that he wrote in Theoderic's name, to rationalize the Gothic role in preserving Roman *vetustas* (tradition) and in guarding what Cassiodorus called *civilitas*—the essence of traditional Roman civic culture. These letters, the *Variae,* are an amazing wealth of information, digressions, learned ramblings about hopelessly obscure points, and learning paraded for its own sake, some of it pompous but much of it infinitely interesting. Cassiodorus also wrote several histories, and in these his concern for a proper understanding of the Goths became even more explicit. In several chronicles, most notably in the lost *Gothic History,* Cassiodorus extended the history of the Ostrogoths back in time until it became as ancient—and heroic—as Roman history. Cassiodorus made an impressive attempt to reconcile Goths and Romans by showing that each was of equal antiquity and that each had been created to collaborate with the other in preserving civilization.

The long war between the Ostrogoths and the Romans that followed the assassination of Amalasuntha, however, proved Cassiodorus's ambitions futile. In the 550s Cassiodorus retired with some friends to his estates near Squillace in south Italy. There he spent his time in devotional readings and assembled his last work, the *Divine and Human Readings,* an encyclopedic survey and analysis of spiritual and secular literature that remained for many centuries a guide for European scholars through the literature of Christian and pagan antiquity.

The *Divine and Human Readings* mark another important feature of late antiquity learning, the process of organizing and classifying knowledge into recognized and labeled subjects. In the first century B.C. the Roman writers Varro and Cicero had developed the idea (from Hellenistic learning) that the proper subjects of study for a free Roman citizen ought to be grouped and classified in terms of their place in the progression of learning and their relationship to one another. Although the proper number of these subjects varied between Varro's time and the fifth century, a very long, obscure, but influential literary work by the fourth-century advocate Martianus Capella numbered these subjects of study as seven and labeled the seven parts of knowledge the "liberal arts." This work, *The Marriage of Mercury and Philology*, is an allegory in verse and prose and extremely difficult to read. Boethius divided the seven liberal arts of Martianus into two groups, the *trivium* and the *quadrivium*. The *trivium* was essentially literary, containing grammar, rhetoric, and dialectic (or logic); the *quadrivium* was essentially mathematical, comprising arithmetic, geometry, astronomy, and music. In the *Divine and Human Readings* Cassiodorus repeated both Martianus Capella and Boethius, thus passing down to later European history a division of learning that remained fundamental until the seventeenth century.

The work of Boethius and Cassiodorus condensed in durable and greatly simplified form much of the intellectual legacy of the ancient world. The people who received that legacy were able, with much difficulty at first, to use it, then to expand it, and much later, in a different world, to recover even more of it.

UNITY AND DIVERSITY IN LATE MEDITERRANEAN ANTIQUITY

The movements of colonization, cultural diffusion, and conquest from the eighth century B.C. on had imposed several different kinds of unity throughout the Mediterranean world and had also brought that world into contact with peoples on its edges. The most easily understandable kind of unity was political: As long as the wealth and strength of the government of the Roman Empire survived, political unity could be maintained. When it weakened, or weakened in part of the empire, political unity began to disintegrate and power relocated itself in different centers and regions. The weakening of imperial authority in the West in the fifth century meant that the East had to assume the burden of attempting to rule the entire empire. The result was a survival of efficient rule in the East and the failure of the East Roman Empire to govern effectively in the West. Although the power of the East Roman Empire survived in Ravenna and Rome in the West, elsewhere sub-Roman Germanic kingdoms appeared in the western provinces—the Visigoths in Iberia, the Franks in Gaul, the Ostrogoths in Italy, and the Vandals in Africa—and these political societies existed side-by-side with older Roman institutions.

One of the most striking features of the early Germanic kingdoms within the old Roman Empire was the degree to which their rulers attempted to preserve many features of Roman civic life. No Germanic ruler failed to recognize at least the nominal authority of the emperors, even when the emperors shifted their concerns to the East. Some forms of civil administration and taxation were retained. Roman aristocrats, churchmen, and courtiers acted as servants to Visigothic, Vandal, Ostrogothic, and Frankish kings. Germanic kings themselves happily accepted titles that indicated that they possessed a place in the hierarchy of imperial service. To understand the increasing diversity in the Mediterranean world of late antiquity, we must also ask what forms of unity survived as well as what lay beneath the disappearance of active imperial governmental administration in the West. One important answer to this question points to the basis of both political authority and the economy in the ancient world: the relation between the imperial government and the inhabitants of the cities and countrysides that sustained it.

The physical fabric of Greco-Roman cities was constructed, maintained, and elaborated by a complex combination of imperial, local, and private donations, of which the last was the most important. Local aristocrats and newly wealthy citizens were expected to contribute heavily, not only to the entertainment, but also to the very urban space of their fellow townspeople. Although some of this generosity may be attributed to public-spiritedness, most of it was the result of what the Greeks called *philotimia* ("love of honor") and the Romans *magnanimitas* ("great spiritedness"), that is, the desire for status, honor, and fame after death that was expressed in a spirit of competition with others who sought the same things. As long as the stimulus survived, the towns and cities of the Mediterranean world benefited greatly and preserved the distinctive functions and "look" that is so striking a feature of the entire Mediterranean world.

Although they were expensively built and usually over-engineered, ancient cities, like modern ones, were physically fragile and required maintenance and repair. Roman donors, however, were usually more inclined to fund new buildings rather than repair older ones, and when donors ceased their public generosity almost entirely in the fourth century, the problem of repairs loomed large, not only in terms of buildings, streets, bridges, and baths, but also in those of town walls and fortifications. When repairs were done in late antiquity, they were expended largely on fortifications or on projects that interested emperors or imperial officials, not those that attracted private interests.

One of the consequences of the third-century crisis and the imperially directed recovery of the fourth century was the reduction in the civic generosity (and perhaps the aggregate wealth) of local aristocrats and civic officials. Increasingly, towns and cities (like provinces) were governed by a network of imperially appointed officials. Exempted from the burdens of local public office themselves, these officials directed their own personal wealth to private projects, while at the same time both reducing the prestige that public generosity had attained before the fourth century and increasing the financial responsibilities and burdens upon the governing class of the cities. Although this process worked more slowly in the area around Rome itself and the vast senatorial lands of southern Italy, it proceeded more quickly elsewhere. Civic finances, never large in themselves, were increasingly diverted to defense and usually not renewed by the influx of new wealth and newly wealthy people desirous of impressing the local population with their importance through civic generosity.

Not only were opportunities of upward social mobility greatly reduced outside of imperial service, but the burden of taxation also grew heavier and heavier during the fourth and fifth centuries. The system of taxation of the fourth and fifth centuries was one more means of unifying the empire: The imperial government reached more deeply into society, directly affecting the lives and property of peasants and merchants as well as landowners, and even exerting a considerable influence on trade and manufacturing. Those who could avoid taxation—very large landowners, immune civil servants, and imperial favorites (as well as, later, the churches)—did so. Peasants also submitted themselves to aristocratic landowning domination by giving up their land in return for dependent (and protected) status under private control and private patronage. The occasional peasant revolts of the fourth and fifth centuries did not slow this process. As large landowners managed to evade many tax responsibilities and increased their wealth and power by absorbing formerly free peasants, their interests and affections ceased to coincide at all points with those of the empire and its rulers.

The costs of empire—the imperial court, the army, the vast bureaucracy, public works, and provisioning of cities—did not decline, but the tax base did, in the fifth century in the West and in the late sixth and early seventh centuries in the East. To many western aristocrats and great landowners, the demands of the empire became too heavy, and accommodation with Germanic rulers (who themselves were largely Romanized in the fifth century) became easier and economically more attractive. Moreover, the Germanic kings of Italy, Spain, Gaul, and North Africa did not require nearly as heavy a system of taxation, because the greatest imperial need for taxes—the army— was supported by grants of land and did not require the immense salaries of Roman soldiers. The mingling of disaffected Romans and Romanized Germans characterizes the fifth and sixth centuries in the West, and so too does the transformation of the basis of wealth from money to land, particularly in the West.

The physical transformation of the city in the late antiquity is the most visible sign of these changes. By the end of the fifth century most of the public buildings in western cities were either in ruins or in severe disrepair, and little reconstruction was taking place. Although Theoderic's Ostrogothic kingdom in Italy attempted with some success to improve both the fairness of tax collection and the state of the urban fabric, neither the resources nor the inclination of most Germanic rulers turned in that direction. Just as the basis of public finance had changed, and the power of the imperial government collapsed in the West, so too the cities of the West needed to find new sources of private patronage and the societies of the West new forms of government as they both emerged from the wreckage of the governmental and economic system of late antiquity.

The great communications network that ran throughout the Mediterranean also reflects the problems of unity and diversity. Although it helped Christianity to disseminate itself (another feature of the enduring power of Mediterranean unity that is often overlooked), the same network also suffered from the linguistic polarization between Greek and Latin as well as from frequent interruptions of trade and food supplies. From the late fourth century on, the empire gradually became polarized into a Greek-speaking eastern part and a Latin-speaking western part. Both aristocrats and churchmen (who were increasingly the same people) focused their attention on their local regions rather than upon the empire as a whole. Intellectuals, too, seemed to be less aware of the empire as a whole, and the old-style bilingual classical education was acquired by a smaller and smaller elite. Individuals who might in earlier periods have served the western imperial court now had to travel to the East to find service, or they could offer their talents to a local ruler, whether Germanic or Roman. Throughout the West in particular, local wealth, talent, and affection were expended locally.

Once it was common to speak of the "decline and fall" of the Roman Empire. Today, historians see rather a "transformation of the Roman world." That transformation occurred at different rates in different parts of the empire. Indeed, some aspects of Mediterranean unity survived into modern times, while others disappeared rapidly or slowly. The idea of the Roman Empire, diplomatic relations between East Rome and the West, and the trade routes across the Mediterranean Sea persisted for many centuries. Christianity, too, constituted for a time a bond throughout that world. The ecumenical Church councils of the fourth and fifth centuries purported to define orthodox Christian belief for all Christians everywhere; in the early fifth century John Cassian brought to the West a vast store of information about eastern monastic practices and greatly influenced ascetic Christianity in the Latin-speaking world. In the East it was easier to preserve both the facts and the fictions of Mediterranean unity. In the West it became more and more difficult to preserve either.

FURTHER READING

In general, see Averil Cameron, *The Mediterranean World in Late Antiquity* A.D. *395–600* (London: Routledge, 1993). On Rome, see Richard Krautheimer, *Rome: Profile of a City, 312–1308* (Princeton, NJ: Princeton University Press, 1980), and Peter Llewellyn, *Rome in the Dark Ages* (New York-Washington: Praeger, 1971).

On the rise of Constantinople, see Richard Krautheimer, *Three Christian Capitals: Topography and Politics* (Berkeley-Los Angeles: University of California Press, 1983); David Talbot Rice, *Constantinople: From Byzantium to Istanbul*

(New York: Stein and Day, 1965); Philip Sherrard, *Constantinople: Iconography of a Sacred City* (Oxford: Oxford University Press, 1965); Cyril Mango, *Byzantium: The Empire of New Rome* (London: Weidenfeld and Nicholson, 1980). For the eastern perspective, see Walter Emil Kaegi, *Byzantium and the Decline of Rome* (Princeton, NJ: Princeton University Press, 1968).

On the migrants and invaders, see Lucien Musset, *The Germanic Invasions* (State College: Pennsylvania State University Press, 1975); Philip Dixon, *Barbarian Europe* (New York: E.P. Dutton, 1976); J. Hubert, et al., *Europe of the Invasions* (New York: Braziller, 1969).

On the Huns, see Otto Maenchen-Helfen, *The World of the Huns* (Berkeley-Los Angeles: University of California Press, 1975).

On the Goths, see Herwig Wolfram, *History of the Goths* (Berkeley-Los Angeles: University of California Press, 1988), and Peter Heather, *Goths and Romans A.D. 332–489* (New York: Oxford University Press, 1992).

On the Franks, see Edward James, *The Franks* (Oxford: Basil Blackwell, 1988).

For the response of the Theodosian dynasty, see Noel Q. King, *The Emperor Theodosius and the Establishment of Christianity* (New York: Westminster Press, 1962); J. F. Matthews, *Western Aristocracies and the Imperial Court, A.D. 364–425* (Oxford: Clarendon Press, 1975).

On the world of Galla Placidia, see Stewart I. Oost, *Galla Placidia Augusta* (Chicago: University of Chicago Press, 1968), and Kenneth G. Holum, *Theodosian Empresses: Women and Imperial Dominion in Late Antiquity* (Berkeley-Los Angeles: University of California Press, 1982).

On Boethius, see Margaret Gibson, *Boethius: His Life, Thought and Influence* (Oxford: Blackwell, 1981), and for Cassiodorus, James J. O'Donnell, *Cassiodorus* (Berkeley-Los Angeles: University of California Press, 1979). Cassiodorus's letters have now been translated: Cassiodorus, *Variae,* Trans. S. J. B. Barnish (Liverpool: Liverpool University Press, 1992).

A brilliant study of the transformation of the city is that of Brian Ward-Perkins, *From Classical Antiquity to the Middle Ages: Urban Public Building in Northern and Central Italy* (Oxford: Oxford University Press, 1984). For the important province of Gaul, see Raymond Van Dam, *Leadership and Community in Late Antique Gaul* (Berkeley-Los Angeles: University of California Press, 1985), and *Saints and Their Miracles in Late Antique Gaul* (Princeton: Princeton University Press, 1993); Claire Stancliffe, *St. Martin and His Hagiographer* (Oxford: Oxford University Press, 1983). On the important genre of saints' lives as historical sources, see now Thomas F. X. Noble and Thomas Head, *Soldiers of Christ: Saints and Saints' Lives from Late Antiquity and the Early Middle Ages* (University Park: The Pennsylvania State University Press, 1995).

Part II TWO HEIRS OF THE ANCIENT WORLD

4

THE MAKING OF BYZANTINE CIVILIZATION

THE EAST ROMAN EMPIRE, 450–527

The success of the emperors Leo I and Zeno in freeing the imperial court at Constantinople from the domination of barbarian masters of soldiers was as remarkable as the emperors' ability to head off threats of invasion into the West. When Odovacar deposed Romulus Augustulus in 476 and sent the imperial regalia back to Constantinople, Zeno was the sole emperor of Rome. No matter how little power he actually exercised in the western provinces, the East Roman emperor claimed a unique character: He was the ruler of the Christian Roman world. Since 450, emperors had been crowned by the patriarchs of Constantinople (*patriarch* was a title given to the ecclesiastical leaders of the cities of Rome, Alexandria, Antioch, Constantinople, and Jerusalem) in a religious ceremony that gave them a quasi-priestly character; the emperor claimed, at least in theory, a kind of authority that no other earthly ruler could match. Moreover, imperial currency remained strong, and even imperial extravagance and high military costs did not impose in the east the crushing burdens they represented in the west. Finally, the core of an imperial civil service survived at Constantinople, and the regulation of imperial government continued in spite of the fact that the East Roman Empire experienced crises similar to those of the West in the sixth and seventh centuries.

Although the empire of East Rome survived Germanic invasions, the decline of ancient patterns of urbanism, and the localization of the economy with greater success than did the West, it experienced one kind of major crisis in the fifth and sixth centuries that the West was generally spared—religious dissension. Although the Arian heresy (except, as we have seen, among the Germanic invaders of the empire) was virtually extinct within the empire by the mid–fifth century, other religious disputes quickly followed it. Most of these dealt with the problem of the relationship between the divine and human natures of Christ, and few of them were restricted to clerics. In fact, the deep penetration of Christianity within the eastern Roman Empire meant that just as more of society was Christianized, so religious disputes touched wider social circles and influenced political affairs as well. One of the most significant of these movements was Nestorianism, named after Nestorius, who became patriarch of Constantinople in 428. Nestorius, and the school of Antioch from which he came, was disturbed by the increasing popularity of the cult of the Virgin Mary and its implications concerning the human and divine natures of Christ. Called *Theotokos* ("Mother of God"), the Virgin was, Nestorius insisted, *Christotokos* ("Mother of Christ"), and Christ's nature was consequently predominantly human rather than divine.

Among the opposition to Nestorianism was a faction led by Eutyches of Constantinople, which insisted on a single (divine) nature (*physis*) of Christ. Monophysitism (from *monos*, "one" and *physis*, "nature"), the name given to the Eutychean doctrine, became a serious social and theological problem.

One response to these powerful dissensions was the calling of Church councils to debate and resolve the issues raised by the dissenters. Thus, the First Council of Ephesus in 431 condemned Nestorianism. The Council of Chalcedon in 451 condemned Monophysitism, stating what became and has since remained the orthodox dogma—that Christ had a completely human and a completely divine nature:

Following the holy Fathers, we teach with one voice that the Son of God and our Lord Jesus Christ is to be confessed as one and the same person, that He is perfect in Godhead and perfect in manhood, very God and very man, of a reasonable soul and a human body consisting, consubstantial with the Father as touching his Godhead, and consubstantial with us touching his manhood; made in all things like unto us, sin only excepted. . . . This one and the same Jesus Christ, the only-begotten son of God, must be confessed to be in two natures, unconfusedly, immutably, indivisibly, inseparably united, and that without the distinction of natures being taken away by such union, but rather the peculiar property of each nature being preserved and being united in one Person and subsistence, not separated or divided into two persons, but one and the same Son and only-begotten, God the Word, our Lord Jesus Christ, as the prophets of old time have spoken concerning him, and as the Lord Jesus Christ hath taught us, and as the creed of the Fathers hath delivered to us.

This ringing definition of orthodox Christology by the Council of Chalcedon denounced a large number of rival beliefs and made clear certain implications of orthodoxy. By insisting on the inseparability of the divine and human natures in Christ, the members of the Council of Chalcedon avoided one of the chief tendencies of early Christianity, that of rejecting the material world as represented in Christ's humanity. On the other hand, they elevated human nature itself, in the Greek philosophical tradition, so that it was deemed capable of sharing a single person and substance with the divinity.

From the Council of Nicaea (325) to the Council of Chalcedon (451), Church councils increasingly undertook to define orthodox Christian belief for all the faithful. But a number of circumstances made the ecumenicity of their decisions problematic, particularly in the West. The emperors played a prominent role in calling and administering the councils. Considerably fewer western churchmen were present, and often those who were could not understand the Greek in which the conciliar agenda were conducted. Many canons (rulings) of the councils were not efficiently or widely distributed, and particularly in the West, the need for translation often led to omissions and incorrect versions of their decisions. Moreover, some bishops, many monasteries, individual holy men, as well as shrines, relics, and sacred pictures (*icons*) could escape orthodox control. Finally, the problem of the different kinds of authority claimed by the different patriarchs within the councils became a pressing issue, as Rome tended to become the voice of the Latin Christian community, opposing, it sometimes seemed, the wisdom and piety of eastern Christians.

Nor did the Council of Chalcedon solve the problems of Nestorianism and Monophysitism satisfactorily. Throughout their reigns, the emperors Zeno and Anastasius were forced to arrange compromises with all sides, and several bishops of Rome, especially Leo I (440–461) and Gelasius (492–496), took up strongly pro-Chalcedon and anti-Monophysite positions. Moreover, the arena of religious dispute was not confined to the formal sessions of the councils, or to the learned (and sometimes physically violent) arguments of ecclesiastical figures. Strongly held heterodox beliefs were stoutly maintained in the provinces, particularly in Syria and Egypt, and in the capital city of the empire, Constantinople, itself. There, religious opinion centered in the factions formed by various groups within the city's population, and found its focus where all broad popular disputes were aired, in the games and chariot races held in the great Hippodrome.

The Christological conflicts also underlined deep regional differences within the provinces of the East Roman Empire. In the fourth century the idea had become widespread that certain cities, because of the founding of their churches directly by the Apostles, enjoyed preeminence in Church affairs; these cities were Jerusalem, Alexandria, Antioch, and Rome. Because Rome was the only city in the western part of the empire to claim apostolic foundation, the prestige of the bishop of Rome was considerable, and this apostolic status contributed to the primacy of the bishop of Rome in western ecclesiastical affairs. At the Council of Constantinople in 381, the patriarch of Constantinople was raised to a level of dignity equaling that of the leaders of the apostolic churches. Thus, a degree of rivalry became evident in the fifth century between the leaders of the other apostolic churches and the patriarch of Constantinople. As we have seen, Nestorius had come to Constantinople from the church of Antioch. One of his opponents, who veered toward heresy himself, was Cyril, patriarch of Alexandria. Alexandria became a center of Monophysite sympathies, and since Alexandria was the ecclesiastical center of Egypt, its dissent represented the alienation of the population of a large and important province from the orthodox capital of Constantinople and from the emperor who resided there. The spiritual alienation of the southeastern provinces of the empire posed a great problem for East Roman emperors until those provinces themselves were lost in the Islamic conquests of the seventh century.

In spite of these profound and enduring religious divisions, the East Roman emperors progressively shaped and structured the Orthodox Church in their dominions. They called councils, appointed patriarchs, often influenced councils' agenda, and considered themselves the protectors of the Church, the patrons of a new Christian capital with no legacy of pagan antiquity, the liberators of Christianity from pagan rule, and the enforcers of ecclesiastical decisions and ecclesiastical discipline. Church councils formally chanted the imperial *laudes* (liturgical veneration) of the emperors, and the emperors were increasingly identified with orthodox Christianity itself.

Zeno's successors, Anastasius (491–518) and the Illyrian soldier Justin I (518–527), managed to calm the worst of the religious quarrels, to reform the imperial fiscal and administrative systems, and to undertake considerable programs of public works and charity. By the accession of Justin's nephew, Justinian, in 527, the East Roman Empire had escaped domination by barbarian masters of soldiers, invasion by barbarian armies, the worst effects of religious dissension, and the strain on the administration and the economy that the events of the fifth century had created.

THE EMPEROR WHO NEVER SLEEPS

Flavius Petrus Sabbatius Justinianus (or Justinian, as he is generally known) was a remarkable ruler in many ways. He was the first emperor since Theodosius II to have been trained in imperial administration. He spent his young manhood observing the machinery of imperial government, and he probably knew it better than any emperor in the past seventy-five years. Justinian was also well educated, and he knew law and theology with the familiarity of a professional. Moreover, he had made an extraordinary marriage with one of the ablest women ever to share a throne in the western world.

Justinian's wife, Theodora, was born not into the aristocracy but into the family of a bear trainer in the circus. Although the sources agree that she was strikingly beautiful and possessed a commanding presence, her role in Constantinople suggests other, more important qualities, including intelligence, great personal bravery, and a strong will. The world in which Theodora grew up was not the equivalent of a twentieth-century "circus world," however. The en-

Theodora and Her Attendants. This mosaic portrait of the empress Theodora and her retinue in the Church of San Vitale at Ravenna suggests the richness and majesty of the imperial court ceremonial and the deliberate invocation of these elements in churches in the
far-flung corners of the empire. (Alinari/Art Resource, NY)

tertainment industry of the sixth century was an unsettling mixture of spectacular performances, athletics, gymnastics, and pornography. It generally included
prostitution and other forms of erotica. Much of our knowledge of Theodora's
early life comes from *The Secret History,* a malicious portrait of Theodora and Justinian written by the court historian Procopius. Procopius, like Theodora's other
enemies, made much of her past life, and the historian John Barker has called
her portrayal in *The Secret History* "probably the most infamous and scurrilous
piece of sustained character assassination in all of literature."[1] Ostensibly, marriage to Theodora might have been a great mistake on the part of the heir to the
imperial throne. As things turned out, the marriage was probably the most sensible act of Justinian's life. Although Theodora held strong Monophysite sympathies, her contribution to the empire far outweighed the religious dissension
she helped to perpetuate.

[1]John W. Barker, *Justinian and the Later Roman Empire* (Madison: University of Wisconsin Press,
1966), p. 68.

The importance of Theodora's presence became dramatically evident during the first great crisis of Justinian's reign, the famous Nika riots of 532. The factions supporting the Blue and the Green chariot-racing teams in the Hippodrome had waged a bitter rivalry through the early years of Justinian's reign, a conflict rendered more serious because the factions had been armed and made into an urban militia some years earlier. In 532, for once disregarding their opposition toward each other, the Blues and Greens erupted in a riot in the Hippodrome directed against Justinian. The riot spread from the arena into the city, destroying most of the old town and killing thousands. Justinian, who fled from the Hippodrome, is said to have contemplated abdication and flight and to have been restrained only by Theodora's firmness, embodied in her alleged remark that "the [imperial] purple makes a glorious winding-sheet." The emperor regrouped his scattered forces and quelled the riot with a force and thoroughness previously unsuspected. He then unleashed reprisals against the aristocrats and their followers that may have killed as many as 30,000 people.

Immediately after the Nika riots (so-called because of the rioters' cry of the Greek word for victory) Justinian began to establish firmly his own imperial authority against the powers of the aristocracy and the urban population. By the middle of his reign he had destroyed most of the traditional powers in the empire and had made himself supreme, basing his strength on the vast fiscal resources of his predecessors and the support of the Christian provincial population of the empire. The necessity of rebuilding the shattered city of Constantinople and the need to reassert the political prestige of the emperor gave Justinian his opportunity.

In rebuilding Constantinople, Justinian gave it the shape it was to have throughout its long history. His triumph was the reconstruction of the great Church of Hagia Sophia (Holy Wisdom), in which the boundless architectural and engineering talent available in Constantinople created one of the greatest buildings in history. Justinian's architects, Anthemius of Tralles and Isidore of Miletus, created an immense quadrilateral of four arches, on the top of which was set a vast dome that seemed to hover lightly over the heads of those far below.

Justinian's architects and engineers completed the physical form of the great city and nearly filled the space inside its eighteen kilometers of fortified wall that had been built by Theodosius II in 450. The city contained a palace complex across the square from Hagia Sophia, many other churches, a hippodrome seating 60,000, and a population of around 350,000. Wide avenues carried ceremonial and commercial traffic through the city. The water and food supplies were supervised by competent city officials, as were the markets, ports, and labor organizations. The public services of Constantinople were greater than those of any other European city before the nineteenth century. Because of its prominence as the imperial capital, the city also thrived economically, becoming a great port and trading entrepôt.

Justinian's passion for thoroughness is reflected in many of his other achievements, particularly in his reform and codification of Roman law. Until

Justinian and His Attendants. This portrait, a twin of that depicting the empress Theodora, stands across the apse of the church from the empress's mosaic. (Alinari/Art Resource. N.Y.)

the reign of the emperor Hadrian in the second century, Roman law had been the archaic Law of the Twelve Tables, the primitive law of the early Roman community. Under Hadrian's reforms, some of the changes that had developed under the pressure of new prosperity and the relations among the new classes were regularized, and the influence of legal philosophy was recognized. The flow of imperial commands increased in the third century, however, and the administration of imperial law had by then fallen into the hands of bureaucrats who appreciated little of Rome's earlier legal history. By the fourth century private collections of imperial edicts were the most commonly used legal reference books, although they varied greatly in quality and availability. In 438 the emperor Theodosius II issued *The Theodosian Code,* an official collection of imperial edicts of the fourth and fifth centuries, systematized according to topic.

In the East Roman Empire the study of law flourished, and Justinian knew it well. He commissioned the jurist Tribonian to assemble a new and systematic collection of imperial edicts. By 529 Tribonian had completed the *Codex,* the first part of what came to be known as the *Corpus Iuris Civilis,* "The Body of Civil Law." In 533 Tribonian and other jurists compiled the *Digestum,* a systematic anthology of the writings of great jurists that had the force of law. In the same year, Justinian's commission produced the *Institutes,* an introductory textbook on Roman law. Finally, throughout the rest of his reign Justinian issued new edicts, the most important of which were included in the fourth section of the *Corpus,* the *Novellae,* or Novels. Justinian's *Corpus Iuris Civilis* formed the basis of imperial law until the end of the Byzantine Empire in 1453, even though later emperors enacted additional collections of law. Moreover, because it was written in Latin, the *Corpus* was accessible to western European societies, although its great influence dates only from the late eleventh century. By the end of the Middle Ages Roman law had influenced every legal system of Europe, and it is arguable that the *Corpus* is Justinian's greatest legacy.

Justinian had many other able servants besides the architects, lawyers, and theologians with whom he surrounded himself. In fact, Procopius remarked that these talented individuals were God's greatest gift to the ruler. Among them Justinian's generals were perhaps the most striking. Under his general Belisarius, Justinian destroyed the Vandal kingdom of Africa in 534, and under Liberius he gained a strong foothold in Spain in 552. In 535 he began a war with the Ostrogoths of Italy that lasted twenty years and caused more damage to the old heartland of the empire than any of the disasters of the fourth or fifth centuries. Justinian's ambition to reunite all the old parts of the empire was perhaps the only area of his reign in which the usually prudent emperor finally overreached himself.

After the great triumphs of the first fifteen years of his reign, Justinian witnessed new threats and disasters and spent the last twenty-three years doggedly trying to cope with them. In 540 the king of Persia broke the long truce that Justinian had so painfully arranged, and the eastern frontier once again became a troubled land—a land, moreover, with few soldiers left to defend it. In 542 a devastating plague struck the empire, weakening the population and dealing the economy a severe blow. In the 540s also, new immigrants to the Danube and the Black Sea began probing the frontiers and making tentative raids into Thrace and the Balkans. The Bulgar, Avar, and Slavic peoples plagued the northern frontier and occupied much of the time, money, and energy of Justinian and his successors.

The emperor's efforts to stem these new disasters and yet preserve something of the triumphs of the 530s shaped the contemporary image of his last years. To the chroniclers, he became "the emperor who never sleeps"—constantly vigilant, eternally deceptive, all day and night directing the vast and intricate process of salvaging an empire. Justinian gained this reputation by cutting costs, exhausting the treasury left by his predecessors, keeping the western armies small, and experimenting constantly with new military organization and new techniques of diplomacy, restructuring the imperial civil service, and drawing the provincial cities more tightly into the imperial fiscal system. At his death in 565 Justinian saw many of his greatest achievements still intact. Constantinople

The Byzantine Empire.

remained the greatest city in the world, and from it the emperor ruled Thrace and Asia Minor, Syria, Palestine, Egypt, and North Africa. Imperial rule was re-stored in Italy, and from the old imperial and Ostrogothic capital of Ravenna, a window on the East and the end of the sea route from Constantinople, a restored imperial Christianity glittered in the mosaics of imperial churches.

THE CITY

Constantinople—the city that Constantine founded, Theodosius fortified, and Justinian rebuilt—remained the largest, most complex city in Europe until its fall to the Ottoman Turks in 1453. Although it was often besieged and twice captured by invaders, it repelled its enemies far more often than it succumbed. Because of the role of Christianity in the life of its founder, Constantinople claimed a novel sort of Christian legitimacy, and its advocates argued that the city was particularly favored by God because pagan rites had never polluted it. If Rome may be said to have become the city of its patron, Peter, and its bishop, the pope, Constantinople must be said to have been the city of Christian imperial rule, the city of the emperor. Thus, a look at the city as it came from the hand of its imperial restorer, Justinian, tells us more than just a piece of early European urban history. Constantinople was the center of the only Christian empire, and it generated great affection and loyalty in its citizens, as well as awe and envy in the hearts of others.

Its easy access to the Black Sea gave Constantinople control of all trade west of the Caucasus Mountains. By the tenth century the grain, fur, gold, amber, and slaves of the Salvic lands sweeping away to the north were flowing through its port, as did later Islamic trade. Its ready access to the Aegean made communications with other Mediterranean cities easy. From Constantinople across Thrace and the Balkans ran a network of roads, defense works, and frontier forts that protected Greece and dominated the eastern Adriatic Sea. Across Asia Minor ran the great road to the eastern frontier on the Tigris and Euphrates rivers. Constantinople became both a political and a commercial center, fed by the rich agricultural and fishing resources of Greece and Asia Minor, drawing on the populations of these lands for its armies and citizens. It proved a far more secure and strategic capital for the emperors of the east than did the city of Rome, the old center of the empire. From the late fourth century its strategic value was proved beyond any doubt, as wave after wave of invading peoples broke through the imperial frontiers, failed to take Constantinople, and invariably moved west to assault the weaker cities of the western part of the empire.

One of the results of the Nika riots of 532 was the destruction of much of the city; indeed, no building earlier than the sixth century can be identified today. One of the consequences of Justinian's success in quelling the riots was his replanning and rebuilding of much of the great city, which gave it the form it had for almost a thousand years, a form that is still detectable in modern Istanbul. Justinian refurbished the great avenues and arcades of Constantinople, and he constructed immense underground reservoirs to improve the city's water supply—several of which are still in existence. Large public buildings, including hospitals and even the great palace complex itself, were rebuilt. Justinian's city, as archaeologists and art historians have reconstructed it, is clearly one of the most important examples of urban design in human history.

Constantinople was a sacred city as well. Its churches and monasteries were as important as its streets, squares, and walls. Justinian shaped the spiritual city as well as the material one. His triumph was the reconstruction of the magnificent Hagia Sophia. The historian Procopius remarked of this striking building:

Reprinted from Cyril Mango. *The Art of the Byzantine Empire 312–1453: Sources and Documents* (Englewood Cliffs, N.J.: Prentice-Hall, 1972), pp. 8–9.

The great door of the new-built temple groaned on its opening hinges, inviting Emperor and people in enter; and when the inner part was seen, sorrow fled from the hearts of all, as the sun lit the glories of the temple. And when the first gleam of light, rosy-armed driving away the dark shadows, leapt from arch to arch, then all the princes and peoples with one voice hymned their songs of prayer and praise; and as they came to the sacred courts it seemed to them as if the mighty arches were set in heaven.

The sense of vast interior dimensions culminating in the great dome was heightened by intricate marble paving of a great variety of colors and designs, and completed in the great eastern and western apses and in the rows of pillars that supported the north and south galleries, which in turn led the eye upward toward the four great arches. In the pendentives, the

Hagia Sophia, Interior. The interior of Justinian's great church, shown here with later Islamic additions, gives some sense of the awe with which its congregants were struck and helps explain its reputation as the greatest church in the Christian world (Byzantine Visual Resources, ©1988, Dumbarton Oaks, Washington, D.C.)

spaces where the arches join, the figures of great angels appeared to loom over the floor far below; with the row of clear glass windows at the base of the dome, the effect created is that the great dome is not supported by the arches, but is suspended delicately from heaven. No other achievement of Justinian captured both the variety of resources and talents available to the emperor and the emperor's intelligence in using them. Procopius summed up the impression the church made on the people of the city and the empire:

Whenever anyone enters the church to pray, he realizes at once it is not by any human power or skill, but by the influence of God that it has been built. And so his mind is lifted up to God, and he feels that He cannot be far away, but must love to dwell in this place He has chosen. And this does not happen only to one who sees the church for the first time, but the same thing occurs at each successive visit, as though the sight were each time a new one. No one has ever had enough of this spectacle, but when present in the church men rejoice in what they see, and when they are away from it they love to talk about it.

The reaction thus described was surely not unanticipated by Justinian, nor was it limited to the sixth century. When in the tenth century Vladimir of Kiev was negotiating with Constantinople for an alliance, his envoys were shown the glories of the city's ecclesiastical centers and were apparently swayed by them toward Constantinople:

The Greeks led us to the edifices where they worship their God and we knew not whether we were in heaven or on earth. For on earth there is no such splendor or such beauty, and we are at a loss how to describe it. We only know that God dwells there among men and their service is fairer than the ceremonies of other nations. For we cannot forget that beauty.

The later strength of Constantinople lay in her economy, in the new armies and military leaders of the seventh through the early eleventh centuries, and in the talents of her government administrators. But when Constantinople reached out, from the sixth century on, to Slavs, Armenians, and Bulgars, it was the spiritual grandeur of such churches as Hagia Sophia that caught and held peoples' hearts in bonds as strong and enduring as the diplomacy of rulers, the wealth of the empire, or the might of her armies.

THE AGE OF HERACLIUS

Against Justinian's triumphs must be set his failures. The great and expensive military campaigns in the west brought few permanent results. The Visigoths in Spain and the Lombards in Italy slowly extended their control over imperial lands. The emperor's insistence on orthodoxy in religious belief deeply alienated several key provinces, including Egypt and Syria. Even the great fiscal legacy of Anastasius and Justin I could not support the vast plans of Justinian; by the end of the sixth century the empire was almost bankrupt. Moreover, natural disasters took their toll. As we have noted, a great plague swept the empire in 542, and throughout the rest of the sixth century and the seventh century the empire underwent a serious population decline. A smaller population meant a smaller tax base, but the need for money did not diminish. As Justinian's successors discovered, new problems on the northern and eastern frontiers—precisely those areas that Justinian had left unattended—increased the need for money and troops. Not only had Justinian neglected the northern frontiers but he had also bought peace with Persia at the cost of a high tribute. The burden of that tribute grew heavier every year. When Justinian stopped paying it, the eastern frontier with Persia became another danger spot.

Justinian's successors thus faced the prospect of expensive wars on two frontiers. They also had to create a new society in the empire, one geared for continual war. The success of this society lay in drawing on the vast reserves of manpower among the populations of Thrace and Asia Minor and maintaining close control over the armies by means of a complex bureaucracy in the capital. This program was to be financed by new forms of social organization and taxation.

Unlike the organized opposition of Persia to the east, the presence of migrating and invading peoples from the north was intermittent and has left few records. Slavic peoples had begun migrating into the empire after the mid–sixth century, and the invasion of the Asiatic Avar people in the late sixth century drove the Slavs further south and westward. By the end of the sixth century the Slavic peoples were exerting steady pressure on Macedonia and Greece. Thessalonica, the second largest city in the empire, was often under Slavic and sometimes under Avar siege. In 617 a combined Slav and Avar force unsuccessfully assaulted the city of Constantinople itself. Besides Macedonia and Greece, Slavic peoples migrated into eastern Bavaria, Moravia, and Bohemia during this period. Further north, Slavic tribes extended along the shores of the Elbe River. The Avar kingdom in southeastern Europe lasted until its destruction by the armies of Charlemagne in 795.

The threats along the northern and eastern frontiers tested both the abilities and resources of Justinian's successors. The greatest of the late-sixth-century emperors was Maurice (582–602). After ten years of war he achieved a temporary peace with Persia. Facing Lombard pressure in Italy and Slav-Avar pressure south of the Danube, Maurice reorganized the western frontiers. He turned the city of Ravenna into a frontier fortification. He created the office of exarch, combining civil and military government in one official. Maurice also created an exarch at Carthage. These steps helped to turn the provinces into defensive societies protecting a frontier threatened on many sides. During the next two centuries the system developed by Maurice spread from troubled frontier provinces into most of the empire and led to the organization of different regions into *themes*, areas whose civilian population was also its defending army, whose military commanders were also its civil governors. This mobilization of social resources was one of the reasons for the survival of the East Roman Empire. But the price of survival was a different kind of empire.

Maurice was assassinated after a military revolt in 602, and a brutal and incompetent military officer, Phocas, usurped the throne. Probably the worst of the East Roman emperors, Phocas fiercely repressed political opposition at home, and his accession signaled a renewal of the Persian wars. After the first decade of the seventh century, the empire was plunged into a crisis that completed its transformation.

In 610 Heraclius, the son of the exarch of Carthage, led a fleet to Constantinople, captured and killed Phocas, and made himself emperor. The renewal of Persian hostilities under Shah Khosroes II (591–628) occupied most of Heraclius's attention. In a series of quick and thorough campaigns, Khosroes conquered Antioch in 613, Jerusalem in 614, and Egypt in 619. From 620 on he assaulted Constantinople directly. In combination the problems posed by the Slav-Avar coalition and the Persians seemed insurmountable. By 618 Heraclius was seriously considering moving the imperial capital from Constantinople to Carthage.

The population of Constantinople, however, resisted. The church and the citizens submitted voluntarily to even more stringent economic measures. They raised enough money to enable Heraclius to hire a new army, which he took into Persia in a dramatic and unexpected move, leaving Constantinople's own citizens to defend their city against the last and greatest combined offensive of Slavs, Avars, and Persians in 626/627. Heraclius's "new model army" carried all before it. His victories in Persia culminated in the defeat of the last Persian army near Nineveh and the destruction of the shah's palace at Dastgerd. Khosroes II, humiliated by the unexpected reversal of his fortunes, was assassinated in 628. As Heraclius fought his way through Persia in 627, the citizens of Constantinople achieved a victory as great as their emperor's. They destroyed the barbarian fleet that lay before the city, and with it the other great threat to the empire's survival.

But victory proved to be immensely costly. It had exhausted the empire economically and militarily, and it proved that Justinian's dream of a restored Mediterranean Roman Empire was gone forever. The western frontiers proved less important than the north and east. Facing the greatest crisis in the history of the empire, Heraclius and his successors turned away from the Latin west, converting the peasantry of Thrace and Asia Minor into a citizen-army and mobilizing the empire for a different kind of life in a new world.

BYZANTIUM

And they did so just in time. With the new threats from Arabs and Bulgars beginning in the seventh century, the empire faced formidable new enemies, one of which remained a threat until the fall of the Byzantine Empire in 1453.

Molded into a new kind of cultural and political force by the religion of Islam (see next chapter), Arab armies began to move out of the Arabian peninsula, and by 636 they posed a threat to both the East Roman and Persian worlds. Disaffected imperial provinces in Egypt, North Africa, and Palestine either could not or would not put up significant resistance to the conquerors, and the shrunken military resources of Heraclius were not sufficient to stem the invasions. The major Arab defeat of an East Roman army at Yarmuk in 636 cost Heraclius the provinces of Syria and Palestine, and shortly afterwards the Arabs swept into the ruins of the Sasanid Persian empire and conquered it entirely. During the next thirty years Arab commanders prepared to assault Constantinople itself. The first major siege came in 674–678, when Arab fleets managed to blockade the city but failed to breach the walls. In 717–718 Arab armies and fleets assaulted the city again. This time an able Syrian general turned emperor, Leo III (717–741), successfully directed the defense of the city. But even such victories as these cost the empire dearly; much of its southern Mediterranean empire vanished. Indeed, as Arab armies and fleets swept across North Africa and into the Iberian Peninsula, which they conquered between 711 and 720, most traces of the Roman southern Mediterranean were obliterated. From the beginning of the eighth century Arab and East Roman forces struggled along a mountainous frontier in southern Asia Minor. The eastern frontier had come to dominate the energies and attention of the East Roman Empire.

In the Balkans another Asiatic people, the Bulgars, established themselves around 680. After having checked the earlier advances of Slavs and Avars, the empire found itself unable to prevent the establishment of a Bulgar kingdom. The defeat of the emperor Constantine IV in 679 by the forces of the Bulgar khan Asparuch guaranteed Bulgar control of the lower Danube valley. With the establishment of kingdom of the Bulgars, the local Slavonic population came under Bulgar domination. Although the new state experienced dynastic conflicts and rivalries for the kingship in the later seventh and early eighth centuries, a strong kingship emerged from the mid–eighth century on, based on a high degree of integration of Bulgar and Slavic elements in the population. The Bulgarian kingdom, like the empire of Islam, became a permanent force in imperial foreign relations.

The crises in imperial defense of the late sixth, the seventh, and the early eighth centuries were not without their internal consequences. The horizons of the empire had shrunk to the eastern Balkans and southern Asia Minor, and the empire had exhausted the last resources of its people to defend and preserve itself. Heraclius had invoked the aid of supernatural powers to defend Constantinople against the Slavs and Avars, and the appearance of yet newer and more threatening enemies seemed to indicate God's anger at the Christian empire. The permanent war-footing of the imperial economy and the importance of orthodox religious observance helped shape the transformation of the East Roman into the Byzantine Empire, a process that was well under way by the early eighth century. An eastern Mediterranean Christian state, the Byzantine Empire depended for its survival on stringent economy and military alertness and religious uniformity. Its horizons were limited to the Black Sea, the Balkans, northern Greece, and Asia Minor.

In spite of the wars, political upheaval, and religious crises of the seventh and eighth centuries, there is striking evidence of a powerful cultural revival that reflects the transformation of the East Roman to the Byzantine Empire. Although many of the greatest cities of the empire were either lost to Islam or suffered from war, Constantinople itself thrived. A core of educated aristocratic civil servants and churchmen in the city preserved some of the traditions of older learning and generated new cultural interests. Greek became the common language of a population that was, in fact, ethnically heterogeneous—"an ethnographic zoo," as one historian of Byzantine civilization has called it. The Greek language and the orthodox Christianity that had been shaped between the sixth and the ninth centuries constituted the basis of Byzantine civilization.

One of the most striking features of Byzantine civilization is the character of its most representative figures. Churchmen and civil servants, they came from the same ranks of urban Constantinopolitan society, received similar educations, and often followed similar careers in the civil service until their paths divided into the church and government. Such similarity between churchmen and government officials was not to be found in the west until much later, and thus it is possible to speak of an educated class consisting of both churchmen and government officials that formed the basis of Byzantine civilization. Schools appear to have increased and improved in the late eighth century, and a new, more efficient form of handwriting appeared. The study of the Greek classics was resumed, and although Justinian had closed the academy of Plato in Athens in 529, influences of Platonic philosophy remained strong in the highly developed philosophical interests of Greek Christian theology.

A second feature of Byzantine civilization is the pouring of artistic talent and innovation into religious ceremonies and church decoration. From the sixth century on, Syrian musicians helped create liturgical services that were marvels of ritual and of aesthetic achievement. In spite of the threat of iconoclasm, the Byzantine genius for pictorial representation survived and indeed triumphed in the new programs for church decoration that were called for in the ninth and tenth centuries. Although Byzantium has sometimes been criticized for its traditionalism and lack of innovation, its culture was, in fact, more integrated into different social levels and tastes than any European culture until the nineteenth century. Imperial court ceremony, like the liturgy of churches, reflected Byzantine philosophy, and the emperors remained great patrons of the arts.

Third, Byzantium had sustained—and survived—what were probably the most sweeping changes that occurred anywhere in the ancient Mediterranean world. In the West, much of the civilization of antiquity was swept away, and rulers and churchmen could create a new world with fewer restrictions and simpler forms. In the East, however, the legacy of both antique and Christian culture managed to survive in spite of transformations that were as profound as those in the West. The old urban aristocracy gave way to a new aristocracy of generals and civil servants; an old society that depended heavily on slave labor gave way to one in which a free peasantry sustained the economic strength of the state. With the removal of the older aristocracy, the imperial government taxed its population directly, and, except for the great city of Constantinople itself, that population was largely ruralized. Many of the great eastern Mediterranean cities declined in the sixth and seventh centuries, and in their place remained Constantinople alone, ruling an empire of villages and towns and defended by an army that was controlled from Constantinople, under the central authority of the state.

In a sense, this transformation may be regarded as the price paid by East Rome for the survival of the state on a new economic and social basis. Under this new state control, orthodox religious belief, directed from Constantinople, became more rigorous against dissent. Even as it lost territories, the East Roman Empire also lost dissidents. Like the Greek language, orthodox Christianity became another support for the state.

The high quality of Byzantine churchmen and their similarity in social background to the governmental civil servants meant that there was less division than there was in the West between ecclesiastical and temporal affairs. It is in this light that Byzantine political theory ought to be understood. Although the Byzantine emperor is often accused of "caesaropapism"—that is, imperial rule of the Church—it is important to note that the highly developed cosmological ideas of the Byzantines provided a special place in God's favor for the emperor, as ruler of the world and "head of the family of rulers" of all peoples. Moreover, the integration of spiritual and temporal culture meant that the emperor, churchmen, and civil leaders were close together. The genius of Byzantine culture lies precisely in the spiritual bonds that held the secular state together. Byzantines considered their state to be the ideal community, charged by divine command to preserve the true faith. This attitude produced the rich ecclesiastical culture that absorbed much of the Byzantine genius that seems so foreign to modern eyes.

The mosaics, icons, sculpture, and architecture of Byzantine civilization should be looked at with these principles in mind. Beneath the glittering, superbly arranged decorative surfaces lies a spiritual ideal, which literally charges each picture with meaning. In the sonorous, intricate liturgy of the Orthodox church is reflected a whole theology. And through ecclesiastical art and liturgy the ideals of Byzantine civilization were expressed to all classes of the empire. Indeed, it may be said that Byzantine civilization was more deeply and thoroughly rooted in its population than either the civilization of the ancient world or that of the Latin west.

FURTHER READING

See the general bibliography under *Byzantine History*. See also John W. Barker, *Justinian and the Later Roman Empire* (Madison: University of Wisconsin Press, 1966); Robert Browning, *Justinian and Theodora* (London-New York: Thames and Hudson, 1987); Robert Browning, *The Byzantine Empire* (Washington: The Catholic University of America Press, 1992); Alan Cameron, *Circus Factions* (Oxford: Clarendon Press, 1977); Averil Cameron, *Procopius and the Sixth Century* (Oxford: Oxford University Press, 1989).

5

THE RISE OF ISLAM

THE ARAB PEOPLES BEFORE MUHAMMAD

In the deserts of the southern Near East there lived Arab peoples, Semitic-speaking desert nomads and intermittent town-dwellers who had long played a role in Near Eastern history. In earliest Arab history the South Arabian kingdom of Saba, whose most famous ruler was said to have been Solomon's queen of Sheba, was wealthy from the trade in incense and from its place as a middle point between India and the ancient Mediterranean world. The Arab peoples are mentioned by the Greeks as early as the fifth century B.C., and they appear in the Old Testament somewhat earlier. During the rise of Rome, the southern Arabian kingdom grew poorer, and the Arabian peninsula came to be dominated by the nomadic tribes of Bedouins that had long flourished in the north of the peninsula. By the sixth century A.D., many Arabs lived in trading cities, and several Arab kingdoms, notably Nabatea and Palmyra, had risen to considerable prosperity. In addition, two of the northern Arab peoples, the Ghassanids and Lakhmids, were important allies of the Roman and Persian empires. In spite of the prosperity of some segments of northern Arab society, however, the majority of Arabs remained Bedouins, and the "Bedouinization" of Arabian society between the fourth and sixth centuries A.D. is a feature marked by all historians of the period. The nomadic tribe under the direction of its elected *shaykh*, became the module of Arab society. The tribe was characterized by its fierce independence, its warlike character, its devotion to tribal gods, its contempt for the life of the urban Arabs, and its adherence to the concept of '*asabiyya*, tribal kinship, later condemned by Muhammad.

In the fifth and sixth centuries A.D., however, the urban Arabs became more prominent and more wealthy. The trade routes between Yemen and Persia, made dangerous by the wars between Rome and Persia, and the trade routes between Ethiopia and Egypt, made dangerous by the attacks of nomadic tribes, declined in importance. The third route of trade between the Mediterranean and Yemen ran down the western edge of the Arabian Peninsula, and this route may have increased in importance as the other routes declined. Although the towns along the western Arabian route were not the equal of the earlier great cities of South Arabia, several of them grew prosperous, and one, Mecca, became a pilgrimage site as well. Growing trade and the presence of a number of important shrines made Mecca attractive to the desert peoples as well as the urban Arabs. The city's most important shrine was a black meteorite kept in a sanctuary called the *Ka'ba*. The desert tribes that came to Mecca brought their fierce independence with them, and the presence of the Bedouins along with the growing commercial wealth and the inability of traditional Arab culture to deal with such pressures made sixth- and seventh-century Mecca a boom town with a highly volatile civil life.

THE PROPHET

Around 610 a middle-aged Meccan caravan manager, Muhammad, began to receive visions and commands from heaven. In the following years Muhammad delivered "recitations" that God had commanded, his *Qur'an*. Muhammad had been born around 570 in Mecca, the son of 'Abd Allāh, a poor member of the important Quraysh clan. An orphan by the age of six, Muhammad was brought up in the lively and turbulent world of Mecca by his grandfather and his uncle. As a young man he became a successful caravan manager and later married his wealthy employer, the widow Khadija. He did not simply retire to the prosperity that his marriage offered, however. He had been religious all of his life, and his experience of Mecca made the spiritual fate of the Arabs in that violent society his chief concern.

Muhammad's revelations directly addressed that concern. He announced that the single god Allah had been his inspiration, and that the substance of his "recitations," the *Qur'an,* was a body of instructions concerning the only acceptable life a subject of Allah was to live. Although Allah had partially revealed himself to Jews and Christians through the prophets Moses and Jesus, Muhammad received the final and ultimate revelation of divine truth. Muhammad was the "seal of the prophets." The *Qur'an,* which was arranged in *suras* (chapters), declared Allah the only god, to whom humans must subject themselves. The religion Muhammad proclaimed, *Islam,* means "subjection to the will of Allah." Like Jews and Christians, Muslims were considered "People of the Book," but only they knew the final revelation of Allah's will. The injunctions contained in the *Qur'an* attacked the ills of contemporary Arabian society and professed to forge all believers into one great *'Umma,* an expanded conception of an Arab tribe, to which all the faithful would feel primary loyalty, regardless of former ties and allegiances.

At first Muhammad gathered around him a few followers from his family and clan, but subsequently he encountered opposition from the ruling aristocracy of Mecca. Possibly fearful of the decline of the city as a pilgrimage center, and certainly disapproving of Muhammad's low social origins, the Meccan rulers were at first indifferent to the new faith and then actively hostile to it. In 622 Muhammad and his followers were invited to the city of Yathrib, where Muhammad had been designated an outside arbitrator of the city's internal difficulties. The flight from Mecca to Yathrib, which thereafter changed its name to Medina, was called the *Hijra,* and the official calendar of Islam is dated from its beginning, September 24, 622.

At Medina Muhammad was able to give his conception of the Islamic *'Umma* a practical form and to begin the alliances among his original followers, the population of Medina, and the neighboring Bedouin tribes. From Medina Muhammad led a triumphant military force back to Mecca in 630, where he was recognized as a religious leader to whom most of the population of the cities and many more of the desert tribes owed allegiance. Using the ethical force of his religious visions to overcome the divisions that separated the desert Arabs from the Arabs of the cities, Muhammad began to forge a new unified Arab society.

THE FAITH

Although it responded to the cultural, social, and political needs of the Arab people, Islam was unquestionably a religious revolution. Like other religious revolutions, it established a new role for religion in the lives of its followers. The old tribal gods, whether worshiped in the desert or in such sanctuaries as the *Ka'ba* in Mecca, either disappeared or were transformed into *jinn* (spirits). The varieties of religious ritual and custom were obliterated, and in their place stood a unified theological and ethical system that bound the individual soul to God and all believers to one another. Unlike Christianity, Islam offered no distracting theological problems, such as that of the Trinity or that of the relation of the two natures in Christ, that might detract from the absolute single majesty of Allah. Unlike Judaism, it possessed no complex history of theological and eschatological movements, nor was its practice limited by intolerant Christian rulers. The intensity and directness of Islamic belief gave the faith the power to appeal to peoples at all levels of social and theological development. The historian D. M. Dunlop has said:

Islam was no doubt accepted at first by the finer natures and the simple-hearted among [Muham-mad's] hearers, then by a process of growth, the exact character of which remains obscure, but which was certainly not unconnected with Muhammad's growing militancy, proved irresistible, so that the most independent of the tribal chiefs and the most hard-headed of the merchants in general found it necessary to give at least a formal assent to the astonishing claims of Muhammad as Messenger of the Lord of the Worlds and accept the new rules of conduct which he enjoined[1]

The attractiveness of Islam to the ferocious Berbers of Northwest Africa as well as to the subtle theologians and country gentlemen of Persia is eloquent testimony to the personal force of Muhammad and the eloquence of his spiritual message.

At the core of Islam is the *Qur'an* and its great message: There is but one God and Muhammad is His prophet. Muhammad appears to have recited portions of the *Qur'an* aloud during the years from 610 to his death in 632. These recitations were memorized and sometimes copied down by his secretaries and friends, perhaps with direction from the Prophet as to which part of the whole each recitation belonged to. Muhammad regarded his recitations as his own repetition of an unwritten heavenly book, uttered at the command of the angel Gabriel. The entire *Qur'an* is believed to have assumed its present shape between 651 and 656. By that time, the language of the *Qur'an* was regarded as sacred and absolutely authoritative. The 114 *suras* in it were considered to have been dictated by God, and therefore no Muslim may read the *Qur'an* for spiritual benefit in any language other than Arabic, nor may the text be altered in any way. The expansion of Arabic political power in the seventh and eighth centuries was accompanied by the spread of the Arabic language as new converts to Islam were made. The *Qur'an* became a spiritual guide, a language manual, and the greatest schoolbook in the Islamic world. It was also a code of law and ethics, a book of political theory, and a guide to conduct.

At the core of Islam is the single truth that Allah is God and Muhammad is His Prophet. Radiating from that core is the dramatically simple ethical law of Islam, the *Shari'a,* a code of law and theology at the same time. The first of the demands of that law was the acknowledgment of Allah and of Muhammad's authentic prophetic role. The ritual prayer said five times a day, with the great public prayer at midday on Friday, was the second element. The third was the observation of the holy month of Ramadan by fasting from dawn to sunset. Visiting Mecca once in a lifetime, if possible, was the fourth. Almsgiving was the fifth demand. These elements of Islam are the same for Muslims today as they were in the seventh century, and the moving passage in *The Autobiography of Malcolm X* describing Malcolm's pilgrimage to Mecca is in the direct tradition of the earliest recorded Arabic pilgrimages. Faithful observance of the law gave the Muslim a place in paradise.

Throughout the Middle Ages—in fact, to the present day—Islam has been much misunderstood and maligned in the West. In particular, the elements

---

[1]D. M. Dunlop, *Arab Civilization to* A.D. *1500* (New York: Longman, 1971), 11–12.

of Islamic law that reflect directly the customs of the seventh-century desert tribesmen—especially the predominance of the male, the abstention from pork and alcohol, and the surprisingly fleshly delights of the Muslim paradise—have detracted attention from other and ultimately far more influential Muslim beliefs. For the Muslim no priest intervenes between the individual and God; there is no Islamic liturgy; the visual representation of living things is restricted; and knowledge of the *Qur'an*—even the memorization of the text—is praiseworthy.

THE PROTECTORS OF THE FAITH AND THE SPREAD OF ISLAM

Muhammad died in 632, leaving no instructions concerning a successor. Because many of the tribes that had submitted to him considered his death the severance of their bond, the problem of a successor became extremely important. Such a leader could not be called Prophet, for that title always designated Muhammad alone. Nor could he be a *shaykh,* which was a tribal title. Ultimately, one of Muhammad's followers, Abu Bakr, was elected by the others as Muhammad's "representative" and given the title *khalifa* (successor). Islamic historians recognize three groups of *khalifas* between 632 and 1258; the "rightly guided" caliphs, from Abu Bakr (632–634) to Muhammad's son-in-law Ali (656–661); the Umayyad dynasty, from Muawiyah (661–680) to Marwan II (744–750); and the Abbasid dynasty, from Abu-l-Abbas (750–754) to the end of the caliphate in 1258.

The "rightly guided" caliphs faced the problems of organizing the Muslim peoples in the absence of Muhammad. The Umayyad dynasty directed the great eastward expansion from their capital at Damascus. The Abbasid dynasty represented the culmination of Muslim expansion and the rise to prominence of nonethnic Arabs in the Islamic world, symbolized by their move of the capital to Baghdad. There occasionally arose rival caliphates (by the tenth century there were two others, in Spain and Egypt) and sectarian leaders who denounced the caliphs. Nevertheless, the caliph, first at Damascus and then at Baghdad, was the official orthodox protector of the faith, interpreter of the *Qur'an* and temporal and spiritual leader of Islamic society.

Muhammad's small community of original followers at Medina bitterly resented their exile from Mecca, and they adopted the old tribal custom of the *ghazwa* (raid or expedition) against those who had scorned them and driven them out. The *Qur'an* calls these activities "striving in the way of the Lord," or *jihad fi sabil Allah*. The *jihad*, misleadingly called the "Holy War" by Westerners, was a Muslim adaptation of the tribal *ghazwa.* Used against persecuters of Muslims, and later against pagans, the *jihad* became one focus of Muslim society under the first caliphs. Raiding against infidels was permitted, then encouraged so that the energies of the warlike desert tribes could be channeled. The purpose of the raids was not to convert the victims, however, but to make them submit to Muslim rule and pay taxes. The plunder of the old *ghazwa* became

The expanding Muslim zone.

the territorial conquests of the new *jihad*. Only Christians, Jews, and Zoroastrians were entitled to the status of protected minorities if they surrendered to Islamic armies; they were called *dhimmis,* and had to pay a smaller tax. For Muhammad and his successors, the conversion of the Arabs to Islam was the primary goal. Others were to be plundered and governed, but they were never faced with the choice of Islam or the sword, as historians once believed. Although many non-Arabs became Muslims, they did not do so because they were forced.

Under Abu Bakr Islam was consolidated among the Arabs, and tribes that had broken off from Islam at the death of Muhammad were brought back into the Islamic federation. Under Abu Bakr's successor Umar (634–644) and the great general Khalid, Arabic armies raided outside the peninsula into the Byzantine and Persian worlds. Exhausted border provinces and disaffected provincials of Palestine, Syria, Egypt, Africa, and Persia passed quickly under Muslim rule. Even the armies of the Byzantine and Persian empires, worn out after the long Byzantine-Persian war, fell before the skillful generalship and superior tactics of the Arabs. The battle of the Yarmuk (Jordan) in 636 destroyed Byzantine resistance, and the battle of al-Mada'in in Persia in 638 virtually wiped out Persian resistance. By 698 Byzantine Africa and Egypt had fallen to Islamic armies.

The direction of the Arab armies was in the hands of able caliphs and their talented generals, supported by an Arab military aristocracy comprising male Arabs who were given a stipend by the caliph if they fought or performed other work for the state. Relieving the Arab military forces of the need for other work and promising a place in paradise to anyone who died a warrior's death, the caliphs and their generals soon created a large, able, and dedicated army. Nothing in the Mediterranean or Persian worlds could match it. Further, the army was kept intact as it cut its way through the south and east of the ancient world. It was contained in separate camps when it conquered territory, isolated from the life of the cities it conquered. The cities of Basra, Kufa, and al-Fustat (the earliest settlement of Cairo) began as such military camps.

Under Abu Bakr and Umar, Arab armies were usually irresistible. Military success was followed by political success, as the Arabs organized their newly won states into wealthy, tribute-paying provinces ruled by the caliphs at Medina. With the reign of Uthman (644–656), however, the problem of succession to the caliphate once more came to the fore. Uthman's successor was Ali, son-in-law and cousin of Muhammad. Ali's rule (565–661) encountered opposition from among Muhammad's old followers and from the great general Muawiyah, who eventually succeeded Ali in the caliphate (661–680) upon Ali's assassination.

The second half of the seventh century was a period of great instability in the central provinces of the Empire. Civil wars and revolts finally drove Ali's dynasty from the throne and replaced it with that of Muawiyah, the Umayyad dynasty, which ruled Islam until 750. The devastation of central Arabia inspired Muawiyah to move the capital of the empire to Damascus, and the displacement of Ali's dynasty contributed to the formation of Shi'ism, the belief that recognizes only Ali's descendants as true caliphs. The victors in the struggle called themselves Sunnites, claiming that they alone followed the orally transmitted commands of Muhammad and were therefore orthodox. From the end of the seventh century to the present, Shi'ite Muslims have been rivals of Sunnite orthodoxy. Politically, Shi'ites recognized lines of successors descended from different wives of Ali. They called the representatives of these lines *Imams,* and they believed that the last *Imam* would appear at some future time as the *Mahdi,* the savior of Shi'ite Islam. Different Shi'ite groups recognized different *Imams* as the future *Mahdi,* and one of these groups established a separate caliphate at Cairo in 973, ruled by the Fatimid dynasty, whose eponym was Fatima, Muhammad's daughter and Ali's first wife.

The internal crises that established the Umayyad dynasty at Damascus and sowed the seeds of Shi'ite-Sunnite dissension in the Muslim world did not, however, slow the process of conquest for long. As early as 647 Muawiyah had begun raids into Asia Minor, and at the same time he began to build an Arab fleet so that Constantinople itself might be assaulted by sea and land. As we have seen, in 678 and again in 717–718, massive Muslim forces assaulted the great city. The frontier between the Byzantine Empire and the Caliphate at Damascus slowly stabilized in southern Asia Minor. At the other end of the Mediterranean, Arab armies swept across North Africa. In the first years of the eighth century one military leader, Tariq, crossed the Strait of Gibraltar into Visigothic Spain, and between 711 and 720 Arab armies destroyed the Visigothic kingdom. Tariq's route has been memorialized in the name Gibraltar, for the Arabic *Jabal-al-Tariq* means "the hill of Tariq." The rapid Muslim conquest of Spain drove the last Visigothic rulers north, where the tiny kingdom of Asturias and the independent Christian Basques maintained their precarious independence.

From Spain Arab raiding armies pushed into southern Gaul, and only the exhaustion caused by the long drive across North Africa and the conquest and settlement of Spain prevented a permanent Arab settlement there. Arab armies regularly raided Gaul until the tenth century, but resistance proved to be stiffer there than elsewhere. After several governors of Muslim Spain had lost their lives in raiding parties, Abd-ar-Rahman, the governor of northern Spain, made an initially successful campaign around Poitiers and then marched on the old city of Tours. Near that city, in 733, he encountered an army of Franks led by Charles Martel, the mayor of the palace of Austrasia. Charles's forces defeated the Muslim army, killing Abd-ar-Rahman and forcing the Muslims to withdraw to Spain for a time. Although Charles Martel's victory has long occupied a prominent place in Western history, it was far more significant in increasing his personal power than in preventing the Arabs from conquering Gaul. In the latter respect, the successful defenses of Constantinople in 678 and 717–718 were far more important in the long run for Christian Europe. As later history shows, the area from the head of the Aegean Sea to the Caspian Sea was the real gateway to Europe, and the centuries-long resistance of Constantinople played a very important part in controlling the northward expansion of Islam.

THE UMAYYAD DYNASTY AT DAMASCUS

Damascus, the new capital of the Muslim Empire, quickly fell under the influence of Byzantine civilization. Greek scientific learning, Syrian art, and the vibrant commercial and social life of Egypt, Palestine, and Syria attracted the conquerors, and until 750 Syria was the first province of the empire. The culture of the conquerors was developed by prolonged contact with that of the old Hellenistic world. Greek and Syrian Christian administrators ruled in the service of the caliph, and subject peoples supported the regime with their taxes. The court of the Umayyad caliphs appears to have been modeled on the imperial court at Constantinople.

The prosperity of the Umayyad caliphate was also reflected in the building and decorative programs undertaken in Damascus itself, as the tribute of a conquered world flowed into the hands of the Arab ruling elite. Although two wars with the Khazars, a Turkic people settled north of the Caucasus, in 642–652 and 722–737, stopped the Muslim advance to the north, Islam moved far to the east with the conquest of Iraq and Persia and victories in Turkestan and Sind. An Arab army even defeated a Chinese army north of the Jaxartes River in 751, but the conquest of China was beyond Muslim resources. From their capital at Damascus the Umayyad caliphs ruled an enormous empire, and they prospered from the material and the cultural gains that empire gave them. Tolerant of other cultures and religions, the Umayyads profited from them too.

The conquests of the late sixth and seventh centuries brought great power and wealth, and also a great stimulus for cultural development, to the Arabs. The rude warriors of the first conquests educated and acculturated their children in the complex and fascinating ways of the world they had conquered. In addition to this slow change in Arabic culture was a change of even greater importance. Although the Muslims did not proselytize among the conquered peoples, many of them converted to Islam nonetheless—so many, in fact, that by the early eighth century the ethnic Arabic element among the Muslims had begun to decline sharply.

THE ABBASID DYNASTY IN BAGHDAD

In 747 a revolt broke out in Iraq against Umayyad rule, and by 750 Abu-l-Abbas had defeated and killed the last Umayyad caliph and exterminated the rest of the family, except for one prince, Abd-ar-Rahman I, who escaped to Spain and founded an emirate (a local principality) and later an independent Umayyad caliphate at Córdoba. The Abbasid dynasty founded by Abu-l-Abbas represented not only a political revolution but also a cultural change in Islam of great importance. The Abbasid caliphs greatly emphasized their religious orthodoxy and criticized the earlier secularizing tendencies of the Umayyads. In addition, they viewed Arab and non-Arab Muslims as equal, regarded the merchant, the judge, and the administrator as ideal citizens, rather than the soldier, and fell under the progressively greater influence of the old Sasanian Persian culture. In 762 the Abbasids built a new city, Baghdad, on the Tigris River, far to the Persian east of Damascus. From the foundation of Baghdad dates the decline of Syria into a second-class province and the rise of Persia as the center of the Islamic Empire. During the first century of the Abbasid reign, large numbers of scientific, philosophical, and theoretical works were translated into Arabic from Greek, Syriac, Persian, and Hindi, and extensive building programs began to create the new face of the Near Eastern world.

The period 750–833 marked the highest achievements of the Abbasid caliphs. Several of them notably Harun-al-Rashid (786–809) and al-Ma'mun (813–833) have become legendary figures even in the West, the former through the *Arabian Nights* and the legends of his wealth and personal style of rule, and the latter from his patronage of learning. But from the late ninth century, the Abbasid caliphs were gradually overshadowed by their powerful advisers and administrators, and local princes often proclaimed their independence of Baghdad. By 1055 a new official called the sultan had become the effective head of the Abbasid state. From the very beginning of the dynasty,

Spain had broken away and later proclaimed its own Umayyad caliph. Other princely dynasties in North Africa proclaimed their independence. As we have seen a Shi'ite caliphate of the Fatimid dynasty was proclaimed in Egypt in 973, and it lasted until 1171.

Political fragmentation of the Islamic world was thus a marked feature of the ninth, tenth, and eleventh centuries. The Abbasid caliphate survived, much weakened, until 1258, when the Mongols captured the city and killed the last caliph, Al-Mustasim. What survived the Abbasid power was not the political unity of an empire, then, but a politically divided world bound by a common religion, language, and culture. Islamic civilization replaced Islamic political unity.

ISLAMIC CIVILIZATION

The desert Arabs who had struck out at the Greco-Roman and Persian worlds in the middle of the seventh century became both their conquerors and their cultural heirs. As early as 700 the intellectual and artistic legacy of those ancient worlds began to influence Arabic culture. By the tenth century Muslims had absorbed and put to their own uses the cultures of the Byzantine and Persian worlds. They had shaped a geographical-cultural world unlike any other ever seen. By extending their culture throughout most of the Mediterranean basin and well onto the Iranian plateau, Muslims assumed some of the older roles of both East Rome and Persia, permitting the interaction among different religious traditions and constituting the main route of long-distance trade between East Asia and the western Mediterranean and Europe.

Islamic civilization conquered worlds and also opened markets. During the Fatimid period in Egypt (969–1171), golden coins called *dinars* circulated so widely throughout western Europe, India, and even China, that they have been called "the dollar of the Middle Ages." Economic exchange went hand-in-hand with agricultural exchange. Muslim agricultural innovation brought many new plant varieties into the Mediterranean world, including hard wheat, rice, sugar cane, cotton, watermelons, eggplants, spinach, artichokes, sour oranges, lemons, limes, bananas, mangoes, and coconut palms. Agricultural engineering techniques developed new and extensive systems of irrigation.

Besides economic and agricultural innovation, Muslim thinkers also appropriated much of the scientific and philosophical legacy of ancient Persia and the Mediterranean world. The Arabic language, given stimulus by the *Qu'ran* itself, possessed a rich heritage of oral poetry, and the development of Arabic prose from the seventh century on made Arabic a flexible and complex language, capable of translating the most complex Greek philosophical and scientific works, including, by 1050, virtually all of Aristotle. Under the caliph Ma'mun (813–833), a regular school of translators operated, translating literary and scientific works from Greek, often via Syriac. The emergence of Islam opened a world of many other things besides conquests.

In terms of material culture, Muslims created a physical "look" to their world that is readily identifiable today. They were great city-builders, and two of their early triumphs, Baghdad and Cairo, are still great cities. Even in modern Spain, the Islamic architectural influences are readily visible. The *masjids* (houses for prayer), with their distinctive courtyards and minarets, the *madrasas* (schools for the study of law), the baths, bazaars, and markets reflect a flowering of urban culture. The life of the cities was supported by a rich agriculture, scientific and innovative, which made material life for the better-off Muslims as comfortable as anywhere in the world. The Islamic development of such architectural features as the pointed arch, traceried windows, and decorative script, as well as fountains, gardens, and secluded courtyards, not only shaped the physical appearance of the Islamic world, but may very well have contributed to important aspects of western European architecture.

Islamic architecture and its highly developed material culture should also be regarded in the light of the Islamic interest in mathematics and the natural sciences, in which Muslims did some of the greatest work the world had ever seen. They studied the logical and scientific works of Aristotle and even surpassed the Greek philosopher in mathematics and astronomy. They adopted and perfected a new system of numeration (the Arabic numerals used today throughout the world), and they introduced the concept of zero. They developed a means of solving mathematical problems by transposing part of the problem to the "zero" side of an equation, calling the process *aljabr,* or algebra. Muslim scholars discussed the possibility of the earth's rotating on its axis, and they mapped the skies, giving many stars and constellations the names they bear today. From their work in mathematics and astronomy Muslim thinkers went on to new studies and discoveries in optics and experimental chemistry. In the latter field they were the first people to perfect the processes of distillation and sublimation.

The remarkable skill that the Muslims displayed in the physical sciences carried into medicine as well. Avicenna (Ibn Sina, 922–1037) produced a medical encyclopedia that outlined the contagious character of tuberculosis and proposed a theory of the etiology of disease based upon the contamination of water supplies. His work was translated into Latin and European vernacular languages and became, along with several other Arabic medical studies, a major medical reference work in the West. Arabic medicine was especially successful in treating eye diseases and plague. In addition, the Arab world saw the earliest development of the modern hospital.

In philosophy, too, Muslim thinkers absorbed and transformed the work not only of Aristotle but of Plato and Neoplatonists as well. The greatest of all medieval commentators on Aristotle was Ibn Rushd (Averroës, d. 1199), many of whose commentaries were made known to the west in Latin translations at the beginning of the thirteenth century.

On less formal levels of culture too, the Islamic conquests produced a thoroughgoing cultural revolution. The *Qur'an* was the basic textbook, as we have seen, for learning the Arabic language. The *shari'a,* the ethical law of the

Qur'an, shaped legal decisions and individual conduct, down to matters of personal hygiene and proper social behavior and responsibility. Thus, in spite of political divisions, the daily life and thought of most of the Muslim world centered on the *Qur'an;* it played an immensely important social and philosophical role as well as a major religious role. As a body of commentary and interpretation grew up around the text of the *Qur'an* and other religious literature that was regarded as pious (such as the *hadith,* words and deeds of Muhammad), schools of formal theology and guilds of law created new intellectual elites who played prominent roles in the Islamic world. Independent devotional movements, such as Sufism, drew their inspiration from the *Qur'an* and created a mystical movement in Islam that proved immensely attractive to many people who had no part in the more formalized intellectual circles of their world.

The economic, intellectual, and spiritual vitality of the Muslim world, particularly between the seventh and the twelfth centuries, is a remarkable part of the rise of Islam. To some extent it is just as remarkable as the appearance of the faith itself, the achievements of Muhammad, and the great early conquests. A religion of desert Arabs created armies, generals, and caliphs, plus a genuine cultural revolution that transformed, once and for all, not only the southern and eastern parts of the old Roman Empire, but the ancient Persian world as well, and extended beyond the Caucasus, India, and even southeast Asia. Where conquest went and religion followed, language went too. The Arabic-speaking world is the world of Islamic belief, and beneath that belief lies a formidable culture. That culture shaped the golden age of Islam and later provided for western Europeans many of the scientific and philosophical tools and economic institutions that contributed to the numerous changes in European society in the twelfth and thirteenth centuries.

FURTHER READING

See the General Bibliography on *Islamic History.* On the Arabian peninsula, see Glen W. Bowersock, *Roman Arabia* (Berkeley-Los Angels: University of California Press, 1983). On the Prophet, see F. E. Peters, *Muhammad and the Origins of Islam* (Binghamton: State University of New York Press, 1990); Hugh Kennedy, *The Prophet and the Age of the Caliphates* (London: 1986). On the holy city and the pilgrimage, see F. E. Peters, *Mecca: A Literary History of the Muslim Holy Land* (Princeton: Princeton University Press, 1994), and F. E. Peters, *The Hajj: The Muslim Pilgrimage to Mecca and the Holy Places* (Princeton: Princeton University Press, 1995). The best study of the early conquests is that of J. Fred Donner, *The Early Islamic Conquests* (Princeton: Princeton University Press, 1981). On material culture and the economy, see Andrew M. Watson, *Agricultural Innovation in the Early Islamic World* (Cambridge: Cambridge University Press, 1988), and George F. Hourani, *Arab Seafaring* (Princeton: Princeton University Press, 1995).

6

CHRISTIAN ROME AND THE NEW EUROPEANS

ITALY IN THE SIXTH AND SEVENTH CENTURIES

The transformation of the East Roman empire in response to the threats posed by Slavic and Persian invasions in the early seventh century and Islamic and Bulgar invasions in the later seventh and early eighth centuries was not the only cause of the growing division between the eastern and western halves of the Roman Empire. In Italy, Gaul, and Iberia a new localism and new political crises also contributed to the division. Some of these circumstances can be seen in the consequences of Justinian's attempt to reunite the empire in the first half of the sixth century.

From 535 to 554 Italy was wracked by Justinian's campaign of reconquest against the Ostrogoths. Early imperial victories under the able generalship of Belisarius provoked stiffer Gothic resistance, and under several kings, notably Totila (541–552), the Goths won back much of what had been lost. The twenty years of war, however, the increasing size of the contending armies, and the refusal of either side to negotiate resulted in the physical and demographic devastation of Italy, far greater than any earlier destruction. In addition to the wars, widespread famine in 538 and the years following, as well as devastating plagues in 542 and 589, and a particularly savage sequence of floods and other natural disasters further reduced the resources and population of Italy. After Justinian imposed a new peace in Italy with his Pragmatic Sanction of 554, Italy enjoyed only fifteen years of peace before a group of new invaders, the Lombards, introduced a new and dominant force in the peninsula that remained aggressive and dangerous for the next two centuries. Lombard hostility to what remained of Byzantine power in Italy (chiefly in the east and south of the peninsula) led the bishops of Rome to assume the role of middlemen between the two hostile powers and eventually to become the focus of the relations among Byzantines, Lombards, and Franks in central and northern Italy.

War, famine, plague, and new invasions greatly affected the social structure of Italy as well. Many Italian aristocrats had fled Italy during the Gothic Wars, either to their estates in Sicily or North Africa or to Constantinople. Many of those who fled did not return. By 600 the Roman Senate had disapeared as a body; the last reported official meeting of a town council outside Rome or Ravenna took place in 565. In those territories still controlled by the East Roman empire, the Byzantine military took the place of the older local aristocracy. Although Justinian's Pragmatic Sanction had envisioned the separation of civil and military authority in Italy, the Lombard invasions and the disappearance of much of the older aristocracy made such a separation impossible. There is no better sign of this failure than the fact that although Justinian sent his new official collection of Roman law to the west, there is no evidence that it was ever used until the late eleventh century. Until then, Roman law in Italy and elsewhere in the west remained the scattered, private, and simplified collections that were adopted and used by local powers, Roman and barbarian both. There arose in Byzantine-controlled Italy a closely integrated military ruling class, at the head of which, from the late sixth century on, was an official known as the *exarch*, who was directly appointed from Constantinople and usually resided at Ravenna.

Side-by-side with the new military aristocracy there emerged the Christian higher clergy. During the sixth and seventh centuries the clergy assumed more and more of the responsibilities for the civil administration of the cities. These included the supervision of urban food supplies, the distribution of charity, the maintenance of walls, gates, aquaducts, and buildings, public spectacles, and the law courts. Although the churches of the leading cities—Milan, Pavia, and Ravenna—prided themselves on their local independence, the long-range consequences of these changes are best reflected in the position of the bishops of Rome.

The case of the city of Rome illustrates better than any other the effects of the sixth-century changes in Italy. Taken by Belisarius in 536, the city was besieged by the Goths and recaptured by them in 546. Much of the city was dismantled and the population scattered before the Goths abandoned the city in 547. The Byzantine reoccupation lasted for only a short time before the Goths once more took the city in 549/550, and not until 552 were they driven out for good. Not only the sieges, but the deliberately destructive policy of the Gothic king Totila, which included prolonged blockades and induced famine, reduced the fabric and life of Rome during fifteen years of unremitting conflict. The population of the city was well along the precipitous decline from nearly one million in the age of Constantine to twenty thousand by the late eighth century. As the population decreased, large formerly inhabited areas of the city became vacant; ancient palaces crumbled, their structural elements often recycled into newer and smaller buildings. With the disappearance of consuls, urban prefects, most of the civil bureaucracy, and the old aristocracy, the clergy undertook to provide what minimal public services were possible. By the late sixth century the city of Rome had acquired the shape and character it was to possess until modern times.

Far from accomplishing the reintegration of the western and eastern parts of the Empire, Justinian's reconquests marked the real transformation of the world of antiquity. The former imperial provinces were now the setting for Germanic kingdoms in Iberia and Gaul. Italy itself was divided among the Lombards and Byzantines, with the clergy acting as a reluctant, uneasy, and often mistrusted mediator between them. The old aristocracy was gone, and the cities themselves were taking on new physical shapes. Civil administration was giving way to ecclesiastical administration—where there were affairs to be administered at all. A new world was emerging, one that can be seen most clearly in the life, writings, and achievements of Pope Gregory I.

GOD'S CONSUL

Gregory I, commonly and accurately designated "the Great," was a Roman noble, born around 540 into one of the immensely wealthy aristocratic Roman families. Part of his childhood was spent on family estates outside Italy, where his family had fled to avoid the dangers of the Gothic wars. Rising in the municipal civil service, Gregory became head of the civil administration of Rome when he suddenly decided to turn his family property over to the Church and to enter as a novice a monastery that he himself had founded, that of St. Andrew on the Caelian Hill. Ordained a deacon in 579, Gregory was designated by Pelagius II (579–590) as *apocrisiarius* (since the early sixth century the office of legate of the bishop of Rome to the imperial court at Constantinople), and in 590 he was elected bishop of Rome.

A number of Gregory's sixty-century predecessors, notably Pelagius II, had continued the ecclesiastical administration of urban offices and services in Rome—large-scale relief for the poor, maintenance of the physical fabric of the city, including its churches, the restoration of dilapidated buildings, and the organization of the increasing territorial wealth of the Church. Gregory I continued and routinized these practices as functions of the Roman episcopal office, but he went much further than this. Loyal to the empire, he sustained diplomatic relations with Constantinople and explored relations with the Lombard rulers of Italy. Finally, he examined in detail the character of clerical life and ecclesiastical office, and he opened new avenues of communication with

Christians scattered throughout the fragmented world of late sixth- and seventh-century western Europe. In many respects he might be termed the inventor of modern Europe.

Such a range of duties carried out by a man with a broad and novel vision of his own world is remarkable. The register of Gregory's letters, the only collection of papal letters besides that of Leo I (440–461) to have survived complete from before the end of the eleventh century, reveals a strong sense of both missionary zeal and diplomatic propriety, and it maps Gregory's attempts to restore communication between Rome and the bishops and kings of western Europe. Gregory's letters contain both theological and administrative instructions, and they may justly be considered among the most important monuments in papal history. Gregory also wrote cautious, discreet letters to barbarian rulers, and to emperors at Constantinople as well. This papal diplomacy constituted the first recognition that the barbarians were here to stay; that, in effect, a new Europe had taken shape.

Gregory's letters depict an ideal of clerical responsibility and conduct that had a great influence on later European civilization. The French historian Jean Gaudemet called these letters and Gregory's treatise *The Book of Pastoral Care* a "mirror for bishops." They embrace the most influential definition of episcopal office written since the work of Ambrose in the fourth century, a definition reflected in later papal regulations, in Church law codes, and in later biographies of saintly bishops. The straightforward and practical *Book of Pastoral Care* has as its theme Gregory's favorite maxim: "The care of souls is the art of all arts." It is largely through Gregory's work that the episcopal ideals of the Church between the fourth and the seventh centuries were transmitted to later centuries, and these ideals still define clerical conduct in most modern episcopal churches. Gregory himself, through his responsibilities for large ecclesiastical properties, knew from experience the practical requirements of ecclesiastical leadership, and, like many talented Roman administrators, he was able to apply his own experience to a treatise written for others.

Gregory also wrote a voluminous commentary on the Book of Job, the *Moralia*. In it he adapted for a far less learned and less sophisticated audience both the fourfold allegorical technique of interpreting Scripture, which had begun with Philo and Origen, and the theological works of his great predecessors Jerome and Augustine. Like *Pastoral Care*, the *Moralia* played an immensely important role in passing down to later centuries the scriptural interpretive techniques and the body of theological knowledge developed in the great age of the fourth and fifth centuries. Gregory has often been accused of thinning out the rich complexities of earlier doctrine and simplifying it, but it may also be said that he passed down these techniques and belief in the only form that people could use easily.

Gregory's Rome had become primarily the Rome of Peter, rather than the Rome of Augustus or Hadrian, or even the Rome of Constantine. Gregory played an important role in the devotional history of the Latin West by his cultivation of the lives and stories of saints and holy places. Gregory's approach to the saints, however, has a far larger aspect of legend and emphasis on dramatic miracles than many earlier saints' lives. In 593/594 Gregory wrote a long work called the *Dialogues,* which, in the form of a series of saints' lives, purports to be conversations between himself and the Deacon Peter about beliefs concerning saints, relics, and miracles. The *Dialogues* too had a great influence on later thought and literature. Gregory's interest in miracle, the drama of sanctity, and the manifestations of God's power in the physical world made his stories simpler, more imaginative, and more widely appealing than many earlier lives of saints, and thus played an important—and as yet unwritten—role in the history of Christian biography.

In his instructions to bishops, his allegorical interpretation of Scripture, his miracle stories, and his letters, Gregory showed great resourcefulness. Although his work has been criticized as reflecting a decline from the theological and intellectual standards of earlier periods, it certainly reflects the concerns of Gregory's age and addresses those concerns with great care and native intelligence. For example, strong anti-Jewish attitudes appeared in the sixth century, and Visigothic kings of Spain issued the first anti-Jewish laws in European history. Gregory, however, fought powerfully against the forced conversion and oppression of Jews.

Although Gregory conceived his world in terms that were consistent with those of traditional Christianized imperial Rome and always deferred to the emperor at Constantinople, the worlds of western Europe and Byzantium were drifting rapidly apart, and nowhere does Gregory's thought reflect this more than in the transformation of his doctrine of conversion. His early statements on the conversion of pagans and heretics are consistent with the view of the Christianized Roman Empire after the fourth century: Christendom and imperial Rome are coterminous, and clerics and holders of power together must bring about the conversion to Christianity of all within the empire. This view had developed at a time when Romans were relatively unconcerned about the Christianization of peoples outside the empire, those conversions being the work of individuals with no imperial support or favor. They characterize Roman attitudes through the sixth century. Gregory continued his loyalty to the empire, but in his handling of the conversion of peoples outside the empire he gradually adapted the earlier and rigid imperial conversion policies to a set of more flexible and adaptable approaches to a problem that was much more complex than that inside the empire. Side-by-side with Gregory's imperial loyalty, his concerns for Rome and Italy, and his respect for fellow bishops in the East and the West, Gregory also perceived that the Christianization of the West posed unique problems and that the transition from paganism to Christianity in western Europe required policies different from those in use in the empire for two centuries. In this sense, the bishops of Rome adapted their policies of conversion to individual novel circumstances and laid the foundations for the idea of Christendom as the unifying bond among the different societies and kingdoms of a fragmented western Europe.

Other aspects of Gregory's thought are equally striking. Sixth-century Christianity demonstrated a heightened interest in demons, miracles, and legend. Although Gregory could not do away with the new fascination with demons and magicians and exotic adventures in devotional literature, his stories could at least show that such forces were always defeated by simple Christian practices. Later, in the fifteenth and sixteenth centuries, when such a simple Christianity no longer satisfied people's fears of demonic power, the new science of demonology led to the great persecutions of magicians and witches that did not end until the end of the seventeenth century. The demons and magicians were a vivid part of Gregory's universe, but they were kept firmly under control by no more than simple Christian practices and demonstrations of sanctity. When the souls of the dead or saints appeared, it was usually to inspire, not to terrify, the living.

Gregory taught by other means as well. At his urging, the visual depiction of scriptural scenes on the walls of churches (and, later, on church windows) took on a new role; they were to become "the scriptures of the unlettered," the teachers of the illiterate. The motifs of Romano-Christian visual art, like the principles of late Roman ecclesiastical administration, were transformed into instructional materials for the new European world. By his death in 604, at the end of a life wracked by physical illness and exhausting concern for the Christian world, Gregory had succeeded in beginning the reorientation of the Latin Church toward its new members. He had taken steps to define principles of missionary work and conversion, re-established papal contact with the far-flung churches from Spain to Britain and from Italy to Alexandria, and shaped the mold of Christian devotion in forms that lasted for a thousand years. His epitaph, a long Latin tribute to his work and saintliness, calls Gregory "God's Consul." There is no more succinct expression of Gregory's Roman and Christian antecedents, nor a better description of his service to his own and future generations.

THE DESERT IN THE WEST: MONKS, MISSIONARIES, AND CULTURE

Among the forms of abandoning the world that emerged in the late third and fourth centuries, monasticism (the word comes from the Greek *monos*, "one," or "alone") was one of the most original, creative, enduring, and influential in later European history. One sign of its creativity has already been noted—the tendency, well underway in the late fourth century, first in eastern, and later in western Christianity, to create communities of monks under the leadership of a single abbot (the word derives from the Coptic *apa*, "father") and following a common rule of life. From the late sixth century on, monasticism became one of the most important institutions in the organization of European social and religious life.

Two of Gregory the Great's major achievements were the sponsorship of monasticism in the Latin Church and—his best-known missionary achievement—

the efforts to convert the pagan and Arian inhabitants of Germanic Europe. Between the sixth and the twelfth centuries, monks and missionaries not only shaped the dominant forms of Christianity and achieved the conversion of Europe, but also passed down the only legacy of the ancient world that early Europeans possessed.

As we have seen, hermits and monks became an important feature of Christianity in the third and fourth centuries, first in Egypt and then in Syria and the eastern Mediterranean. The appeal of a life of isolation and prayer spread quickly, and in the fourth century a number of individuals withdrew from the world, seeking such a life in the wilderness of Italy and Gaul. Martin of Tours (ca. 335–397) was a striking and influential example of such a person. Martin was a Roman soldier who converted to Christianity, left the army, wandered through several Roman provinces, and settled in Gaul, where he soon attracted followers and began to convert the rural population around Tours. He became bishop of Tours in 372 and patronized the spread of other monastic communities.

In the early years of the fifth century, a Gallic Roman named John Cassian (385–440) made a journey to the monastic centers of the east and returned to Gaul with a plan for an ideal monastery and a large literature on monastic life that he had acquired in his travels. John Cassian introduced ideals of monastic organization that had developed in Egypt, Syria, and Cappadocia. His own influential writings, the *Institutes,* attempted to homogenize the different rules and practices that he had found into a single ideal system. By the sixth century there was no single kind of monastic life; individuals and groups followed a wide variety of practices throughout Latin Europe.

The most substantial contribution to Latin monasticism was that of the community founded by Benedict of Nursia (480–547) at Monte Cassino, south of Rome. Benedict came from a prominent Roman family, but he rejected the education and plans for a public career that his family had made and withdrew to live a hermit's life in central Italy. Benedict, like many other holy men, soon attracted followers, and early in his life he demonstrated considerable organizational ability, as well as penetrating insight into the minds of those who wished to become monks. He established a successful community on Monte Cassino, and for it he wrote his *Rule,* one of the most remarkable documents in Christian history and one of the most influential organizational programs in the history of human society, although its greatest influence was not widely felt until the ninth century and later.

Between 400 and 800, a large number of monastic rules flourished side-by-side in western Europe. Some of them reached out to influence the ecclesiastical life of Gaul and, later, lands beyond even the old imperial frontiers.

Another sign of the creativity of monasticism in the West was the range of its appeal to very different kinds of people. The appeal of Martin of Tours, for example, rested not only upon his effective conversion of the Gallic countryside, the last bastion of rural paganism in Gaul, but also on the immensely popular *Life* of Martin written by Sulpicius Severus, which depicted Martin as a devout bishop-monk and a model for the religious life of bishops as well as monks. Another kind of appeal struck the Frankish king Clovis, who saw in Martin not only a saintly warrior, but a personal patron who aided in battle. Clovis's sponsorship of the cult of Martin dramatically increased the appeal of the *Life* and the dedication of more communities to Martin's ideal.

The monasteries founded under the influence of John Cassian (particularly that of St. Victor at Marseilles) and his contemporary Honoratus on the island of Lerins at the mouth of the Rhone River presented yet another kind of appeal. Both Cassian and Honoratus were extremely learned, and their communities appealed especially to aristocrats, particularly those displaced by the turmoil in northern Roman Gaul. The intellectual influence of these Rhone-area monasteries was considerable. Monks from these centers were often chosen as bishops and archbishops by neighboring communities, and some of them produced impressive and influential theological literature, introducing the important component of learning to religious communities that were best suited to preserving it during periods of political and religious turbulence. A monk of Lerins, for example, and later bishop of Arles, Caesarius, produced the first rule of monastic life for women, and female religious communities sprang up quickly in Gaul, located near shrines and churches containing the relics of a venerated saint and often under the protection and authority of the local bishop. The Lerins tradition, too, emphasized the subordination of the monastic community to the local bishop. The relations between monastic communities and episcopal religious authority became a continuing source of tension throughout the early history of Europe.

The appeal of such figures as Martin and Benedict and such institutions as Lerins was spread by patronage, texts, and cult, from levels as different as that of Gregory the Great and that of the itinerant holy man Martin. Their effectiveness in converting local rural populations, offering sanctuary to dislocated Gallo-Roman aristocrats, and developing new forms of the religious life for bishops helps to explain much of their effectiveness. Their role in the conversion and the organization of the religious life of key areas of northern Europe, particularly Ireland and Britain, suggests an even greater importance from the late fifth century on.

THE CONVERSION OF IRELAND

In the fifth century A.D. Ireland remained outside the worlds of the Roman Empire and the Germanic invaders. Other Celtic Europeans had been absorbed into the empire in Italy, Gaul, Spain, and Britain. Thus, by A.D. 500 Celtic culture had been reduced to the "Celtic Fringe" of western Europe—Ireland, Scotland, Wales, Cornwall, Brittany, and Galicia—where it is ethnically traceable today.

Irish society on the eve of Christianization was very different from the societies around it. The Irish were organized in clans, which were dominated by a military aristocracy and ruled by petty kings. The aristocracy measured its status in fame and wealth, usually in land and cattle. Although the kings lived on a somewhat larger scale than the aristocracy, their authority and power were limited. Customary law and the aristocrats actually ruled the Irish people. The law was preserved in memory by a class of men known as *brehons,* who were specially trained in law schools and able to establish the procedures for adjudicating the legal relations of feuding clans and powerful aristocrats. Besides the *brehons,* noble houses also patronized the *fili,* a class of poet-historians who composed oral histories of their patrons and songs praising their bravery and generosity. This pastoral, aristocratic society of clans suggests a very old form of European culture. Irish society in the fifth century has been called "a window on the Iron Age."

The first evidence of Christianity in Ireland is the record of Palladius, a priest who appears to have gone to Ireland from Gaul in 431. But the best-known figure of the fifth-century conversion is Patrick. Patrick was the son of Romano-British Christians, and in his short autobiography, the *Confessions,* he states that he was kidnapped as a child and kept as a slave in Ireland for six years before escaping and returning home. In a vision, Patrick states, he heard the Irish people calling for him to return. He did this shortly after 431, and began the conversion of the island. In spite of many dangers, Patrick appears to have had great success, and by the seventh century a strong cult claimed him as the founder of Irish Christianity. His popularity has not declined since.

Although Patrick may have been trained and sent to Ireland by Germanus, bishop of Auxerre in Gaul (who probably sent Palladius as well), the details of the mission and the process of conversion are obscure. It is clear that the first organization of Irish Christianity was modeled on Continental patterns; bishops and priests led the people, and the church at Armagh emerged as a central authority. Yet Continental Christianity had been shaped by Roman society, and ecclesiastical institutions by the administrative institutions of Rome. Ireland, however, had no cities, no provinces, none of the structures that had supported the spread and established the character of Christian organization elsewhere. Moreover, the culture of Ireland soon imparted distinctive characteristics to Irish Christianity. One of these characteristics was the Irish passion for asceticism—a life of austerity. A second feature was the growth of family monastic settlements, perhaps as a result of asceticism combined with the technical difficulties of Irish land law, which made monasteries easier to establish than bishoprics. These two features soon made Irish Christianity predominantly monastic, and made the abbots of family monasteries the most important ecclesiastical figures in Ireland. The bishops were relegated for the most part to subordinate sacramental roles within the monastic community.

By the middle of the sixth century large monastic foundations were being built. Clonmacnoise on the River Shannon was founded around 550, Bangor in the north around 560, and Clonfert around 570. By the end of the sixth century Irish monasticism had absorbed most other forms of Irish asceticism and had begun to reflect another distinctive characteristic of Irish culture, its fascination with learning. The Irish had never had to fight the fierce intellectual battle against learned paganism that the churches and churchmen in Italy, North Africa, and Gaul had, and the Irish took eagerly and quickly to Greek and Latin learning. After the monks at Lerins, Irish monks were the first in European history to make schooling and learning a major part of the monk's life. Learning, of course, entailed writing, and with Christianity writing entered Irish life. The distinctive handwriting and decorated manuscripts produced by Irish monasteries testify to the resources, learning, time, and talent of Irish monastic culture.

Another distinctive feature of Irish monasticism was the emergence of penitential exile. Because Ireland was a society of clans, the identity of an individual was established by the place he or she held in the structure of a clan. One of the greatest punishments in Irish law was exile from the clan, for exile meant a removal of part of a person's identity, since one could never attain full membership in another clan. In monastic communities such exile was undertaken voluntarily as a sign of penitence—"exile for the love of God." Irish monastic exiles, however, did not simply go off alone into remote regions for a life of isolation.

In 565 a monk named Columcille, better known as Columba, left Ireland to found a monastic settlement in exile on the island of Iona, off the coast of Scotland. From the community at Iona a missionary movement moved into northern England and began one phase of the conversion of the Angles and Saxons. Shortly after the founding of Iona, Columbanus, a rigorous ascetic driven to missionary work, moved onto the Continent itself, wandering through eastern Gaul and founding monastic communities in what is now Switzerland and northern Italy. Bobbio, a community he established in the latter area, became one of the most important devotional centers of the seventh and eighth centuries. The impact of Columbanus's form of monasticism was considerable. Columbanus did not withdraw from the world, but maintained contact with powerful lay patrons. His form of monasticism asserted the independence of the monastery from the local bishop, and it offered a kind of Christian clerical life to the Franks that was not based on the culture of the Gallo-Roman aristocracy that had monopolized ecclesiastical office until the seventh century. Through the influence of Columbanus, the Frankish aristocracy began to take its place in the network of ecclesiastical offices, acquiring saints in its families, and taking a family interest in the establishment and patronage of ecclesiastical foundations. Columbanus was buried at Bobbio when he died in 615, eleven years after Gregory the Great, the other great representative of the rich and varied religious culture of the early seventh century. The distinctiveness of Irish Christianity, both in Ireland itself and on the Continent, suggests a new experience of European cul-

Medieval Christianity.

ture—the adaptation of monasticism and Continental forms of Christian devotion to the customs and minds of a non-Roman and non-Germanic society.

ANGLES AND ANGELS

Among the many pressing concerns of Gregory the Great was his vision of bringing to Christianity all the peoples of Europe. In 596 Gregory began his best-known attempt at conversion, the mission of Augustine of Canterbury to England. Gregory may have felt particularly compelled to conversion missions because Lombard pressure on Christianity in Italy had recently increased, and in 590, the year Gregory became bishop of Rome, King Aistulf had forbidden orthodox Christians to be baptized. Gregory had already urged Italian bishops to use preaching more intensively as a means of converting the Arian Lombards. At first, Gregory was not wholly opposed to the use of coercion, especially with those who had slid from orthodoxy to heresy and those who lived under Christian rulers. During the conversion of England, however, Gregory adopted a more moderate approach and rejected the use of force as a means of conversion to Christianity.

When Gregory set about planning the mission to England, so legend has it, he was inspired by the sight of some Anglo-Saxon prisoners in Italy being sold in the slave market. Asking who these striking people were, Gregory was told that they were Angles. "Not Angles," Gregory is supposed to have replied, "but angels."

Gregory undertook the mission to England seriously. All Gregory knew of the island, however, was what was said in late Roman geographical lore and administrative literature—and that was not much. Gregory's younger contemporary, Isidore of Seville, wrote a large encyclopedic work called *The Twenty Books of Etymologies,* in which he noted that Britannia "is an island set in the sea, wholly separated from the world." Besides such information as this, Gregory knew only of England's provincial organization under the late Roman Empire, an organization that had been totally destroyed by the end of the sixth century.

In the invasions of the 440s Roman Britain received the first challenges of Germanic invaders from the continent. Although subsequent British resistance was stiff—the great British victory at Mount Badon around the year 500 is only one indication of this—the invaders finally began to carve out small kingdoms throughout the island. Of these many kingdoms Gregory chose that of Kent, in southeastern England, as the first target for his mission.

For that mission Gregory selected Augustine, prior of the monastery of St. Andrew in Rome. Dispatched in 596, Augustine and his companions traveled through Gaul and arrived at Kent in 597. Kent was ruled by the pagan Anglo-Saxon king Ethelbert, who was married to Bertha, a Christian Frankish princess. Permitted to settle and preach, Augustine and his companions soon converted the king and a large part of his following. In several letters of 601, Gregory announced that he was sending Augustine more help, wrote to Ethelbert concerning the duties of a newly converted Christian king, and described for Augustine the principles of establishing a church in newly converted lands. In these last letters Gregory abandoned force as a motif in conversion and urged Augustine instead to convert people gradually by persuasion, using their old shrines and sacred places as new Christian church sites. Gregory's close supervision of the mission to England and his urging of what seem to us to be anthropologically sound means of organizing Christianity in a pagan land suggest something of his vision of Christianizing the world.

As Roman Christianity spread from Kent northwards into other kingdoms, notably Northumbria, in the middle of the seventh century, it encountered Celtic Christianity already at work in the north of the island. The resulting form of Christianity that took shape in England drew heavily from both Celtic and Roman traditions, and marks a second distinctive example of the role played by Christianity in the transformation of the life of the new Europeans. Among the conflicting issues that divided Roman and Celtic Christianity were the Celtic concept of individual, rather than public, communal confession of sins, and penitentials—books of meticulous lists of penances to be performed for various sins. In addition, the tonsuring of Celtic monks differed in form from that used in Rome, and the Celtic churches celebrated important Church feasts, notably Easter, according to a calendar different from the one in use at Rome.

These differences led to friction between Celtic and Roman Christians, and their disagreement came to a head at the court of Oswy, king of Northumbria (641–670). Oswy, a Celtic Christian, and his wife, a Roman Christian, found themselves celebrating religious feasts at different times, and they therefore sponsored a debate between representatives of Celtic and Roman Christian practices. At the Synod of Whitby, held in Northumbria in 663, the authority of Rome was recognized by the king and by many of the Celtic clergy. The first encounter of two varieties of Christian practices outside the Roman Empire had been resolved in favor of Rome.

From 663 until the end of the eighth century, the fusion of Celtic and Roman Christianity under the guidance of Roman ecclesiastical organization produced a church that was thoroughly loyal to Rome, yet retained many of its distinctively Celtic features. Like Celtic Christianity, English Christianity developed a powerful monastic culture, although under the influence of an episcopal organization. At the head of the English church was the archbishop of Canterbury, Augustine's own center. Later a second archbishop was added at York. Dioceses for bishops, which had not taken root in Ireland, did so in England, although several centers were changed or abandoned before the late eleventh century. Asceticism and learning became features of English monastic life as well. So did the ideal of exile and missionary work among pagans.

In the eighth and ninth centuries, a stream of English missionaries carried Romano-Irish learning and devotion to the Continent. The results of those missions included not only the conversion of still-pagan peoples but the beginnings of the reform of the Christian church in Gaul. The English loyalty to Rome gave the popes a new voice in northern Europe, and laid the foundations of ecclesiastical renewal among the Franks and other Germanic peoples that so marked the age of Charlemagne in the late eighth and early ninth centuries.

These developments in Ireland and England suggest the extent of the transformation of the Roman world by the middle of the seventh century. They also reflect the new organization of European life and culture that permitted the circulation of Roman influences under the direction of churchmen long after the direct rule of Rome had been forgotten.

FURTHER READING

On the political structure of Italy in the period, see T. S. Brown, *Gentlemen and Officers: Imperial Administration and Aristocratic Power in Byzantine Italy*, A.D. *554–800* (Rome: 1984); Chris Wickham, *Early Medieval Italy: Central Power and Local Society* (London: Macmillan, 1981); Thomas F. X. Noble, *The Republic of St. Peter* (Philadelphia: University of Pennsylvania Press, 1984). Neil Christie, *The Lombards* (Cambridge, MA: Blackwell, 1994).

The best introduction to the world of Gregory I is R. A. Markus, *The End of Ancient Christianity* (Cambridge: Cambridge University Press, 1990). On the popes, see Jeffrey Richards, *The Popes and the Papacy in the Early Middle Ages 476–762* (Boston: Routledge & Kegan Paul, 1979); Jeffrey Richards, *Consul of God* (Boston: Routledge & Kegan Paul, 1980). The best study of Gregory's thought and writings is Carole Straw, *Gregory the Great: Perfection in Imperfection* (Berkeley-Los Angeles: University of California Press, 1988).

On the conversion and ecclesiastical establishment in Iberia, Gaul, and Italy, see J. N. Hillgarth, *Christianity and Paganism, 350–750: The Conversion of Western Europe* (Philadelphia: University of Pennsylvania Press, 1986), and E. Peters, *Monks, Bishops, and Pagans* (Philadelphia: University of Pennsylvania Press, 1975). On Martin, see Stancliffe, *St. Martin and His Biographer* (cited above).

On Ireland, see Michael J. O'Kelly, *Early Ireland: An Introduction to Irish Prehistory* (Cambridge: Cambridge University Press, 1989); R. F. Foster, *The Oxford History of Ireland* (New York: Oxford University Press, 1989); Kathleen Hughes, *The Church in Early Irish Society* (Ithaca: Cornell University Press, 1966). On Britain, see Charles Thomas, *Christianity in Roman Britain to A.D. 500* (London: Batsford, 1981), and Henry Mayr-Harting, *The Coming of Christianity to England* (1972; reprint edition University Park: Pennsylvania State University Press, 1991).

On the Iberian Peninsula, see Edward James, ed., *Visigothic Spain: New Approaches* (Oxford: Clarendon Press, 1980), and Roger Collins, *Early Medieval Spain: Unity in Diversity, 400–1000* (New York: St. Martin's Press, 1983).

On Gaul and Germany, see the brilliant study by Patrick Geary, *Before France and Germany* (New York: Oxford University Press, 1988).

On thought and literature, see Pierre Riché, *Education and Culture in the Barbarian West* (Columbia: University of South Carolina Press, 1976).

7

THE ENVIRONMENT OF
NORTH TEMPERATE EUROPE

THE PHYSICAL GEOGRAPHY OF
TRANSALPINE EUROPE

The geographical focus of this book so far—and of the history of the ancient world generally—has been the Mediterranean basin, the societies around it, and the frontiers drawn by Romans to defend it. By the beginning of the eighth century the Mediterranean basin no longer housed a universal society, but rather three contending societies, those of Islam, Byzantium, and the Latin West. Thus, its role in medieval and modern history is different from its centrality in the history of the ancient world. In addition to the transformation of the Mediterranean, northern Europe for the first time ceased to be either a frontier province of a Mediterranean empire or the setting of an Iron-Age, preliterate Germanic culture. The growth of settled societies that began to increase the agricultural production of northern Europe was well under way by the eighth century. It is therefore necessary to survey the land of the new Europeans in order to understand something of the nature of their achievements. Whatever else the history of medieval Europe may be, it is certainly the story of the opening of north temperate Europe to extensive agricultural production by peoples whose descendants still inhabit it.

On the physical map of Europe, unencumbered by familiar but often misleading political, cultural, and linguistic boundaries, three broad areas, each with distinctive characteristics, are prominent: (1) the Mediterranean basin, (2) the mountains and plains of central and eastern Europe, and (3) the western parts of transalpine Europe. These areas constitute the three great geographical and climatic zones of the European world. Considered together, they remind us of the proximity of Europe and the western part of Eurasia generally to the great sweep of the Baltic and North seas, the Atlantic Ocean, the Mediterranean Sea, and the Black Sea. Few places in Europe are far from one of these bodies of water, and the remarkable systems of navigable rivers that reach out from the deepest parts of the land mass bring much of European society even closer to the sea. Coasts and rivers, valleys, mountains, forests, and plains offer different physical landscapes in each of our three major areas, but the elements they have in common must be kept in mind as we consider their distinctive features.

Among the movements of peoples that can be detected from prehistory and recorded in history, that from western Asia to transalpine Europe is one of the best known. The route from western Asia led through the narrow gate between the northern edge of the Caspian Sea and the southern tip of the Ural Mountains. From southern Russia a few routes led southward toward the Mediterranean, around or over the Balkans. Due west of this area, the protective ring of the Carpathian Mountains offered settlement areas for a number of different peoples, notably the Avars. Beyond the Carpathians the upper Danube Valley carries a Mediterranean-type climatic area into what is now the Czech Republic, Slovakia, and Austria.

For the most part, however, western Europe consists of a vast plain slowly rising from west to east, its southern border lying along the great chains of mountains that begin with the Pyrenees in northern Spain, continue east and south along the Alps and the Dinaric Alps, and end with the Balkans and the Black Sea. North of these mountain ranges Europe consists generally of a great fan-shaped plain that begins in southern France and opens out north and east all the way to Russia. This great plain is crossed by many navigable rivers and by low mountain ranges rich in minerals. South of the plain the long ridges of the Pyrenees, Alps, and Balkans lie in an east–west axis that separates western and central Europe from the Mediterranean. The maritime and riverine character of western Europe gave access to the sea and, for sea people ranging from Bronze Age migrants to the Vikings, access to the land. Surrounded by the sea, the fan-shaped plain of western and northern Europe extends east to Russia and includes southern England and southern Sweden in its sweep. The rivers that cross it are evenly flowing and suitable for navigation. From the Atlantic coast of France to western Russia, the Garonne, Loire, Seine, Meuse, Thames, Rhine, Weser, Elbe, Oder, Vistula, and Duna systems offer both transportation and agricultural possibilities perhaps unequaled anywhere else in the world. Some of these systems extend even beyond the western European geographical region. The Rhine-Danube corridor offers virtually unimpeded routes from the North Sea to the Black Sea, and the Duna-Dnieper system nearly constitutes a water route from the Baltic to the Black Sea.

Physical map of Europe, Western Asia, and Northern Africa.

In western Europe rainfall is plentiful and generally even. This area does not experience the sharp differences of hot dry summers and cold wet winters of the Mediterranean. European soil, which is heavy and wet, can produce two crops per year instead of the Mediterranean one. The heavy soils of western Europe tend to leach out mineral content and retain excessive moisture unless they are plowed deeply and turned so as to afford good drainage for fields. Drainage and fertilization are thus two essential elements in maintaining the soil of western Europe. Forests grow thick and usually consist of hardwoods. Although much of the economic history of early Europe is the history of agricultural development, the presence of these great, thick forests is a constant in European history until the modern age, and the forest economy played an important role in the early Middle Ages.

Of all the physical features of Europe, the last to be adapted to the will and needs of humans was the ocean. Atlantic civilization did not begin to replace Mediterranean civilization until after the sixteenth century. Yet even the Atlantic and the North Sea, far more stormy and capricious bodies of water than the Mediterranean, Black and Baltic seas, offered Europeans advantages that they were quick to accept. The North and Baltic seas (like the Grand Banks off Newfoundland) teem with fish, and the European Atlantic coast is not so difficult to sail that maritime cultures from as early as the Bronze Age could not exploit the ocean itself as a means of transportation. The Gulf Stream (which Europeans call the North Atlantic Drift) warms the Atlantic very far north in Europe; even the winter water temperatures off the North Cape of Norway are no lower than those off Boston, Massachusetts (35°F). The Gulf Stream contributes to the cool summers and rarely bitter winters of Europe. When Europeans began to cross the Atlantic they had two easy corridors. In the tenth century the warmer North Atlantic and the reduced drift ice allowed Scandinavian sailors to reach and colonize Iceland and Greenland and to touch North America. In the late fifteenth century Columbus and his successors had only to sail south to meet the easterly trade winds that blow steadily across the Atlantic. But for even the best-rigged and manned sailing ships, travel to the east is far more difficult.

LANDSCAPE AND FOLKSCAPE

Ancient and medieval sources and modern scientific techniques, such as the study of glacier movements, pollen analysis, and the examination of tree rings, have contributed to our knowledge of climatic history in the ancient and medieval periods. From 100 B.C. to A.D. 400 the climate of Europe seems to have slowly become warmer and dryer. From A.D. 400 to around 1250, the Atlantic Ocean was relatively free of drift ice and great storms. Mediterranean writers noted that it was possible to cultivate the vine and the olive, the characteristic Mediterranean crops, much farther north than they are found today. A mean summer temperature several degrees higher than at present reduced the dangers of May frosts and produced milder Septembers, the two crucial periods of the agricultural year. Between 1200 and 1400, however, mean temperatures dropped and rainfall increased considerably. The Northern Hemisphere as a whole appears to have grown colder, and records indicate erratic seasons of drought and flood, abundance and famine. During the crucial period of the opening of transalpine Europe to agricultural activities, however, the climate was ideal.

The fragile balance between population levels and agricultural production in the Mediterranean region was upset by disease, war, and social turmoil, but the world of northern Europe was little better off. In that world of heavy forest and rivers, in which less than 10 percent of the land was under cultivation, societies remained small and lived precariously. Both Romans and Germans suffered high infant- and maternal-mortality rates and very low life expectancy. Both societies produced many children, most of whom died very young. The survivors were exposed to high mortality risks throughout their youth, as well as the general shortcomings of medical science and the risks of the warrior's or farmer's life.

Even for those who survived birth and youth, the physical experience of life itself was different from that of people in modern industrialized nations. Many people were familiar with prolonged periods of illness, including low-grade fever, blood poisoning, and pain from improperly healed wounds. They were unable to correct defective eyesight and hearing problems, and they were subject routinely to intestinal sickness, including worms. Skin disorders and other forms of disfigurement were common, and there were very few effective painkillers. Moreover, the results of illness and other physical disorders were everywhere visible; people saw the worst results of the human condition before them in both rural and urban areas, and they accommodated themselves to what they saw more readily than modern people do.

Much of transalpine Europe was thinly settled, with small, densely populated communities of farmers and warriors widely separated by thick forest, swamp, and ridge. Until after the eleventh century, the hardships of the transalpine environment set firm limits to population growth and increased agricultural productivity. A glance at the population trends in England from the Roman period to the seventeenth century (see graph) suggests the difficulty of sustaining population growth and the vulnerability of population to natural disasters, such as the invasions of the fifth century and the wave of plague in the fourteenth century. Although England is not typical of the European demographic experience in all details, it does reflect some common elements. The population

England: Population in Millions, 100–1850

remained small, averaging no more than two to ten persons per square kilometer. Small villages, tiny markets and fairs, small areas of rational, careful cultivation, and large areas of wasteful, unproductive cultivation constituted the physical profile of transalpine Europe between the sixth and tenth centuries.

The small societies of early medieval Europe sustained themselves by cultivating at first a very small portion of the land available to them. Their productivity was low, and their resources—from tools to theory—were few. For most people the village or the isolated farmstead constituted the social horizon, and growing and finding food the principal occupation. Economic historians have suggested that in the early Middle Ages not enough land was in cultivation to feed even the small population of Europe, and that hunting and fishing played an essential part in forming the European diet. The bulk of that diet was cereal-grain products. Meat and fish were not as common. Studies of skeletons reveal considerable dietary deficiency, and the diet appears to have been relatively uniform throughout most social ranks. One difference between rich and poor was that the rich ate more, but not necessarily better or different food.

Because of the difficulties of plowing the heavy soil of northern Europe, cultivated acreage remained small. Because there was generally no fertilizer, fallowing (letting a field lie idle for a season) was the chief way of restoring at least some of the land's fertility. These limitations point to the very low ratio of yield to seed, the standard index of agricultural productivity. Throughout the Middle Ages one measure of seed yielded about three measures of grain, a ratio that rarely changed. Twentieth-century farmers are accustomed to getting twenty measures of grain for one measure of seed. In addition, agricultural tools were few and generally of poor quality. They usually had to be made locally. Although the eleventh and twelfth centuries saw the development of the water mill and windmill on a relatively large scale, the period before the eleventh century knew only animal power as a supplement to human effort.

The rhythm of the agricultural calendar is the oldest and most wide-ranging of Europe's social rhythms. The agricultural calendar dominated individual and social life, but local agricultural and landholding customs varied considerably from place to place. Thus, there was not only great seasonal variation in Europe but considerable regional variation as well. The need of small communities for the cooperation of all their members at critical times during the agricultural year imposed great solidarity, but at the price of restricting personal choice.

Above all, these societies were prone to a wide scale of natural disasters. A bad harvest brought the threat of starvation for many. A series of bad harvests brought the threat of famine. Dietary deficiencies made early Europeans more vulnerable to many more diseases than later Europeans. Too much rain drowned fields and vineyards; too little brought drought. Because early Europeans depended for most of their life support on field and forest, they tended to overuse the land they had. Indeed, inefficient early medieval agriculture required large areas of land to support relatively few persons. The land also had to produce trees for building and tool making, hay and oats for animal feed (there were no fodder crops), and grazing land for sheep and areas for flax growing—the latter two needed for the production of wool and linen clothing.

Although the agricultural riches of northern Europe were beginning to increase by the eighth century, they did not yield much, and they did not yield it easily. The archaeology of population and settlement in this area reveals a small world living precariously on a limited agricultural economy, subject to the ravages of disease and the blows of natural disaster. This world was hard, and making it marginally less hard took centuries of labor.

FAMILIES, *GENTES,* AND KINGDOMS

The material limitations—in terms of population levels and technology—on early medieval transalpine society contributed to the shape and structure of that society. So too did the historical experience of migration and settlement in the Roman provincial world of Gaul, Iberia, and Italy and the emergence of new political and social structures as a result of these. The old "tribes" were greatly transformed by the migrations across Europe, into and out of the Roman Empire, and by the pressure of other peoples who were also migrating. Contact with the empire itself offered new models of social organization. Not only were the political structures of the empire, the Roman armies, and the Roman provincial governments available for imitation, but the pattern of life suggested by Roman landholding systems, agricultural technology, communities, and cities offered prospects that had been unthinkable in the world beyond the imperial frontiers. The decay of Roman institutions and the formation of a sub-Roman culture among the Germanic immigrants meant that both societies were becoming more like each other and less like their own individual remote and even recent pasts. And just as the late Roman Empire barely resembled the empire of the first and second centuries, so the Germanic peoples of the fifth, sixth, and seventh centuries bore little resemblance to their predecessors, whose way of life had been described so extensively by the Roman writer Tacitus at the end of the first century.

For most of the Germanic inhabitants of seventh-century Europe the most important social bonds were those between lords and followers and that of the kin-group. Early Europeans used several different words to describe what moderns would call the "family," and these words possessed distinct meanings. *Parentes* or *parentela* designated a group of relations, or kin, while *familia* (the word from which the modern term "family" is derived) designated the individual household, including blood-relations, other dependents, and slaves, but it could also designate the entourage of a bishop or a monastic community.

Whether grouped in villages or isolated in farmsteads, those who worked the land thought in terms of household work-units and wider groups of kinfolk. Those who did not work the land thought in terms of gifts, plunder, and warfare.

The legal texts of Germanic peoples reflect some of the chief features of the social structure. Much of the terminology that describes military service or tax assessment tends to measure society in terms of households. In several early law codes the *hide,* or land required to support a single household, and the *mansus,* meaning the land and possessions required to support a household, are terms used frequently. These may be considered the elemental social forms of early medieval society.

In the legal codes, the kingroup and household are generally assumed largely to comprise and certainly to be ruled by free individuals, that is, fully fledged members of "the people," the largest group to which any individual professed loyalty. Freedom entailed the right to carry weapons in the wars of the people, the right to participate in the settlement of legal cases and disputes according to the laws of the people, and the right to participate in community decisions. In other words, freedom meant full membership in a group larger than the family. In day-to-day experience the free peasant was a fully privileged member of an agricultural community. Membership in the village community also meant full membership in the larger people, which was signaled by the right to be judged by the law of the people, whether Visigothic, Frankish, Burgundian, or Lombard, no matter in whose territory a legal dispute was heard. It also meant the right and obligation to fight, either in the expeditions of occasional war-leaders or in the wars of the king. Throughout the Middle Ages one sure sign of personal freedom was the right to carry weapons.

The settlement of Roman provincial Europe and non-Roman Europe contributed also to various social orders that conspicuously lacked freedom. Both the ancient Mediterranean world and the early Germanic world knew the institution of slavery, the possession of one human being by another as a form of chattel property. Roman slaves and even Roman freemen who had taken on servile status constituted part of the slave population, as did Germans or other non-Roman peoples captured in war or purchased. The early Middle Ages also knew several statuses that are generally described as "half-free." Lombard law, for example, recognized the *aldius,* a person who did not have the full legal status of a freeman and was tied to the land he worked, rather than regarded as the personal property of someone else. The Lombard *aldius* seems similar to the Frankish *litus,* also a person of half-free status. One point of origin of such a status seems to have been the dependent free laborers on the vast estates of Roman Gaul and northern Italy who had conceded much of their freedom in return for the protection of the great landowner. From the fifth through the eleventh centuries, however, formerly free Germanic individuals also appear to have lost considerable freedom and themselves become dependents of powerful landlords. The process seems to have worked at different rates of speed in different parts of western Europe, and its causes, rate of occurrence, and geographical distribution are not yet matters of scholarly agreement.

We know far more about those at the top of society during these centuries than we do about those at the middle or bottom. One way to recognize the different statuses below the nobility is to look at the institution of wergild in the early law codes. Wergild (literally, "the money for a man") was the assessed value of individuals of different social status. Because most Germanic law was personal (the members of a people could be judged only according to the law of that people), and because most legal disputes were treated as matters involving personal injury (or tort, in modern legal terminology), the focus of Germanic law was compensation rather than punishment. Thus, the way by which compensation was determined reveals the "worth" of different members of society. The slave (or rather the slave's owner) received the lowest amount of wergild, the *aldius* somewhat more, the freeman much more, and the noble—in some instances the noble in the king's service—most of all. Formally, at least, the law codes give us an approximate profile of social rank and offer rudimentary terminology for distinguishing among members of society.

The society of the codes, however, was not fixed forever. As the conquests slowed down and stopped, as society was transformed by settlement, and as individual circumstances changed, the fixed categories of law had to be adapted to new circumstances. One general trend after the seventh century was the gradual emergence of the institution of lordship and the "dependence" of different kinds of individuals on a lord. A second trend was the general lessening of formal slavery and the general depression of many peasants of technically free status. With this general leveling at the bottom of society, the dependent agricultural worker, or serf, tied to the land and under the rule of a local lord, became a characteristic social type. The process is complex and certainly occurred more rapidly in some areas than in others, but by the eighth century at the latest, the institution of serfdom was in the process of formation.

The *gens* (plural *gentes*), or "people," was the aggregate of all free individuals who lived under the same law and fought in the same armies. Roman writers had used the term *gens* to describe either a family clan or, more frequently, a people organized on a level just below that which the Romans considered fully civilized. *Natio* (plural *nationes*) was a Roman category whose status in Roman eyes was well below that of *gens*. Roman writers and Germanic writers using Latin referred to the Germanic peoples of Europe as *gentes*. Thus, one could speak both of the *gens Merovingorum* as the dynasty of Clovis, or the *gens Francorum* for the Frankish people as a whole; *gens Langobardorum* was the proper term for the Lombards.

The term *gens* meant something more than a "tribe" and something less than a state. It reminds us that the focus of Germanic culture was the individual and his membership in a larger group, reflected in personal law, rights within that group, and recognition of a common king. The *gentes* were loosely structured, however, and membership in them was not the same as either citizenship or subjecthood in a later form of kingdom. In general, public organized life existed on a small scale.

As many free peasants shrank into half-free status, the idea of freedom came to be restricted to powerful men who dominated others, the first European nobility. Originally, the Germanic nobility consisted of the most successful warriors, the richest men, and relatives and favorites of the kings of the *gentes*. If families managed to retain their wealth, connections to royalty and to each other, and remained prominent over several generations, they were considered *nobilis*, or noble. As one writer put it, "They had a known name." The wergild of their members was far higher than that of other persons. One means of maintaining noble status was marriage to members of other powerful families. Another was the benefits derived from royal favor and service. Powerful men who served the king and acted as his representatives could easily dominate others and pass to their heirs at least some of the wealth they had acquired. Although the seventh and eighth centuries witnessed family fortunes rising and falling, the most powerful, wealthy, and fortunate great families of the Germanic kingdoms came slowly to constitute a generally recognized social rank having special wergild and privileges, a special name or set of names that they alone used, and an increasing consciousness and general recognition of their superior status.

At the head of these societies stood the king, but the office of king had also changed from its tribal status. It too had been subjected to the cultural pressures of migration, war-leadership, models of Roman office, and the demands of ruling a newly settled society. Thus, by the eighth century kings were no longer priests and symbolic tribal chiefs, nor were they simply successful war-leaders who had managed to conquer a territory and hold on to it for a sufficient length of time. One justification for kingship was descent from a single family from which the kings had long been chosen. Dynastic right, rather than individual right, was one of the most important bases of early medieval kingship. Second, kingship was regarded as distinguishing a people, a *gens*, from other societies that did not have kings or had different kings. The Merovingian kings of the Franks wore their hair long and flowing as a visible sign of their royal rank. They and other kings were expected to give gifts to their loyal followers, an echo of the division of booty in the war band. One source of royal treasure was inheritance from the previous king, but another was tribute paid by neighboring peoples and plunder from those they conquered. The kings, and their guardianship of the law of the *gens*, were living embodiments of the common origin and history of their peoples, however recent that history might have been, and they were rulers of peoples, not of land. Early medieval monarchy was generally not based on territory, as in the modern state. Although the king could and sometimes did make new laws for the *gens*, he was regarded far more as the protector of the people's law. This law, as we have seen, remained essentially private, settling disputes between equally free litigants.

With the Christianization of the Germanic peoples, kingship began to be regarded partly in terms of Old Testament institutions and partly in terms of the late imperial concept of the Christian emperor. The figures of David and

Solomon frequently appear in the sources as bases for comparison with sixth- and seventh-century Germanic kings, and such Old Testament practices as anointing the king at his accession and creating prayers specifically for the king slowly appeared in the ceremonies of early medieval kingship. The new, larger territories of the kings of the Franks and Visigoths in the sixth, seventh, and eighth centuries strengthened the concept of kingship, and the use of Latin in royal documents and in the writing of law codes suggests the Roman influence on Germanic institutions in a changing social and political world. The two influences of Christianity and Roman imperial ideas and institutions worked on the kings of the seventh and eighth centuries in their new circumstances in settled kingdoms far larger than ancient Germanic tribal societies.

The role of king also came to include the protection and patronage of the Church, and the royal office and its functions were often included in liturgical prayers. Sometimes kings themselves or members of their families were venerated as saints, thereby adding luster and sanctity to the whole dynasty, and Christian chroniclers held before contemporary kings both historical and contemporary examples of good and bad royal behavior. In Bede's *Ecclesiastical History of the English People,* finished in 731, the figure of King Oswald of Northumbria is held up as that of an ideal monarch, whereas other kings are held up as examples of evil rule. Although one cannot say that the chroniclers' world-views directly influenced royal conduct, through them we may observe the formation of new kinds of political communities in seventh- and eighth-century western Europe. Superimposed on the social realities of family and *gens,* the idea of a Christian people ruled by a Christian king came to be a commonplace by the eighth century.

GENDER IN EARLY MEDIEVAL EUROPE

The biological differences between men and women have not changed through human history, but the extrapolation of biological differences to the definition any culture makes about what constitutes masculine or feminine identity—the problem of gender—has changed considerably. Some of these changes were reflected in later Roman history and in the ideals of masculinity and femininity in the early Christian communities, at least until the assertion of a definition of masculinity that coincided with the location of authority within the church, around the sixth century.

The law codes also tell us something of gender differences. They indicate that Frankish women, for example, were valued by men chiefly for their ability to bear children. The ideal Frankish woman was the obedient spouse, and obedient female spouses and unmarried women were protected by the laws. Insult, rape, and the seizure of free women, particularly those unmarried and those of childbearing age were harshly punished, not only because they violated a woman's greatest value, but because they also violated the woman's father's or husband's *mundium,* his right of protection. Marriage transferred this right from the woman's father to her husband, usually in return for the dowry—originally the price paid by the groom's family to the bride's father, and the main support for the bride's widowhood if the husband predeceased her. The morning-gift, also paid from the groom to the bride, was presumably a price for her virginity. *Mundium* was not only a right of protection, but the right to represent the woman in court and to manage her property.

Masculine identity, then, was construed as that of a protector, lord, and disposer of women. Masculinity was a gender to which violence was permitted and even expected, just as sexual activity such as concubinage with a free woman not his wife or sexual activity with female slaves was permitted to men, but not to women. Men were also expected to be generous gift-givers to friends and followers.

In spite of the powerful restraints imposed on early medieval women by gender definition, they were not entirely without resources, and on occasion power. As converters of pagan husbands to Christianity, founders or patrons of monasteries and churches, patrons of candidates for appointment to a bishopric or abbacy, or functioning as links between different kingroups, women were certainly capable of exerting influence. In royal marriages queens were given considerable authority in managing the affairs of the royal household, the palace, the royal estates, representing absent royal husbands, and guarding the treasure of the royal house.

More than queens, however, female holy women suggest an inversion of the very characteristics that defined most early medieval European women. The lives of female saints are relatively abundant from the fifth through the eighth centuries, and they reveal a creative adaptation of the very features that defined and limited women in the world. The female saint preserved virginity because she rejected the lusts of the flesh; her humility conquered pride; her meditation on scripture suppressed the desire for visual delights. She chose an immortal, rather than a mortal husband. And although she might leave normal feminine roles in the world, she might also take property with her into the religious life, often serving as a kingroup's representative in controlling monasteries or churches that the kin wished to keep in its possession. The holy woman, too, gave gifts—but to the poor and to the churches, and she and her ecclesiastical property offered shelter and hospitality. Also, holy women could construct communities of spiritual kin: JoAnn McNamara has pointed out that,

While the physical mothers of saints are commonly called "genetrices," the word "mater" [Latin for "mother"] was reserved for the role of the abbess within the spiritual family. Similarly, "soror" [the Latin word for "sister"], opposed to the more physical "germana," was reserved for sisters in the community.

Women generally had a shorter life expectancy than men, and throughout the early Middle Ages the practice of men about to be married to bring gifts and payments to their bride's family on marriage, may serve as evidence that women were not only fewer in number but also shorter-lived than men. Women were also a means of enhancing a man's social status by marriage, and a number of prominent families in the early Middle Ages listed their descent from a female rather than a male, even naming their children according to naming-patterns in the female line rather than the male. At the highest levels of society, women could control property, and by the eighth century (and probably even earlier) queens undertook a number of responsibilities in the management and disposition of royal property. The first coronation ceremonies for queens occurred in 856.

In the religious life, women in early Frankish and Anglo-Saxon society enjoyed considerable power and status, not only as wives of bishops and priests (the active and successful enforcement of clerical celibacy dates only from the eleventh century), but also as patrons and founders of monasteries. Such figures as Hilda of England and Radegund of Poitiers played crucial roles in the spread of literacy, the transmission of intellectual traditions, and the patronage of unmarried women—women who deliberately chose a celibate life, women who had persuaded their families that they preferred the cloister to marriage, or women who were deliberately cloistered by their families in order to keep them from an undesirable marriage market. Although the formal ecclesiastical orders of widows and the female diaconate were abolished in early medieval society, the presence of women in religious life remained significant, and the works of a number of women writers constitute a small, but no less important literature than those of male writers.

From celibacy and widowhood, women also experienced a variety of different forms of association with males. The early Merovingian rulers of the Franks appear to have practiced polygamy, and the older Roman form of concubinage also survived, as well as the Germanic institution of *Friedelehe,* a form of marriage conspicuous among Frankish royalty when they married socially inferior women, in which the woman remained under the rule of her own family, along with her children. In spite of the ecclesiastical restrictions on the ministry of women and the formal male control of women in the law codes and legislation, it is clear that both the status and the function of women were considerably higher and more varied than the sources immediately reveal. As guardians of minor children, as patrons of monastic and other ecclesiastical institutions, as wives of powerful men whose own status protected that of their wives, and as religious scholars, women in the early Middle Ages experienced a series of exclusions from formal authority in ecclesiastical and lay environments, but at the same time their status and the informal exercise of power on their part reflected the transformation of late antique and early Germanic society and offered opportunities for control over much of their own lives, usually in spite of the dictates of gender distinctions and the legal limitations on female independence.

RELIGION AND CULTURE

The emergence of a concept of Christian kingship among the Germanic peoples of sixth- and seventh-century western Europe is one striking sign of the fusion of Christian-Roman and Germanic cultures that marks these centuries. When Clovis, king of the victorious Franks, called a meeting of the Gallic clergy in Orleans in 507, he began a tradition of royal patronage of the Church—and royal interest in seeing that the Church was properly organized—that ran through the Middle Ages and early-modern European history. But regular meetings of Church councils were not a sustained feature of seventh-century life, either among the Franks or among any other Germanic people, except the Visigoths in Spain, where frequent councils met at Toledo until the extinction of the kingdom in 711. Although kings and their clerical advisers might preserve the ideal of a well-organized church, the actual state of Christianity and paganism in the sixth and seventh centuries was far from anyone's ideal.

The battle with paganism was not yet won, especially in the countryside and in the lands not conquered by Christian rulers. Many sermons of the sixth and especially the seventh centuries were based no longer on the Bible, with which most Christians were generally unfamiliar, but on proverbs, moral stories, and the histories of saints and martyrs. They were also directed against surviving pagan beliefs and practices. Much of the tone of Christian culture in this period is combative—designed to prove the superiority of Christianity over pagan beliefs or to Christianize pagan practices. Thus, as we have noted, much pagan practice was simply redesignated as worship of demons, although the muscular Christianity of the seventh century always showed the demons defeated by Christian holiness. Lists of "superstitions" forbidden to Christians appeared regularly down to the twelfth century. Among the most original legislation of Germanic kings was that dealing with violations of Christian practices on the part of their people. One result of such legislation was the imposition of Christian values on older non-Christian customs. Thus, the legal procedure of the ordeal, according to which an individual was subjected to physical injury and later examined to see if the injury had miraculously disappeared, slowly acquired Christian liturgical patronage. Because the outcome of the ordeal "proved" guilt or innocence of a criminal charge, and because Christians, like pagans, believed in "immanent justice"—that is, in the direct intervention of God in human life—a Christian liturgy for preparation, execution, and interpretation of ordeals slowly developed in the early Middle Ages.

The hierarchy of the clergy, developed in late Rome and based on an urbanized empire, was originally ill-suited for the Germanic kingdoms. Too often archbishops and bishops were poorly trained, not entirely separated from the noble classes from which they came, and out of contact with Rome. In fact, through the mid–ninth century the bishops of Rome were regarded much more as local high priests and guardians of the tombs of Peter and Paul and preserving ideal forms of Christian worship than as in any sense the directors of a universal church.

The canons of Frankish Church councils always represent an ideal state of the Christian community, but rarely do they describe actual practice. The purest forms of devotion were to be found in monasteries, which survived less touched by the world than did the higher clergy who were still in it. But even monasticism was fragmented by a multiplicity of rules and by the problem of monastic subjection to the local bishop. The creation of rural parishes brought religion to some of the population, but it fragmented the unity of the diocese. Bishops on the whole were inconsistent in their devotion and inept in their administration. Therefore, the chief concern of the clergy was to impose uniform religious practices on the people. By substituting orthopraxy (correct religious practice) for the ceremonial aspects of paganism, seventh-century churchmen could influence conduct, even if they were generally unable to exert as much influence over popular beliefs.

It is in the realm of popular belief that early medieval Christian culture is most striking. Christians, like pagans, wanted above all security in this world and salvation in the next. Security in this world was a matter of appeasing the proper god, and much of the tenor of missionary Christianity in this period was to prove the superiority of the Christian God in providing help in this life in terms of more abundant harvests, fewer natural disasters, and protection from the forces of the other world. Such fears were overcome by changes in practice, not changes in belief. Even the saints came to acquire specialized functions and to be localized; each region venerated its own proven saintly patrons, and those patrons in turn protected those who venerated them. Just as certain kinds of conduct distinguished a member of a *gens* from members of other *gentes,* so certain kinds of conduct marked off a Christian from non-Christians. Early medieval Christianity is characterized by behavior rather than by belief, and the king's insistence on proper behavior in the Church was the sole guarantee of preserving divine favor in a turbulent world.

The image of God in the early Middle Ages was that of a remote and terrible judge, always ready to strike down humans for their sinful lives, yet willing to show mercy if attempts at reform were made. By extension, the theory of immanent justice applied to divine wrath as well, and the causation of events was seen as a manifestation either of divine favor or of divine anger. God was a power to be appeased rather than loved, for only by faithful observance of His commands could a society expect earthly peace and some assurance of heaven, however slight. In a world characterized by the worst effects of a fallen human nature, plagued by demons, full of uncertainty and insecurity, the Christian first wanted help and protection. In their search for help and protection for everyday cares, men and women turned to the local saints, through prayers and liturgies, and then to God, remote and barely approachable. Saints' and holy men's triumph over demons, illustrated in sermons and stories and art, was the visible proof of God's mercy in a world that regarded itself as existing precariously under the dominion of Satan.

FURTHER READING

On geography and the environment, see the Bibliography under the headings Historical Geography, The Physical Environment, and Demography.

In addition, see Georges Duby, *The Early Growth of the European Economy: Warriors and Peasants from the Seventh to the Twelfth Century* (Ithaca, NY: Cornell University Press, 1974); B. H. Slicher van Bath, *The Agrarian History of Western Europe, A.D. 500–1850* (London: Edward Arnold, 1963).

On the forms and structures of society, see Jack Goody, *The Development of the Family and Marriage in Europe* (Cambridge: Cambridge University Press, 1983). This is an ambitious and fascinating survey, but it should be read with Suzanne Wemple, *Women in Frankish Society* (Philadelphia: University of Pennsylvania Press, 1981).

On the complex question of rulership, see D. A. Binchy, *Celtic and Anglo-Saxon Kingship* (Oxford: Clarendon Press, 1970); J. M. Wallace-Hadrill, *Early Germanic Kingship in England and on the Continent* (Oxford: Clarendon Press, 1971); P. H. Sawyer and I. N. Wood, eds., *Early Medieval Kingship* (Leeds: School of History, University of Leeds, 1977); Janet L. Nelson, *Politics and Ritual in Early Medieval Europe* (London: Hambledon Press, 1986); Patrick Wormald, Donald Bullough, and Roger Collins, eds., *Ideal and Reality in Frankish and Anglo-Saxon Society* (Oxford: Basil Blackwell, 1983).

On women in early medieval society, see the work of Wemple previously cited as well as Christiane Klapisch-Zuber, ed., *A History of Women in the West*, Vol. II, *The Silences of the Middle Ages* (Cambridge, MA: Harvard University Press, 1992), and Jo Ann McNamara and John E. Halborg, with E. Gordon Whatley, *Sainted Women of the Dark Ages* (Durham and London: Duke University Press, 1992), a superb collection of annotated documents in English translation. A fine example of one of the most important legal collections in translation is Katherine Fischer Drew, *The Laws of the Salian Franks* (Philadelphia: University of Pennsylvania Press, 1991). See also the General Bibliography under the heading Women and History.

8

THE BOOK AND THE SWORD

THE LONG-HAIRED KINGS

In the sixth and seventh centuries, the old Roman provinces in western Europe were slowly transformed into new kingdoms, each of which developed a distinctive culture, and each of which had a distinctive history. The Lombard kingdom in Italy, initially hostile to Roman civilization, nevertheless developed a number of precocious public institutions and preserved a good deal of Roman learning, not least the use of formal documents in governmental affairs, until its conquest by Charlemagne in 774. The Visigothic kingdom in the Iberian peninsula represented yet another type of state development, closely integrating ecclesiastical and secular authority, until its absorption by Arabic invaders between 711 and 720.

The two kingdoms on which most research in the period has focused, however, are those of Anglo-Saxon England and Frankish Gaul. The distinctive intellectual, religious, and political culture of England, long viewed as growing out of Irish missionary efforts and the mission of Augustine of Canterbury in 596, was once thought to have reinvigorated the culture of Gaul, which had declined from its high levels in the fifth and sixth centuries into political weakness, ecclesiastical corruption, and aristocratic chaos. Recent research, however, has tended to regard the kingdom of the Franks as an essential element in the conversion of England, and to see in the Merovingian dynasty, "the long-haired kings" as contemporaries called them, not the series of despots and incompetents that their Carolingian successors portrayed, but energetic kingdom-builders on whose work the later, far better documented kingdom ruled by the dynasty of Charlemagne (769–814), creatively built. This chapter will begin with an account of the development of Anglo-Saxon culture and will then turn to the Frankish kingdom under the Merovingian and Carolingian dynasties.

AN ISLAND SET BEYOND THE WORLD

The link that Gregory the Great forged between Rome and England with the mission of Augustine in 596 resulted in the conversion of the Angles and Saxons to Christianity and was strengthened by the victory of Roman customs at the Synod of Whitby in 663. The English church was the first northern European community to have been shaped by both Roman and non-Roman Celtic influences. As such, it exerted great influence on the communities near it, particularly the still-pagan Germanic peoples in northwest Europe and the Frankish kingdom. The influence of English churchfolk on the Frankish kingdom in the first half of the eighth century set the stage for the later reforms of Pepin III and the later triumphs of Charlemagne.

In 668, five years after Whitby, Pope Vitalian consecrated Theodore, a native of Tarsus in Asia Minor, as archbishop of Canterbury. Theodore traveled to England with Hadrian, a north African monk, and together they completed the organization of the English church and gave great impetus to monastic development. Both learned men, Theodore and Hadrian brought considerable classical learning with them, and they established a series of monastic schools that became the best in western Europe. Theodore ruled the English church for twenty-one years, and his influence was felt in diocesan organization and was reflected in the greatly heightened intellectual level of monasticism. Hilda, a contemporary of Theodore and Hadrian and the founder of the abbey of Whitby in 657, raised learning and study to a major role in the monastery at Whitby and in other ecclesiastical centers where her influence reached. By the end of the seventh century, the English clergy was probably the most learned and best trained in western Europe. Study of the Scriptures was, of course, the focus of monastic and cathedral schools, but in addition it constituted a framework for the preservation of the liberal arts. It also influenced the devotional lives of those who knew no Latin. Hilda patronized the first known poet in vernacular English, Caedmon. Under her patronage Caedmon produced Old English poems on religious topics, thereby bridging one of the gaps between the literary Latin culture of ecclesiastics and the oral, vernacular culture of Christian lay people.

The influence of these individuals is seen in the next generation of ecclesiastical leaders, particularly in the careers of Benedict Biscop and Wilfrid of Ripon. Benedict Biscop was born around 628 and spent his youth in the service of King Oswy of Northumbria. About the time he turned twenty-five Benedict left the royal service, distributed his goods, and undertook a pilgrimage to Rome. He traveled with Wilfrid of Ripon, another wealthy young noble who became a controversial and influential churchman. Benedict made five pilgrimages to Rome during his life, and he traveled to monastic communities on the Continent, where he observed different customs and took monastic vows himself. He was in Rome when Theodore was made archbishop of Canterbury, and he accompanied Theodore back to England. Benedict founded a monastery at Wearmouth in 673 and a second monastery at nearby Jarrow a few years later. Under the abbacy of Ceolfrid, another Northumbrian nobleman who left secular life to become a monk, the two monasteries founded by Benedict Biscop exerted spiritual and intellectual influences as far away as Ireland and the Continent.

The extraordinary intellectual and spiritual vitality of late-seventh-century England is exemplified by the careers of Aldhelm and Bede. Aldhelm was born around 640 and studied with Celtic Christian teachers until he was about thirty. He then went to Canterbury and studied under Abbot Hadrian, acquiring great learning and proficiency in Greek and some Hebrew. Late in life Aldhelm became abbot of Malmesbury, an important monastic community, and throughout his life he produced literary works of considerable learning in an extremely ornate and difficult Latin style. Poems, letters, and theological treatises flowed from his pen, and his career suggests the high level of ecclesiastical culture that characterized England in the late 600s.

Bede (ca. 672–735) was born a few miles from Benedict Biscop's monasteries of Wearmouth and Jarrow, which he entered as a small boy around 679. He spent his entire life at Jarrow, chiefly as a teacher of young monks, and most of his literary works were pedagogical. He wrote, around 701 or 702, an essay on versification, as well as other works introducing students to the technical problems of the primarily literary subjects that they studied. Bede later wrote two longer works on chronology, as well as many biblical commentaries and lives of saints. His greatest work, however, and one of the greatest histories ever written, was his *Ecclesiastical History of the English People,* which he completed in 731. The culture that produced Bede and his *History* is clearly remarkable. In it, the reform of monasticism, including the introduction of Benedictine influences by Benedict Biscop and Wilfrid, the diocesan organization, and the high level of learning mark an important moment in European history and constituted a threshold for the reforms of Charlemagne later in the eighth century.

Bede's *History* is in many ways the climax of that movement in learning, devotion, and the arts that distinguishes late seventh- and early eighth-century England. Bede consciously shaped a unified history of his England within the framework of England's conversion to Christianity. But Bede's England is also Roman, and the figure of Gregory the Great, whom Bede calls the "apostle" of the English, clearly dominates the early part of the history, which preserves many of Gregory's original letters to the members of the English mission. From the early martyrdoms, through Saint Augustine's mission, to the portrait of Oswald of Northumbria as the ideal Christian king, Bede's *History* is a remarkable intellectual document. The level of learning achieved by Bede in a life spent at a small monastery in a remote part of "an island set beyond the world" was equaled elsewhere in England during his lifetime—at Hexham, Ripon, Malmesbury, Canterbury, and York. This cultural revolution marked English society for centuries and greatly influenced the Continent as well. Indeed, it may be considered the first European culture. It is reflected in the epithet that Boniface applied to Bede later in the eighth century—*candela ecclesiae,* "the light within the Church."

The society of England between the arrival of Augustine of Canterbury in 596 and the death of Bede in 735 was divided into a number of kingdoms descended more or less from the leaders who had conquered sub-Roman Britain by the early sixth century. The kingdom of Kent, where Augustine landed and began the conversion of the south, shows in its archaeological remains a willingness to adapt older British arts and crafts and in its fewer literary records extensive contact with the Franks in Gaul. The wife of Aethelberht, king of Kent, for example, was the Frankish princess Bertha.

Letters of Gregory the Great and later bishops of Rome to the kings of Kent and their successors reflect the ecclesiastical attempt to turn pagan kingship into a Christian office with predominantly moral and legal responsibilities. This became a powerful theme in the later writings of Bede and other Anglo-Saxon churchmen. Aethelberht issued a code of laws for his kingdom, the first laws written in a European vernacular language—Old English. Although not all of Aethelberht's successors subscribed to Gregory's ideals, the history of a number of English kingdoms in the seventh and eighth centuries is marked by close cooperation of rulers and churchmen and the literary sources, particularly Bede's *History,* regard this collaboration as essential to the stability of the kingdoms.

Like the contemporary and later laws of the Franks, Aethelberht's Kentish laws and later English collections reflect special concerns with the security of ecclesiastical property rights, violent acts, and trade. Wergild in these laws reflects the higher status of the noble, and the laws of Ine of Wessex (688–694) recognize three or four levels of society below the king, each indicated by the amount of wergild that must be paid for killing a person at each level. Other offenses besides killing also reflect different social ranks. The breaking of a promise of surety, or the breaking of protective rights (the English version of *mundium*) also were graded according to the status of the victim.

The highest status in the English kingdoms after the kings were the ranks of *ealdorman* and *thegn.* The *ealdorman* was a royal officer, apparently responsible for much local government and military service, progressively bound closer to the kings in the late eighth and ninth centuries. The *thegn* was originally a servant, but as in other kingdoms, the term was gradually transformed into the designation of an official who possessed respectable wealth and was responsible for some military matters, the maintenance of the peace, and took a leadership role in local assemblies.

Below the *earldorman* and the *thegn* were the free *ceorl* and the merchant. Both these latter groups could achieve *thegn*-status if they acquired enough wealth and property. Throughout free society, the kingroup was an important element in social structure, particularly in raising compensation for injury, or *wergild,* and in pursuing the feud with enemies of the kin. Along with the ties of blood and responsibility that connected members of the kingroup, there also existed the ties that bound leaders and their followers together. Much early English literature deals in one way or another with the rituals, responsibilities, and heroic ideals of the fighting group of leaders and followers.

In the ninth and tenth centuries, the kings of England increasingly dealt with their kingdoms as collections of geographical units that gradually took over many of the public functions that had once been performed by kingroups. The bonds of lord and follower, collective military service, defense, and tithing all contributed to the weakening of the kingroup and the consolidation of the local territorial unit directly under the higher nobility and the kings.

Although the ideals of rulership preached from Gregory the Great to Bede did not always guide the organization of English society, they did influence kings and nobles, created close ties between rulers and churchmen and shaped the changes in English society from the seventh century through the tenth.

THE LAST OF THE LONG-HAIRED KINGS

The distinctive religious and political culture of late seventh- and early eighth-century England contrasted sharply with that of the rest of northern Europe. In 711, as we have seen, the Visigothic kingdom in Spain was swept away, confined to small pocket-kingdoms in the north of the Iberian peninsula by Arab invaders. The slow conversion of the Lombards in Italy from Arianism to Catholicism delayed the growth of a strong Lombard Catholic Christian culture, although the Lombards did adopt and modify a number of elements of Roman public institutions. The travails of the Byzantine Empire during the attacks of Bulgars and Muslims and during the ensuing iconoclastic controversy played havoc with the Byzantine enclaves in Italy and weakened the position of the popes. Only the Frankish church and society appeared to resemble the great success of England, but the great resources of the Frankish kingdom required a political and cultural revolution in order to be mobilized in the direction of extensive social change. The English developments of the late seventh and early eighth centuries constitute one essential part of the background for this revolution. The history of the Frankish kingdom constitutes the other.

The kingdom created by Clovis before his death in 511 was a wholly new entity in the experience of the Franks. Clovis had to create an adequate form of kingship, and he had to come to terms with the Gallo-Roman inhabitants of his new kingdom, including the powerful aristocratic churchmen. His conquest gave him all of the formerly imperially owned land in Gaul and the income from the Roman fiscal system. Even though he and his successors passed along much of this wealth to their servants, favorites, followers, and to the church, they often replenished it by means of conquest, plunder, tribute, and the confiscation of the wealth of their internal enemies. Clovis and his successors also based their administrations on the old Roman *civitas*-districts, and they continued many of the forms of Roman taxation. Finally, Clovis issued the first written law code of the Franks, in this instance too, imitating both earlier Roman rulers and later Germanic kings.

Clovis was also faced with the problem of Christianity. His wife was an orthodox Christian rather than an Arian, however, and her influence, along with that of the Christian bishops and Clovis's own estimate of the advantages of becoming an orthodox Christian led to his conversion and baptism in 508. Clovis immediately began to call meetings of churchpeople, and until the late seventh century Frankish church councils played a prominent role in the religious and political life of the kingdom.

Clovis also had to determine the succession to his own royal title. The problem of succession was a new problem. Although Frankish law stated that privately owned land had to be divided equally among the surviving sons of a deceased father, there is no indication that the Franks considered the kingdom as property in quite this way. It is likely that contemporary political and dynastic considerations dictated the solution—a division of Clovis's kingdom into four parts, each ruled by one of his four sons as king. Except for brief periods between 558 and 561 and between 613 and 639, when a single ruler governed the whole kingdom of the Franks, the realm was usually divided among three or four rival, and usually hostile, kings.

During the reigns of the first generation after Clovis, new territories were added to the Frankish orbit, particularly Thuringia and Burgundy. During the sixth and seventh centuries some of the divided kingdoms acquired a sense of regional continuity and identity. Gradually, three divisions became customarily recognized. The territory known as Neustria, with its capital at Soissons, emerged out of the Romanized western Frankish lands. The kingdom of Austrasia took shape out of the more Germanic eastern Frankish lands; its center was at Metz. The third kingdom, Burgundy, was generally dominated by one or the other of the remaining two kingdoms. From 623 on, the separate identities of Neustria and Austrasia became a fact of Merovingian Frankish political life.

All three kingdoms were ruled by descendants of Clovis—the members of the Merovingian dynasty were marked by their long hair and their royal wealth. But no individual ruler was entirely secure, either in inheriting a kingdom or in holding on to one once he acquired it. A combination of membership in the ruling dynasty and approval by the powerful clergy and magnates of the realm assured succession, but civil war, rebellion, or assassination might as quickly remove a ruler, particularly when these resulted in the prospect of the total loss of wealth or prestige on the part of one or more factions of the aristocracy. When heirs were minor children, Merovingian queens played prominent political roles in the succession. Also, the powerful individuals surrounding the ruler and the court, members of wealthy families, always played a role in distributing the royal power as well.

Royal favorites were appointed king's representative—whether count, duke, or patrician—to look after royal interests in different parts of the kingdom. Command of the king's army was usually in the hands of one of the Merovingian dukes. Beneath the military and supervisory ranks of dukes and patricians, counts carried out most of the daily responsibilities of the rudimentary administration of the kingdom. Although the titles of the nobility appear to have derived from royal service, most of the great families found it to their advantage to attempt to consolidate their royally delegated powers with their own lands, wealth, and rights and in this way increase their own wealth from the resources of the monarchy and enhance their own status. In at least one area they were successful: as royal service became regionalized in the seventh century, families were able to consolidate their own lands with the lands they administered for the king.

Even in the royal household, the position of *major domus,* "mayor of the palace," began to overshadow that of the king. But the process by which the Merovingian aristocracy increased its wealth made it generally independent of the mayor of the palace, as well as of the king. Especially in the lands on the edges of the kingdoms, virtually independent noble families came to dominate both their regions and their rivals. During the late seventh and early eighth centuries, both the mayor of the palace and the regional nobility began to increase their wealth and power at the expense of the kings. A succession of minor children to the thrones of Neustria and Austrasia in this period helped both these new forces to assert increased power.

Until the end of the seventh and the beginning of the eighth centuries, the Merovingian church and kingdom were the largest and most articulately developed in Europe. Although the kingdom produced no intellectual figure comparable to Bede and no king as saintly as Oswald, its achievements were considerable. It produced—and left—a substantial documentary legacy, not only of literary and public documents, but of ecclesiastical legislation, monastic organization, and a rich literature of saints' lives. But from the late seventh century on, its political direction was drastically transformed.

Of the two main Frankish kingdoms, Neustria remained the more powerful, particularly under Ebroin (657–683), the mayor of the palace, or chief adviser of the kings. Ebroin's power depended on the loyalty to him, rather than to the king, of the prosperous and increasingly powerful and self-conscious regional aristocracy. In Austrasia, too, a regional aristocracy was forming. The most prominent of its families was the Arnulfings, whose leader, Pepin II of Herstal, asserted his military supremacy over Neustria at the Battle of Tertry in 687. Pepin's son, Charles Martel, who succeeded him as mayor of the palace of Austrasia in 714, greatly strengthened that office and began to impose his own rule over many provinces that had slipped out of the hands of the weak later Merovingian kings. In addition, Charles led a successful attack on an invading Muslim army in 733. At his death in 741 Charles Martel was virtually the undisputed ruler of the Franks in Austrasia, Neustria, and Burgundy. He had assembled and enriched his supporters by confiscating church lands and ignoring the rights of the legitimate king. He left his office and his power to two sons, Carloman and Pepin III.

The rise of the aristocracy and the family of Charles Martel in the kingdoms of the Franks coincided with a vigorous missionary movement launched by the English church. Their primary purpose was to convert the still-pagan Germanic peoples in Frisia, Saxony, and Thuringia.

In 718 a monk from Wessex, Winfrid, also undertook a mission to convert the Germanic pagans. In 719 he went to Rome to receive official sanction from the pope, and at that time he changed his name to Boniface. Between 719 and 722 Boniface worked in Frisia, Bavaria, and Saxony. In 722 he went once more to Rome, where he was made bishop, and in 739 he became an archbishop. At the pope's recommendation, he received the protection of Charles Martel. During the next several years, Boniface's independence and the hostility of the Frankish clergy often blocked his attempts to further his missionary work and reform the Frankish higher clergy. Nevertheless, under Charles Martel's sons, Pepin III and Carloman, an alliance between the English missionaries and the Frankish mayors of the palace was forged. In 742 Boniface presided over the first of the reform councils of the Frankish church. In 746, with Pepin's blessing, the Frankish bishops sent a series of ecclesiastical questions to Rome, and in 747 Pepin and the Frankish aristocracy sent a declaration of faith to Rome.

Through the work of the English missionaries a new contact between the Franks and Rome was slowly being forged. During the 740s and early 750s, Boniface was the most prominent churchman on the Continent. He laid the missionary groundwork for the Frankish expansion to the east, as well as leading the reform movement inside the Frankish church. Focusing on his Frisian mission once more, Boniface was killed by the pagans in 753. After his death he was revered as the apostle to the Germans. He had called himself *exul Germanicus*— "the exile in Germany." In him we see the full power of recent English tradition carried to the Continent, not only to the still-pagan Frisians and other Germanic peoples but to the decayed Frankish church. Missionary and reformer, Boniface brought to the Continent a sense of proper ecclesiastical order and secular religious responsibility, as well as the link to Rome that contributed to the shaping of the kingdom of the Franks after Pepin's revolution and throughout the life and reign of Charlemagne.

In 751 Pepin III, son of Charles Martel and mayor of the palace of both Neustria and Austrasia, deposed the last Merovingian king of the Franks and ascended the Frankish throne in his place. To effect his revolution, which had immense consequences in Western political history, Pepin used his own power, an alliance with some of the Frankish aristocracy, and his relationship with Boniface. The association between the new Frankish rulers, Pepin III and Carloman, and the English missionaries—brief as it had been, and intermittent as well—contributed several important elements to the new conception of kingship. A chronicle entry gives what must have become the "official" version of Pepin's revolutionary act:

Burghard, Bishop of Wurzburg, and the chaplain Fulrad of St. Denis were sent by Pepin to Pope Zachary to ask him about the kings in Frankland, who at that time had no royal power. Was this right or not? Pope Zachary replied to Pepin that it was better for the man who had power to be called king rather than one who remained without royal power, and, to avoid a disturbance of the right ordering of things, he commanded by apostolic authority that Pepin should become king.

The seeming naturalness of this text must not cloud its genuinely revolutionary character. Pepin invoked ecclesiastical support to overturn the Merovingian claims to kingship by blood right. His supporters devised a new kind of liturgical ceremony to make him king. He consulted the pope in a matter about which no pope—or any churchman—had ever been consulted before. In short, Pepin transformed the character of Frankish kingship. A near-contemporary account suggests the diverse elements he and his supporters combined to create the new model monarchy of the Franks: "Pepin was a pious king . . . raised to the throne by the authority and order of Pope Zacharias . . . by anointing with the holy chrism at the hands of the blessed bishops [and] by the choice of the Franks." No longer did simple blood right make a Frankish king, but energy and zeal for the welfare of his people and his church. If he is indifferent to power, dissipates wealth, and neglects his people's spiritual welfare, he loses his title to legitimacy. Much of the interpretation of the history of the Merovingian dynasty has derived from Pepin's and later Carolingian propagandists' smearing of the reputations of the last long-haired kings. Only recently has that reputation begun to be restored.

Pepin's revolution was not merely a coup d'etat among the Franks, but the creation of a new theory of society and power entailing new standards for rulership, or at least reasserting some of the standards enunciated by Gregory the Great a century and a half earlier. According to those standards, the Merovingian kings were anachronisms, and a new line of Frankish kings ascended the throne.

THE EXPANSION OF FRANKISH POWER

From the reign of Pepin (751–768) to that of Charles the Bald (848–877), the Carolingian kings of the Franks stabilized and increased the monarchy's resources within the kingdom of the Franks and expanded Frankish power throughout Europe on a scale not seen since the days of Roman expansion. Within half a century, the Franks controlled all of western Europe except for the

British Isles, most of the Iberian peninsula, and southern Italy. Their frontiers marched against those of the pagan Frisians, Saxons, Danes, Balts, northern and southern Slavic peoples, Christian Greece, and Muslim Spain. The immediate driving force behind this expansion was the Frankish army, but the organization of the kingdom by Pepin and his son Charlemagne (768–814) played an equally important role. From their reorganization of the royal household, which they grandly called the "royal palace," to their institution of counts and dukes as royal representatives throughout the kingdom, and their patronage and support of the Frankish church, the kings reshaped the political order of Frankish society.

Among the royal resources available to govern the kingdom, the greatest was land. The income, often in food and goods, that the land produced supported the king, his household, and his officials. In order to obtain the regular services of the nobility, the king granted lifetime tenure of part of the royal lands to those who served him. When the person so rewarded was a bishop, the lands and income he received were called the *epsicopatus*. When the servant was a count, the total was called the *comitatus*.

The count (*comes*, or *grafio*) was the essential unit of royal administration outside the household itself. Counts had existed under the Merovingians, and in old Roman territories they had come to control the former public services and sources of income that had become the property of the Frankish king. They combined the functions of judge, provincial governor, military commander, court clerk, and royal representative. Under the later Merovingians many counts had assimilated their royal duties and resources to their own personal and family property, thus alienating much of the royal wealth. Under Pepin and Charlemagne the counts were controlled more effectively. They were made to serve in areas where they had no personal connections, their offices ceased to be heritable by their children, and their duties were spelled out in directive after directive issued by the royal court. Traveling circuit inspectors called the *missi dominici* ("those sent by the king") reviewed the counts' activities and corrected them when necessary. Charlemagne also made the counts work harder, especially in administering the law courts. They were also responsible for the local contingents of soldiers and supplies for the army campaigns of the summer. The counts had small staffs of assistants, including the *vicecomes*, or viscount, and the *scabini*, or *judices*, men learned in the law. But the count, like the king, worked out of a household rather than an office.

Although the system of administering the kingdom by counts (and in particularly troublesome places by margraves and dukes, counts with increased powers and resources) is clear enough in theory, it had many shortcomings, even under Charlemagne. Ideally, the system would have required around 2500 officials to operate efficiently, but it is doubtful that Charlemagne ever assembled nearly that many. Many of the ills that had plagued Merovingian governance could only be checked, not overcome. Long distances, the tendency of counts to localize themselves, the inefficiency of supervision and communications—all worked to reduce efficiency, and the kings often reiterated their demands that loyalty be the count's primary virtue.

Fidelity—and its opposite, treachery and breaking faith—dominate the literature of the ninth century. The limitations of the ethical world of these royal servants are shown nowhere more clearly than in the constant emphasis on personal loyalty to the king. As late as the thirteenth century, treason was understood chiefly in terms of personal disloyalty to a lord to whom one had taken an oath of allegiance.

Out of these limited resources and on the tenuous foundations of personal oaths of loyalty, the Carolingian rulers of the Franks built their extensive kingdom. Its fabric consisted of the church and the palace household, the local courts, the *scabini,* the vicars, and the counts. The great frontier lords were conceived as a kind of supercount, and the seven marches that they ruled—Spain, Brittany, Bavaria, Pannonia, Friuli, Nordgau, and Swabia—guarded the edges of the expanding but always threatened kingdom. Through these territories traveled the kings *missi,* his household servants, ecclesiastical officials going back and forth to Rome, pilgrims, and strangers.

The new and insistent tone of the Frankish king's ecclesiastical mission makes the ecclesiastical reforms under Pepin and Charlemagne an illuminating aspect of the character of Carolingian kingship. The divisions of ecclesiastical administration created in the last years of imperial rule in the Roman West had virtually disappeared by the late seventh century. Episcopal offices were left vacant for long periods or given to royal relatives and favorites without consideration of personal qualifications or the ecclesiastical legality of elections to ecclesiastical offices. The ecclesiastical reforms urged by Boniface changed the course of the Frankish church in the late eighth century, but the power of Pepin and Charlemagne prevented the Church's establishment of an autonomous hierarchy. Part of the royal mission was the assumption of responsibility for a Christian people, and the Carolingians retained considerable power in the matter of ecclesiastical appointments. The reorganization of the Church, however, was now sponsored powerfully by the kings themselves, and the restoration of the old archbishoprics, the subordination of bishops to their metropolitans and of local clergy to bishops, and the frequency of ecclesiastical synods and councils contributed to the restoration of administrative order within the Frankish church and constituted simultaneously a new kind of organized support for the king. Not only were older sees reconstituted, but new ones were founded and some such as Salzburg in 798 were raised to metropolitan status–that is, they were ruled by archbishops. This vigorous, newly organized episcopate, many of whose members were drawn from the greatest families of the kingdom, became one of the strongest supports of the monarchy and eventually a nearly independent group in the complex ecclesiastical and political atmosphere of Charlemagne's son and successor, Louis.

Besides the bishoprics, Pepin and Charlemagne restored and enriched the monasteries of Gaul and founded new ones in other parts of their territory.

The monasteries, whose reform was continued brilliantly through the reign of Louis, provided the norms of religious life in the rough Frankish kingdom, personnel for royal service, scribes, advisers, and allies to the ruling dynasty. Such monasteries as St. Denis, near Paris, Corbie and its daughter house to the east, Corvey, St. Gall in Switzerland, and especially St. Martin at Tours are the best-known of Charlemagne's day. Under Louis's ecclesiastical adviser, Benedict of Aniane, the influence of the Benedictine rule grew much greater in the Frankish kingdom.

The internal stability created by the king's use of counts and dukes, bishops and abbots, enabled Pepin, and still more Charlemagne, to turn to the expansion of the kingdom. The frontiers moved slowly outward toward Spain, Italy, Germany, the Slavic lands, and the Netherlands. Territories that had been in the kingdom but had continually proved restive whenever a crisis troubled the royal authority—areas such as Aquitaine, Bavaria, and Brittany—received particular royal attention, and the commanders of the marches were in a state of almost continuous military preparedness. The Carolingian kings also developed the ability to conduct different military operations on different fronts at the same time. During the period 752–759, Pepin fought both the Lombards in Italy and the Arabs in Septimania in northeastern Spain. Later, kings were often recalled from one area of military activity in order to quell a local rebellion or defend another frontier from invaders.

The driving mechanism of Frankish expansion was the 8000-man military force that the Frankish kings could assemble every spring, after a winter's military planning. The army consisted primarily of infantry, well armed and highly disciplined, and some cavalry, wearing mailed coats and helmets and armed with sword and spear. Depending on the area of campaigning, some parts of the kingdom contributed more fighting men, some less, from year to year.

After putting down local revolts in Aquitaine, Brittany, and Bavaria, Pepin and then Charlemagne directed Frankish power primarily toward Spain, Saxony, and Italy. In 778 Charlemagne entered Spain. His failure to take Saragossa became the kernel for the epic poem *The Song of Roland,* but he captured Gerona in 785 and Barcelona in 801–803. In addition, he established the Spanish March, a durable enclave of Frankish power south of the Pyrenees that protected the frontier against the Muslim forces to the south.

The conquest of the Saxons proved to be Charlemagne's longest and most costly campaign. The nobles from the eastern parts of the kingdom and the missionary churches along the eastern border had long faced the power of this Germanic people settled between the Elbe and the North Sea. Charlemagne directed a substantial campaign into Saxony virtually every year between 772 and 785. Frankish victories were followed by Saxon rebellions, and Charlemagne's early policy of forcing Saxons to convert to Christianity helped to maintain their resistance. By 804, however, Charlemagne was able to add the vast territories of Saxony to his domain. The fall of Saxony made it easier for Charlemagne's

Charlemagne's Palace Chapel at Aachen. Borrowed from Roman imperial buildings at Ravenna, the design for this chapel (now a part of Aachen cathedral) suggests visually Charlemagne's heightened sense of Christian rulership. *(Ann Munchow, Aachen)*

armies to overcome Frisian resistance in the Netherlands, and the conquest of these two areas brought Charlemagne's borders to the base of the Jutland peninsula and face to face with the Danes.

To the southeast, Charlemagne defeated Tassilo, duke of the Bavarians, in 787 and incorporated his realm into the Carolingian kingdom. The conquest of Bavaria led Charlemagne to Carinthia, and thereby into the affairs of the southern Slavs and the Avars. The Avars, as we have seen, had entered the Danube valley in the sixth century, divided the Slavs and incorporated many of them into their kingdom, and participated in the great assault on Constantinople in 626. Their military capabilities had been considerably reduced by the late eighth century, however. Charlemagne's armies destroyed their capital in 796, removing the great Avar treasure to Aachen and causing the Avars to disappear from history.

The military reforms of Charles Martel, the political revolution of Pepin, and Charlemagne's single rule for forty-three years after 771 contributed to the development of a new type of power under Charlemagne. The weaknesses of surrounding peoples, the remarkably wide base of support that Charlemagne received from the Church and the laity, and the effectiveness of the Carolingian army all contributed to the expansion of the kingdom. The kingdom was held together by the only successful means known—loyalty to a single ruler who was sufficiently powerful to enforce loyalty or submission when they were not voluntarily forthcoming. The kingdom itself, particularly in the newly conquered lands, underwent no governmental revolution, and the common Christianity of the whole kingdom cannot have been expected to constitute the bond that it became only much later. The kingdom of the Franks was still the kingdom of the Franks. But it was also the kingdom of Charlemagne, and it could only have been ruled, its particular loyalties and local and regional senses of independence only overcome, by a ruler as able, vigorous, and fortunate as Charlemagne. But no other such king of the Franks was forthcoming. Even in Charlemagne's old age, the kingdom began to come apart.

THE CAROLINGIAN RENEWAL

Charlemagne accompanied his successes as a king and a warrior by a heightened conception of himself as having a divinely ordained mission that included responsibility for the quality of spiritual as well as temporal life. The quality of spiritual life turned on the quality of the clergy, and Charlemagne's clerical reforms gave rise to a vigorous Latin literary and artistic culture often called the Carolingian renaissance, but perhaps more properly designated the Carolingian renewal. Charlemagne's first steps were to continue his family's patronage of Frankish church reform and to secure accurate texts of essential items of Christian literature—the Bible, canon law, a reliable sacramentary, and the Benedictine rule. From this essentially practical emphasis on proper learning for the purpose of improving the quality of ecclesiastics, there quickly grew up active book-producing centers that copied the works of classical writers as well as those of church fathers, borrowing books to copy from Spain, Italy, Ireland, and England and in turn circulating copies to other monastic and episcopal centers. If not the intellectual profundity or originality, then certainly the sheer volume of book production in the late eighth and early ninth centuries characterizes the reigns of Charlemagne and Louis as critical in the intellectual history of Europe.

The Carolingian literary renaissance was marked not only by the increasing circulation and standardization of basic Christian literature, but also by striking changes in the techniques of book production, particularly decoration and handwriting. Book covers of jewels and precious metals adorned the most important sacred writings. A new and much clearer form of handwriting, the Carolingian minuscule, replaced the irregular and difficult-to-read Merovingian script, and durable vellum and parchment replaced papyrus. The organization of the scriptoria (writing rooms) of the monasteries included the selection of works to be copied, the assignment of works to copyists, and the training and supervision of new scribes. The head of the monastic scriptorium became an important figure in the monastery and not uncommonly, when the abbot himself happened to be a learned man, produced literary works whose importance cannot be overestimated. The Carolingian bishops constituted administrative and disciplinary support for the new Frankish monarchy, and the monasteries constituted its intellectual and literary complement. In order to promote these intellectual reforms, Charlemagne developed the palace school, transforming an older institution for the training of young boys into an academy where literary learning and other forms of training were combined under the watchful care of the king himself and the scholars he brought to court.

Carolingian scholars' search for authentic texts of fundamental documents had important consequences. The Dionysio-Hadriana, the collection of ecclesiastical law sent to Charlemagne by Pope Hadrian I in 774, became the foundation for later collections of canon law. The copy of the Roman Sacramentary that the king received in 786 became the foundation for Continental liturgical practice. The copy of the rule of Benedict that Charlemagne ordered from Monte Cassino in 787 became the basis for the monastic reforms of the next several centuries.

The Carolingian choice of the Rule of Benedict had momentous consequences. It gave most of Latin monasticism a single pattern to observe, and it brought into the mainstream of European thought and sensibility one of the most remarkable influences they ever experienced. The rule of Benedict differed from earlier monastic rules in several ways. First, most eastern monastic rules were aimed at the individual monk, whereas Benedict's was directed at the monastic community. Second, many early rules were noted for their ruthless breaking of the human spirit by a rigid pattern of self-denial; Benedict's rule struck a remarkable balance between penitential discipline and human relations within the community. Third, many earlier rules reflected their regions of origin; Benedict's rule is clearly patterned on the needs of Latin Christians in general and reveals strong traditional Roman influences. Finally, many earlier rules were aimed at cultivating an exotic piety that frequently exceeded human endurance; Benedict's rule aimed at shaping the devotional life of the monk within the context of an organized community, carefully and conscientiously administered by its leader, the abbot, and intended to keep the monk from falling into vices rather than cultivating devotional excesses.

The chief emphasis in Benedict's rule is on the cornerstone of monastic life: the vows of poverty, chastity, and obedience. The individual monk owns nothing, is celibate, and gives up his individual autonomy to the community under the abbot. Thus prepared, the monk, by living a temperate life characterized by a balance of contemplation, prayer in community, and manual labor, could avoid some of the extremes of eccentric behavior that were sometimes encouraged by other rules. By setting the monk's sights lower, Benedict prevented the despair that individual hermits or extreme communities experienced when they could not live up to their often unrealistic expectations.

The Rule of Benedict is as important a document in the history of psychology as it is in the history of religion. It shows considerable concern for what today we would call the monk's personality. Its main thrust is toward a kind of psychological conditioning, dependent on a careful balance of different kinds of activity, sensible dietary regulations, and strict but charitable discipline. Regularity, consistency, order—these are the keys of Benedictine monasticism. The earliest use of the concept of revolution in modern Western thought, in fact, comes from this monastic environment. Here it meant, not social disorder or reversal, but the repetition day after day of the same patterns of monastic devotional life. Indeed, one reason for the later success of the Benedictine rule may have been that it helped create the most stable personalities in the West between the sixth and the eighth centuries.

Charlemagne sought out scholars from the far reaches of his empire and beyond. Peter of Pisa and Paulinus of Aquileia, both grammarians, and Paul the Deacon, the historian of the Lombards and of the church of Metz, all came from Lombard Italy in the 770s and 780s. Theodulf of Orleans was a Visigoth. Dicuil, the geographer, and Dungal, the astronomer, came from Ireland. The man associated most closely with the Carolingian renaissance, Alcuin of York, also came from a great distance. Alcuin was intellectually a product of the great growth of learning in England in the late seventh and eighth centuries. On a trip to Rome he met Charlemagne at Parma in 781 and was invited to the king's court. From 782 to 796 Alcuin was Charlemagne's major ecclesiastical adviser and perhaps the greatest scholar in the kingdom. His influence can be seen in the intellectual tradition of his students who administered the great ninth-century monastic schools and their teachers. For twenty years the most powerful ruler in the West and the English scholar who, probably more than anyone else, was his guide and consultant on the most important intellectual issues of his day shared an extraordinarily close relationship.

In 793 Einhard, a young layman from the Main valley, came to Charlemagne's court, participated in its intellectual and administrative life, and much later, after Charlemagne's death, paid the king the tribute of writing his biography, the first biography of a layman in many centuries. Although much of Einhard's style and approach derived from Roman and later Latin sources, his portrait of Charlemagne is invaluable. In it one can see a semiliterate barbarian prince, a second-generation king who rose from a coup d'état of doubtful legitimacy, dressing and acting much like those around him, fond of hunting and baths and fighting. One can see something more, too. Something in Charlemagne's imagination made him view his conquests and power as more than private acquisitions. With his conquests there grew in him a mighty sense of personal responsibility for the lives and the souls of his subjects. The legacy of this vision influenced the thought of Europe for centuries to come. Warrior and king, Charlemagne was also Christian Europe's first great lay patron of religion and the arts, and perhaps its first political idealist.

Some of Charlemagne's intellectual legacy is tangible. Around 8000 manuscripts survive from the late eighth and ninth centuries, and many more are known to have been produced. These books are usually clearly written— many of them in the new style of handwriting called the Carolingian minuscule, which spread throughout Europe in the ninth century—usually well edited, and sturdily made. They consist not only of the expected ecclesiastical treatises, saints' lives, and chronicles, but also of the work of earlier Latin writers, many from the classical period.

Two examples may suggest the range of the revival of learning under Charlemagne. In the first half of the ninth century, several collections of Church law appeared that are known to have been forgeries. The most famous of these is the collection attributed to Pseudo-Isidore. Many of them purported to contain documents as old as the second and third centuries. Although they were forgeries, the skill of those who made them, the wide range of ideas they contain, and their sheer bulk testify to the technical and intellectual abilities even of the forgers, themselves a product of the Carolingian renaissance. Many of the documents they fabricated played a prominent part for centuries in European intellectual history.

A second indicator of the renewal of learning is the degree of sophistication found in the theological disputes of the ninth century. One of the most prominent participants was the Irish scholar John Scotus Erigena, who taught at the court of Charlemagne's grandson, Charles the Bald, learned Greek, and translated the important sixth-century treatise *On the Celestial Hierarchies* by Pseudo-Dionysius into Latin. The disputes ranged from the nature of sacraments to predestination, reflecting the continuing influence of Carolingian educational reforms in the monastic and court schools through most of the ninth century. The Carolingian intellectual and artistic renaissance played as important a role in European history as the political and military achievements of the eighth-century Franks.

THE "KINGDOM OF EUROPE" AND THE EMPIRE OF THE ROMANS

Around 776 the Anglo-Saxon monk Cathwulf referred to Charlemagne's kingdom as the *Regnum Europae,* "the kingdom of Europe," reviving the obscure Roman geographical designation *Europa* to indicate the breadth of his new power. In the last decades of the century Charlemagne's relations with the kings of Northumbria and Mercia indicated their sense of inferiority to him, as did the tribute from the increasingly powerful King Alfonso II of Asturias in northern Spain. Shortly after 780, Empress Irene of Constantinople negotiated with

Charlemagne concerning a marriage between his daughter Rotrud and her son Constantine VI. This recognition, along with the embassies from Harun al-Rashid, the caliph of Baghdad, and the overtures from the Christian inhabitants of Jerusalem that reached Charlemagne in 800, indicate one level of his position. The prestige of the king of the Franks was greater than that of any other Christian ruler.

Charlemagne's immense prestige and power in northern Europe were also well known to the popes, and during his reign the link between the Franks and the popes grew considerably stronger. To understand Charlemagne's unique position in papal eyes, we must consider some important crises in papal history during the second half of the eighth century. Of these, the most important were generated by the Lombards and the iconoclastic controversy in Byzantium. From the early eighth century a restored, ambitious Lombard monarchy, first under Liutprand (712–744) and then under his more ruthless successors Ratchis (744–749) and Aistulf (749–756), moved against the powerful and largely independent Lombard duchies of Spoleto and Benevento, to the east and south of Rome. The tactical importance of the position of Rome and the weakness of the unsupported Byzantine garrisons in central Italy made the independence of Rome precarious, and when in 751 Aistulf finally captured Ravenna, which had been for two centuries the chief seat of Byzantine imperial power in Italy, he threatened to place Rome under his own authority.

The popes, who were unable and perhaps unwilling to treat with the Lombards, sought allies beyond the Alps. As we have seen, the middle of the eighth century was a period of crisis and instability in many parts of Europe, and the papal approval of Pepin's revolution in 751 drew the bishop of Rome and the king of the Franks closer together. In 754, when the Synod of Heireia pronounced firmly against the cult of images, when only Byzantine emissaries, not troops, were forthcoming from Constantinople, and when Aistulf's forces were threatening Rome more ominously, Pope Stephen II (752–757) made his way to the kingdom of the Franks. There he anointed Pepin again and implored his aid, which he obtained in spite of considerable resistance among the Frankish magnates and Pepin's doubtful security so soon after his revolution. Stephen had also crowned Pepin's sons Carloman and Charles kings in perpetuity, making Pepin *patricius Romanorum,* a title implying the status of special protector of Rome. The relationship between the pope and the king of the Franks—tentatively begun earlier in the century, established firmly by the approval of Pepin's revolution in 751, and cemented by the meeting between Pepin and Stephen II in 754—had enduring consequences, both for the future history of Italy and the papacy and for the concept of Frankish protection of the Latin church. The lands that Pepin guaranteed to the pope comprised large parts of the old Exarchate of Ravenna. Pepin's donation of these lands, confirmed by Charlemagne, became the Papal States, a block of territory in central Italy under the direct rule of the bishop of Rome. They played an important part in medieval history and survived until the invasion of Rome in 1870. Not until the papal concordat with Mussolini in 1929 did the popes formally acknowledge the loss of these territories, although they preserved Vatican City as a sovereign state.

Around the middle of the eighth century, perhaps as late as 778, a document began to be cited by papal scribes that had a great bearing on the constitutional history of European Christian society. This document, the Donation of Constantine, professed to be a deed issued in the year 313 in which the Emperor Constantine extended many privileges to the pope and clergy, chiefly in the matter of rank, possessions, and privileges. The most important statement in the document, however, was a passage that could be interpreted as granting rule over the entire western part of the Roman Empire to the bishop of Rome. The document probably was intended to provide independent legitimacy for the Papal States and to shore up the position of the bishop of Rome in the face of Byzantine, Lombard, and Carolingian pressures. Although little used in the eighth and ninth centuries, the Donation became a key document in twelfth-century collections of Church law and a foundation for later papal claims to control the rulers of Europe. Its authenticity was not formally disproved until the critical work of the scholar Lorenzo Valla in the fifteenth century. The donation of Pepin and the Donation of Constantine both contributed to the strengthened relations between pope and ruler of the Franks in the later eighth century.

Between 754 and 790 the popes ceased sending notification of their election to the emperors at Constantinople and sent it instead to the kings of the Franks. Imperial portraits disappeared from Roman coinage and were replaced with portraits of the issuing popes; popes ceased dating their official documents in terms of imperial reigns, doing so instead in terms of their own. In spite of continuing Byzantine difficulties and Lombard resistance, the papacy in the second half of the eighth century reconstituted itself as a distinctly Latin power and slowly removed the lingering traces of imperial authority from central Italy.

By 780 new negotiations appear to have temporarily restored good relations among the pope, Charlemagne, and Byzantium. The Papal States had come into being, and the extension of Charlemagne's power had brought him not only the iron crown of the Lombards but a newer and closer relationship with the pope and a renewed official status in the eyes of Rome and the Roman church. This aspect of the expansion of the Frankish kingdom opened the way not only to a double royal title, "King of the Franks and the Lombards" and the Roman title *patricius Romanorum,* but also to the idea of a new title appropriate for all of the lands Charlemagne ruled, a renewed imperial title in the west.

We have already seen how Charlemagne's concern with ecclesiastical questions began early in his reign and, if anything, increased markedly toward the end of the century. The 780s witnessed extensive ecclesiastical reforms in the capitularies (ordinances issued by Charlemagne). The first suppression of iconoclasm in

Carolingian Empire and Anglo-Saxon England.

Byzantium had taken place in the Council of Nicaea of 787, whose canons, agreed upon by Pope Hadrian I but badly translated into Latin, reached the Frankish kingdom and elicited a complex response written principally by Theodulf of Orleans but signed by Charlemagne. This response, the *Libri Carolini*, strongly criticized the iconodule position, challenged the right of Irene, as a woman, to rule the empire, and undercut the claims to universality of imperially sponsored church councils in Constantinople. At the same time, it reiterated the traditional orthodoxy of the

Franks, Charlemagne's conversion of infidels, and the traditional ties between the Franks and the pope, the true authority for the determination of orthodox beliefs.

At the Council of Frankfurt in 794 the Carolingian king and high churchmen dealt with the heresy of Adoptionism, a dispute concerning the natures of Christ that reflected a rivalry between the Christian churchmen of Muslim Spain and those in the Christian kingdom to the north. Throughout the 790s the correspondence of Alcuin, Charlemagne's closest adviser during these years, reflected a great concern for the survival of orthodoxy and the dangers to orthodox belief posed by various movements in Spain and Italy. In 797 Charlemagne issued the *Capitulare Saxonicum,* a broadly conceived and diplomatic approach to a program for the peaceful introduction of Christianity among the Saxons and Slavs, a program very different from the earlier, more brutal policies of Christianization that the king had insisted upon.

From 795 on, another ecclesiastical crisis confronted the king. Pope Leo III, Hadrian's successor, encountered formidable opposition in Rome, was accused of crimes, and was ultimately kidnapped. Both Alcuin and Charlemagne were particularly concerned about the situation of the pope and the consequent welfare of the Church. These ecclesiastical concerns, which show a steady sharpening of Charlemagne's concept of his own role, as well as the influence of articulate advisers, occurred at the same time as the first successes of Carolingian educational reforms and the building of the palace at Aachen, which had been under way since 794 and reflected a new concept of a palace-capital for the king. Echoes of the difficulties of both Byzantium and Rome resound in a remarkable letter written by Alcuin to Charlemagne in 799, at the height of the crisis:

Until now, there have been three men of highest rank in the world. The first is the apostolic sublimity, governing from the throne of the blessed Peter, prince of the apostles, as his vicar. . . . The second is the imperial dignity and power of the other Rome [Constantinople]. . . . The third is the royal dignity which by the dispensation of our Lord Jesus Christ is conferred upon you as the governor of the Christian people.

After remarking upon the present weakness of the papacy and the crimes of the empress Irene, he concludes:

The royal dignity is more excellent than the other dignities in power, more shining in wisdom, more sublime in rank. Now on you alone rests the tottering safety of the churches of Christ. It is for you to avenge crimes, to guide the erring, to console the sorrowing, and to raise up the good.

In Alcuin's view at least, Charlemagne, the just king, must now act alone and imperially.

Pope Leo was kidnapped in April of 799, but he escaped and made his way to Charlemagne at Paderborn. In November 800 Charlemagne arrived outside Rome and was greeted by the pope with the ceremonial procedures appropriate for an imperial entrance into the city. In December Leo cleared himself of all charges by an oath of purgation, and the ensuing synod that he held probably decided to crown Charlemagne emperor, possibly at the urging of Frankish clerics then present. On the evening of December 25, 800, following the third mass of Christmas, Pope Leo placed a crown on Charlemagne's head and declared him emperor of the Romans. The imperial *laudes* were chanted, and the pope prostrated himself in the *proskynesis* (ritual prostration) before the emperor.

The coronation, acclamation, and public veneration of Charlemagne as emperor of the Romans has long vexed historians as a problem of interpretation. Its primary sources consist of texts that themselves describe liturgical acts. These acts contained meaning for those who performed them and for those who witnessed them or heard about them. From late antiquity, the public life of the empire had been conducted according to an increasingly elaborate ceremony, and from the fourth century on, that ceremony had acquired a religious dimension, including participation by the clergy. Such a ceremony influenced the early Germanic kingdoms, from that of the Visigoths in Spain to those of Anglo-Saxon England, and Francia as well. In addition, inauguration ceremonies existed in the East Roman Empire. In Charlemagne's world—and for long after—many basic political ideas were expressed rather through ceremony and the pictorial representation of ceremony than through explicit texts. Significant stages in human life—marriage, birth, coming of age, entering one state of life or another, coronation and formal visits (*adventus*) in the case of kings, and death were all accompanied by rituals whose meaning was understood by all concerned. The coronation of Charlemagne was part of that process of the ritual expression of significant sacramental, social, and political stages of life that characterized Europe from late antiquity until early modern times.

The ritual order of Charlemagne's coronation differed from that of contemporary Byzantine rulers. In Constantinople, the ruler-to-be was first acclaimed by the Senate and the army (originally in a military camp), then crowned by the patriarch (originally in a palace or public square, later in the Church of Hagia Sophia), and finally was publicly "worshiped" by the people in the ritual of *proskynesis*. In Charlemagne's case, the coronation by Leo III preceded the acclamation (the imperial *laudes* that were chanted by Romans and Franks together in St. Peter's basilica). These were followed by the *proskynesis*, which was also performed by Leo III himself. From 801 on, Leo III issued documents dated from Charlemagne's coronation, and he issued coinage in Rome with Charlemagne's portrait. By May of 801 Charlemagne and his court had settled on the exact form of the imperial title: "Charles, Most Serene Augustus, crowned by God, great and peaceful emperor, governing the Roman Empire, and, by the mercy of God, King of the Lombards and the Franks."

In the eyes of some, at least, of Charlemagne's followers, his coronation as emperor was the result of the recognition that God had so favored Charlemagne that Charlemagne had created a new era of peace and just government that so far extended beyond the traditional achievements of the Frankish and

Lombard kings that it deserved the renewal of the old imperial title. Charlemagne probably shared this view, as well as the extraordinary and novel responsibilities it imposed. In the years after 801 he made a particular effort to organize the ecclesiastical and secular legal systems of his empire and to intensify the Christianization of his subjects. Later diplomatic negotiations with Constantinople also emphasize the legitimacy of Charlemagne's status as emperor and the identity of his title with that of the early Christian emperors. In 802 Charlemagne required a new oath of allegiance from his subjects—this time to him as emperor—and throughout the last decade and a half of his life, many of his accomplishments and aims are phrased in terms of a *renovatio*—a renewal—of idealized earlier times.

Although the coronation conferred no additional rights, lands, or wealth on Charlemagne (except, conceivably, in parts of central Italy), it did serve as a contemporary recognition of his extraordinary career and the impact it had on a wide variety of late eighth-century peoples, from Frankish aristocrats to churchpeople and a pope. And it added new dimensions to the idea of rulership itself.

FURTHER READING

On England and conversion, see Henry Mayr-Harting, *The Coming of Christianity to Anglo-Saxon England* (University Park, PA: The Pennsylvania State University Press, 1991). For the late seventh and eighth centuries, see H. R. Loyn, *Anglo-Saxon England and the Norman Conquest* (New York: St. Martin's Press, 1962. On the religious context, see David Rollason, *Saints and Relics in Anglo-Saxon England* (Oxford: Basil Blackwell, 1989); Nicholas Brooks, *The Early History of the Church of Canterbury* (Atlantic Highlands, NJ: Humanities Press, 1984); S. J. Crawford, *Anglo-Saxon Influence on Western Christendom, 600–800* (reprint ed., Cambridge: Cambridge University Press, 1966); Wilhelm Levison, *England and the Continent in the Eighth Century* (Oxford: Clarendon Press, 1946); Peter Hunter Blair, *The World of Bede* (London: Secker & Warburg, 1970); Paul Meyvaert, *Benedict, Gregory, Bede and Others* (London: Variorum, 1977); James Campbell, *Essays in Anglo-Saxon History, 500–1100* (London: Variorum, 1986); and H. R. Loyn, *The Governance of Anglo-Saxon England, 500–1087* (Stanford, CA: Stanford University Press, 1984).

On early Frankish history, see the classic studies by J. M. Wallace-Hadrill, *The Long-Haired Kings* (New York: Barnes and Noble, 1962), but the new revisions of Merovingian history are best followed in Patrick Geary, *Before France and Germany* (New York-Oxford: Oxford University Press, 1984) and especially Ian Wood, *The Merovingian Kingdoms, 450–751* (London-New York: Longman, 1994). The most comprehensive recent survey of Carolingian political history is that of Rosamund McKitterick, *The Frankish Kingdoms under the Carolingians, 751–987* (London-New York: Longman, 1983). Two different, but provoking studies of Carolingian rulership are Karl F. Morrison, *The Two Kingdoms* (Princeton, NJ: Princeton University Press, 1964), and Walter Ullmann, *The Carolingian Renaissance and the Idea of Kingship* (London: Methuen, 1969). Rosamund McKitterick, *The Frankish Church and the Carolingian Reforms, 789–895* (London: Royal Historical Society, 1977) is a detailed study of the ecclesiastical side of the period. An important, and visually stunning account of one aspect of Carolingian culture is the masterpiece by Walter Horn and Ernest Born, *The Plan of St. Gall* (Berkeley and Los Angeles: University of California Press, 1979). See also Janet Nelson, *Politics and Ritual in Early Medieval Europe,* and, for Italy, Thomas F. X. Noble, *The Republic of St. Peter,* and J. T. Hallenbeck, *Pavia and Rome: The Lombard Monarchy and the Papacy in the Eighth Century* (Philadelphia: American Philosophical Society, 1982).

On Carolingian Europe, see Donald Bullough, *The Age of Charlemagne* (New York: Putnam's, 1966); Bullough, *Carolingian Renewal: Sources and Heritage* (New York: St. Martin's Press, 1991); Heinrich Fichtenau, *The Carolingian Empire* (reprinted., Toronto: University of Toronto Press, 1978); Pierre Riché, *Daily Life in the World of Charlemagne* (reprinted., Philadelphia: University of Pennsylvania Press, 1988); Riché, *The Carolingians: A Family Who Forged Europe* (Philadelphia: University of Pennsylvania Press, 1993); H. R. Loyn and John Percival, *The Reign of Charlemagne* (New York: St. Martin's Press, 1976); F. L. Ganshof, *The Carolingians and the Frankish Monarchy* (Ithaca, NY: Cornell University Press, 1971); Louis Halphen, *Charlemagne and the Carolingian Empire* (Amsterdam: North Holland Publishing Co., 1977).

On broad aspects of intellectual life, see Rosamond McKitterick, ed., *Carolingian Culture: Emulation and Innovation* (Cambridge: Cambridge University Press, 1994), and Bernhard Bischoff, *Manuscripts and Libraries in the Age of Charlemagne* (Cambridge: Cambridge University Press, 1994). Janet Nelson, *Politics and Ritual;* Ernst Kantorowicz, *Laudes Regiae* (Berkeley and Los Angeles: University of California Press, 1946).

The most detailed study of the imperial coronation of Charlemagne is that of Robert Folz, *The Coronation of Charlemagne, 25 December 800* (London: Routledge & Kegan Paul, 1974).

Two important studies of the ceremonial aspects of early medieval kingship are: Michael McCormick, *Eternal Victory* (Cambridge: Cambridge University Press, 1985), and Michael J. Enright, *Iona, Tara and Soissons. The Origin of the Royal Anointing Ritual* (Berlin-New York: Walter de Gruyter, 1985).

9

EUROPE EMERGES

EMPIRE, KINGDOMS, AND THE LAST INVADERS

Charlemagne's triumphs did not guarantee political or military stability to the Franks and other subject peoples of his empire, nor was Charlemagne under any delusion that they would. Toward the end of his life he is even said to have asked "whether we are truly Christians." Throughout his last years he faced the reality that the imperial title (and the imperial idea he shared with Alcuin) had been chiefly the concept of a small aristocratic and ecclesiastical elite close to Charlemagne personally, and not widely, if at all, understood or accepted by most of his subjects. Others, including the rest of the aristocracy and clergy, still thought in terms of a more traditional Frankish monarchy and society. Louis, the Pious (814–840), Charlemagne's son and successor, faced this difficulty, and his successors faced new invasions from Vikings, Magyars, and Arabs that the Frankish armies proved to be less and less able to resist.

Charlemagne was succeeded by his one surviving legitimate son, Louis. He personally crowned Louis king and emperor. Not until a few years later did Louis permit Pope Gregory IV to anoint him emperor as Leo III had anointed Charlemagne. But Louis's independence, native intelligence, and unquestioned devotion to the responsibilities of being a Christian emperor were offset by problems his father had never had to face. The costs of war rose, and there were fewer clear-cut victories. The Frankish armies were far better on offense, when they could plan long campaigns, than on defense, when they might be called unpredictably to different parts of the empire.

Finally, Louis, unlike his father and grandfather, faced the problem of dividing his empire among several sons. There is no better test of the differing concepts of the empire in the generation following that of Charlemagne than the problem of a divided succession to the Frankish kingdoms and the imperial title. Civil wars among Louis's sons and between his sons and himself clouded the last years of Louis's reign. After his death in 840 further fighting among his sons, Louis, Lothair, and Charles, led to the Treaty of Verdun of 843, when three kingdoms were cut from the old Frankish kingdom. These divisions signaled the resurgence of independent kingdoms and hence the fragmentation of the empire.

Of Louis's three eventually surviving sons, Charles the Bald (d. 877) received the western part of Louis's territories, which became the kingdom of West Francia. Louis the German (d. 876) received the eastern portion, the kingdom of East Francia. Lothair (d. 855) received the central portion, the "Middle Kingdom," extending from Rome to the North Sea, as well as the imperial title. But the division of the empire according to the politics of inheritance meant that these kingdoms, too, could be subdivided among the surviving sons of their own rulers. The most dramatic instance of this was the division of the Middle Kingdom upon the death of Lothar I in 855 into a northern kingdom, ruled by Lothar II and called after him ever since, Lotharingia, or Lorraine, and a southern part, the kingdom of Italy, ruled by Louis II. The division and ultimate disappearance of the Middle Kingdom played a powerful role in the later history of France, Germany, the Low Countries, and Switzerland.

In the years that followed the Treaty of Verdun, a strong new sense of regional loyalties displaced the idea of central royal authority. The grandsons and greatgrandsons of Charlemagne surrounded themselves with local nobles in their kingdoms. This nobility was not as mobile and was much more territorially bound than its Carolingian predecessor-nobility. The kings of West Francia, East Francia, Lorraine, and Italy could not move their royal servants across as broad an expanse of territory as could Charlemagne. Therefore, the nobility from the ninth century on found itself localized and committed to a limited territory; its interests could best be served by acquiring specific lands and powers in a single territory, preserving these for their heirs, and beginning the process of narrowing the kingroup to a patriarchal lineage focused on particular properties and succession to them, increasingly in opposition to the interests of the kings. In addition, as in Aquitaine and Bavaria, old ethnic memories provided a cultural framework for this new sense of localism. Because the new kings were increasingly dependent on their local nobility, noble families increased their power, often by combining lands received from the kings with lands they owned privately, as had the wealthy Merovingian families two centuries before. In this way they laid the base for large territorial principalities—when and if their descendants could keep them.

The title "Emperor of the Romans" usually went to the strongest of these kings or, failing strength, to the one who seemed most likely to protect central Italy. Thus, the imperial title followed Louis II to Italy when the Middle Kingdom was divided in 855 and remained at the disposal of the later ninth-century popes, who tended to award it to whichever Carolingian (and later, non-Carolingian) candidate appeared to offer the best chance of protection and order to central Italy. As early as 862 a Frankish monastic chronicle referred to Louis II only as the "emperor of Italy." Not until the papal coronation of Otto I in 962 did the imperial title once more evoke the idea of a transalpine empire.

After 888, the disintegration of the late Carolingian kingdoms proceeded swiftly. Non-Carolingians assumed crowns in West Francia and Provence. The imperial title itself was assumed by non-Carolingian warlords in Italy. In 911 the last Carolingian king of East Francia died, and the local dukes elected one of their own number, Conrad of Franconia, as king. In 987 the last Carolingian king of West Francia died, and a non-Carolingian, Hugh Capet, was elected ruler of the shrunken kingdom in his place. Although the later kingdoms of Germany and France did not yet exist, their origins lie in the disintegration of the Carolingian monarchy in the late ninth and tenth centuries.

During the ninth and tenth centuries the nobility grew stronger still, as a new wave of invasions pierced the once secure Carolingian world. During the late eighth and ninth centuries Muslim sea power had grown considerably stronger, and from bases in North Africa, Spain, and southern Gaul Muslim raiders penetrated most of the southern coasts of Europe, reaching even the passes of the Alps. By 900 Sicily had fallen to the raiders and most of the Carolingian defenses in northern Spain were in ruins.

In eastern Europe another people, the Magyars, proved even more deadly than the Muslim raiders of the Mediterranean. The Magyars were a Finno-Ugrian people from western Asia (their later name, Hungarians, derived from the name of one group of them, the Onogurs). In 896 the Byzantine Empire urged the Magyars to attack the Bulgars. But the Bulgars invited another Asiatic people, the Pechenegs, to attack the Magyars, and the latter fled west into central Europe, established themselves in the Carpathian basin, and launched lightning cavalry raids into Germany, France, and Italy. Between 898 and 920 Magyar war bands descended into Italy, Burgundy, eastern France, and especially Germany. Magyar warlords dominated their people until the end of the tenth century, when the Arpad dynasty began to establish its own superiority, converted to Christianity, and began to stabilize the kingdom of Hungary.

Invasions of Europe, seventh through eleventh centuries.

THE VIKINGS

The raids of Muslims and Magyars hastened the political disintegration of ninth- and tenth-century western Europe. The raids of the Vikings nearly completed the process. The third and ultimately the most influential group of invaders were the Vikings, bands of Scandinavian warriors who sailed south in their long wooden ships in the summer, looted and pillaged freely along the coasts and river valleys of western Europe, and sailed home in the autumn. Scandinavian traders and fighters had been known in eighth-century Europe and Asia, but in the ninth century their raids became more frequent. Their superbly built ships were not only the finest oceangoing vessels of the age, but their shallow draft allowed them to sail far up the western European rivers, attacking Rouen and Paris on the Seine and Trier on the Moselle, as well as the Frisian ports of Quentovic and Duurstede. The Viking dragon ships, carrying 50 to 100 men and propelled by a single great sail and banks of oars, devastated the European seaboard. They ravaged undefended ecclesiastical lands, defeated the small armies that local lords and kings sent against them, and sacked the little towns that lay in their path.

The weakness of local resistance to these raids gave plenty of opportunities to powerful local lords to protect weaker people from the Vikings and, in return, take over several of the functions of governance that had once been only the king's to give. In many cases, what the Vikings left, or never even touched, also fell into the hands of powerful warlords, including ecclesiastical property. This secondary effect of the Viking, Magyar, and Arab raids should not be overlooked. Carolingian Europe was defenseless, but this situation did not exclude opportunities for strong and ruthless warriors to increase their own power at the expense of both the victims of the Viking raids and their own neighbors.

The paths of Scandinavian expansion were many. Norwegians moved chiefly into Ireland and western England. Swedes moved into the eastern Baltic and across northwestern Russia to Lake Ladoga, then down the great north-south river systems of Russia and the Ukraine to Novgorod and Kiev, trading and raiding alike, until they came into contact not only with Byzantium across the Black Sea but with Arab merchants on the Volga and the Sea of Azov. The Danes attacked eastern England, Frisia, and the Rhineland and then penetrated up-river into the heart of the old kingdom of Francia itself.

By the middle of the ninth century, the patterns of raiding had changed. Groups of Scandinavians established winter quarters in Europe, and the raiding parties grew larger. They turned, in fact, into expeditionary armies seeking land to take and settle. By the 850s there were Norse settlements in Ireland, and in 865 the famous Great Army landed in England and stayed. By 878 a substantial part of northeastern England had fallen under Danish rule; it was known for centuries afterward as the Danelaw. English kings raised large sums of money by taxation to offer to the Danes as tribute. The *Danegeld,* as this money was called, played an important role in later English royal finances.

The Vikings clearly knew something about the lands they raided and captured. There is strong evidence that they had advance intelligence on defenses and military preparations and raided accordingly. By the tenth century they had begun to settle on the Continent as well as in the British Isles. In 911 the king of West Francia, Charles, the Simple, formally ceded to one Viking leader, Rolf, some land at the mouth of the Seine. Under Rolf and his successors, this territory was greatly expanded to become the eleventh-century Duchy of Normandy.

The Vikings did not confine themselves to Britain and the Continent, however. Between 860 and 865 they sailed westward across the North Atlantic, and in 874 they settled Iceland. Not only did the strong egalitarian sensibility of the Icelandic settlers survive the settlement, but their privately owned farms,

The Oseberg Dragon Head. Viking artistic skills are strikingly evident in this dragon's head on a cart found in the Oseberg ship burial. (*Copyright University Museum of National Antiquities, Oslo, Norway*)

their great seamanship, and their public assembly laid the foundations for the oldest democratic community in western Europe. In 984 Erik, an exile from Iceland, discovered the island of Greenland, and small settlements sprang up there as well. In 1000 Erik's son Leif sailed even farther west and made a landfall at a place he called *Vinland,* which scholars now agree was located in North America. The archaeological evidence, principally from L'Anse aux Meadows ("Jellyfish Creek") in northern Newfoundland, discovered in 1960, strongly indicates an eleventh-century occupation by Vikings. By the end of the tenth century, western Europe had been subjected not only to the ravages of Viking raids but also to the pressure of Viking settlements. It had received a new maritime vocabulary and been drawn closer to the northern Atlantic than ever before, and it had been expanded enormously by the wide-ranging voyages of the Vikings.

From the mid–ninth century on, royal dynasties in Denmark, Norway, and Sweden began to increase the authority and control of the king over the marauding bands of pirates and raiders. Some Viking leaders fled to England, the Continent, or Iceland rather than live under a royal rule that increasingly tended to direct and limit their raiding activities. With the expansion of royal authority and the Christianizing of the Scandinavian kings in the late tenth century, the great age of Viking expansion came to an end. By the twelfth and thirteenth centuries, the early tales of the Viking period, particularly of Iceland, had begun to be worked into heroic tales called *sagas,* the last genuine European epics. Preserving their rough history in this form, the Scandinavians joined the Magyars as the newest peoples on the edge of Christian Europe.

KINGS AND WARLORDS

The most successful defenders of western Europe in the tenth century were the kings of England and East Francia on the one hand, and on the other, the tough warlords of West Francia who protected their little territories with ruthlessness and skill. Late Carolingian-style monarchs and illiterate warriors, kings, and lords survived with the help of churchmen and the labor of peasants, and in their age the history of Europe dissolves into the histories of two successful monarchies and several hundred territorial principalities. In these territories were the beginnings of recovery. Old landholding systems, archaic social forms, and much custom had been swept away by the shock of the invasions. The land was fertile, however, and the little populations of warriors and peasants, tied to the land more closely than ever but secure once more, began to increase. Lords, once the greatest military threats to their rule had been removed, began to explore ways to assert and legitimize their titles and powers. Churchmen sought ways of ensuring peace in a society that had become more warlike than ever before.

The tenth century has long rivaled the seventh for the title of the "darkest" of the "Dark Ages," but recently historians working with very different kinds of sources have changed the conventional picture of this period, just as historians have begun recently to rehabilitate the seventh century. The economic historian Robert Lopez, basing his case on the signs of steady population growth and new economic developments, even postulated a tenth-century renaissance. In a book dealing chiefly with political culture, Geoffrey Barraclough notes:

The ninth and tenth centuries were a formative period in European history, every bit as much as the better known periods which preceded and succeeded them, and it was out of the anarchy and tribulation which men and women of that generation suffered that a new Europe took shape.

Indeed, the great debate between historians of early Europe centers largely on the problem of the emergence of a distinct and continuous European culture—in the eighth or the late tenth and early eleventh centuries.

Because political history has long offered readers an attractive organizing theme for different periods in the past, it has been tempting for historians sometimes to interpret other aspects of life in terms of political stability and instability. Thus, the experience of most of the peoples of tenth-century Europe (England and East Francia excepted), having been largely that of decentralized political institutions, it has been tempting to see social and economic aspects of tenth-century society in much the same light. However, social and economic growth do not always require political stability over large areas, and the tenth-century growth of Europe is most easily traceable in small areas. In the early tenth century there was a swamp outside the gates of Paris (which consisted solely of the island in the middle of the Seine and a small bit of territory on the right and left banks) and forests and unworked fields inside the walls of Rome and Milan. Cultivatable land did not have enough hands to work it. But by the end of the tenth century, population growth is traceable in the expansion of cultivated land. The older Carolingian landscape of densely populated settlements separated by forest and waste slowly gave way to a more regularly developed landscape devoted in greater proportion to agriculture, the founding of new villages and monasteries (themselves capable of stabilizing agricultural demand and production), and the appearance of local fairs. Such growth of population and expansion of cultivated land constituted the strong substructure for the political and longer-range trade developments of the eleventh and twelfth centuries, and those who first benefited from it were not kings and emperors, but the secular and clerical lords of the land.

In two notable instances, however, those of England and East Francia, strong central rulers began to take advantage of the ending of the invasions and the stirrings of local growth and expansion.

THE EMERGENCE OF "ENGLALAND"

The tide of invasion began to turn in Anglo-Saxon England with the victory of Alfred the Great (871–899) over a large Danish army in 879. Alfred, originally the king of Wessex only, proceeded to consolidate his authority in other English kingdoms, and his tenth-century descendants proved to be strong, able monarchs. By the reign of Edgar (959–975), the English monarchy was the most highly developed in Europe. England was now a single kingdom, which its ruling groups began to refer to as *Englaland*. The kings and the nobility cooperated, and the old units of local government, the hundreds and shires, provided a broad base of support. The English church, under the leadership of a remarkable group of prelates, notably Dunstan of Canterbury (lived 909–988) and Aethelwold of Winchester (963–984), patronized learning and the arts and placed their skills at the service of the monarchy. During the tenth century the Old English language, the most precocious vernacular language in Europe, experienced its greatest age. Epic and lyric poems, sermons and scriptural commentaries, and the first vernacular national history—the Anglo-Saxon Chronicle—were produced, as were continuing compilations of royal laws and even translations from such Latin writers as Gregory the Great and Boethius.

But the strength of England depended on the cooperation of the kings and the nobility, and continuing Scandinavian threats weakened that cooperation at the end of the tenth century. Ethelred II, the "Ill-Counseled" (978–1016), lost his nobles' loyalty when he proved incapable of resisting a renewed Danish threat. England was conquered by Cnut, king of Denmark. Cnut, however, was not a Viking. He continued the English-style monarchy and preserved English laws, language, and other institutions.

When Cnut's line died out in 1042, Edward the Confessor (1042–1066), the last surviving son of Ethelred II, became king. But Edward's reign did not stabilize the relations between king and nobles, and it attracted the attention of still other peoples to the English scene. During the reign of Cnut and his sons, Edward had been raised at the court of the Dukes of Normandy—the precocious state-builders descended from the Viking invaders of the ninth and early tenth centuries. The continuing connection with Edward the Confessor, gave the rulers of Normandy a unique interest in the fortunes of the English crown, and at Edward's death in 1066, the Norman invasion marked yet another transformation of the English state.

THE PUZZLE OF "NATIONAL" ORIGINS

It has long tempted politically minded scholars and politicians with a taste for historical scholarship to see the beginnings of more modern nation-states in the patchwork of kingdoms and territorial principalities that succeeded the Carolingian empire. But the limited scope of tenth- and eleventh-century political life warns against such anachronistic interpretations. Late-Carolingian forms of kingship survived until the late eleventh century, and late-Carolingian kingship consisted of personal and symbolic relations among great men, whether kings or territorial princes, with such elements as ethnicity and wide-spread public consciousness coming into play only much later.

Those relationships no longer reflected the empire-wide kingship and imperial aristocracy that had characterized the world of Charlemagne and Louis, but smaller and more regional circles of rulers and nobles with narrower horizons. Although many bonds linking rulers and nobles across regional frontiers continued to exist, the nature of kingship itself was reduced, as non-Carolingian rulers found that they could not exercise power in the same way as their predecessors—too many people remembered when they had not been kings at all. The kingdoms of East and West *Francia* offer contrasting examples of the long political process that eventually produced the proto-modern nation-state.

The Carolingian kingdom of East Francia was the part of Charlemagne's empire that had been most recently conquered—not completely until the first years of the ninth century—and still preserved a distinct sense of folk-identity on the part of the different peoples that had been brought under Carolingian power at different times. Bavaria and Saxony had been worked into the fabric of the Frankish kingdom slowly, but deliberately, in the late eighth and ninth centuries. Having had a substantial tradition of independence, both territories preserved a sense of Bavarian and Saxon identity, and Charlemagne recognized the distinctive legal customs of Saxon and Bavarian law.

Frankish rulers had also recognized the identity of some eastern peoples when they assigned officials known as *duces* (dukes) to govern them rather than the ordinary *comes* (count). Although many of the duchies were suppressed at the end of the late eighth century, they appeared again a century later, with men using the old ducal title now firmly identified with the people (or tribe) the duchy was originally constituted for. The ducal title was also worth fighting for among rival great families. In Franconia and Swabia, such competition was prolonged into the tenth century; in Bavaria and Saxony, the dangers of exposed borders may have hastened the process, for strong ducal families appeared in both territories in the ninth century.

With the death of the last Carolingian, Louis the Child, in 911, the dukes of the Saxons, Bavarians, Franconians, Thuringians, and Swabians elected one of their own number, Conrad I of Franconia, as king. Conrad's reign was ineffective and short, however, and in 919 Henry the Fowler, duke of Saxony (919–936), was elected by Franconians and Saxons, Swabians remaining aloof, and the Bavarians electing their own duke as king and only later recognizing Henry. Henry founded the Saxon dynasty, which lasted from Henry I to Henry II (1002–1024) and achieved considerable success, but it never molded Germany into the compact kingdom that England became. Henry I and his vigorous son and successor Otto I (936–973) both had to rule with far less autocratic power than Carolingian kings had wielded. Also, behind even the royal self-awareness of Otto I there lay a world of consensus politics, and alongside the basis of royal wealth and noble support in Saxony there survived the general independence of the other duchies and their own local nobility. Carolingian kingship could not be reconstructed in the east, and it took considerable time to discover precisely what kind of kingship could.

The Saxon kings had to defend a very large kingdom against both outside invaders and local rebellions, and they had to create a new kind of legitimacy, for they were not Carolingians. The Saxon kings faced other problems: They could not, unlike the Carolingians, reward their local followers with lands and titles throughout a large kingdom, as Charlemagne had; they were not individually wealthy enough to be able to partition the kingdom among their sons; much of the Saxon nobility that might have aided the kings in other parts of Germany could not be spared from the wars with the Slavic peoples on the eastern border of Saxony. Moreover, other dukes as well as local nobles did not forget that the Saxon kings had once been dukes themselves. Their only resources for ruling all of East Francia were the lands and incomes they owned personally as dukes. Lacking regular sources of men and money, the Saxon kings turned to the church of East Francia, and that institution became one of their most important sources of support. To maintain themselves, therefore, the Saxon dynasty had to acquire other duchies or control appointments to high church offices. Usually they tried to do both. The vast size of their kingdom, and their widely scattered possessions throughout it, meant that they spent most of their lives in the saddle. Their only means of imposing their rulership was to travel constantly throughout East Francia, being seen by their subjects, giving judgments, bestowing rewards and punishments as best they could, and trying to stem the strong sense of independence, particularism, local rivalries, and resistance to their rule.

The most successful Saxon king was Otto I (936–973). In 955 on the river Lech, Otto led an army that annihilated a large force of Magyar invaders, thus turning the tide in favor of East Francia. In later successful campaigns against pagan Slavic peoples Otto founded a chain of missionary bishoprics that played an important role in Christianizing the pagan Slavic and Scandinavian peoples. Otto I also intervened in Italy, and his immense personal prestige led to his coronation as emperor of the Romans in 962 by Pope John XII. For the remainder of his own reign and those of his son Otto II (973–983) and grandson Otto III (983–1002), the Saxon kings faced the difficulties of managing the large and difficult-to-control kingdom of Germany as well as the smaller but historically very different kingdom of Italy.

Unlike the kings of England and East Francia, the kingdom of West Francia had shrunk considerably by the late tenth century. From 987 the early Capetian kings of West Francia directly ruled only a small territory surrounding Paris. Although their titles made them the nominal lords of the powerful territorial princes whose lands surrounded theirs (and in some cases were far larger), they possessed no effective control over the warlords and noble territory-builders of their kingdom. These men were the real powers in West Francia.

The nature of their lordship reached back into the Roman and Germanic past, but it took on new significance and shape in the ninth and tenth centuries. Many powerful Roman landowners had controlled large armed followings dependent on them. In early Germanic society powerful and popular war leaders were surrounded by their *comitatus*—a group of young fighting men who had taken an oath to follow them into battle, share the spoils of victory, and share death, too, if they lost. To return from a battle in which the lord of the *comitatus* was slain shamed the warrior forever. The rise of royal power among the Franks in the eighth and early ninth centuries had prevented the independent survival of such private followings. But the emergencies of the late ninth and tenth centuries offered a new opportunity for the warlord to surround himself with military followers and acquire new independence, borrow the legitimacy of a royal title such as count, and make service to him attractive by virtue of the prestige of his noble blood.

Although the idea of dependence and service had originally been repugnant to free Germanic warriors, the wealth, glory, and prestige derived from serving a Carolingian king or other powerful lord slowly overcame such cultural reluctance. The very terms that came to designate the institutions of lordship—*dominus* (lord) and *vassus* (vassal)—reflect the humble roots of the bond between fighting men and between fighting men and their war-leaders. The English word "lord," for example, derives from the

Old English term *hlaford*, "the giver of the loaf," or provider of food. *Vassus* is a Latinization of an old Celtic word meaning "boy" or "menial servant." One psychological root of lordship and vassalage, then, is reflected in the acceptance by members of relatively high social status of a terminology that once designated functions of a very low social status. Even in Carolingian royal household service, performed by men of very high social status indeed, such terms as constable, marshal, and seneschal all derived from older Latin and Germanic words designating menial domestic service. The language of lordship described an old domestic relationship between superiors and inferiors that rose in social esteem and increased in acceptability as it became a specialized description of relationships among powerful persons.

The strongest and sometimes the only bond between lord and follower was the power of the mutual oath of loyalty. The vassal commended himself to the lord by offering acts of homage (becoming the *homo*, or man, of the lord) and later fealty (from the Latin *fides*, meaning faith or loyalty). Upon receiving homage, the lord swore to protect the vassal and be loyal to him in turn. The lord might signal his favor by conferring a conditional gift of land, money, or rights on the vassal. Such a gift was called a *beneficium* ("good deed" or "benefice") or a fief. In theory, this mutual assertion of personal loyalty could be breached by either party, if either thought that the other did not fulfill his promises.

Upon the vassal's death or breaking of faith, his benefice reverted to the lord, who might then grant it to another vassal. On the lord's death, the old vassals had to become vassals of the lord's successor. Increasingly, pressure from vassals led to the custom of the vassal's son (or, in some cases, daughter) succeeding the vassal in the benefice. The complex bonds of these personal relationships were often confusing, especially when land received as benefice was confused with land held privately, or when lands held from two different lords became the object of mixed loyalties.

Originally, the chief value of a vassal was his military ability. As vassal of a lord (whether supported within the lord's household, or perhaps as the domestic lord of a large household himself), he was able to maintain the expensive equipment and specialized training of a mounted warrior and to take the time to fight in his lord's wars. Socially, lords and vassals constituted the class of fighting men that came to dominate the composition of the European nobility in the eleventh and twelfth centuries. The turbulent character of these warlords led churchmen to try to impose the sanctions of morality on their relationships with each other, and the oath of lord and vassal came to be surrounded by liturgical rites.

The growth of the ninth- and tenth-century nobility and of territorial principalities is as much a chapter in the history of European communities as is the segment of the history of European invasions and post-Carolingian "anarchy." In imposing their own rule, the small and great lords, who controlled lands ranging from tiny single castles in Castile to the great Duchy of Saxony, made themselves responsible for the keeping of the peace, maintaining the privileges of diverse communities, and the safety of the Church. In return they received, sometimes grudgingly, loyalty and prestige. They ruled the most manageable territories that the tenth and early eleventh centuries could create. They also patronized the beginnings of the agricultural revolution and the eleventh- and twelfth-century spiritual revolutions as well. Often enough, they were brutal, suspicious, abrupt, and ferocious. Yet they were also devout after their own fashion, efficient, and ambitious for their dynasty and their territories. Often possessing no family history, they had histories made up; lacking traditional legitimacy, they invented titles for themselves, and they cultivated and patronized the monasteries and the holy men of the tenth century. Unlike the newly Christianized kings of Norway, Poland, and Hungary, they did not become saints. But they cultivated those saints they could find, and they did become pilgrims. William the Bastard succeeded to the dukedom of Normandy in 1035 because his father, Robert, had died on a pilgrimage to Jerusalem. Some lords went two or three times, and to Compostela and Rome as well as to Jerusalem. They ransacked land and labor alike for their fortresses, but they also gave away favorite hunting lodges to monks, allowed exceptional privileges to colonizing peasants, and sometimes entered the religious life themselves after a lifetime of looting and fighting. In practice they became successful warlords; in theory they retained spiritual horizons and ideas of loyalty to higher powers that held the germ of wider social bonds.

The fragmentation and very different circumstances of England, East *Francia,* and West *Francia* graphically illustrate the variety of political paths from the Carolingian world to that of the territorial monarchies of the twelfth and thirteenth centuries. As western European kings, nobles, and peoples explored those paths, it is worth considering at the same time the circumstances of the two other civilizations that had emerged out of the old Mediterranean world, those of Byzantium and Islam on the eve of the western European economic revolution and the age of the crusades.

SAILING TO BYZANTIUM

The Byzantine Empire was also troubled by invasions and internal revolts in the ninth century, as well as divided by the iconoclastic controversy. But it survived these threats and reached its greatest development between 829 and 1025, the golden age of Byzantine civilization. The reign of the emperor Theophilus (829–842) witnessed the beginnings of Byzantine recovery. However, the iconoclastic controversy and the Photian Schism later in the ninth century also revealed how deep the divisions were between Greek and Latin Christendom. The revival of Byzantium did not herald a restoration of harmonious relations between Greek east and Latin west. Indeed, the problem of Christianizing the still pagan Slavic and Balkan peoples of eastern Europe made the question of Greek and Latin spheres of religious influence become even stronger than it had been in the days of Charlemagne.

Under Theophilus's son and successor, Michael III (842–867), iconoclasm was abolished and Michael's great minister Bardas succeeded in mobilizing the resources of the empire and introducing remarkable reforms in secular education, ecclesiastical life, the military, and the peasant economy. The school at Constantinople came under the direction of Bardas himself, and under his great contemporary, Patriarch Photios (858–867, 877–885), a new energy was given to religious studies as well. Such men as Bardas, Photios, Leo the Mathematician, and the linguist and missionary Constantine (Cyril) led an intellectual renaissance easily comparable in importance and influence to the military and social reforms of the imperial administration.

The Byzantine revival of the 860s was not, however, without its darker side. From the reign of Irene to that of Basil I (867–886) ecclesiastical problems became hopelessly intermingled with politics. The end of the iconoclast controversy in 843 did not end the difficulties within the Greek Church nor did it lead to improved relations with the Latin Church. Internal struggles over the office of patriarch of Constantinople at the accession of Photios in 858 led to a Byzantine faction of the clergy appealing to Pope Nicholas I (858–867), a brilliant and ambitious man. The problem of Photios and a letter from the khan of the Bulgars, Boris, in 864, asking the pope about Rome's view of certain liturgical and theological problems, led to a clash between pope and patriarch. In the course of the dispute Photios accused the pope of heresy, on the ground that the Latin Church had erred in making the Nicene Creed state that the Holy Spirit proceeded from the Father and the Son rather than from God the Father alone—an issue that sill divides the Greek Orthodox and Roman communions. The Photian Schism, as the division between pope and patriarch is known, shows the strains in the relationship between the eastern and western branches of the Church and the increasing tendency of both pope and patriarch to make claims that were very close to universal authority.

The ecclesiastical difficulties of the 860s were rivaled by new military crises. In 860 a fleet from Kiev attacked Constantinople, but was repulsed—the first hostile contact between Byzantium and the society out of which the first Kievan principality grew. Under the powerful khan Symeon (893–927) a new Bulgar attack on the empire was launched, and between 911 and 925 the Bulgar threat loomed very large on the Byzantine horizon. The Arab domination of the eastern Mediterranean, their occupation of Sicily, their landholds in south Italy, and their control of the island of Crete also posed a threat to Byzantium. In 895 Byzantine diplomacy introduced the Magyars to the west, inviting them to attack the Bulgars from the rear. As we have seen, however, Symeon of Bulgaria induced the Pechenegs to attack the Magyars, and in their flight the Magyars drove not south toward Bulgaria but west toward Moravia. Between

896 and 909 the Magyar hordes destroyed the Great Moravian Empire and settled on the plains of Transylvania, from which they proceeded to raid Germany, Italy, and Poland. The Pechenegs moved west to take the place that the Magyars had vacated. In 904 Arab raiders sacked Thessalonica, the second city of the empire, and as the tenth century opened, Byzantium appeared to be threatened by overwhelming external enemies and severe internal religious and social dissent.

Byzantine civilization, however, proved extraordinarily resilient. The new Macedonian imperial dynasty, led by Leo VI (886–912), Constantine VII Porphyrogenitus (913–959), and Basil II (976–1025), succeeded in reducing the power of the empire's external enemies and restoring internal stability to the troubled cities and provinces.

The foundation of new themes, the expansion of missionary activity and diplomacy, the collaboration of the patriarchs of Constantinople with the emperors, and the great patrician civil servants of the ninth and tenth centuries constituted the foundations of Byzantine survival and triumph. Palace revolutions, usurpations of the throne and military blunders in the face of new enemies failed to undo the work begun in the mid–ninth century. The administrative and legal genius of Leo VI and Constantine VII was augmented by skillful generals, several of whom even usurped imperial rank temporarily, yet at the same time strengthened the defenses of the empire. Under the first of these, Romanus I Lecapenus (920–944), the threat of the Bulgarian ruler Symeon was finally turned back. In 911 and 945 trading treaties were signed with the rulers of Kiev. During the last years of Romanus's reign Byzantine forces defeated the Bulgars, the Muslim forces from Syria, and the attacks of the Kievans and participated in operations in South Italy and even in southern France against the Arab raiders. Romanus also resisted the growing powers of the landed aristocracy and legislated in favor of the farmer-soldiers, the settlers of the themes, on whom most of the Byzantine military success had long rested. Under Basil II the final period of Byzantine triumph was ushered in with the conversion to Christianity of Vladimir, prince of Kiev, in 988, and the final war to suppress the Bulgars, which took place between 986 and 1019.

The successful defense of the empire and, after the first quarter of the tenth century, the rapid and virtually unopposed expansion of its power to the Euphrates, Crete, South Italy, Hungary, and Russia reveals both the great strength and the ability of its ninth- and tenth-century rulers. A series of successful, learned, and able emperors, generals, churchmen, and scholars, an ecclesiastical administration that skillfully included missionary activity alongside diplomatic negotiations, and a talented civil service of urban aristocrats constituted the resources of imperial policy.

The basis of that strength consisted of the farmer-soldiers of the themes, the busy merchants and artisans in the cities, and the most successful mobilization of state resources since the fourth century Roman Empire in the West.

Spread of the Slavs and the Kievan Rus.

Besides its military, political, and economic survival, Byzantium continued its renaissance of scholarship and literary activity, its remarkable innovations in the liturgy and in religious art and music, and its creation of a style
of urban life that astonished ally and enemy alike. From Hagia Sophia and the
imperial palace, the influence of Constantinople extended throughout the empire and into the lands beyond it. The city became as much a legend to the
traders and warriors of Scandinavia and northern Russia as to those of eastern
Persia and North Africa.

THE GARDEN OF ISLAM AND THE HOUSE OF WAR

The revolution that overthrew the Umayyad dynasty and brought the Abbasids to the caliphate in 751 resulted in the increasingly autocratic character of the caliphate, a greater degree of parity between ethnic Arabs and non-Arab Muslims, and a period of considerable social and economic growth in the Islamic world. The eighth, ninth, and tenth centuries were a period of cultural development as well. Although during this period the single caliphate broke up into separate kingdoms, a distinctive Islamic civilization emerged to influence the lives of all who lived under it. The *Qur'an* recognized two kinds of world: Dar-al-Islam, the house, or garden, of Islam, and Dar-al-harb, the non-Islamic world, the house of war. Muslims referred to Persia as "a garden protected by our spears." The important changes within the Muslim world in the ninth, tenth, and eleventh centuries and the relations between the garden of Islam and the house of war outside it suggest that the changes in western Europe and the Byzantine Empire in the tenth century were not the only important changes in the lands around the old Mediterranean world.

The immense wealth controlled by the Abbasids at first transformed the Islamic world. The rich agricultural areas of North Africa, Spain, and the Tigris and Euphrates valleys produced food supplies in abundance, and speculation in foodstuffs was forbidden, thereby keeping food prices low. The conquests brought under Islamic control rich resources in precious metals and jewels, as well as productive copper and iron mines. Damascus steel remained prized for weapon making for centuries. The public works of the Abbasids produced irrigation projects and the draining of swamps. Domestically produced textiles, particularly linen and cotton, contributed to trade, and the acquisition of papermaking skills from captured Chinese papermakers around 751 led to the extensive use of paper throughout the Islamic world; by 900 it had reached even Spain. It took nearly three hundred years for papermaking technology to come to the attention and control of western Europeans. Paper provided material not only for government use but for commercial and literary purposes as well.

Baghdad grew more important as both an imperial capital and a center of a vast trading network. It controlled not only local imports but a growing re-export trade connecting the edges of the Islamic world with each other and with the most remote corners of Asia and Europe. Muslim ships plied the Indian Ocean regularly and even entered the China Sea, and developed lucrative trading relationships with the Khazars and Bulgars in the region of the Black Sea. Muslim coins have been found along the shores of the Baltic, and northern trade goods, particularly furs and amber, moved south to the Muslim world. Muslim traders reached sub-Saharan Africa, and with them went the religion of Islam.

The range and scale of trade and the high degree of government interest in it, the wide variety of rates of exchange and prices of precious metals, and the problems of commercial relations throughout a vast community accelerated the development of commercial institutions such as banking and the branching out of trading families to different parts of the Islamic world. It has often been noted, for example, that by the ninth century a check drawn on a bank in Baghdad could be cashed in Morocco. The double revolution of paper record-keeping and long-range commercial and financial transactions had a great impact on the upper levels of Islamic society.

Above even the traders and bankers, however, was the aristocratic group of families close to the caliphs. These families combined personal wealth and official government appointments to make themselves the most affluent and powerful ruling class in the world.

The growth of wealth and governmental activity, coupled with the immense size and resources of the markets inside and outside the Islamic world, made the civilization of Islam more cosmopolitan and diverse than it had ever been. Arabic-speaking Muslims were accepted everywhere, whether they were ethnically Arab or not. The *Qur'an* and the Islamic law, the *Shari'a,* contributed further to the homogeneity of Islamic society from India to Spain.

The economic, political, and social changes in the eighth and ninth centuries were accompanied by important intellectual changes. The Arabic language was slowly expanded and adapted to the rich intellectual and religious legacies of Persia, the eastern Roman Empire, Egypt, Palestine, and Spain. Arabic, originally the language of an ethnic conquering elite and of a religious faith, slowly became the chief cultural medium of expression of the southern Mediterranean and Near Eastern worlds. Even such non-Semitic languages as Persian and Turkish came to be written in Arabic script and to borrow many Arabic terms. Although the *Qur'an* condemned poetry, pre-Islamic Arabic poetry survived and a rich rhetorical and poetic culture grew up, not only among the ethnic Arabs but in Persia and elsewhere in the Islamic world. The study of the *Qur'an* became a starting point for the study of law, history, and theology.

One of the most profound experiences of Islamic civilization was the encounter of the Arabic language with the literary and scientific legacy of ancient Greek. Little translation had been done from Greek to Latin or from Latin to Greek in the ancient world, and the only case of a local written language adopting translation from one or the other of these languages to any large extent was that of Syriac (a version of Aramaic). From about 400 A.D. on, Syriac translators turned a considerable amount of Greek philosophical and scientific material into their own language and, as Islam expanded northward and eastward, Muslims encountered among their Syriac-speaking subjects a vast literature, originally Greek, which began to be translated into Arabic during the Abbasid dynasty from the eighth century on. Not only did the series of translations from Greek to Syriac to Arabic represent the largest effort at translation from one written language to another in human history to that date, it also forged written Arabic into a literary language that was secular as well as sacred. As a result of this process, Arabic thinkers acquired a degree of familiarity with the philosophy and scientific literature of classical Greece, particularly that of Aristotle, much earlier and far more thoroughly than their western European counterparts.

For example, between 750 and 1050 all of Aristotle and much of the work of his ancient commentators were translated into Arabic. Muslim thinkers did not simply accept the works of ancient Greek writers; they corrected them, commented on them, and made their own original and brilliant discoveries. The development of Islamic scientific and philosophical literature was one of the most striking intellectual achievements of the ninth and tenth centuries. By the time new intellectual channels of communication opened up between Arabic and Latin in the twelfth century, Islam had much to offer the Latin West, and the Latin West happily and scornfully accepted it.

The rich and varied culture of the Muslim world was not, however, exempt from the stresses of rapid expansion and dramatic social and cultural change. The increasingly autocratic character of the caliphate and the increasing luxury of the caliph's court generated hostility on the edges of the Muslim world and financial weakness at the center. In the ninth century the caliphs took to awarding anticipated revenues to favorites and making the favorites governors of provinces. In this way the power of the caliphs slowly dissipated and the actual rule of territories fell under powerful local families. The military commanders also increased their power at the expense of the caliphs. In 945 one such military dynasty assumed control of the caliphs. After that date the caliphs themselves became largely figureheads, while the real power in the Islamic world was increasingly localized.

The weakening of the caliphate was not the only important political problem the Muslims faced. The social and economic changes generated a number of revolutionary movements throughout the eighth and ninth centuries. All of these were primarily religious in character, for the *Qur'an* was a code of public and private conduct as well as of religious belief. Indeed, the *Qur'an* has been appealed to by Muslim revolutionary movements from the eighth century to the present day. Not only did slave and peasant revolts plague the Islamic world, but sectarianism also became a problem in the ninth century, especially in the rise of the radical and esoteric Ismaili movement. Such movements formed the background for the separatist states that appeared to challenge the unique authority of the caliph in the tenth century. By the end of that century, the Muslim world and civilization had developed on a vast scale, and the faith of Islam and the homogeneous Arabic culture it carried with it became the unifying forces in a world that was in the process of political and economic fragmentation.

As comparison with the Byzantine and Islamic worlds around the year 1000 makes clear, western Europe was by far the least developed of the three and had preserved the least of its ancient intellectual and artistic legacies. The following two centuries saw a dramatic reversal of these conditions.

FURTHER READING

On Louis, the Pious, see Peter Godman and Roger Collins, eds., *Charlemagne's Heir* (Oxford: The Clarendon Press, 1991). For the later history of Carolingian Europe, see Rosamund McKitterick, *The Frankish Kingdoms under the Carolingians, 751–987* (London, New York: Longman, 1983), and for particular divisions, Timothy Reuter, *Germany in the Early Middle Ages, 800–1056* (London-New York: Longman, 1991); Jean Dunbabin, *France in the Making, 843–1180* (New York: Oxford University Press, 1985); Barbara M. Kreutz, *Before the Normans: Southern Italy in the Ninth and Tenth Centuries* (Philadelphia: University of Pennsylvania Press, 1991).

Studies of individual rulers vary in availability and quality. Charles the Bald, has attracted more recent scholarly attention than others. See Margaret Gibson and Janet Nelson, eds., *Charles the Bald: Court and Kingdom* (London: British Archaeological Reports, 1981), and Janet L. Nelson, *Charles the Bald* (Harlow: Longman, 1993).

Recent early histories of modern nations have begun to cast off twentieth-century spectacles and analyze ninth- and tenth-century society in terms more consistent with ninth- and tenth-century mentalities: see Josef Fleckenstein, *Early Medieval Germany* (New York: North Holland, 1978). The most important aspect of this period, however, is the self-awareness and power of the aristocracy. For the most important collection of studies of the aristocracy, see Timothy Reuter, ed., *The Medieval Nobility* (New York: North Holland, 1979).

Geoffrey Barraclough's book, *The Crucible of Europe* (Berkeley and Los Angeles: University of California Press, 1976), has a distinctive and clearly argued point of view. Eleanor Shipley Duckett's study, *Death and Life in the Tenth Century* (Ann Arbor: University of Michigan Press, 1971), is lucid and informative.

On the Vikings, see Gwyn Jones, *A History of the Vikings* (New York: Oxford University Press, 1973); P. H. Sawyer, *Kings and Vikings: Scandinavia and Europe, A.D. 700–1100* (New York: Methuen, 1982); David M. Wilson, ed., *The Northern World: The History and Heritage of Northern Europe, A.D. 400–1000* (New York: Harry N. Abrams, Inc., 1980); Peter Foote and David M. Wilson, *The Viking Achievement: The Society and Culture of Early Medieval Scandinavia* (New York: St. Martin's Press, 1990).

On the character of Ottonian East Francia, see Karl J. Leyser, *Rule and Conflict in an Early Medieval Society: Ottonian Saxony* (Bloomington: Indiana University Press, 1979), and Boyd H. Hill, Jr., *Medieval Monarchy in Action* (New York: Barnes & Noble, 1972). Important studies are collected in Karl J. Leyser, *Medieval Germany and Its Neighbours, 900–1250* (London: Hambledon Press, 1982), and in Fredric L. Cheyette, ed., *Lordship and Community in Medieval Europe* (New York: Holt, Rinehart, 1968). On mental life and social orders, see Heinrich Fichtenau, *Living in the Tenth Century,* trans. Patrick Geary (Chicago: University of Chicago Press, 1991).

On the golden age of Byzantium, see Romilly Jenkins, *Byzantium: The Imperial Centuries, A.D. 610–1071* (New York: Vintage Books, 1969).

On Islamic civilization, see the General Bibliography under Islamic History. On the translation movement from Greek to Arabic, see F. E. Peters, *Aristotle and the Arabs* (New York: New York University Press, 1968), and in general two studies by Norman Daniel; *The Arabs and Medieval Europe* (London: Longman, 1975), and *The Cultural Barrier: Problems in the Exchange of Ideas* (Edinburg University Press, 1975).

Part IV CHRISTENDOM: AUTHORITY AND ENTERPRISE, 950–1150

10

MATERIAL CIVILIZATION

THE POPULATION GROWTH OF MEDIEVAL EUROPE

Between Scandinavia and Spain, Ireland and Kiev, late-tenth-century Europe probably numbered around 38 million people, most of them living in irregularly spaced, isolated, and densely populated rural communities. Most of these communities lacked the resources to make their agriculture more efficient, and they required extensive cultivated land to feed a very small number of people. By the mid–fourteenth century the population of Europe stood at around 75 million, before it was decimated by the wave of drought, famine, and plague from which it did not fully recover until the seventeenth century. The population of mid–fourteenth-century Europe cultivated far more land than that of tenth-century Europe, and it did so far more efficiently. The food surplus helped the population to grow, to break the old Carolingian patterns of settlement, to undertake the cultivation of new lands, and to build much larger cities. Thus, the population growth between the tenth and the fourteenth centuries transformed the way of life of late Carolingian Europe and rearranged the demographic and economic map of western Europe.

The population growth after the tenth century did not occur at the same rate all over Europe. A glance at an approximate population table for different areas of Europe between the years 500 and 1500 reveals two striking features of this population growth: first, the population grew most rapidly between 1000 and 1300; second, the repopulation after the disasters of the mid- to late-fourteenth century occurred even more rapidly. But these figures alone do not suggest the full importance of European population growth between 1000 and 1500. One of the leading demographic historians of medieval Europe, J. C. Russell, has noted that, while the population of Europe was increasing from around 27 million in the sixth century to around 38 million in the year 1000, the population of the Islamic world was falling from around 22 million to around 12 million. Such a contrast sets off Europe's population growth even more dramatically.

In preindustrial traditional societies population growth may occur because fertility rates increase, because sexual activity coincides closely with a woman's actual childbearing years, because mortality rates decrease, or because of a combination of these factors. For growth to be sustained, children who are born must survive, and the amount of food per person must either remain the same or increase. For social diversification to occur on an appreciable scale, significant numbers of people must be freed from the time-consuming task of producing their own food. All of these elements played important roles in European population growth after the tenth century.

However, the circumstances of population growth are not the same in all cultures. In Europe some distinctive features, both natural and cultural, must also be taken into account. Monogamy, the sexual union of one man with one woman, whether institutionalized in marriage laws or simply practiced voluntarily, usually acts as an element of population control, even when the probability of illegitimate births remains strong. The amount of landed wealth conventionally required to support a married couple may grow or shrink, thus lowering or raising the age of a couple at marriage. If mothers breast-feed their own children, the time between pregnancies is lengthened; if wet-nurses are used, the same time is shortened. If women's mortality rate declines and life expectancy increases, the production of children is likely to increase. Although medieval people appear to have used few methods of contraception and not to have used abortion on a significant scale, it appears that infanticide occurred regularly, usually in the cases of sickly infants and in terms of gender, more often in the case of female infants. Celibacy, too, played a role in population control. From the eleventh century on, clerical marriage as well as clerical cohabitation of any kind with women was not only more widely denounced, but it actually appears to have declined.

Although early Europeans were fertile and prolific, infant mortality remained high, and many women died in pregnancy and childbirth or succumbed to related diseases shortly after giving birth. In addition, mortality rates remained high for both sexes through adolescence and into early adulthood. Although cemetery evidence is always very localized and must be used with caution, some of it indicates that in the age group 14 to 19 there were 114 women for every 100 men, a relatively small ratio. But the proportion of women to men in regional populations changed over time and from place to place. The usual ratio that demographers find to be the norm is around 104 men to 100 women. Mortality differed between the sexes in terms of age groups. Male mortality after age 20 was greatest in the age group 40 to 59, whereas female mortality after age 20 was greatest in the age group 20 to 39—the ideal childbearing years. Statements about average life expectancy can be extremely misleading, particularly when they sometimes include the very high mortality rates of birth, infancy, and childhood. Better evidence comes from the studies of J. C. Russell and others on the life expectancy of men and women over age 20 in terms of the percentage of each sex that survived to age 60. Russell's results are set out in the following table:

Average Percentages of Males and Females Aged 20
and Older Who Survived to 60 Years of Age

PERIOD	MALE	FEMALE
1–540	15.9	17.4
541–750	6.0	5.1
751–1000	16.9	16.4
1001–1345	9.3	10.5
1346–1500	7.9	10.8

Better diet, less abandonment of female children, and less succumbing to disease probably account for much of the increased balance in favor of women after age 20 beginning around the year 1000. The greatest age might be extremely advanced; we know by name a great many individuals who lived into their eighties and nineties and a few who reached 100.

Besides celibacy and monogamy, other elements contributed to the specific profile of age and sex in medieval Europe. Europeans tended to marry later than other peoples, and the high rates of mortality in different age groups meant that frequently an older man might marry a younger woman and that an older woman, often a widow, might marry a younger man. This too influenced the pattern of female childbearing. A number of religious regulations, notably specified periods of abstention from sexual relations, probably reduced the childbearing period even further. In general, the population of Europe remained far younger in the aggregate than that of the modern world. In 1980 about 25 percent of the population was under 14 years of age. In the thirteenth century this figure was as high as 40 percent.

The high proportion of the young meant that a smaller percentage of the population was economically productive. On the other hand, it meant that the young had to be included in the work force early. The birthrate tended to stay just slightly ahead of the mortality rate, and people tended to remain in the work force late in life. If too many people in a society grew too old to work, the burden on the work force increased because it had to support both youth and age.

The second element in medieval population growth, the availability of food per capita, will be discussed in the next section of this chapter. Here it may be noted that food production did, in fact, increase considerably, that new lands were brought under cultivation, and that the generally mild European climate during the period 1000–1300 may well have improved agricultural conditions. So too did the ending of the tenth-century invasions and the return of security, perhaps the essential requirement of a peasant society.

The final element, the freeing of part of the enlarged population from the necessity of producing its own food, led to the possibility of social diversification, to the growth of the nobility and clerical orders, and to the expanding population of towns. It also permitted new settlements to grow up within the vast, largely empty lands of western and central Europe. Forests could be cut down, swamps drained, lands reclaimed even from the ocean (as occurred in the Netherlands). Scholars have estimated that by the end of the thirteenth century more land in Europe was under cultivation than at any time before or since. Specialized crops began to be grown, because people could depend on markets to provide them with the food they did not grow themselves. The population expansion between the tenth and the fourteenth centuries is the basis for the development and articulation of medieval European civilization, from the specialization of agriculture to the diversification of the nobility, clergy, and urban centers and crafts.

THE AGRICULTURAL REVOLUTION

Agricultural communities were the basis of European society and the original centers of population growth. Essential to survival, trampled over by invaders and defenders, worked by serfs and free peasants, they altered the rhythm of county and kingdom alike. Their essential product was grain, which in the forms of bread, porridge, and ale constituted the primary diet of Europeans. The more land that was cleared and the better the cleared land was worked, the more grain was grown. The increased availability of grain sustained population growth, and slowly vegetable proteins, meat, and fish supplemented the grain diet. Improved methods of planting led to the introduction of vegetable proteins and soil-renewing crops at the spring planting. Markets traded in food as well as craft and luxury goods. Dairy and stock herds were sustained by increased grain production, and some regions were able to cultivate single crops, such as grapes, because other elements in their diet could be provided from elsewhere.

There was much work to be done, but from the eleventh century on there was also a new kind of help. From this century date the earliest references to the new sources of nonhuman power and the new labor-saving devices that constitute such a distinctive feature of western European history from the seventh to the nineteenth century. By the sixth century there is evidence of the increased use of waterpower. At first used chiefly to turn mills, by the twelfth century it was employed in a remarkable variety of ways. The sixth-century volume of saints' lives by Gregory of Tours mentions one of the earliest examples of its use:

The Abbot Ursus (d. ca. 500) . . . had the idea of [diminishing] the labor [of his brethren] by establishing a mill in the bed of the river Indre. Fixing rows of stakes in the river, with heaps of great stones to make dams, he collected the water in a channel and used the current to make the wheel of the machine turn with great speed. By this means he diminished the monks' work and one brother could be delegated to this task.

The water mill had been used sparingly by the Romans. In the tenth century it began to be used more regularly for a variety of tasks.

As important as the wider use of the water mill was the revolution in the use of animal power for plowing. The development of the stirrup and the breeding of the great and expensive war-horses that appeared in Europe early in the eighth century represent another new power source. Less spectacular but ultimately more important were two further ways in which the horse was employed in society. Widespread use of the faster and more versatile horse in agriculture had been hampered under the Romans and in the early Middle Ages by the limitations on the weight a horse could pull, limitations imposed by the traditional system of harnessing. A tight collar around the horse's neck choked off the animal's air supply if too great a weight were attached to it. The great French historian Richard LeFebvre des Noëttes discovered that a new system of harnessing horses had appeared during the tenth century. The new horse collar allowed the pressure points of the load to be placed on the horse's shoulders instead of the throat, which increased the pulling power of the animal. The horseshoe, too, appeared around this time. It complemented the increased pulling power of the horse by improving both footing and traction and by protecting the hooves against the damp, heavy clay soils of northern Europe. Thus, an animal of hitherto limited military and domestic use suddenly became the second great non-human power source available to Europeans. The third source of power was wind. By the end of the twelfth century windmills had appeared. The power revolution of the tenth through the twelfth centuries was the first major development of nonhuman sources of power since the domestication of oxen and the invention of the ship, and the most important before the discovery of steam power in the eighteenth century.

These new sources of power were soon put to work. By the twelfth century water mills and windmills were used in different phases of the process of cloth manufacture, and soon after they were turning saws and driving triphammers. The horse and the ox were used in front of an equally important machine, the heavy plow. The plow of the Mediterranean and the Near East had been developed for the soils of that world—light, sandy soils that were easily broken and pulverized. The agricultural engineering of the ancient world was not concerned with plowing techniques, but with water engineering—the complicated business of keeping the dry soils moist, either through irrigation or planned flooding—and with terracing and supporting fragile hillside fields. But the Mediterranean scratch plow proved barely effective against the heavy, poorly drained clay soils north of the Alps. Although literary references suggest that the sixth century witnessed the appearance of a new kind of heavy plow, archaeo-logical research indicates that it may have been invented even earlier. This new plow, called *carruca* by the sources (as opposed to the Mediterranean *aratrum*), appears to have begun to circulate widely after the ninth century.

Several features of the new plow bear closer examination, because they helped transform social as well as mechanical relationships. The new plow con-sisted of three parts: The coulter cut the sod, the plowshare lifted and turned the earth to a considerable depth, and the mouldboard shaped the turned earth into a furrow. These three parts, in other words, cut the earth, raised important soil elements to the surface, and provided for essential drainage. In order to op-erate efficiently, the new plow required considerably greater power than the older plow; not one or two oxen or horses but six or eight were needed to pull its load. The thinness of early medieval population and the unlikelihood that a single peasant would possess eight oxen suggest that a pooling of plow teams was necessary. Second, the ideal way to plow a field was to move in a straight line as far as the pitch of the field would permit. The long narrow fields of the world of the heavy plow contrasted sharply with the square fields cultivated by the cross-plowing techniques utilized with the older scratch plow. Thus, the heavy plow in-troduced a degree of peasant cooperation, a redesigning of fields, and an increase in labor productivity that made faster headway in lands hitherto unset-tled or vacated rather than in lands crowded with peasants who had divided their fields in traditional ways. The new plow required a long field (measures of field lengths varied greatly), a headland at the end to permit the plow to make its great turn, and a layout of fields that saved time for peasants going to and from work.

The old and new systems of plowing operated on land whose use had been developed over centuries. Because animals were few and were often turned out to graze when not working, much animal manure was lost. The necessity of fertilizing the heavy soils of Europe or letting them rest fallow in order to restore their fertility directed that early plow lands generally be divided into two parts. One field was planted in the fall and the other left fallow, the process being re-versed every year. Thus, half or all the arable land lay fallow at any one time. The fallow field was restored in part by animals grazing over it, leaving their manure to restore its soil. Around the eighth century, however, possibly earlier, another system appeared. Instead of two fields, one of which lay fallow, the new system provided for three. One field was planted in the fall with grain, one was planted in the spring with spring grain and peas, beans, and vetches, and the third lay fallow. Both winter and spring plantings were harvested in the summer, at which point the cycle altered: the fallow field became the winter field, the winter field became the spring field, and the spring field turned to fallow.

The advantages of the three-field system are obvious: The amount of land that was out of use was reduced from one half to one third; the varieties of vege-table protein from the spring planting improved and varied the diet; the beans yielded by the same spring planting returned valuable nitrogen to the soil; and the rotation of crops made less likely the exhaustion of the land by exclusive grain growing. The two- and three-field systems were not, of course, separate in time. Both systems coexisted with other kinds of agricultural practices. Land might be cleared, sown for a few seasons, and then left fallow indefinitely; some land might be cultivated intensively and continuously while most of the rest was cultivated and left fallow in alternate years, or planted one year and left fallow for two or three. To impose uniformity on medieval agricultural practices, whether in the form of an "ideal" manor or a single system of cultivation, is to distort seriously the variety reflected in, and the chronology of, agricultural history.

Agricultural life consisted, of course, of far more than plowed fields and woodland, meadow, and pasture lands. Rural household economy also played a fundamental role, and this role was largely directed and undertaken by women. In great and small households, women generally controlled domestic management, the accumulation and distribution of food supplies, and the rearing of young children. But women's role in the household economy did not end there. If men plowed, sowed, and reaped the fields, women made hay, sheared sheep, milked animals, and sometimes harvested grapes and other fruits. In the house proper, women assured the absolutely essential supplies of fire and water, maintained the hearth—which moved into or close to the house in the eleventh and twelfth centuries, and often milled grain before baking it into bread. They also worked the household, or kitchen-garden, where much of the household's food was produced. Outside the house, women congregated at the local mill, at the point where community laundry was done (by themselves), and at communal ovens, when the hearth had not yet moved into the house. Agricultural societies do not live by plowing and reaping alone, and medieval writers always recognized the autonomous sphere of what they termed *opera muliebria*—the respected work of women.

MANOR AND VILLAGE

The agricultural economy of medieval Europe bound lords and peasants alike into communities of enterprise and management. The term *manor* describes the holding of a single lord and the laboring community of serfs and free peasants who worked his land. A manor might be so small as to be part of a village, or so large as to include several villages. The manor and village were also legal communities, and the customs of the manor, ruled on in the lord's manor court, constituted the only law that most rural people knew.

The village church also constituted a community. It compelled the parish community's attendance at religious feasts, baptisms, marriages, and funerals. After the Fourth Lateran Council in 1215, the parish also compelled yearly confession and communion. The patron saint of the church was also the patron of the village community. Most villages also possessed at least one rural confraternity—a religious organization whose members banded together to care for their sick, bury and pray for the dead, and celebrate its annual feast together, distributing food and clothing to their members once a year. Manor, village, and parish thus overlapped and together constituted the social framework for almost every person's life and death. At the end of the eleventh century in England, for example, 90 percent of the population lived in rural communities; four centuries later, even in highly urbanized areas, more than 60 percent of the population continued to live in such communities. The world of developing western Europe was emphatically and predominantly rural. Its history can be constructed from (generally few) written documents, archaeological remains (buildings and cemeteries), the modern earth-sciences, and place-names. Its dimensions are social, economic, legal, and religious.

The lands of the manor, of course, stretched beyond the village center, extending out into, and including, the woodland, forest, and meadow that surrounded and were essential resources for the economy of rural villages. These lands were usually linked by a path or rough track, rarely by roads. In theory, each manor consisted of enough land to support a lord's household and peasant tenant farmers; in fact, many lords had several manors, and traveled from one to another throughout the year. The manor required not only a house for the lord and houses and barns for the lord's tenants, but cultivated land, pasture, meadow, and woodland as well. The outer woodland provided kindling, rooting ground for the village pigs, berries, timber, and hunting—the last a privilege usually reserved for the lord alone. The lord commonly controlled the appointment of the village parish priest. This person was obliged to cultivate his own plot of ground, which was given him by the lord in return for his services. On most manors the lord took a percentage of the harvest, since his own land was scattered throughout the manor fields. Villagers took their own percentages, based on the number of pieces of land they held.

Although manor and village can often be discussed as if they were ideal types, it is inaccurate to consider rural society as static and uniform. The character of European agriculture and the historical development of rural society made for much diversity in village economic, legal, and spiritual institutions and hence in village life.

In spite of the rough similarity of manors and villages, the European landscape was socially diverse. Several features of eleventh- and twelfth-century life contributed to this variety. First, large areas beyond the local village woodland began to be opened up for greater agricultural production. Second, lords' new interest in exploiting the economy of their property often led to changes in peasant status and obligations. Third, the settlement of hitherto sparsely populated lands along the edges of Europe offered new opportunities for lords and peasants alike. The eleventh and twelfth centuries saw both the internal and the external colonization of western Europe.

As new regions in settled areas were opened for cultivation, and as unsettled areas attracted settlers, the shape and structure of manor and village slowly changed to accommodate the new character of agricultural enterprise. Such changes often benefited both lords and peasants. When lords with uninhabited lands supervised their colonization, as they did in northern Germany, Ireland, and northern France, the patterns of settlement in the new lands resembled those of the old and involved similar conditions of service and social status. When lands were let by remote lords and ecclesiastical establishments, individual entrepreneurs would be empowered to offer attractive terms to the colonists, acquire such concessions as milling and baking rights for themselves, and guide the new inhabitants to their new land, rather like the wagon masters in the nineteenth-century United States. Cities, too, required a steady increase of settlers from the countryside. Traditionally, cities do not replace their own populations; steady immigration is required if urban populations are to sustain their numbers or grow. Migration to the cities—indeed, the entire urbanization of early Europe—took place between 900 and 1300.

SERVITUDE AND FREEDOM

The agrarian development of western Europe also poses problems of personal status. These focus on the categories of servitude and freedom. Until recently, conventional wisdom stated that ancient slavery gave way after the seventh century to several distinctively medieval European forms of limited servitude, generally known as serfdom, which in turn gave way to increasing personal liberty and the substitution of wage labor and rents for obligatory labor and precarious land tenure. Since the pioneering work of Marc Bloch and Georges Duby, however, this picture has been drastically revised. What has replaced it is the recognition that slavery survived in much of western Europe until the eleventh century, and that it often existed side by side with various conditions of limited freedom as well as large numbers of free peasant proprietors. Scholars have also recognized that such a mix of statuses could vary immensely depending on the particular area considered. The organization of servitude and freedom on great estates ruled by kings or churchmen was far different from that in a region consisting largely of free peasant households or a manor ruled by a single lord and consisting of slaves, half-free serfs, and independent peasant proprietors.

Moreover, the history of personal status was not everywhere one-way: in Catalonia and in Eastern Europe free peasant populations were reduced to servile status between the eleventh and the fifteenth centuries, and in Catalonia only a substantial fifteenth-century revolution reversed a process that lasted in parts of eastern Europe until the nineteenth century.

Another aspect of the problem is the nature of those who held power over others. Slaves held by ecclesiastical establishments or by those possessing public authority had a far better chance of improving their unfree status than slaves owned by private persons. Conversely, it was far less degrading for a free peasant to convert himself and his family into the serf of a great monastery (usually in return for the right to work the land) than into that of a private person, unless he was forcibly coerced.

Generally, from the year 1000 on, actual slavery does seem to have disappeared, and much of the free peasant population did experience the depression of its status to that of half-freedom. But as early as the twelfth century, the movement towards full freedom slowly developed throughout most of western Europe, and with it went the creation of a free peasant society. But not all of that society remained peasant—much of it moved into towns and cities.

TOWN AND CITY

The small rural village and the slightly larger country market-town were the largest societies in which most medieval people lived. But in the eleventh and twelfth centuries the differences between villages on the one hand, and cities on the other, began to stand out more sharply as the latter began to grow larger and form different kinds of societies from those in the countryside. The most striking feature of the early medieval landscape was probably the ruins of old Roman cities. Even they housed only very small populations, but they made useful fortifications in time of invasion. In the eighth and ninth centuries these fortified towns grew more attractive to both lords and merchants, and many a *portus,* the center of transportation and market facilities, grew up at their edges. Especially along the great rivers of France and Germany, trade, communications, and fortifications all contributed to the continuation of some forms, at least, of urban life.

Outside of northern Europe, however, city life survived in more clearly marked ways. The Islamic cities of Spain and Syria thrived at the two ends of the Mediterranean. In southern Italy, particularly after the Byzantine reconquest of the ninth century, such towns as Bari, Amalfi, Salerno, and Naples remained in contact with northern Italy and Byzantium. In central Italy, Rome remained a shell of the old imperial city, although the papacy, the troops of pilgrims, and the ecclesiastical affairs of the city sustained its concentration of population. Such port towns as Genoa and Pisa recovered slowly from the Lombard and Arab domination, but by the end of the tenth and the beginning of the eleventh centuries the small fleets of both cities had begun to regain some maritime success.

One extraordinary example of urban growth took place in the West. A region of lagoons, islands, and marshes at the head of the Adriatic Sea had long sheltered a population of fishermen and small marine towns. The invasion of the Lombards late in the sixth century drove many wealthy Italians into these regions, and by the end of the eighth century the town of Venice had emerged. Under Byzantine control (except for its capture by Charlemagne's forces in 809), and always maintaining its close maritime and commercial ties with the Byzantine Empire, Venice developed a mercantile fleet. Throughout the ninth century it engaged in trade with Byzantium and the Islamic world and with the hinterland of the Po Valley. Salt and slaves constituted the earliest bases of Venetian prosperity, and by the tenth century Venice was the central trading depot in the West for Byzantine and Islamic commerce.

Other medieval cities, however, were much more a part of the economic and political life of their surrounding regions than was Venice. They drew on the rural areas close by for population, food, and labor. Towns also existed as parts of larger territorial lordships, and many lords failed to treat the cities any differently from the way they dealt with their other lands. However, the lords quickly found that cities desired greater autonomy and different treatment from other forms of society. From the eleventh century on, associations of nobles and urban patricians, sometimes helped by rebellious clergy, often wrested administrative and legal control of their cities from the counts or bishops.

The new communes, which were often bitterly and savagely resisted, regulated town law and institutions, appointed their own town officials from among an urban aristocracy, and distributed their new authority across a system of offices and powers that aimed to increase the prosperity of at least that part of the population that counted as citizens. By the twelfth century, communes had begun to acquire charters from royal and episcopal authorities that specified their newly won rights and powers. Within the cities there was an increasing regulation of both economic and political affairs, as well as the beginnings of a new kind of social mobility.

Some lords, however, saw an advantage in granting to cities those rights and privileges that the citizens wanted. London, for example, was an old Roman city that had fallen on hard times after the fifth century, being displaced as the capital of Britain by Winchester in the Anglo-Saxon period. By the end of the eleventh century, however, London had begun to grow, both as a commercial center and as the center of royal government in the kingdom. At the death of Henry I in 1135, Londoners proudly proclaimed that it was they alone who determined who would be king of England. More important (and less exaggerated), Henry I issued a charter of privileges to London's citizens during his lifetime. This charter freed the city from the jurisdiction of Middlesex County and permitted its leading citizens, as a municipal corporation, to be solely responsible for paying all fees and taxes owed by the city to the king. In the twelfth century London won the privileges of burgage tenure (the right to transfer ownership of land, usually as collateral for credit) and the farm of the town (to arrange internally the collection of all dues owed by the city), and the right to administer its own law courts.

The kings of England, however, like many other lay and clerical lords in the twelfth century, were never quite comfortable with town liberties. William, the Conqueror (1066–1087) built the Tower of London to assure that he could control the city when he needed to. But English and French kings also found it to be to their advantage to increase the liberties and privileges of townspeople, especially since grants of liberties increased their own revenues and offered allies in the king's dealings with the landed nobility. By the end of the twelfth century London had a population of 30,000, a charter, a corporate seal, a mayor, more than 130 churches, and a growing collection of neighborhoods, trades, and crafts. It was the greatest city in England.

The movement for town independence in Europe was greatest where the rule of lords was weakest—in northern Italy, southern France, the Netherlands, and the Iberian peninsula. The hardy frontier society of Castile and Aragon needed settlers and fighters more than it needed traditional forms of lordship, and the towns of the Iberian peninsula won considerable rights and privileges as a result. The urban Spanish *fueros* (municipal codes of local law) and the powers of municipal representatives in the *cortes* (representative institutions of the kingdoms of Castile and Aragon) made Spanish towns precocious examples of virtually independent municipal corporations. In southern France, where traditional territorial lordship was difficult to establish because of the large number of small, ferociously independent lordships and because of the survival of Roman cities, towns also showed a remarkable degree of independence. The city of Narbonne, for example, was governed by its own consuls as early as 1056. In Flanders, the organization of wool and cloth production developed a number of precocious cities—notably Bruges, Arras, Lille, and Ghent, which took advantage of the superb network of waterways and the agricultural and pastoral resources of the surrounding countryside in order to assert their predominance.

The most striking examples of the movement toward urban independence are to be found in the cities of northern Italy, in Lombardy and Tuscany. The northern Italian cities were generally ruled by a count, a bishop, or both. The cities' resistance to the invasions of the ninth and tenth centuries often permitted urban groups to bypass the powers of count and bishop and undertake corporately the defense of the city. In the eleventh century, the citizens of the northern cities played prominent roles in instituting ecclesiastical reforms, and this experience permitted the citizens to reduce the authority of the local bishop. In general, the lords of the northern Italian cities were not as powerful as the kings of England and France or the counts of Flanders or Champagne. During the eleventh and twelfth centuries municipal corporations took over more and more rights of governance, usually with a charter from their bishop or the emperor authorizing them to do so.

The new municipal corporations, with their roots in recent military, political, and religious change, invented new political offices through which to rule themselves. The office of consul, for example, appears in many northern Italian towns from the late eleventh century: in Pisa around 1085, in Asti in 1095, in Milan in 1097, in Arezzo in 1098, and in Genoa in 1099. The consuls ruled what came to be called the *commune.* They were elected by those citizens possessing the franchise (members of the municipal corporation) and served as rulers of the cities for a specific period. Votes on important matters were often presented to the citizens at larger assemblies, and the consuls were frequently more like city managers than city rulers. The need for the municipal corporation to delegate authority to consuls, or to representatives of the city in its dealings with other cities, the pope, or the emperor, created a precocious constitutional climate in which corporate authority, delegated power, representative government, and other aspects of a new political order became highly developed. Although none of the communes was democratic and all continued to be ruled by a corporate patrician elite, the nature of political authority in them was novel in the eleventh and twelfth centuries.

By the end of the twelfth century urban corporate lordship was far advanced in northern Italy, and its experience widened the political horizons of Europeans for centuries to come. Not yet democratic, barely republican in a classical sense, the northern Italian cities nevertheless were genuinely new and disturbing political communities. Even though they were closely governed, their political power was distributed more widely and used more versatilely than anywhere else in Europe. With the new political order came increased population growth, a commercial revolution, and even new forms of urban spirituality and lay culture. In the fourteenth century, the Italian jurist Bartolus of Sassoferrato coined a formula that seemed to a world of kings, lords, and princes the troubling embodiment of urban freedom: *civitas sibi princeps*—"the city is a prince unto itself." The new reality of independent city-republics was thus cast in the constitutional language of medieval Roman law.

THE ADVENTURE OF TRADE

In the Byzantine and Islamic worlds, trade played an important and recognized role in social, legal, and economic life. Merchants' journals, their correspondence, and descriptions of trade and travel conditions from North Africa across the Middle East as far as the Baltic Sea illuminate whole regions and classes of people about whom no western source speaks until the late tenth century. In the matter of trade, as in many other areas, eleventh-century western Europe was far less developed than Byzantium and Islam.

The strangers who came to trade in the small western European markets and fairs were sometimes pirates and thieves (as were the Vikings), more often hard-working small-scale traders in wool, foodstuffs, and craft goods. *Homines duri* ("hard men") they were called, and their lives involved far more risks than pleasures. Like all strangers in the early Middle Ages, they possessed no legal identity and at first received little protection from local authorities. They had to overcome the infinite variety of weights and measures, which differed from region to region and were an important sign of the particularism of eleventh-century Europe. Their activities were confined to specific places; they might sell their goods only for the duration of a fair; they had to deal fairly, pay their bills, and leave when their work was done. Before the eleventh century European communities had no place for people who possessed no local identity, who had no status (in the anthropologist's sense of the word), who were not part of the local community. By the end of the eleventh century, trading conditions had im-

Medieval cities and trade routes.

proved. Some lay and clerical authorities worked out the rudimentary structure of markets and fairs and began to create a protected identity for merchants. The *homines duri* became a more common sight, and the image of the merchant began to change from that of a "hard" man to that of a "sly" man. Ecclesiastics worried more about the moral consequences of the merchant and his money than about his sword and his wrath. The changing adventure of trade in the period between the tenth and the twelfth centuries reflects not only economic growth and diversity, but also the alteration of a warrior and peasant society into a society with room for merchants, administrators, and townspeople.

Lords and communities that did not accommodate merchants soon found themselves at a disadvantage with those who did. The most striking example of aristocratic patronage of trade is the series of great fairs held annually in Champagne, where the trade of southern Europe could meet that of northern Europe. The counts of Champagne, ambitious territorial princes, offered protection to visiting merchants, having devised novel legal procedures for this purpose, and regulated the practice of commerce carefully. In the twelfth and thirteenth centuries Champagne developed a cycle of six fairs a year, from the fair at Lagny in early January through fairs at Provins and Bar-sur-Aube to the "cold fair" at Troyes in December. These fairs represent the first regular large-scale commercial enterprise in European history. With the development of the Champagne fairs, luxury goods and exotic items became part of a large-scale trading network that included raw and finished wool, furs, crafted goods, grain, and wine. The variety of regions represented at the fairs helped begin the long process of standardizing weights, measures, and coinage. Mercantile law spread from developed fairs to places just beginning to establish their own markets. Like the travels of pilgrims, those of merchants opened new routes of communication and exchange throughout most of western Europe. The fairs held by the monks of the monastery of Saint Denis, near Paris, combined the pilgrimage to the shrine of the saint with the sale of the wine produced on the monastery's lands.

European agricultural conditions and the European climate both created demands that could be satisfied only by manufactured goods. Iron tools, wine, building materials, and wool for clothing were not usually produced locally; they had to be bought from their manufacturers or traders. More than the expensive consumption of luxury goods by aristocrats and high clergy, this necessary domestic trade marks a distinctive change in European life. Sometimes the two kinds of trade were combined. Venice began its great commercial career by trading salt from its own region, then by shipping grain and timber to Constantinople, and then by bringing back luxury goods from the East.

In many areas of Europe the towns signaled the new importance of trade. In Flanders, northern Italy, and southern France, urban centers became centers of economic exchange. The rich wool of England and Flanders was processed in the Flemish cities and sold at fairs. It even passed through northern Italy, whose merchants then transported it to the Near East and traded it with Muslim merchants. Both the urbanization of trade and the kinds of goods being manufactured at this time help explain another feature of European economic development—technological innovation and its rapid influence on all forms of life.

The early history of the water mill reflects this characteristic of European culture. By the eleventh century, not only had this method of grinding grain spread more widely than ever before but new applications of its physical principles were continually appearing. The principle of water-powered rotary motion was adapted to the creation of reciprocal motion from the same power source. Thus, by the twelfth century water mills were being used for the fulling of cloth and the powering of sawmills. The extent of the use of these new devices suggests a propensity for the application of technological developments to industrial use very quickly, more so than in earlier periods and in other civilizations. The organization of new monasteries and settlements in former wasteland, the increase in the demand for such products as cloth, iron, and spices, and the existence of a complex market system all contributed to the spread of technological developments and their application across a broad band of the labor spectrum. Although the scale of such development was very small by modern standards, its mere existence is significant. Agriculture on a very large scale and small local centers of industrial and commercial enterprise were the driving forces of the medieval economy.

FURTHER READING

Besides the references in the bibliography under Social History, Economic History, and Demography, and the references at the end of Chapter 7, see Norman J.G. Pounds, *An Economic History of Medieval Europe* (New York: Longman, 1974); Robert L. Reynolds, *Europe Emerges* (Madison: University of Wisconsin Press, 1961), and C.N.L. Brooke, *Europe in the Central Middle Ages, 962–1154* (New York: Longman, 1975).

There is a large literature on medieval rural life and the status of those who worked the land. J.A. Raftis, ed., *Pathways to Medieval Peasants* (Toronto: University of Toronto Press, 1981), is an excellent collection of studies dealing with many aspects of peasant life. On households, see David Herlihy, *Medieval Households* (Cambridge, MA: Harvard University Press, 1985), and on houses and settlements, see Jean Chapelot and Robert Fossier, *The Village and House in the Middle Ages* (Berkeley and Los Angeles: University of California Press, 1985). Del Sweeney, ed., *Agriculture in the Middle Ages* (Philadelphia: University of Pennsylvania Press, 1995).

On peasant life, see Leopold Genicot, *Rural Communities in the Medieval West* (Baltimore: Johns Hopkins University Press, 1990), and Robert Fossier, *Peasant Life in the Medieval West* (Oxford-New York: Basil Blackwell, 1988).

On the vexing question of personal status, see Pierre Bonnassie, *From Slavery to Feudalism in South-Western Europe* (Cambridge-New York: Cambridge University Press, 1991); Guy Bois, *The Transformation of the Year One Thousand* (Manchester: Manchester University Press, 1992); Ruth Mazo Karras, *Slavery and Society in Medieval Scandinavia* (New Haven-London: Yale University Press, 1988); Paul Freedman, *The Origins of Peasant Servitude in Medieval Catalonia* (Cambridge-New York: Cambridge University Press, 1991); William Chester Jordan, *From Servitude to Freedom: Manumission in the Senonais in the Thirteenth Century* (Philadelphia: University of Pennsylvania Press, 1986).

There is considerably lucid discussion of the communal and corporate character of both villages and cities in Susan Reynolds, *Kingdoms and Communities in Medieval Europe, 900–1300* (Oxford: Clarendon Press, 1984). On cities, see Susan Reynolds, *An Introduction to the History of English Medieval Towns* (New York: Oxford University Press, 1977), and Edith Ennen, *The Medieval Town* (New York: North Holland, 1978). Different approaches and perspectives are reflected in Harry A. Miskimin, David Herlihy, and A.L. Udovich, eds., *The Medieval City* (New Haven, CT: Yale University Press, 1977). On the continuity of European urban history, see Paul M. Hohenberg and Lynn Hollen Lees, *The Making of Urban Europe, 1000–1950* (Cambridge, MA: Harvard University Press, 1985).

11

POWER AND SOCIETY

LORDSHIP AND KINGSHIP

The most common formula that medieval people used after the tenth century to describe the structure of their society was that of the three orders. These orders first appeared in King Alfred's translation of Boethius's *Consolation of Philosophy:* "A king's raw materials and instruments of rule are a well-peopled land, and he must have men of prayer, men of war, and men of work." This idea of a tripartite society reflected both an idealized conception and a prescriptive norm.

The prayers of the clergy, in an age when most lay people were considered too sinful and inarticulate to pray for themselves, were essential for the spiritual well-being of the men of war and the men of work. In turn, the kings and lords fought to protect the men of prayer and the men of work. Finally, the men of work labored to feed the men of prayer and the men of war.

About a century after Alfred, Abbo of Fleury took up the theme again:

Concerning the first order of men, that is laymen, it must be said that some of them are farmers, others warriors. Farmers sweat at agriculture and other crafts in a rustic manner, whereby they sustain the multitude of the whole Church. The warriors, supported by the dues of military service, ought not contend with each other in the womb of their mother [the Church], but by their military skills contend against the enemies of the holy Church of God.

For Abbo, the men of war and the men of work were two subdivisions of the laity in "the Church," parallel to the other order, the clergy. There were no women in Abbo's social schematic.

In spite of its conventional popularity, however, the image of the tripartite society concealed great differences among men of war and among men (and women) of work. It is true that bearing arms was common to kings and great lords as well as to poor knights. Not only the expense and character of military expertise, but also the institution of knighthood bound the men of war together and contrasted them with the men of work. In order to understand the character of eleventh- and early twelfth-century political power, it is first essential to understand the social divisions among the men of war.

In the preceding chapters we saw a new nobility take shape in the late ninth and tenth centuries. These individuals often combined the social status of high birth with old royal titles of service (count, duke, viscount) and landed wealth that enabled them to attract and bind subordinates to them by oaths of vassalage. The creation of this new lordship transformed older social relations and made the bond between lord and vassal more important than that between king and subject. In order to rule effectively, kings had to control lords, who in turn controlled their vassals. One way for kings to do this was to make themselves the lords of the lords. But to do this was to transform the older Carolingian and Anglo-Saxon ideas of kingship. Such a step required assistance—from the clergy, who emphasized the sacred character of kingship, and from the nobles themselves, who had to recognize the king's superiority over them partly in order to assert their superiority over others. Kings first had to become effective lords in the lands they ruled personally—their royal domain—before they could hold sway over distant and independent lords who preferred to exercise their inherited or usurped authority untroubled by royal interference.

This authority of the eleventh- and twelfth-century nobles derived from the older private and public wealth and offices that they had accumulated from the wreckage of Carolingian kingship. In addition to consolidating and perpetuating land and income, they assumed control of older public legal and financial powers that had once belonged to the king and his servants. Such rights, from the collection of fines in the courts that they ruled to the collection of old and sometimes forgotten taxes, made the aristocracy of the eleventh and twelfth centuries a mixture of private lords and "public" authorities.

In order to break down the somewhat simplistic notion of "public authority in private hands" as a criterion for identifying "feudal" society, some historians have distinguished the kinds of lordship that were exercised. Three in particular are worth noting. *Domestic lordship* was a relationship between a lord and individuals who were directly attached but infinitely subordinate to him, generally serfs. A second type, *landlordship,* was based on control of land rather than individuals. Tenants of a lord's land owed him services and rents because they held land that owed these things, not because they were personally bound to him. A third type was *banal lordship*. Here, the rights of lordship that had been usurped from older public authority were wielded by individual lords for their own benefit. When differentiated in this manner, lordship is seen as the essential basis of the different kinds of power that the "men of war" had come to exercise by the eleventh and twelfth centuries.

Although warfare had been one of the phenomena that created the noble order, the changing character of warfare helped give that order shape. From the tenth century on, in a number of different places, movements of clergy and laymen had sprung up with the intention of curbing the violence of private warfare. It was not for nothing that warlords gave lands and income to the Church, undertook penitential pilgrimages, and sometimes became members of monastic communities at the end of their lives. The nobility that saved Europe from the invasions of the late ninth and tenth centuries was hardly better than the invaders at enforcing its own rights and wants, whether real or imagined.

The idea of peace had been surrounded with spiritual legitimacy in the Gospels and the writings of the Church fathers, and it echoed in the canons of ecclesiastical councils down to the tenth century. At a council at Charroux, near Poitiers, in 989, an assembly of bishops pronounced a solemn condemnation, over relics, of anyone who attacked a cleric or robbed the poor. From this date on, longer and longer lists of specific prohibitions against attacking certain classes of people were issued by ecclesiastical assemblies, frequently with local laymen joining in the pronouncements. By the mid–eleventh century, the Peace of God had become formalized; it designated protected classes of persons and regulated the character of violence. The Truce of God, which soon followed, protected certain times. At first the periods of Easter, Lent, and Advent and later the period every week from sundown Wednesday to sunrise Monday were declared to be free of violence.

These movements did not consist simply of pious pronouncements by ecclesiastics. Laymen joined in the acts of proclamation, and by the end of the eleventh century the peace associations had emerged as powerful local groups, joined by a common oath and secured by a willing armed force. In some areas these groups grew powerful enough to be considered local governments in themselves, and in strong local principalities such as Normandy the Peace of God became the Peace of the Duke, a new means of expanding the local ruler's power over independent nobles. The emperor Henry III publicly preached a peace sermon in Constance in 1043. As the end of the century approached, peace movements, peace associations, and the concept of the Peace and the Truce of God themselves acquired great emotional and institutional strength. The lords against whom many of these movements were directed often found themselves either facing strong resistance or being invited to participate in the movement themselves. In the latter instance, lords could further legitimate their military prowess by casting an air of sanctity over themselves as warriors and over their particular warlike functions.

Although the peace movements reduced one early prerogative of the nobles, they did so by justifying the use of limited violence against breakers of the peace and large-scale warfare against infidels. Along with the private and banal rights of the aristocracy there emerged a new form of legitimizing noble status—that of protector of the peace of the Church. It is in the light of such movements and the nobility's efforts to justify its social superiority that the institution of knighthood ought to be understood. Once the skills of the fighting man were dedicated to a set of values approved by the clergy, one obstacle to the elevation of his status was removed—the traditional Christian ban on violence. From the tenth century on, in art, saints' lives, chronicles, and cult, the figure of the warrior dedicated to God became very prominent. The act of receiving arms was ritualized into a religious ceremony, and weapons and other accoutrements of war were blessed and dedicated to Christian service. Thus, the men of war—whether wealthy hereditary rulers or simple knights—constituted something more than a functional "order" within a tripartite society. They created social and economic divisions among themselves but at the same time linked the highest and wealthiest group with the lowest and poorest. They transformed the character of political power within society, and they posed to kings the problem of transforming lordship over territorial principalities into territorial monarchy.

EAST *FRANCIA*, GERMANY, AND THE IMPERIAL TITLE

Under the first four Saxon kings, the kingdom of East *Francia* achieved a sense of identity that was not substantially weakened by the frequent revolts on the part of members of the royal family and the leading nobles of the kingdom. Even the frequent attention paid to the affairs of Italy and Rome by Otto II and Otto III and their pronounced interest in the imperial title did not alter the separate conceptions that their most powerful subjects held of the kingdom and the empire. The failure of later Ottonian policies in Italy, however, did cause unrest in the kingdom of East *Francia*, and Otto III's successor, Henry II (1002–1024), the last of the male line of Saxon kings, adopted as his motto the phrase "the renewal of the kingdom of the Franks" and devoted much of his reign to affairs north of the Alps.

The last Saxon rulers managed to establish generally stable territorial frontiers to the west, through negotiations with the new Capetian dynasty of the kingdom of West *Francia*, and in the east by establishing diplomatic and ecclesiastical relations with the rulers and the churches of Poland and Hungary. Within the East Frankish kingdom, Henry II added his own domains in Bavaria to the older Saxon and Franconian resources of the Saxon dynasty. He also laid the groundwork for the successful claim of his successor, Conrad II, to the throne of the kingdom of Burgundy. During his reign, Henry II relied heavily on the Church, supporting monastic reform programs, but at the same time exploiting ecclesiastical property for the purpose of service to himself. In return, churchmen regarded Henry with particular affection, and since he and his wife Kunigund had no children, some assumed that the couple had deliberately lived a life of married celibacy and therefore deserved to be venerated as saints.

But Henry II, in spite of his two titles of king and emperor, also faced difficulties that were characteristic of Saxon East *Francia.* He had to be careful about delegating power and territory, for these tended to slip away from the kings and into the private control of those who received them. Lacking a consistent system of communication with his officials, the king had to travel constantly—and over a much larger territory than that of any other ruler in Europe. In East *Francia,* where ducal power was strong and growing stronger and where the inhabitants were acutely conscious of their own local legal traditions, the frequent physical presence of the king was essential. Although Bavaria naturally saw much of the king, Saxony was the duchy in which Henry II traveled the most. The rich ceremonial trappings that accompanied the king's travels were enhanced by the support of ecclesiastical ritual, giving every possible sign of the divine grace and favor that were often invoked to distinguish the kings from powerful nobles who were otherwise little different from them.

In spite of their attempts to set themselves off from the dukes and great nobles, the Saxon kings were regularly drawn into private feuds, revolted against, and forced to compromise with mighty subjects. Lacking adequate institutions—given the size and peculiar structure of their kingdom—they were forced to work personally, usually against formidable opponents and interests. The Saxon dynasty had to conciliate, honor, and use members of different ethnic groups—Saxons, Franconians, Bavarians, Swabians, and others—and therefore no single group could claim a monopoly on royal closeness, service, or benefits. Because of this, particularly in Saxony, loyalties tended to remain local rather than be extended to the kingdom as a whole. Paradoxically, as the king and some of the high churchmen became less localized and spoke more regularly from the eleventh century on of a "Kingdom of Germany," the powerful inhabitants of the duchies remained local-minded and could only with difficulty be persuaded or coerced into thinking in kingdomwide terms.

When Henry II died in 1024, leaving no male heir and designating no successor, he raised the possibility of the elective principle becoming an instrument against the power of a singly dynasty. But both candidates for the throne were connected by blood to the Saxon dynasty, and the election of Conrad II (1024–1039), the first Salian emperor, was peaceable. In addition, Conrad won the imperial title in 1027 and successfully established his claim to the kingdom of Burgundy in 1033. Geographically, Burgundy greatly strengthened Conrad's access to Italy, and the possession of the three crowns of Germany, Italy, and Burgundy, as well as the imperial title, greatly added to the prestige of Conrad II.

No matter how great his titles and prestige, however, Conrad II also faced the divided great nobility and new groups that asserted themselves as possessing rights that the nobility could not fail to oppose. In a dispute in northern Italy in

1035, Conrad came out in full support of the lesser nobility against the greater nobility and the powerful churchmen, assuring the lesser nobility that its own family interests would be protected by making landholdings heritable and by assuring them that their relations with greater lords would be regulated by courts of their own equals. During Conrad's reign a class of men who performed knight-service to greater lords but were themselves unfree, the ministerials, claimed certain rights in spite of their unfree status, rights that derived from the dignity of the kinds of service they performed. Although the rise of the ministerials was slow and unsteady, here too a new force was located in the lesser nobility and service-knights that later shaped the internal political culture of the kingdom.

In a dispute with the people of Pavia at the beginning of his reign, Conrad II had argued that "If the king is dead the kingdom remains, just as the ship remains even if the helmsman falls overboard." In this assertion of the indivisibility and continuity of the kingdom apart from the lives of individual kings, Conrad was recognizing the character of kingdoms in eleventh-century thought. The kingdom was an entity apart from local ducies and leading families; apart, too, from the normal patterns of inheritance and division of property common in many legal systems. This awareness of the existence of the kingdom, and an equal awareness of the existence of the empire, marks the reign of Conrad II and his son and successor, Henry III (1039–1056). The first two Salian kings of the *regnum Teutonicorum,* the "Kingdom of the Germans," continued the policies of their Saxon predecessors, elevated the ideal of kingship to the highest in Europe, and acknowledged their responsibilities in ecclesiastical and imperial affairs. But the cases of the lesser nobility and the ministerials indicate that there were other forces in the kingdom as well, forces that included the great "tribal" dukes and the higher nobility, as well as reform-minded churchmen and disruptive local interests. Beyond the Salian triumph and the emergence of the term and the reality of the "Kingdom of Germany" there lay problems that the kingship was ill equipped to solve.

FROM WEST *FRANCIA* TO FRANCE

Unlike East *Francia,* which contained five "ethnic" duchies whose leaders drew their authority from private lands, the old royal title, and the ethnic solidarity of the assembled peoples they ruled, West *Francia* possessed few territories in which a comparable ethnic identity gave a regional sense of identity to local inhabitants. The territories of Brittany and the Basques possessed both an ethnic character and former royal designations as marches; Aquitaine and Burgundy possessed a strong historical and political identity. Other territories, however, were the products of the successful ambitions of holders of the royal title of counts and dukes and of the progressive divisions and redivisions to which West *Francia* had been subjected after the death of Louis the Pious in 840.

By late tenth century the term *Francia* might mean one of the three broad sections into which the old Carolingian kingdom was divided (along with

Aquitaine and Burgundy), or, more commonly, it referred to that part of the old kingdom of West *Francia* that had shrunk to the region around Paris and Orleans, ruled by the last Carolingian kings but largely under the control of powerful local nobles. Aside from the kings, the nobility of tenth-century West *Francia* was largely biologically descended from the earlier Carolingian nobility, although its concept of its place in the kingdom, its relation to its own local lands, its strategies for dealing with neighbors (whether more or less powerful than itself), and its attitude toward the king and the kingdom were all different from those of the eighth and early ninth centuries. Other divisions separated the old Carolingian West *Francia* from the tenth-century kingdom, including those of vernacular language and the different experience of outside invasions.

The last Carolingian king of West *Francia,* Louis V, ruled only a fraction of the former West *Francia,* and even within his own lands was rivaled by other families, notably that of the Robertines, the *"duces* of the Franks," who had already provided a king in West *Francia* earlier in the tenth century. But even in the diminished territory known as *Francia* the kings faced further erosions of older royal authority. Some of the great peripheral territories—Normandy, Brittany, Aquitaine, and Burgundy—had broken away under their own rulers. Large territories in the east were disputed with the kings of East *Francia.* Still other territories, under leaders who proclaimed themselves princes, dukes, marquesses, or counts—Flanders, Maine, Blois, Champagne, and Anjou—existed in virtual independence of the king, and sometimes of other large territorial rulers. They rarely visited the royal court, and the king never entered their territories. Their signatures are conspicuously absent from the witness-lists in royal documents. Territorial and banal lordship was also claimed by rulers of even smaller territories, namely castellans and simple knights. In many parts of the kingdom, bishoprics and the estates of monasteries fell into the hands of ambitious territory-building families.

When the last Carolingian king died in 987, the Robertine family, unlike Conrad I of Franconia or Henry I of Saxony, had already seen several of its members on the throne of West *Francia* since 888. The only Carolingian claimant, Charles of Lorraine, the uncle of Louis V, was not attractive to the nobles and prelates who had to decide on a king. The election of Hugh Capet in July 987 permanently changed the dynasty of West *Francia,* although that fact could not have been known at the time.

Hugh Capet (987–996), his son Robert II (996–1031), and his grandson Henry I (1031–1060) had to fight hard to preserve the shrunken royal possessions of West *Francia.* Chronicles and official documents suggest strongly that the kings were surrounded by local subjects only, with few distant lords appearing at their courts. Ties of vassalage to the king weakened among higher clergy as well during the first half of the eleventh century.

During this period, the kings of *Francia* were effective kings only where they were effective lords, and this meant strictly the royal demesne lands around

Paris. The counts or dukes of Champagne, Blois, Chartres, Anjou, Maine, Normandy, and Flanders were far more powerful than the kings of *Francia* but they were also rivals among themselves, and they never collaborated against the weaker kings. Even this nominal recognition of the distinctiveness of the royal title helped preserve the kingship of *Francia*, however. In theory at least, some of the traits of late Carolingian theocratic kingship differentiated the kings from the other great lords. During the reign of Robert II, for example, the legends of the king's power to cure certain diseases by his touch began to circulate, and the ecclesiastical literary patronage of Robert managed to preserve some of these important traditional attributes even in the most difficult days of the kings, when they were hard put to establish their lordship even in the heart of their own demesne.

Hugh Capet and Robert II spent their reigns trying without marked success to enforce their lordship over their own territories and to expand their dominion over neighboring lands. Elected to the kingship, the early Capetians strengthened their hand by associating their sons (and later their wives as well) in their rule. Thus, although the monarchy of France was not formally declared hereditary until 1223, the Capetian dynasty was strengthened by the continuity provided by the genetic good fortune of eleven monarchs having sons usually old enough to share power from the beginning of a reign and formally crowned during the lifetime of their fathers. Indeed, much of the legitimacy of the Capetians was acquired through sheer dynastic endurance.

The reign of Philip I (1060–1108) marked the advance of effective royal attempts to establish lordship securely in the region of Ile de France, to establish royal justice against arbitrary local lords, and to establish royal authority within the royal demesne. This process of creating a strong lordship within the compact territory ruled by the king was the real beginning of the French monarchy. Exploiting both ecclesiastical and temporal resources, Philip paid little attention to the wider movements for ecclesiastical reform that stirred Europe within his lifetime. Unlike William the Conqueror, he had little to gain by supporting the reformers, and like his other contemporary, Emperor Henry IV, he had much to lose. Excommunicated from 1092 to 1108, Philip went on no crusade and kept his political horizons narrow. He made himself lord in his small domain, and his descendants built on that lordship in expanding the horizons of French kingship.

The struggles between popes and emperors in the last quarter of the eleventh century and the first half of the twelfth (discussed in the next chapter) made the kingdom of France an attractive ally for the papacy. Philip's son and grandson, Louis VI, the Fat, (1108–1137) and Louis VII (1137–1180) cultivated this relationship. The close connection between France and the papacy lasted until the end of the thirteenth century. It increased greatly the strength and prestige of the royal dynasty while affording the popes sure allies in their imperial struggles. During this period the Capetian dynasty also profited from the dynastic crises among the neighboring nobility. England, Flanders, and Normandy were all affected by French royal interference in their dynastic affairs. Such accidental opportunities, the consolidation of power within the royal demesne, the connection with the papacy, and the stubborn retention of the trappings of monarchical authority—often without the power to make them effective—constitute in large part the first century and a half of Capetian lordship and the slow creation of the kingdom of France.

ANGLO-NORMAN ENGLAND

The last Anglo-Saxon king of England of the house of Wessex, Edward the Confessor (1042–1066), succeeded to the throne after the extinction of the Danish dynasty of Cnut. Edward had spent much of his life outside of England, a good deal of it at the court of the duke of Normandy, with whom he maintained generally good relations. Edward was not able to hold the loyalty of the greatest magnates of England, and some of the most powerful English families increased their independence during his reign. Harold Godwinson, a member of the greatest of these families, claimed the kingship of England for himself upon Edward's death without heirs in 1066. Across the English Channel, William, duke of Normandy, claimed to have been designated Edward's legal heir and prepared to back his claim by force.

In September 1066 William of Normandy assembled a fleet and a large army, crossed the Channel, and challenged Harold for the Crown. Harold, who had just routed a Scandinavian invasion in the north of England, hurried south, gave William battle at Hastings, and fell under the swords and spears of the Norman invaders. At Christmas William was crowned king of England in London, and a new era of English history began.

The reign of William the Conqueror (1066–1087) began as a continuation of the reign of Edward, but William soon imposed a different style of kingship. His need for resources, his obligations in Normandy, and the turbulence of his subordinates forced him to impose a stronger personal rule than that of the last Anglo-Saxon kings. In doing so, William created a stronger English monarchy. Not only had he inherited the lands formerly owned by Anglo-Saxon kings and the lands confiscated from rebellious nobles, but he had conquered the island and become lord of England in a novel way. Keeping about one fifth of England under his personal rule, William gave the rest to his nobles and churches, thus ensuring that every piece of land in England was held as a fief, directly or indirectly, from the king. The Anglo-Norman aristocracy stood in a different relation to the Norman kings of England than had the Anglo-Saxon aristocracy to the Anglo-Saxon kings. About 180 great lords held land directly from the king (making them tenants in chief), and several hundred lesser nobles held land from the king's tenants in chief. The massive transfer of nearly all the land of England from Anglo-Saxon kings with limited territory and great independent landed families to a hierarchy of nobles holding ultimately from the king himself transformed the nature of English kingship and nobility. Whether deliberately or simply by marrying his nobles to Anglo-Saxon heiresses—whose landholdings were scattered throughout the kingdom, William's disposition of the landed wealth of England gave to the new Norman aristocracy a perspective more "national" in character than that of the Norman or French aristocracy. In addition, William's decision permitted earlier English units of local government, such as the shire and hundred, to survive and become integral parts of the Anglo-Norman state. William also preserved the most unique device of Anglo-Saxon kingship, the royal writ, as his chief means of communication with his subjects, although William's writs were now written in Latin rather than Old English.

Although much of the old Anglo-Saxon culture was preserved in local administration and law, much was swept away in the twenty years following the Conquest. The genius of the Old English vernacular literary language slowly withered in the face of the conquering aristocracy's Norman French; the unique calendar of Anglo-Saxon saints and liturgy in some instances gave way to the continental reform ecclesiology of the Norman churchmen. The tough and troublesome Old English aristocracy slowly disappeared before the numerous and powerful Normans. Nor was the kingship of England the only concern of William and his successors. Normandy and the Continent occupied them routinely. Not until the thirteenth century did England by itself become the primary concern of its kings. But England was not simply an appendage of Normandy. If Old English slowly gave way before Norman French, the English language nevertheless reasserted itself and developed into Middle English, the immediate ancestor of modern English. Anglo-Saxon culture was never entirely wiped out or forgotten. Royal writs remained the distinctively English means of expressing the king's will. Even the size of William's conquest required a novel exercise of royal enterprise. In 1086 William ordered a literal inventory of the land and property in England—which became the famous *Domesday Book*, the first inventory of a kingdom in European history.

Upon William's death in 1087, his possessions were divided among his sons, in keeping with the Norman law of inheritance. William II Rufus (1087–1100) inherited England, Robert inherited Normandy, and Henry received some land and money. At William Rufus's death in 1100, Henry inherited England and made a strong bid for the control of Normandy as well, which he achieved by 1106. The reign of Henry I (1100–1135), the last of the Conqueror's children, witnessed the strengthening of royal lordship in England and the shaping of a system of governance that later came to characterize English monarchy and the role of kingship in English society. Faced with pressing financial needs for his defense of Normandy, Henry I raised a group of men from the lower nobility—or sometimes from no nobility at all resembling the ministerials of Germany,—to serve his interests in England. These royal servants, dependent solely on the king's favor and backed solely by his power, turned their attention and energies not to traditional structures of privilege and the acquisition of great landed fortunes, but to the institutions of uniquely royal governance—the courts, tax systems, wardship, and administrative privilege—in order to funnel as much money as possible to the king. As a result, they strengthened these institutions and made the royal court focus on governance and administration as well as power and prestige. By making the royal law courts recognized centers of recourse for injuries, the servants of Henry I offered wider opportunities to those who resorted to law and created a structure that was easily supervised by the king and his chief servants. With few exceptions, the strength of the English monarchy was built up by royal servants working for hard taskmasters.

The energy and skill of William the Conqueror and Henry I managed both to preserve Anglo-Saxon monarchy and to impose a Continental-style lordship on England. By the middle of the twelfth century a native English culture had begun to revive, a culture that lacked the earlier brilliance of Anglo-Saxon culture but was distinctive in its own right and drew more heavily on French and Mediterranean influences. Moreover, in the late eleventh and twelfth centuries the Continental concerns of England's kings drew the country more and more into Continental affairs and created for it the role of treasury for Continental enterprises. Not until the thirteenth century did England's role among its king's possessions change significantly.

Henry I, who had lost his one legitimate son in a shipwreck in 1120, entrusted his kingdom and duchy and their cares to his daughter Matilda, who had been successively the wife of the Roman emperor Henry V and of Geoffrey Plantagenet, count of Anjou. At Henry's death in 1135, however, his nephew Stephen of Blois (the son of William, the Conqueror's daughter Adela and Stephen, count of Blois) assumed royal authority and kept it for the rest of his life. The nobles who had chafed under Henry's strong rule took the opportunity offered by Stephen's easy going disposition and his need for support to rebel against him and encourage his rivalry with Matilda. A final compromise established Matilda's son Henry Plantagenet Fitzempress as the successor to Stephen. Upon Stephen's death, Henry II Plantagenet (1154–1189) became king of England. Far more than his grandfather Henry I, Henry II had extensive possessions on the Continent. He was count of Anjou, duke of Normandy, king of the English, lord of Ireland, and, through his marriage to Eleanor of Aquitaine, duke of Aquitaine. The history of England in the later twelfth century is inextricably bound up with the Continental empire of the Plantagenet house.

THE IBERIAN PENINSULA: CONQUEST OR RECONQUEST?

The Muslim conquest of the Iberian peninsula between 711 and 720 had destroyed the kingdom of the Visigoths and brought all but the extreme northern mountains and coast into the economic, cultural, and religious orbit of the vast southern Mediterranean and Iranian empire of Islam. *Iberia* was the name the

Greeks had given to the peninsula; the Romans and their Visigothic successors had called in *Hispania* (whence modern *España,* Spain), and its Islamic rulers termed it *al-Andalus* ("the land of the Vandals"). Although the contrast between al-Andalus and Hispania is a convenient one, neither Islamic nor Christian Spain was a unified and focused whole. Dissent within the Islamic community and rivalry among the Christian princes of the north reveal profound dissensions within each part of the peninsula. The great vision of the reconquest, the *Reconquista,* of formerly Christian Spain from its Muslim invaders inspired a number of Christian writers (and a large number of modern historians of medieval Spain) to designate Spanish history from the late eighth century on as largely or exclusively the progress and momentary setbacks of the Reconquista. Such a view, however, neglects the actual circumstances of the peninsula between the eighth and the midtwelfth centuries.

The early decades of the new Muslim state witnessed severe conflicts between Arab and Berber Muslims, and not until the reign of Abd-al-Rahman (756–788) was there a single emirate in Spain. Abd-al-Rahman established his capital at Córdoba and began the construction of the Great Mosque, one of the monuments of Islamic architecture. During the eighth century occasional Muslim attempts to secure the far north of the peninsula were checked, as were Muslim incursions into southwestern Gaul. In 721 Odo, duke of Aquitaine, repelled a large Muslim raid. In 733 Charles Martel, mayor of the palace of the Frankish kingdom, defeated a Muslim expeditionary force. In the late eighth century Charlemagne established a Frankish buffer zone, the Spanish March, north of Barcelona, which became the territorial basis for the later county of Catalonia, which itself was later absorbed into the Crown of Aragon. To the west of the Spanish March lay a number of small territories governed by petty Christian rulers: the county of Aragon, the largely Basque county of Navarre, and the larger and more important kingdom of Asturias, with its capital at Oviedo.

Under the vigorous rulership of Abd-al-Rahman III (912–961), al-Andalus became a full-fledged caliphate, rivaling Baghdad in its claims to legitimacy within the Muslim world. From the reign of Abd-al-Rahman to that of al-Mansur (977–1002), al-Andalus reached the height of prosperity and power. The cities of Córdoba, Valencia, and Seville boasted great wealth and large populations, Córdoba itself approaching the size and splendor of Constantinople and Baghdad, with a population over 300,000. The city contained many mosques, schools, public baths, libraries, bazaars, and lavish private homes. The productivity of Muslim agriculture was legendary, and al-Andalus, too, began to grow rice, melons, oranges, lemons, and other new European crops in abundance. Leather, steel, and other manufactured goods became known as the best of their kind in both the Muslim and Christian worlds. Wool, cotton, and silk fabrics came from Andalusian looms, and papermaking was introduced to Europe there. Spanish Muslims recognized Jews and Christians as *ahl al-kitab* ("People of the Book"), possessing legitimate revelation from God in their religious traditions, and therefore treated as a special class of subjects, *dhimmis* ("protected ones") and taxed at a different rate from infidels.

Although Muslims in Spain, as elsewhere, were generally tolerant of Jews and Christians, not many conversions to Islam appear to have taken place. Thus, substantial populations of Jews and Christians survived in al-Andalus and shared some of its material prosperity and rich cultural life. Some Christians adopted Muslim culture, if not Islam itself, and spoke Arabic. These individuals were called *Mozarabs.* Although they developed their own unique liturgy and Christian culture, they were regarded with suspicion by the Christians in the north of the peninsula and by Christians elsewhere. When the Muslim powers in the Iberian Peninsula were overthrown between the eleventh and the sixteenth centuries, the population of non-Christians (Jews and Muslims) in Iberia was the largest in any western European state, and it posed problems of assimilation that characterized later Spanish culture from the late fourteenth century on.

Muslim Spanish devotion and learning were well known in the Islamic world. Extensive libraries and large schools preserved in Spain and Muslim versions of Greek philosophy and scientific thought. Ibn-Rushd (Averroës to the Latins), the greatest of all commentators on the works of Aristotle, lived in al-Andalus. With devotion and learning and prosperity went art and architecture, particularly the latter. Such buildings as the Alhambra at Granada and the Great Mosque at Córdoba, with their delicate structural elements, brilliantly colored and arranged tiles and mosaics, and exquisite ivory and rare wood inlays, have survived to the present and give even modern Spain its characteristic Muslim architectural flavor. In spite of the political rivalry between al-Andalus and Baghdad, Muslim Spain continued to be nourished by contact with the rest of the Islamic world. In the early eleventh century, internal dissensions led to the downfall of the caliphate and to the emergence of a number of small states and rulers, the *reyes de taifas,* in Muslim Spain. The fragmenting of the caliphate gave opportunities to the rulers of the small Christian states to expand at the expense of the Muslims. These small, tough states, whose force depended on an alliance between fighting kings and small-proprietor freemen, enabled some kingdoms to grow and change. The old kingdom of Asturias became absorbed in the larger northwestern kingdom of León, and in the course of the twelfth century León was absorbed into the north-central county, and later kingdom, of Castile. Growing population pressures, especially in the north, brought Muslims and Christians into frequent military contact during the late ninth and tenth centuries. The northern Christian kingdoms, particularly Castile, began to press south against the frontiers of the Muslim caliphate. The rule of al-Mansur proved to be the last of the great Muslim reigns in the peninsula. In the eleventh century, the Muslims lost about a third of their territory in northern Spain, and the young Christian kingdoms of Castile, Aragon, León, and Navarre emerged as substantial Christian powers, calling their expansion a *Reconquista,* a "reconquest" of Hispania from the Muslims. Under the patronage of the apostle Saint James (*Santiago Matamoros*), whose cult was centered in the northwestern town of Compostela, they appealed for aid from Christians across the Pyrenees and mobilized their own forces for expansion to the south.

The Reconquista provided a focus for the expansion of these northern Iberian kingdoms, and its publicizing north of the Pyrenees appealed to fighting men and pilgrims who were beginning to see, in war against the infidels, a means of legitimating their own warlike inclinations. During the eleventh century legends of "Saint James the Killer of Moors," of Pelayo, the legendary successor of Roderigo, the last Visigothic king, and of Fernán González, a great warrior of Castile, helped develop the Iberian consciousness of the sacred character of the Reconquista.

Navarre, under Sancho I (1000–1035), achieved considerable success and preeminence in the north. The division of Sancho's lands at his death in 1035 made kings of his three sons, and the kingdoms they created—Navarre, Aragon, and Castile—became strong Christian powers. The earlier kingdoms of Asturias and Galicia united to form León, and the old Spanish March became the county of Barcelona. The division and recombination of these small kingdoms continued into the later eleventh century. Under Ferdinand I of Castile (1035–1065), León and Castile were united into a single kingdom.

The reign of Alfonso VI of Castile (1065–1109) proved Castile's endurance and ability. The Muslim south paid tribute and yielded booty to Alfonso's warriors. Alfonso also opened communications across the Pyrenees; French aid, warriors, monastic foundations, and clergy assisted his efforts in the south. In 1085 Alfonso captured the city of Toledo, the old Visigothic capital and ecclesiastical center of Spain, a triumph that increased his reputation at home and in the north.

Alfonso's greatest servant, Rodrigo Diaz de Vivar, who was called *El Cid* (from the Arabic word *siddi*, meaning "chief"), led his master's armies heroically, but other aspects of El Cid's career suggest the kind of life northern Spain offered in this period of turbulence. El Cid fell out with Alfonso in 1081, entered the service of some Muslim princes, was briefly reconciled with the king, and then undertook to conquer Valencia for himself. The independence and occasional indifference of El Cid to Alfonso's political difficulties, his willingness to serve under Muslim leaders, and his political adventurousness in Valencia suggest that the ideal of a Christian warrior fighting God's war was not his unvarying self-image. The epic poem in the Castilian vernacular produced in the late twelfth century, however, *El Cantar de Mio Cid*, tried to mold the frontier adventurer and local warlord into a model Christian warrior.

The enemies against whom Alfonso VI and El Cid fought were no longer the great caliphs of al-Andalus. With the collapse of the caliphate in the first half of the eleventh century, about the same time as the Abbasid caliphate collapsed in Baghdad, petty rulers of small regions and individual cities, the *reyes taifas* ("kings of parts") now constituted the political and military strength of al-Andalus. Strong at home, they were nevertheless vulnerable to the forces of Christian expansion, and with the fall of Toledo several of these kings invited the puritanical warrior sect of the Almoravides into Spain from North Africa. The victory of the Almoravides over Alfonso VI at Zalaca in 1086 temporarily halted the Reconquista and briefly unified al-Andalus under Almoravid rulers, but they did not win back much territory from the Christians.

Even this temporary unification of al-Andalus could not prevent the kings of Castile, Navarre, and Aragon from consolidating their earlier gains and even expanding more slowly. In 1139 a noble adventurer named Afonso Henriques established Portugal as an independent lordship and began to build it into a monarchy with himself as king. With the slowing of the Reconquista after 1086, the rulers of the Christian kingdoms consolidated their newly expanded realms and laid the foundations for the next phase of expansion.

During the late eleventh and early twelfth centuries, the rudimentary institutions of governance and the rivalry among different Christian rulers make it difficult to see the ideal of Reconquista as anything more than an occasional rallying cry in particular instances. With the increasing interest in the Iberian peninsula on the part of other continental Europeans and the papacy, however, particularly under the influence of the Franco-Roman idea of crusade as it developed slowly during the same period, by the late twelfth century it is possible to see the idea of reconquest shaping royal policies over time and influencing the self-consciousness and self-definition of Castilians and Aragonese, as well as Portuguese. Before the late twelfth century, however, during the reigns of Alfonso VI, his talented and able daughter Urraca (1109–1126), and Alfonso VII (1126–1157), population pressures, the economy, and individual ambition account for both internal relations among the Christian rulers of Spain and their relations with their Muslim counterparts.

FROM LORDSHIP TO KINGSHIP IN SOUTH ITALY AND SICILY

One of the most spectacular instances of the shaping of royal lordship was the creation of the Norman kingdom of Sicily and South Italy, not out of older Visigothic, Anglo-Saxon, or Frankish traditions, but out of fragments of Byzantine and Lombard institutions through the dynamism and ruthlessness of an able Norman dynasty. "The Other Norman Conquest," as historians sometimes call it, created a state where none existed before, a state whose wealth, character, and power made it the most powerful kingdom in Europe by the end of the twelfth century and a major point of contact among Christian, Jewish, and Muslim cultures.

In the tenth century Byzantium had regained control over much of South Italy, including its restive Lombard principalities and its largely Greek population. The eleventh-century crisis in the Byzantine Empire (see Chapter 12), however, weakened Byzantine control and sparked a Lombard revolt. The Lombard rebels hired a number of Norman pilgrims as mercenary warriors, and between 1017 and 1029 Norman military power led the Lombard resistance to Byzantine authority. In 1029 Rainulf, a Norman leader, won for himself the countship of Aversa, and in the following two decades other Norman leaders also carved out territories for themselves.

In 1053 Pope Leo IX sent a military force into South Italy, intending to displace the Normans and reassert papal claims to the territory south of Rome. The papal force was soundly beaten by the Normans at Benevento in that year, however, and the pope himself was taken prisoner. In the negotiations that followed, Leo recognized certain Norman rights in South Italy, and in 1059 Robert Guiscard, the Norman count of Apulia, formally became the vassal of Pope Nicholas II. In return the pope recognized Robert's title as duke of Apulia and Calabria. From 1059 until his death in 1085, Robert Guiscard continually enlarged his territory and consolidated his control in South Italy. Robert's younger brother, Roger, "the Great Count," wrested Sicily from its Muslim overlords between 1061 and 1091. In 1071 Bari, the last Byzantine stronghold in South Italy, fell into Robert's hands. In 1081 Robert Guiscard launched an attack against the western coast of Greece itself, but the campaign had to be interrupted when Guiscard was called back to Italy to rescue Pope Gregory VII in his struggle with the Emperor Henry IV (see Chapter 12). Robert Guiscard died shortly after his rescue of the pope, and his lands went to his son, Roger Borsa.

At his own death in 1101, Roger the Great Count left his widow Adelaide and a young son, Roger II (1095–1154). Adelaide, one of the most remarkable noblewomen of the late eleventh century, maintained a successful regency for her young son until he legally came of age and was knighted in Palermo cathedral in 1112. During the first years of the rule of Roger II Sicily was welded into a territorial principality. In 1129 Roger II succeeded Roger Borsa, thus uniting all of Sicily and South Italy under a single ruler. In 1130 the antipope Anacletus II pronounced Roger king of Sicily, Apulia, and Calabria, and on Christmas day 1130 Roger was crowned in Palermo. More effectively and dramatically than any other twelfth-century ruler, Roger II had transformed lordship into kingship.

FURTHER READING

On the concept of the three orders of society, see Georges Duby, *The Three Orders: Feudal Society Imagined* (Chicago: University of Chicago Press, 1980). The term *feudalism* is now properly on the wane among historians of medieval Europe. See the essays in Fredric L. Cheyette, ed., *Lordship and Community in Medieval Europe* (New York: Holt, Rinehart, 1968), and especially Elizabeth A. R. Brown, "The Tyranny of a Construct: Feudalism and Historians of Medieval Europe," *American Historical Review 79* (1974), pp. 1063–1088. The best collection of studies on the transformation and continuity of the aristocracy is that of Timothy Reuter, ed., *The Medieval Nobility* (New York: North Holland, 1979).

On the Peace and Truce of God, see Thomas Head and Richard Landes, eds., *The Peace of God* (Ithaca: Cornell University Press, 1992), and the essays in H. E. J. Cowdrey, *Popes, Monks and Crusaders* (London: Hambledon, 1984).

On East *Francia,* see, beside the works in the Bibliography under Political History: Regional, Timothy Reuter, *Germany in the Early Middle Ages, 800–1056* (London-New York: Longman, 1991).

On West *Francia,* see Jean Dunbabin, *France in the Making, 843–1180* (New York: Oxford University Press, 1985), and Elizabeth M. Hallam, *Capetian France, 987–1328* (New York: Longman, 1980).

On Anglo-Norman England, see the works of David C. Douglas, *William the Conqueror* (Berkeley and Los Angeles: University of California Press, 1967); *The Norman Achievement and the Norman Fate* (Berkeley and Los Angeles: University of California Press, 1969; 1977), and John Le Patourel, *The Norman Empire* (Oxford: Clarendon Press, 1976). On the kings, see Frank Barlow, *William Rufus* (Berkeley and Los Angeles: University of California Press, 1983), and Judith A. Green, *The Government of England under Henry I* (Cambridge: Cambridge University Press, 1986).

On Iberia, besides the works by Collins and O'Callaghan, see Bernard F. Reilly, *The Kingdom of León-Castilla under Queen Urraca* and *The Kingdom of León-Castilla under Alfonso VI* (Princeton, NJ: Princeton University Press, 1982, 1988), and the excellent cultural histories of R. A. Fletcher, *St. James's Catapult: The Life and Times of Diego Gelmirez of Compostela* (Oxford: Clarendon Press, 1984). On stress between Muslims and Christians, see Kenneth Baxter Wolf, *Christian Martyrs in Muslim Spain* (Cambridge: Cambridge University Press, 1988).

On southern Italy and Sicily, see Barbara Kreutz, *Before the Normans: Southern Italy in the Ninth and Tenth Centuries* (Philadelphia: University of Pennsylvania Press, 1991), and Donald Matthew, *The Norman Kingdom of Sicily* (Cambridge: Cambridge University Press, 1992), as well as the older but readable work of John Julius Norwich, *The Normans in the South* and *The Kingdom in the Sun* (London: Longman, 1967, 1970). An important scholarly study is that of H. E. J. Cowdrey, *The Age of Abbot Desiderius* (Oxford: Clarendon Press, 1983), as is that of G. A. Loud, *Church and Society in the Norman Principality of Capua, 1058–1097)* (Oxford: Clarendon Press, 1985).

12

CHRISTENDOM EAST AND WEST

THE IDEA OF REFORM

From the fifth to the eleventh century in western Europe lords and churchmen recognized two main goals: the conversion of pagans to Christianity and the establishment of proper order within the Christian community. The expansion of Frankish power and Christianity under Charlemagne, and Charlemagne's insistence on clerical reform and education, illustrate both goals at a moment in early European history when they first seemed closest to achievement. In spite of the disasters of the late ninth and tenth centuries, the process of conversion went on, including that of the Viking and Hungarian invaders and the peoples of Slavic and Baltic Europe. By the end of the eleventh century, most western European pagans had become converted to Christianity and one of the religious aims of the early Middle Ages had been accomplished. One sign of this change is the decreasing frequency with which ecclesiastical writers described forbidden pagan customs and superstitions in their works on penance in the twelfth century; they concentrated instead on the proper attitudes of Christians within Christian society.

The period between the tenth and the late twelfth centuries, designated Romanesque by historians of art, witnessed a new stage of European religious consciousness, one that reflects a heightened awareness of the proper ordering of Christian society. At the end of the long duel with paganism, Romanesque religion faced the problem of order inside the Christian world. Among the main aspects of this problem were the role of the monastic life, the perception of abuses within the Church, the relation between lay and clerical authority, and lay piety.

One problem was that of terminology. The breaking of Carolingian unity led to the increasing usage of the term "Church" to apply more and more exclusively to the clergy. The term "Christendom," *Christianitas,* was used more frequently to designate both laity and clergy as a divinely validated community. The role of the laity was to provide personnel for the clerical order, alms to support it, and swords to defend it. This role had led to what has been called the "lay domination of the church"; that is, in terms of clerical personnel, for example, not to send excess offspring into the church, but to provide clerical specialists who would see to the family's spiritual benefits while living the religious life. Families identified themselves with particular ecclesiastical centers and often controlled the policies of those centers—monasteries, houses of regular or secular canons, or cathedral chapters. Finally, the laity often dominated high ecclesiastical appointments and participated in rivalries between ecclesiastical centers. From the late tenth century, a new clerical movement gathered force in opposing this role of the laity in religious affairs.

The process was not sudden, nor did all ecclesiastical institutions react the same way. Some of the first signs of the new temper are to be found in the strongest centers of early medieval Christianity, the monasteries. Perhaps the most influential and best known center of monastic reform was the monastery of Cluny in Burgundy. Established in 910 by Duke William the Good of Aquitaine, Cluny was exceptional from its very origins, for the duke gave the monastery not to an individual abbot, bishop, or lay protector but directly to Saint Peter. The monastery was therefore independent of all local ecclesiastical and lay authority and directly subordinate only to the pope. The power of the spiritual attraction of Rome was considerable even in the dark days of the tenth century, and some of Cluny's early prestige may have derived from its particular connection with Rome.

A series of extraordinarily distinguished abbots—Berno (910–927), Odo (927–942), Aymard (942–954), Mayeul (954–993), Odilo (993–1048), and Hugh (1048–1109)—supervised the development of Cluny into a reformed and remarkably influential monastery. The closely regulated life of the monks at Cluny made them models of monastic devotion. The monastery greatly emphasized liturgical reforms, and its liturgy became a model for monastic liturgies throughout western Europe. The rich Cluniac liturgy, however, removed monks from their earlier labors in the fields and barns and required a close dependence on the nobility in order to acquire land and workers for its support. Local and distant nobles came under the influence of this dynamic institution, and asked for instructions about reforming their own monasteries along Cluniac lines. Many other monasteries were slowly put under the direct control of Cluny, and the Cluniac influence began to reach out into corners of Europe where there had been little previous interest in ecclesiastical reform.

The abbot of Cluny was the only abbot in the order; all other monasteries controlled by Cluny were governed by subordinate officials called *priors*. The fact that the abbot could select his own successor and that he was the single abbot among the 1500 or so monasteries that were attached to Cluny enabled the houses of the Cluniac system to work together for reform and to coordinate their activities closely. The abbots traveled extensively, and they were as familiar in Rome and northern Italy as they were in France. The kidnapping of Mayeul by Arab raiders in the Alps appears to have been the rallying point for the final southern French assault that destroyed the powerful Arab stronghold of La Garde Freinet toward the end of the tenth century.

There is no greater monument to the synthesis of aristocratic reform monasticism represented by Cluny than the great monastic church, now destroyed, called Cluny III. Begun in 1088 and financed largely by gifts of King Alfonso VI of León-Castile, the building was completed after many delays in 1130. Until the rebuilding of St. Peter's Church in Rome in the sixteenth century, Cluny III was the largest church building in Latin Christendom. It was a church in which not only monks but clergy and laity alike could see God worshiped with devotion, elegance, and purity that were achieved in few other places in western Europe. In a culture that valued the purity of ritual highly and was all too aware of the distractions of secular life on other "men of prayer," Cluny and its great church offered the fulfillment of the Carolingian ideal of enlightened lay patronage and protection that enabled disciplined men of religion to perfect the art of liturgical prayer, to struggle against the forces of darkness in their increasing liturgies, and to accept and shelter the bodies of their patrons and pray for their souls after death.

The abbots of Cluny were not only the only monastic reformers of the late tenth and eleventh centuries, nor was their form of monasticism the only model followed by their contemporaries. A second kind of monastic reform took a more ascetic direction. At Camaldoli in Italy and elsewhere a rigorously ascetic form of monasticism was developed and, in conjunction with this, new forms of the religious life of hermits and anchorites. These practices often sacrificed the earlier ideals of study and manual labor (and, in later forms, even the liturgical richness of Cluny) in favor of a life of silence and contemplation. In order to fulfill the material needs of some of these rigorous communities, groups of lay brothers were admitted. These figures, the *conversi,* became a major part of monastic life in the late eleventh and twelfth centuries.

Besides the life of the "new desert" yet other centers of monastic reform worked more closely with the reforming elements in secular society. The Norman monastery of Bec, for example, was extensively patronized by the eleventh-century dukes of Normandy and became the source of much ecclesiastical reform after William I had conquered England. William's first two archbishops of Canterbury, Lanfranc and Anselm, were both former monks of Bec. At Gorze, near Metz, an important reform monastery remained closely tied to local episcopal and noble society, exerting its influence especially in Lorraine and southwestern Germany. Emphasizing the necessity of cooperation with pious earthly rulers, Gorze gave great impetus to the reforms of the Church in Germany and Italy on the part of the later Salian emperors and their servants.

Reform monasteries at Cluny, Gorze, Camaldoli, and other centers offered models of the devotional life that influenced other clergy and much of the laity, and their influence sharpened the perception of the need to carry reform even further than the monasteries themselves. Abuses in the clerical life outside monasteries were now perceived more sharply. Among these, two in particular stand out: clerical sexual purity and clerical dependence on lay power.

Although the Church had prohibited the clerical marriage of altar priests as early as the fourth century, the circumstances of clerical life between the fifth and the eleventh centuries made the prohibition relatively a dead letter outside of monasteries, although few monks were priests. With the demand for a purer and more authentic clergy that emerged in the eleventh century, however, and with the increased influence of monastic standards on reformers' thought, there rose the question of clerical marriage and concubinage. The charge of "Nicolaitism," the technical term for clergymen who were married or kept mistresses, was hurled with increasing vigor at clergy throughout the eleventh and twelfth centuries. Popes legislated against it, councils forbade it, and individual bishops were urged to combat it. In many cases clerical marriage became a weapon with which lay people attacked nonreformed clergy, and the problem generated a large literature in the twelfth century. This movement may also be understood as a result of heightened concern with sexuality in general and with the role of women in Christian society in particular. Behind the growing distaste for clerical marriage was the ideal of a pure clergy, separated sexually as well as sacramentally from laity.

Of equal importance was the second great abuse of the century, the problem of the dependence of the clergy on the laity. Several elements had contributed to the lay domination of the clergy. One of them, obviously, was the clergy's need for defense and protection against rapacious neighboring lords or invaders. A second was the influence of Old Testament thought on early medieval political theory and the resemblance of early medieval kings—at least in their own and the clergy's minds—to David and Solomon, the great kings of Israel. Other elements were technical and legal. Germanic law had permitted privately owned churches, called *Eigenkirchen*, (literally, "churches of one's own"), whose owners appointed clergy, often in return for a gratuity or fee. In the larger world, kings and emperors often appointed bishops and abbots, either as their vassals or because of customary right. The altar, according to this view, was the province of grace and of God, but the church building, property, and income were the province of the patron. As we have seen in the case of Cluny and elsewhere, the power of a reform-minded lay patron could be the easiest path toward reform; on the other hand, an indifferent or wicked lay patron could cripple the devotional life of many people. In the eleventh century, the general practice of laity dominating clergy came to be called *simony,* after the figure of Simon Magus, the charlatan who allegedly attempted to buy religious power from Saint Peter.

By the second half of the eleventh century two distinct attitudes toward reform had become predominant. The first, traditionally Carolingian, left it to the emperor and his clergy to rectify abuses, even, if necessary, to the point of removing from office canonically consecrated prelates, from abbots to popes. This great responsibility was considered to be justified by the emperor's status. The second view, which necessarily possessed political as well as spiritual dimensions, attacked the whole concept of lay authority of any kind over clergy, whether that of a local lord or that of the emperor himself. This view was maintained by radical reformers in the name of *libertas,* the freedom from interference of any sort that was guaranteed by God to the Church so that it might carry out its sacred mission. In the first half of the eleventh century the two views did not necessarily find themselves in conflict, for the agenda of reform was vast, and imperial and other lay help was badly needed. From the middle of the century, however, their ways divided, and the one view opposed the other with increasing sharpness. The polarizing of views on Church reform, and the great conflict between spiritual and temporal authority that they generated toward the end of the eleventh century, constituted a major departure from the spiritual ideals of Carolingian Europe and opened new horizons for both government of Christian society and the character of religious sensibility.

POPES, EMPERORS, AND CHRISTIAN SOCIETY

The first centers of religious reform had been the monasteries of France, Germany, and northern Italy. The high standards of some imperial German churchmen and emperors and the popular religious sentiment in Flemish and Italian towns contributed other elements to the reform movement. However, the papacy had been slow to change. From the reign of Otto III, however, emperors had attempted to install reform-minded churchmen in the throne of Peter. In 1046, when a particularly offensive scandal produced three claimants for the papal title, the emperor Henry III (1039–1056) convened the Synod of Sutri, at which he and a group of sympathetic higher clergy declared all three claimants deposed from the papacy and installed the first of a series of German reformers as pope. Although the first two reform popes after Sutri died soon after their election, in 1049 Henry III's cousin, Bruno of Toul, was elected and took the papal name of Leo IX (1049–1054). Leo brought with him to Rome representatives of the reform movement in Lorraine and Burgundy, traveled back across the Alps to hold reform councils and synods in France, and by his own reputation for holiness greatly increased the prestige and presence of the papacy in the reform movement of the late eleventh century.

Among the reformers who rose to prominence under Leo IX and his successors was Humbert, Cardinal of Silva Candida, the most articulate and radical proponent of reform. Humbert's treatise Against Simoniacs argued not only that bishops who had purchased their ecclesiastical offices be deposed, but that ordinations to the priesthood that they had performed not be recognized as valid. Other reformers, such as Peter Damian (1007–1072), an outstanding representative of ascetic monasticism and a supporter of a strong lay ruling presence in the world, argued a more charitable position. On a mission for Leo IX to Constantinople in 1054, Cardinal Humbert excommunicated the patriarch of Constantinople, Michael Kerularios, and abruptly launched one of the many schisms that further separated Latin and Greek Christendom.

The sense of mission on the part of the reform papacy is illustrated by Alexander II (1061–1073), who sent a papal banner to William of Normandy as he was departing to conquer England, urging him to reform the English church and thereby link Normandy and England with Rome. The church of Aragon adopted the Roman liturgy in place of the older local Mozarabic liturgy, thereby forging another kind of link with Rome. Nor did the reform papacy neglect the workings of the church in Rome. During the vigorous pontificate of Nicholas II (1059–1061) a new rule for electing popes was adopted. Henceforth, only the cardinal clergy and the people of Rome itself were to have the right of designating and electing the pope, although the "due honor and reverence" owed to the emperor were to be respected. The decree of 1059 also forbade for the first time a cleric's acceptance of a church from the hands of a lay person.

The most active and controversial of the reform popes was Gregory VII (1073–1085). Unlike some of his predecessors, Gregory saw the causes of abuses in the Church not in specific faults that might be corrected one by one, but in the defective ordering of the Christian world. Gregory's pontificate launched a great debate about the nature of Christendom, *Christianitas*, between the two great powers that claimed responsibility for the ordering of spiritual and temporal life, the pope and the emperor. Against the old Carolingian idea of the emperor's ultimate responsibility for Christian society, Gregory set an alternative vision of two contending societies on earth— Christian society and the city of Satan—thus echoing one aspect of Augustine's fifth-century work *The City of God*. According to Gregory and his supporters, only the pope at the head of Christian society, strengthened by the authority and merits of Peter, could fulfill God's plan for the world. Any challenge to such a plan was a threat from the forces of Satan and had to be countered by whatever force was required.

Thus, a large part of Gregory's career was devoted to outlining as systematically as he could the nature and history of papal authority. To this end he had some of his subordinates search out old collections of laws and treatises to substantiate his case. The work of earlier eleventh-century reformers in building a doctrinal basis for the attack on clerical marriage and simony had already produced a significant body of research on doctrinal and papal history, and some of it had begun to be organized in the form of legal texts. *The Collection in 74 Titles,* compiled in Rome, first established papal authority over the entire Church in the form of a legal code. Earlier searches, various collections, and the renewed efforts of Gregory VII turned up a vast amount of literary material, and much of the late eleventh and twelfth centuries was spent in shaping it into a constitutional theory of Latin Christendom, largely through the increasingly important discipline of canon law. Some of this material came from the great ninth-century collections of forged material, particularly that of Pseudo-Isidore, which, as we have seen, contained the text of the Donation of Constantine. The *Dictatus Papae,* a list of papal privileges and powers intended to serve as an index of the diverse aspects of papal authority, was produced by Gregory VII and included in the official register of his correspondence, the first full surviving register of papal correspondence since that of Pope Gregory I, who died in 604. In the process of organizing the theory of papal authority, describing it in collections of canon law, and building an administrative system through which it might be distributed and applied regularly and effectively everywhere, Gregory VII contributed substantially to the foundations of papal power in the twelfth and thirteenth centuries. Not only did he increase the workload of the staff of the papacy in Rome, but he dispatched papal legates, representatives for special diplomatic and legal missions throughout Europe; in some places he established permanent legates. The clergy of the city of Rome, hitherto important chiefly for its role in assisting the popes in their many liturgical functions throughout the city, grew into an administrative body. The cardinals, priests, deacons, and bishops of old and originally privately-owned Roman churches slowly grew into an administrative body that directly handled papal affairs. In both the realm of ideas and the translation of those ideas into institutions and programs of action, Gregory VII transformed the papacy and made himself the spokesman for a new vision of the ordering of Christian society.

Although Gregory VII began his pontificate on good terms with the emperor Henry III's successor, Henry IV (1056–1106), the pope's vision of the respective places of pope and emperor soon led to direct conflict. Gregory, for example, supported the reform-minded citizens of Milan who rejected Henry IV's candidate for archbishop, although the position of archbishop of

Milan was a crucial imperial office in northern Italy. Moreover, resistance to Henry's methods of governance in Germany had grown stronger, and Gregory found allies among the German nobility when he pressed further with new regulations against the lay investiture of clergy. In 1076 Gregory declared Henry excommunicated and suspended from the imperial office after Henry and a synod of imperial bishops at Worms had announced Gregory himself deposed from the papacy. In the winter of 1077, in one of the wisest and most dramatic moves of the conflict, Henry IV suddenly crossed the Alps and presented himself as a penitent at the Tuscan castle of Canossa, where Gregory VII was staying, asking forgiveness from the cleric who had excommunicated him. Gregory agreed to absolve Henry, thus weakening the opposition to Henry in Germany, which nevertheless proceeded to elect an antiking on its own and wage civil war against the emperor for the next three years.

Relations between Gregory and Henry quickly broke down again, but Gregory's censures had far less effect the second time they were used, and by 1080 Henry had overcome his opponents in Germany and turned his full wrath on Rome. The synods of Bamberg and Mainz in 1080 renounced obedience to Gregory and elected an antipope, the archbishop of Ravenna, in his place. With the antipope in his train, Henry IV invaded Italy in 1084 and forced Gregory to flee Rome and go to Salerno, where he was protected by the Norman dukes of Apulia. Gregory died in Salerno in May, 1085. After the brief pontificate of the former abbot of Monte Cassino, Odo of Cluny was elected pope and took the name Urban II.

Urban II (1088–1099), unlike Gregory, was a nobleman and had been prior of the monastery of Cluny. By compromise, diplomacy, and a reorganization of the administration of the papacy, Urban II undercut much of the support of Henry IV and greatly strengthened the prestige of his own office. The intransigence of Henry IV, who died in 1106 and of his son and successor Henry V (1106–1125), dragged out the formalities of the conflict between pope and emperor. Not until the pontificate of Calixtus II (1119–1124) was the formal aspect of the conflict finally resolved. In 1122 pope and emperor agreed to a treaty, the Concordat of Worms, according to which the emperor retained the right to oversee the election of high churchmen, to decide between disputed candidacies, and to confer the temporal privileges of ecclesiastical office by means of the scepter. He gave up the right to invest prelates with the ring and the crozier, precisely these ceremonial rights that had appeared to confer spiritual as well as temporal authority on a churchman.

The Concordat of Worms formally ended the Investiture Conflict, but it did not conceal the real triumph of Gregorian ideals that the papacy and its supporters had achieved. Never again could an emperor successfully invoke the old Carolingian idea of the emperor as God's vicar on earth, responsible for laity and clergy alike. Only the popes could now make such a claim. The image of a

Church of St. Peter, Moissac: Tympanum. The Tympanum is the part of the church façade just above the doors. Romanesque tympanum imagery is particularly striking. In this tympanum Christ in Majesty is represented as in the Apocalypse with the symbols of a widely understood pictorial religion. (*H. Roger-Viollet*)

tripartite society comprising men of prayer, men of war, and men of work became less important than that of a bipartite society. "There are two kinds of Christians," said a popular text often quoted by churchmen in the twelfth century, "laity and clergy." Of the two, the clergy now claimed the ultimate responsibility for the spiritual welfare of humanity. This legacy of Gregory VII led to a widening of the idea of reform, new monastic and clerical movements, and a new search for lay piety.

NEW MONKS IN A NEW DESERT

By the late eleventh century a new ascetic spirit was inspiring a number of monastic leaders to try once more to remove monks from close contact with the world and restore the rule of Saint Benedict to its place of supremacy over local privileges, customs, and diverse practices. The most successful of these movements was that begun at Cîteaux in Burgundy. Founded in 1098 by a group of monks who sought a stricter application of the monastic rule than existed at their old monastery of Molesmes, Citeaux (*Cistercium*) in Latin, whence the common name for the order, Cistercians) prospered under the directorship of Stephen Harding (1070–1134) and the immense prestige of Bernard of Clairvaux (1090–1153). By the late twelfth century there were nearly three hundred Cistercian religious houses, as well as several hundred more that followed one variation or another of the Cistercian rule. That rule, drawn up by Stephen Harding in 1114 and called *Carta Caritatis* (The Charter of Love), was a modification of the rule of Saint Benedict. It organized and regularized the liturgical life of Cistercian houses, their relationships with one another, and the relations between the order and the world outside. The Cistercians did not receive child oblates, and their rule and forms of devotion emphasized the development of the spiritual discipline of the monks.

Principles of monastic organization were not, however, the greatest legacy of the Cistercians. The order offered not merely a rigid austerity and a puritanical view of the dangers of worldly temptation, but the prospect of a new interior spirituality, a wholly new relationship between humanity and God. In their scriptural commentaries and devotional writings, the Cistercians opened new avenues of spiritual awareness that exerted profound and enduring influences on the world around them. Both in organization and spirituality, the Cistercians illustrate the role of monasticism in the age of Gregorian reform.

One of the most striking features of the *Carta Caritatis* was the constitutional principle of Cistercian organization that it laid out. The abbot of Citeaux was, as was the abbot of Cluny, the head of his order, but there were far more checks on the former than upon the latter. First, Citeaux developed a strong sense of the relationship between motherhouse and daughterhouses. The abbot of any Cistercian monastery that had directly sent out monks to found other monasteries had to inspect those monasteries and in turn be inspected by their abbots at the motherhouse. The abbot of Citeaux, for example, had the right to inspect the four daughterhouses of La Ferté, Pontigny, Clairvaux, and Morimond, and the abbots of those four houses had the right to inspect Citeaux. In addition, all Cistercian abbots were to convene annually at Citeaux to make collective decisions about the order, a reflection of a considerable corporate awareness in the governance of the order.

Cistercian recruitment was also versatile. Those who seemed less suitable than others for participation in the full austerity of the monastic program were enrolled as *conversi*, or lay brothers. They came to operate the farms and granges of the order and to live a regulated life separate from that of the monks. For the Cistercian monks themselves, life was strict. Only the most severe decorations were permitted in Cistercian churches. Clear glass alone filled the windows. Bright colors, intricate sculpture, bell towers, metal crucifixes—all of these were banned from Cistercian churches. The cloisters too were stripped of their architectural ornament. A "typical" Cistercian style of church architecture carried the aesthetic and devotional principles of the order into the farthest corners of Europe as the order itself spread south to Italy and Spain, northwest to England, and northeast to Germany and Poland.

The greatest attraction of the Cistercian movement, however, was its creative role in developing the new spiritual outlook of twelfth-century Europe. Traditionally, monasticism was a defensive institution, consciously isolating its members from the temptations of a fallen world by placing them, through self-discipline and community life, in a tiny earthly duplication of heaven. In Cistercian spiritual writings there appears less emphasis on the defensive character of monastic life and much more on its role of developing the inner spirit of the monk, enabling him to reach out and grasp God's love for humanity. This new spirituality is also reflected in the way artists from the tenth century on depicted the crucifixion of Jesus. Instead of a remote, majestic being graphically superimposed upon a cross, they depicted a suffering figure who aroused the viewers' sympathy and affection, not merely their awe and dread. Depictions of the Virgin and the infant Jesus, originally a Byzantine motif, became more popular at the same time. No longer in art and spirituality was all of humanity depicted as fighting a hopeless rearguard action against the inevitable triumph of the devil. Rather, people were said to follow a path, conduct a quest, or climb a ladder—all of these images appear frequently in the devotional literature of the twelfth century—toward inner spiritual growth. This new sense of God's affection for humanity and the obligation of interior spiritual development was largely an invention of twelfth-century Cistercian writers.

The most prominent individual in the Cistercian movement—indeed in the religious life of all western Europe—in the twelfth century was Bernard (1090–1153), abbot of Clairvaux. Part of the importance of Bernard lies in the extent of his personal influence outside as well as inside the cloister. Bernard was born to a noble family near Dijon. In 1112, with his brothers and a large group of other young noblemen, Bernard suddenly left the lay life and joined the still young community of Citeaux. Bernard's arrival traditionally marks the surge of the order; indeed, it greatly increased the attractiveness of the order throughout France. In 1115 Bernard was sent out to found the third daughterhouse of Citeaux, at Clairvaux. Throughout his life he remained devoted to the ascetic ideals of the Cistercian program. In spite of continually debilitating illness, his physical austerities became well known throughout Europe. His flawlessly ascetic character, the burning lyricism of his devotional works, his concept of human dignity, and his explorations in the psychology of devotion establish him securely in the great exemplary tradition of Benedictine monasticism. Yet, Bernard was also the most widely respected holy man of the twelfth century, and it is as one of the last and most outstanding examples of the holy man, a type that developed in antiquity, that Bernard is perhaps best understood.

Cathedral of Autun, Tympanum: The Torment of Souls. The great tympanum of Autun depicts salvation and damnation. In this detail, the signed work of the sculptor Gislebertus, demons are tormenting the souls of the damned. (*Photographie Bulloz*)

Bernard played a role outside the cloister as extensive as his role in it. In 1128, for example, he was the secretary for the Synod of Troyes, where he composed a work in praise of the new orders of monk-knights in Jerusalem (see following section). In 1130 his prestige determined the outcome of a disputed papal election. In 1140 he attacked the new theology of Peter Abelard at the Council of Sens. In 1144 he preached the Second Crusade and even traveled to Germany to put a stop to the persecutions of Jews and to persuade King Conrad III to join the crusading expedition. In the last decade of his life he wrote an influential handbook for his protegé, the Cistercian pontiff Eugenius III (1145–1153), on how to be a pope. In 1145 Bernard traveled to southern France to preach against heresy. In addition to these personal journeys, Bernard poured forth a stream of correspondence, treaties on devotion, prayers, and meditations, and instructions to diverse groups and individuals in European society.

The success of the Cistercians and similar monastic movements inspired other clerics to reform their lives outside of strict monasticism. Because individual clerics often found it impossible to live reformed lives without support of a religious community, groups of pastoral clergy (those actually serving the spiritual needs of lay people) began to organize themselves in communities.

There they lived according to a rule, as monks, but served the laity as priests. One such group, the Augustinian Canons, took their rule of communal life from the rule for religious that Augustine had produced in the fifth century. As Canons Regular (pastoral clergy who lived like monks), they became a very effective branch of the clergy. The Premonstratensian Canons, founded by Norbert at Laon in 1120, were a second important group of Canons Regular. The form of life of both groups of canons greatly improved the quality of the ministry in areas where they worked, and they began the long labor of improving the quality of the secular clergy. They thereby made themselves a bridge between the new monasticism and the ill-educated and poorly trained parish clergy that ministered to lay people.

THE EXPEDITION TO JERUSALEM

Throughout the early years of his pontificate, Urban II (1088–1099) made extensive reforms in the operation of papal government and continued the diplomatic struggle with the excommunicated Henry IV. He also entered into favorable relations with the emperor at Constantinople, Alexius I Comnenus, attempting to heal the breach caused by the mutual excommunications of pope and patriarch that had taken place in 1054. In 1095 Alexius sent legates to the Council of Piacenza in northern Italy, requesting papal aid in enlisting mercenary soldiers for the defense of the Byzantine Empire. As Urban moved across southern France during the summer of 1095 he decided on his response to Alexius. At the Council of Clermont in November 1095 Urban made no call for mercenary recruits. Instead, he appealed to a large assembly of laity and clergy to impose peace everywhere in Christian Europe and to turn Christian weapons only against infidels. Urban proposed a large armed pilgrimage to Jerusalem, offering forgiveness of sins to those who undertook the journey from pure motives. In proposing the armed pilgrimage (which he and his successors always called a "journey," "expedition," or "pilgrimage"), Urban II created the ideal vehicle for the expression of the growing piety of the lay warrior class in the wake of the restrictions on its ecclesiastical activity urged by the Gregorian reform movement. Indeed, the First Crusade, which Urban's plea created, was first and foremost a vehicle for lay warriors to participate in a renewed Christian society in the one capacity for which they were ideally suited, controlled violence in God's service against non-Christians.

By the late eleventh century the Byzantine Empire had been wracked by political rivalry between the imperial civil servants and the landowning rural aristocracy. The extinction of the Macedonian dynasty in 1056 had given rise to a series of civil wars, which only the accession of Alexius I (1081–1118) had been able to stop. Byzantine economic and military power had declined, moreover, at the moment when new invasions threatened the empire again. The greatest threat had come from the Seljuk Turks, an Asiatic people who had converted to

Islam and risen to control Iran. In 1055 a Turkish leader even entered Baghdad, proclaiming himself a "deliverer" of the caliph, and assumed effective control of the Abbasid Empire. Turkish leaders called themselves sultans, and two of them, Alp Arslan (1063–1072) and Malik Shah (1072–1092), threatened both the Byzantine Empire and the Fatimid caliphate of Egypt. In 1071 the armies of Alp Arslan destroyed a Byzantine army at Manzikert, and for the next two decades Byzantine foreign policy was dominated by the twin threats of the Normans in South Italy and the Seljuk Turks in Baghdad. With the death of Malik Shah in 1092, however, Seljuk power became briefly decentralized, and Alexius I's request for western mercenaries was made with a view of exploiting the breathing space that Islamic disunity had given him.

The response to Pope Urban's proclamation of the "expedition to Jerusalem" also was not that of a mercenary army. The very first groups to march east were not chiefly knights, but an ill-assorted assembly of fighting men, townspeople, and peasants led by a number of self-appointed leaders, including the independent preacher Peter the Hermit. The "Crusade of the Poor," as Peter the Hermit's expedition is often called, suggests the depth of response stirred by Pope Urban's call for a campaign in the Holy Land. Peter's army terrorized the Rhineland and Hungary as it passed through, massacring Jewish communities in the Rhineland and elsewhere, and looting its way east until it passed through Constantinople and met its destruction in Turkish Anatolia.

In 1096 four well-organized armies of western fighting men set out for Constantinople. They were led by great nobles and directed by Adhemar, bishop of Le Puy, Pope Urban's legate, or representative, on the expedition. Alexius I Comnenus, a skillful diplomat, worked out treaties of agreement with each leader, forcing some of them to swear allegiance to him personally. He then escorted the huge army across the Bosporus, where it captured the city of Nicaea. After marching south through Anatolia, the westerners encountered and defeated a Turkish army at Dorylaeum and marched east to Antioch. The siege and subsequent defense of Antioch lasted from late 1097 to the end of 1098. Not until January 1099 did the final march to Jerusalem begin. Led by Raymond of St. Gilles, count of Toulouse, who was clad as a penitent and a pilgrim, the armies first sighted Jerusalem on June 7. After a fearful five-week siege the city fell on July 15. Two principalities had already yielded to the Crusaders before the siege of Jerusalem began. Antioch had fallen into the hands of Bohemund, son of Robert Guiscard of Sicily. Edessa, an Armenian principality to the east of Antioch, had fallen to Baldwin, brother of Godfrey of Bouillon, one of the expedition's leaders. The capture of Jerusalem and the existence of two other independent principalities immediately raised the question of the organization of the captured territories. Many members of the expeditionary army left Palestine and Syria to return to Europe, their mission completed. The occupying forces remaining in the Holy Land shrank dangerously. Byzantium made several claims concerning its own rights to captured territories, especially Antioch. In 1099 Godfrey of Bouillon was elected advocate of the Holy Sepulcher, but that title could not be made to work effectively as a force of governance. When Godfrey died in 1100 his brother Baldwin of Edessa formally became king of Jerusalem. By 1111 most of the important coastal cities had been taken by the Crusaders; the last, Ascalon, fell to them in 1153. During the reign of Baldwin I (1100–1118), four principal Crusader states took shape: the principality of Antioch; the county of Edessa; the county of Tripolis in the center of the Holy Land; and the kingdom of Jerusalem in the south.

The turbulent Crusader states rarely agreed on a single policy, and Muslim resistance grew measurably after 1125. In 1127 a talented Seljuk prince named Zangi established a strong Muslim principality in the city of Mosul and expanded his territory at the expense of Muslim and then Christian leaders. In 1138 Zangi captured Damascus, and in 1144 he assaulted and captured Edessa, the first Christian principality to fall back into Muslim hands. The capture of Edessa stimulated the pope to call another armed pilgrimage and to send out preachers and promise spiritual benefits on a large scale. As we have noted, among the preachers of the Second Crusade was Bernard of Clairvaux, whose fiery eloquence stimulated many, including King Conrad III, to go to the East. The Second Crusade of 1147 was very different from the First. Led by Conrad the German King, and King Louis VII of France, the two main armies were virtually uncoordinated and far worse organized than the noble armies of the First Crusade. In addition, dissension in the lands that the Europeans had begun to call simply *Outremer* ("Overseas") prevented any significant action except a futile assault on Damascus. Both king and emperor headed home without any of the glory that had covered the leaders of the First Crusade half a century before. Human sinfulness, said Bernard of Clairvaux, had lost the Crusaders God's favor. Human wickedness and cunning, said apologists for the king of France, had betrayed the Crusaders. Louis was particularly enraged at the Byzantine emperor Manuel I, whom he believed had betrayed him in alliance with Conrad III. This attitude sharpened the Latin dislike of Greek Christians and contributed to the deteriorating relations between Byzantium and the West, already aggravated by the frictions caused by the First Crusade and the rise of Venice. Of all the effort expended in the Second Crusade, only two elements are worth noting. First, some forces from eastern Germany were permitted to fight against the still pagan eastern European Baltic and Slavic peoples. Thus was crusading legitimacy added to the old conflict between expansionist Christian states and non-Christians in northeast Europe. Second, the city of Lisbon was captured by a mixed army of English, Flemish, French, and Portuguese soldiers in 1147, an important step in the history of the Reconquista.

The four Crusader states in Palestine, Lebanon, Syria, and Armenia were Christian principalities situated precariously in a turbulent and disunified but still powerful Muslim world. As relations between the Crusaders and Byzantium had begun to deteriorate quickly, the new lands were especially dependent on the Italian maritime cities for their lifeline to western Europe. Genoa, Pisa, Lucca, and Venice grew wealthy from the concessions they won in Palestine and Syria, and their new wealth played an important role in their drives toward independence from domestic powers. The prominence of Venice in both the Crusading and Byzantine worlds grew particularly quickly in the twelfth century, and Venice, like the Crusader states, experienced a deterioration of relations with Byzantium, although Venetian importance in Byzantine commerce grew during the same period. One result of the new energies of the Italian cities and the Crusader states was the economic undercutting of Byzantium. The loss of lands and manpower, the continuing high expenses of Byzantine imperial government, heavier taxes drawn from a diminishing tax base, and a debasement of Byzantine coinage weakened Byzantium considerably during the twelfth century. Besides threats from Norman Sicily and South Italy, Byzantium faced the economic ambition of Venice and the sullen distrust of the Crusader states. Although the twelfth-century Byzantine Empire profited from the abilities and good sense of the Comnenian imperial dynasty from Alexius I to Manuel I (1143–1180), it failed to recover fully from the crises of the eleventh century and the shift in wealth and power to the Latin West.

Although Zangi was assassinated in 1146, his son and successor Nur-ad-Din (1146–1174) assisted in the defense of Damascus against the armies of the Second Crusade, and by 1154 he had acquired Damascus for himself. For the next twenty years Nur-ad-Din strengthened his state and profited from the dissensions and political crises in Outremer, which put the Christian states at a distinct disadvantage. Disputes over the succession to the kingship of Jerusalem, conflict between the noble families and the kings, and the important role played by the Military Orders, especially the knights Templars, (communities of knights who took monastic vows and lived a life of war and prayer) all weakened the stability and strength of the Crusader states in the face of growing Muslim resistance.

Although some collaboration between the kingdom of Jerusalem and the Byzantine Empire held off Muslim forces in the 1150s and 1160s, their combined efforts were achieved only at great expense. In 1176 the Byzantine army under the emperor Manuel was crushed at Myriocephalum by the Seljuk Turks, a defeat that lost the whole of Anatolia and exposed the Crusader states to a powerful Muslim enemy. In addition, the forces of Nur-ad-Din grew stronger elsewhere in the Muslim world. Under the vigorous leadership of one of Nur-ad-Din's officers, Saladdin (1137–1193), a Muslim army conquered Egypt. After Nur-ad-Din's death in 1174 Saladdin succeeded him and directed his combined forces at the Crusader states. In 1187 at the Battle of Hattin Saladdin routed the Crusader forces, and shortly afterward he captured the city of

The Crusades.

Jerusalem. The Christians were left with a few coastal cities and the island of Cyprus, to which the kings of Jerusalem moved.

The triumph of Saladin ended the century of the Crusader states, but it did not stop the Crusade movement. The vigor of the early Crusades had created an image in European minds that the disasters of the twelfth century did little to diminish.

FURTHER READING

In general, see Gerhart Ladner, *The Idea of Reform* (Cambridge, MA: Harvard University Press, 1959), and Gerd Tellenbach, *The Church in Western Europe from the Tenth to the Early Twelfth Century* (Cambridge-New York: Cambridge University Press, 1993). A number of themes are discussed in the studies in Adriaan H. Bredero, *Christendom and Christianity in the Middle Ages* (Grand Rapids: William B. Eerdmans, 1994), and M.-D. Chenu, *Nature, Man, and Society in the Twelfth Century* (Chicago: University of Chicago press, 1968).

On monasticism, see Giles Constable, *Medieval Monasticism: A Select Bibliography* (Toronto: University of Toronto Press, 1976). Two general surveys are especially valuable: Wolfgang Braunfels, *Monasteries of Western Europe: The*

Architecture of the Orders (Princeton, NJ: Princeton University Press, 1972), and C. H. Lawrence, *Medieval Monasticism* (New York: Longman, 1984).

On Cluny, see Barbara Rosenwein, *Rhinoceros Bound: Cluny in the Tenth Century* (Philadelphia: University of Pennsylvania Press, 1982), and H. E. J. Cowdrey, *The Cluniacs and the Gregorian Reform* (Oxford: Clarendon Press, 1970).

Two useful studies of other forms of religious life are Henrietta Leyser, *Hermits and the New Monasticism: A Study of Religious Communities in Western Europe, 1000–1150* (London: Macmillan, 1984), and Ann K. Warren, *Anchorites and Their Patrons in Medieval England* (Berkeley and Los Angeles: University of California Press, 1985).

On the Investiture Conflict, see now Uta-Renata Blumenthal, *The Investiture Controversy: Church and Monarchy from the Ninth to the Twelfth Century* (Philadelphia: University of Pennsylvania Press, 1988). A classic work is that of Gerd Tellenbach, *Church, State and Christian Society at the Time of the Investiture Contest* (Oxford: Basil Blackwell, 1948). A detailed balanced account appears in Karl F. Morrison, *Tradition and Authority in the Early Church, 300–1140* (Princeton, NJ: Princeton University Press, 1969). On the period after Gregory VII, see H. E. J. Cowdrey, *The Age of Abbot Desiderius: Montecassino, the Papacy and the Normans in the Eleventh and Twelfth Centuries* (Oxford: Clarendon Press, 1983). On the polemical debates, see I. S. Robinson, *Authority and Resistance in the Investiture Contest* (New York: Holmes & Meier, 1978).

On pilgrimage and Crusade, see Vera and Helmut Hell, *The Great Pilgrimage of the Middle Ages* (New York: Clarkson N. Potter, 1967); Jonathan Riley-Smith, *The First Crusade and the Idea of Crusading* (Philadelphia: University of Pennsylvania Press, 1986), and, by the same author, *The Crusades: A Short History* (New Haven, CT: Yale University Press, 1987). For the Muslim perspective, see Amin Maalouf, *The Crusades Through Arab Eyes* (New York: Schocken Books, 1985), and Francesco Gabrieli, *Arab Historians of the Crusades* (Berkeley and Los Angeles: University of California Press, 1969).

Part V CULTURE AND SOCIETY
IN THE HIGH MIDDLE AGES 1150–1325

13

NEW ART AND NEW LEARNING

A WHITE ROBE OF CHURCHES

The spiritual concerns of reformers and new forms of devotion were not the only signs of a revived religious culture in the eleventh and early twelfth centuries. Writing in the early eleventh century, the chronicler Radulphus Glaber noted that around the year 1000 Europe began to be covered with "a white robe of churches." A new wave of church building and a new consciousness of the meaning of the church building and the priestly order accompanied the spiritual concerns of the eleventh and twelfth centuries and gave them an important visual dimension.

The new and larger churches that appeared in the eleventh-century Europe were based on several tenth-century architectural innovations and a new awareness of late imperial Roman architectural technique. Among the former influences is the appearance in several tenth-century churches of stone vaulting, the construction of a church ceiling completely out of stone arches instead of the timber that had characterized Carolingian architecture, especially in northern Europe. Among the latter influences are the size of late Roman buildings, particularly the basilicas, the use of the rounded arch, and the dignity and solemnity of late antique architecture. The early eleventh century also reveals the earliest sources for ceremonies surrounding the dedication of a church, as well

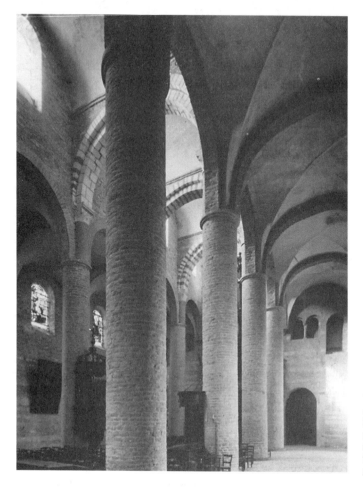

The Church of St. Philibert, Tournus: Interior. This is a good example of Romanesque church architecture. Note particularly the rounded vaults and small windows, as well as the ambitious formality of the design. (*Archives photographiques, Paris*)

as depictions of the role of the priest in art that suggest a new respect for the sacramental powers the clergy claimed. This enhanced sense of the dignity of the church building and the person of the priest helps to explain the enthusiasm with which church builders constructed their new churches in the eleventh and early twelfth centuries.

Late-tenth- and eleventh-century builders also considered church building a penitential act, as did William the Conqueror, when he built Battle Abbey at the site of his victory over the forces of King Harold at Hastings in 1066. In thanks to God, the monks who had escaped from the Vikings and settled at Tournus built the church of St. Philibert shortly after 950. The patronage of the German emperors and the ambitions of imperial German churchmen accounted for a wave of large, new churches appearing in Germany throughout the eleventh century. These churches were deliberately modeled on late Roman basilicas, and their large naves, high, rounded stone arches, and

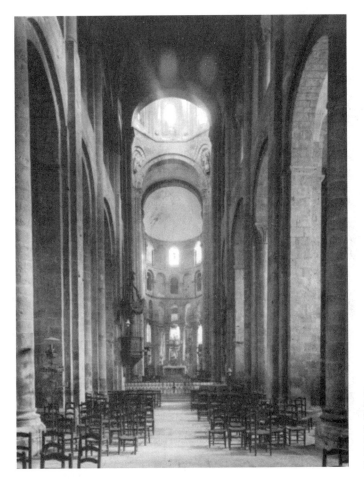

Church of Ste. Foy, Conques: Interior. An important pilgrimage church, the Church of Ste. Foy suggests the increased architectural solemnity of Romanesque church architecture and an impressive command of building techniques. (*Marburg Art Reference Bureau*)

generous interior spaces were livened by a lavish use of color in their interior decoration. One of the most striking of these is the Church of St. Michael at Hildesheim, which was begun in 1010.

Still other churches were the result of rebuilding programs. That of the monastery of St. Savin-sur-Gartempe, rebuilt in 1021, had its ceiling covered with remarkable frescoes depicting scenes from the Old Testament. Such churches as these, first in Germany, then in France, Spain, and Italy, and finally in England, reflect not only the development of tenth-century techniques and an imitation of Roman monuments and ruins but also internal influence within western Europe and architectural influences from the Byzantine and Muslim worlds.

The new churches of Romanesque Europe are testimony to the new ease of communications and the popularity of pilgrimage during the period in which they were built. As the pilgrimage to the shrine of St. James at Compostela in

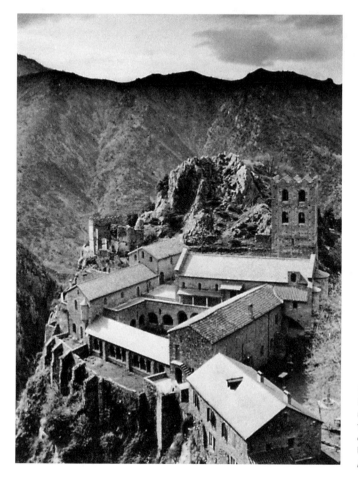

Monastery of St. Martin, Canigou.
Perched high in the Pyrenees, this
monastery and others like it witnessed
the monastic reforms of the tenth and
eleventh centuries. It was founded by a
layman, Wilfred of Cerdaña. (*Photo Re-
portage*)

northwestern Spain became more and more popular, many towns along the
routes to Compostela built, or rebuilt, churches to accommodate the large numbers of pilgrims who wished to visit as many holy places and venerate as many
relics of saints as possible on the long and dusty road to their destination. A fine
example of one such church is that of St. Sernin in Toulouse, begun in 1060 and
consecrated in 1096. Churches of this type were constructed in the form of a
cross, with a nave large enough to hold a considerable crowd. The high side
aisles of the nave continue around the north-south arms of the cross and meet
in the apse at the east end of the building. This route inside the church is called
an *ambulatory,* and it was a prominent feature of Romanesque church architecture. Its purpose was to offer a path for pilgrims walking around inside the
church that would take them as close as possible to the relics they had come to
venerate. The new appearance of churches, their size, and the increased degree
of veneration people felt for them contributed an important visual dimension to
an age of spiritual unrest and reform.

SCHOOLS AND SCHOLARS

The new churches of western Europe were chiefly those of monasteries and bishops. So was the custody and direction of learning. The intellectual history of medieval Europe is closely bound with the character of medieval schools. From the monastic schools of the tenth century to the great universities of the thirteenth, institutions of learning and their curricula constituted a setting for intellectual development of far greater influence than any comparable process in the ancient world and different from the circulation of ideas in other civilizations. One reason for this aspect of medieval thought was the important role that monastic schools, libraries, and scriptoria had played in Charlemagne's revival of ancient Christian learning. In Carolingian monasteries the old curriculum of the *trivium* and *quadrivium* governed the primarily literary education that monasteries provided. From the tenth century on, changes in thought took place largely in the context of monastic literary education.

The first change was the increasing sophistication of grammatical and rhetorical education. The high literary quality of eleventh- and twelfth-century monastic literature is eloquent testimony to the improved status of these traditional subjects. The second change was the growing interest in the study of dialectic, or logic. An example of both changes may be found in the monastery of St. Emmeram at Regensburg, which boasted in the eleventh century of being a "second Athens" because of the reputation of its schoolmaster, Otloh. A passage in Otloh's autobiography suggests how early and in what manner logic had begun to challenge grammar and rhetoric for primacy:

[Dialecticians are] simple enough to hold that Scripture should be construed according to the authority of dialectic, and to believe in many passages in Boethius, rather than Scripture. Following Boethius, they reproach me for ascribing the name of "person" to anything but rational substance.

Otloh was a great teacher and a sensitive and troubled spirit. He was also a good prophet, for the formal study of logic challenged traditional ways of understanding Scripture. It also offered critical means of comparing apparently conflicting statements in Scripture and the writings of the Church fathers. Throughout the eleventh and twelfth centuries considerable tension existed between the logical and literary analysis of key texts, especially in the monastic world and the study of scripture.

Outside that world, in the schools attached to cathedrals and in the schools founded by private individual teachers in the eleventh century, the study of logic moved faster, partly because it could be applied in areas of study and thought that were not always prominent in monastic curricula. These schools became more and more popular in the late eleventh and twelfth centuries, and represent a second stage of the transformation of the setting for European learning. Under talented and dedicated bishops and individual teachers, such cathedral schools as those at Reims and Chartres, Laon and Paris, took advantage of their urban setting and their wide appeal to build an educational tradition that did not always rival but certainly complemented that of the monastic schools.

In the absence of widespread lay literacy and with limited means of communicating ideas, the schools of the eleventh, twelfth, and thirteenth centuries played a more prominent role in the history of thought and literature than modern schools usually do. As the relationships between literary and oral culture became more complex, the schools influenced wider areas of society and even lay thought. This influence may be seen in the thought of prominent theologians at monastic schools, the private schools of the twelfth century, the appearance of new subjects, and the universities.

ANSELM OF BEC/CANTERBURY

The career of Anselm (1033–1109) reflects many facets of the learning of the eleventh century. Born in Aosta in northern Italy, Anselm withdrew from the world and sought the contemplative life in the monastery of Bec in Normandy, then newly patronized by the rulers of Normandy. He eventually became schoolmaster and abbot of Bec, and then archbishop of Canterbury. Anselm was primarily a monastic theologian, and his literary works focused on the monastic life and monastic devotion. But in some of those works Anselm gave considerably more importance to the use of reason in devotion than had earlier monastic theologians. His best-known expression of this use of reason is the phrase *fides quaerens intellectum,* "faith seeking understanding." Anselm proposed logic not as a road to faith or as an alternative to it, but rather as an important dimension of human nature that could be used only in conjunction with faith: "I do not seek to understand in order that I may believe," he once wrote, "but I believe in order to understand, for I also know that if I did not have faith, I would not be able to understand anything." Or, as he wrote elsewhere, "I want my understanding to comprehend in a certain way that same truth that my heart believes and loves."

Although he subordinated reason to faith, as all medieval thinkers did, Anselm greatly opened the role of reason in theological discourse. In a work called the *Proslogion* Anselm demonstrated that the truths of faith were not incompatible with reason. In his famous "ontological argument" about the proofs of the existence of God, he claimed to discover a proof of God's existence that needed no further proof outside itself. Here again reason reaches the same conclusion as faith and revelation.

PETER ABELARD AND HELOISE

Peter Abelard (1079–1142) was the son of a knight in the service of the count of Brittany. Instead of taking up his father's profession of arms, he left the little

The Faces of God: Christ in Majesty. The image of Christ in majesty, triumphant and serene, was a popular theme in early medieval art. It is shown here on the ninth-century Lorsch Gospels.

town of Le Pallet and traveled through northern *Francia* studying under private teachers, including Anselm of Laon, a student of Anselm of Bec and a prominent logician. Having a quick mind and a striking personality, Abelard claimed to have surpassed his own teachers. He became a professional teacher himself and moved to Paris. Although Abelard belonged to no monastery and had no formal right to teach theological matters, he began to lecture on precisely that subject. He soon became the most popular teacher in *Francia,* attracting students from England, Germany, and Italy as well as from the provinces of *Francia* itself.

But Abelard made enemies as well as friends and admirers, as much because of his sometimes abrasive personality as because of the novelty of his thought and teaching. Fulbert, a canon of the Cathedral of Notre Dame in Paris, invited the famous Abelard to tutor his niece, Heloise, a brilliant student and later an eloquent and important writer. The relationship between student and teacher turned into passion. After she became pregnant by Abelard,

Heloise and Abelard were secretly married. Fulbert, outraged at the secrecy of the marriage and Heloise's pregnancy, hired a gang of thugs, who broke into Abelard's living quarters and beat and castrated him. Both Heloise and Abelard withdrew from the world and took religious vows, Heloise at the convent of Argenteuil and later at Abelard's own foundation of the Paraclete, and Abelard at the monastery of St. Denis. After a brief retirement, however, Abelard resumed teaching, and again students flocked to hear him. Although some of his theological ideas were condemned at the Council of Soissons in 1121, he became once more the most popular teacher in Europe. Condemned again at the Council of Sens in 1140, Abelard made plans to go to Rome and plead his case directly before the pope, but he died as a monk at a dependent priory of Cluny before he could do this. He recounted his earlier career in his autobiographical *History of My Troubles*.

Individual teachers of logic had stepped into theological speculation before Abelard, but none had acquired his reputation or encountered as violent an opposition. During Abelard's own lifetime such theological doctrines as the Eucharist (the presence of Christ in the consecrated bread and wine of the Mass), the reasons for Christ's Incarnation and Crucifixion, and the nature of conscience all attracted much discussion, some of it traditional but some of it extremely novel. The most important novelty in the new theological literature was the question later called that of realism and nominalism, or the problem of universals. Late antique Neoplatonic thought had speculated on whether individual things, species, and genera exist as substances or as mental abstractions. In one influential work, the sixth-century thinker Boethius had followed Aristotle and stated that existence can be predicated only of real things; mental categories were mere abstractions, convenient cognitive devices and nothing more. In another work, however, Boethius followed Plato, arguing that such categories as species and genera were real things that existed in the mind of God, and that this existence was superior to the material imperfection of earthly things. This problem had troubled Otloh of St. Emmeram, and it continued to trouble thinkers in the twelfth century. Some twelfth-century thinkers argued for the Aristotelian approach: Only individual things have reality; the groups into which we classify them are simply *nomina* (names) and possess only a cognitive reality. Others argued for universalism, the Platonic notion that only the ideas in the mind of God were real, that individual things possessed only an inferior reality. Nominalism in its broadest sense argued that truth could be discovered only by the study of individual things and material creation; realism argued that the truth could be discovered only by the contemplation of universals. Abelard himself adopted a modified nominalist position. Begun in the late eleventh century, this debate continued throughout the Middle Ages. It was one of the most significant frameworks for theological and philosophical discourse down to the seventeenth century.

Abelard's most important works were the *Ethics* and the *Sic et Non*. The former is subtitled *Know Thyself,* and it was this knowledge that Abelard regarded as the cornerstone of good and evil actions. Echoing the current theological emphasis on the love of God for humanity and the necessity for humans to participate actively in achieving their own salvation—the latter a topic in Anselm's writings—Abelard stressed the importance of human intention in any estimate of the gravity of a sin or the virtue of a good act. He thereby contributed to the psychology of the twelfth century a view of human motivation that greatly widened the concept of the human personality. In addition to his emphasis on intention and consent, Abelard stated that internal sorrow for sin was the essential stage of penance.

The *Sic et Non* ("Yes and No") is a teaching manual in which apparently contradictory passages from Scripture and the writings of the Church fathers are placed side by side. Thus was revealed the problem of reconciling the diverse texts on which Christianity based its beliefs. In his preface to *Sic et Non,* Abelard laid down the criteria for systematically reconciling the apparent contradictions and, as in many of his other works, insisted that the application of logical method was the key to understanding the self, the self's relation to God, and the complexities of revelation. Aside from the colorfulness of his career, it is in this insistence on the supremacy of logical method that Abelard's originality lies and his influence is seen most clearly. Indeed, in his logic, his moral theology, and his autobiography we see one of the most remarkable and original thinkers in European history.

The case of Heloise reflects another aspect of twelfth-century learning—the perceived dangers of learning when the learned person was a woman, and the limited circumstances in which learned women might express their thought. Whatever her domestic background, Heloise came from a family with ecclesiastical connections, and her uncle's invitation to Abelard to tutor her indicates a respect for at least some learning on the part of women in such families. It is also clear, from Abelard's own account and from other sources, that Heloise's learning was widely known and admired. Heloise's own first letters to Abelard in response to *The History of My Troubles* reflect a powerful mind, lively emotions conveyed in excellent Latin prose, and a wide range of literary references. They also reveal a determined and highly individualized perspective on their relationship and on Abelard's duties to Heloise and her sisters.

The correspondence then focuses on the role of religious women, a role that Heloise accepted reluctantly and appears to have exercised brilliantly. In the twelfth century the convent offered a place, not only for unmarried women and widows, but also for female study and writing. Religious women who possessed and expressed distinctive personalities appear in many convents in twelfth-century Europe. These women were literate, could write and illustrate manuscripts, commission literary works, give and receive dedications of literary works, and read aloud to their sisters in the convent. They were also considered more likely (and safer because of their communal and often cloistered life) to receive special revelations from God. Although Heloise never professed to receive divine visions, a number of professed religious women did.

Hildegard of Bingen (1098–1179), from a noble family in the Rhineland, followed the religious life from childhood, chiefly at the convent for noble women she founded at Rupertsberg near Bingen on the Rhine. There she produced a series of encyclopedic literary works, including three books of visionary writings that had wide influence and brought her into contact with the rulers and popes of her time.

Hildegard's visionary writings were recognized and approved by Pope Eugenius III, chiefly because they were orthodox and explicitly attacked contemporary heretical movements and because Hildegard posed no threat of independence to the structure of the Church and Empire. The same was true of her friend and correspondent, Elizabeth of Schönau (1128/9–1164/5), also a member of the Rhineland nobility, whose visionary works also circulated widely.

The cases of Heloise, Hildegard, and Elizabeth indicate something of women's participation in the intellectual world of the twelfth century. Noble families in courts and convents could offer women both access to and a distinctive role in the new learning. Their work did not alter clerical misogyny or improve the status of women in society, but it did express a feminine mind and voice that achieved considerable recognition from the twelfth century on.

LAW AND LEARNING IN THE TWELFTH CENTURY

The development of early European legal institutions had produced a body of law very different in complexity and purpose from Roman law. From the earliest Germanic law codes to the customary legal arrangements of individual manors, villages, and towns, early European law possessed little of the philosophical and professional attraction of Roman law. In addition, the fragmenting of political authority in the ninth and tenth centuries had tended to turn legal institutions into the private property of lords who controlled law courts, pocketed the fines they awarded, and administered a heavy-handed kind of local justice. Some legal systems such as that of Anglo-Saxon England were relatively highly developed, but Anglo-Saxon law was subsumed under the oppressive legal practices of William the Conqueror's Norman aristocrats. In most of the principalities that made up eleventh- and twelfth-century France, regional customs determined legal practice. Moreover, much law operated under heavy procedural limitations and according to the theory of immanent justice—the belief that in certain cases divine intervention is required to indicate the guilt or innocence of the accused. Thus, various forms of the ordeal and trial by combat were practiced because it was believed that in them the will of God was revealed.

Christ Pantocrator. The image of Christ Pantocrator, "the Judge of all," was of Byzantine origin. This dome mosaic from the church at Daphni, near Athens, influenced the West at a time when church decoration was being developed in order to overawe the spectator. (*J. Powell, Rome*)

However, the same intellectual revolution that had affected rhetoric and logic, bible study and philosophy, also came to influence the law. The revolution had both ecclesiastical and secular sides. On the secular side, the revolution of learned law is generally attributed to the Bolognese rhetorician Irnerius (1088–1125), who began to expound to his students the recently rediscovered text of Justinian's *Digest,* the great volume of Roman philosophical jurisprudence. As the explanation of this lawbook grew beyond the stage of simply explaining the meaning of obscure words, the great achievements of Roman law began to generate independent interest, and schools devoted exclusively to the study of Roman law began to grow up, first at Bologna and later throughout western Europe.

By the midtwelfth century the "Four Doctors," Martinus, Bulgarus, Jacobus, and Hugo, had developed the techniques of explaining the texts of the law by writing marginal glosses, composing short treatises on legal reasoning, and writing summaries of individual titles in Justinian's collection. Medieval teachers of Roman law believed that the law was binding throughout Italy and the Empire, although students studied it as much for its scientific character as for its alleged authority, and the cities of Pavia and Bologna became especially well known as centers of Roman legal study. After more than a century of scholarship on Roman law, the jurist Accursius (d. 1260) arranged the long tradition of commentary on the law into a single systematic commentary that became known as the *glossa ordinaria,* the ordinary gloss, of Roman law. In time the *glossa ordinaria* was routinely taught in schools of Roman law along with the text of the law itself.

The rediscovery of Roman law threw traditional practices into sharp relief. Twelfth-century teachers of Roman law tried to fit it into the law of the towns of northern Italy, southern France, and parts of the empire. Naturally, they encountered a great many difficulties, but their efforts tended to make law more rational and systematic. In Ranulf de Glanvill's treatise *On the Laws and Customs of England* (1188), it was suggested for the first time that English law was susceptible to explanation in an orderly and logical manner, just as Roman law was. At the same time, King Henry II of England was engaged in sweeping away the variety of jurisdictions and practices in English law and imposing instead the law practiced in the royal courts, which later came to be called the common law of England. In the thirteenth century a royal justice, long considered to be Henry De Bracton, wrote the most sophisticated and rational analysis of a national legal system in European history, *On the Laws and Customs of England*. Between 1279 and 1283 Philippe de Beaumanoir wrote a treatise *On the Customs of the Beauvaisis* (the region around the city of Beauvais in northern France) that showed mastery of the principles of Roman law and applied them to a body of regional law totally different in origin and development. During the same time, the actual officers of the law became more specialized and headed toward the creation of a legal profession.

The revival of Roman law coincided with a growing distaste for the confusion and archaism that many thinkers found in eleventh- and twelfth-century European law. Even in those legal systems that formally remained outside the orbit of Roman law, such as the common law of England, the rationality, systematization, and regularity of Roman law made a great impact. Twelfth-century theologians protested against the use of the ordeal and the trial by battle, on the grounds that they tempted God and were a kind of blasphemy. When the Fourth Lateran Council in 1215 forbade clerics to participate in the administration of the ordeal, the older legal procedure was well on its way to becoming a dead letter. In its place civil and canon lawyers insisted on the collection of evidence, its analysis, and a decision based on rational process. So did the teachers and students of Roman law, who also worked as scribes, agents, judges, lawyers, and consultants for the towns, principalities, and monarchies of western Europe. Even those students who did not intend to become lawyers often studied Roman law for a time in order to acquire the intellectual training and discipline that the study of Roman law offered. The recovery of Roman law in the late eleventh and early twelfth centuries was one of the most important changes in the schools and the judicial systems of Europe. It touched abstract legal learning, helped rationalize the practice of law throughout Europe, and habituated many to solving disputes by rational procedures, supported and supervised by public authorities, not for their private benefit, but for what a number of legal thinkers came to call the common good.

CANON LAW AND THEOLOGY

The revival of Roman law and the slow spread of its influence to the customary laws of different regions in Europe illustrate the appeal that systematic, consistent thought exerted on a society that had suddenly become aware of its own lack of system and the inconsistencies of its own law. The growth of theology and canon law in the twelfth century also reflect that perception.

With the spread of learning and the production of more texts and new works, thinkers became aware of the inconsistencies that also existed in the vast body of religious literature that the eleventh and twelfth centuries had inherited from the past. Peter Abelard's *Sic et Non* was an ambitious attempt to illustrate the conflicts in interpretation in the sources and to devise a reliable method for resolving them. In spite of opposition to Abelard's theology, his method attracted more and more followers, because it offered an irresistible tool for solving the problems that thinkers had become more acutely aware of. In addition to Abelard's logical study there was, as we have seen, a transformation of the substance and temper of theology, illustrated in Anselm's linking of reason and faith and in Abelard's sophisticated psychological analysis of intention and consent. Moreover, such theologians as Bernard of Clairvaux paved new ways in devotional literature, sharing with Anselm and even with Abelard a new sense of the love between God and humankind, a fascination with the human nature of Jesus, and a new emotional dimension to theological thought. It is in the light of these three developments that the rise of the study of theology and canon law ought to be considered.

Others besides Abelard had long worried about the apparent conflicts that seemed to exist when equally ancient and authoritative texts appeared to contradict each other. Ivo of Chartres, a contemporary of Abelard, prefaced one of his own collections of ecclesiastical legal texts with a set of interpretative rules that was very similar to that of the *Sic et Non*. In 1140 Gratian, a monk at Bologna, compiled a collection of ecclesiastical texts arranged in such a way that apparently conflicting statements dealing with the laws of the Church could be reconciled with each other. He arranged these conflicting texts in a logical sequence in order to solve a systematic set of problems of ecclesiastical law, and he called his book *The Concordance of Discordant Canons*, or the *Decretum*. More than Abelard's work, Gratian's *Decretum* was informed by a mind both legally acute and devout. From the beginning to the end of his work, Gratian imposed order, principle, and coherence on the previously undigestible materials of ecclesiastical law. He marshaled over four thousand different texts from dozens of authors, sometimes using as many as seventy to clarify and illuminate the diverse sides of a single topic. Between the texts, introducing them, and bringing each topic to a conclusion, is Gratian's own commentary, a model of lucidity and economy. Although it always remained unofficial, the *Decretum* became the model for later official collections of canon law and for the system, used in subsequent theological works, of grouping thematically related texts and analyzing them.

Around 1150, and probably under Abelard's and Gratian's influence, Peter Lombard, a master in the Paris schools and later bishop of Paris, produced his book of *Sentences,* a systematic collection of scriptural texts and writings of Church fathers and masters that dealt topically with theological problems. The works of Gratian and Peter Lombard became the schoolbooks for the study of law and theology, and in some cases they were used until the beginning of the twentieth century. Arising in the schools and from masters such as Abelard, Gratian, and Peter Lombard, the principles of selecting, ordering, and typologizing diverse texts were now applied to the disciplines of law and theology.

Thus, the masters of theology in the schools moved further and further away from traditional methods of explaining Scripture. The language of theological definition and explanation became more and more that of the schools of logic and the philosophers, and less that of the meditative and literary traditions of the past. Not only did the new language and the new systematizing of thought and exposition explore further dimensions of the relationship between God and creation, but they also opened vistas in the definition of the human personality and in the analysis of society and social obligations.

As the tools of logic and philosophy became the tools of theology, specialization, training, and formal expression became necessary for theological study. At the Fourth Lateran Council in 1215, the number of the sacraments was finally set at seven and their nature was defined; the complex questions of nature, grace, sin, and salvation now received firm definitions. When teaching theology, the master now proceeded to treat texts, no matter how traditionally authoritative, in terms of the questions they illuminated, and the choice of these questions and their complexity directed the thrust of study. In time, such questions became the principal form of theological exposition.

The creation of canon law was as significant as the development of the new theology. From Gratian's *Decretum,* through the unofficial and later official collections of papal legal decisions that appeared in 1234, 1298, and 1314, scholars and popes shaped a body of law that laid down a new, juridical view of the relationship between the individual Christian and the Church. This body of law remained valid and in use throughout Christian Europe until the Reformation of the sixteenth century and in the Roman Catholic Church until 1918. Part of its influence lay doubtless in Gratian's organizing principles, which displayed clearly where the greatest legal problems lay, and in the fact that the lack of a fundamental organization comparable to that of the *Corpus Iuris Civilis* left teachers and students much room to add their own thought to the body of scholarship on the law or to criticize Gratian's. From a course in the liberal arts, including dialectic, students moved on to read Roman law. They might then proceed to canon law, their minds sharpened by logicians, Romanists, and their own teacher of canon law. The first commentaries on Gratian's collection are hesitant and elementary. Longer commentaries quickly appeared, however, modeled on those produced by teachers of Roman law—*summae,* questions, and rules. Several of the early canonists, or decretists, greatly influenced later approaches to the teaching and the creation of Church law. Such twelfth-century figures as Rufinus, Stephen of Tournai, and, the greatest of all, Huguccio of Pisa, were followed in the early thirteenth century by Richard of England, Alan of England, Tancred, and Johannes Teutonicus, who composed the *glossa ordinaria* to the *Decretum* around 1215.

THE UNIVERSITIES

The schools of Paris in the days of Peter Abelard and for decades afterward consisted of assemblies of students grouped around individual masters who owned the schools. These assemblies came under the ecclesiastical jurisdiction of the bishop of Paris and his chancellor. In Paris and Bologna the experience of individuals coming together to study in a strange city far from their homes was a social and legal novelty, and the very presence of the schools and their lack of legal status rendered the students vulnerable to much of the hostility generated by the inveterate localism of the twelfth century. Unprotected by citizenship, status, or privilege, students were subject to price and rent gouging, a lack of legal protection, and the perennial distresses of under-financed strangers.

In 1158 the emperor Frederick I Barbarossa, whom we will meet again in Chapter 15, issued the *Authenticum Habita,* in which he extended his protection to students in imperial territories. In particular the document granted students free travel and legal immunities, and it acknowledged that their study profited the emperor and his subjects. As a professional social consciousness grew among teachers and students, so did formal recognition of the status that formal study conferred. In the late twelfth century there appeared the ceremonial inception, a public defense of one's learning that has parallels in the formal rites of initiation into the order of knighthood, the oath of citizenship in the corporation of citizens of a town, and the ritual recognition of the status of master in a craft guild.

Thus, students and teachers slowly created a collective place for themselves in a society that jealously guarded its status ranks and left unprotected the stranger without status. They formed corporate bodies called *guilds,* which were similar to religious fellowships and craft associations. These defensive measures taken by the late-twelfth-century schools consisted of creating for scholars a recognized corporate status. *Universitas,* the Latin term used to designate the schools, was a common word indicating any collectivity, from craft guild to confraternity to body of citizens, and the formal designation of the universities was *Universitas societas magistrorum discipulorumque,* "the university, or society, of masters and students."

The term *schola,* from later Roman imperial and Byzantine tradition, meant many different groups regarded simply as groups. *Schola* in academic terms remained the designation of a master and his students together. A group of *scholae* working in close proximity and having a similar character was called a *studium,* and certain *studia* were given the exalted status of *studium generale.* These terms possessed no collective legal status, however, and privileges such as the *Authenticum Habita* applied to scholars individually, giving them no collective rights and recognizing no collective legal existence. The key events in the history of the universities occurred between 1200 and 1220, when the issuance of papal, imperial, and royal privileges entitled the scholars to act as a legal corporation, a *universitas.* They thereby had the right to be represented legally as a corporation, to possess a seal, to collect and administer common funds, and to sue and be sued collectively in courts of law. In some places as in Paris, the *universitas* was one of the masters alone; in others such as Bologna, the students constituted a *universitas.* Through such societal and juridical changes, the universities came into legal as well as social existence by the middle of the thirteenth century.

In 1200 King Philip II Augustus of France provided an extensive charter of privileges to the *universitas* at Paris, a document generally regarded as the foundation charter of the present university. In 1231 Pope Gregory IX issued the decree known as *Parens scientiarum,* "the mother of knowledge," which afforded ecclesiastical privileges to the University of Paris. The universities of the thirteenth century, possessing legal existence, often suffered from the organizational problems that other "universities" suffered from: disputes between masters and students, among masters, students, and the officials of the diocese, and between scholars and townspeople. Possessing legal identity, universities could leave a city, negotiate with another city for accommodations and move there, supervise lower schools in the vicinity, issue collective pronouncements on public questions, and regulate areas as diverse as the book trade and the rate of rents charged to students and teachers. For the universities existed only legally, and not physically, except for their members. There were no university campuses, no libraries, no buildings that were distinctly and exclusively a university's. Lecture rooms were rented in private buildings. Masters took students into their homes for residence and instruction; students who did not live in a master's house had to find other private lodging. Only slowly, through gifts, did individual buildings become university property. Even the earliest colleges consisted simply of endowed funds that paid for the housing, feeding, and instruction of poor students under masters' supervision; they were more charitable trusts than physical places. For example, the Sorbonne, the popular designation of the University of Paris, derived from the gift by Robert de Sorbonne in the thirteenth century of a charitable endowment for the support of poor scholars. The first buildings belonging to Oxford, Merton College, were left by Robert Merton. He had acquired them from the Oxford Jews, who had renovated them and thus helped originate what is commonly called the Gothic style of college architecture.

Within these legal and physical circumstances, the schools developed their curricula and played out their role in terms of the new and the old learning. The triumph of logic, the subordination of the subjects of the *trivium* to the increasingly professional disciplines of theology and law, and the creation of the degree, the *licentia ubique docendi*—"the license to teach anywhere"—shaped their internal intellectual processes, just as their privileges, legal status, and endowments shaped their physical and social character.

The universities prospered because society needed them. The Church, faced with increasing business at Rome and in the great dioceses after the Investiture Conflict, felt an increasing need for capable, loyal, specially trained assistants, and it had the great power to attract the men it needed. The twelfth century was probably no more fond of legal disputes than the eleventh, but the new law courts of the towns and the courts of kings and princes and prelates had to be staffed. Moreover, lesser princes and prelates began to find that when their clerical business was not kept up, their revenues and status declined perceptibly. All of these potential patrons helped generate a new demand for learning and letters.

When Abelard returned to Paris in 1136, one of his students was a young man who had been born about 1115, raised in the old episcopal town of Salisbury, and then sent to Paris to study. In 1147, after completing his studies, John of Salisbury joined the papal court. He remained there until 1153 (during which period he wrote an important and fascinating account of papal history), when he became the secretary of Theobald, archbishop of Canterbury. Europe in the 1140s and 1150s was full of opportunities even for men from places as remote as Salisbury, or, for that matter, England. The chancellor of the papacy in 1146 was Robert Pullen, the English theologian, and from 1154 to 1159 the pope himself was the Englishman Nicholas Breakspear (Hadrian IV), who had previously spent many years in papal service throughout Europe. John of Salisbury worked closely with Theobald and his successor, Thomas Becket. Exiled in the 1160s, John was present at the murder of Becket in 1170. In 1176 he was elected bishop of Chartres, a post he held until his death in 1180. Becket, a friend and patron of John, was the son of a prosperous Norman citizen of London and also went to Paris to study. Becket, too, became a clerk of Theobald's, and became chancellor of England and then archbishop of Canterbury under Henry II.

Such careers as these—and there were many more as striking—illuminate the changing conditions and new opportunities in the world of governance and power. Learning now could lead to a kind of success until now greatly restricted, although many students failed to achieve careers they sought and hurled bitter charges against those they thought prevented it. Even successful men such as John of Salisbury condemned the intellectual extravagance and bombast that sometimes passed for learning; they and others complained that true learning was bypassed and that flashy superficial talents seemed to make all the headway. These criticisms have much substance, as did the twelfth-century complaint that "Galen gives riches, and Justinian gives wealth"—the complaint about excessive study for professional purposes and the gaining of wealth—in this case the study of medicine and law. But they also remind us of the explosion of the new learning and the new institutions that came along with it as well as what they offered to ambitious, brilliant, or merely glib and aspiring scholars and officials.

Nor were the new scholars only those whose social origins made them more mobile and adventurous than the rest. John of Salisbury and Heloise came from ecclesiastical surroundings. Abelard from a knightly family in the backwoods of Brittany, Becket from London urban prosperity. One of Becket's contemporaries at Paris was probably Rainald von Dassel, a noble who later became provost of the cathedrals of Hildesheim and Münster and Archbishop of Cologne and, after 1156, Chancellor of the emperor Frederick Barbarossa, whose own uncle and biographer, Otto of Freising, had also studied at Paris.

Such opportunities afforded ambitious students considerable incentive to seek out the best (or the most popular) schools and teachers and to cultivate among their contemporaries those who gave promise of one day being able to dispense patronage. This early example of "networking" contributed to the patronage of learning and the spread and attractiveness of the schools. The schools and universities imparted a new style to learning to the centers of power, and they patronized others like themselves. In a world that had hitherto been one of orders, ranks, and carefully graded statuses, they invented the professional career. In doing so they shaped the intellectual circumstances in which both educational and political institutions dealt with day-to-day problems, formed theories of law and governance, and contributed a new intellectual format for the reconsideration of old questions and archaic structures.

FURTHER READING

On Romanesque art, see Gustav Kunstler, *Romanesque Art in Europe* (New York: Norton, 1973), and Kenneth John Conant, *Carolingian and Romanesque Architecture* (Baltimore: Penguin, 1974). Walter Cahn, *Romanesque Bible Illumination* (Ithaca: Cornell University Press, 1982) is an excellent study of nonarchitectural Romanesque art.

On schools and scholars generally, see Robert L. Benson and Giles Constable, eds., with Carol Lanham, *Renaissance and Renewal in the Twelfth Century* (Cambridge, MA: Harvard University Press, 1982); Peter Dronke, ed., *A History of Twelfth-Century Philosophy* (Cambridge: Cambridge University Press, 1988); John Marenbon, *Early Medieval Philosophy (480–1150): An Introduction,* and *Later Medieval Philosophy (1150–1350)* (London-New York: Routledge, 1988, 1987).

On Anselm, see R. W. Southern, *Saint Anselm: A Portrait in a Landscape* (Cambridge: Cambridge University Press, 1991), and on Lanfranc, see Margaret Gibson, *Lanfranc of Bec* (Oxford: Clarendon Press, 1978). On Abelard, see Leif

Grane, *Peter Abelard* (New York: Harcourt Brace Jovanovich, 1970), and D. E. Luscombe, *The School of Abelard* (Cambridge: Cambridge University Press, 1969).

On Heloise and the letters, see *The Letters of Abelard and Heloise,* trans. Betty Radice (Baltimore: Penguin, 1974), and on women writers and the epistolary genre, see Peter Dronke, *Women Writers of the Middle Ages* (Cambridge: Cambridge University Press, 1984), and Karen Cherewatuk and Ulrike Wiethaus, *Dear Sister: Medieval Women and the Epistolary Genre* (Philadelphia: University of Pennsylvania Press, 1993). On Hildegard and Elizabeth, see Barbara Newman, *Sister of Wisdom: St. Hildegard's Theology of the Feminine* (Berkeley-Los Angeles: University of California Press, 1987); Sabina Flanagan, *Hildegard of Bingen, 1098–1179, A Visionary Life* (New York-London: Routledge, 1989); Anne L. Clark, *Elisabeth of Schönau: A Twelfth-Century Visionary* (Philadelphia: University of Pennsylvania Press, 1992).

The centrality of biblical study is studied in the classic work of Beryl Smalley, *The Study of the Bible in the Middle Ages* (Notre Dame: Notre Dame University Press, 1964).

On the complex matter of dispute settlement and law, see the essays in John Bossy, ed., *Disputes and Settlements: Law and Human Relations in the West* (Cambridge: Cambridge University Press, 1983); Wendy Davies and Paul Fouracre, eds., *The Settlement of Disputes in Early Medieval Europe* (Cambridge: Cambridge University Press, 1986). On the ordeal, see the fine study by Robert L. Bartlett, *Trial By Fire and Water: The Medieval Judicial Ordeal* (Oxford: Clarendon Press, 1986). On law and literacy, see Michael Clanchy, *From Memory to Written Record,* 2nd ed. (Cambridge, MA: Blackwell, 1993).

The much broader question of literacy is analyzed in the brilliant book of Brian Stock, *The Implications of Literacy* (Princeton, NJ: Princeton University Press, 1983).

On learned canon and Roman law, see the essays in Benson and Constable, *Renaissance and Renewal in the Twelfth Century.*

The great works on universities are Hastings Rashdall, *The Universities of Europe in the Middle Ages,* 3 vols, eds. F. Powicke and A. B. Emden (Oxford: Clarendon Press, 1936), and Lynn Thorndike, *University Records and Life in the Middle Ages* (reprint ed., New York: Norton, 1975). The best new history is *A History of the University in Europe,* Vol. I, *Universities in the Middle Ages,* ed. Hilde De Ridder-Symoens (Cambridge: Cambridge University Press, 1991). On the origins, see Stephen C. Ferruolo, *The Origins of the University* (Stanford: Stanford University Press, 1985). On one interesting case, see Beryl Smalley, *The Becket Conflict and the Schools* (Oxford: Basil Blackwell, 1973).

Two general and indispensable works are Anders Piltz, *The World of Medieval Learning* (Totowa, NJ: Barnes & Noble, 1981), and Alexander Murray, *Reason and Society in the Middle Ages* (Oxford: Clarendon Press, 1978).

14

RELIGION AND SOCIETY

THE RISE OF PAPAL AUTHORITY

From the first movement to reform the papacy in 1046 until the end of the twelfth century, the popes exerted an increasingly active and successful headship in Christian society. Depending originally on the support of the emperor Henry III, and then, during the Investiture Conflict, upon that of prominent lay nobles and kings, the papacy slowly transformed its administration and strengthened its claims to supremacy in Christian society. By the second half of the twelfth century it was the real leader of the Church.

Among the most important stages of this process were the reform of the papal *curia* (the immediate servants of the pope in Rome) by Pope Urban II, the growth of papal prestige through the Crusade movement, the establishment of papal legates (officials sent by the popes to different parts of Europe with special legal and political authority), and the frequent holding of church councils to publicize and legislate the ideals of reform. In addition, the appearance of such works as Gratian's *Decretum* and later canon-law scholarship strongly emphasized the constitutional and legal authority of the popes. The papacy also gained in its ongoing struggles with kings and emperors, for in the twelfth century neither of these powers could marshal arguments as sophisticated and persuasive as those of papal lawyers. Finally, the areas from which popes were recruited also changed. The interpretation of episcopal status in the early Church was that a bishop had to remain in the diocese in which he became a bishop—he was "married" to his see. Early medieval popes therefore tended to come from diverse backgrounds in clerical life and not frequently from the ranks of the bishops. From the mid–twelfth century on, however, this older view was relaxed (in part because of the work of canon lawyers) and more popes came from the ranks of bishops and servants of the papal curia. Many of these men also had experience and training as lawyers, and thus their early lives prepared them very differently from their predecessors for taking an active role as pope.

Among the popes of the twelfth century who helped transform the papacy into a great power were Alexander III (1159–1181) and Lucius III (1181–1185). Significantly, both had spent long periods in papal service: Alexander III had been in charge of the papal chancery (the office for writing documents) and Lucius III had been a cardinal whose name appeared frequently on documents from the mid–twelfth century on. This experience was important for men who came to occupy an office that grew more complex every year. Not only did the popes have to communicate actively with church officials and lay people throughout Europe, they had to govern the city of Rome and the papal states in central Italy as well.

The furtherance of reform on the one hand and the eradication of heresy on the other became the twin goals of the papacy at the end of the twelfth and beginning of the thirteenth century. One means of achieving these ends was the frequent holding of Church councils, both on a European scale and regionally when necessary. In 1123, for example, the year after the Investiture Conflict was ended by the Concordat of Worms, Pope Calixtus II called the First Lateran Council in Rome. There were many other councils during this century, among them the Second Lateran Council of 1139, the Council of Rheims in 1148, the Council of Tours in 1163, the Third Lateran Council in 1179, and the Fourth Lateran Council of 1215. These councils put the full force of the papacy and the rest of the Church hierarchy behind the reform movement, the organization of the Church, and the new developments in theology and canon law. The canons passed by the councils were copied by the attending prelates and taken back to their own dioceses, where they were translated into legislation tailored for each diocese. Thus was the work of the universal Church brought down to the level of the parish and individual monastery.

Not every churchman was pleased at the new influx of business that occupied the time and the minds of the twelfth-century popes. Bernard of Clairvaux bitterly denounced the volume of legal business handled by the chancery, the legates, and the popes. The legal dimension of papal activity increased throughout the late twelfth and early thirteenth centuries and imprinted itself on the concept of the community of the Church. Popes of the late twelfth century, in fact, may be seen to alternate between thinkers who desired to maintain papal authority to the letter of the law (and sometimes beyond it) and those who were willing to compromise with opponents, to check some of the consequences of an excessively legalistic conception of papal authority, and to cultivate devotion and piety rather than administration.

This dichotomy was more complex than it at first appears. The career of perhaps the most active of the popes, Innocent III (1198–1216), reflects both of these aspects of the papacy. In decretal after decretal Innocent laid down with striking precision supported by juridical reasoning the principles of papal authority, assembling throughout his pontificate a formidable body of legislation that gave concrete legal shape to papal authority. Yet Innocent possessed a second side. His biographer devotes considerable attention to Innocent's care for the well-being of the Church, and of individual churches, on the restoration and decoration of which Innocent spent much money and time. He responded with surprising swiftness to the new devotional movements of the early thirteenth century, and should not be viewed solely as a lawyer and administrator acting within a narrow, legalistic tradition.

In the decretal *Sollitae* to the Byzantine emperor (1201) Innocent made vague but serious claims to universal authority. In two decretals of 1202, *Venerabilem* and *Per venerabilern,* Innocent further defined his authority in cases subject to temporal jurisdiction. At the same time, and for a while after, Innocent negotiated with the excommunicated king of England, John. The pontificate of Innocent III, the busiest if not the greatest of medieval popes, revealed the broad spectrum of jurisdictional areas across which the theories of papal authority could be spread and the extraordinary ability of the pope and his curia to make such theories the basis for practical decisions in hundreds of particular cases.

THE FOURTH LATERAN COUNCIL
AND THE COMMUNITY OF THE FAITHFUL

The work of twelfth-century theologians, canon lawyers, Church councils, and popes culminated in the canons of the Fourth Lateran Council, held at Rome in 1215. The council is a good focus for understanding the life of the faithful as it was envisioned by ecclesiastical specialists at the beginning of the thirteenth century. Making the ideas and rules of theologians and canon lawyers understandable to ordinary believers was generally accomplished in three ways: by the legislative and teaching authority claimed by pope and bishops; by the creation of new religious organizations directly aimed at the religious life of the average believer; and by the work of a remarkable group of moral theologians, many of them in Paris, who adapted the large and abstract theories of learned theologians and lawyers to everyday situations, which could become the teaching materials of confessors, preachers, and other ecclesiastics. The laity was reached by authority, by pastoral reforms, and by teaching.

The first canon of the Fourth Lateran Council was a general statement of Christian belief, a form of the *credo,* or creed, that all Christians were expected to memorize, just as they did the two most common prayers, the *Our Father* and the *Hail, Mary*. The creed insisted on both the unity of God and the Trinity of three Persons, the Father, Son, and Holy Ghost; on God's creation of the world from nothing; and on Christ's divinity, humanity, and sacrifice in order to save humanity. It insisted on a single, universal Church, the repetition of Christ's sacrifice in the Mass, and the efficacy of other sacraments (which the Fourth Lateran Council was to number at seven). It asserted the spiritual and bodily resurrection of the dead. Some Christians would be eternally saved in Heaven, and others would be eternally lost in Hell.

Moral theologians did not expect ordinary Christians to understand the complex workings of theology, but they did expect assent to simple statements of doctrine, and they also expected regular participation in the sacraments, those liturgical acts that facilitated the reception of divine grace. Baptism signaled the rebirth of the individual into the Christian community, providing him or her with spiritual kindred (godparents, or god-sibs, whence the English word *gossip*), which included the saints, particularly the saint after whom one was named, which was the general practice from the thirteenth century on. The baptized Christian might marry (marriage was declared one of the seven sacraments at the Fourth Lateran Council) or enter the religious life. Whether married or a celibate religious, Christians were expected to confess their sins at least once a year (a rule instituted by the Fourth Lateran Council) and to perform the necessary penance. Sins were generally categorized in terms of the vices to which humans were subject, and the theme of the Seven Deadly Sins was a popular organizing motif for the ordering of conscience. It was also a schematic that differed for women and men. Of these, those sins that led to hostility against others—Pride, Anger, Avarice, and Envy— were considered most serious. Penance for these might be harsh and prolonged and might include a long pilgrimage or a public display of penitential status. For some sins, exceptionally grave or public ones, private penance assigned by a confessor in the "internal forum" of conscience and the confessional was considered insufficient, and a hearing in the "external forum" of a canon law court was required. In some cases, excommunication might be required. Although by the thirteenth century excommunication might mean no more than exclusion from the sacraments for a specified period, on some occasions it could entail severe spiritual and material penalties.

Death, too, was surrounded by ecclesiastical assistance, from individual counseling to the Last Rites and to burial in consecrated ground. The ritual surrounding death was as elaborate as other rituals and, on the whole, the entire apparatus of belief and Christian life and death represented a joining of high doctrine and authority and the earthly affections and expectations of a large body of believers. Even the spaces of the church building were used in versatile ways to reflect both the differences between spiritual and material life on the one hand and their merging on the other. On some occasions—marriage, the seeking of sanctuary, baptism, religious drama—the porch, doorway, or side of the church building was used; on others, the interior of the building was used. The varied uses of the church building suggest the versatile ways in which the spiritual demands of Christianity accommodated themselves to the needs and expectations of the ordinary Christian. Besides the visible authority of popes and the enactment of rules in such events as the Fourth Lateran Council, we must also appreciate the expectations of the laity that the events of this life and this world also demanded sanctification, and that spiritual dignity and even holiness might be located in the actions and thoughts of everyday people, whether noble or not.

Although most Europeans were Christians, not all Christians were thought of in the same ways. Medieval thinkers regarded men and women as being far more different from each other than mere biological and physiological differences might indicate. From the beginnings of biblical history, Eve was considered to have first succumbed to temptation herself, and then, through what some writers termed "women's language" persuaded Adam to sin. As temptress and deceiver, women were nevertheless also considered fragile, inconstant, and weak. Against the image of woman as Eve, the twelfth century had cultivated the image of the Virgin Mary, but many of the most devout adherents of Mary did not extend their devotion past her uniqueness. Marian veneration did not much change the situation of the daughters of Eve.

But contemporary women could (and often were urged to) achieve a life of virginity, and theologians continually asserted that the spiritual rewards of the virginal life were far greater than those of the widowed or married life. Although the Fourth Lateran Council included marriage among the sacraments, theologians were reluctant to abandon the conventional misogynistic image of women. During the twelfth century, for example, the legend of Mary Magdalene was created as the epitome of feminine lust and weakness who had transformed her sinful life into one of virginal purity. The cult of Magdalene, centered on the monastery church at Vézelay, was, like that of the Virgin, much more a cult of spiritualized ideals than a consideration of the nature and spiritual needs of real women.

But misogyny alone was not the whole story of women in the late twelfth and thirteenth centuries. The sacramental status of marriage stubbornly asserted the spiritual dignity of the married life, even though the nature and extent of advice to married women from confessors and preachers insisted in locating them within rigid and narrow frameworks usually based on a denial or restriction of women's sexuality. Freedom of movement for women was thought to give dangerous rein to the characteristic female vices of inconstancy and curiosity. Women were frequently discouraged from undertaking pilgrimages and were vehemently forbidden to go on crusades. Therefore, custody and restraint were urged upon women, in the household, especially in public, in costume, bodily comportment, and speech. With the new interest in the spirituality of marriage there also emerged the image of the good wife. Again, an idealized type who was expected to be as much the "preacher to her husband" as his sexual and social companion and household manager.

Since most female marriage partners were considerably younger than their husbands, even the principle that consent made a marriage usually was understood to mean the young girl's consent to her parents' choice of a husband for her. Those who objected were generally coerced, and only a few remarkable figures like Christina of Markyate were later venerated for their determined resistance to a forced marriage. Even Christina was venerated because she sought a higher spiritual life, that of the cloistered virgin.

Thus, even changes in cult and devotional modes—like the cults of the Virgin and Mary Magdalene—and the new spiritual dignity attributed to marriage did not realistically define the life of a Christian woman. But the cloister, as the cases of Heloise, Hildegard, and Elizabeth of Schönau indicate, might indeed offer a setting for a feminine theology and what has been termed "women's religion." Not only in cloistered convents, but in communities of religious women who lived and worked in the world— these begin to appear in the late twelfth century—women found considerable freedom to explore the spiritual life generally unrestrained by male authority or presence.

It is in these settings—the cloister and the community of women who took no vows and continued to work in the world—that the most original manifestations of the feminine experience of the medieval Christian religion has been found. Besides the controversies over sex and wealth that influenced both the image of women and male definition of their material and spiritual natures, there were also other foci of religious experience. Some of these were located in religious symbolism, particularly that of food. The work of Caroline Bynum, for example, has suggested that food was central in women's material and spiritual existence because it was one of the few elements over which women had control, that fasting on the part of women was, for example, the counterpart to the renunciation of wealth on the part of men. The stories of female saints involve intense eucharistic devotion, the giving of food to the poor, and the undergoing of extreme physical privations (including the denial of food to themselves) as a means of fusing their own humanity to the suffering of Christ. Such arguments imply that women in the twelfth and thirteenth centuries did not reverse gender roles to assert themselves as males, but elevated feminine nature by identifying it with the nutritive, redeeming, and suffering body of Christ. Thus, although the canons of the Fourth Lateran Council reflect some of the transformations of Christianity from the ninth through the early thirteenth centuries, they are not exhaustive guides to such topics as personal devotion and the individual experience of religion. However, they did reflect another movement that seemed at the time more complex and dangerous than the nature of feminine devotion—the threat of substantial dissent and the reawakening of the older terminology of heresy to characterize it.

DISSENT AND HERESY

The religious movements of the eleventh and twelfth centuries reflect the deepest strata of European language, consciousness, and culture. The successful struggle against paganism was virtually over by 1100. Monastic reforms, reform of the clergy, and the new prominence of the popes in European ecclesiastical and lay life all marked a new stage in the development of Christian society. However, the clergy were not the only ones whose lives were touched by change. The transformation of lay piety was as important a phenomenon, and it was more complex. But for some clergy and laity even the reforms of the eleventh and twelfth centuries and new expressions of devotion were not sufficient. These centuries witnessed the first recorded surge of popular religious dissent since the later Roman Empire. Religious dissent among the laity and clergy that reveals some evidence of popular interest and support appears in a few sources between 1000 and 1050, in virtually none between 1050 and 1100, and then in a great number and variety of manifestations from 1100 on.

Not only does religious dissent occur more frequently in the sources, but it occurs against a background of heightened religious sensibilities, new forms of devotion, the popularity of pilgrimage, the construction of new churches designed for large crowds, and the formalizing of beliefs and conduct by the emergence of theology and canon law. The theology of Anselm, Abelard, and Bernard, the elevation of marriage to sacramental status, the new prominence of the virtuous warrior on Crusade or in the service of the Church, and the expansion of such doctrines as that of Purgatory (which held out the hope of salvation even after a sinful life) combined to offer both clergy and laity more hope of eventual salvation and more aids to devotional life than had been offered in the preceding five hundred years.

Much of the dissent, as we have seen, was directed at unreformed clergy, particularly during the Investiture Conflict, and was concerned with one form or another of clerical purity. Married or concubinous clergy and clergy who had polluted themselves by paying for their offices were the main targets. In the twelfth century a broader and deeper heretical movement swept through Christian Europe. Not surprisingly, its roots have been the subject of much scholarly and confessional controversy. The term *haeresis* came into Latin from Greek, where it had originally designated the general concept of choice; later it referred specifically to the different beliefs of the philosophical schools. In Christian Latin usage it gradually acquired the meaning of doctrines held contrary to the teaching of the Church. The thirteenth-century definition of Robert Grosseteste conveys both the contemporary and the original meanings of the term: "Heresy is an opinion chosen by human faculties . . . contrary to sacred scripture . . . openly taught . . . pertinaciously defended. Heresy in Greek, choice in Latin." These meanings are important to remember in considering the development, content, and spread of heretical beliefs and the Church's response to them. The individual whose opinions ran counter to those officially proclaimed by the Church was not immediately guilty of heresy. One might be instructed, cautioned, asked to change one's mind, or, in the manner used by Bernard of Clairvaux, publicly denounced. For heresy to exist, it had to be openly maintained and taught; the concealed heretic did not emerge as a problem until later. Finally, the true heretic was one who, after being admonished and corrected, openly maintained and defended one's opinion against all opposition.

The use of the word heresy was extremely loose in the early twelfth century. Abelard applied it to persons who held incorrect theories of grammar, and much of the conflict between him and Bernard of Clairvaux leading to the condemnation of some of Abelard's doctrines at the Council of Sens in 1140 used the term in a way more reminiscent of the correction of an erring monk than of its later twelfth-century meaning. But the worlds of the cloister and the Paris schools were slowly drawing apart, and such conflicts grew sharper in the late twelfth and early thirteenth centuries.

As far apart as they were drawing, however, the worlds of Abelard and Bernard were still closer to each other than either of them was to the popular world of devotion, which was becoming more intense day-by-day. Indeed, "learned heresies" were rarely attacked as bitterly as the spreading popular heresies, and scholars retained a considerably greater latitude in their teachings than did popular preachers or heretical societies. One of the strongest condemnations made by the early Church, for example, was directed at astrologers. This hostility, which is reflected in the writings of the influential twelfth-century thinker Hugh of St. Victor, did not prevent astrology from becoming a popular learned pastime. Receiving the imprint of the Islamic thinkers whose popularity grew as the twelfth century wore on, astrology slipped in the door of orthodoxy, as it were, just before that door slammed shut against heresy and other forms of the occult.

The roots of popular heresies, however, were more complex than scholars' disputes or monastic unorthodoxy. Just as the tenth century had witnessed a turn to the more human aspects of the crucified Christ and the depictions of the Mother and Child, so the tenth, eleventh, and twelfth centuries saw increased veneration of the Virgin. Yet side-by-side with this new sensibility and the new doctrine it inspired, another set of attitudes appears to have evolved, attitudes that savagely attacked what was considered to be the confining of divine power in earthly material symbols. In the eleventh and twelfth centuries groups led by preachers attacked churches, overturned altars, burned crosses, and bitterly denounced the clergy. The general crisis concerning the extent of the reform movement, which worked itself out in the twelfth-century decrees of popes and councils, engendered uncertainty in the believing public. Moreover, both progressive reformers and hostile, traditionalist critics heaped scorn on the burgeoning legal business of the papal chancery and the administration of the Church. Bernard's attacks on the extravagance and materialistic Christianity of Cluny and the diversion of the papacy into the law courts found many ears and

The Faces of God: The Suffering Christ. One way to trace the changing forms of Christian piety is to study the depictions of Christ and the different moods they invoke. One of the most moving and revolutionary images is that of the suffering Christ crucified, an image that gained popularity after the tenth century. This is one of the earliest of such images known, the crucifix of Archbishop Gero of Cologne, from around 975. (*University of Pennsylvania*)

were echoed and distorted by many minds. Some scholars have drawn the distinction between movements of reform and movements of heretical unorthodoxy. Reform and dissent that became heretical were defined as sharply by the definitions of orthodoxy with which church leaders met their challenges as they were by their own internal development.

Throughout the first half of the twelfth century, the sources describing heresy and dissent tend to reflect certain traditional views of their subject. First, they tend to assume that twelfth-century movements were simply revivals of what Bernard of Clairvaux called "the heresies of old," that is, the movements of dissent and heresy that marked the first six centuries of the Church. Thus, most groups who believed in two supernatural powers, one good and one evil, were labeled Manichees. By the middle of the twelfth century, however, writers appear to have known much about the new movements and to have regarded them more as "novelties," than as older heresies revived. In addition, historians have long debated the influence of heretical movements from outside of Europe. The most controversial of these was Bogomilism. Emerging as a heresy in the Byzantine Empire, Bogomilism found a home in

Bulgaria and moved west on trade routes and Crusade routes in the early twelfth century. The Bogomils attacked much of the fabric of Christian orthodox belief. They echoed Manicheism by denouncing material creation and the creator as evil gods and in emphasizing the exclusive goodness of spiritual beings. Bogomil influence has generally been regarded as having arrived late in western Europe, however, and the roots of all Latin heretical movements have been located in the religious excitement of the twelfth-century conscience.

The two best-known types of heresy in the twelfth and thirteenth centuries—Waldensianism and Catharism—flourished primarily in Provence and Languedoc in the south of France, although Waldensians were also widespread in Austria and Bohemia. Waldensianism, named for the merchant Valdes of Lyons, held the doctrine of the corruption of the Church, the priesthood of all believers, the necessity of preaching and reading Scripture in the vernacular, and apostolic poverty. This group, which resembled in many aspects other voluntary groups later accepted by the Church, differed from similar sects in its intransigence rather than in doctrine. Admonished, they would not accept ecclesiastical conditions; they were, in Grosseteste's term, pertinacious. Catharism, whose name derives from the Greek word meaning "pure," was more complex. Sharing the Bogomil concept of a material universe created by an evil spirit, Cathar doctrine may also have shared the antimaterialistic revulsion that we have noted accompanying the growth of a "humanized" relationship between God and humans. The Cathars held that human spirits were imprisoned in flesh, and for them the greatest sin was procreation, imprisoning another spirit in the material world. God sent Jesus, who only appeared to take on the characteristics of a human being, to show humans the way out of the trap of material creation. None of the "human" aspects of Jesus—not the cross, not the passion, not the Church that was built on those symbols—had anything to do with God. The Church was a creation of Satan, and hell was earth, imprisonment in the material world.

One of the bitterest charges leveled by reformers, dissenters, heretics, and even high churchmen and female visionaries alike was at the ineptitude and immorality of the clergy. Such charges had lain behind the success of the reform movement of the late eleventh century and the church councils and local prelates of the twelfth. To a large extent, many of these charges were true. Yet it is difficult to know where to lay blame for what is, after all, an anachronistic charge. There were no training schools for clergy; bishoprics often were awarded for purely temporal reasons and with ecclesiastical connivance or the clergy's submission to temporal power. The lowest clergy came untrained from the same class of people whom they served. Moreover, the rapid growth of towns and the settlement of new lands tended to make for a shortage of clergy, especially at the parish level. The growth of dissent and heresy posed acute problems to the Church and, because the Church touched the lives of all, to European society as a whole. Besides the problem of ongoing Church reform and that of the relation between spiritual and temporal powers, the problem of ordering the Christian life loomed large as the twelfth century came to an end.

THE ATHLETES OF GOD

Part of the Church's response to dissent and heresy was to develop new approaches to pastoral theology—the care of souls. A group of moral theologians at Paris under the leadership of Peter the Chanter, adapted twelfth-century theology to specific cases and social needs, thereby bridging the philosophical theology of the schools and the problems of daily living. By 1200 there were handbooks for helping preachers and confessors perform similar functions. The papacy also turned to traditional institutions within the Church, particularly to the Cistercian monks. But in spite of the occasional successes of a Bernard, monks proved unable to win a hearing from the busy lay and clerical world. Some lay people and clerics, however, began a new kind of pastoral movement. Realizing that the heretics had adopted preaching in the vernacular languages, they too began to preach. In 1206 one of the canons regular of the Spanish diocese of Osma, Domingo de Guzman (1170–1221), having witnessed the ineffectiveness of Cistercians attempting to refute heretics in Montpellier, decided to organize a group of clerics who would be trained to preach and to live in strict poverty. For ten years Domingo—or Dominic—worked with a small group of trained preachers, and between 1215 and 1217 the group dispersed to carry out its mission in different parts of Europe.

Later thinkers saw a close parallel between Dominic and Francis of Assisi (1182–1226). Born to a wealthy merchant family in central Italy, Francis spent his youth and young manhood in the military and literary secular pastimes of his society. Suddenly, at the age of about twenty, he began to reject his own background and to circulate more and more freely with poor priests, lepers, and beggars. In 1206 he received his mission in a vision and began to preach. Francis and his first companions preached as laymen, rejected the ownership of property for themselves, and drew up a simple rule that attempted to translate the gospel into a program of action. Pope Innocent III, who was, as we have seen, both a capable and ambitious administrator and a pope of great vision, accepted Francis's rule and became a particular patron of the new group.

Both Dominic and Francis discovered in preaching and poverty two of the most effective keys to the pastoral needs of their age. Because of their poverty, the orders each man founded reached out to those who criticized the wealth of the established Church. By bringing the license to preach, hitherto a prerogative of bishops alone, to priests who were specially trained for the task, they finally began to equal the appeal of the heretical preachers. In addition to the rights to preach of Dominic's Order of Preachers (popularly, the Dominicans) and Francis's Order of Friars Minor (the Franciscans), other individuals, even some lay people, were enabled to preach, although in doing so they were limited to exhortation to penitence rather than the exposition of dogma. The wave of preachers over the thirteenth and fourteenth centuries had an incalculable impact, and the literature of preaching influenced thought and secular literature for several centuries.

Yet another consequence of the development of the Mendicant Orders was the creation of second orders, cloistered communities of religious women following the rules of Dominic and Francis. The most famous of these, the Franciscan convent at San Damiano, was directed by Clara di Offreducio, the first female follower of Francis, but Franciscan religious women were cloistered and not given the freedom of movement of those in the first order. But the Franciscans also generated a third order, one of lay men and women living in the world but following Franciscan rules in their personal and public conduct. The emergence of these third orders helped to shape the communities of religious women living in the world—generally termed Beguines—that took shape in northern Italy and the Low Countries from the late twelfth century on.

HERESY, CRUSADE, AND THE INQUISITORIAL OFFICE

The new orders of Franciscans and Dominicans captured the essence of the Church's new spirituality and employed it in a pastoral context. There was another side to the thirteenth-century church, a juristic one, and it was also called into play, particularly when the orders seemed less than successful. As we have seen, the work of episcopal and papal courts had grown in the twelfth century. The procedure they used borrowed more from earlier ecclesiastical procedure and Roman law than from the kinds of law used in the lay courts of the twelfth century. Early European law, both temporal and ecclesiastical, was based on the accusatorial process, in which a private accuser made charges before a judge and the accused party responded. This was the format of all trials, criminal and civil, including those decided by ordeal, by judicial duel, or by compurgation. Another process was sometimes used, however, one that allowed the judge to act independently of an accuser when the accused was guilty of public notoriety. Episcopal visitations—a bishop's formal visits to subordinate churches—throughout a diocese used this procedure. In the twelfth century those newly familiar with Roman law discovered the complexity of the inquisitorial procedure, in which, unlike the accusatorial procedure, the judicial authority itself might begin a case and inquire into its facts. The decretal *Ad abolendam,* issued by Pope Lucius III (1181–1185) in 1184, ordered all bishops to inquire after heretics within their jurisdictions, to conduct, in effect, an inquest. Early legislation against heresy aided the spread of the inquisitorial process, but that process was still used loosely, and the chief punishment was anathema or excommunication.

In 1199, however, Innocent III published the decretal *Vergentis,* in which he increased the punishment of convicted heretics to include the confiscation of goods and property. The chief importance of this text lies in its specific application of the old Roman legal concept of treason to heresy. In this decretal heresy became treason to God, and the forefeiture of worldly possessions and excommunication were consistent with the penalties prescribed for treason in Roman law, though they did not yet lead to the death penalty. In 1208, however, the papal legate Pierre de Castelnau was murdered in Toulouse, and Innocent decided to launch an all-out attack on the center of Catharism. Thus began the Albigensian Crusade against the heretics and their indifferent rulers, the counts of Toulouse.

The Albigensian Crusade lasted from 1209 to 1229; it destroyed the heretical culture of Occitania (the lands of southern France) and marked the turning of the Crusade against inhabitants of Christian Europe. Innocent recruited an army from the north of France. For two decades of intense military conflict, acts of brutality on both sides, and the slaughter of heretics and orthodox Christians alike, the knights of the north battered and ultimately destroyed the rich and varied civilization of the south.

But the military campaigns did not wipe out centers of heresy, and Innocent's successors, particularly Gregory IX (1227–1241), doubled their efforts to urge bishops and councils to use inquisitorial techniques to discover hidden heretics. By 1233 Gregory had begun using the Dominicans and Franciscans as inquisitors, granting them powers that traditionally belonged to the bishops, particularly in those districts in which bishops seemed ineffective. By entrusting inquisitorial powers to the orders, Gregory moved a long way toward establishing a series of judicial functionaries directly under papal authority for discovering heresy by means of the inquisitorial process.

The continuous role of the Dominicans and Franciscans as inquisitors developed the inquisitorial process quickly. Although most of their earlier coercive power had been psychological, financial, and sacramental, the inquisitors discovered the technique of "relaxing" or "releasing" recalcitrant defendants to "the secular arm," the lay magistrates who could use physical force without violating their canonical status. The inquisitorial procedure soon developed its first oppressive features: the concealment of the identity of witnesses and the specifics of evidence, the refusal of counsel, the obligation to identify accomplices as a sign of repentance, the admission of evidence from hitherto unacceptable witnesses, and, in Innocent IV's decretal *Ad extirpanda* in 1252, the admission of torture.

Judicial torture made its first appearance in Europe since the Roman Empire early in the thirteenth century in the city-states of northern Italy, where it probably derived both from new kinds of crime and law enforcement and from the revival of Roman law. By 1252 it had become an instrument of inquisition and from that date until the nineteenth century, judicial torture spread from the town courts of Italy and the inquisitor's chambers into most of the criminal courts of the Christian world. Within a century, the newly armed inquisitorial office had crippled heresy in Occitania, and the Church had acquired a formidable and terrifying instrument for detecting and rooting out heresy. The new coercive powers of the Church were felt by others besides heretics, particularly by the Jews of Christian Europe.

CHRISTIAN ATTITUDES TOWARD NON-CHRISTIANS

Most medieval Christians shared the ignorance of the wider world beyond Europe and the Mediterranean that characterized late Roman geography and anthropology. They generally believed that the equatorial zone was so hot that humans could not pass through it into the Southern Hemisphere; also, since Jesus had come to save all people, there could not be people in that hemisphere, which was sometimes called the *Antipodes*. Within the inhabitable Northern Hemisphere, however, there were many wonders and monsters, many of them drawn from the literary tradition of Pliny, Strabo, and other Roman geographers. These images of monstrous humans and humanoids survived into the Renaissance, and even Shakespeare's audience recognized the tradition when Othello told of

> my travels' history;
> Wherein of antres vast and deserts idle,
> Rough quarries, rocks, and hills whose heads touch heaven,
> It was my hint to speak—such was the process;
> And of the Cannibals, that each other eat,
> The Anthropophagi, and men whose heads
> Do grow beneath their shoulders.

Such creatures survived in literature, particularly travel accounts, long after the Middle Ages, but speculation on distant and unknowable humans was not a major concern of medieval thinkers. More important were those yet to be converted to Christianity such as the pagan Baltic and Slavic peoples, who were not converted until the fourteenth century, or pagans who might be converted by Muslims or Jews, as Christians feared the Mongols would be in the thirteenth and fourteenth centuries. Most important were those peoples—Muslims and Jews—who were neither pagans nor Christians and who lived both inside and outside of Christian Europe. Christian attitudes toward non-Christians were shaped primarily with Muslims and Jews in mind. Because Christian relations with Muslims took place generally in the areas of trade and crusading warfare, Christian official attitudes are best discovered in the writings of canon lawyers. By the twelfth century these legal comments had replaced the earlier literary and purely theological ideas and put Christian-Muslim relations on a new footing.

The late eleventh and early twelfth centuries witnessed distinctly new forms of anti-Muslim and anti-Jewish expression. Christian attitudes toward the Muslims were a mixture of curiosity and persistent misinformation. To Bede, the eighth-century English chronicler, the Muslims were the descendants of Hagar and Ishmael, the Old Testament outcasts. To others they were a schismatic Christian sect whose doctrines were a perversion of Christian doctrines (some even constructed an imaginary Muslim "Trinity" consisting of Muhammad, Apollo, and Termagant). For those in Spain, Sicily, and the Crusader states who dealt with Islam on a day-to-day basis, however, there was much mutual understanding and even cultural sympathy; Carolingian attitudes toward Islam had been marked, one historian has observed, by "caution and sobriety." El Cid, as we have seen, could casually feud with Alfonso VI of Castile and enter the employment of Muslim leaders without apparent pangs of conscience, and so could many others. Away from the frontiers, however, the new Christian selfconsciousness generated strong anti-Muslim attitudes.

By the thirteenth century, popes and canon lawyers had laid down a theory justifying Christian invasion of Muslim lands in Syria and Palestine and used that justification as an approach to the question of whether Muslims could exercise any kind of just dominion over humans. That is, could a non-Christian polity be considered a legitimate polity? Such questions as these greatly widened Christian legal and political thought, although they would not have provided much comfort to a Muslim who read them. By forcing questions of international relations into a religious framework, Christian attitudes toward Muslims greatly influenced the later development of Christian European attitudes toward non-Christians generally. The attitudes of Christians toward Muslims developed largely in the atmosphere of Crusade propaganda and legal discussions. Most Muslims lived out of the reach of Christian authorities—except for those in conquered parts of Spain and south Italy and in the Crusader states—and the problems of dealing with them were similar to those of dealing with foreigners generally.

JEWS IN CHRISTIAN EUROPE

In spite of increasing Christian hostility and the political weakness that followed the failed revolts of 66–70 and 131–135, the Jews of the Roman Empire preserved both their Roman citizenship and the privileges that their faith had been given from the days of Julius Caesar on. Settled in the cities of the Mediterranean world—their religious lives centered on both the rabbinic teaching of the law and the synagogue—Jews practiced the trades and crafts of the Mediterranean world as long as the Roman Empire survived in the East and West. Christian antagonism was expressed not only in terms of religious hostility, but probably in fear of conversions of Christians to Judaism, of which enough are documented to indicate Christian insecurity as long as the fourth-century emperors sustained the Jewish legal status within the empire. Rules against different forms of social intercourse with Jews were first made inside the Christian community, as the canons of the Council of Elvira in 312 indicate. Imperial law, however, although it tended to restrict Jewish rights in regard to Christians, tended to preserve

other Jewish rights, even in the face of increasing Christian hostility and the beginnings of a Christian anti-Jewish literature. Although such acts as the Christian destruction of synagogues in several Roman cities were individual
expressions of violence, several emperors insisted that the synagogues be rebuilt.
As the fourth century ended, however, the attitudes toward Jews on the part of
such figures as Ambrose of Milan reflected an ambivalence. On the one hand,
Ambrose preached against what he considered the errors of Judaism and the in-
sults to Christ that Judaism constituted, but he did not demand the abolition of
Judaism, nor did he permit bishops to lead attacks on Jews. On the other hand,
he appears to have urged imperial indifference to manifestations of popular
Christian hostility toward Jews and to have thought that the Roman state should
prevent the growth and development of its Jewish population.

With the disappearance of the Roman Empire in the West after the fifth
century, privileged Jewish legal status became a matter for individual Germanic
kingdoms either to preserve or destroy. Various kingdoms acted differently in
this matter. In Spain, for example, a number of rulers issued harsh, restrictive
anti-Jewish legislation, although in other Germanic kingdoms there is little
proof of this and even evidence of a continuation of distinctive Jewish status.
During the same period several formal doctrines regarding the Jews were
adopted by Church councils and individual bishops of Rome, the most notable
and enduring being the observation of Gregory I around the year 600 that,
"Just as license ought not to be allowed for Jews to do anything in their
synagogues that is not permitted by law, so also they ought to suffer no injury in
those things that have been granted to them." This legal doctrine was later
joined by a theological-historical doctrine: Because prophecies of the Second
Coming of Christ and the end of the world indicated that only at that time would
the Jews be converted, Jews had to be preserved in their religion until that time,
and therefore not forced to convert to Christianity or leave Christian lands.
Together, these doctrines came to represent a formal Christian position, and
until the twelfth century they seem to have been partly responsible for the
growth of the Jewish community in Europe as the only non-Christian population
of any significant size to be permitted to exist in Europe regularly and even to
grow at times into economic prosperity.

From the fifth century on, Jewish communities originally clustered in
southern Italy, Spain, and southern Gaul began to expand north and east, particularly, into *Francia* and the Rhineland. By the eighth century, southern Italy
witnessed a Jewish revival of Hebrew studies, and Jewish population growth increased and became largely urbanized. Such scant evidence as exists suggests
that the Jewish household consisted of parents and two children, and that rabbinic households, at least, were proudly aware of their lineage and of the learning and piety of their ancestors. Decisions of rabbinic courts indicate that the
conjugal unit was the chief and primary social bond in Jewish society. Landowning, trade, artisanship, medicine, and moneylending, all largely urban economic

activities, characterized most of the Jewish population of Europe, but it should be noted that these activities were more generally urban than particularly Jewish. Historians have long overrated Jewish prominence exclusively in trade and moneylending.

The application of family law also indicates the urban character of European Jewish society. Especially in rabbinic families, which are usually the best documented, women married only with their own consent and preserved rights pertaining to dowry and domination by the husband that were significant. Women in rabbinic families were usually literate and might teach the law to other women and attend synagogue, and in many families women possessed somewhat more legal and economic autonomy than comparable women in Christian families. The cooperative character of the urban working family thus reinforced the distinctive characteristic of women's status in the rabbinic family.

The religious life of Jews in western Europe centered on the twin institutions of the synagogue and the rabbinic school. Prohibited from access to political power and increasingly restricted as to mobility and choice of profession, the Jewish communities developed strong domestic and communal bonds, and the level of Jewish devotional life and scholarship became extremely high. The *responsa,* decisions of individual rabbis and rabbinic courts, illustrate both the character of Jewish communities and the high level of religious and legal scholarship they enjoyed. The great traditions of biblical and Talmudic scholarship culminated in the work of Rashi of Troyes (1040–1105) and—through Rashi's successor, Joseph Bekhor Shor—influenced the revival of Christian biblical studies of Andrew of St. Victor in the twelfth century, Hugh of St. Cher in the thirteenth, and Nicholas of Lyra in the fourteenth. The role of Talmudic scholarship and the work of a philosopher such as Moses Maimonides (1135–1204) played in shaping thirteenth-century scholastic Christian philosophy were especially significant. During the twelfth and early thirteenth centuries, the domestic and urban stability and prosperity of Jewish communities, the high levels of biblical and Talmudic scholarship, and the expression of Jewish thought in poetry and philosophy—as well as the widely recognized Jewish skills in a number of professions, including medicine—marked the high point in Jewish social and cultural life in western Europe between the fourth and the nineteenth centuries.

Christian society did not regularly or frequently express powerful and violent anti-Jewish attitudes until the eleventh century. From that time on, signaled by the massacres associated with the crusading pilgrims in the Rhineland in 1096, when entire Jewish families and communities destroyed themselves rather than undergo forced conversions to Christianity or were slaughtered by enraged warriors, Christian behavior toward Jews changed. Although the formal doctrines guaranteeing protection to Jewish belief, life, and property were preserved and frequently reissued, the fury of individual Church and lay people usually ignored them.

Two clear ideas appear to date from the early twelfth century: the principle that Jews had no legal rights except those granted them by the king, first outlined in England after 1135, and the necessity for firm pronouncements guaranteeing the safety of Jews from high ecclesiastical authorities. In 1120 Pope Calixtus II issued a decretal, *Sicut Judaeis,* reminding all Christians of this responsibility, and Bernard of Clairvaux had to hurry to Germany in 1144 to stop the new persecutions of Jews that attended the preaching of the Second Crusade.

By the second quarter of the twelfth century, the danger to the Jews appears to have distinctly increased. The new self-consciousness of Christendom, described in earlier chapters, may well have played a role in this new hostility. Certainly the anti-Muslim attitudes developed in the eleventh century came in part from the new Christian self-confidence. The new humanizing of the figures of Christ and the Virgin may also have contributed to the hostility to Jews, whose imaginary atrocities in twelfth-century literature surely derive from this new devotional sentimentality. Finally, the treatment of Jews in the twelfth and thirteenth centuries must be considered in terms of the broader religious and social turbulence of the period. Ruling and governed elements in a society and culture develop their own distinctive insecurities, which produce fear and hatred, and this fear is projected into whatever groups are the aliens of the moment. However deeply rooted and however indistinguishable from Christians Jews were, in law, religion, and culture they were the most visibly alien group, more alien than the heretics.

Those who had long been acknowledged to have an obligation to protect Jews—the emperors, kings, and popes—began in the late twelfth century to issue formal statements of protection, but also to exact from the Jews what the letter of the law (most of which dated from the fifth and sixth centuries) permitted. The need for money on the part of thirteenth-century monarchies, the popes' furious attack on heretics and dissenters, and such legislation as the requirement that Jews wear identifying marks on their clothing, which dates from the Fourth Lateran Council of 1215, made these "protectors" less useful than a reading of the law and the theory about the protection of Jews might lead one to expect. Kings and popes, as it turned out, were very dubious protectors at best. What Gavin Langmuir has called "the balance of contempt and toleration laid down in the Church's doctrines" was impossible to maintain. And when it was overthrown it was always on the side of contempt, brutality, and sacrilege. The twelfth and thirteenth centuries marked not only a new hostility toward individual Jews and Jewish communities, but the development of anti-Semitism in its most manifold and wide-ranging aspects.

From the twelfth century on, two other significant transformations characterize Christian attitudes toward Jews. In the rhetoric of traditional Christian anti-Jewish literature, Jews were usually depicted as blind, stubborn, rooted in the flesh, unchangeable in time, and insulting to Christ and to Christianity. In the twelfth century, however, as Christian thinkers elevated reason to a greater

Strasbourg Cathedral: Ecclesia and Synagoga. (left) The figure of *Ecclesia* (Church), suggests the power of personified images and the techniques of Gothic sculpture. The female
figure symbolizing the Church stands crowned, with cross and cup. (right) The figure of
Synagoga (Synagogue), a personification of the Jews, holds a broken spear and disused
book, items that correspond in symbolic value to the cross and cup of *Ecclesia.* Such visual
juxtaposition of images reflects the anti-Semitism of thirteenth-century Europe, suggesting
the paradox of art conveying social assumptions. (*Marburg Art Reference Bureau*) on this
image in medieval art and literature, see Wolfgang S. Seiferth, *Synagogue and Church in
the Middle Ages: Two Symbols in Art and Literature* (New York: Frederick Ungar, 1970).

height among the disciplines of learning—and identified reason and reason-
ableness with Christianity—anti-Jewish polemic now attacked the Jews as unrea-
soning and irrational, no longer merely blind and stubborn humans, but
humans deprived of reason. In addition, increasing Christian familiarity with
postbiblical Jewish literature, particularly the Talmud, led Christians to argue
that the Talmud contained not only blasphemies against Christ and Christian beliefs and practices, but also heresies against biblical Judaism.

    In addition to the new attacks from learned Christians, the twelfth cen-
tury witnessed a new intensity in popular anti-Semitism. Charges were made
more frequently that Jews committed unspeakable crimes against Christians and
the items sacred to Christians; that Jews murdered Christian children and used
their bodies in abominable rituals; that Jews were an underground enemy of
Christian society. The occasional popular outbursts of earlier periods now in-

creased in frequency and savagery. Jewish quarters in cities became targets for rioting mobs, and individual Jews, marked out by distinctive costume and badges, became more routinely visible as Jews at the same time.

Late in the 1230s much of this new hostility culminated in a series of trials of the Talmud in France and elsewhere. Nicholas Donin, a former Jew, accused the Jews before Pope Gregory IX of having replaced Scripture with Talmud. In several trials, alleged Talmudic excesses were condemned, and only edited versions of the Talmud were permitted to be used in Jewish communities. At the same time, Christian definitions of "forced" baptism of unwilling Jews became extremely restricted, to the point that only physically forced immersion into the baptismal water accompanied by specific verbal protests on the part of the unwilling "convert" constituted technical forcing. By the fourteenth century, charges of performing magic were leveled more frequently against Jews, and in 1324, when a millennialist panic seized France, Jews and lepers were accused of poisoning water supplies, charges that were repeated after the onset of the Black Death in 1348/1349.

In the wake of intellectual and emotional changes in the character and intensity of Christian anti-Semitism, the large and prosperous Jewish communities of the eleventh and twelfth centuries were drastically transformed. As Jews lost rights and lives, wore distinctive clothing and were restricted to distinctive quarters of cities, were persecuted by sporadic mob violence, and exploited by greedy and hostile rulers, Christian doctrinal obligations often became virtually a dead letter. Afflicted with Talmudic censorship, exiled from England in 1290, from France in 1306 and in 1394, from some territories in Germany by 1350, and from Spain in 1492, the Jewish communities of Europe were attacked, herded, and forced into the role of a despised and largely impoverished minority. By the fourteenth century Jewish religion, humanity, and culture had been brutally caricatured in the earliest wave of anti-Semitic literature, art, and propaganda.

FURTHER READING

The rise of papal authority is a complex subject with a large literature. The most recent account is that of Bernhard Schimmelpfennig, *The Papacy* (New York: Columbia University Press, 1992). Richard Krautheimer's book, *Rome: Profile of a City* (Princeton, NJ: Princeton University Press, 1980) is a good account of papal Rome, and Kenneth Pennington, *Pope and Bishops. The Papal Monarchy in the Twelfth and Thirteenth Centuries* (Philadelphia: University of Pennsylvania Press, 1984) studies the problem from the side of canon law. As a central theme in a larger history of Christianity, see Colin Morris, *The Papal Monarchy: The Western Church from 1050 to 1250* (Oxford: Clarendon Press, 1989), and for detail, see I. A. Robinson, *The Papacy 1073–1198* (Cambridge: Cambridge University Press, 1990). On the papal state, see Peter Partner, *The Lands of St. Peter* (Berkeley and

Los Angeles: University of California Press, 1972). On Innocent III, see Helene Tillmann, *Innocent III* (New York: North Holland, 1980).

There are a number of good introductions to the topic of the religious life of the laity in medieval Europe: Bernard Hamilton, *Religion in the Medieval West* (London and Baltimore: Edward Arnold, 1986) offers a handy survey of doctrine, institutions, and the life of ordinary Christians. Rosalind and Christopher Brooke, *Popular Religion and the Middle Ages* (London and New York: Thames and Hudson, 1984) discusses a variety of popular religious practices. Benedicta Ward, *Miracles and the Medieval Mind: Theory Record, and Event, 1000–1215* (Philadelphia: University of Pennsylvania Press, 1982) is a detailed and enlightening study of one category of devotion. Jacques Le Goff, *The Birth of Purgatory* (Chicago: University of Chicago Press, 1984), studies another. The lively work by R. A. Fletcher, *Saint James's Catapult* (Oxford: Clarendon Press, 1984) deals with pilgrimages generally and particularly with those to Compostela. Patrick Geary, *Furta Sacra: The Theft of Relics in the Central Middle Ages* (Princeton: Princeton University Press, 1978) studies a particular aspect of devotion and economics. On marriage, see Christopher Brooke, *The Medieval Idea of Marriage* (Oxford: Oxford University Press, 1988).

On one important aspect of the relationship between the spiritual and the social identity, see Joseph Lynch, *Godparents and Kinship in Early Medieval Europe* (Princeton, NJ: Princeton University Press, 1986).

On dissent and heresy, see the extensive references and texts in Edward Peters, *Heresy and Authority in Medieval Europe* (Philadelphia: University of Pennsylvania Press, 1980). There are good discussions in R. I. Moore, *The Birth of Popular Heresy* (New York: St. Martin's Press, 1975); R. I. Moore, *The Origins of European Dissent* (New York: St. Martin's Press, 1977 2nd ed.); Malcolm Lambert, *Medieval Heresy* (New York: Holmes & Meier, 1977 Oxford-New York: Blackwell, 1995). An excellent detailed study is Walter L. Wakefield, *Heresy, Crusade and Inquisition in Southern France, 1100–1250* (Berkeley and Los Angeles: University of California Press, 1975).

On the Mendicant Orders, see Rosalind B. Brooke, *The Coming of the Friars* (New York: Barnes & Noble, 1975).

The problem of new forms of coercion has been taken up in different ways in Edward Peters, *Inquisition* (New York: Free Press, 1988), and R. I. Moore, *The Formation of a Persecuting Society* (Oxford: Basil Blackwell, 1987). A regional study of high quality is that of Richard Kieckhefer, *Repression of Heresy in Medieval Germany* (Philadelphia: University of Pennsylvania Press, 1979). On various other uses of the Crusades, see Benjamin Z. Kedar, *Crusade and Mission* (Princeton, NJ: Princeton University Press, 1984), and, on papal diplomacy, see James M. Muldoon, *Popes, Lawyers, and Infidels* (Philadelphia: University of Pennsylvania Press, 1979).

On the Jews in Europe, see the General Bibliography, under Judaism.

15

THE POLITICAL CULTURE
OF CHRISTIAN EUROPE

THE POLITICAL COMMUNITY

The "history" of modern states is often extended backwards in time to remote periods and based on an idea of the political community that was developed only in the nineteenth and twentieth centuries. The main components of modern political societies are continuity in space and time (and the memory of these in geography and history), community of language, impersonal institutions of governance and the impersonal loyalty of subjects and citizens, political sovereignty, and the various aspects (some nonpolitical) of ethnicity or "national consciousness." Neither nationalism nor the modern sovereign state appeared in the twelfth and thirteenth centuries, but some extremely important elements of them did. These were strengthened over the enormous span of time in which European political communities could develop without massive outside interference. Such diverse elements of a political community as the awareness of a common history and language, uncritical loyalty to a legitimate ruler, and even the common notion of being subject to a king coalesced with the claims of kings and helped to identify kingship with the idea of the state. The mobilization of state resources, a general test of modern states, occurred on a far smaller scale and for shorter periods of time in medieval polities. The concept of patriotism and, conversely, that of a state with resources so great that universal coercion was possible for its rulers were both far in the future. The words *politics, polity,* and *policy* appeared in most Western languages in the late thirteenth and fourteenth centuries, but it took them a long time to become part of people's common vocabulary.

By the end of the tenth century the older tribes, war bands, *gentes,* and *populi* of early medieval society had virtually disappeared as political societies. The idea of a single Christian people, the *populus Christianus,* one of the legacies of the age of Charlemagne, still survived, and both popes and emperors claimed certain ordinary governmental rights (and at the very least a kind of honorific preeminence) in respect to it. But neither the regional principalities nor a universal Christian society constituted the dominant political forms of Europe between the twelfth and the fourteenth centuries. That distinction was reserved for the city-republics, especially those of northern Italy, and the territorial monarchies of England, France, Sicily, and the Iberian peninsula, which emerged with a new kind of political culture. Apart from these examples of early development and failure, some kingdoms simply disappeared, as did the old Carolingian Middle Kingdom and Burgundy, which was absorbed into the Roman Empire. Other kingdoms, many of them much smaller and with fewer resources, survived vigorously into early modern times. A good example is Scotland, which developed strong national feelings in spite of its relative size and weakness in comparison with England or France.

For much of the twelfth century, such great territorial principalities as Normandy, Lorraine, Bavaria, Poitou, Flanders, and Champagne remained strong and proved indigestible to centralizing monarchies. This is but one indication that the road from medieval monarchy to modern nation-state was long and difficult. The transformation was not inevitable. In the examples considered in the rest of this chapter, which focuses on kings and their servants, the two streams—political and nonpolitical—in the evolution of a political society should be kept in mind. For only by developing monarchical power on the one hand, and on the other a collective consciousness of belonging to a political community on the part of a widening circle of classes and individuals, did the medieval kingdom lay the foundations of the modern state.

Early European states also developed with one further key element. In spite of the strength of arguments on behalf of monarchical power—whether of emperors, kings, or popes—a second major theme was the theme of law. However autocratic many early European rulers might seem in practice, and however much they seem to have used what we would call public resources to further dynastic and personal ends, no ruler professed to rule without the law. Even in cases where lawyers argued that "the Prince is above the law," or "what pleases the Prince has the force of law," they usually referred only to the positive law that the rulers themselves had made. But no ruler could fail to be subject to the law of nature, divine law, and even in some areas, custom. If law and lawfullness was one of the supports of monarchical authority, it was also, perhaps paradoxically, one of its great checks.

The twin developments of monarchical authority and the rule of law shaped early European political culture. In them lay the kernel of both power and individual rights. In the twelfth and thirteenth centuries an old political order was transformed into a new one.

THE OLD ORDER: PAPACY AND EMPIRE

The Concordat of Worms of 1122, the First Lateran Council of 1123, the death of Pope Calixtus II in 1124, and the death of the emperor Henry V in 1125 brought to a close several aspects of the Investiture Conflict and inaugurated a new stage in the relationship between popes and emperors. The Investiture Conflict had generated a large literature of political theory and propaganda, most of it supporting or attacking the claims of popes or emperors to supremacy within Christendom. In the course of the conflict, the old Carolingian-Ottonian imperial ideal was defeated. Theorists of papal authority transformed the figure of the pope from the chief liturgical officer of the holy city of Rome to a legitimate constitutional authority supreme in many respects over all other Christian powers. Although new claims for and against papal or imperial authority were made for the next century, the rivalry between the two became a less significant focus of political theory and discussion. After the mid–thirteenth century, the old polarity between papacy and empire gave way to a consideration of the rights and powers of princes, city-republics, and territorial monarchies, even against the rights of popes and emperors themselves. By the late thirteenth century a new political order, one that considered the respective spheres of authority of popes and territorial monarchies and republics, had become the framework of European political culture.

We have already traced some of the routes by which the papacy of the period 1000–1300 was transformed from an institution of the early Middle Ages into a juridical and constitutional authority. Supported by canon law and the formal study of theology, this new papacy extended its claims to legitimacy throughout Christendom. It controlled a vast system of ecclesiastical provinces and institutions, was increasingly well financed, and balanced its legal supremacy with its liturgical powers. At the highest levels of Christian society, no imperial claims could match the combination of articulate claims made on behalf of the pope as the leader and in some ways the personal embodiment of the Christian Church and society. But the redefinition of the legal and constitutional authority of the papacy, as well as its new style of administration, governance, and diplomacy, cost it must of its popular appeal. Earlier popes had been numbered among the fathers of the Church. They were widely revered, chiefly on the grounds that they were holy men and teachers of their people, guardians of the tombs and relics of Peter and Paul, high priests of the holy city of Rome, and mediators between God and the Christian people. By the mid–twelfth century, though, supporters of the papacy were complaining about the pressing routine of legal and financial business that took up the popes' time and attention. Even Bernard of Clairvaux complained to his protegé, Pope Eugenius III (1145–1153), that papal piety seemed to be giving way to papal administration. Dissident movements also complained about the new institutional character of the Church, as did literary satirists, whose stinging verses accused the popes of venality, hunger for power, and neglect of their holy office. Few popes between the mid–eleventh and late thirteenth centuries were regarded as saints after their deaths.

Although the popes of this period were no less devout and no less concerned about the spiritual welfare of Christian society than their predecessors had been, the demands made upon them were very different from those of an earlier period. As the social and political structures of European society had changed, so too had the concept of the Church and the expectations people had of its leaders. Many of those who complained the loudest about the "new Pharisees" of Rome also flooded the Roman curia with legal appeals, petitioned it for office and placement, and became its official theologians, lawyers, tax collectors, and administrators. The last major phase of the conflict between empire and papacy, then, saw a different kind of papal office on one side of the polarity.

The imperial office also changed during the later part of the struggle. The emperors of the Romans were also the kings of Germany, and the Investiture Conflict had revealed that the two offices were not as separate in fact as they might be in theory. The needs of the kingdom of Germany colored both the functions of the imperial office in the later twelfth and thirteenth centuries and the policy of the kings of Germany, emperors of the Romans. Although much of the earlier prestige and memory of the emperors from Charlemagne to Henry V survived in imperial policy and propaganda, the actual facts of imperial rule changed nearly as much as the actual problems of papal governance.

Let us recall some characteristics of the German monarchy and the imperial office in order to clarify the changes in both during the twelfth century. In an age when the physical presence of the king counted for much, the very size of Germany, five or six times that of England, meant that the king of Germany had to be constantly on the move. Tracing the itineraries of these rulers is an important part of the historian's work, not only because the itineraries reveal how often and how extensively the kings traveled, but *where* they could travel, where they had enough personal property or loyal subjects to afford them hospitality. The kings of Germany relied on their personal wealth to pay the costs of governing the kingdom. This wealth, usually in land, was not distributed evenly throughout the kingdom. In some areas, notably the eastern borders of Saxony, nobles had opened up extensive lands in which the kings had never possessed any property or claims at all, and thus were virtually excluded from visiting. The limits on royal resources left the German kings two sources of support: the royal ministerials and the local church and aristocracy.

The ministerials were unfree knights who administered royal property. Like the lowborn royal servants of the kings of England and France, they tended to rise into the local nobility as time went on. In order to control them efficiently, the German kings would have had to possess a sophisticated system of supervision, but they were never able to develop one. What some historians have called the "low intensity" of the Germany monarchy meant that kings rarely had systematic or efficient communications with, or effective control over, their local servants. The German aristocracy, unlike the aristocracy of England and France, possessed extensive lands that it owned privately and therefore did not hold from the kings. Most of the aristocracy's power base was out of the king's reach, and many nobles had no need even of nominal contact with the king. One way for the kings to achieve some control over the aristocrats was to give them lands that carried obligations of service, but many families were reluctant to accept these. Even when they did, they tended to merge the new lands with lands they already owned privately. Indeed, dynastic territory-building characterized many noble German families in the twelfth century. Even the old tribal duchies, while retaining their former names, became the territories of princely families in the twelfth century and bore little resemblance to what they had been before.

Ultimately, the kings of Germany had to leave a great deal of power in the hands of the higher aristocracy, upon whose alliances they depended. This necessity, coupled with the expansion of German power to the east, created a powerful class of princes who effectively governed their smaller territories and expanded their lands into areas in which the kings had less and less authority. The best example of this aristocratic independence is the famous *Drang nach Osten,* the "push to the East," which developed steadily in the twelfth and thirteenth centuries, but under the direction of the princes, not the kings.

The long history of northern Germany as a base for territorial expansion to the east and or missionary efforts to convert pagan Scandinavians, Balts, and Slavs is the main political and cultural theme of northern European history from the tenth to the fifteenth century. With the foundation of the archbishopric of Lund in 1108, Scandinavian Christians developed an independent ecclesiastical center, free of German episcopal control. The German bishoprics of Magdeburg, Bamberg, and Hamburg-Bremen all launched missionary efforts in pagan Slavic lands, sometimes creating friction with the Christian Slavic kingdoms of Poland and Bohemia. In 1147 Bernard of Clairvaux obtained papal permission for German Crusaders to battle the pagan Wends in Central Europe instead of going to Jerusalem.

Warriors followed missionaries, as did merchants and settlers. The expanding population of western Europe permitted not only the internal colonization of older territories but expansion into new ones. The Cistercian monks were particularly zealous in settling remote lands. The founding of Lübeck in 1158/1159, the development of a community of merchants in Gotland during the twelfth century, the success of Albert, bishop of Livonia (1199–1229), in founding bishoprics and monastic orders in the newly conquered lands and establishing military orders to support them, and the territorial ambitions of

Henry the Lion, duke of Saxony and Bavaria, and the margraves of Branden-burg furthered the expansion. By the early thirteenth century, trade was flour-ishing in the North Sea, the Baltic Sea, and the Rhine Valley. This trade linked England, the Low Countries, Denmark, Sweden, the towns along the Baltic coast, and Novgorod in northern Russia. The economic developments attend-ing this trade, the growth of towns along the Baltic shore, and the large markets of Poland and Russia underwrote the great financial cost of the new German ex-pansion and colonization.

In 1226 the Teutonic Knights, one of the many military orders in the Holy Land, moved to northeastern Germany, where, with the support of Em-peror Frederick II and under the leadership of the Grand Master Hermann von Salza, they conquered and occupied Prussia. In 1236 the Knights incorporated the Livonian orders, and from the mid-thirteenth century on they governed Prussia and pushed frequently into Poland and Russia. In 1309 the city of Marienburg became their headquarters and the seat of the grand master.

The military aspect of German eastward expansion was not dominant everywhere, nor did conquest allow the mass immigration of German settlers. Migration and settlement were more often peaceful than forceful, and the com-petition for settlers was brisk among lords of all sorts. By the thirteenth century a specialized group of men known as *locatores* were organizing movements of set-tlers in western Europe and being rewarded with privileges in the new settle-ments. By the end of that century the balance of wealth and political power in Germany had shifted from its Rhineland origins far to the east. This movement was signaled by the rise in power of the King of Bohemia, the growth of Prussia, the influence of Cistercian institutions and ideas on eastern Germany, and the rapidly growing wealth of the Baltic and Rhenish cities and the city-foundations of Danzig, Riga, and Breslau. The rise of the Bohemian and Polish kingdoms and the eastward expansion of Germans during the twelfth and thirteenth centuries was thus a complex process, one that has far more political and economic char-acteristics than ethnic or racial ones. Dynastic difficulties and a limited economy, more than German hostility or influence, contributed to the weakening of the Polish Piast dynasty in the thirteenth century and the growing local Bohemian resistance to the Premyslid dynasty in the fourteenth century.

A second difficulty—perhaps less initially important than the conse-quences of dynastic territory-building—was the constitutional problem of elec-tion versus dynastic succession in the kingship. In spite of the electoral character of the early East Frankish monarchy, the Saxon and Salian dynasties had estab-lished the facts, if not the principle, of dynastic succession of son to father in the kingship. The death of Henry V without an heir in 1125, however, permitted the great nobility and clergy to decide between two particularly powerful families, the Staufer and the Welfs. Their choice of the Welf-sponsored candidate Lothar III (1125–1137) suggests that the electoral principle was becoming more active, as did the election of Conrad III (1138–1152), a Staufer, after the death of

Lothar. The elections of 1125 and 1138 appear to have been an attempt on the part of the higher lay and clerical nobility to balance the power of two great families that themselves were rivals on other fronts as well.

The election of Frederick I Barbarossa (1152–1190), who had both Welf and Staufer blood, appears to have been a compromise designed to satisfy both dynasties. Moreover, the electoral process now came to mean that the elected king had to make compromises with his electors in matters of property, privilege, and even usurped rights. The electoral principle may have been less dangerous as a "constitutional" principle than it was as a practical means of the ambitious territorial nobility's assuring itself that royal power could not be used to dislodge it from its expanded possessions and powers. The rivalry between the Welf and Staufer families endured long after the election of Frederick Barbarossa, coloring Barbarossa's long reign, and influencing royal politics and papal relations into the first quarter of the thirteenth century. It was a large-scale echo of other family rivalries that marked German aristocratic society through the thirteenth century.

The imperial title gave the German kings opportunities to exploit territorial and financial resources in Burgundy and Italy, which were not available to them as kings only of Germany. The reign of Frederick Barbarossa suggests how skillfully (although with only limited success) the imperial title might increase the resources of the German monarchy. Because Barbarossa needed the financial resources of the northern Italian cities, he boldly asserted his imperial rights, not only claiming the Saxon and Salian traditions of imperial rule but also invoking Roman law and Roman history. These imperial claims encountered stiff opposition from the independent Italian cities, which formed the Lombard League against him in 1167, and from the popes, particularly Alexander III (1159–1181). Barbarossa had to compromise with both forces at the Peace of Venice in 1177 and later at the Peace of Constance in 1183. Barbarossa also attempted to forestall the growth of some of his aristocratic opponents, particularly Henry the Lion, duke of Bavaria and Saxony. By allying himself with other nobles, enriching them, and enhancing their power, Barbarossa succeeded in destroying the vast power of Henry the Lion, but even this triumph resulted in the emperor's recognition of the growing power of the German princes. Although Barbarossa kept control over the German church, one of the chief resources of the monarchy, here too the aristocracy began to acquire considerable authority during his reign.

In 1186 Barbarossa's son, Henry VI married Constance, heiress to the kingdom of Sicily. When Barbarossa died in 1190 on a Crusade to Jerusalem, Henry VI succeeded him in Germany, as emperor of the Romans, and, in his wife's right, as king of Sicily. Although Sicily proved a difficult kingdom to govern, it promised the German kings precisely that base of financial and military power that had largely eluded them in Germany and northern Italy. But the death of Henry VI in 1197 plunged Germany, Italy, and Sicily into a succession

Medieval Germany and Italy.

crisis. Henry left a three-year-old son, Frederick II, to succeed him, but Frederick's minority and the unleashing of rival forces in Germany and northern Italy and Sicily plunged both royal offices and the imperial office into chaos.

In 1198 a Welf-dominated electorate chose Otto IV as king. Otto was the son of Barbarossa's old enemy, Henry the Lion. Supporters of the Staufer dynasty revolted, and for ten years the political worlds of Germany, Sicily, and Italy were plunged into discord. In 1201 Pope Innocent III recognized Otto's election, thus drawing the papacy into the dynastic struggles around the German crown.

The growing ambitions of Otto troubled the peace of Italy and the empire virtually from the moment of his imperial coronation in 1209. When, contrary to his promise, Otto's forces crossed into the Sicilian kingdom in 1210, Pope Innocent III excommunicated the emperor. Pope Innocent, with the cooperation of some of the princes in Germany, then approved the candidacy of his ward, Frederick II, son of Henry VI and insecure ruler of the beleaguered kingdom of Sicily. Frederick quickly traveled to Germany, rallied more support, and was crowned king at Mainz at the end of 1212. In 1213, with the consent of the German princes, Frederick issued the Golden Bull of Eger, in which he confirmed the autonomy of the papal states, echoed promises made earlier by Otto IV, and gave up those rights in the selection of bishops and abbots that the Crown had retained in the Concordat of Worms.

Otto IV was defeated by the king of France, Philip Augustus, at the battle of Bouvines in 1214 and was formally deposed in 1215. He died in 1218. After promising to keep the German and Sicilian kingdoms separate, Frederick II was crowned emperor of the Romans at Rome in November 1220.

Frederick's insecure boyhood in Sicily and the difficulties of restoring order to the old Norman kingdom posed severe difficulties, and from 1220 on, the emperor directed his immense energies and considerable talents to the restoration of the southern kingdom. Frederick founded the University of Naples in 1224, chiefly to provide his kingdom with the scholars and administrators he needed. Naples was the first university to be established purely out of monarchical interest. In 1231 Frederick issued a remarkable law code for his Sicilian kingdom, the *Constitutions of Melfi*. With the issuance of this document, the development of a strong military and naval force, the recruitment of able administrators, and the imposition of a sound and efficient financial system, Frederick II shaped the kingdom of Sicily and South Italy into the most thoroughly governed, secularized state in Europe within little more than a decade. A symbol of this achievement was Frederick's striking of gold coinage—the magnificent *Augustalis*—in 1232, the first gold coinage struck in Europe since the early ninth century.

Frederick's spirit of adventurous calculation is also reflected in his crusading policies. Although he had agreed to go on Crusade, Frederick was forced to postpone the expedition several times, and in 1227, when he had to postpone it because of illness, Pope Gregory IX (1227–1241) excommunicated him. Undaunted, Frederick sailed to Jerusalem the next year and won a remarkable treaty with the sultan al-Kamil of Egypt in 1229. According to the treaty's terms, the holy sites of Jerusalem, Bethlehem, and Nazareth, along with a strip of coastal territory and certain other rights in the city of Jerusalem, were ceded to Frederick. The excommunicated emperor had won more rights in the Holy Land than any other crusader in the past century. The dissension between the pope and the crusading emperor, however, became one of the elements that helped to mute the ideal of the Crusade in western European thought.

Relations between pope and emperor continued to deteriorate, and Frederick's concentration on South Italy and Sicily weakened his power in Germany and led the papacy to forge alliances with the Lombard cities of northern Italy, who also felt their autonomy threatened by Frederick's energies and ambitions in the south. In addition to these political circumstances, Frederick's own royal style tended to cost him sympathy in the north. This splendid court and life in Sicily and South Italy appeared alien and exotic both to Germans and to the citizens of the northern Italian towns. The emperor surrounded himself with immense wealth and splendor, ranging from Muslim bodyguards and a multiethnic court population to the imperial zoo with its elephants and other strange beasts.

Frederick gave wide rein to his considerable intelligence and curiosity. Learned men from all parts of the Mediterranean world—Muslims, Jews, and Christians alike—thronged his court. Michael Scot, a well-known translator of Arabic works and a reputed sorcerer, was Frederick's constant companion. Speaking several languages with ease, Frederick was an integral part of the intellectual life of his court, not merely its pageantry-loving master. He corresponded with the mathematician Leonardo Fibonacci of Pisa. A poet himself, Frederick supported a school of court poets among his courtiers and administrators. So influential was the court poetry of Frederick II and his school that at the end of the century the poet Dante proclaimed Frederick the father of Italian vernacular poetry. A patron of the arts as well, Frederick left a powerful personal legacy throughout South Italy in his castles, public works, and sculptures. Frederick's new golden coins, the *Augustales,* reveal a quality of minting art and a metallic purity of an extraordinarily high character. To his subjects as well as his enemies, Frederick II was a remarkable and enigmatic man who was regarded more in awe and fear than in affection and respect.

Frederick's ambitions in the south led him to make concessions not only to the popes but also to the German princes. In 1220 his *Confederation with the Ecclesiastical Princes* recognized the territorial lordships of the ecclesiastical princes, and in 1232 his *Statute in Favor of the Princes* removed several important imperial rights over the great magnates. Although these concessions were not of vital importance as long as Frederick's personal political power was intact, they became immensely influential after the emperor's death and strongly influenced the growth of virtually independent princely power in Germany from the late thirteenth century on.

In 1237 war broke out between Frederick II and the great northern Italian cities. Although Frederick was initially successful, destroying the Milanese army at the Battle of Cortenuova in that year, Pope Gregory IX, alarmed by his ambitions and victories, excommunicated the emperor for a second time in 1239, and Frederick turned his forces against Rome itself. Gregory died in 1241, and his short-lived successor failed to deflect Frederick's ambitions. But the election of the Genoese canon lawyer Sinibaldo Fieschi as Pope Innocent IV (1243–1254) seemed to indicate a change in imperial-papal relations. A member of a proimperial family, a superb jurist, and a man wholly lacking in what Frederick II considered the irritable majesty and mystical intractability of Gregory IX, Innocent IV appeared to be an ideal candidate for compromise.

Innocent turned out instead to be Frederick's greatest opponent. Turning the full energies of his mind and office against the emperor, Innocent rallied the Lombard cities and Frederick's other enemies. Escaping to the city of Lyons, he called an ecumenical council and announced the excommunication and deposition of the emperor in 1245. Innocent's decretal deposing Frederick, *Ad apostolice,* summed up fully and eloquently the canon-law tradition of papal authority over the emperor. In spite of a battle of pamphlets designed to wear down papal support—and even a series of complaints against Innocent's action by other European rulers—Frederick was unable to overcome Innocent's opposition. He resumed the war in northern Italy in 1248 and even began a march on the city of Lyons in the same year. But military reversals in the Italian campaign prevented Frederick from capturing the pope, and when the emperor died in 1250 the great German-Sicilian polity began to disintegrate.

Frederick's son, Conrad IV (1250–1254), failed to hold his father's inheritance together. The German imperial electors, freed from the power of the Staufer dynasty, turned to non-German candidates for the imperial office. The system of electors reflects the transformation of German aristocratic society in the thirteenth century. The succession crisis of 1198–1215 and the conflict of 1245–1254 between popes and emperors permitted many lords, clerical and lay, great and small, to assume virtually sovereign power over their own territories while holding only a nominal obligation of allegiance to higher authority. After the death of Frederick II, the *Confederation with the Ecclesiastical Princes* and the *Statute in Favor of the Princes* gave the nobility a free hand. Groups of cities formed mutually protective leagues. The Hanseatic League dominated the trade of the Baltic Sea and the North Sea; the Rhenish League and the Swabian League, founded in 1254 and 1331, respectively, dominated western and southern Germany. With local princes and towns increasing their local authority, the power of the nobles whose votes officially elected the king of Germany increased greatly, although the number of official voters was reduced to seven: four lay and three ecclesiastical princes. With the elimination of the Staufer dynasty, the electors turned to candidates who could buy votes or submit to control by the electors.

The papacy, now able to separate Sicily from Germany, formed an alliance with Charles of Anjou, brother of Louis IX of France, promising him the Sicilian crown if Charles could drive the last Staufer, Frederick II's illegitimate son Manfred, out of Italy. At the battle of Benevento in 1266 Manfred's forces were defeated, and Charles of Anjou accepted the crown of South Italy and Sicily. The German electors, with a confusion of imperial candidates, simply left the kingship vacant from 1254 to 1273 and then elected a series of weaker rulers in the late thirteenth and fourteenth centuries. The old order had come to an end.

ENGLAND: FROM ANGEVIN EMPIRE TO ISLAND KINGDOM

The reign of Henry II Plantagenet (1154–1189) illustrates both the building of royal institutions of government and law in England and the wider, less specifically English interests of a continental lord. Henry II's titles reflect the personal empire of an ambitious and fortunate king in the late twelfth century. Henry inherited the county of Anjou from his father Geoffrey in 1149. He became duke of Normandy in 1151. He became duke of Aquitaine as a result of his marriage to Eleanor, heiress to that territory, in 1152. He inherited the throne of England from his mother in 1154. Later in his reign Henry received the title of lord of Ireland from the pope. In addition, Henry held other territories as a vassal of the king of France: He was lord of Maine, Brittany, Touraine, Berry, Poitou, La Marche, Auvergne, Quercy, and Gascony. As king of England in his own right and as vassal of the king of France for the rest of his lands, Henry II assembled a vast personal empire that included the entire western part of what later became France. He ruled territories that extended unbroken from the Scottish border to the Pyrenees.

Henry's father had advised him to permit local customs and governmental institutions to survive, and in fact Henry's different titles and different rights in different parts of his empire prevented him from creating a homogenized state. Nevertheless, he was a talented and ambitious ruler. His judicial and administrative reforms in England and Normandy began the creation of some degree of uniformity between the two most important territories of his empire. Even though he was a vassal of the king of France for much of his territory, Henry treated his relationship casually. On the other hand, he watched his lands like a hawk. He spent twenty-one years of his thirty-four-year reign as king of England on the Continent, and he spent his energies where he spent his time. If Henry had succeeded in establishing his rule on the Continent more securely, and if his sons had been able to hold his territories together, the present-day political maps of France and England might look very different. But Richard I Lion-Heart (1189–1199) and John (1199–1216) could not hold Henry's empire together. Not only did they have personal shortcomings as rulers, but they encountered the stiff and successful opposition of two remarkably able and persistent kings of France, Louis VII (1137–1180) and Philip Augustus (1180–1223). The relations among these five kings from 1154 and 1216 shaped the internal growth of both France and England and defined the territorial sphere of each king's authority.

The story of the growth and disappearance of the Angevin Empire of Henry II is the framework for the political history of England in the twelfth and thirteenth centuries. Within that framework Henry's governmental reforms and King John's formidable political concessions to his nobles transformed the governance of England. At the outset of his reign Henry faced the immense task of reconstructing royal authority in England after the nearly two decades of civil war and political anarchy caused by the succession contest between King Stephen and Henry's mother, Matilda. Royal power had eroded drastically during this period. The English nobles, by changing sides and demanding royal concessions at opportune moments during the conflict, had acquired a degree of independence greater than any the Anglo-Norman aristocracy had enjoyed. In addition, the English church had become involved in the dispute. But with his astute judgment of royal servants, his ruthless drive to impose his authority, and his sophisticated concept of kingly power, Henry reshaped the governance of England and laid the foundations of a new monarchical constitution for the kingdom.

One way of measuring the effects of the anarchy created by the wars between Stephen and Matilda is to note that by 1154, at the outset of Henry II's reign, the royal income had fallen to around ten thousand pounds per year. Not until Henry II's death in 1189 did it attain the level of thirty thousand pounds per year reached in Henry I's reign. In addition, the great magnates who held their lands directly from the king, the tenants in chief, had grown independent between 1135 and 1154. They had also had time to develop a strong hereditary interest in their holdings, regarding their fiefs as a family right that ought to descend to no one but a child of the grantee. These two developments made the Anglo-Norman nobility much more dangerous in 1154 than it had been twenty years earlier, as did the fact that most of the 180 tenants in chief also held lands in Normandy as well as in England. Furthermore, the movement for ecclesiastical independence associated with the Gregorian reform principles came to England early, during the tenure of Anselm as archbishop of Canterbury (1093–1109). During the civil wars of 1135–1154, the English church grew even more independent of royal control.

The royal response to these movements within the nobility and the Church was at first one of concession. In 1153 the Treaty of Winchester recognized certain hereditary rights among tenants in chief and all vassals of the crown. Henry I had earlier tried to maintain control of the Church after the death of Saint Anselm in 1109. But the influence of reform made a strong impact on England, and most of Henry's senior clergy, even though he appointed them from his own household and from ecclesiastical establishments that he patronized, were imbued with reform ideals. During Stephen's reign the Church added a practical degree of independence from the king to the theoretical independence that reform ecclesiology had already given it.

Henry II's first task as king was to establish the rudiments of public order in England. From the outset he insisted on the destruction of unlicensed castles and the curtailment of private warfare. His second problem was that of royal finance. Henry first recovered and then reorganized the income from the lands he ruled directly, the royal demesne. Then he turned his attention to the money due him as overlord of his tenants in chief. He successfully converted the personal military service owed him into scutage—"shield money" paid to the overlord in lieu of this service. Although the costs of war rose rapidly in the second half of the twelfth century, Henry's financial basis for military affairs made him less dependent on the uncertain resources of his vassals. Henry also made selective grants from his own lands in return for payment, and he increased the fees charged to those who collected taxes locally throughout the kingdom. He sold charters to municipal corporations, although he always distrusted cities and their populations. His legal reforms greatly increased the royal income from fines and pardons. Henry also brought more and more judicial business into his own courts, and thereby helped weaken the judicial powers of his vassals. Henry knew well that royal officials might be even more rapacious than the king, and he supervised them closely. In 1170, for example, he held an investigation of sheriffs, dismissing and fining heavily those whom he found either incompetent or excessively greedy.

Henry also developed an institution begun by Henry I. In 1156 his treasury, the Exchequer, was permanently established at Westminster, outside London, and its practices regularized. By the end of Henry's reign the institution was so efficient in keeping accounts of money paid to the king that one of its officials wrote a treatise about its operations, *The Dialogue of the Exchequer,* the first analytical treatise on institutional operation in European history. Henry's reign witnessed another mark of administrative significance. From 1156 on, the records of royal government survive for the most part in unbroken sequence, and for the period 1156–1220 they are very numerous. Henry II's administrators proved to be able and inventive servants of the king. We can trace their work from year-to-year in thousands of documents, whose existence makes the reign of Henry II qualitatively different for study from any previous reign in England or elsewhere.

His finances revamped, regularized and slowly growing, Henry II turned simultaneously to legal and ecclesiastical reforms. Of course, the profits of justice and income from the church were part of the royal finances, and Henry's motives for his reforms in these two areas were financial as well as political. Henry II's legal reforms, however, did not consist simply of restoring to the king those judicial rights that most of his predecessors had possessed and had let slip from their hands. As we have seen, the late twelfth century witnessed changing ideas about law and legal procedure in general, and the revived study of Roman law and the increasing sophistication of canon law also influenced legal reform in England. Occurring when they did, Henry II's legal reforms greatly transformed English law in ways that would have been impossible several decades earlier.

The pattern of English law at the accession of Henry II reflects the pattern of the Conquest. Ancient local courts of shire and hundred (some of which had fallen into the private hands of great laymen or ecclesiastics) existed side-by-side with the banal courts of the Anglo-Norman aristocracy, for with most grants of land from the king had also gone the grant of jurisdiction on that land. Justice was local, and even the king's courts resembled the courts of any lord, dealing only with those matters that touched upon the king's rights as lord. Judges made their decisions according to local custom or on the basis of extremely limited modes of accusation and proof. For any cause it was necessary for one person to accuse another and for the court to decide between the litigants not on the basis of evidence, but on the oath of one or the other or the successful outcome of an ordeal, when the procedure called for one. Such courts and procedures were much more instruments of social consensus and control than rational courts of law. For the most part, they regulated personal relations; they cannot be said to have administered "justice" in any modern sense of the term.

The king's court was like that of any other lord with two exceptions. Because in England the king was everyone's ultimate overlord, and because he was the king, possessing certain extraordinary rights, he had slightly more freedom to claim jurisdiction in some cases than any other lord in England or Normandy. Henry I had begun to exploit these conditions, but it remained for Henry II to make a major transformation in the law of the land. In 1166 Henry II issued a set of instructions to a group of royal judges about to set out on a tour of the kingdom. These instructions, the *Assizes of Clarendon,* are a landmark in English law and reflect the knowledge of the law that Henry and his servants had acquired during his twelve years as king of England. The *Assizes of Clarendon* and other enactments of Henry's reign greatly increased the number of offenses that had to be tried in the king's own courts. In this way Henry II brought a great deal of criminal law under his own jurisdiction. Moreover, he required that a local group of landholders in each locality publicly testify under oath as to the criminal activities in their district since the last visit of the royal justices. This finding jury, the predecessor of the modern grand jury, removed the necessity of a private person's having to bring an accusation against a criminal and put the burden of supervising the peace on the community itself.

The legal procedures that Henry II developed for the courts of royal demesne became models of superior efficiency and lesser cost to litigants. By emphasizing the rights of royal officials in shire courts, Henry associated these courts with the procedures in effect in the courts of the royal demesne. This slow legal revolution tended to homogenize the law of the two kinds of courts and constituted the basis of what later came to be called the *Common Law of*

England. By the end of the twelfth century, a royal justice named Ranulf de Glanvill found English law to have become sufficiently rational and systematic that he wrote a treatise *On the Laws and Customs of England.* Like the *Dialogue of the Exchequer,* Glanvill's treatise—and the superior treatise of the same title attributed to Henry De Bracton in the thirteenth century—reflects the systematization of one of the most important social institutions of twelfth-century England. The large numbers of royal personnel who had to administer English law also testifies to the institutional importance of the laws, as does the establishment of a permanent Exchequer office in Westminster in 1156 and the settling of the Court of Common Pleas at Westminster in 1178. The court of Henry II, like that of the kings of Germany, was largely itinerant, and the placement of these two institutions in a permanent home indicated that the character of monarchical government was in an important process of transformation. Soon the kings themselves would cease to travel and would rule from a capital city.

Not all of Henry's high officials proved as docile as Ranulf de Glanvill and the author of the *Dialogue of the Exchequer.* Thomas Becket, the son of a landowning knight of London, attended the schools of Paris and entered the service of Archbishop Theobald of Canterbury, where he rose quickly to a position of prominence. When Henry II ascended the English throne he made Becket his chancellor and then archbishop of Canterbury. But Becket proved to be more devoted as a churchman than a king's servant. He experienced years of exile between 1164 and 1170 and earned Henry's hostility for his refusal to conform the English church to the king's legal reforms. In 1170 Becket was assassinated by four of Henry's knights, although without Henry's knowledge or approval. Henry undertook a severe penance for the murder, but his reform legislation overcame both Becket's opposition and the immense popularity of the cult that formed around his martyrdom and sainthood.

Henry's sons nearly ruined their father's work. Richard devoted himself to continental affairs, to the Crusade of 1187, and to his rivalry with Philip Augustus of France. In Richard's prolonged absences from the kingdom, however, the real strengths of Angevin governance became apparent. The busy, loyal agents who governed England in the king's absence developed the institutional character of English governance considerably. Richard's brother and successor, John, was energetic and intelligent, but a bad general and a tactless and capricious king. John also had the misfortune to lose much of England's continental possessions to Philip Augustus, including Normandy in 1204, thereby giving his barons an immediate reason for opposing the king such as they had not had since the days of Stephen and Matilda. To make matters worse, John's interference in the election of the archbishop of Canterbury in 1206 permitted Pope Innocent III to intervene and choose Stephen Langton, a brilliant and popular theologian at the University of Paris. When John refused to accept Langton, Innocent placed England under an interdict—an ecclesiastical discipline imposed on a region. While the interdict was in force, from 1208 to 1213, few religious services were permitted and Christian life was publicly suspended.

Having alienated his barons by the loss of Normandy and the pope by his rejection of Langton, John brought further difficulties on himself by his rapacious attempts to raise money for the recapture of Normandy. When John's allies were defeated at the Battle of Bouvines in 1214 the barons turned against John and, in 1215 on the field of Runnymede, forced him to issue a charter of privileges that promised to restrain the most offensive features of Angevin governance. The Great Charter, Magna Carta, was surely no Declaration of Independence, and it proved offensive to the pope, to whom John had given England in 1213. In its sixty-three clauses, however, even those dealing with technical problems of lordly rights, it is possible to discern some important principles. Subjects must be allowed to enjoy their customary liberties in peace; government might be hard, but it must not be capricious, and it must use regular procedures in collecting taxes and administering justice. In short, the king must be consistent, and he must recognize the myriad rights and liberties of his greater subjects. If he was not yet under law, he was now under custom. Although Angevin-style governance was not destroyed, it was brought face-to-face with principles that rendered its most offensive aspects less harsh.

John was succeeded by his young son Henry III (1216–1272), during whose long minority control of the government was disputed by great barons and papal legates. When Henry came of age he proved to be an ambitious but incompetent ruler. The public servants of the crown became more efficient, and the king took lower-ranking nobles into his service and extended his governance deep into the countryside. But the very efficiency of Henry's government and his use of low- or continental-born servants outraged many of England's great nobles. Their response went much further than that of their predecessors at Runnymede; they forced the king to accept the Provisions of Oxford of 1258, which permitted royal governance to be controlled by groups of barons. Disputes between the king and the barons led to the intervention of Louis IX of France in favor of Henry III, but the barons, led by Simon de Montfort, rebelled and captured the king at the Battle of Lewes in 1264. A year later, however, Henry triumphed over the rebels at the Battle of Evesham and reasserted the king's supremacy in governance. Henry was succeeded by his son Edward I (1272–1307), one of the strongest English kings. Edward took Wales, fought in Scotland, developed the few continental possessions left to the English king, and systematically enforced the royal common law of the land. He continually investigated baronial titles to jurisdiction and restricted the acquisition of land by the Church.

By stressing the law, rather than royal whim, as the test of rights and liberties, Edward greatly strengthened the political order of England. He continued Simon de Montfort's innovative practice of calling a Parliament—an assembly made up of two knights from every shire and two burghers from every town—to learn of the king's business and assent to his actions. These assemblies had roots in the full sessions of the royal court, which had been held from the twelfth century on. At first Parliament met to give the king advice and to approve royal requests for taxation, but it was also the highest court in the kingdom, and it taught its members something about their common interests, sometimes against the wishes of the king. In the end, the reigns of Henry III and Edward I led England out of the difficulties created by the Angevin style of governance without capitulating to the self-interest of the great nobles or depending on individual royal whim. Perhaps the phrase that best expresses the character of English governance in the thirteenth century is one that the people of that century invented: "the community of the realm."

The concept of the community of the realm is not as precise as that of the nation-state, but it accurately reflected the results of the innovations of Henry II and the crises under Henry III and Edward I. The scattered communities of early-twelfth-century England had been forced into what some historians called "self-governance at the king's command." Royal justices sat and administered the same law in all parts of the kingdom. Representatives of boroughs and knights of the shires attended Parliament, which was both a court and a representative assembly of the politically aware and financially responsible subjects of the king. In England the law was the medium through which the king and his subjects arrived at definitions of their respective rights and responsibilities. Together, below the law, they constituted the community of the realm. That unique constitutional creation had been shaped by shrewd and greedy kings out of the rough mix of tradition and autocracy that survived the eleventh century. The association of local communal consciousness with a national monarchy was the great result of the Angevin experiment.

THE IBERIAN PENINSULA

Twelfth-century Iberian Christian rulers were able to continue expanding southward, although at a slower rate. Sometimes they had remarkable success. Alfonso I of Aragon and Navarre (1104–1134) had to face both civil wars and the Almoravids, but he managed to capture several important towns in a series of able campaigns. In 1118, with help from southern France, he captured Saragossa. In 1119 Tarragona fell to him, and in 1120 Calatayud. This continued expansion and consolidation of territories already conquered created in Iberia a tough, highly mobile frontier society that developed differently from societies in England and France.

In 1229 James the First of Aragon captured Majorca and the other Balearic Islands. In 1236 Ferdinand III of Castile captured Córdoba. In 1238 James captured Valencia, and in 1247 Ferdinand captured Seville. By 1247 only the Nasrid kingdom of Granada was left under direct Muslim rule, protected by its contacts with the strong Moroccan kingdom and the many enclaves of Muslim power and population in reconquered Christian Spain. By the middle of the thirteenth century the *reconquista* was nearly complete. The remaining Christian triumphs extended over two centuries—the capture of Algeciras in 1344 and the capture of Granada itself in 1492.

The *reconquista* was attended everywhere by two problems—a shortage of people for repopulation and the need of the kings for money to finance their long and often costly campaigns. Apart from these common problems Castile and Aragon produced very different political cultures, and it is worth taking a look at how they developed.

The development of Christian kingdoms on the Iberian peninsula may be seen as a result of the ways in which land was conquered and became available for settlement and governance and the particular characteristics of Iberian societies. Almoravid power lasted in Spain until the 1140s, when another Muslim sect, the Almohades, invaded the peninsula. They remained the dominant force in Islamic Spain until the Christian victory at Las Navas de Tolosa in 1212. With this battle Muslim power in Spain was broken, except in the south, and Iberian society began to develop its distinctive forms.

In Castile the powers of the warrior aristocracy and the privileged towns and associations of sheepherders grew great at the expense of both large-scale agriculture and commercial trade. The kings of Castile, lacking a permanent administrative class of servants, were subject to a rebellious aristocracy and an ambitious church. They did control the *Cortes,* the representative assembly that had met since 1188, and occasionally succeeded in demonstrating potentially extensive power. Alfonso X El Sabio (1252–1284), for example, issued elaborate and ambitious codes of law, patronized a cultural revival, and offered himself as a candidate for the imperial title. But his reign ended in succession quarrels, and once again the privileged aristocracy and the economically underdeveloped countryside and towns failed to provide a workable basis for political centralization.

In spite of Aragon's expansion into the Mediterranean, to Sicily, and even to Greece and the Levant in the fourteenth century, its nobility and townspeople regularly opposed the king, limited royal authority severely, and defended their local immunities and customs. Two institutions in particular limited the authority of the king. The office of *justicia,* created in 1265, was a legal mediator between the nobility and the king of Aragon. The *Cortes* of Aragon, unlike that of Castile, also limited royal authority. Such restraints on the ruler constituted an important aspect of early European political culture.

Political instability, succession crises, and economic disorder plagued the Iberian kingdoms in the fourteenth and fifteenth centuries. However, the small frontier principalities in the northern part of the peninsula that had set out to "reconquer" Iberia from the Muslims in the eighth century had managed to create large, generally prosperous kingdoms. Under the banner of *reconquista* these kingdoms slowly became diverse political communities possessing the most complex ethnic and historical legacy in Europe.

THE MOST CHRISTIAN KINGS OF FRANCE, 1108–1328

At the beginning of the twelfth century France was a large kingdom in theory but a small and poor one in fact. Although the kings of France were technically the overlords of the great territorial princes whose vast, thoroughly governed domains surrounded the small royal domain in the Ile de France—the dukes of Normandy and Burgundy and the counts of Anjou, Blois and Chartres, Champagne, and Flanders—their overlordship was usually recognized as a mere formality; most of their reigns were spent trying to impose order on their tiny personal territories. Unlike the kings of England (who, as Dukes of Normandy, were among their most powerful and troublesome vassals), the kings of France possessed no land that they ruled directly outside the small royal domain; they controlled the appointment of few bishops and abbots outside the royal domain; and their courts were peopled by their own local vassals. Few signatures of powerful lords from the south, west, or east of the kingdom appear on royal documents from the eleventh or twelfth centuries. The best-known image of this diminished royalty is the remark said to have been made by King Louis VII when someone praised the great wealth of Henry II of England: "Now in France, we have only bread and wine and our heart's desire."

At the end of the thirteenth century France was the largest, wealthiest, and most thoroughly governed monarchical state in Europe. Its king contended successfully with the pope and ruled directly a state that was forty times larger than it had been in 1100. Royal officials and relatives ruled most of the old territorial principalities; of the vast holdings of the Angevin Empire only Gascony remained in the hands of the king of England. The city of Paris was an international center of learning and culture, and the kings of France had made it the first capital in modern political history. Toward the end of the thirteenth century, the lawyer Jean de Blanot proudly recognized that the king of France had come to possess qualities that had hitherto been attributed to the Roman emperor: "The king of France is emperor in his own kingdom, for he recognizes no superior in temporal affairs." By the end of the century the king of France was indeed emperor in his own kingdom, ruling from a rich capital over a talented and energetic provincial administration, possessing most specialized instruments of governance, and, in spite of his conflict with papacy, recognized by a title that set him off from all other kings and even the emperor: He was the "most Christian king," ruling a people universally regarded as defenders of the true faith. The bond between king and people in this most Christian kingdom was as strong as that reflected in the English phrase "community of the realm." The great transformation of the kingdom of France was the result of seven generations of hardworking kings and their servants, the particular configuration of

French provincial governments and centers of power, and the rivalry between the kings of France and their powerful vassals who were also the troublesome kings of England.

The reign of Louis VI (1108–1137) illustrates both the limited power and rudimentary governmental institutions of the early kingdom of France and some characteristic features of royal policy. Louis struggled chiefly to make his authority recognized throughout the Ile de France, a land full of independent warlords living in virtually impregnable towers and owing no allegiance to anyone. Louis's household was ruled by the great officers whose titles ran back to Carolingian Europe: the seneschal, chancellor, butler, chamberlain, and constable. These offices were hereditary in great local families, and the men who held them controlled the local royal administrators, the *prévots*. Such a system had more ceremonial value than practical effectiveness, however, and Louis relied on two other aspects of his authority much more heavily: cooperation with the Church and unremitting warfare within the royal domain. By claiming to be a defender of the Church Louis preserved his own interests and invoked growing ecclesiastical support, witnessed by Abbot Suger's biography of him as a saintly defender of the faith.

The work of pacifying the royal domain and continuing the association between the king and the clergy was brilliantly accomplished by Louis VII (1137–1180) who also greatly increased the financial resources of the king and began to make royal authority directly felt outside the royal domain. Louis's patronage of the monastery of St. Denis and its abbot, Suger, gained the monarchy a strong source of support. Louis VII also made frequent expeditions outside the domain in order to defend ecclesiastical establishments elsewhere. As a result he acquired as fiefs several important ecclesiastical holdings, and several lay lords as well formally recognized his overlordship. Louis's role as a defender of the Church was reflected in his reputation as a crusader, for although the Second Crusade (1147/48) covered no one with glory, the portrait of Louis that emerges from Odo of Deuil's *Journey of Louis VII to the Orient* is an admiring one. Louis also helped protect Pope Alexander III from the emperor Frederick Barbarossa.

Besides supporting the Church and receiving its support in turn, Louis began to develop Paris as the royal capital. He gave privileges to the Paris shipping merchants. (Their seal, bearing the picture of a ship, is still the official seal of the city.) Although Louis ruled the rest of the royal domain by the old system of household officers and *prévots,* he defined the powers of officeholders more sharply toward the end of his reign. By then he had increased his income to sixty thousand pounds per year, making himself the wealthiest territorial prince in the kingdom. Although Louis used no administrative institutions outside the royal domain, his presence as king was felt more regularly and with greater impact than that of any other early Capetian ruler.

Louis's son and successor Philip II Augustus (1180–1223) benefited from his grandfather's and father's efforts and greatly increased royal rule and royal wealth in his own right. He is usually regarded as the first great king of France. Only fifteen years of age when he inherited the crown, Philip Augustus had already been associated in the kingship, during the last year of his father's life. By 1190, when Philip Augustus issued instructions for the operation of the kingdom while he was away on Crusade, several marked changes in royal governance are noticeable. First, the *prévots* were instructed to come to Paris to render their accounts three times a year. Second, a new official, the *bailli,* was created to hear cases within the royal domain. Like the *prévots,* he reported three times a year to Paris. Together, the *prévots* and *baillis* brought in royal revenues of around 100,000 pounds for the year 1202/03, according to the first records that survive. Philip's *baillis,* then, were roughly comparable to the traveling justices of Henry II in England. In using Paris as a center of fixed governmental supervision, Philip Augustus continued the tradition established by his father. He made all citizens of Paris free townspeople, governed by a council of six and a provost. In 1185 Philip called an assembly of townspeople to discuss paving the streets of Paris, a considerable achievement of urban development at the end of the twelfth century.

Upon his return from the Crusade, Philip Augustus began to transform the archaic institutions of the royal household into a more modern system of governance. He ceased to fill the great household offices of chancellor (after 1185) and seneschal (after 1191). He drew more on the services of lesser nobles and less on those of the great families of the royal domain or nearby principalities. Other great household positions became merely honorific. Philip's increased use of *baillis* and low-born servants created a small, efficient, and loyal central royal court that was very well suited to the new and much larger administrative duties that the last two decades of Philip's reign imposed on it.

In 1202 King John of England married Isabella of Angoulême, who had been betrothed to another royal vassal, Hugh of Lusignan. Hugh accused John of bad faith before the royal court, and Philip hailed John to appear at a hearing conducted by Philip's other vassals. John refused, arguing that the king of England could be no man's vassal, and Philip, invoking lordly privilege, declared all John's holdings from him forfeited and invaded Normandy. Philip's able generalship and financial resources soon wore down John's opposition, and Normandy was lost to the English in 1204.

Philip enforced his rule in two other parts of the Angevin Empire, Anjou and Touraine, in 1206. Shortly afterwards Philip acquired the large territorial principality of Vermandois and increased his powers in Flanders. These new and very large additions to the territories directly ruled by the king posed considerable problems for Philip. However, by adapting his rule to local customs, adopting sophisticated Norman institutions, and sending his *baillis* to supervise the operation of provincial government in the new territories, Philip Augustus developed a full-fledged provincial administration and immensely increased both royal wealth and the prestige of the king of France.

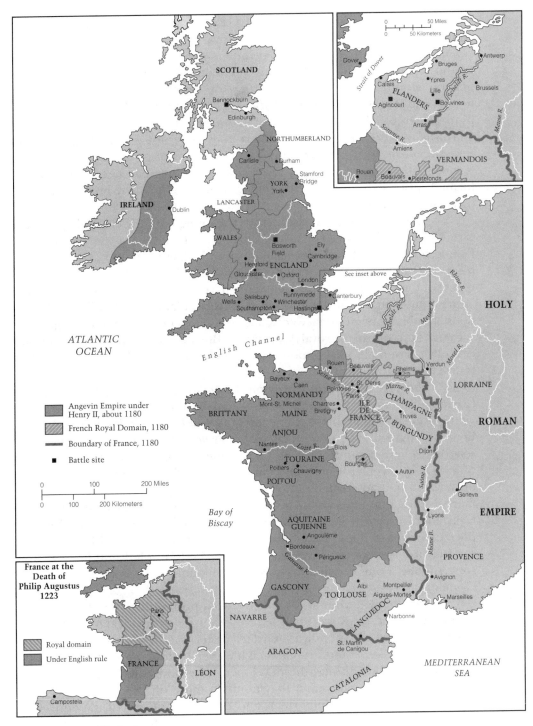

Medieval France and England.

Under Philip's son Louis VIII (1223–1226) and his remarkably able and talented queen, Blanche of Castile, royal institutions of governance were extended even farther into the old independent territorial principalities of Poitou and Languedoc. By the reign of Louis VIII there were three levels of royal administrators. The older offices of *prévot* and viscount had dropped to a second-level status. The new offices of *bailli* and *sénéschal* constituted a senior rank of officials. Drawn from the lower nobility, they were paid a salary and usually posted in provinces where they were not native. At the bottom were numerous local royal servants called *servientes* or *gardes*. By the early thirteenth century, then, the royal governance of France had been greatly transformed, just as the territory directly and indirectly ruled by the king had increased immensely.

The early death of Louis VIII left the young Louis IX (1226–1270) in the care of Queen Blanche. For nearly thirty years Blanche was the real ruler of France, both during Louis's formal minority, which lasted until 1234, and during his young manhood. When Louis departed on a Crusade in 1248 Blanche was regent of the kingdom, and she remained in control during Louis's capture and imprisonment in Egypt, which lasted until 1254. Blanche had to fight off coalitions of nobles anxious to take advantage of Louis's minority and the regency of a woman and control the royal government. But together Blanche and Louis successfully resisted baronial opposition and developed even further the administrative reforms of Philip Augustus.

Louis IX depended heavily on the *baillis,* and in 1247/48 he began to rearrange several of their jurisdictions, making them regularly territorial, dividing some into more manageable territories, and redesigning others. In 1247 Louis also introduced a new office, that of *enquêteur* (inquisitor), a royal official sent out to hear complaints of illegal activities on the part of *baillis* and other officials. Louis relied heavily on Dominicans and Franciscans to perform this duty, which he had created out of conscience and piety as well as a desire for more institutional supervision. So thoroughgoing were Louis's *enquêteurs,* especially after his return from Crusade in 1254, that Rutebeuf, a satirical French poet, complained that if Louis investigated his Dominicans and Franciscans as carefully as his *enquêteurs* investigated others, he too would find faults and errors. Among Louis's *enquêteurs* was Gui Fulquois, who later became Pope Clement IV.

Personally devout and imbued with a profound sense of royal moral responsibility, Louis IX was regarded for centuries as the ideal medieval ruler. His patronage of the Mendicant Orders, his crusading activities, his passionate desire for justice, and his personal life overshadowed even his administrative successes. Even though he developed his grandfather's institutions and increased royal revenues until they doubled those of Philip Augustus, Louis was remembered as a saintly ruler, and he was canonized at the end of the thirteenth century. Louis's canonization culminated the tradition of ecclesiastical support of the French monarchy. At Louis's death on yet another Crusade in Tunis in 1270, not only did the territory and wealth of the king of France surpass those of every other European ruler, but the prestige of the Capetian dynasty and its most recent saintly representative had been vastly and permanently increased.

Philip III (1270–1285) continued to develop both the royal administration and the royal crusading policy. However, it was during the reign of Philip IV the Fair (1285–1314) that the achievements of the Capetian monarchy were put to their most severe tests. Although the kings of France had added to their territory by warfare in Normandy in 1204 and defended their gains at the Battle of Bouvines in 1214, they fought no major wars for the rest of the thirteenth century. Although their revenues had grown, costs had risen also, and the French king was in no position to make extraordinary military expenditures out of his normal revenues. Finally, France and the papacy had always been particularly close, and the French church had readily cooperated with the French kings without papal interference. But during the reign of Philip IV war broke out once again on a wide scale. Royal finances were strained to the utmost, and the king of France and the pope entered a great contest to determine who in fact ruled the Church in France.

The king who experienced these crises has always been in enigma to historians. Some have argued that Philip the Fair was a rational, calculating ruler who closely supervised all governmental activities; others argue that he was a nonentity whose policies were those of his assistants, particularly the many lawyers with whom he surrounded himself. One school of history regards Philip as a "constitutional" king who recognized his duties to the law; another regards him as an autocrat who respected neither tradition nor law. Some regard him as an antireligious tyrant who tried to destroy the papacy and the faith, others as a devout Christian who merely resisted papal encroachments on his traditional rights. Not only the crises of Philip's reign but the problem of his character make his reign at once fascinating and ambiguous. In 1271 the crown of France had been augmented by the acquisition of Languedoc, and in 1285, upon Philip IV's marriage to Jeanne of Navarre, the crown acquired the rich counties of Champagne and Brie. These immense territorial gains continued the meteoric expansion of the kingdom, but they put considerable strains on royal institutions and finances and involved Philip more closely in the affairs of English Gascony and in the urbanized region of Flanders. From the outset of his reign Philip had to prepare for war, and his many campaigns against the English in Gascony and the Flemings in Flanders consumed his resources at a great rate.

Not only did Philip ruthlessly push his *baillis* and *sénéchaux*, but he also turned the *enquêteurs* into financial agents, whose new functions continued into the fourteenth century. Philip tightened control over his financial office, and laid the foundations for its reorganization and permanent settlement in Paris as

Thirteenth-century Paris.

the *Chambre des Comptes*. He also systematized his royal court of appeals, the Parlement of Paris, which became the judicial center of the kingdom. Philip drew into royal service townsmen and professional lawyers, usually of urban background and fiercely royalist in their sympathies and loyalties.

In order to increase revenues, Philip began to regularize the principle of the royal right to tax his subjects, at first in cases of the defense of the realm in emergencies, and later on a routine basis. In matters of taxation Philip and his agents dealt with provincial assemblies, because of the strongly localized traditions of legal and financial administration that had prevailed in France during the acquisition of so many new territories. Thus, the large national assemblies that Philip called in Paris in 1303 and 1308—the Estates-General—never acquired the financial or judicial powers of the English Parliament.

Philip IV's financial demands strained every royal resource and led him into areas where no French king had acted before. Although the status of the Jews in France had sharply declined under Louis IX, it became much worse during Philip's reign. In 1306 Philip confiscated Jewish money and property and expelled the Jews from the kingdom, as his contemporary Edward I had done in England in 1290. Philip increased his demands for money and even claimed the right to tax the clergy. Pope Boniface VIII protested Philip's actions, and after a long, drawn-out battle between the two (discussed later in this chapter), Philip gained the power to tax the clergy as well as the laity.

Yet for all of his fiscal rapacity and opposition to traditional clerical privileges, Philip IV was not irreligious. Rather, his sense of religion appears to have been inseparable from his awareness of the mission of Christian France and the spiritual obligations of his kingship imposed on him. Cold, impersonal, and distant, he was nevertheless driven by a vision of France as a holy land and its people and king as particularly loved by God. His propagandists and also his subjects appear to have agreed with him. His great appeals to the kingdom were answered favorably by a population whose resources were strained to the utmost by royal demands. The people's acceptance of regular royal taxation marked an important step in the creation of new royal resources and in the growth of their loyalty to the king and the kingdom.

When Philip died in 1314, the kingdom had survived the military, financial, and ecclesiastical crises of his reign, testimony to the achievements of Philip and his royal ancestors. But within a few years the kingdom faced as great a crisis, one from which it was not able to extricate itself quickly as it had in the early years of the fourteenth century. Philip was succeeded in order by his three sons, Louis X (1314–1316), Philip V (1316–1322), and Charles IV (1322–1328). At the death of Charles IV in 1328, the succession to the throne was a major problem. The aristocracy's resistance to royal centralization complicated the issue, and sent France into the fourteenth century facing what the historian Raymond Cazelles has termed the "crisis of royalty" at the end of the eleven generations of Capetian kings.

A NEW ORDER: THE CONFLICT BETWEEN THE PAPACY AND THE TERRITORIAL MONARCHY

The Great Interregnum of the kingdom of Germany ended with the election of Rudolf of Habsburg as king of the Romans in 1273. Rudolf and his imperial successors, with the striking exceptions of Henry VII and Louis of Bavaria (1314–1347), remained content to exercise their powers in Germany and Austria and to build their family domains and influence. The popes had succeeded in removing Sicily from the Staufer dynasty in 1268 through the agency of Charles of Anjou, brother of Louis IX of France, who became king of Sicily in that year. But Charles's rule in Sicily and South Italy excited fear of his power on the part of the Roman curia and resentment on the part of his Sicilian subjects. In 1282 the population of Palermo massacred the French garrison and precipitated a general conflict throughout the northern Mediterranean world. This conflict lasted until the Treaty of Caltabellotta in 1302, which awarded the island of Sicily to the royal house of Aragon and mainland South Italy to the successors of Charles of Anjou.

Charles of Anjou's grandnephew was Philip IV the Fair, who, in addition to the considerable debts inside his kingdom, faced popular resentment toward France's participation in ecclesiastical vendettas and the diplomatic intricacies of the papal elections of the years 1292–1305. After a two-year vacancy following the death of Pope Nicholas IV in 1292, the saintly hermit Peter Morone was elected pope. Although many hopes were pinned to Morone, who took the papal name of Celestine V, the burden of the papacy was too much for him, and he resigned the office in December 1294. His successor was an old, wily, and talented papal bureaucrat, Benedetto Gaetani, who took the name Boniface VIII.

It was precisely over questions of royal financial needs and practices that the great quarrel between Philip and Boniface was launched. Although papal permission had long been required in order for temporal rulers to tax their clergy (and even then only in cases of dire necessity), thirteenth-century rulers had often neglected this rule. Facing a war with England and a vexing problem in Flanders, Philip issued new demands for taxes from the clergy in 1296. Boniface responded with a papal letter directing the French bishops not to pay. This letter, *Clericis laicos,* condemned the abuse of temporal authority, and although its legal provisions were on solid ground, its tone was rather more categorical than suited Philip. In the same year, Philip prohibited the export of any money at all, including papal revenues, from France. In 1297, in the letter *Romana mater,* Boniface qualifiedly suspended the provisions of *Clericis laicos* for France, and in a later letter of the same year, *Etsi de statu,* he withdrew slightly from his earlier position.

In 1297 Boniface faced difficulties on several fronts. An influential segment of the college of cardinals denounced him as a usurper, and Boniface resorted to the unfortunate device of proclaiming a Crusade against them. Supporters of Celestine V further accused Boniface of canonical irregularity. In 1298 Boniface published his great lawbook, the *Liber Sextus,* part of which included texts justifying papal resignation and the procedures for providing a successor to a still-living former pope. In 1297 Boniface had proclaimed the canonization of Louis IX of France, and in 1300 he announced the Jubilee Year, a period in which the pilgrimage to Rome was rewarded with particular spiritual benefits. By 1301 both parties appeared to have recovered from the earlier encounter, and the success of the Jubilee Year must have been encouraging to Boniface.

Later in that same year, however, the second conflict broke out. Philip arrested the bishop of Pamiers, Bernard Saisset, for treason and heresy, condemned him, and wrote to Boniface requesting papal confirmation of his action. Boniface could legitimately have modified his position on taxation, but he could not relax the canonical sanctions against any layman who presumed to try to convict a bishop. Boniface therefore refused, called a council at Rome for 1302, and wrote Philip a long letter, *Ausculta fili,* in which he carefully cautioned the king against abusing the age-old liberties of the Church. Philip's agents circulated a forged version of the letter in which Boniface was made to appear to have claimed complete temporal and spiritual authority. This was one of the first documents in modern propaganda warfare. In addition, in 1302 Philip called a large assembly of nobles, clergy, and people—the first Estates-General in the history of France—to solicit public support in his quarrel with the pope. By the end of the year Boniface had replied with the bull *Unam sanctam,* a long, detailed, and wholly traditionalist exposition of papal authority. This bull, one of the most famous documents in the history of the relations between the papacy and the monarchy, elicited no counterarguments from Philip's supporters. Instead, Guillaume de Nogaret, Philip's chief minister, denounced Boniface as a heretic and blasphemer and marched into Italy, where he took the pope captive at Anagni and attempted to force him to repudiate his earlier statements and renounce the papacy. Although he was released before he was forced to do this, Boniface died a few weeks later, and the questions of the relations between France and the papacy were momentarily suspended.

With the accession of Clement V (1305–1314) the relations between France and the papacy were slowly restored, but at a formidable price to the latter. The excommunications against Nogaret and others were lifted, and Philip was formally praised for his devotion in the bull *Rex Gloriae* of 1311. Some of Boniface's arguments in *Clericis laicos, Ausculta fili,* and *Unam sanctam* were formally repudiated by the pope, and Clement had to work very hard to prevent Philip from engineering a church council that would pronounce Boniface VIII an antipope. These concessions seriously weakened the direct authority of the popes after Clement V, and they presaged an even more remarkable incident, the destruction of the Order of the Templars.

In one sense, Boniface's concern over Philip's claim may well have come from his fear that the territorial monarchies in general were acquiring too much direct power over the clergy in their kingdoms. After all, the machinery of governance and communications was more direct and influential within England or France than throughout all of Christendom, and events of the fourteenth and fifteenth centuries proved such that monarchical control over clergy was a significant threat to the universal claims of the papacy.

No event suggests more clearly the threat constituted by a temporal power than the affair of the Templars. This order, having earned an attractive reputation in the Holy Land, had expanded its role in Europe, particularly in the fields of banking and Crusade financing. The wealth of the Templars and their virtual independence from governmental institutions made them an attractive target for the needy Philip, and their growing concern with financial affairs and their own privileges had doubtless weakened their standing in the eyes of many Christians. Between 1307 and 1314 Philip undertook to destroy the order and confiscate its property. In 1307 his campaign began with the arrest of the Templars on charges of heresy and unspecified but enormous and horrible vices. By 1310 a number of Templars had been burned at the stake as heretics, and in 1314 the grand master of the order, Jacques de Molai, was executed. The financial resources of the Templars were confiscated by the crown, and papal approval was elicited with difficulty after pressure was exerted on Clement V in the matter of Boniface VIII and the troubles of the first decade of the fourteenth century. Although not all subjects of Philip IV, clergy and laity, concurred in the destruction of the Templars, the king's success marked, along with his successful conflict with the papacy, one moment in the rise of temporal authority in European history. The powers of the king, enhanced by new administrative agents, financial resources, unquestioned Christian orthodoxy, and the growing cult of the kingdom of France itself, were both more immediately visible and more directly effective.

The relations of the papacy with Charles of Anjou and Philip the Fair, the complex problems of the reigns of Boniface VIII and Clement V, and the French king's destruction of the Templars, one of the last vestiges of a kind of supranational Christian society, an event that heralded the civil theology of territorial monarchy, did not of course destroy the traditional authority of the pope. The struggle between the two powers was not that between an archaic church and the "modern" state, but rather between spiritual and temporal authorities in the new circumstances of the late thirteenth and early fourteenth centuries. In this sense both powers were still traditional powers. The authority of the clergy and the papacy still counted for much throughout the fourteenth century, and continued to do so until the eighteenth century. Temporal authority, with its resources, claims, and spiritual justification, defined the terms of the new relationship, but still left much room in which spiritual authority could function.

FURTHER READING

In general, for individual states, see the General Bibliography under the heading Political History: Regional. Recent research in political history has focused on both the development of political theory and doctrines and the establishment of communities at different social levels. On theory, see the concise summary of Brian Tierney, *Religion, Law, and Constitutional Thought, 1150–1650* (Cambridge: Cambridge University Press, 1982). Tierney's work may be supplemented by Joseph R. Strayer, *On the Medieval Origins of the Modern State* (Princeton, NJ: Princeton University Press, 1970), and there is a fine study of the alternatives available to medieval Europeans in Antony Black, *Guilds and Civil Society in European Political Thought from the Twelfth Century to the Present* (Ithaca, NY: Cornell University Press, 1984). Although it deals primarily with the period 1300–1500, there is much important information in Bernard Guenée, *States and Rulers in Later Medieval Europe* (Oxford: Basil Blackwell, 1985). The extensive survey of political theory in J. H. Burns, ed., *The Cambridge History of Medieval Political Thought c.350–1450* (Cambridge: Cambridge University Press, 1988) is essential for the entire period covered by this book. The most recent general study is Kenneth Pennington, *The Prince and the Law 1200–1600: Sovereignty and Rights in the Western Legal Tradition* (Berkeley and Los Angeles: University of California Press, 1993).

On papacy and empire, see the works previously cited, and Horst Fuhrmann, *Germany in the High Middle Ages, c. 1050–1200* (Cambridge: Cambridge University Press, 1986), and the classic work of Ernst H. Kantorowicz, *The King's Two Bodies* (Princeton, NJ: Princeton University Press, 1957).

On England, see W. L. Warren, *Henry II* (Berkeley and Los Angeles: University of California Press, 1973), and Frank Barlow, *Thomas Becket* (Berkeley and Los Angeles: University of California Press, 1986).

On France, see the works of Jean Dunbabin and Elizabeth Hallam, cited earlier and John W. Baldwin, *The Government of Philip Augustus* (Berkeley and Los Angeles: University of California Press, 1986); William Chester Jordan, *Louis IX and the Challenge of the Crusade* (Princeton, NJ: Princeton University Press, 1979), and Joseph R. Strayer, *The Reign of Philip the Fair* (Princeton, NJ: Princeton University Press, 1980).

On the Iberian Peninsula, see Bernard Reilly, *The Medieval Spains,* and Joseph F. O'Callaghan, *The Learned King: The Reign of Alfonso X of Castile* (Philadelphia: University of Pennsylvania Press, 1993).

On the papal side of the conflict, see T. S. R. Boase, *Boniface VIII* (London: Constable, 1933).

16

REASON AND IMAGINATION
IN THE GOTHIC WORLD

THE TRIUMPH OF ARISTOTLE

One of the most important aspects of the new learning of the twelfth century was western Europeans' interest in Muslim and Greek scientific and philosophical thought. With the Christian capture of Toledo in 1085, clerical scholars in Spain and then in Sicily began the process of translating the works of some of the most important thinkers in both alien cultures, first from Arabic and later directly from Greek. Peter the Venerable, abbot of the monastery of Cluny, even commissioned a translation of the *Qur'an* in the mid–twelfth century. Among the works of Arabic scholars available to Europeans in Latin versions by the end of the twelfth century were those of Ibn Sina (Avicenna to the Latins: 980–1037) on medicine and philosophy, al-Khwarizmi (d. 850) on mathematics, and Al-hazen (d. 1039) on optics. In turn, the Latins received from the Arabs much Greek scientific and philosophical literature, particularly the scientific and philosophical works of Aristotle with the great commentary of the Muslim philosopher Ibn Rushd (Averroës to the Latins: 1126–1198).

The new Aristotelian studies also affected the curriculum. The study of ethics was joined to that of grammar, while the new natural philosophy of Aristotle was attached to logic. Gradually, dissatisfaction with the conventional schema of the liberal arts led to two major changes. First, some of the liberal arts, notably grammar and rhetoric, became preliminary subjects and eventually dropped out of some university curricula altogether. Second, the subjects of the quadrivium, along with logic, grew in importance. In addition, by the thirteenth century the "sciences"—physics, ethics, and metaphysics—became subjects in their own right and were added to the arts. Thus was created the category of "arts and sciences." By the early thirteenth century not only was academic learning a corporate profession with specialized professional curricula and technical vocabularies, but the old arts curriculum was wholly dominated by the study of logic and natural philosophy. Those old liberal arts that did not lend themselves to the requirements of the new disciplines of theology and law tended to be downgraded into merely preparatory subjects; those that did grew to dominate the study of the arts and sciences and to shape European thought in many areas.

In different medieval universities the new subjects produced different results. Oxford became prominent in natural philosophy and mathematics, chiefly through the influence of its first chancellor, Robert Grosseteste; Paris concentrated on theology and metaphysics. Orleans, on the other hand, maintained a respected school of rhetoric, and the University of Bologna became the greatest of medieval schools of law. Not only the flood of new knowledge but the importance of methods of analysis and disputation shaped the thirteenth- and fourteenth-century schools. In general, the faculties of the arts and sciences, by now separated from the faculties of theology and law, treated their own specialized subjects with a new freedom and disregard for both tradition and theological caution.

Thus, several thirteenth-century thinkers came under attack from theologians who accused them of sharing not only Aristotle's beliefs in natural philosophy but also his pagan ideas about the uncreatedness of the world. They were also charged with failing to account properly for such doctrines as that of the Trinity. Growing friction between theology and philosophy led to several incidents of rivalry within the thirteenth-century universities. In Paris, for example, secular arts masters bitterly resented the arrival of Franciscan and Dominican scholars in university teaching chairs of theology. This rivalry was one of the dominant themes at Paris throughout the century. In addition, the arts faculty was censured several times during the 1200s for teaching philosophical doctrines that ran counter to Scripture and Christian truth. In 1277 Etienne Tempier, the bishop of Paris, issued a condemnation of 219 propositions that he claimed were erroneously being taught at Paris by the arts faculty. This action played a very important role in redirecting philosophy away from pure Aristotelianism, although a strong and articulate school of philosophers committed to the teaching of Aristotle and his Arabic commentator Averroës flourished through the fourteenth century.

The logical works of Aristotle that had not been translated by Boethius, notably the *Posterior Analytics,* had been integrated into curriculum of the eleventh- and twelfth-century schools under the subject of dialectic. But the remainder of Aristotle's corpus of writings—and the important Arabic commentaries upon it, as well as original works of Arabic science and philosophy (some of which Europeans attributed erroneously to Aristotle)—dealt with subjects that were not so easily accommodated to the standard academic curriculum. Natural philosophy, ethics, metaphysics, and politics required an expanded curriculum, just as they influenced learned attitudes toward the naturalness of the created universe and the dignity of nature and humanity. They challenged the Platonic-Augustinian tradition of thought that disparaged material reality and human effort and focused on the invisible forms and ideas in the mind of God that were more perfect, and hence more "real," than their crude and imperfect earthly copies. The new material from Greek and Arabic thinkers argued instead for the regularity, coherence, and intelligibility of material creation and the institutions of human life.

Because much of the thought of late antiquity that had originally transmitted Aristotle to the Latin West had been devoted to proving that Aristotle and Plato were in essential agreement, there was little initial resistance to the reception of more Aristotelian texts from the middle of the twelfth century onward. Aristotle's works of natural philosophy offered a systematic and consistent set of physical principles that were then applied elsewhere to different aspects of human nature and activity. Aristotle's *Physics,* for example, analyzed motion in terms of changes in some of the logical categories that the texts of logic had established. It then considered innate tendencies in terms of actuality and potentiality in matter that were realized by motion. In Aristotelian physics, motion was a key concept, and the doctrine of motion and of movers (including that of the "unmoved mover," which appealed to both philosophers and theologians) laid the groundwork for both physics and mechanics. Aristotle's other works of natural philosophy—*On Generation and Corruption, On the Heavens, On Meteorology,* and *On the Soul*—offered an account of the physical universe, its structure, and its inhabitants that appealed very strongly to thirteenth-century thinkers. Aristotle divided the "skies" into a realm of nature, *physis,* and one of meta-nature, the heavens. His doctrines of motion and matter accounted for the movement of planets and apparent lack of movement of the stars, and they also accounted for the possibility of an "unmoved mover" beyond the stars. Aristotle's treatises of natural philosophy made both the earth and the heavens intelligible without apparently violating major Christian beliefs.

His treatise *On the Soul* distinguished among the different life-forces of sentient, animate, and rational beings. For Aristotle, the soul and body are one, as are form and content. Only in the function of the active intellect, which is not localized, do humans have a power of conceptualization and reasoning that distinguishes them from other life forms. Aristotle's praise of both the reasoning and the sensory process in humans drew wide appeal after the twelfth century.

For Aristotle and his followers, metaphysics was the supreme science. It is the study of being and virtue, as well as that of the four causes of all things: the material formal, efficient, and final. These "causes" are related to Aristotle's sense of the purposefulness of all change in nature.

Aristotle's Arabic commentators were often not distinguished by Europeans from Aristotle himself. Islamic philosophers had already identified the "unmoved mover" with God and the active intellect with the prophetic spirit of Muhammad. Avicenna had added the dimension of necessity and contingency in distinguishing between God and creation. This theological-philosophical approach to Aristotle by the Arabic natural philosophers and theologians appealed equally to Christians, and not only Aristotle's natural philosophy, but his work on metaphysics, ethics, and politics was swept along in its train.

In short, Aristotle had offered the picture of an intelligible universe, the heavens distinguished from the realm of nature, the operation of sentient, animate, and rational beings, the nature of the intellect, and the structure of being itself. At first, his teachings seemed richly to complement earlier Christian doctrines, to give to creation itself a dignity and worthiness that it had hitherto lacked. The "Arabized" Aristotle became the presiding genius of the created world.

The texts of Aristotle generally served thirteenth-century Europe well. They argued for the dignity and intelligibility of the material world, the naturalness of human society and the state, and the secular virtue of social obligations and the rational use of public power. But, although they were long held authoritative, they were not always accurate, and they and their popularity troubled thinkers from the late thirteenth century on (see Chapter 18). In other areas they reinforced ideas that were already too powerful. One instance of this is the popularity and authority of Aristotelian biology, astrology, and gynecology.

Aristotelian biological doctrine held that the material generation of the human being began when menstrual blood was given form by male semen, the perfect union of the two producing a male, the imperfect union producing a female. The male seed represented the Aristotelian concept of form, which created being when it was imposed on matter, in this case the menstrual blood. The male seed was also assumed to impose rational characteristics to the fetus, which developed a soul slowly, absorbing both astrological and divine influences because of its combination of material and spiritual existence. Christian theologians read Aristotle on human gestation in the light of the long history of their theories of female inferiority to the male and their fear of unbridled lust and the passions generally, which they thought disordered reason.

This ambiguous attitude toward sexual reproduction colored virtually all discussions of both human sexual relations and the psychological and physiological character of men and women, consistently to the disadvantage of women. When the masculine was identified with the mind and spirit—the nobler parts of the human being—the feminine was identified with the flesh and carnal passions, considered the least noble aspects of human nature. Aristotelian physiology even offered directions for being assured of begetting male children: intercourse immediately following the menstrual period tended to beget males; intercourse later in the cycle tended to produce females, monsters, or no children at all, for it was thought to impose male form on unfresh and tainted matter.

Menstruation was regarded as a form of pollution, and many of the rules of Jewish and Islamic scripture regarding sexual purity and pollution were adopted by Christian theologians and canon lawyers. Women were regarded as enjoying twice the sexual pleasure of men, and of possessing far more intense carnal desires than men. The act of sexual intercourse was considered more fatiguing and injurious for men, since it was also thought that women had the alternative means of purging their bodies by menstruation.

In this instance, the new science of Aristotle and his Arabic commentators served to confirm the highly ambiguous and frequently misogynistic attitudes of learned European males. What about female medical practitioners? Statistics are hard to come by and unreliable when found, but those that are most respected suggest that in France and England about 1 percent of known medical practitioners were women, and perhaps half of 1 percent midwives. At the important medical center at Salerno, a number of women practitioners and medical writers are recorded, the most famous of whom was the twelfth-century Trota, to whom were later attributed a great number of medical treatises that passed under the general name of "Trotula." These female practitioners were not limited to gynecology, nor were they limited to the treatment of women exclusively; and male practitioners certainly undertook to deal with at least some gynecological problems, particularly fertility.

But the experience of actual practitioners, male or female, does not seem to have affected the view of human gestation confirmed in the Aristotelian biological writings. In his errors Aristotle was as influential as in his virtues. And his influence spread quickly, widely, and through orthodox religious and philosophical channels.

It is against this background that the career of Albert the Great, or Albertus Magnus (1193–1280), can best be understood. Albert was born at Lauingen in Germany, entered the Dominican order, and lived at the Dominican convent in Cologne until he was sent to Paris in 1240, where two years later he assumed the Dominican chair of theology. From 1242 until his death, Albert became virtually the model of a learned churchman. From Paris he returned to Cologne to lecture to the Dominicans. He traveled up and down central Europe, from Rome to the Baltic Sea, as head of the German province of the Dominican order. He became bishop of Regensburg and served in other administrative capacities throughout Europe. He attended the Second Council of Lyons in 1274, where he defended some of the work of his greatest pupil, Thomas Aquinas, and he repeated his defense at Paris during the attacks on Aquinas associated with the condemnations of 1277. Although Albert occupies a central place in the history of medieval thought, his career was also that of a competent administrator and experimental scientist.

Albert's greatest efforts were directed at assimilating the body of Aristotle's natural philosophy into a plan of Christian learning without conflicting with revelation and dogma. To do so, Albert distinguished two spheres of knowledge. Theology, he said, dealt with supernatural things and was reached by faith; philosophy dealt with natural things and was reached by reason. Albert argued that these two kinds of knowledge and two ways of knowing were not incompatible, for they led to the same faith and the same truth. Although Albert thought that much of revelation lay outside the realm of reason, he argued that certain topics could be studied by both theology and philosophy. Albert taught in the faculty of theology at Paris from 1242 to 1248, and his most important works are theological. His *Commentary on the Sentences* of Peter Lombard is one of the landmarks of thirteenth-century theology. In his later works, which tended to treat philosophy more than theology, Albert attempted to create a system of natural philosophy that could be tested by reason and experience and proved by purely rational means without dependence on revelation and theology. By sharpening the distinction between theology and philosophy, Albert, heavily influenced by Aristotle, created one sphere in which reason could claim legitimate autonomy.

THOMAS AQUINAS AND BONAVENTURE

The new mendicant orders of the thirteenth century produced not only preachers, saints, and pastoral missions to the populations of the towns, but also scholars. By the 1250s the theology faculty at the University of Paris was dominated by teachers who were members of these two orders. Of these the two greatest were Thomas Aquinas, a pupil of Albert the Great, and Bonaventure, the most influential representative of Franciscan learning in the thirteenth century.

Thomas Aquinas was born around 1225 to the family of the lords of Aquino in southern Italy. He studied at the monastery of Monte Cassino from 1230 to 1239 and in the arts faculty of the University of Naples. In 1244, against his family's opposition, Thomas joined the Dominican order, began his theological studies under Albert the Great at Cologne, and was sent to Paris as a bachelor in Scripture in 1245. After lecturing on the text of Scripture, Aquinas went on to lecture on Peter Lombard's *Book of Sentences,* just as Albert and other theologians had. Aquinas's *Commentary on the Sentences* was his first great work. Although Aquinas was prepared to be received by the higher faculty of theology, both he and the Franciscan Bonaventure had to wait, because of secular masters' opposition to the rise of the orders in the university.

Bonaventure was born Giovanni di Fidanza in Italy in 1221. He took his religious name when he entered the Franciscan order around 1240, and he studied at Paris with the great English Franciscan theologian Alexander of Hales (1170–1245). After a distinguished teaching career at Paris, Bonaventure was elected minister-general of the Franciscan order, was the official biographer of

Francis of Assisi, and was made a cardinal in 1273. He died at the Second Council of Lyons in 1274.

Although Thomas and Bonaventure were both affected by the resentment against the rise of the orders in Paris, they were not similar thinkers. Aquinas followed his teacher Albert in taking the path of Aristotle and in creating a sphere of activity in which reason was supreme and perfectly consistent with faith. Bonaventure, on the other hand, was far less an Aristotelian, adhering instead to the older tradition of Augustinian Platonism. Thomas, for example, argued that the question of whether the world was created or eternal could not be answered by reason and therefore had to be answered by faith, which stated that God had created the world. Bonaventure, on the other hand, argued that reason can and does prove that the world was created and could not be eternal. Bonaventure scorned many of the claims made for reason by the Aristotelians, and argued for the primacy of mystical knowledge.

The two thinkers also revealed their differences in their works. Those of Aquinas were chiefly either academic treatises or occasional pieces dealing with philosophy. His *Summa Against the Gentiles* was requested by Raymond of Peñafort, the great Spanish canon lawyer who turned missionary, in order to provide missionaries to the Muslims with logical arguments for Christian faith that did not depend on revelation. His *Summa Theologiae* was a vast compendium of both philosophy and theology, the monument to Aristotelianism in its Christian form. Bonaventure, besides his academic works, was also a contemplative theologian, and his little work *The Mind's Journey to God* is a monument of contemplative theology. Even so, his work as minister-general of the Franciscan order took him out into the world and its affairs more than the restricted academic career of Aquinas.

The careers of Aquinas and Bonaventure reflect merely two of the many sides of the rapidly changing world of thirteenth-century thought and testify to the enduring influence of Plato, Aristotle, and Augustine on that world. In spite of their differences, however, which also reflect some of the differences between their two orders, these two thinkers together suggest much of the variety and power of the philosophical revolution of the thirteenth century.

GOTHIC ARCHITECTURE AND ENGINEERING

One result of the triumph of Aristotelianism was a new degree of confidence in the assertion made by many thinkers that the created universe was intelligible in terms of geometry and mathematics. The appearance of a new interest in mathematics (and the slow introduction of Arabic numerals and mathematical place notation in the late twelfth and thirteenth centuries) influenced aesthetics and carried the concept of the intelligibility of nature into yet other areas. Twelfth- and thirteenth-century thinkers and artists often considered God as a kind of geometer-craftsman using mathematical principles and aesthetic criteria to make physical objects. A famous manuscript illumination of the twelfth century, in fact, shows God setting out to create the world with a geometer's compass in his hand; another of the thirteenth century shows two angels rotating the universe by means of celestial cranks. Neither of these depictions is naive; both represent a courageous attempt to represent immaterial reality in terms of rational principles.

This elevation of the dignity and intelligibility of the material world carried over into theology as well, as the art historian Erwin Panofsky has noted:

The human soul, though recognized as immortal, was now held to be the organizing and unifying principle of the body itself rather than a substance independent thereof. A plant was thought to exist as a plant and not as the copy of the idea of the plant. The existence of God was believed to be demonstrable from His creation rather than à priori.[1]

The impact of Aristotelian natural philosophy and metaphysics on Christian theology was not so much a revolution as a shift in emphasis. Chapter 57 of the *Rule* of Saint Benedict had permitted monks who were craftsmen to work at their crafts as long as they had their abbot's permission and did not take excessive pride in their work. Around 1120 Theophilus, a monk who believed in the inherent dignity in all labor dedicated to God, wrote a rational account of many artistic processes, *On the Various Arts*. Perhaps the most eloquent expression of this new respect for material creation is the sculpture on the north porch of Chartres cathedral showing a seated, infinitely compassionate and tender God molding Adam out of amorphous clay; Adam's human nature takes physical shape in God's own hands. In this portrayal of creation the soul and body of a human being are undifferentiated visually. Thus, Aristotelian influences extended into theology and the arts, taking up an old strand of Christian thought and making it a dominant theme of philosophy, theology, and the visual arts.

Theophilus's treatise reveals a wealth of artistic talent and rationality in the ideal monastery, but that talent was exercised chiefly on manuscript copying, illumination, painting, metal sculpture, and the coloring of glass. The greater building arts were probably beyond the capacities of a single group of monks or a single chapter of a cathedral, except for some aspects of design and later decoration of the finished church building. The achievements of Romanesque architects and engineers, however, had revolutionized architecture. In addition, other aspects of building craftsmanship had greatly improved. The increasingly professional use of geometrical principles of design, the development of complex tools such as cranes and hoists, and improved jointing work and stone dressing all contributed to the high quality of the building crafts in the twelfth and thirteenth centuries.

---

[1]Edwin Panofsky, *Gothic Architecture and Scholasticism* (New York: Meridian Books, 1957), pp. 6–7.

The Faces of God: The creation of Adam. This sculptured group, from the north porch of Chartres cathedral, is a stunning expression of the Creator's love for his creation, and emphasizes its physical and material aspects. (*Archives and Photographiques, Paris*)

The high degree of technical expertise worked out in Romanesque church architecture was enhanced by new design elements in such Romanesque buildings as the cathedrals of Autun in France and Durham in England. At Autun (1120–1132) the pointed arch, contrasting with the round arches of traditional Romanesque style, first appeared in a major church building in western Europe. The Durham cathedral (1093–1104) featured the ribbed vault. Thus, two of the most characteristic features of the style called *Gothic* appeared in late Romanesque churches. The first church to combine these two elements, which permitted the height of the building to increase greatly and the structural role of walls and columns to be transformed, was the new church at the monastery of St. Denis, constructed by Abbot Suger around 1140.

Durham Cathedral, Nave. The nave of Durham cathedral is a fine example of the transition from Romanesque to Gothic church architecture. (*Courtesy of the British Tourist Authority*)

The monastery of St. Denis was the religious institution associated most closely with the kings of France. Suger himself, while still abbot, was made regent of the kingdom during the absence of King Louis VII on the Second Crusade. The chronicles of St. Denis were the closest to an official history of the monarchy that France possessed. Therefore, Suger's decision to build a new church was an act of public importance; he was the regent of the kingdom, the biographer of the late King Louis VI, and one of the ablest churchmen and councillors in the kingdom. The new church was to be no mere monastic center; it was the spiritual center of royal France, a pilgrimage site, and the physical illustration of the new twelfth-century spirituality.

Suger was moved to his task by the great churches that most twelfth-century western Europeans knew or knew of—Hagia Sophia at Constantinople and the Temple of Solomon. As he built, almost certainly with the aid of a master builder, the inspiration of these remote buildings became embodied in a structure that employed the newest and most effective techniques that the twelfth century knew. By building the vaults on cross-ribs (arches that stretched diagonally from one column to another and crisscrossed at the center of a bay supported by four columns), Suger was able to lighten the load of the ceiling. By using pointed arches, he was able to deflect the weight of the roof directly onto much thinner support columns. The use of these two techniques meant that the height of the church could be greatly increased and that the thick, formidable walls, piers, and columns of the Romanesque churches could be replaced with slender walls pierced by windows and light, slender columns, and greater length. The aesthetic experience was wholly different from that of the earlier Romanesque style.

The problems of organizing a large-scale building project are illuminated not only by this great new church itself but by Suger's *De administratione*, in which he recounts the story of its creation. Suger tells of the decision to renovate an older, sacred church, the problems of getting stone of the right quality and timbers large enough for his purposes, and of course raising the necessary monies. Organizing the labor on this church and others like it was a considerable task. A master builder had to be found with the technical expertise and the managerial skills to administer the whole project. Masons, carpenters, roofers, metalworkers, glassmakers, and sculptors had to be brought together, often from great distances. For them, the work site became a living site for several years. By the mid–twelfth century practical geometry was essential, not necessarily for the patron of a project like Suger, but certainly for the master builder. He had to translate suggestions into sketches and mathematically perfect them by basing them on a single modular measurement, multiples and subdivisions of which became the actual measurements of the design. Sometimes other buildings besides the older church had to be demolished for a new, larger church. The entire project, from plans and early demolitions to the final consecration, could take as long as thirty years.

The organization and financing of the work, the integration of the new building with others nearby, and the quality of engineering and building techniques were striking. A finished Gothic church such as St. Denis, or the slightly later cathedrals of Chartres and Notre Dame, was the result not only of a new spirituality and aesthetic sense but of applied geometry, engineering, and construction skills of a very high order. The historian Lynn White, Jr., has pointed out that these cathedrals and monastic churches were the first examples of monumental architecture produced by free, paid laborers in the Western world. The professional dignity, literacy, and cosmopolitanism of the Gothic architects and master builders help explain the spread of Gothic architectural principles and the high regard in which the technical achievements of great builders were held.

The aesthetics and engineering of Gothic architecture are its most striking aspects to one unfamiliar with them. Less clear, but no less important, is the spiritual ideal that the aesthetics and engineering skills of the patrons and builders shaped into physical form. Beneath their high roofs, whose weight was distributed onto slender columns and external buttresses, Gothic churches were

The Choir and South Transept of Notre Dame, Paris. The most famous, if not the most beautiful of all Gothic churches, was, like many others, an urban church. A long structure, its short transept is barely noticeable. The towered façade, pointed arches and great rose window are characteristic of the Gothic style. (*Trans World Airlines Photo*)

full of light. The walls were filled not with thick stone and small windows but with great windows of stained glass, providing images of light and color to those inside. The ceilings soared far higher than any most people had ever seen or could imagine. The naves reached as high as 160 feet, the ultimate physical height of stone architecture before the development of structural steel in the nineteenth century. Light and the impression of fragility of the church fabric, immense height, and the delicacy of window traceries and sculpture are the aesthetic dimensions of Gothic architecture.

In twelfth-century theology the church building was symbolic both of the Church as a whole and of paradise. The elaborately decorated west fronts of twelfth- and thirteenth-century churches were specifically designed to lead the eye and mind of those entering them into a spiritual state in which they could benefit from the experience of the liturgy. The two main features of Gothic

Reims Cathedral, Façade. One of the richest Gothic façades, that of Reims cathedral held particular meaning, since it was the church in which the kings of France were crowned. (*Marburg Art Reference Bureau*)

architecture, light and the visibility of structural elements, also played a spiritual role. The light suggested the principle of creation and the gifts of the Holy Spirit; the visible structural members emphasized the order, unity, and coherence of the Church, of belief, and of the spiritual community. The dignity and majesty of the greatest Gothic churches conveyed as well the gifts and richness of a loving God. As a work of art, of engineering, and of spirituality the Gothic church illustrates the link between reason and imagination in the Gothic world.

THE KNIGHT BETWEEN THE WORLD AND GOD

The new schools and the new churches of the late twelfth and thirteenth centuries were not the only institutional expressions of reason and imagination in the Gothic world. Cities and aristocratic and royal courts also developed new cul-

Chartres Cathedral, Nave. The opening of the walls, the great height of the interior, and the rose window all suggest the great enthusiasm for Chartres that is reflected in literature from the twelfth century to the twentieth. (*Marburg Art Reference Bureau*)

tural forms, which are reflected in the arts and literature, in building styles, and in styles of life. The style of behavior, status, and values among the higher and lower nobility in the late twelfth century acquired a name of its own, which appeared first in France and quickly spread to the rest of Europe: *courtois, höflich, cortese,* "courtly." Courtly manners, ethics, dress, skills, and values grew out of the rough life of the warrior and warlord. Next to the man who was brave, *preux,* there emerged the ideal of the man who was properly behaved, the *prudhomme.* By the thirteenth century the way of life of the ideal courtier, whether wealthy lord or individual knight, was considered by such different figures as King Louis IX of France and the German poet Wolfram von Eschenbach to be the layman's counterpart of the monk's daily round of prayer and liturgy.

But courtly life and values represented something more than a cultural style. The configuration of noble households and families was changing in the twelfth and thirteenth centuries, and to a certain extent the rules of courtly behavior accommodated this transition and institutionalized new social and emotional dimensions of noble life.

One instance of this is the emergence of the noblewoman as the object of erotic and amatory pursuit and conquest. In many of the poems, tales, and longer romances that courtly society generated is the motif of the young man whose heart is kindled with passion, usually for the lady of his lord. Since conjugal love was thought to be more restrained than passionate, erotic love, these tales gave a respectable dimension to eroticism—coming (as it was thought to) from an uncontrollable passion generated by the vision of the feminine object of the masculine gaze. The motif indeed allows for the social and domestic superiority of the woman and the submissive status of the lover, but it also allows for the woman to subject the lover to a highly intricate code of etiquette and to tests, which the lover fulfills and thereby earns a reward from the lady. Because of the lady's superior status and the dangers of being discovered, the lovers are compelled to an elaborately deceptive code of public behavior, although the conclusion of the lover's passionate courtship is clearly intended to be sexual.

This motif, cultivated by courtly society and written in the vernacular (and hence understandable even to those who could not read) may represent a shared fantasy of high- and lower-born members of that society and may have also served as often as a focus for proper behavior as a fantasy of knightly males. It allowed for a temporary role-reversal in the initial domineering female and the submissive male, and this reversal allowed for the depiction of psychological states and public behavior that reflected the interests and psychology of important aspects of courtly society.

Courtly society dealt with far more than experimental eroticism. The existence of courtly households required the articulation of statuses and the status of one court versus that of others. The late twelfth and thirteenth centuries saw elaborate definitions of noble status, and the development of coats of arms and rules for knightly conduct may all be regarded as manifestations of the efforts of both the higher and lower nobility to come to terms with a rapidly changing world. In these courts a secular lay life, an ideal for knights possessing a dignity equal to that of the clergy, was first expressly enunciated. The heavy-handed fighting man of the tenth century and the greedy warlord of the eleventh, who had to do hard penance for killing and whose hopes for salvation were few, slowly turned into the knight, whose initiation into knighthood paralleled the entry into religious life of the clergy. The knight's brotherhood with all other knights discreetly obliterated real social and economic differences among the nobility. The character of a *prudhomme,* as Louis IX once observed, was so dignified and meritorious that merely to say the word "filled the mouth."

The elevation of knightly status and the elaboration of courtly culture are perhaps best reflected in the term *gentleness.* In the late thirteenth and early fourteenth centuries this concept, with its complex earlier meanings in the literature of love and knightly conduct, became imbued with an ethical dignity that was close to virtue and constituted a major landmark in the history of social ideas and relationships. This slow process of transformation of the human concept of self had some of its roots in the changing conceptions of the relations be-tween man and God in the devotional revolution of the eleventh and twelfth cen-turies, and other roots in the formulation of a secularized ideal of gentlemanly conduct. In this process, which later extended from the courts to the towns and contributed much to an increasing emphasis of human dignity, courtly culture played a considerable role. The knight, like other social types, made a contri-bution far greater than his picturesqueness, quaintness, and archaic dignity; he helped in his own way to seek a measure of lay life that satisfied both material circumstances and the high demands of moral theology. The knight and the court, just as much as the townsman, merchant, free peasant, and ecclesiastical critic, constitute part of the variety of secular experience that established the le-gitimacy of lay status in early Europe. Far from being remote, idealized, pic-turesque institutions, the courts of the thirteenth century legitimated with a new ideal of the self a life of hard activity and much insecurity. Lords, courtiers, re-tainers, clergy, and poets in these courts absorbed influences from the world out-side and created a sense of order and ethical conduct that accommodated their own status and an increasingly secularized world.

The Latin and vernacular love poetry of the twelfth and thirteenth cen-turies has several themes in common with other kinds of literature, much of it originally clerical in its emphasis on self-knowledge, whether that knowledge was to be found in Peter Abelard's interest in the role of intention in judging the sin-fulness or innocence of an act, or in the treatises on friendship by such monas-tic writers as Ailred of Riveaulx, the English Cistercian monk who turned Cicero's views on friendship into the language of twelfth-century spirituality. For the clerics too, self-knowledge necessarily meant self-improvement. The individ-ual who explored the inner life, whether that of the emotions or that of the con-science in confession, was regarded as superior. Theologians valued passionate repentance more than routine penance; devotional writers insisted on the emo-tional bonds between humans and God, not merely on the formal bonds of wor-ship and obedience to the law. The surprising number of twelfth-century autobiographies also reflects a heightened awareness of an inner life, and thus a new kind of psychology.

Part of the new vernacular love poetry of the twelfth century can thus be understood as one further reflection of a concern for the self, its relation to oth-ers, and the changes made in it by different emotions. The sophisticated erotic po-etry of southern France (along with the bawdy songs and stories that the same poets often turned out) found in the amatory emotions a topic eminently suited to the values of an aristocracy whose life and culture were changing from the harsh and crude ideals of the eleventh century to a more mannered and stylized court life.

Birth, training, and the acceptance of a place among the vassals of a great lord made a knight; but knightly status alone was not sufficient to prove a man's quality. Certain virtues had to be added to noble birth in order to make a true knight. Constancy in love, the capacity for love itself, gentleness, humility, bravery, and above all the capacity of the "gentle" heart to experience these emotions made the nobly born knight worthy of the love of the nobly born lady. Proponents of such a view argued that love in the courtly setting indicated that the heart was gentle; a gentle heart indicated elevation above the common run of human beings. When a knight loved "gently" he became a better person, and his superiority had to be recognized by others in his society.

A literary setting different from those of the *chansons de geste* (epic poems of heroism and war) was needed for the expression of these values. Writers began to adapt Greek and Roman stories, and then they discovered King Arthur. The legends of King Arthur, scattered obscurely through saints' lives and piecemeal histories, suddenly began to attract a great interest after the mid–twelfth century. The Champagne poet Chretien de Troyes wrote a number of remarkable works in which the court of Arthur served as a focus for knightly adventures that had far more to do with what a modern critic would call the search for an identify than with battles with Saracens or endless feuds over property and privilege. In this world personal identity was discovered through the solution of problems posed by adventure. The court represented order, stability, established identity, and public recognition. Outside the court—in the forests, lakes, and deserts of the literary landscape—lurked the elements of temptation, disorder, uncertainty, paradox, and unintelligibility. There, outside the court, the knight discovered who he was, and his trials legitimized him when he returned to the court to tell his story. In the thirteenth century the stories of Arthur's court expanded. The theme of the Holy Grail, introduced under Cistercian influence, reflects the elevation of knighthood to sacral status. By the early thirteenth century the great *Prose Vulgate* had begun to piece together all the stories linked to Arthur. Versions of this work are found in most European languages. By the mid–fifteenth century in England the Arthurian corpus had become a great mine of secular themes, one that contributed political as well as emotional dimensions to Thomas Malory's great epic *Morte d'Arthur.*

The romance based on Arthurian materials expressed a spectrum of courtly concerns. Early in the thirteenth century Gottfried von Strassburg produced the brooding *Tristan und Isolde.* Among his contemporaries were the great German poets Wolfram von Eschenbach, whose *Parzival* and *Willehalm* contained new speculations on secular values and personal doubts, and Hartmann von Aue, whose *Der Arme Heinrich* and *Gregorius* included analyses of the layman's devotion and the conflict between role and conscience. The love lyrics of Languedoc, the center of lyric vernacular poetry in southern France, were echoed in Germany, Italy, Sicily, and England.

The history of the tenth-century explorations and settlements in Iceland and Greenland fed a Scandinavian literature of adventure and social concerns— the sagas. Scandinavian mythology, from pagan antiquity to the thirteenth century, contributed to the *Eddas*, long, complex poems exploring the remote past in the light of thirteenth-century concerns. In Kievan Russia the *Song of Igor's*

Campaign was the twelfth-century counterpart to the heroic literature of Scandinavia, early Germany, northern France, and the Spain of the *Song of El Cid.*

Folk literature circulated throughout the European world. Its stories, including those from Islamic, Byzantine, and Buddhist sources, made their way into Latin as well as the vernacular literatures, and they contributed to the language of emotional discourse. In the thirteenth century the Franciscan influence, reflected in the *Little Flowers of St. Francis,* a collection of unique stories about the personality of that individual, extended to other forms of narrative. As we have seen, the new devotional revolution of the twelfth and thirteenth centuries produced different types of saints and holy men, clerical and lay, such as Bernard, Thomas Becket, and Francis of Assisi. Their distinctive lives and personalities expanded the genre of biography. The lives of women saints contributed to the continued exploration of the self in an otherwise traditional genre. *Fabliaux* — comic stories that satirized both townsmen and knights—laid the foundation for the wide range of humorous and moral tales of the fourteenth century, particularly those of Boccaccio, Sachetti, and Chaucer.

There existed also a vast body of literature of which much less is known. Popular songs, tales, verses, and moralizing stories are often neglected by scholars because of their dubious value as "great literature." Yet to the historian of culture they reflect life and interests no less than do the more formally recognized works. The collections of miracle stories written for young monks by Caesarius of Heisterbach at the beginning of the thirteenth century and those of saints' lives by Jacobus of Varagine at the end of the century were read by Europeans for centuries. The *exempla,* moral tales used to illustrate and enliven sermons, offer frequent insights into popular life and interests. The stories, jokes, and scurrilous verses quoted in chronicles and memoirs of such thirteenth-century writers as Salimbene offer glimpses of general life that are found nowhere else. From moralizing tales to outright scatology, medieval vernacular literature is a widely varied, rich, and wonderful genre. For the interested reader, these materials heighten and illuminate a level of culture that is attained only incompletely in more formal documents and works of philosophy.

Perhaps two final examples will serve to illustrate these remarks. The *Song of the Nibelungs* is a thirteenth-century epic poem written in Bavaria and based on materials that date, in their Latin form, from the sixth and seventh centuries. It is the tale of the warrior Siegfried and his people and his wife, Kriemhild, the sister of Gunther, Siegfried's enemy. Following Siegfried's murder Kriemhild plots revenge upon Gunther, and the ensuing action involves the whole world; Attila the Hun, Theoderic the Ostrogoth, and the heroes of the old Latin and German sagas are all drawn together. Yet the Nibelung poet does not revel in the wealth of legend, literary tradition, folklore, and violence he presents, but focuses the action and diversity in a masterly way on the theme of Kriemhild's revenge. The classification of this marvelous work somewhere among the sagas, *chansons de geste,* and romances reflects both the high command of literary skill that had been reached throughout Europe by the thirteenth century and the complex relationships between medieval vernacular literature and early European society.

The *Song of the Nibelungs* preserves some of the older aspects of heroic literature while emphasizing many of the newer, particularly in its depiction of Kriemhild's psychology. Another work, written around the same time in France, shows another side of courtly values. Around 1235 a French poet named Guillaume de Lorris wrote the first 4000 lines of a poem that he called *The Romance of the Rose*. The poem was in the popular form of a dream-vision, in which the poet dreams he is in a garden peopled by personifications of human behavioral traits — characters with such names as Sir Mirth, the lord of the garden, his lady Dame Gladness, and a helpful aide named Fair-Welcome. The dreamer falls in love with a rose in the heart of the garden (the symbol of a young woman), but his attempts to reach the Rose are blocked by the vices of Shame and Jealousy. These abstractions in the allegorical garden are in one sense all part of a refined analysis of the psychological state of what the author considered the proper way of falling in love.

The Romance of the Rose was immensely popular throughout the thirteenth century. At the end of the century another poet, Jean de Meun, completed the poem with another 18,000 lines. But the two approaches were remarkably different. Guillaume de Lorris was a gentle idealist. His figures are painted lightly and gracefully, and the theme of proper love is linked to the theme of the proper social life. Jean de Meun, however, knew other kinds of twelfth- and thirteenth-century thought, and his long continuation of the poem drew on the methods and interests of academic and legal culture as well. Personifications of various psychological states and human attributes give long and contradictory speeches and argue violently. As the modern English editor Charles Dunn points out, "the entire work portrays an intellectual chain reaction among scholarly specialists occasioned by the Lover's dogged determination to persevere in his pursuit of Love." At the end of the poem, after a military siege of the Rose's castle described by a master of the language of military siege tactics, the Lover wins the Rose, and elevated though they are by the bizarre courtship, the conclusion is clearly sexual. Jean de Meun brought a different mind and different values to the elegant poem of Guillaume de Lorris. It is nevertheless striking that the courtly setting, developed by twelfth-century poets and continued by thirteenth-century romancers, became an appropriate background for his scholastic diatribe.

The *Song of the Nibelungs* and *The Romance of the Rose* encompass a wide range of thirteenth-century courtly literature. Its knightly characters, caught between God and the world, developed an ethos that appeared for a time to satisfy the demands of both, based as it was on the creative power of love, personal loyalty and conduct, and devotion to God. Even though other cultural values soon clamored for recognition in different settings, courtly literature survived until the eighteenth century. In it the European aristocracy had found its perfect mirror.

THE WORLD OF DANTE

Others besides the courtly nobility found new sets of values in the twelfth and thirteenth centuries. In northern Italy, France, Flanders, and Germany towns-people created a distinctly urban culture, the liveliest manifestations of which may be found in the large cities of northern Italy—in Lombardy, Tuscany, and Venetia. The term that people used to describe this new urban culture—the *vita civile*, or civic life—is as important as the new courtly culture. Like that culture, with which it shared many values, the *vita civile* represented a predominantly lay approach to the definition and ordering of the good life.

The cities of northern Italy present a variegated picture at the turn of the fourteenth century. They differed widely in size and constitutional structure, in dependence upon other, more powerful towns, in financial, commercial, and diplomatic affairs, in the degree of city control of social and economic life, in the degree of civic consciousness, in relations with the countryside and neighboring towns, and in levels of education and artistic patronage. They were small societies, but the degree of political energy required to mobilize their resources and conduct policy, their high consciousness of the dangers of the surrounding world, and their control of ecclesiastical authority all reflect their precocious development as political societies. The wealth brought in from trade, industry, and finance, the necessity of having a "foreign" policy and a militia, the needs of public financing, and the sense of independence reflected by what a later lawyer called "the city, a prince unto itself," made many of these cities resemble later kingdoms. The political instability and constitutional crises to which the cities were usually prone reflect not so much political immaturity as political creativity. After the Church, the northern Italian towns may be said to have created the first European states.

Population and economic growth, the long struggles for independence, and the very experience of living within the physical city contributed to the development of an urban culture that expressed itself in various ways, from education to history writing, from architecture to public ceremonies. The necessities of town government produced the great town halls that still survive in many of even the smallest towns, as do the carefully planned and maintained public squares. Pride in the physical appearance of the city dates from very early in communal history, and statutes protecting the physical city, from measures concerning hygiene to those dealing with aesthetics, appear on the statute books of many towns. The towns were responsible too for church building. Citizen committees managed the work and commissioned the artists who decorated the churches. The contacts many cities had with Byzantium and the east and with France and the north and west brought many diverse influences into the towns, and those contributed to the selection and planning of buildings and the artistic themes embodied in them. The cities knew of individual artists by reputation, and many of the greatest works of Duccio di Boninsegna, Arnolfo di Cambio, and Giotto were done on civic commissions. The decoration of churches expressed the spiritual values of the town, and the decoration of public buildings expressed the town's sense of its own history and self-image.

There is no more striking example of the liveliness of urban artistic patronage than the series of frescoes produced by Ambrogio Lorenzetti in the Palazzo Publico of Siena in 1338–1340. His frescoes on the subject of good and bad government offer a vast and extraordinarily detailed exposition of the self-image of the city of Siena. Theological personifications and political abstractions are set against a highly intricate depiction of the life of the city and its inhabitants, from masons and carpenters to farmers, traders, hunters, and governing officials. Outdoors, in the towns themselves, fountains, piazzas, public buildings, streets, and bridges provided opportunities for the city to enhance its beauty and reinforce visually and physically the sense of belonging to a well-ordered society.

Ideas, artistic and literary styles, and new forms of urban devotion were other contributors to the *vita civile*. The courts of southern France and Frederick II of Sicily gave birth to literary influences that, adapted by urban Italian poets, shaped the *dolce stil nuovo,* "the sweet, new style," in which amatory, ethical, and philosophical themes were blended in Italian vernacular poetry of a very high order. Lively satirical lyrics and short tales found eager audiences in the towns. So did the stories about Francis of Assisi and his followers, as well as the Latin and vernacular town histories that began to appear early in the thirteenth century. The earliest and one of the greatest of these was the *Chronicle* written by the Franciscan Salimbene of Parma about the events of his day. At the end of the thirteenth century Dino Compagni (1266–1324) of Florence wrote a *Chronicle of Events Occurring in His Own Time,* a vivid account of personalities and political crises in Florence at the end of the thirteenth and beginning of the fourteenth centuries. Another Florentine, Giovanni Villani (1270–1348), wrote a *Chronicle* of Florentine and world history that constitutes an important landmark in the lay writing of history.

This lively cultural world appealed to the eyes, ears, and especially the minds of townspeople in the thirteenth and fourteenth centuries, and it appealed to their spirits as well. Eminent laymen listened to lectures in the Dominican church of Santa Maria Novella in Florence or the Franciscan church of Santa Croce. These two great churches, the cathedral of Santa Maria dei Fiore, and the third circle of the city walls of Florence were all built in the lifetime of Dante Alighieri (1265–1321), the greatest of all Italian poets and men of letters. At the turn of the fourteenth century cities such as Florence had an air not of antiquity but of striking modernity. Florence literally took shape under the eyes of the writers, artists, and preachers who were the most eloquent praisers of the city and its life.

Associations for the building of churches, drinking and gaming clubs, youth associations, masters' guilds, literary circles, and religious confraternities—communal organizations of piety—divided and subdivided the social and cultural life of the towns. By the fourteenth century, the life of the city had come to include urban religion as well. The culture of the townsman as well as the culture of the knight and noble acquired a spiritual dimension that enhanced the secular activities that sustained the worlds of court and city.

No single figure represents—indeed transcends—the cultural world of the northern Italian towns more strikingly than Dante Alighieri, and no single literary or artistic work reflects the intellectual and political movements between 1150 and 1300 in greater detail and artistic force than his great poem, *The Divine Comedy*. Dante was born in 1265 to an impoverished family that claimed descent from the earlier Florentine nobility. Though in Dante's youth it had experienced a brief period of economic prosperity through moneylending, its status certainly remained modest. This is indicated by Dante's marriage to Gemma di Manetto, a member of only a minor branch of the great Donati family. Even minor respectability afforded many opportunities to Florentine citizens, however. Dante pursued a course of studies, probably in Florence, and in 1289 he participated in the Florentine defeat of Arezzo at the Battle of Campaldino. By that date his earliest literary work, several lyric poems, had attracted the attention of a talented and influential group of Florentine writers, and his friendships with the great lyric poet Guido Cavalcanti, and the encyclopedist Brunetto Latini date from these years.

Dante was thus exposed both to a wide literary circle and to the new sensibility expressed in contemporary love lyrics. In his own life the figure of Bice Portinari, who was to become the wife of Simone dei Bardi, a prominent citizen of Florence, became his personification of ideal womanhood. After her death in 1290 Dante wrote a short account of her role in his personal spiritual and intellectual development in verse and prose, *La Vita Nuova* (*The New Life*), which he completed in 1292. Not only are the verses in this work the indication of a major poetic talent, but the development of Bice into Beatrice, Dante's own spiritual guide, foreshadows her role in the *Comedy* and represents a highly original transformation of the older courtly motif of passionate love between a man and a woman, this time into a powerful spiritual force through which the woman raises the man spiritually to heights he would be unable to achieve without her.

Dante's development during this period was not solely that of a poet and philosopher. Between 1295 and 1300 he held various political offices and, like other men of letters, enrolled in the guild of apothecaries and physicians. Membership in a guild was essential for holding political office, and there is no evidence that Dante was ever a practicing pharmacist or physician. The fortunes of Florence were insecure during Dante's terms of public service. Boniface VIII, the Black faction of the Guelf party that dominated Florence, and the royal house of France were involved in complex intrigues, and Dante's term of prior in June and August 1300 revealed to him the dangers surrounding the city. In 1301, while Dante was serving as the Florentine ambassador to Rome, the Black Guelfs seized power, attacked their enemies, and banished Dante from the city *in absentia,* citing several charges of political corruption on his part that would have sufficed for his execution had he returned.

From 1302 to 1304 Dante wandered throughout northern Italy, serving as an adviser to the exiled White Guelf faction in its quest to restore itself to power in Florence. However, Dante broke with his fellow exiles, whose short-sightedness, greed, and self-interest he later denounced bitterly in the *Comedy.* Between 1304 and 1310 he wandered even more widely, moving from court to court and experiencing both the pain of exile and the fitful patronage of local princes. When Emperor Henry VII descended into Italy, Dante joined his cause and became a spokesman on his behalf. The early years of his exile had produced the unfinished treatise on the Italian vernacular, *De vulgari eloquentia,* and the long, unfinished collection of philosophical poems and commentaries, *Il Convivio.* Dante's letters on behalf of Henry VII contain a more prophetic strain, and his later letters, written when Henry's cause had failed, contain bitter denunciations of those whom Dante held responsible not only for the emperor's failure but for the chaos of Italian life.

From 1310 to his death in September 1321 Dante lived at the courts of various patrons, most notably that of Can Grande della Scala at Verona and that of Guido da Polenta at Ravenna, where he died and is buried. During the last decade of his life, and possibly earlier, he worked on the *Comedy,* a vast vision of hell, purgatory, and heaven in which he organized and analyzed the events of his life and his time with a vast intelligence and one of the greatest poetic voices the world has ever known.

Several times he attempted to negotiate with Florence for his return to the city, but the parties never reached terms that Dante could accept. His exile and pilgrimage became for him a metaphor of justice; *exul immeritus,* "an undeserving exile," he called himself, condemning in passionate and eloquent language the disorder of justice that in his vision prevented humankind from governing itself properly. From his exile there emerged the great poem that embodies his visionary genius. Citizen, scholar, man of letters, philosophical lover, and exile, Dante illuminates, not as a type but as a distinctive, compelling individual, the life of the cities in which he lived and the force of the culture that he shared and helped shape.

MEDIEVAL WOMEN IN CITY AND CONVENT

The reform movement of the eleventh and twelfth centuries completed the exclusion of women from priestly orders and from positions of authority within the church. But demographic figures reveal that women in the same period began to outnumber men, and Albertus Magnus observed that, contrary to the teaching of Aristotle, women had a longer life expectancy than men. The redefinition of women's place in the Church and the increasing numbers of women living to an older age posed a substantial problem for both women and men in thirteenth-

and fourteenth-century Europe. Although demographic conditions had improved for women, they also posed new problems.

One problem was the religious life of women, and a number of reforms were instituted with this problem in mind. As M.-D. Chenu has shown, one consequence of the heightened religious consciousness of the late eleventh and twelfth centuries had been a new interest in the *vita apostolica*—the apostolic life. This interest was not confined to males or to clerical authorities alone. A number of new religious institutions were designed primarily with women in mind, not all of them with official support. Robert of Arbrissel, for example, formed religious houses of reformed women in which a woman governed both women and men. The English Gilbertine Order was designed specifically for women. Several of the major religious orders (sometimes reluctantly) accepted houses of women under their patronage and direction, as did the new Mendicant Orders of the thirteenth century. Even in the cases of individual religious women, the number of anchorites and their social function linked women to the new eremitism that continued for several centuries. At the turn of the thirteenth century Jacques de Vitry, an astute and sensitive observer of much of Europe, praised the activities of a group of religious women in Lorraine and their leader Mary of Oignies (d. 1213) as new "mothers of the Church." In some cases, notably that of the prophet and mystic Hildegard of Bingen (1098–1179), the writings of religious women exercised a profound influence on both clerical and lay rulers. As a number of historians have shown, the imagery and religious sensibility of medieval women broadened and enriched the religious and psychological sensibility of religious language and emotion.

The Franciscan Third Order represents one new option for female devotion. The movement known as that of the *Beguines,* which emerged in the late twelfth century in the lower Rhineland and the Low Countries, represents another. Although Beguine communities were associated with no notable male founder-figure, received no papal approval, and were often misinterpreted by other churchmen—a condition illustrated by the remark of the Franciscan Gilbert of Tournai in 1274: "There are women among us whom we have no idea what to call, because they live neither in the world nor out of it." This anomalousness in the eyes of the clergy led to considerable opposition to Beguine life, accusations of heresy, and to a temporary decline in the practice in the early fourteenth century.

Beguines appear to have come from an urban setting and from the class of the urban patriciate. They developed unique devotional forms and cultivated mysticism—the direct communion between the individual and God. Beguines lived communally—a number of cities in modern Belgium have preserved these communities, *Beguinages,* or *Begijnhofen*—and often worked during the day in the urban textile industry. The devotional literature—including the lives of a number of Beguine saints—offers a rich complement to other works of the thirteenth and fourteenth centuries.

In spite of the new dimensions that the status of religious women offered in the late twelfth and thirteenth centuries, the status and perspectives of medieval women must be understood in other terms as well. Although a number of clerics and lay rulers respected female spirituality, others drew on biological doctrines and moral theology to fear and despise women. Yet just as religious women demonstrated a versatility and inventiveness in matters of spirituality and religious sensibility in spite of the increasingly oppressive weight of biological and theological theory, at the same time women's position in lay society also changed.

A sufficiently high social status, whether in the case of religious or lay women, could allow a woman to avoid some of the most hostile and misogynistic views of medieval society, although she could not avoid them completely. Queens and female members of royal or noble families, although they did not possess explicit constitutional authority, nevertheless could defend themselves against the most conspicuous aspects of misogyny. Yet their own choices of a form of life remained restricted: with the exception of the Beguines and a small number of extraordinary and distinctive individual holy women, marriage and the cloister were the principal choices for most aristocratic women, because their social value demanded that their marriages serve diplomatic or political purposes.

Below the high nobility, married women were both more vulnerable to misogny and, at the same time, more supported. In the towns, marriage too was a means of uniting family and fortune and passing property down through the next generations. But it was also the association with another family in the relatively small confines of a city, and desirable marriages occupied much of the time and minds of parents and children. The literature that is devoted to the topic of "the good wife" in the thirteenth and fourteenth centuries is considerable, and highly restrictive.

The sacamentalization of marriage in 1215 generated much of this literature, evoking much more frequently than earlier the institution of marriage by God in the Garden of Eden and the wedding at Cana, the site of Jesus' first miracle. Aristotle was pressed into service, not only as a biological and gynecological authority, but as the philosopher of the well-ordered household. This literature commanded the wife to respect her in-laws in order to establish and preserve social peace, love her husband (but with the restrained conjugal affection that did not weaken the marriage, as spousal passion was thought to), be submissive to her husband, and indeed educated by him, who would return the moderate and tempered affection proper to a man. The wife should not look for wealth or status in a husband (although a husband could do so in seeking a wife). The wife was to manage the household, produce and supervise the early raising of children, care for the family, and above all live an irreproachable life, so that no word could be said against her inside or outside the household.

Also in spite of its sacramental status after 1215, marriage remained chiefly an important social and economic transaction. As the ratio of women to men increased sometime after the tenth century, the dowry became a more important aspect of the marriage contract, replacing bride-price. Throughout the thirteenth century in Italy demands for dowries appear to have grown greater, and Dante, in his *Divine Comedy,* criticizes the high price demanded by suitors' families when they sought a bride. At the same time, women could inherit, own, acquire, and dispose of their own property. Women worked in family businesses, and they often controlled them. Although they did not hold public office, and thus had a very limited public role, nonnoble urban women exercised considerable independence, sometimes rivaling in this regard the women at the very highest reaches of society who also controlled much of their own lives.

In a scene of such variety and rapid change, the courtly literature that appeared to venerate women, must be taken critically. Literary works—lyric poems and romances—that praised the virtues of women, their worthiness as objects of love, their inaccessibility to all but the most polished and worthy suitors—indeed constructed a female ideal that was later transformed by Dante and others into a vehicle for spiritual enlightenment and salvation itself. However, such literature merely created another form of ideal and hardly affected the status or views of women in the life outside of literature. In the twin figures of Mary and Eve, theorists found a view of women that contained both the best and worst aspects of the female—indeed, the two figures were virtually irreconcilable. But beyond Mary and Eve, in the worlds of courts, religious sensibility, urban life, and rural households, medieval women worked out other roles and other identities. To understand these one must go beyond the cliches of courtly love and the polemics of clerical misogynists to explore the growing interest in and evidence for the history of women, the history of gender differences, and the nature of feminine experience.

FURTHER READING

In general, see *The Cambridge History of Later Medieval Philosophy,* eds. Norman Kretzman, Anthony Kenny, and Jan Pinborg (Cambridge: Cambridge University Press, 1982).

On Aristotelian and other theories of sexuality and gestation, see the essay "The Nature of Woman," by Claude Thomasset, in Klapisch-Zuber, *A History of Women in the West,* Vol. II, *The Silences of the Middle Ages,* 43–69, and the references in the General Bibliography under Women, and History and The Body and Sexuality. The most recent survey is that of Monica Green, "Women's Medical Practice and Health Care in Medieval Europe," *Signs* 14 (1989), 434–473, with extensive further references. Green is presently translating the text of Trota.

The literature on philosophy and theology in the thirteenth century is vast, and the beginning student will want as easy a guide through it as possible. M.-D. Chenu, *Toward Understanding St. Thomas,* trans. A.M. Landry and D. Hughes (Chicago: Henry Regnery, 1964), is an ideal student's guide to the period in general as well as to Aquinas himself. A good recent biography of Thomas is Jean-Pierre Torrell, *Saint Thomas Aquinas,* Vol. I, T*he Person and His Work* (Washington, D.C.: Catholic University of America Press, 1995). For Bonaventure, see J. Guy Bougerol, *Introduction to the Works of St. Bonaventure,* trans. Jose de Vinck (Paterson, NJ: St. Anthony Guild Press, 1965).

An excellent general introduction is that of John Marenbon, *Later Medieval Philosophy (1150–1350): An Introduction* (New York: Routledge & Kegan Paul, 1987).

On Gothic architecture, see Jean Bony, *French Gothic Architecture of the 12th and 13th Centuries* (Berkeley and Los Angeles: University of California Press, 1983). For a single example, see Robert Branner, *Chartres Cathedral* (New York: Norton, 1969). The wonderful children's book by David Macaulay, *Cathedral: The Story of Its Construction* (Boston: Houghton Mifflin, 1973), is a mine of easily accessible information.

On the complex problem of knighthood and chivalry, see Georges Duby's essays, *The Chivalrous Society* (Berkeley and Los Angeles: University of California Press, 1980). The essential study of the origins of courtly culture is now that of C. Stephen Jaeger, *The Origins of Courtliness: Civilizing Trends and the Formation of Courtly Ideals, 939–1210* (Philadelphia: University of Pennsylvania Press, 1985). On chivalry as a topic of research, see Maurice Keen, *Chivalry* (New Haven, CT: Yale University Press, 1984).

On the *vita civile* and Dante, see John Larner, *Italy in the Age of Dante and Petrarch, 1216–1380* (New York: Longman, 1980); *The Cambridge Companion to Dante,* ed., Rachel Jacoff (Cambridge: Cambridge University Press, 1993), and Charles T. Davis, *Dante's Italy and Other Essays* (Philadelphia: University of Pennsylvania Press, 1984). A contemporary account of Dante's city is now available: Daniel E. Bornstein, ed. and trans., Dino Compagni's *Chronicle of Florence* (Philadelphia: University of Pennsylvania Press, 1986). A good detailed study of the interweaving of poetry and politics is Joan M. Ferrante, *The Political Vision of the Divine Comedy* (Princeton, NJ: Princeton University Press, 1984). The best general history of thirteenth-century Europe is that of John H. Mundy, *Europe in the High Middle Ages, 1154–1309,* reprint ed. (New York: Longman, 1973).

Mundy's study of the High Middle Ages also contains important aspects of the history of women, as does the volume of essays made in his honor: Julius Kirschner and Suzanne F. Wemple, eds., *Women of the Medieval World* (Oxford: Basil Blackwell, 1985). See also the General Bibliography under the heading Women and History.

17

MATERIAL CIVILIZATION: CRISIS AND RECOVERY

APOCALYPSE THEN: THE FOUR HORSEMEN

In the book of Apocalypse, or Revelations, the last canonical book of the Christian Bible, the Four Horsemen let loose to afflict the earth were identified as death, famine, pestilence, and war. The art of the fourteenth and fifteenth centuries abounds with depictions of these figures, and in the fourteenth century famine, pestilence, and war plunged material civilization into a crisis. Population levels fell, land turned to waste, and the overextended system of agricultural production virtually collapsed.

The mild climate that Europe had enjoyed since 100 B.C. began to change in the thirteenth century. This did not mean instantly colder temperatures, shorter summers, and more severe winters. The signs of change came, rather, in increasingly unpredictable weather patterns. Extremely good years were followed by inexplicably bad ones; a series of heavy rains that rotted crops and leached the earth might last for several years, to be followed by improved weather for a decade or more; intermittent severe conditions might freeze or inundate vineyards and grain fields for a season or two.

The effects of such changes were felt most quickly in the former marginal lands that required intensive cultivation and whose margin of productivity was small in the best of times. Famine had been a constant danger, even in periods of prosperity, and from 1290 on, it appears to have occurred more regularly. Although from 1309 to 1314 extremely poor crops and a series of long, destructive rains posed a threat of famine in a few places, the general shortage of food everywhere and the immediate impact of climatic change on marginal land mark the first of the fourteenth-century crises. The tenuous balance between population and agricultural productivity was particularly threatened. The seed-to-yield ratio of even the best-tended and most productive fields was relatively low, and even a small decline in that ratio had serious consequences for the total agricultural output of a region. On lands requiring intensive labor for prevention of erosion or maintenance of drainage, a higher population level was needed than elsewhere; agricultural output had to remain high if it was to sustain that population.

The famine was greatest from 1315 to 1317. Grain prices soared astronomically. Regions that depended on distant places for their food suffered a drastic population loss—as high as 10 percent in some towns, and the seed-to-yield ratio fell, in some cases by half. The 1315/17 famine was the greatest that Europe experienced, but it was not the only one. The fragile agricultural system, even if it had not achieved its potential output, had nevertheless proved incapable of feeding Europe without profound revision. Moreover, nearly every succeeding decade of the fourteenth century witnessed either regional or more widespread famine, and hunger became a universal and perennial scourge for the first prolonged period since the end of antiquity.

Hungry people die or move. In the fourteenth century, land that could no longer be worked—because of soil exhaustion, population loss, the ravages of war, or the frequency and extent of pestilence—was abandoned. The fourteenth century produced an increasing number of deserted farming settlements, many of which were never settled again. People moved to monasteries, towns, or more productive regions, there to seek food through charity, wage labor, or the assumption of servile status. The migrations provoked by famine raised other problems. The new arrivals could contribute little to the quality of town or city life, and they strained urban food supplies. As we will see later in this chapter, fourteenth and fifteenth century warfare also disrupted agricultural life. And on the heels of famine and war followed pestilence.

The dangers of reduced harvests, rising grain prices, and widespread famine are many. Death by starvation is not the only consequence of famine, nor is it the most far-reaching. Medieval people knew little about the different properties of foods, and medieval nutrition was barely adequate even in the best of times. The wealthy tended, even as late as the seventeenth century, to eat more animal protein and fewer vegetables than they needed, and the poor tended to eat far less animal protein. Because these foods were more readily available, the poor ate far more vegetables and starch. Animal protein, always expensive, was usually available only in late fall and early winter, when animals were slaughtered.

The Labors of the Months. Scenes showing the different occupations appropriate to different months of the year often decorated astronomical manuscripts, as in this tenth-century example. (*Bild-Archiv der Osterreichischen Nationalbibliothek, Vienna*)

As winter progressed meat was salted more and more heavily and spiced to prevent rancidity.

Besides producing such diseases as gout, an unbalanced diet of too much meat raises the dangers of a host of other diseases and severe vitamin deficiency. Wealthy or moderately prosperous Europeans ran these risks until well into modern times. On the other hand, a deficiency of animal protein produces tuberculosis, dysentery, and other maladies, and stunts growth substantially. Vitamin deficiency generally produces enormously painful and prolonged physical conditions—scurvy, rickets, gallstones. Thus, the European diet, even in the most prosperous of years, created physiological imbalances that afflicted many people, although their causes were not generally known until the eighteenth century. Starvation and malnutrition raised equally severe problems. The period between 1300 and 1850 witnessed the greatest effects of malnutrition on the greatest number of people. Starvation and malnutrition kill the old and the weak and, as we now know, damage those who experience them in childhood. They produce a drastic change in the demographic composition of society. The number of old and sick drops, infant mortality increases, and the birth rate decreases. Women die during their most fertile years. Those who survive leave the area, taking with them another generation, one that will be born elsewhere. Thus, the depopulation of many farms, villages, and towns does not last merely for the duration of the period of famine, but for two or three generations, and sometimes forever.

THE PALE HORSEMAN: PLAGUE IN LATE MEDIEVAL EUROPE

Those who suffer malnutrition lack resistance to disease. Widespread starvation and malnutrition had already begun to reduce the population of Europe when the next of the Four Horsemen—pestilence—struck with unprecedented fury. It struck a population weakened by hunger and lack of resistance, crowded into cities, more mobile than in any period of Europe's history since the fifth and sixth centuries, and thus extremely vulnerable to contagion—a principle it did not understand—carried by a bacillus that was not identified until 1918.

The history of widespread epidemic disease and human society has only recently begun to be written. The great plague described by Thucydides in Athens during the Peloponnesian War, the plague brought back to Italy by Marcus Aurelius's troops in the late second century A.D., and the great plague that struck Constantinople and the West in 542/43—these were the most striking, best-known, and remembered epidemics in early European history. Although the great epidemics of cholera, smallpox, and influenza in nineteenth- and twentieth-century Europe have been better described and analyzed than earlier epidemics, the plague of 1348/50, and its subsequent outbreaks between the mid–fourteenth and the late seventeenth centuries, stands as the most memorable and destructive of all. Although its ravages were regional, it reduced the population of Europe by one third, completely depopulated some regions and towns, and further aggravated the earlier effects of agricultural disaster, famine, and population loss that had begun by the last years of the thirteenth century. It was also a prodigious test of the resiliency of European society. The recovery of fifteenth-, sixteenth-, and seventeenth-century Europe in terms of population, agricultural output, and living conditions offers eloquent testimony to the vigor and recuperative powers of that society. The roots of this recovery surely lay in the agricultural, technological, and economic innovations of the tenth through the early fourteenth centuries.

Bubonic plague is the product of the bacillus *yersinia pestis*, which lives in the blood stream of the flea, *xenopsylla cheopsis*, which in turn lives in the coat of the black rat (*rattus rattus*). This combination thrived best in warm and moist environments, and it appears to have grown and disappeared historically in cycles, from cycles of twenty, and up to three hundred years. The etiology of the plague begins when the flea, whose suckling mechanism is blocked when laden with *yersinia pestis*, repeatedly bites a human in order to consume the blood it needs. The repeated bites transmit the bacillus into the human, which produces a pustule (a bubo, hence the name bubonic plague for this form of the disease) which necroses to a blackish placque after a day of high fever. In the following days large abscesses form in the lymphatic system nearest to the original innoculation. The patient is then subject to neurological and psychological disturbances as the nervous system is afflicted; digestion becomes difficult, and dark blotches appear on the skin as a result of subcutaneous hemmoraging. If the buboes supurate within a week, the patient may survive. If they do not, 30 to 40 percent of those infected die by the second day; 50 to 90 percent die by the end of the first week, and 80 to 90 percent die by the third week.

When the plague creates abscesses in the lungs, the pneumonic form of plague is contracted. After a one to three-day incubation the fever is not as high as in the bubonic form, but the pulse varies drastically, respiratory difficulties ensue, sputum increases, neurological disorders are manifested, the patient falls into a coma and gradually suffocates. All those infected in this way die within two to three days, with an average life expectancy of 1.8 days. Pneumonic plague is highly contagious. Coughing, expectoration, and sneezing spread the bacillus into the air (in cool and damp atmospheres, the bacillus can linger in the air), creating a zone of contagion up to four meters. When the bacillus infects the bloodstream directly, the plague assumes its septicemic form, and the patient dies before buboes have a chance to form. In its three forms—bubonic, pneumonic, and septicemic—the plague was until the twentieth century the most devastating epidemic disease known to humans. The cycle that struck in 1348 did not end until the late seventeenth century, and the black rat was not driven out of Europe and replaced by the less plague-hospitable

Spread of Black Death.

brown rat until the eighteenth century. Only the invention of modern antibiotics has made the possibility of breaking the great plague cycles possible.

The cycle of plague that struck western Europe in 1348 seems to have originated in Asia and to have struck first in China around 1333. By 1340 it had reached Lake Baikal in Siberia, and by 1346 it has crossed the Caucasus and struck the Crimea, at Caffa, the great port center on the Black Sea. Carried by the rats on an Italian fleet from the Black Sea to the Mediterranean, the plague struck first in Europe in Messina and Sardinia in 1347. The next year it hit Genoa and Venice, the greatest ports of the west, simultaneously. From the ports the plague followed the trade routes. In February 1348 both Lucca and Avignon reported outbreaks, and two months later Siena and Perugia in Italy and Cercana and Rousillon in southwestern France were struck. In May, Ancona, Orvieto, and Rimini in Italy and Barcelona and Catalonia in Spain were afflicted, followed in July by Paris and Antioch and a year later by Germany and Tunisia. By September of 1349 the plague had reached England, by 1350 Prussia, Bremen, and the eastern Netherlands, and by 1351/52 western Russia. The indescribably swift spread of plague, its erratic destructiveness of human life, and the utter incomprehension of European society not only provoked severe loss of life and economic disruption on a vast scale but struck the European Christian mind and imagination with a terrible force. The consequences of the plague were echoed in literature, devotional styles, and the visual arts, as well as in depopulated farms and villages, devastated cities, and disordered economic institutions. Moreover, survival of the 1348/51 crisis did not guarantee immunity to later outbreaks.

Quickly joining the widespread bubonic form of plague were the vastly more contagious and deadly pneumonic and septicemic strains. In these three forms the plague attacked a population that was crowded into towns and ecclesiastical centers under the worst possible hygienic conditions, possessed uncertain food supplies, and already lacked a full complement of women of childbearing age. Those who survived one attack of plague were, of course, vulnerable to other infectious diseases, such as tuberculosis.

The years 1362 and 1375 witnessed epidemics as severe as that of 1348, and plague returned at least once in every decade until 1497. The great plague cycle begun in 1348 did not end until the late seventeenth century. Pestilence, then, followed hunger and malnutrition in the experience of fourteenth- and fifteenth-century men and women.

The birth rate usually increases after great population losses, as if to offset them. After the mid–fourteenth century, however, the frequent recurrence of plague and famine prevented the birth rate from increasing the population. Indeed, most of the population increase in Europe after 1100 was wiped out. But such population loss did not occur uniformly everywhere. Population densities were redistributed considerably, villages were deserted for centuries, new villages were founded, and the proportion of urban to rural dwellers increased. Cities recovered their populations faster, not through an increased birth rate but by drawing off the rural population increase. The countryside had to populate both itself and the cities.

THE RED HORSEMAN: WAR AND SOCIETY

Famine and plague strike most severely at those least able to provide for themselves. In fourteenth- and fifteenth-century Europe, a society in which material resources had been stretched to their limits, a series of wars broke out between 1337 and the late fifteenth century. Their duration and character were different from those of earlier wars, which had consisted generally of infrequent pitched battles between small armies that were not assembled for long periods of time. Such wars usually troubled the noncombatant population relatively little, because they did little permanent damage. The wars of England and France, Castile, and northern Italy in the fourteenth and fifteenth centuries, however, had a different character. Recurring campaigns made battlefields out of plowed fields year after year. Some elements of agricultural life such as mills and barns could not be quickly replaced, because they required substantial capital and labor investment. The temporary but often regular destruction of crops and the prolonged effects of the destruction of mills and barns framed the circumstances of warfare. An invading fourteenth-century army, rather like a small expeditionary force, struck into enemy territory on a swift raid, a *chevauchée* supporting itself from enemy land capturing enemy towns, and destroying opposing forces. The invaded country, its inhabitants temporarily crowded into fortified towns and castles barely large enough to contain them, could only destroy the food in its own fields so that it did not fall into enemy hands, and hold out until the invaders, frustrated and hungry, moved on. The open country of northern France was particularly vulnerable to this kind of warfare, and the frequent slowing down of military campaigns by prolonged sieges increased the dangers to the noncombatant population considerably. Enemy armies, particularly when they wished to demoralize a hostile population, could themselves destroy fields and crops, exact large ransoms and bribes, and fail to keep their armies from looting.

The duration, frequency, and style of warfare proved particularly disastrous to noncombatants, and so did the composition of fourteenth-century armies. Soldiers were paid little, and their pay was frequently late if it came at all. Soldiers were usually recruited from the poorer and less stable elements of society, and regarded military activity as a means of self-enrichment. Prisoners were taken for ransom, towns and castles were plundered, and agricultural lands were held for tribute. Financial needs usually demanded that armies be disbanded as soon as possible, and large bands of discharged soldiers wandered around the countryside during truces, plundering and terrorizing the population. These groups, called *routiers* in the fourteenth century and *écorcheurs* in the fifteenth, posed continual problems. Sometimes they were reabsorbed into armies when the wars broke out again, and sometimes they sold themselves to the highest bidder in local conflicts. France and Italy were plagued the most severely by them, until the end of the fifteenth century.

Closely related to the activities of discharged or deserted soldiers was the increasing prevalence of banditry in the late fourteenth and fifteenth centuries. *Écorcheurs* took over territory around fortified places they had captured on their own, demanded ransom from those they kidnapped, demanded entire harvests, and required "protection" payments from all whose lives they touched. Impoverished and undisciplined lords of castles found it profitable to raid neighboring areas, particularly after acquiring some military experience—and probably some military personnel—in the numerous wars of the fourteenth century. Both nobles and displaced peasants sometimes formed their own bands or joined larger gangs in the French provinces and the north of England. Finally, robber bands seem to have formed among the poor, as well as among individuals of yeoman status. From the fourteenth century to the nineteenth, banditry became a ubiquitous and, to those already ravaged by famine, plague, and war, a particularly dangerous aspect of life.

A final aspect of late medieval warfare ought to be discussed. Earlier wars had been fought by professional knights and men-at-arms, and were caused by the arguments of princes and kings. They were small in scale and generally short. By the fourteenth century, however, wars touched the noncombatant population more regularly, not only through their destructiveness but through their financing and recruitment as well. The affairs of kings and princes drew upon a wider circle of resources and personnel. The organization of late medieval warfare and its power to mobilize extensive social and material resources made war a more prominent part of both social and economic history and an important part of political and constitutional history as well.

Philip IV the Fair of France won his first conflict with Pope Boniface VIII on the grounds that a king's obligation to defend his kingdom overrode his conventional obligations to churchmen and their finances. As other kings and rulers found that financing warfare was growing more and more expensive, they too tended to neglect traditional restraints in their dealings not only with the Church but with their other subjects. Royal administrators, judges, and tax collectors had made the king's power known throughout his kingdom; so now did military recruiters and suppliers. In this way, then, late medieval warfare made people more aware that they were the subjects of a territorial monarch and that this status entailed certain obligations.

THE BLACK HORSEMAN: FINANCIAL COLLAPSE AND RECOVERY

Among the earliest consequences of the changes in material life between 1270 and 1350 in the agricultural sector of the economy were the stabilization and decline of cereal-grain prices, a rise in the prices of manufactured or crafted goods, a considerable jump in the prices of commercial agricultural products, and an increase in the size of sheep herds at the expense of agricultural land. The new mobility of peasant families and the new demands for labor contributed to changing patterns of inheritance among the peasant population and to the practice of leasing vacant land at a fixed rent for a short period and subcontracting a laborforce to work it. High urban labor costs and the search for cheap sources of power of the urban craft guilds led entrepreneurs to take different stages of wool production into the countryside, where they found an unregulated labor force in need of income. In much of England, western Germany, the Low Countries, and Savoy the growth of rural craft industry became prominent. The material crises of the fourteenth century opened much land to the profitable vocation of sheep raising, and in Castile an organization of wealthy sheepherders, the *Mesta*, grew quickly after 1273. Great herds of fine merino sheep were driven north across the vast Castilian tableland in the Spring and south in the Fall, and this restricted the development of the Castilian agricultural economy.

To the peasants who survived famine, plague, and war, the new economic opportunities were in some places considerable. The price of labor in a reduced labor force had gone up. If old lords were unwilling to renegotiate the price and conditions of service, other lords or prosperous peasant proprietors would. Statutes against wage increases proved incapable of controlling labor costs, and there appeared thriving peasant agricultural entrepreneurs who became employers of the available rural wage labor. The old haphazard scatterings of settlements on good land and bad that had spread unchecked between the tenth and the fourteenth centuries began to be tightened into compact new villages. Field systems were reorganized. Large farms appeared, owned and worked by a single peasant family with its own employees and servants. These peasants were increasingly resentful of demands made by old lords and royal tax agents, and of the successful enterprise of townspeople and middlemen that seemed to keep grain prices down and allow the towns to grow rich at the expense of rural labor. The new conditions of rural enterprise and the markets of the wider world contributed to the heightened tensions of society.

The good fortune of some peasants must not obscure the miserable lot of others. Wage laborers had been forced to trade the security of servile tenure for the instability of a world in which there was opportunity both to earn and to lose money. The increase in the number of wage laborers in the countryside who had no possessions or security led to a widening of the spectrum of the peasant population and to a differentiation of social and economic relationships. For instance, the cereal-grain farmer was generally closer to his employees and servants than the commercial farmer or the stock raiser. The new conditions of economic exchange further eroded the old social and economic bonds of dependence and security that had characterized much of rural society before the mid-fourteenth century.

The crisis in grain prices and the growth of industry in the fourteenth and fifteenth centuries increased the spread of commercial agriculture. Barley and hops for the brewing of beer brought better prices than wheat and rye. Flax, hemp, woad, madder-fiber, and dye crops all increased in value as wheat prices remained stable or declined. Some of the changes in late medieval agriculture ultimately proved beneficial. The retreat of grain cultivation to good land rather than marginal or poor land concentrated the remaining labor force on the most productive lands. The increase in crop rotation and the generally greater proportion of leguminous crops meant that the soil received more nitrogen, animal and human diets improved, and land that grew grain crops after having produced legumes required somewhat less animal manure to fertilize it. The cultivation of fodder crops, which increased after the fourteenth century, decreased the frequency of necessary fallow periods, in many areas from one year in three to one year in five or six.

The city was the module of nonagricultural society, and although its population remained small and its political significance often dwindled in the face of the increased power of royal authority, it remained the hub of the European economy. Moreover, between the fourteenth and the seventeenth centuries the city replaced the rural castle as the seat of royal government. In spite of the catastrophes in the agricultural, industrial, and commercial sectors of the fourteenth- and fifteenth-century economy, the importance of the city increased. While territorial monarchies were being shaped, the cities became the critical components of larger states, and the life of the late medieval city influenced the psychology, politics, and economy of larger regions. The study of the nonagricultural sectors of the late medieval European economy begins, then, with the cities.

The density of population in a medieval city permitted the concentration not only of a productive labor force but of economic activities on both a large and a small scale. Venice, Genoa, Milan, and Florence became the principal centers in Italy of international trade and finance; in England, London and Bristol; in Germany, Cologne, Nuremburg and Augsburg; in Flanders, Ghent and Bruges; in the south of France, Marseilles and Avignon; and in the north, the Hanseatic towns of Dansig, Riga, Stralsund, Rostock, Lübeck, Hamburg, and Bremen. These were the international as well as the regional centers of the European economy, and they controlled the economy in their immediate vicinity: Venice, the Adriatic Sea and increasingly the towns in the Trevisan March; Genoa, the Ligurian coast and what is now the Riviera, with a growing influence in southern Spain; Milan and Florence, the center and north of Italy; London and Bristol, the productive wool trade of southeastern and southwestern England. In international affairs these cities prospered because of their strong coinage, the exclusivity of their control, and the supporting services they offered their merchants and bankers. In regional affairs their strong political control of the countryside and their relative prosperity made them local capitals as well. Powerful rulers of large territories transformed such cities as Paris, London, Dijon, Avignon, and Naples into political capitals, thereby enhancing their economic prominence and drawing people to them. Although many medieval cities preserved their traditional character and their customary political divisions, the economic boom of the twelfth and thirteenth centuries, the growing concentration of political authority, and the stabilizing of local and long-distance trade and finance caused the greatest cities to grow even greater.

Sophisticated and extensive recording and accounting systems created new kinds of information about the economy. Public as well as commercial finances were watched more carefully and more expertly. In the fifteenth century the kingdom of France produced the first modern budget constructed according to sound accounting principles. A good example of this new economic instrumental rationality is to be found in the history of late medieval banking. The word "bank," like the legal term "bench," derives from the Latin *bancus*, the

The Walled City Carcassonne. Built in the thirteenth century primarily as a trading and manufacturing center, Carcassonne was extensively restored in the nineteenth century. The restoration has perhaps given it a more quaint and romantic look than it originally possessed; it was far more busy than picturesque. (*Peter Buckley*).

bench on which simple bankers and judges did their work. But neither law nor finance remained simple. Large amounts of capital in the hands of Italian merchant bankers of the thirteenth century were let in the form of large loans, sometimes to individuals or companies but more often to those who could offer more substantial security—the rulers of the principalities and territorial monarchies. As we shall see, the fiscal and political crises of the early fourteenth century caught European rulers with antiquated fiscal systems in a dilemma: Rulers had come to depend on large loans as a regular part of their revenue, and the retarded development of public finance in the late thirteenth and early fourteenth centuries met the new flood of private commercial capital and engorged it indiscriminately.

One of the most striking political changes in the late fourteenth and fifteenth centuries was the restructuring of public finances and their influence on political life.

The large amounts of capital available to underfinanced rulers in the late thirteenth and early fourteenth centuries led them to borrow on anticipation of revenues, to assign future revenues to their creditors, and to issue monopolies inconsiderately. Even these unwise measures failed to produce enough money for repayment of debts, and they further decreased operating revenues. Consequently, the kings of England and France, faced with extensive financial needs because of their mobilization for war, refused many of their obligations to the Italian and Flemish bankers who had loaned them money. Thus, in addition to demographic, epidemic, and military crises Europe experienced a financial crisis of previously unheard-of dimensions. Banks whose revenues had been committed to government loans quickly failed. The great banking houses of Siena collapsed in 1339; in 1343 and 1346 the great Florentine banks of the Peruzzi and the Bardi went under. The crisis of the great early banking houses not only incapacitated public finance for most of the century and turned the rulers of Europe to new means of raising money; it also transformed banking itself. Investments in even the most wealthy territorial monarchies had proved to be no more secure than investments in private enterprises. Banks had to take two steps: first, to find a way of minimizing their risks, and, second, to find new investments for their diminished capital.

Until the seventeenth century, the banking houses that survived the crash of the mid-fourteenth century operated generally on a smaller scale than their great predecessors had. The new banks that rose in the wake of the mid-fourteenth-century failures—in Italy, those of the Medici, the Casa di San Giorgio in Genoa, and the Banco di San Ambrogio in Milan—became semipublic, absorbing shares of the increasingly common funded debts (publicly guaranteed, interest-paying bonds) of the cities and acquiring political power that made their investments more secure than they had been in the thirteenth century. The surviving banks and the newer institutions were aided by an increasing tendency to make monetary values homogeneous over wider regions. With this alignment of currencies one of the most vexing and time-consuming activities of early medieval money changers and bankers was slowly overcome. Some areas also insisted on evaluating different currencies according to a stable gold standard determined according to weight. Currency speculation had long provided a profitable area of investment, but unstable currency had increased economic risks, and "bad money" persisted in driving out "good money." The great stable coins of the twelfth and thirteenth centuries—the Byzantine *solidus*, the Venetian *ducat*, the Florentine *florin*—all succumbed in the fourteenth century. By the end of the fourteenth century Italian banks had begun to issue paper currency, but the spread of this new form of money was slow and uneven. Early modern Europe operated on a metallic currency, and the scarcity or promiscuity of bullion altered considerably the economic activity of regions, cities, and kingdoms.

The history of the wool industry in the fourteenth and fifteenth centuries illuminates one aspect of late medieval trade: shifts in the areas of production, finishing, and sale and the consequent economic, social, and political changes in those areas that lost and those that gained from such shifts. The rise of the English cloth industry, its relative freedom from restriction, the decline of Flanders, and the weakening of Italian trade all suggest an aspect of late medieval economic life that has long been misunderstood—the economic reorganization within a complex system that many historians have insisted must be

The Market. In Italian towns no aspect of social life was too modest to be depicted in bright frescoes. The stalls, shops, and houses of merchants were anchors of civic life. The shops depicted here are from two fourteenth-century frescoes in northern Italy. (*L'Italia Magazine, Rome*)

labeled uniformly as a decline. To be sure, there is remarkable evidence of many sorts of decline—from financial to agricultural—during this period. But there are also compelling indications that the rearrangement of the European economy—from finance to agriculture—not only increased prosperity in some places and among some social groups, but ultimately laid the groundwork for the social and economic changes of the seventeenth and eighteenth centuries. The new freedom of different kinds of entrepreneurs, new means of record keeping and accounting, the increasingly prominent role of political authority in economic activity, and the rapidly changing prosperity of many areas offer a confusing picture, but not one that can casually be labeled as uniform decline. Regional variations were still the predominant characteristic of European economic life until well into the eighteenth century, and the decline of one region, town, or family usually meant the rise of another.

Most of these economic changes were misunderstood: They were interpreted as acts of God, as signs of the corruption of political or ecclesiastical authority, as the result of greed (the predominant vice in late medieval moral philosophy), or as the consequences of a world turned upside down. Economic complaints were joined indiscriminately to other kinds of complaints and sometimes to the literary or artistic preoccupations of late medieval society. The resulting picture of unrelieved gloom and totally unchecked self-interest is a common portrayal but certainly not a uniformly accurate one. It does little justice to those who in bettering their lot, however novel and incomprehensible their activities, did attempt to be useful to society, to serve their rulers loyally, to be good Christians, and to accommodate as best they could the deepest and most enduring values their society held.

FURTHER READING

See especially Denys Hay, *Europe in the Fourteenth and Fifteenth Centuries* (New York: Longman, 1966); George Holmes, *Europe: Hierarchy and Revolt, 1320–1450* (New York: Harper & Row, 1975); John Hale, Roger Highfield, and Beryl Smaller, eds., *Europe in the Later Middle Ages* (Evanston, IL: Northwestern University Press, 1965); Margaret Aston, *The Fifteenth Century* (New York: Harcourt Brace Jovanovich, 1968); F. R. H. Du Boulay, *An Age of Ambition* (New York: Viking, 1970); and Johan Huizinga, *The Waning of the Middle Ages* (New York: Doubleday, 1953; new trans. Chicago: University of Chicago Press, 1995.).

On the plague and its consequences, see Philippe Ariès, *Western Attitudes Toward Death* (Baltimore: Johns Hopkins, 1975); Philip Ziegler, *The Black Death* (New York: Harper & Row, 1969); William McNeill, *Plagues and Peoples* (New York: Doubleday: 1976); Robert S. Gottfried, *The Black Death* (New York: The Free Press, 1983), and the brilliant cultural study by Millard Meiss, *Painting in Florence and Siena after the Black Death* (New York: Harper & Row, 1964). On a particular region, see John Hatcher, *Plague, Population and the English Economy,*

1348–1530 (London: Macmillan, 1977), and for a fine collection of sources, *The Black Death*, ed. and trans. Rosemary Horrox (Manchester-New York: Manchester University Press, 1994).

On warfare, see Philippe Contamine, *War in the Middle Ages* (Oxford: Basil Blackwell, 1986); for the ecclesiastical doctrines, see Fredrick H. Russell, *The Just War in the Middle Ages* (Cambridge: Cambridge University Press, 1975). Other studies include: J. F. Verbruggen, *The Art of Warfare in Western Europe During the Middle Ages* (Amsterdam: North Holland Publishing Co., 1977); John Keegan, *The Face of Battle* (New York: Random House, 1977); Kenneth Fowler, ed., *The Hundred Years' War* (New York: St. Martin's Press, 1971); and John Barnie, *War in Medieval English Society* (Ithaca, NY: Cornell University Press, 1974). The most exhaustive history of the hundred years war is the work by Jonathan Sumption, *The Hundred Years War: Trial by Battle* (Philadelphia: University of Pennsylvania Press, 1990). See also Kelly De Vries, *Medieval Military Technology* (Lewiston, NY: Broadview, 1992), and Randall Rogers, *Latin Siege Warfare in the Twelfth Century* (Oxford: Clarendon Press, 1992).

On commerce and finance, see the General Bibliography.

18

THE CHURCH AND THE WORLD

CHRISTENDOM AND EUROPE

From the time of its coinage by Popes Nicholas I and John VIII in the ninth century, the term *christianitas*—"Christendom"—had been used to designate any individual's Christian identity as well as the common identity of all who professed Christianity. It also came to mean those lands where Christians lived—Carolingian writers had termed Charlemagne's lands the *imperium Christianum,* "the Christian empire." By the beginning of the thirteenth century it was thought to have boundaries and was regarded as territorial.

    The term *Europa*—"Europe"—on the other hand, was not used in the same sense during this period. Originally, a purely geographical term designating one of the three parts of the earth—along with Africa and Asia, the latter thought to be as large as Europe and Africa combined—the term "Europe" originally designated the island of Crete, and later the Greek mainland and the lands to the west and north. Christians read the biblical story of Noah's three sons as meaning that Japheth and his descendants were the first humans in Europe. The term also acquired a ceremonial and cultural connotation. Writers who wanted to praise Carolingian and later rulers often mentioned them with Europe as a backdrop for their achievements. Rome and its bishop were said to represent the spiritual center of Europe.

The conversion of northern and parts of eastern Europe, the conquests by Christian rulers and peoples in the Iberian Peninsula, the Crusader States, and, briefly, parts of the North African coast, also suggested that Christendom could expand and that it had expanded already. But it did not exactly coincide with Europe. But thirteenth- and fourteenth-century Europeans also discovered that Christendom could shrink, that some lands once confidently thought Christian ceased to be so. Most important, from the late thirteenth century on, the actual territory controlled by Christians coincided more and more exactly with the geographical ideas about the boundaries of Europe. From the fifteenth century on, the term Europe began to replace Christendom in common usage, having acquired both a cultural and a geographical meaning.

There were many reasons why Europe replaced Christendom. Among them are the loss of territory outside continental Europe, the changing relations between Christian and non-Christian peoples within Europe, the appearance of a new people, the Mongols, and both the threats that they posed to the wealth and abundance of Europe and the avenues that they opened into eastern Asia, and an increasing geographical sense of just how vast the world was and how small a part of it the Christian peoples of Europe occupied.

The kingdom of Jerusalem had fallen to the Muslims in 1187. The Third Crusade, launched in 1187, failed to recapture it. Although many plans for Crusades were drawn up and several were launched in the thirteenth century, the movement failed. With the fall of the city of Acre to the Muslims in 1291, the last Christian territory in the Holy Land was lost. The kings of Jerusalem moved to the island of Cyprus. Some of the military orders also moved. The Teutonic Knights shifted their activities to the Baltic and northeastern Europe. The Knights of the Hospital of St. John conquered the island of Rhodes in 1308 and held it until the sixteenth century. The Templars, as we have seen, remained in France, where they were destroyed by Philip IV the Fair between 1307 and 1312. The great idea of Pope Urban II, the event that the historian Edward Gibbon termed "the world's debate," had indeed brought Latin Christians into a new world, but it failed to keep them there.

In 1198, when Pope Innocent III preached yet another Crusade to recover Jerusalem, an army assembled and sailed from Venice. The army's inability to pay the fleet of Venice for its transportation to the Holy Land, however, and several political intrigues led the Crusaders not to the Holy Land but to Constantinople, which they conquered in 1204. A Latin Empire was established, and Latin rites and observances were forced on the Greek Christians. Further deterioration of relations between Latin and Greek Christians was the result. The Latin princes who carved out territories for themselves behaved ruthlessly toward their Greek subjects. The city of Constantinople was looted of both its wealth and its treasury of relics. But the Latin Empire failed too. From 1204 until its collapse in 1261 it struggled with its own rebellious Latin subjects and with Byzantine resistance, kept up in a few territories that the Latins had not managed to capture. In 1261 the emperor Michael VIII Palaeologos recaptured the city of Constantinople and drove the Latins out of part of his empire. But Greece itself was lost to the Byzantines. From 1261, the weakened and shrunken Byzantine Empire struggled between pressure from the Latins and pressure from the continuing power of the Islamic world close by.

In spite of propaganda and the urging of popes and preachers, the Crusades that followed 1291 tended to be smaller in scale and limited in purpose to defending the frontiers of Europe, matters that were of greater importance to those who lived near the frontiers than to those who, having no hope of recapturing Jerusalem, grew less inclined to participate in Crusades that brought them to no Holy Land. With the failures in North Africa, and Syria-Palestine, a new boundary had been drawn for Christendom. With the fall of Constantinople to the Ottoman Turks in the middle of the fifteenth century (see Chapter 20), the ambiguous Byzantine presence was also removed from the orbit of Christendom. Its southeastern limits had been redrawn.

In other parts of southern Europe, however, Christian rulers and peoples gained territory. From the eighth century on, the Iberian Peninsula had been one of the very few places in Europe in which large non-Christian populations lived side-by-side with Christians, in both the Islamic kingdoms and in those of the Christians. From the twelfth century on, the pace of the Christian conquest quickened, and over the next three centuries much of the Peninsula had been won by Christian kings and their armies. If North Africa, Syria-Palestine, and much of Anatolia and Greece were removed from Christian hands, most of the Iberian Peninsula came into them.

The most dangerous challenge to the frontiers of the Christian world in the early thirteenth century was the rise of the Mongol Empire. Under the inspired leadership of Genghis Khan, several central Asian peoples joined together in a vast military empire that struck at China and Europe simultaneously. Moving westward, the Mongols destroyed Kiev in 1240 and struck deeply into Hungary and Poland. Mongol armies also assaulted the Islamic world, and the destruction of Baghdad in 1258 indicated the presence of a threat to the Christian and Islamic worlds alike. But the unity of the Mongol Empire broke up after 1258. One part of the empire, the Golden Horde, established itself in Russia, where it remained until the fifteenth century. In 1266 Kublai Khan established a powerful Mongol empire in China, with its capital at Beijing. Kublai's brother Hulagu Khan established the empire of the Ilkhans of Persia and was responsible for the sacking of Baghdad. He was prevented from moving farther west by his defeat at the hands of the Mamelukes of Egypt at the great battle of Ain Jalut in 1260. Although Mongol power weakened after the middle of the fourteenth century, the Mongols had transformed the world of western Asia.

As was the case along the southern edge of Christendom, however, in northern Europe there was a gain of both territory and Christians as well as a loss. Although Christian kingdoms had existed in Hungary, Bohemia, and

Poland since the tenth century, the large territories extending northward to the Baltic Sea had not been Christianized, either by Slavs or by the expanding northern German territorial principalities. From the thirteenth century on, German princes launched military enterprises in the form of crusades against the Prussians, Livonians, and Estonians. In addition, with the marriage of the Polish princess Jadwiga to Prince Jagiello of Lithuania in 1383, the Christianization of Lithuania began and was quickly completed. The last substantial non-Christian territory and people in the north of Europe had now become Christian. By the late fourteenth century, Christendom and Europe, with the exception of the Mongol presence in Russia, had become virtually identical.

The drawing together of Christendom and Europe cast the world beyond those borders in a new light. No longer was there a realistic hope of expanding the powers of Christian rulers, but there was the hope of exerting the spirit of Christianity in an effort of conversion. Moreover, legends of Christian peoples beyond the lands ruled by Muslims and Mongols remained attractive, particularly those centered on the legendary Christian ruler Prester John. But as Christians began to travel overland to Asia, they found no Prester John, although they did find large numbers of peoples they had never heard of before. In this context, a new missionary and conversion spirit arose, heightened by a sense that prophecies circulating through Europe since the twelfth century were about to be fulfilled.

Arnald of Villanova, a lay theologian, physician, and counselor of popes and kings, wrote on prophecy and the coming end of the world. Among the strongest influences on Arnald was the conviction that a new age of the world had begun when new spiritual men would convert Jews and Muslims without the need of the sword or temporal power. The historical failure of the Crusade movement and new idealistic hopes about the immediate future converged to create a new vision of the future, a vision whose emphases on reform, the coming of the millennium, and the miraculous conversion of non-Christians became common topics of discussion in many clerical and lay circles.

One of the most striking figures in this movement was the Catalan noble Ramon Lull (1232–1316). A gifted poet and a prosperous man, Lull was moved by the example of Francis of Assisi around 1263. Renouncing marriage and the world, he learned Arabic, founded training schools for missionaries and teaching them Arabic, and became a missionary to Muslims himself, and produced many literary works of great influence. He died, possibly in North Africa, on a conversion mission. His ideas and works continued to circulate widely, and he is one of the most important figures in late medieval devotional literature.

Such aspects of Christian practice and theory as the problem of the rights of non-Christians, the conversion movements, and the problem of the reunion of the divided Greek and Latin churches dominated much of the Christian thought from the midthirteenth to the midfifteenth century. The emotional pitch of this concern was very high, for lay people and clerics alike feared that their efforts had been too few and that hope for reform had dawned too late. The Council of Vienne in 1312 decreed that schools of Arabic and other non-Christian languages ought to be established, and popes and lawyers attempted to institutionalize these concerns in their decretals and administrative practices. At a very different level, such laymen as Arnald of Villanova and Ramon Lull responded to these same concerns in their own inventive ways. Behind both institutional and personal activity lay the fear that the last age of the world was coming soon, or was already upon humanity. A prophetic mentality was echoed in many places in the fourteenth and fifteenth centuries, and it forms a characteristic background to the hope, fearful anticipation, and sense of duty that mark the efforts of so many thinkers between the midthirteenth and midfifteenth centuries. It also shaped the attitudes with which people responded to the crises of the later fourteenth century—the failure of Greek and Latin reunion, the Avignon papacy, the Great Schism, the conciliar movement, and the new forms of devotion that were to grow up in the fifteenth century.

THE REVOLT AGAINST ARISTOTLE AND AQUINAS

From the first appearance of Aristotle's works of natural philosophy and metaphysics in the late twelfth century, opposition to Aristotelian thought developed among Christian theologians, just as it had among earlier Muslim theologians. Aristotle's picture of an uncreated universe and a single collective intellect for the human race, the failure of this theology to account for the Trinity, and his theory that God acted from necessity rather than freedom encountered bitter opposition from theologians and led to the condemnation of many of his works and ideas (and their Arabic commentaries and developments) from 1210 to 1277. Indeed, the condemnation of many Aristotelian and Averroistic theses by Stephen Tempier, the bishop of Paris, in 1277 has often been considered the watershed of medieval intellectual history. But others besides theologians had attacked Aristotle, and even the expositions of Albertus Magnus and Thomas Aquinas came under heavy fire, from outside and inside the Dominican order.

Roger Bacon (1214–1292), a teacher of natural philosophy and a lay member of the Franciscan order, bitterly attacked Parisian scholars for their unthinking acceptance of Aristotelian natural philosophy. Other natural philosophers, including Robert Grosseteste, developed original scientific approaches to problems that Aristotle had generally left unsolved or had treated inadequately, such as the nature of rainbows and the problem of local motion. The condemnations of 1277, which were primarily theological and aimed at restoring the liberty of God from Aristotelian necessity, were also important for prying loose Aristotelian authority in general and consequently permitting the work of such natural philosophers and Grosseteste and Bacon to be continued in the schools with much greater independence.

The condemnation of many Aristotelian and Thomistic principles at the University of Paris in 1277 produced a revolt not only against a theology based on Aristotle, but against Aristotelian natural philosophy as well. Although a few schools, notably those of theology and natural philosophy at the University of Padua, remained close to Aristotelianism and Averroism (too close, many thought), and although the Dominican order tried (ultimately successfully) to preserve the authority and reputation of Thomas Aquinas, a number of thinkers set off in new directions in both theology and natural philosophy.

John Duns Scotus (1265–1308), an immensely complex theologian in the Augustinian and Franciscan traditions, criticized the Aristotelian tendency to make God less transcendent by attributing to him rationality and a kind of intelligibility that made him accessible to human reason. Duns Scotus argued that such a view of God diminished God's transcendence and majesty. He therefore emphasized the divine will, rather than divine reason, and the ultimate unknowability of God. Reason, Duns Scotus argued, can give no reliable information about God at all.

Although William of Ockham (1285–1349) criticized much of Duns Scotus's work, he agreed that God was transcendent, omnipotent, and infinitely free. Only faith and revelation tell us about God's nature and will. Reason, on the contrary, informs us only of the observable world. Although Ockham's rationalism may appear to represent a step backwards in its reversion to a mystical theology from a rational one, it is probably wiser to regard his and Scotus's theology as correcting a theological movement toward rationalism that had gone too far. On the other hand, by insisting upon the supremacy of reason in the field of observable phenomena, Ockham gave a new and separate degree of authority to rational and scientific analysis. Having deprived reason to all power to inform us about God, Ockham gives it every power to inform us about the phenomenal world. Since in Scotus's and Ockham's theology God's will may interrupt the phenomena of the material world at virtually any time, reason describes only the regular operation of that world before God intervenes.

Out of this division of religious and philosophical consciousness, reflected in other theologians and scientists between the fourteenth and the seventeenth centuries, there emerged the twin currents of divine voluntarism and rational authority in explanations of the material world. In the case of voluntarism, God's will, unbounded and incomprehensible, characterized the Divinity. Mystical theology, mystical devotion, pious private prayer, interior spiritual development, a revival of symbolic thought and expression, and a new interest in contemplation came to characterize religious sensibility after the midfourteenth century. Some of its most dramatic manifestations may be seen in the writings of the German Dominican Meister Eckhart (1260–1328) and in the Flemish mystic Jan Ruusbroec (1293–1381), in the writings of the school known as the *Devotio Moderna,* "the modern devotion," and in the writings of a number of Beguines in the Low Countries, particularly Hadewijch and her followers.

In the case of rational natural philosophy, Scotus and Ockham opened the door to the idea that if reason is of no value in ascertaining truths about God, it may be of supreme and uncontestable value in ascertaining truths about the observable world. If reason has no validity in clarifying the spiritual realm and must thereby defer to faith, revelation, and mysticism, conversely these three may not validly ascertain truths about the material world. This last point, developed more fully by thinkers of the fifteenth and sixteenth centuries, created a much smaller realm, but a much more manageable and verifiable one, for rational empiricism. Finally, both voluntaristic theology and rational empiricism, having developed in common as a reaction to Aristotelianism and Aquinas, were mutually acceptable to each other. One finds many late medieval thinkers of a strongly mystical theological bent holding obviously rational ideas about the material world. By separating reason from theology, Scotus and Ockham made it acceptable to both theologians and natural philosophers.

While Franciscans were attacking Aristotle and Aquinas, several fourteenth-century thinkers revived the thought of Augustine into a dominant influence. Thomas Bradwardine, archbishop of Canterbury (d. 1349), relied heavily on Augustine's writings in his treatise *On the Cause of God Against Pelagius*, which emphasizes the importance of faith in the achievement of salvation.

Bradwardine was also associated with a group of mathematicians at Merton College, Oxford, and in his scientific studies of dynamics and local motion he strongly criticized Aristotelian dynamics and brought to bear on Aristotle's generally nonmathematical physics a new mathematical sophistication that further eroded the prestige of Aristotelian natural philosophy.

Thus, the revolt against Aristotle and Aquinas gave new impetus to the evolution of theology and natural philosophy alike. The marvelous synthesis of Aquinas came under attack from many directions, and the vast resources of theological thought and feeling, as well as the new interest in experimental natural philosophy—incompatible as these movements may appear to a modern mind—shaped the spiritual and scientific direction of late medieval thought and began to forge the links (which historians are still exploring) between the late medieval and modern worlds.

THE POPES AT AVIGNON

Not only did Greek and Latin Christianity fail to find union, but internal changes in the Latin Church itself marked the fourteenth and fifteenth centuries. The Avignon papacy was perhaps the most striking manifestation of these changes.

Boniface VIII died at Rome in 1303. His successor, Benedict XI (1303–1304), died at Perugia. Benedict's successor, Clement V (1305–1314), was not in Italy when he was elected, and was crowned pope in Lyons. Mediation between the kings of England and France and the Council of Vienne in 1311/12 kept Clement out of Italy, and the press of business and turbulence in Italy kept his successor, John XXII, in the south of France. From the pontificate of John XXII (1316–1334), the popes took up residence in the city of Avignon, in which they purchased first the bishop's palace and in 1348 the city itself from its owner, the king of Naples, a papal vassal.

To a great extent the Avignon residence aided the papacy in its task of directing the spiritual life of Christendom. It is ironic that although the popes at Avignon were more disposed, better equipped, and more efficiently financed for the task of directing Christian society than ever before, their residency there was regarded by many as the "Babylonian captivity" of the papacy. There were reasons for this. The increasing friction between the kings of France and England always tend to place the mediating popes in great disfavor with parties who opposed their activities. The struggle between the Avignon popes and the emperor Louis of Bavaria (1313–1347) has often been regarded as high-handed and autocratic on the part of the popes. Indeed, the Avignon residency was long widely heralded by contemporaries and later historians as the symbol of the breakup of medieval Christendom. Only recently have scholars clarified its real accomplishments, estimated the dedication of popes and curia, and begun to appreciate the work of some of the fourteenth-century popes as highly as it deserves.

The Avignon popes put papal financial, and administrative practices on a sounder footing than ever before. The Palace of the Popes at Avignon appears to have been designed and built specifically to facilitate papal business; it may be regarded as the first building in Europe devoted to large-scale administrative functions. The care with which papal archives and records were kept, the intelligent design and decoration of the palace, and the increasing consistency of papal policy during this period mark the Avignon papacy as a time of vigorous application of rationality to the stubborn problems of rule rather than a captivity, a concession to the kings of France, or the expression of a frustrated monarchical political theory.

As the fourteenth century wore on, pressures on the popes to return to Rome grew stronger. But the enormity of the task of moving the papal administration, household, and records postponed such a move (except for a very brief visit by Pope Urban V) until 1377, during the papacy of Gregory XI (1370–1378). The conflicting opinions concerning the return of the papacy to Rome proved to be the prelude to a great crisis, the double papal election of 1378.

THE GREAT SCHISM AND THE COUNCIL OF CONSTANCE

The pressures on the conclave of cardinals voting in Rome after the death of Gregory XI in 1378 were strongly in favor of an Italian pope. Conflicting opinions between Italian and French cardinals led to the election of an Italian from outside the curia, Bartolomeo Prignano, archbishop of Bari, who took the title of Urban VI. But Urban's high-handed treatment of the curia led a dissident group of cardinals to flee Rome, denounce the papal election as uncanonical, and elect as their own pope, Cardinal Robert of Geneva. These two popes, the "Roman" Urban VI (1378–1389) and the "Avignonese" Clement VII (1378–1394), divided the Christian Latin world into two conflicting camps. Their rivalry destroyed the nonpartisan status of the papacy in mediating international conflicts, diverted the papacy's attention from the needs of Christendom to those of personal predominance, and led to a virtual duplication of papal governing apparatus as each pope strove to force his rival and his rival's supporters to capitulate.

In spite of widespread efforts at mediation between the two parties, the schism endured. Catherine of Siena (1347–1380) wrote bitter letters denouncing those who sustained the Avignon residence and those who perpetuated the Schism, including the male ecclesiastical hierarchy. A number of individuals also left the path of ecclesiastical careerism to establish new devotional movements, including Gert Groote, who established the Brothers and Sisters of the Common Life and the Congregation at Windesheim, the center of the *Devotio Moderna*. Various steps were also taken by kings, theologians, canon lawyers, and prelates to pressure the two sides to compromise. Between 1399 and 1403 the king of France declared a "subtraction of obedience" from both sides and gave the French church an early experience of that independence from Rome that, in the form of special agreements between the king of France and the papacy, was to help create the highly autonomous Gallican church of the sixteenth and seventeenth centuries. In 1409 a council at Pisa deposed both papal rivals and elected yet another pope, thereby widening the contest to a field of three. The next six years were spent in a series of dramatic attempts to resolve their conflicting claims, and only the persistence of a number of prelates, the universities, and the emperor Sigismund (d. 1437) determined the direction in which a solution to the dilemma might be found. It was decided that this, the greatest of all ills in the history of the Church, must be solved—could only be solved—by an ecumenical Church council. The council, called to meet at Constance in 1415, was to be the Church's last opportunity to restore unity to a faction-ridden world and to place once more a single universal pope on the Throne of Saint Peter.

The Council of Constance (1414–1418) managed to remove the three contending popes and elect a fourth pope, Martin V (1417–1431), who spent his pontificate trying to restore the pope's rights and security in the city of Rome and recover the papacy's lost prestige throughout Europe. The council also executed by burning the Bohemian ecclesiastical reformer John Hus, who was accused of unorthodox views on the Church hierarchy, excessive criticism of clerical abuses, and heresy. Hus had been a major figure in Bohemian spiritual and cultural life, however, and after his execution Bohemia was torn by civil wars until 1434.

Finally, the council voted that general councils be called regularly. But the suggestion of the most extreme supporters of this view, the Conciliarists, that a general council might be superior to a pope, generated papal opposition to the notion of regular councils. From the pontificate of Martin V on, the popes grew more preoccupied with settling affairs within the Papal States and Italy, ruling the Church alone with the help of the curia, and, by opposing councils, thereby turning the loyalties of many churchmen to local temporal powers instead of to Rome. Up to the beginning of the sixteenth century these popes found that the return to Rome and the local political rivalries in central and northern Italy occupied far more of their time and attention than they could readily spare from dealing with the remnants of a universal Christian society and its pressing spiritual and material needs.

VARIETIES OF DEVOTION ON THE EVE OF THE REFORMATION

The idea of Christendom as geographic term designating those lands in which king and clergy supported a set of common religious beliefs and observances was only one meaning of the term. Another meaning was that of the quality of being a Christian, and for most people that quality was learned and practiced in one's immediate locality. By the late Middle Ages, this locality was organized as the *parish*. The parish supervised the beginning and end of the Christian life in its administration of the sacraments of baptism and the last rites and burial. The parish and its priest taught the rudiments of the religious life through the medium of confession, after 1215 a mandatory annual practice for all Christians, and penance. The content of belief was reiterated in simple creeds, taught by memorization to a largely nonliterate public. Beyond this sacramental life, the sermons of popular preachers played a more and more important role. The Dominican Order had been founded as the Order of Preachers, and dynamic individual preachers appeared throughout Europe in the fourteenth and fifteenth centuries. The individual experience of becoming—and *being*—a Christian was also a common experience throughout most of Europe. The organization of the religious life—from the observance of the ecclesiastical calendar to baptism, confession and penance, marriage or holy orders, feast days, and the last rites—was also a common and public experience, shared by whole communities with the exception of Russia, where the Mongol presence made Russia, with parts of the Iberian Peninsula, the only places in Europe in which non-Christians mingled with predominantly Christian populations.

By the fourteenth century the world of ordinary lay people, ecclesiastical specialists such as parish priests, preachers, canon lawyers, and theologians, and the mediating and regulating offices of the ecclesiastical hierarchy had shaped a religious culture that paid attention to the affairs of this world and also defined and aspired to the sacred. The mental images in which people conceived of such issues as sin and penance, baptism and salvation, were those of kin and fraternity—kinship with Christ, the Virgin, and the saints, and fraternity with fellow Christians on an earth that abounded in occasions for hostility and violence. The sins of avarice, pride, and anger were particularly worrisome because they tended to drive people apart. Unity and fraternity dominated the perception of the sacraments and the lives of people who received them.

Images of unity and fraternity also defined sharply those who were not brothers and sisters—Jews, Muslims, heretics, and those thought to practice magic or witchcraft on their fellow Christians. The late Middle Ages witnessed ferocious attacks on the outsider—the enemy—just as it emphasized the brotherhood of true Christians in sacramental and social bonds.

Attempts at Church reform are surprisingly numerous after 1350, and the intensity of the lay people's search for spiritual comfort and assurance is notable. Fourteenth-century English bishops, for example, made substantial attempts to administer their dioceses and care for the spiritual life of their congregations. The appearance of such guides for parochial clergy as William of Pagula's *Occulus Pastoralis* in the fourteenth century and John Mirick's *Instructions for Parish Priests* in the fifteenth marks the first stage of the slow process by which thirteenth-century theology, morality, and canon law began to filter down to the parish level, and there generate a pastoral revolution, just as the influence of the Franciscans and Dominicans was beginning to wane. The early fourteenth-century compendium by John of Freiburg, the *Summa Confessorum*, became the standard handbook of theology for most fourteenth- and fifteenth-century clergy with any pretense to learning at all. In the mid–fourteenth century Pope Benedict XII made an extensive effort to reform monasticism, the first such attempt since the Cistercian revolution two centuries before, and the last until the mid-sixteenth century. In a number of instances particular religious houses or groups of houses within a religious order transformed their way of life into a much more strict form, which they called "Observant."

In the fourteenth century a pastoral ideal took shape that is perhaps best illustrated by the parson in Chaucer's *Canterbury Tales*, a figure certainly not invented by Chaucer himself. A genuine sense of responsibility for the souls of individual Christians at all levels of society—aided by ideals of clerical behavior, handbooks of instruction for laity and clergy alike, and helps for sermon writing and delivery—was one of the greatest legacies of the thirteenth century. That sense of responsibility was sometimes impossible to activate, however, and it is more remarkable in isolated centers than in dioceses with consistently applied and supervised regulations.

The fourteenth and fifteenth centuries also witnessed a new sophistication and acuteness of conscience on the part of many individuals, laity as well as clergy. Confraternities spread through the towns as urban spiritual needs came to be perceived as different from the needs of the rural population. The Brethren of the Common Life at Deventer in the Netherlands offer a different example. A devoted organization of lay people from all walks of life, they explored the inner spiritual life by means of pietist contemplation, the most popular example of which was the little book called *The Imitation of Christ*, by Thomas à Kempis. Brigit of Sweden, Catherine of Siena, Bernardino of Siena, and Thomas à Kempis—some of the most remarkable religious figures of the fourteenth and fifteenth centuries—shared this concern for devotional purity and its pollution by secular abuses.

Another powerful force in the religious sensibility of the later Middle Ages was the growing sophistication of the European vernacular languages. Although prayers and sermons had always been part of vernacular expression, Latin Christian society heard masses and other forms of the liturgy in Latin, and the formal administrative affairs of the Church, as well as all higher learning and much law, were conducted in that tongue. The universality of the Latin language made it easier for universal institutions such as the papacy and universities to draw on a wide range of peoples for administrators and staff members. It was also a linguistic reflection of a kind of Christian European unity. Finally, it permitted sophisticated thought to find expression at a time when vernacular languages were not sufficiently developed to do so.

The European vernacular languages developed quickly and irregularly after the eighth century. Two generations after Charlemagne the Frankish language was giving way to Old French and Old High German. In the Strasbourg oaths of 842, the grandsons of Charlemagne swore mutual oaths of respect in the Old French and Old High German languages of their followers, and the chronicler Nithard recorded these vernacular statements. But medieval linguistic development reflected the particularization of Europe. In the territory of France, for example, the language of the north, the *langue d'oïl,* was very different from the language of the south, the *langue d'oc.* But dialects and smaller regional differences also survived, as did the different languages of Catalan in the southwest and Breton in Brittany.

A variant of the *langue d'oil* traveled with the Normans to England in 1066 and helped create the Anglo-Norman language of the Norman aristocracy, which displaced vernacular Old English to a socially inferior status. The Anglo-Norman tongue contributed to the shaping of yet another language, Middle English, which appeared in the twelfth century. Not until the reign of King John (1199–1216) could a post-Conquest king of England speak English. Not until 1349 was English used as a medium of teaching, and not until 1362 was it made the language of law. In the latter year English was first used in a speech in Parliament. What has been called the triumph of English took place between 1350 and 1400.

The slow development of vernacular languages made churchmen hesitant to permit translations of Scripture into European vernaculars on the often justified grounds that theological errors and mistranslations might crop up as a result of linguistic incapacity. But much devotional literature, especially after 1200, did make its way into common languages. Stories about Francis of Assisi, stories for use in sermons, meditative literature, and poetry all conveyed religious sentiments to wider circles of people. By the fourteenth century the hunger for vernacular Bibles had led to several English translations and versions in other languages as well. John Hus wrote several pieces of religious literature in Czech, thereby doing for literary Czech what Martin Luther's German bible would do for literary German early in the sixteenth century. Vernacular biographies of Jesus also appeared, supplementing the Latin Gospels. The coming of age of the European languages had a great impact on religious sentiment and expression during the fourteenth and fifteenth centuries. Joan of Arc, for example, although she was illiterate, could articulate her powerful sense of her religion and her keen awareness of what it meant to be a subject of the king of France.

A heightened sense of pastoral obligation, a broad awareness of the need for reform, the insistence on self-awareness through confession, the spread of religious fraternities and devotional movements, the growing self-consciousness of the laity, and the rise of vernacular religious literature—all are eloquent testimony to the spiritual condition of Europe on the eve of the Reformation. The fragmented ecclesiastical organization of the fifteenth century could not deal adequately with these movements as a whole and had only occasional contact with them in particular localities. The death of the learned and humanist Pope Pius II (1458–1464) as he was setting out on a crusade against the Ottoman Turks—the first great humanist pope setting out on the last Crusade—may well have marked an end to one formal phase in the history of the idea of Christendom.

FURTHER READING

On the changing concepts of Christendom and Europe, see Denys Hay, *Europe: The Emergence of an Idea* (New York: Harper, 1966), and Karl J. Leyser, "Concepts of Europe in the Early and High Middle Ages," *Past & Present* 137 (1992), 25–47. On the changing territorial character, see Robert Bartlett, *The Making of Europe: Conquest, Colonization and Cultural Change 950–1350* (Princeton: Princeton University Press, 1993).

On the Crusades and the Near East, see Donald Queller, *The Fourth Crusade* (Philadelphia: University of Pennsylvania Press, 1977); James M. Powell, *The Anatomy of a Crusade, 1213–1221* (Philadelphia: University of Pennsylvania Press, 1986) and Maureen Purcell, *Papal Crusading Policy, 1244–1291* (Leiden: Brill, 1975), and, for criticism, Elizabeth Siberry, *Criticism of Crusading, 1095–1274* (Oxford: Clarendon Press, 1985). On the fourteenth century, see Norman Housley, *The Avignon Papacy and the Crusades, 1305–1378* (Oxford: Clarendon Press, 1986).

On the Baltic, see William Urban, *The Baltic Crusade* (DeKalb: Northern Illinois University Press, 1975), and Urban, *The Prussian Crusade* (Lanham, MD: University Press of America, 1980); Michael Burleigh, *Prussian Society and the German Order* (Cambridge: Cambridge University Press, 1984). On the great Baltic-Rhineland trading network, see Philippe Dollinger, *The German Hansa* (London: Macmillan, 1964).

On the Iberian Peninsula, see the General Bibliography under the heading Political History: Regional.

For the peoples of Eurasia and North Africa generally, see Archibald R. Lewis, *Nomads and Crusaders* (Bloomington and Indianapolis: Indiana University Press, 1988).

For the Mongols in western Asia and Russia, see David Morgan, *The Mongols* (Oxford: Basil Blackwell, 1986); Paul Ratchnevsky, *Genghis Khan* (Oxford: Blackwell, 1991), and Charles J. Halperin, *Russia and the Golden Horde: The Mongol Impact on Medieval Russian History* (Bloomington: University of Indiana Press, 1987). See also *The Secret History of the Mongols,* trans. Francis Woodman Cleaves (Cambridge: Harvard University Press, 1982), and Christopher Dawson, *Mission to Asia* (Toronto: University of Toronto Press, 1980).

Most general histories of late medieval Europe deal in some way with the problems of reform, reunion, and prophecy discussed in the first section of this chapter. Several works, however, are good guides to some of the most interesting aspects of the period. E. Randolph Daniel, *The Franciscan Concept of Mission in the High Middle Ages* (Lexington: University Press of Kentucky, 1975), and Marjorie Reeves, *The Influence of Prophecy in the Later Middle Ages* (Oxford: Oxford University Press, 1969), offer sensitive treatments of the prophetic mentality from a wide variety of sources. Delno C. West, ed., *Joachim of Fiore in Christian Thought,* 2 vols. (New York: Burt Franklin, 1975), is a good collection of essays on different aspects of one influential thinker. An example of the popularity of prophecy is Robert E. Lerner, *The Powers of Prophecy: The Cedars of Lebanon Vision from the Mongol Onslaught to the Dawn of the Enlightenment* (Berkeley and Los Angeles: University of California Press, 1983).

On formal thought, see John Marenbon, *Later Medieval Philosophy* (London-New York: Routledge, 1987), which contains an excellent bibliography. A good recent study of Ockham is that of Marilyn McCord Adams, *William Ockham* (Notre Dame, IN: Notre Dame University Press, 1987), 2 vols.

On the Avignon papacy, see Yves Renouard, *The Avignon Papacy, 1305–1403* (London: Faber & Faber, 1970). See also Walter Ullmann, *The Origins of the Great Schism* (reprint ed., Hamden,, CT: Archon Books, 1973); W. A. Pantin, *The English Church in the Fourteenth Century* (reprint ed., Toronto: University of Toronto Press, 1980); Louise Ropes Loomis, *The Council of Constance,* John H. Mundy and K. M. Woody, eds. (New York: Columbia University Press, 1961); and Matthew Spinka, *John Hus: A Biography* (Princeton, NJ: Princeton University Press, 1968).

Fine recent general studies of the period are Francis P. Oakley, *The Western Church in the Later Middle Ages* (Ithaca, NY: Cornell University Press, 1980), Steven Ozment, *The Age of Reform* (New Haven: CT: Yale University Press, 1980), and most recently John Van Engen, "The Church in the Fifteenth Century," in Thomas A. Brady, Jr., Heiko A. Oberman, and James D. Tracy, eds., *Handbook of European History 1400–1600: Late Middle Ages, Renaissance, and Reformation*, Vol. I

(Leiden-New York: E. J. Brill, 1994, pp. 305–330). On the pastoral concerns of the period, see Leonard E. Boyle, *Pastoral Care, Clerical Education and Canon Law, 1200–1400* (London: Variorum, 1981).

The theme of fraternity is well laid out in John Bossy, *Christianity in the West, 1400–1700* (New York: Oxford University Press, 1985). Some of the most important devotional literature is translated and analyzed in Bernard McGinn, *Meister Eckhart and the Beguine Mystics* (New York: Mahwah: Paulist Press, 1994); Mother Columba Hart, *Hadewijch: The Complete Works* (New York-Ramsey-Toronto: The Paulist Press, 1980); James A. Wiseman, *John Ruusbroec: The Spiritual Espousals and Other Works* (New York-Mahwah: Paulist Press, 1985), and John Van Engen, ed., *Devotio Moderna: Basic Writings* (New York-Mahwah: Paulist Press, 1988).

On vernacular languages, see the General Bibliography. The general framework of the place of religion in medieval life has also been reassessed in the excellent and wide-ranging study by John Van Engen, "The Christian Middle Ages as an Historiographical Problem," *American Historical Review* 91 (1986), 519–552.

19

POWER AND ORDER

THINKING ABOUT POLITICS

By the thirteenth century the various intellectual specialties of Christian Europe—rhetoric, theology, canon law, philosophy, learned law, and the writing of history—had each come to deal with problems of the proper ordering of society and the place of legitimate political authority in it. Although each specialty approached political theory from a different perspective and asked different questions about it, most political theory now agreed with the observed facts of political life and the religious and ethical theories that usually framed discussions of the legitimate sources and uses of public power and the earthly, as well as the spiritual, purpose of human society.

To most political thinkers, monarchy, tempered by divine law, was the ideal form of human government. Most political thinkers also recognized that monarchy might be misused—either by tyrants or by incompetent kings—and that some constraints on monarchy were a part of theories of legitimacy. The king's duty was increasingly thought to include both the maintenance of Christian society and the well-being of society: the maintenance of justice, peace, and prosperity on earth. The impact of Aristotle's ideas on politics in the thirteenth century was great precisely because twelfth-century thinkers had already begun to consider such topics as the naturalness of society and the state, the common good, the limits of legitimate authority, and the rights of subjects in the face of injustice or oppression. Dante's *Divine Comedy* carried a profound political message, and the late thirteenth and fourteenth centuries produced a number of innovative and original examples of constitutional experiments as well as works of theory.

One of the best examples of the potential of political discourse in the late thirteenth- and fourteenth-century Europe is Marsiglio of Padua's treatise *The Defender of the Peace.* Marsiglio (1275–1342) set out to solve the problem of the loss of civil peace in the Italian cities of the late thirteenth and fourteenth centuries, a problem that inspired some of the most dramatic and influential political discourse in European history and gave Italian writers a predominance in political theory until the end of the sixteenth century. In his greatest work, *The Defender of the Peace* (completed in 1324), Marsiglio drew upon the political thought and culture of the northern Italian cities, which had had to justify their independence not only from ecclesiastical authority (as had Philip the Fair of France), but from imperial authority as well. The Italian city-republics, consequently, made greater and wider use of Aristotelian political theory than did most transalpine thinkers, and they discovered and wrote much earlier than others about an organic concept of the political community. The *Defender of the Peace* is therefore the first European political treatise to offer a comparative vocabulary of political concepts and constitutional principles applicable to all political communities in general, not merely to particular monarchies, the Holy Roman Empire, or individual city-republics.

For Marsiglio, political order is a natural and beneficial attribute of human society. Its end is the formation of a new kind of political community, one whose members participate freely and productively in a society ordered on the basis of civic peace. Marsiglio's analysis of such a society is certainly not "liberal" in the modern sense of the term, but it may truly be called philosophically liberal. He drew on many diverse strands of earlier political thought and the unique experience of Italian city-republics to describe a universal set of political principles based on the overriding rights of an essentially lay community.

Others besides Marsiglio of Padua addressed political questions, and they usually wrote with a sense of urgency, a need to provide legitimate doctrine for real societies with real problems. It is in the fourteenth century, for example, that arguments about the nature and character of citizenship appear with great frequency in works of political theory, following on the theologians', lawyers', and philosophers' distinctions between the individual, mortal body of the king and the representative, immortal body politic of the realm, which the king also possesses. At the level of the individual and the state, late medieval political thought reflected both real theory and real life, speculation and experience, their issues, and the stakes at risk. The political culture of the fourteenth and fifteenth centuries gave them even more opportunities to do this.

KINGS, PRINCES, AND CITIES IN GERMANY, 1250–1519

The disappearance of the Staufer dynasty left the Empire without an emperor and Germany without a king. The period between the death of Frederick II in 1250 and the election of Rudolph I of Habsburg in 1273 is generally termed the *Great Interregnum,* although two rival candidates were simultaneously elected in 1257 and one of them, Richard of Cornwall, brother of Henry III of England, pressed his claim until his death in 1272. During this period a number of elements dramatically transformed the constitutional structure of the kingdom of Germany, giving it a shape that lasted far longer than the end of the Middle Ages. One of the most striking of these elements was the breakup and dissipation of the vast Staufer properties throughout Germany. These properties and the public rights attached to them consisted of lands, certain rights of taxation in cities, a number of fiscal rights in particular districts, a number of forests, taxes from Jews, and the revenues of a number of courts of law. As these were taken over by individuals and cities, they constituted a steady drain on royal resources. Later rulers also contributed to this drain by selling imperial offices, pledging lands to creditors, and failing to develop alternate revenue such as taxation. From 1273 on, the kings of Germany were forced once again to depend on their own personal resources and those they could acquire through legal, military, or dynastic policies.

A second important element was the regularization of the number and character of those who elected the king and emperor into a recognized electoral college, ultimately a separate order of nobles within the kingdom, lower only than the king himself, and in many ways sharers in the royal power. The first mention of a specific group of people empowered "by law" to elect the king occurs in a document written on behalf of the candidacy of Otto IV in 1198. In 1198 fifteen nobles claimed to be the legal electors, but by the late thirteenth century the number came to be set at seven: three ecclesiastical electors and four lay electors. The ecclesiastical electors were the archbishops of Mainz, Trier, and Cologne, who were also the chancellors of Germany, Burgundy, and Italy, respectively. The four lay electors were the Count Palatine of the Rhine, the Duke of Saxony, the Margrave of Brandenburg, and the King of Bohemia. The four lay electors had also performed certain ceremonial functions in the royal court, those of steward, marshal, chamberlain, and cupbearer. The final number of four lay electors has long posed a problem for historians: Why these four and not, for example, the Duke of Bavaria (who in fact contested an electoral role until the fourteenth century) or other powerful nobles? The most recent argument put forth to explain the number of lay electors is very persuasive. The historian Armin Wolf has argued that these were the surviving descendants of the female line of the Ottonian, or Saxon, royal dynasty that ended in the male line in 1024, thus casting the old debate about election and inheritance in a new light: Although the kings became clearly electable, they were elected by electors whose position was hereditary. From 1257 until the publication of the *Golden*

Bull of 1356, the powers of the electors, their status among the nobility, their relation to the king, and the inviolability of their lands were made more and more
precise at law. By the middle of the fourteenth century they constituted an order
that had no parallel elsewhere in Europe.

Thus, the tasks that faced Rudolph of Habsburg (1273–1291) were formidable, and they were increased by the powerful rivalry of King Ottakar of Bohemia, who had added to his domains the large and important territories of
Carinthia, Lower Austria, and Styria. During a long conflict, Rudolph declared
these territories to be vacant imperial fiefs, and Ottakar refused to pay homage
to the king for them. At the battle of the Marchfeld in 1278, Rudolph was victorious, and he transferred these territories to his son, Albert, thus beginning the
Habsburg rule in Austria that lasted until 1918. From 1273 on, the Habsburgs,
although not an electoral dynasty, became one of the most powerful German noble families, providing kings in Albert I (1298–1308) and Albert II (1438–1439)
and an emperor, Frederick III (1440–1493). But the success of Rudolph of
Habsburg also determined the electors to seek out other candidates for the
throne, and throughout the fourteenth century the Wittelsbach and Luxemburg
dynasties contended with the Habsburgs and with each other as the rulers of
Germany, Austria, and Bohemia. Imperial history became the history of the rivalry among these three families.

From the death of Rudolph I in 1291 a series of emperors invoked grand
ideals, but they achieved their greatest successes as dynasty-builders. The history
of the Habsburg, Wittelsbach, and Luxemburg dynasties is much more important in their own lands—Austria, Bavaria, and Bohemia—than in the history of
the German kingdom or empire.

By the middle of the fourteenth century the "German lands," as the kingdom was commonly called, had been constitutionally and territorially transformed. On the frontiers as well, new pressures were felt. The sons and
successors of Charles IV, Wenzel (1378–1400) and Sigismund (1411–1437), the
dynasty of Luxemburg, concentrated largely on Bohemian and Hungarian affairs. Sigismund's involvement in the attempts at Church reform and reunion at
the Council of Constance, efforts which were recognized as the emperor's
unique responsibility as the head of Christian society, nevertheless cost him
dearly in prestige and power. At the western edge of the empire, the growing influence of France and the power of the Duchy of Burgundy (see further in this
chapter) eroded royal power there and alienated considerable noble loyalty.

For all of its economic vitality, the settlement of new lands in the north
and east, the planning of towns and villages, and the establishment of a lively and
productive trading network, the kingdom of Germany remained fragmented
politically, and the developments in the late thirteenth and fourteenth centuries
preserved and regularized that fragmentation. Even the more ambitious reigns
of Frederick III (1440–1493) and Maximilian I (1493–1519), which established
the Habsburg dynasty firmly on the imperial throne, failed to consolidate the

divided kingdom. The political experimentation of the fourteenth and fifteenth centuries left hundreds of principalities, towns, and greatly weakened emperors to divide the riches and the people of a vastly expanded Germany. The political vigor that in other states focused on centralizing governance and the development of various sentiments of national identity remained focused in the German lands on local princely and ecclesiastical authority.

THE HUNDRED YEARS' WAR: ENGLAND AND FRANCE

Rivalry among Italian city-republics, the conflict between the Wittelsbach emperor Louis of Bavaria and Pope John XXII, and the political growth and development of most territorial monarchies in the fourteenth and fifteenth centuries are all manifestations of the political problems that concerned Marsiglio of Padua and other political theorists. However, there is no better or broader example of the relation between old and new political theory and old and new political experience than the long war between the rulers of England and France that lasted from 1337 to 1453 and acquired the dramatic but erroneous name of the Hundred Years' War. Like most medieval conflicts, it began as a private war between rival kings. It ended by consuming resources and people on a national scale, transforming the political culture of its participants, and influencing the affairs of other powers drawn into it.

The heavy hand of Edward I of England had suppressed rebellions against his father, Henry III, controlled the turbulent English aristocracy during his own reign, established (for a short time) the supremacy of the English king in Scotland, and intervened in the affairs of the turbulent French province of Flanders. Flanders, with its prosperous cities of Ghent, Bruges, and Ypres, was a key trading partner for English wool, and its wealthy and independent-minded citizens regularly contended with both the count of Flanders and his lord, the king of France for their economic and political independence. In 1302, for example, an army organized by the Flemish cities defeated the army of Philip IV at Courtrai. Although the king of France reasserted his authority in 1305 in the treaty of *Atlis-sur-Orge*, the territories in Flanders remained ready to revolt any time they considered their economic and political interests threatened. The counts of Flanders themselves often turned to England when threatened by the power of their own lords, the kings of France. English intervention in Flanders, particularly during the struggle between Edward I and Philip IV, had far greater consequences than English intervention in Scotland. One reason for this was the location of Flanders. The northernmost province of the kingdom of France, Flanders was also the gateway into the counties of Holland and Zeeland to the north and to the territories of Brabant and Hainault to the east and south—the latter two technically part of the old duchy of Lower Lorraine and belonging, in theory at least, to the jurisdiction of the king-emperor of the German lands.

The Hundred Years' War and English rule in France.

But the death of strong kings was inevitably the signal for a resurgence of the aristocracy and a reconsideration of both domestic and foreign policy, especially when faced with the prospect of a weaker successor. Upon Edward's death and the increasingly perceived political incompetence of his successor, Edward II (1307–1327), the Scots under Robert I (1306–1329) successfully asserted independence from England. Aristocratic discontent and the alienation of the queen, Isabella, led to Edward II's deposition and murder and the placing of his young son, Edward III (1327–1377), on the throne in his place.

In France the succession crises of 1314–1328 led to the replacement of the Capetian dynasty by the Valois dynasty in the person of Philip VI (1328–1350). The instability in England and the lack of unanimity in France about Philip's legal title to the throne exacerbated a number of structural elements in the governance of France and led to war with England. Large segments of France were ruled by virtually independent dynasties of nobles—Brittany, Aquitaine, and Flanders. Other large territories were given as appanages to royal children, especially the duchies of Burgundy and Bourbon and the counties of Artois, Alençon, and Evreux. The financial resources of the kings of France were thus considerably reduced at a moment when the number of wars they fought increased, royal expenses rose, royal arsenals—particularly those at Narbonne and Rouen—became more costly, the pay of soldiers rose, and taxation collections failed. One resource of the kings of France had been gross confiscations—of the property of expelled Jews in 1306 and of the Order of Templars in 1313. Kings had also attempted to manipulate the metallic content and value of the coinage. Several historians have argued that at the death of Philip IV in 1314 the kingdom of France was at the zenith of its power—but also at the absolute limits of its economic and political capacities.

The succession crises of 1314–1328 emphasized the limited resources of the French crown and the structural dangers to the kingdom. The three territories of Brittany, Aquitaine, and Flanders were closely tied to the interests of the king of England, and in 1337–1338 Edward III undertook a campaign against the king of France in Flanders, the most expensive military enterprise of any English king in history to that date. The opening salvos of the Hundred Years' War took place in Flanders, culminating in the combined naval-infantry victory of the English at Sluys in 1340.

But Flanders did not long remain the main theater of war. In 1337, and again in 1340, Edward III claimed the crown of France as his own, since his mother had been a daughter of the French king. His claims to legitimacy were made in a period of financial crisis and aristocratic ascendance, and they influenced governmental policy in such territories as Gascony and Brittany, which, although they were in France, were either ruled or strongly influenced by England. In 1341 a disputed succession to the duchy of Brittany created another arena for English and Frency royal conflict, as did the pressing of the French king's claims to Gascony, the English-ruled enclave in southwestern France.

The English occupation of Gascony represented virtually all that was left of the once extensive Angevin empire. Technically, the king of England was vassal to the king of France for his lordship of Gascony, but the roles of lord and vassal became very strained in the thirteenth and fourteenth centuries when both happened to be kings. Theorists on both sides argued that "the king shall be no man's vassal." The kings of England had long administered Gascony in much the same way that they administered other Crown possessions to which they had absolute authority. Moreover, Gascon wine was part of a complex English economy that included free access to Flemish wool centers, Breton salt processing, and Portuguese trade. The conflict between lord and vassal over Gascony is simply one way of looking at a set of problems that possessed equally critical economic and diplomatic dimensions. The lord-vassal relationship, if pressed too strictly, was no longer capable of accommodating these problems successfully.

The French pressure on Gascony and the English claim to the French throne heightened tensions between the two monarchs, which were exacerbated by the French alliance with Scotland. In 1340 the English destroyed a French fleet at Sluys, and from then until the Treaty of Bretigny in 1360 the English had the upper hand in the war. England launched armed expeditions into France, winning pitched battles at Crécy and Poitiers in 1346 and 1356, capturing the Channel Islands in 1345 and the great port of Calais in 1347.

The war proved difficult to control and very expensive. Moreover, both kingdoms were devastated by the Black Death of 1348. The early English triumphs helped strengthen the prestige and the power of Edward III, but the French losses, culminating in the capture of King John II in 1356, precipitated intense factionalism among the nobility and in 1356–1358 a social revolution in Paris itself, led by Robert LeCoq, bishop of Laon, and Etienne Marcel, provost of the merchants of Paris.

The reign of Charles V (1364–1380) witnessed significant improvements for France. Between the capture of his father John II and John's death in 1364, Charles was the regent of France. In that capacity he first subdued the rebels of 1358 and then successfully negotiated his father's ransom and release. By 1369 Charles's administrative and financial reforms had allowed him to resume the war, in which he profited from the senility of Edward III, the deaths of Edward's son the Black Prince in 1376 and of Edward III himself in 1377, and the minority of Richard II (1377–1399) to gain a truce. Charles's fiscal and military reforms were only part of his success. His artistic and literary patronage helped inaugurate the role of the French crown as a leader in intellectual and artistic as well as political life.

However, Charles's son Charles VI (1380–1422) was a minor at his accession, and his long reign was also troubled by his periodic insanity after 1392. While the great noble families were contending for power over Charles VI, John the Fearless, Duke of Burgundy (1401–1419), in a dramatic step against his rivals for control of the French king, allied with England. Because the Duchy of Burgundy had been linked to the County of Flanders through the marriage of John's father Philip the Bold (1384–1404) and Margaret de Male, hereditary countess of Flanders, the potential for a new and greatly expanded Burgundian state considerably upset the conventional balance of power (see below in this chapter). Upon the English resumption of the war in 1415, then, France was plunged into far greater misery than it had experienced from 1340 to 1360.

England had made little use of its early victories in the war, and forces of discontent built during the last years of the disabled Edward III. The loss of the king's popular and widely admired son, the Black Prince, and the troubled minority of Richard II permitted great nobles, particularly Edward III's younger brother John of Gaunt, duke of Lancaster, to assume ascendancy over the crown and the young king and create the economic policies that helped precipitate the Peasants' Revolt of 1381. Richard II's peace policy and his intelligent but autocratic attempts to restore royal control over the government and nobles led to his deposition and murder in 1399, the usurpation of the throne by Henry IV (1399–1413), son of John of Gaunt, and the beginning of the royal house of Lancaster.

Henry V (1413–1422), facing rebellions in the north and discontent at home, reopened the war with France in 1415, and the English forces sustained a major victory at Agincourt in 1415. At the Treaty of Troyes in 1420, Henry V's title to the trone of France was guaranteed. When Charles VI of France died in 1422, he left a shattered kingdom with an English king on its throne, an empty treasury, bitter resentment against the Crown and the higher nobility, and a legally disinherited son, the Dauphin Charles, ruling a small part of southern France from an empty, borrowed palace in the old city of Bourges.

Between 1415 and 1453 the tone of the war changed. The length of the conflict, its social and economic costs and consequences, the political instability that ensued, and the character of the fighting made it considerably more savage than earlier wars, and France, the invaded land, bore the brunt of these effects first. The complete and efficient occupation of a conquered nation is difficult in the twentieth century, and it was impossible in the fifteenth. Although England began the fifteenth century by ruling most of northern France, it had neither the population nor the ability to "occupy" the kingdom, nor could it support indefinitely an expensive expeditionary force in an economically depleted country. Intimidation of the population had become a matter of English policy, and the economic and social consequences of this intimidation influenced the character of English rule. Thus, as the character of the war changed and the costs of war mounted, opportunities for dissension increased considerably, whether over traditional problems such as privilege and status or over novelties such as the burden of taxes and the less tangible circumstances of shifting fortunes. France's internal stresses between 1340 and 1430 prefigured the internal conflicts of 1380 to 1480 in England. The shifting aims of war, changing political circumstances, and the mutual reluctance of France and England to surrender, respectively, sovereignty and the claim to the French throne, revealed that there was no clear way of ending the conflict that might satisfy all interested parties.

PATTERNS OF RECOVERY: FRANCE

In spite of England's initial triumphs, the toll of prolonged war and the poverty of English institutional response to its social and economic crises threatened its hold on France. Not the least important element of French resistance was the disinherited prince himself. Charles VII (1422–1461), weakened by the Treaty of Troyes and suffering from the added imputation of illegitimacy, was an unlikely reformer. Sickly, personally unattractive, completely unwarlike, and dominated by ruthless favorites, he helplessly witnessed the English armies proceed south from 1422 to 1428 through Maine and Anjou toward his temporary residence in Bourges.

But in 1428 French military resistance stiffened. Among the complex causes for this new resistance was the appearance of a young peasant woman named Joan "of Arc" from a small town on the frontier of Lorraine and Champagne. Arriving at Charles' court at Chinon in 1429, Joan claimed that Saints Michael, Catherine, and Margaret had "told me of the pitiful state of France and told me that I must go to succor the King of France." In April, Joan and the leaders of the French army relieved the English siege of Orleans, and in July Charles was able to proceed to Reims for his coronation. But Joan was captured by the Burgundian allies of England (see next section), tried by an irregular court, condemned as a relapsed heretic, and burned at the stake in 1431.

In 1434, the legitimacy of Charles VII's birth was affirmed by the Council of Basel, and in 1435 at the Council of Arras he was formally reconciled with Philip the Good (1419–1467), successor to John the Fearless as duke of Burgundy. By 1453 Charles had won back northern France, Normandy, and Gascony and had begun to restore many of the reforms instituted by his grandfather, Charles V. In 1456 he initiated the overturning of the verdict of heresy on Joan of Arc. The last years of Charles's reign were spent restoring royal fiscal and political dominion over a drastically weakened kingdom against the discredited nobility and the rebellious burghers. When he died in 1461, Charles VII had laid the foundations for the growth of monarchical power and national order.

Joan was the most dramatic but not the most efficient servant of Charles VII. Over the long process of recovery and reform Charles was also served by the great financier Jacques Coeur. A wealthy merchant of Bourges, Coeur traveled and traded in the Mediterranean and returned to France to be made master of the royal mint at Paris in 1436. In 1437 Charles made Coeur his treasurer, and in this post Coeur became the king's chief commercial and financial entrepreneur. Coeur helped restore the financial stability of the French Crown, and his own private trading network helped open the Mediterranean to French trade, in which Coeur also had a hand, trading cloth, salt, silver, copper, leathers, and furs. Like many successful traders, he operated money exchanges as well. Coeur grew so wealthy that he was personally able to lend Charles 200,000 gold crowns in 1449, enabling the king to begin the reconquest of Normandy. The services of Joan and Jacques Coeur gave Charles VII the epithet by which he is known to history, Charles *le Bien Servi*—Charles the Well-Served.

Charles's son Louis XI (1461–1483) built upon his father's successes in striking ways. A rebel against Charles as a youth, Louis had lived a complex and anxious life for many years. Of this period Louis's biographer Philip de Commines once remarked: "What he did in his youth, when he was a fugitive from his father under the Duke of Burgundy, was very valuable to him, for he was compelled to please those of whom he had need, and this benefit taught him the meaning of adversity." Louis's capacity for finding out information, dissembling his real intentions, and controlling the French nobles gave him the nickname of "the Spider King," a reputation that Louis himself did little to discourage.

However, Louis also worked. Commines elsewhere remarked: "I think that if all the good days he enjoyed during his life, days in which he had more pleasure and happiness than hard work and trouble, were carefully numbered, they would be found to be few; I believe one would find twenty days of travail and worry for every one of ease and pleasure." Louis fully developed the use of royal authority to alleviate the economic problems of his kingdom. He encouraged industries and domestic trade, continued his father's practice of abolishing internal tolls and tariffs, and sponsored fairs that brought the money of others into France and prevented a financial drain on the kingdom. On the other hand, Louis continually collected old taxes and levied new ones. He waged economic warfare abroad and practiced economic protectionism at home.

Louis XI was one of the first monarchs in European history to possess an accurate sense of the potential economic power of the royal government in alliance with a national economy. At his death in 1483 France had greatly improved its economic position, both internally and in relation to other kingdoms, the great nobles had generally been humbled, and the income of the Crown had nearly quadrupled. Charles VII had left Louis an income of 1,800,000 pounds per year. Louis left his successor Charles VIII an income of 4,700,000 pounds per year, a full treasury, a strong diplomatic position, a kingdom at peace, and a restored throne.

"I, A WOMAN, DARE . . . "

The case of Joan ("of Arc" was her father's surname, but she did not use it, calling herself only "Joan the Maid"), an illiterate young peasant woman from Domremy, not only stirred the sluggish Charles VII of France and greatly vexed the

English, but it also inspired a poem, the *Ditié de Jehanne d'Arc,* written by one of the most distinctive writers in early European history, Christine de Pizan. Christine was born either in the Venetian Republic or in Bologna, probably in 1365. She went with her father to France in 1368, where he had been invited as astrologer to Charles V. She married a minor official at the royal court in 1380. Upon the death of her husband in 1390, Christine was left a twenty-five-year old widow with three small children to raise and very little money.

Christine had come from and married into a circle of literate, educated men, and was literate and learned herself, although apparently without formal education. But she was a remarkably quick student, having read both Boethius's *Consolation of Philosophy* and Ovid, as well as a substantial learned and popular literature. She may at first have become a copyist of manuscripts for patrons, a profession that required an accomplished and well-trained script, and occasionally wrote verses for her own spiritual consolation. Soon, however, certainly by the 1390s, her lyric poems began to attract a wider audience, some of them criticizing the male-dominated themes of courtly love by focusing on the theme of deceived and abandoned women, and on the sorrows of being a widow—at the time, an original topic. In 1402 Christine participated in a literary dispute over the *Romance of the Rose,* taking the position that it slandered women, and leading her into more ambitious literary ventures. She was one of the first writers in France to mention the work of Dante, and her great work, *The City of Women,* continued her defense of women, this time by emphasizing their contributions to civilization and extensively discussing the problems they faced in organizing their world. These and Christine's other works inspired her to write what was probably her last work, a poem in praise of Joan, who seemed to her an ideal subject for her long argument on behalf of women and feminine identity.

The *Ditié* had another purpose. Written in 1429, when it appeared that Joan and Charles VII would soon occupy Paris and permit Christine's return to her city from which she had been exiled since 1418, the poem praises Joan for raising Christine's own prospects of return and praises Charles VII for promising a period of peace and prosperity to France. The poem is thus political on the large scale as well as in praise of Joan the individual. Christine says that Joan's career reflects not only divine providence, but God's particular favor toward France. Joan is identified with a number of Old Testament heroines; her achievements are miracles, and thus a proof of divine favor. But Christine also raises the political theme; not divine providence alone, but the character of France and its monarchy are also her theme. For Christine displays a broad and complex political vision, comprised of anti-English sentiments, but also devotion to France and its kings and her expectation of the recovery of the prosperity of France.

Christine links her theme of the defense of women to her other political concerns. She emphasizes Joan's youth in order to show how Joan surpasses all other heroines. Joan's achievements have not only saved France, but have saved womankind, as well as exemplifying the importance of women in their own right, rather than as appurtenances to the male-dominated chivalric world. The *Ditié* was a kind of summing-up of Christine's long concerns with philosophy, politics, religion, and the defense of women with a woman's voice. As Christine once wrote, anticipating much of the criticism that she foresaw her work and thought might generate:

Let no one accuse me of unreason, of arrogance or presumption, for daring, I, a woman, to chal-lenge and answer back so subtle an author [Jean de Meun, the author of the Romance of the Rose] *or for diminishing the praise due his work, when he, one man on his own, has dared to slan-der and reproach the entire female sex without exception.*

The figures of Joan and Christine illustrate other aspects of the partial recovery of France—and, in a wider sense, of Europe—from the silences that had been generated by a long tradition of misogyny and the concealment of women and women's lack of a feminine and public voice.

PATTERNS OF RECOVERY: ENGLAND

England recovered politically less quickly than France, and in a different way. The overstrained English governmental institutions were not improved by Lancastrian rule, and the collapse of the English occupation of France, coupled with the early death of Henry V in 1422 and the long minority of Henry VI (1422–1461), precipi-tated political and military struggles that lasted nearly to the end of the fifteenth century. The costs of the wars had been enormous compared with the returns from English victories, and the resulting strain imposed on English royal finances had led to violent clashes within the high aristocracy. The reign of Henry VI witnessed fiscal and political collapse, and the reversals of English fortune in France plunged Eng-land into the dynastic conflicts commonly called the Wars of the Roses (1454–1485).

But the economic, military, and social consequences of these overro-manticized wars turned out to be quite small. The changes of dynasty that placed Edward IV on the throne in 1461 and then Henry VII in 1485 were accompanied by the increasing ability of the English monarchs after 1461 to capitalize on the end of expensive foreign wars and to reorganize both royal finances and aristo-cratic factionalism in favor of a stable but not particularly strong royal rule. Eng-land's recovery was achieved at the expense of the vast English territorial claims in France. The Channel became the dividing line for the two kingdoms from the late fifteenth century on.

THE GREAT DUCHY OF THE WEST: THE BURGUNDIAN NETHERLANDS

The scope and pressures of the Hundred Years' War, especially in the County of Flanders and the western German territories of Hainault and Brabant help to ac-count for the appearance of a remarkable state in the late fourteenth and fif-teenth centuries, Burgundy, "The Great Duchy of the West." Almost from the outset of the great conflict between France and England, other powers were drawn into the contest. England attempted to interfere in Flanders and France in Scotland. England and France both interfered in the struggle between Pedro the Cruel of Castile and the successful rebel, Henry of Trastamara. The king of Bohemia, John of Luxemburg, son of the emperor Henry VII and father of the emperor Charles IV, was killed by the English at the battle of Crecy while fighting on the side of France. But no greater example exists than that of Burgundy of the opportunities, as well as the new kinds of alliances, that the Hundred Years' War offered to ambitious princes.

One of the techniques developed by the French monarchy in the thirteenth and fourteenth centuries in order to bind together the different children of the king was the creation of the *appanage*. The appanage was an extraordinary territorial lordship, sometimes over a recently acquired province, given to younger sons of the royal family as a means of maintaining for them a respectable status in the world while at the same time binding the new territories more closely to the royal dynasty. After the rule of several generations descended from the original recipient, however, some of these appanages became as troublesome to the kings as the other great principalities of other great families not related to the dynasty. The story of fifteenth-century Burgundy is a classic example of an appanage run wild.

Ever since its days as a virtually independent territory at the end of the Carolingian period, Burgundy had been a prosperous, largely rural principality, part of which came under the rule of the German kings and emperors, and part of which was ruled by dukes who were often very closely related to the royal house of France. Its rulers expanded their territory piecemeal, and in the course of the fourteenth century the French duke acquired the neighboring imperial county of Burgundy, thus greatly expanding his territory.

At the death of Duke Philip de Rouvres in 1361, King John II of France claimed the duchy and got part of it, although another part descended to Countess Margaret of Flanders. When John II died in 1364, he left his part of the duchy of Burgundy to his youngest son, Philip the Bold, who married Margaret of Flanders in 1369, thereby not only reuniting Burgundy but also adding the immensely wealthy and troublesome territories of Flanders to his lands and creating two great principalities extending nearly from the Alps to the North Sea between the kingdoms of Germany and France, separated only by Lorraine. Philip, nicknamed the Bold (1364–1404), became one of the great princes of France, a strong influence on his royal brother, Charles V, and on his young and unstable nephew, who later became Charles VI (1380–1422).

Philip's son and successor, John the Fearless (1404–1419), inherited his father's wealth and power. Philip's other children married into neighboring noble families, and both Philip and John the Fearless received enormous revenues from the French Crown as well as their various princely revenues from their possessions in Flanders and Burgundy.

Bitter rivalry arose between John the Fearless and the other great princes of France, particularly over the question of who was to control Charles VI during that king's increasingly frequent periods of insanity. John the Fearless was apparently responsible for the assassination in 1407 of his greatest rival, the Duke of Orleans, and John's bitter hatred of his other opponents led him to support Henry V of England when Henry invaded France in 1415. In 1419 John himself was assassinated. His son, Philip the Good (1419–1467), continued the English alliance, cemented at the Treaty of Troyes in 1420 in which Henry V's claim to the throne of France was recognized. After the death of Charles VI in 1422, Philip the Good, Duke of Burgundy, was a vastly more powerful figure in France than the young and uncrowned Charles VII, who possessed only an empty treasury, few allies, and had been legally disinherited by Charles VI, who had also denied the legitimacy of Charles VII's birth. The young "King of Bourges," as Charles VII was sarcastically called, appeared insignificant compared to his prosperous and successful cousin, Philip of Burgundy.

Although the many different territories ruled by Philip the Good in his different (and entirely distinct) capacities of Duke of Burgundy, Count of Flanders, and other titles posed all of the problems of localism, variety, and inconsistency that often accompanied personal empire-building in the later Middle Ages, the dukes of Burgundy were generally successful in establishing their customary rights of governance and revenue throughout their lands, and they devised an impressive court to rule over all of them. They used some of the governmental techniques developed in the kingdom of France, which had also grown strong by acquiring territories with different histories, institutions, and traditional forms of limitation on the powers of their princes.

The combination of territories that the Dukes of Burgundy inherited, acquired by marriage, and conquered was the most diverse of any medieval state. The Duchy of Burgundy itself was largely rural and agricultural, already famous for its wines, and was not very urbanized. Its chief city, Dijon, was small.

The County of Flanders, however, was part of the most densely populated area north of Italy. Its two major cities, Ghent and Bruges, were the second and third largest cities north of the Alps (the first was Paris). The County held still other substantial cities, and these were largely merchant-dominated, contained a substantial manufacturing base and served as centers of commerce with the cities of northern Italy, as well as the great trading network along the Rhine and the Baltic Sea. Such a territory was difficult to rule, as the long history of struggles between the cities and the counts, as well as those between the counts and the kings of France, indicate. The Flemish towns were ruled by a broader group of citizens than anywhere else in Europe, were difficult to govern, and had long worked out principles of insisting on their own consent to taxation—and often rebelling when their liberties were infringed. Both in Flanders and Brabant the cities prided themselves on the custom of the *Joyeuse Entrée*, the *Blijde Inkomst*—the formal promise to respect the town's liberties and privileges made by a new count upon his first formal entry into a city. In 1356 a *Joyeuse Entrée* was forced upon the Duke and Duchess of Brabant by the entire territory. The terms of this agreement required that the duchy not be divided, that only Brabanters could hold government office, and that the prince could not make war or coin money without the consent of his subjects.

In addition to Flanders, the Dukes of Burgundy slowly acquired comital and ducal rights over other territories, notably Brabant (with its cities of Brussels and Leuven) and Hainault. They usually managed to place candidates of their choice in the Prince-Bishopric of Liège, and they exerted influence on the important northern Netherlands counties of Holland and Zeeland, the Duchy of Guelders, and the Prince-Bishopric of Utrecht.

To balance all of their different titles, rights, and complex territories was an immensely difficult task for the Dukes of Burgundy, but the rewards for doing so successfully were great—the ducal income was enormous. By the early fifteenth century the Dukes of Burgundy were as powerful and respected as any rulers in Europe. Their prestige in turn helped them to govern their various territories.

The greatest creation of the dukes of Burgundy was the ducal court. A successful and prestigious court was one of the most important tools any ruler had, both for display and admiration and for asserting control over a varied and often violent and ambitious nobility. By the beginning of the fifteenth century many of the royal courts that had dominated Europe earlier were either in decline or politically divided. The Bohemian court of Prague declined after the death of Charles IV; that of Vienna was still being developed; that of Paris had been greatly diminished by warfare and political rivalry. The creation of the ducal court of Burgundy gave the dukes access to most of the political talent in their territories, and their patronage supported some of the greatest artists of fifteenth-century Europe. The decline of other courts made it seem even more brilliant than it was. Located in the city of Dijon, the court of the dukes of Burgundy became an instrument of administration as well as display, patronage, and diplomacy. Its reputation grew rapidly, and its style and manner influenced the other courts of Europe down to the sixteenth century. The dukes developed in addition a talented and loyal cadre of educated noble and non-noble servants, an able and salaried group of domestic officials, and an efficient and usually full treasury, usually managed from the city of Lille in Flanders.

The administrative side of the court was complemented by its social side. The dukes attracted the nobility from throughout their dominions and abroad, thus weakening local resistance to their centralizing powers, and they blended the various regional nobilities by arranging their marriages. The Dukes also created the knightly Order of the Golden Fleece in 1430, the most prestigious military order in Europe, thus creating yet another means of tying their different noble subjects more closely to their own rule. The rich ceremonial life of the court, marked by formal banquets, its own religious calendar, tournaments, and spectacles, impressed its visitors and subjects and created stronger bonds among the leading figures of the different territories the dukes ruled. The court's attendants, when they returned to their own homes throughout the dominions, were expected to explain ducal policies to their neighbors, and they brought home tales of the court's brilliance, from the specially trained and recruited singers and musicians, to the gardeners and architects and painters who decorated its spaces.

Poets, chroniclers, and writers of romances all found patronage at Dijon, and visual artists, then still considered mere domestic servants in most of the rest of Europe, were treated with respect by their ducal master. Some of the best examples of early Netherlandish painting, for example, the sculptures by Claus Sluter and the great Baerze-Broderlam altarpiece for the Charterhouse at Champmol, were produced for the ducal court of Burgundy. The painters Jan Van Eyck and Rogier Van Der Weyden did some of their greatest work on ducal commission. And the duke's officials followed suit. His great Chancellor, Nicholas Rolin, not only had his own portrait painted by Van Eyck, but commissioned the great *Last Judgment* from Van Der Weyden for the hospital he founded at Beaune, not far from Dijon. The striking mobility of talent—from royal officials to artists—that the dukes generated is a particularly important feature, not only for the resources it suggests, but for the history of pictorial art throughout Europe.

But the success of the Great Duchy of the West also depended on the weakness of France and the indifference of the empire. When the tide of war turned in favor of France, the dukes lost much of their influence at the French royal court. From the reign of John the Fearless, the Dukes of Burgundy turned their attention more and more toward their northern territories, the Burgundian Netherlands. With each new acquisition of territory in the Netherlands, the interests of the dukes increased. John the Fearless and Philip the Good spent most of their time in their Netherlands territories, staying variously at Ghent, Bruges, Mechelen, and Brussels.

In 1435 Philip the Good was formally reconciled with Charles VII of France at the Congress of Arras. With the growing strength of the French recovery, Philip's successor, Charles the Bold (1461–1477), turned his attention to the lands on his eastern flank and engaged in immensely expensive military campaigns, draining the ducal treasury and alienating many of his taxpaying subjects. Charles the Bold's agreement with Edward IV of England to invade France in 1461 alienated Louis XI of France, who stirred up further resistance to Charles within Charles's own dominions. Louis XI allied himself with Charles's enemies in Austria and Switzerland, and after a series of dismally unsuccessful military campaigns, Charles was killed at the Battle of Nancy in 1477.

But Charles's death did not diminish the cultural splendor of the ducal court or cause the disappearance of Burgundy. He left an heiress, his daughter

Mary of Burgundy, who lost some of her lands to Louis XI, but who also married Maximilian of Austria, the future emperor. Although much of the great dynastic lordship forged by Philip the Bold, made powerful and independent by John the Fearless and Philip the Good, was dismantled as an independent state by the laws of lordship and inheritance, Mary of Burgundy brought her rich northern lands into the Habsburg orbit. When the children of her marriage to Maximilian married those of the union of Isabella of Castile and Ferdinand of Aragon, they set the stage for yet another dynastic union whose consequences troubled and largely dominated Europe for the next two hundred years: the vast Habsburg territories that combined part of the old duchy of Burgundy with the mighty Crown of a united Spain and allied its rulers by blood to the emperors and their domains in southern Germany, Bohemia, Austria, and Hungary. Although the Great Duchy of the West had passed into history more quickly than it had arisen, it had greatly influenced the internal dynamic and resources of the southern Netherlands, a dynamic that long survived it and that underlies the later history of the Netherlands and Belgium. Its dismemberment influenced the diplomatic shaping of western Europe until well into early modern times.

FURTHER READING

There is a large literature on Marsiglio of Padua. The work may be used in the translation of Alan Gewirth, *Defensor Pacis* (reprint ed., Toronto: University of Toronto Press, 1980). Antony Black, *Politieval Thought in Europe 1250–1450* (Cambridge: Cambridge University Press, 1992), and Brian Tierney, *Religion, Law, and the Growth of Constitutional Thought, 1150–1650* (Cambridge: Cambridge University Press, 1982) are the best introductions to the transmission of late medieval political theory through the early modern period and are important correctives to most studies of the political theory of the Renaissance and Reformation. Ernst H. Kantorowicz, *The King's Two Bodies* (Princeton: Princeton University Press, 1957), is a classic work, as is Margaret Aston, *The Fifteenth Century* (London-New York: Thames and Hudson, 1968). An excellent recent topical study is J. H. Burns, *Lordship, Kingship, and Empire: The Idea of Monarchy 1400–1525* (Oxford: Clarendon Press, 1992).

On Germany, see the works of F. R. H. Du Boulay, *Germany in the Later Middle Ages* (New York: St. Martin's Press, 1983), Joachim Leuschner, *Germany in the Late Middle Ages* (New York: North Holland, 1980), Gerald Strauss, *Manifestations of Discontent in Germany on the Eve of the Reformation* (Bloomington: Indiana University Press, 1971), and Gerald Strauss, ed., *Pre-Reformation Germany* (New York: Harper & Row, 1972). For one aspect of social history, see John B. Freed, *Noble Bondsmen* (Ithaca, NY: Cornell University Press, 1995).

For the Hundred Years' War, see the classic work of Edouard Perroy, *The Hundred Years' War* (New York: Oxford University Press, 1951); Christopher

Allmand, *The Hundred Years War* (Cambridge: Cambridge University Press, 1988), and Kenneth Fowler, ed., *The Hundred Years' War* (New York: St. Martin's Press, 1971). John Barnie, *War in Medieval English Society* (Ithaca, NY: Cornell, 1974) describes the social impact of the war. The new history begun by Jonathan Sumption, *The Hundred Years War: Trial by Battle* (Philadelphia: University of Pennsylvania Press, 1991), will be the most complete narrative account.

On Joan see Regine Pernoud, *Joan of Arc* (New York: Stein and Day, 1966); there is an exhaustive bibliography by Nadia Margolis, *Joan of Arc in History, Literature, and Film* (New York: Garland, 1990). Christine's *Ditié* is available in Angus J. Kennedy and Kenneth Varty, *Ditié de Jehanne d'Arc* (Oxford: Society for the Study of Mediaeval Languages and Literature, 1977). For Christine herself, see Christine de Pisan, *The Treasure of the City of Ladies,* trans. Sarah Lawson (Harmondsworth-New York: Penguin, 1985), and Charity Cannon Willard, *Christine de Pizan: Her Life and Works* (New York: Persea Books, 1984).

For France's recovery, see P. S. Lewis, ed., *The Recovery of France in the Fifteenth Century* (New York: Harper & Row, 1972). On England, see J. R. Lander, *The Wars of the Roses* (New York: Capricorn, 1967), and H. S. Bennett, *The Pastons and Their England* (Cambridge: Cambridge University Press, 1970).

There is much value in the work of P. S. Lewis, *Essays in Later Medieval French History* (London: Hambledon, 1985); M. G. A. Vale, *Charles VII* (London: Eyre Methuen, 1974); Richard W. Kaeuper, *War, Justice, and Public Order: England and France in the Later Middle Ages* (Oxford: Clarendon Press, 1988).

On courtly culture generally, see the essays in A. G. Dickens, ed., *The Courts of Europe: Politics, Patronage and Royalty, 1400–1800* (New York: McGraw-Hill, 1977), and Ronald G. Asch and Adolf M. Birke, eds., *Princes, Patronage, and the Nobility: The Court at the Beginning of the Modern Age, ca. 1450–1650* (Oxford: Oxford University Press, 1991).

There is now an excellent history of Flanders: David Nicholas, *Medieval Flanders* (London-New York: Longman, 1992). Johann Huizinga's classic work, *The Waning of the Middle Ages* (1919; English trans. 1924; reprint Garden City: Doubleday, 1953; new trans. Chicago: University of Chicago Press, 1995), must be read with both caution and skepticism, and M. G. A. Vale, *War and Chivalry* (London: Duckworth, 1981) should be consulted for its critique. On the lively character of the towns, see Barbara Hanawalt and Kathryn Ryerson, eds., *City and Spectacle in Medieval Europe* (Minneapolis: University of Minnesota Press, 1992). On the culture of Holland, see the brilliant work of Frits Pieter Van Oostrom, *Court and Culture* (Berkeley-Los Angeles: University of California Press, 1992).

The best studies of Burgundy in English are those of Richard Vaughan: *Philip the Bold* (New York: Barnes & Noble, 1962); *John the Fearless* (New York: Barnes & Noble, 1966); *Philip the Good* (London: Longman, 1970); *Charles the Bold* (London: Longman, 1973); *Valois Burgundy* (London: Allen Lane, 1975).

On Valois Dijon, see William R. Tyler, *Dijon and the Valois Dukes of Burgundy* (Norman: University of Oklahoma Press, 1971). Recent scholarship is reflected in the essays of C. A. J. Armstrong, *England, France and Burgundy in the Fifteenth Century* (London: Hambledon, 1983).

A major work, superbly illustrated, is that of Walter Prevenier and Wim Blockmans, *The Burgundian Netherlands* (Cambridge and New York: Cambridge University Press, 1986).

20

FRONTIERS AND HORIZONS

THE WORLD ON THE LAST DAY

In the late fourteenth and fifteenth centuries a new Turkish invasion swept into Asia Minor and the Balkans, and in 1453 Constantinople, the last, shrunken symbol of the idea of a universal Christian and Roman empire, fell to the Turkish armies of the Ottoman Sultan Mehmet II. Byzantine resistance to western demands for ecclesiastical reunion and the vastly diminished resources of the restored empire of Michael VIII Palaeologos after 1261 had reduced Byzantine power considerably. A fifteenth-century English chronicler who had observed Emperor Manuel II's visit to the west asking for aid sadly commented, "How grievous it was that this great Christian prince should be driven by the Saracens from the furthest East to these furthest Western islands to seek aid against them. . . . Oh God, what dost thou now, ancient glory of Rome?" In the fourteenth century the vigorous kings of Serbia, particularly Stephen Dusan (1331–1355), had already threatened the empire's existence, and the growth of Catalan and Aragonese power at the same time in the eastern Mediterranean also reduced Byzantine strength. In the early years of the fourteenth century the Catalan Grand Company brought the first Ottoman Turks to Europe as mercenaries, and in the next several decades the expansion of the emirate in Anatolia and the growing reputation of the Ottoman sultans as supporters of Sunnite orthodoxy increased Ottoman power and prestige in the Islamic world.

In 1354 the Turks conquered Adrianople, the site of the emperor Valens's defeat at the hands of the Visigoths nearly one thousand years before. The powerful and well-organized Ottoman armies assaulted Constantinople in 1396 and 1422. In 1453, when Mehmet II assaulted the city by sea and land with vast armies and massive artillery pieces, the city was defended by only five thousand troops and two thousand foreigners. The assault breached the great Theodosian walls on May 29, and Constantine XI, the last emperor, died fighting in the streets of the sacred city. The principalities in the Peloponnesus and Trebizond capitulated to the Turks shortly after the fall of Constantinople, and the great city became the capital of a new Turkish empire. Control of the Black Sea and new influence in South Russia and Poland, as well as in the Balkans and most of Hungary, passed into the hands of the Sultan. The eastern borders of Europe had suddenly become very clear indeed.

In a famous letter, Pope Pius II (1458–1464) complained of Europe's failure to restore Constantinople and blamed the particularism of the Latins for their reluctance to challenge the new Turkish lords of southeastern Europe: "Who will understand the different languages? Who will rule the diverse customs? Who will reconcile the English with the French, or join the Genoese to the Aragonese, or conciliate the Germans to the Hungarians and Bohemians?" The resources of Christendom as a collective society seemed to have disappeared with Constantinople. Latin Europe indeed fought later battles against the Turks, but these were largely defensive battles. The last emperor was dead, and the new Christian patriarch of Constantinople, George Scholarios Gennadios, was an appointee of the Sultan.

In spite of papal urging and diplomatic activity it became clear during the next century that Constantinople would not be won back and that the Turks would advance even further into southeastern Europe. Only very small enclaves preserved something of the vanished Byzantine past. But the power of Byzantine civilization survived in other places: in Venice, whose very fabric was built from Byzantine influences; in Russia, which became the heir of Byzantine religious orthodoxy and culture; in the new concern for the Greek language and Greek scholarship in western Europe; in the somber and mysterious pictures painted in faraway Spain in the sixteenth century by the Greek painter Domenikos Theotokopoulos—El Greco. The Byzantine writers themselves preserved a different memory—a vision of the sacredness of the city that not even the Turkish conquest could pollute. Several later chroniclers tell of the last free religious service held at the Church of Hagia Sophia, on the day the Turks took the city. The crowd huddled together and the service began. But the Turkish soldiers burst through the doors of the great church and began to slaughter the congregation. The priests, however, continued the service, and at the last minute took up the sacred instruments of the Mass and walked toward the wall of the sanctuary. The wall, the chroniclers say, then opened to let the priests in. Legend has it that they will emerge to finish their service when Constantinople is once again a Christian city. Such is the power of legend in the face of history.

Mongol and Ottoman Turkish invasions of eastern Europe.

THE THIRD ROME

The Mongol occupation of Russia had virtually cut that land off from both Byzantium and the West. In 1300 the metropolitan of Kiev established himself in Vladimir, to the north of Kiev, and then in 1328 in the town of Moscow. The Russian revival of the fourteenth century that brought it once again into active contact with Byzantium began with the rise of the principality of Muscovy and signaled a change in the relations between the Russians and the Byzantines. Muscovy's greater distance from Constantinople, its long period under Mongol domination, and its ecclesiastical rivalry with Lithuania all helped weaken the bonds between Byzantium and the most faithful of its cultural dependents. The alternations between Greek and Russian metropolitans of Kiev after 1250, however, helped maintain relations between the two peoples, and the steady stream of Russian pilgrims to Constantinople continued to testify to the great city's religious attraction in the north. In addition to its rivalry with Lithuania over the question of the metropolitan, however, Muscovy also began to criticize Constantinople itself after 1439. The Council of Florence, at which union between the Greek and Latin churches was proclaimed, seemed to the Russians a breach of the faith. The Greek metropolitan of Kiev, Isidore, was arrested after his attempts to introduce the Latin rite on his return to Muscovy. In 1448 a synod of Russian bishops took the unprecedented step of electing a metropolitan of Kiev without Byzantine initiation. Although this step must be considered in terms of Russian resistance to Byzantine unionization, it may also be considered as a reflection of the vigor of the Russian church.

The rule of Grand Duke Ivan III (1462–1505) traditionally marks the full coming of independence to Muscovy. Under Ivan's energetic and ambitious rule, the breakup of the Mongol khanate and the western interests of Lithuania were both exploited to Muscovy's advantage. By the midfifteenth century the Golden Horde had splintered into three separate khanates, one at Kazan, one in the Crimea, and a third on the lower Volga. Ivan III became the first grand duke of Muscovy to assume his rulership without Mongol permission, and he soon began to exert Muscovite control over other northern Russian principalities. Between 1456 and 1473 the great city of Novgorod, hitherto dependent on its economy and its Lithuanian neighbors for support, fell to Ivan's armies. The rise of Muscovy to the domination of all Russia had begun.

The strained ecclesiastical relations between Russia and Byzantium in the fourteenth and fifteenth centuries, the vigor of the principality of Muscovy, and the success of Grand Dukes Vasili (1425–1462), and Ivan III in the face of Lithuanian, Polish, Mongol, and other Russian opposition all led to the development of considerable economic and political power within the Muscovite state, as well as to a fierce sense of pride and divine approval. Thus, in 1460 the metropolitan of Moscow could firmly observe that Constantinople had fallen because of God's disapproval of the union of the churches at the Council of Florence. Certainly, the new Muscovite dominance was a heady experience, and the success of the grand dukes of the fourteenth and fifteenth centuries had acquired for them a preeminence even among the boyars, which hastened political consolidations. Like the earlier rulers of Serbia, Bulgaria, and the Romanian principalities, the grand dukes of Muscovy began to adopt the outward signs of Byzantine imperial rule. In 1472, partly through the agency of the pope, Ivan III married Zoe Palaeologina, the niece of the last Byzantine emperor. Although the pope may have hoped through this marriage to effect the 1439 provisions in Russia, Ivan and the empress, renamed Sophia, adopted an elaborate Byzantine court ceremonial and the imperial device of the double-headed eagle. Under this rule the grand dukes of Muscovy began to evolve into the tsars of Russia (*tsar* is the Byzantine equivalent of *Caesar*). Muscovite self-confidence went even further in certain areas. In 1492 Moscow was proclaimed the "New Constantinople"; in 1510 the monk Philotheus of Pskov declared it the "Third Rome."

THE FIRST ROME

As the Muscovite principality claimed its place in the sequence of centers of Christendom many western European thinkers also turned to the idea of Rome, but not in search of a successor state to old Rome and Constantinople. From the twelfth century on, western Europeans had begun to acquire a greater appreciation of some of the achievements of ancient Roman culture and civilization. This new appreciation was not exclusively the result of greater familiarity with ancient Latin literature, although reading the classics was certainly one important part of it.

R. W. Southern has suggested some of the conditions of twelfth- and thirteenth-century western European culture that supported a new interest in the Roman past. Among them are a concern with the dignity of human nature and the dignity and intelligibility of the natural order. The new twelfth-century devotional exercises that led to the search for God into the soul and the inner self are one consequence of the new attitudes. The recognition by theologians and pastors of the spiritual life of the laity, particularly that of the lay population of the growing cities, is another. The increasing complexity of legal relationships made the rationality, order, and systematic character of Roman law appealing to judges and political leaders as well. In short, as medieval European society grew more complex, the old and profound differences between the new Christian world and ancient pagan Rome appeared to be less important than other elements that the two societies were perceived to have had in common: a respect for precise language, a search for civic morality, principles of political order, and a new and wholesome respect for the intellectual rather than the purely religious virtues of classical Latin literature and the writings of the early Fathers of the Church.

Thus, the considerable literary achievements of European writers in the twelfth century had led some writers to take great pride in the achievements of their own time. Chrétien de Troyes, the greatest of the French writers of knightly romances, went so far as to claim for France the sum total of all the virtues of the past:

> Greece once had, for chivalry,
> The greatest honor, and of clergy.
> Then chivalry passed on to Rome,
> And clergy too. But now their home
> Is France.

Next to the papal ideal of the *translatio imperii,* the translation of legitimate empire from Rome to Germany, and the university ideal of the *translatio studii,* the translation of learning from the east to the west, there emerged the secular idea of the translation of culture, not merely from the lands of the east to those of the west but from the societies of antiquity to those of twelfth- and thirteenth-century western Europe.

Europeans also discovered that antiquity held treasures that had not yet been understood. Among these were the writings of the fourth-century Church Fathers, particularly Jerome and Augustine. Besides the theology of the Fathers, however, fourteenth-century thinkers discovered their Latin prose style, which was modeled on the clarity and elegance of earlier Latin writers such as Cicero. Just as philosophers were drawn away from Aristotle toward Plato, so theologians and writers were drawn from the thirteenth-century scholastic thinkers to the eloquent Church Fathers. Because the Fathers themselves had been strongly influenced by Plato, the works of that philosopher began to be translated. The fifteenth century saw the acquisition of other Greek manuscripts by Latins, some of them from Constantinople and from Greek scholars traveling in western Europe. This new interest in the thought of Plato and other Greeks also led to greater study of Greek language in western Europe, first in northern and southern Italy and later across the Alps.

However, the primary linguistic focus of fourteenth- and fifteenth-century thinkers was Latin, and their initial coloring was moral. Perhaps the most characteristic of the new thinkers was the Florentine scholar and man of letters Francesco Petrarca (1304–1374), whose importance lies as much in his later influence as in his own considerable achievements. Petrarca was raised in Avignon and was sent to study law at the universities of Montpellier and Bologna. Unlike many of his contemporaries, however, Petrarca felt no love for the law or for what he perceived as the immorality of most lawyers. Indeed, he bitterly criticized the flat technical jargon not only of legal studies but of logic and medicine as well. Petrarca's ambitions were literary rather than legal, and he never finished his legal studies. From early in life he had studied Latin, particularly the prose of Cicero, which he admired immensely and read more carefully than anyone before him. Petrarca's excellent ear for the intricacy and subtlety of Ciceronian Latin was matched by a careful eye and a critical intelligence of considerable merit. As he read he became aware of the errors that had crept into ancient texts because of scribal carelessness or incomprehension over many centuries of recopying. With other scholars in Avignon, Petrarca began to search for more and more manuscripts, developing his study of Latin philology and textual editing into a fine art. These two activities led to Petrarca's own development of a fine Latin prose style, flexible and elegant, which stood in sharp contrast to the dullness and formality of the academic and professional language he had come to despise. Petrarca's interest in searching out manuscripts turned up not only more Latin literature than had previously been known to exist, but brought to light literary works that had been little used since the twelfth century.

The renovation of Latin prose and the beginning of the search for antiquity through the study and collection of ancient manuscripts were two of Petrarca's most important achievements. But his real greatness lay in two other areas. Having rejected the profession of law—and indeed the very idea of a profession in the fourteenth-century sense—Petrarca became a poet and man of letters, perhaps the first such figure in European history. However, he did not do so solely out of a love for literature. In Cicero's and Augustine's works Petrarca found a personal and social moral theory that appealed to him far more strongly than the theology and social ideas of his contemporaries, and he insisted that the study of Latin and the practice of letters had primarily a moral end. His own early works investigate his own personality. Petrarca was not reluctant to reveal his shortcomings as well as his virtues. Indeed, this search for the true self, inspired by Cicero and Saint Augustine, was one of the Petrarca's great contributions to the history of European thought. Besides seeking the true self Petrarca searched for the ideal society, and he claimed to have found it in the civilized, moral world of Cicero's Rome. Clarity, eloquent language, friendship, and cultivated leisure—these for Petrarca were the elements of the ideal life, and he pursued them in his own life and writings, particularly in his many letters and treatises. In so doing he opened a new vista not only upon scholarship and literature but on individual and social morality.

This practical use of the Latin classics, coupled with Petrarca's thoroughgoing Christian values, immensely influenced the next several generations of scholars and writers north and south of the Alps. By claiming for Roman morality a degree of virtue that no Christian writer had ever accorded it, Petrarca opened new avenues for later generations to explore, especially in literature and moral thought. This combination of literary study, exact scholarship, and the ideal of the life of dignified leisure has generally been labeled humanism, and Petrarca was acclaimed the first humanist by later scholars. As we have seen, Cicero himself had defined the liberal arts, and chiefly literature, as those arts befitting a free man, that is, a leisured, conscientious Roman citizen with aristocratic status and good taste. Cicero's idea of human studies strongly appealed to Petrarca's secularized psychology, and although strong claims have been made for a medieval ideal of humanism, tradition still attributes to Petrarca the title of the first humanist.

Petrarca's interest in ancient Rome did not end with imitating its literary language and appreciating its morality. On his visits from Avignon to Rome (where he was awarded the ancient laurel crown for poets in 1341), Petrarca was stunned by the desolation of the city, abandoned by its popes as it had once been abandoned by its ancient emperors. When a young Roman, Cola di Rienzo (1313–1354), created a revolutionary government in the city and designated himself its *tribune*—the ancient civic title of Rome's Republican leaders—Petrarca praised Cola eloquently. Even Cola's early death and the failure of the "Roman Republic" did not dissuade Petrarca from his fascination with the ancient greatness and present desolation of the city. Rather, it led him to the study of history. In 1343, two years after his poetic coronation amid the ruins of Rome, Petrarca wrote to his friend Giovanni Colonna:

As we walked over the walls of the shattered city of Rome, or sat there, the fragments of the ruins were under our very eyes. Our conversation turned toward history, which we appear to have divided up between us in such a way that in modern history you, in ancient history I, seemed the more expert. Ancient were called those events that took place before the name of Christ was celebrated in Rome and adored by the Roman emperors. Modern, however, were called the events from that time to the present.

Petrarca's sense of a major division of history, marked by the Christianization of the Roman Empire in the fourth century, was the result of his veneration of ancient Latin literature and morality. But it proved to be very influential in the following three centuries, when Petrarca's own role in "reviving" the culture of antiquity was regarded as the beginning of a rebirth—in French, a *renaissance*—of the world of antiquity. As closely related as his thought was to the devotional and scholarly trends of the fourteenth century, Petrarca's vision of history was later regarded as itself beginning a new age in European civilization, the "Age of the Renaissance."

But the rediscovery of the first Rome was not an achievement of Petrarca alone, nor of Italian scholars exclusively. Richard de Bury, (1281–1385), tutor to King Edward III of England and author of the *Philobiblon,* was also a fine Latin scholar, collector of manuscripts, and connoisseur of Roman civilization. In France the great moralist Nicholas de Clamanges shared the literary and cultural interests of Petrarca, Richard de Bury, and other humanists. By the end of the fourteenth century, the new interest in Latin literature and the morality of ancient Roman and Greek civilization that had been created by Petrarca and others had brought the first Rome before the eyes of curious and interested Europeans. By revealing, sometimes painfully, the differences between the civilization of ancient Rome and that of fourteenth- and fifteenth-century western Europe, the humanists sharpened Europeans' sense of the complex nature of the past as they began to provide more accurate information about that past.

The image of the first Rome gradually became grander, more dignified, and more profound than contemporary culture, and European thinkers began to speak of Petrarca's "modern history" as if it were a great decline from the glories of Rome. For the next three hundred years that period of the European past extending from the fourth to the fourteenth century had to defend itself against the formidable attacks of the humanists as one-by-one its own achievements were either ignored or dismissed as errors. With the rediscovery of the first Rome there also occurred the invention of the "Middle Ages".

ANCIENTS AND MODERNS

Those writers who praised the virtues of ancient Greece and Rome at the expense of the Middle Ages made possible another point of view, one that regarded the fifteenth century and later as superior even to the glories of Greece and Rome. Such a view, which did little to change the attitude of people toward the Middle Ages, grew out of certain late-medieval achievements in culture and technology. By the seventeenth and eighteenth centuries the debate between those who praised Greece and Rome as the greatest cultural achievements of humanity and those who claimed that distinction for the period between the fifteenth and eighteenth centuries had produced a literary and philosophical argument that is generally called the Quarrel Between the Ancients and the Moderns. Although ancients and moderns both used examples from literature, morality, the arts, and the sciences in their arguments, the moderns had an edge that the ancients could not claim—the results of late-medieval and early-modern developments in technology.

As we have seen in earlier chapters, one of the most distinctive features of early medieval society was its free use of new techniques and machines to open the forests and scrublands of northern Europe to extensive agricultural development. The spread of the water mill from the sixth century, the heavy plough after the seventh, the three-field system after the eighth, and the new developments in the breeding, shoeing, and harnessing of horses after the ninth enabled northern Europeans to make great strides toward the settlement of hitherto empty parts of Europe and increased the productivity of settled parts. After the tenth century, developments in agricultural technology began to influence other areas of economic activity, chiefly manufacturing. The water mill produced about three and a half horsepower, which after the tenth century was applied to the brewing of beer, the fulling of cloth, the sawing of wood, and the making of paper. The windmill, which appeared in western Europe around 1200, generated around twenty-five horsepower. Mounted on a large shaft, it could be turned to face the wind. The power of the windmill was also applied in other areas besides the grinding of grain. Sixteenth-century writers were well aware that the Romans had not known of the windmill, and they took pride in this achievement of the "moderns." But the development of new techniques in agriculture and new sources of nonanimal and nonhuman power was not the only medieval contribution to the arguments of the moderns against the ancients. Much more striking was the application of machines from one area of economic activity to others—from the farm to the cloth mill, from the rural monastery to the smithy, from the grain mill to the sawmill. The best historian of medieval European technology, Lynn T. White, Jr., has argued persuasively that one of the most distinctive features of medieval European culture is precisely this machine-mindedness, the assimilating ability and willingness of Europeans that made them the most technologically developed people in the world at the end of the Middle Ages: "During the later Middle Ages there was a passion for the mechanization of industry such as no culture had known. . . . The Europe which rose to global dominance about 1500 had an industrial capacity and skill vastly greater than that of any of the cultures of Asia—not to mention Africa or America—which it challenged."[1] The windmill and the printing press were simply two of the many machines that made Europeans, however great their reverence for Greece and Rome, vastly different from their ancient predecessors.

"Every day new arts are discovered," observed a Florentine preacher in 1306. Friar Giordano da Pisa particularly admired (as scholars have ever since) the invention of eyeglasses, which had taken place around 1280. He went on to note:

There are [even] many [arts] which have not yet been discovered. Every day you could find one, and there would still be new ones to find. . . . It was not twenty years since there was discovered the art of making spectacles which help you to see well, which is one of the best and most necessary arts in the world. I myself saw the man who discovered and practiced it, and I talked with him.

As White concisely observes, "Here was a mood without historical precedent: . . . the invention of invention as a total project. It was the mood of Europe's technicians from the later thirteenth century onwards."[2] Although White and other historians of technology and science have differed over which qualities in European culture of the period between the sixth and the fourteenth centuries made Europeans so machine-minded, most agree that the causes are cultural, the product of distinctive human attitudes toward labor, the material world, mathematics, and efficiency. Not only did Europeans borrow, modify, and invent machines, but they also put them into works of art and imagination. As they discovered Roman ruins and artistic monuments they found that they possessed cultural traits that the Romans lacked, and they took pride in them.

And they spread them. Individual technological developments were spontaneously invented in several different places. Communication was another integral part of European technological development. From the thirteenth to

---

[1]Lynn T. White, Jr., *Medieval Religion and Technology: Collected Essays* (Berkeley and Los Angeles: University of California Press, 1978), p. 221.

[2]Ibid.

the seventeenth century most of the improvements in land communication and transport consisted of refinements of techniques that had been developed in the twelfth and thirteenth centuries. New techniques in harnessing and shoeing horses, more maneuverable wagons with better suspension, and improvements in road and bridge building brought European technology in this field to a state that remained essentially static until the extensive road-building programs and the development of the steam engine in the eighteenth century. Networks of information, in merchants' companies and in kingdoms and other political units, improved the regularity and speed of some communications. By the early fourteenth century cart roads were being built in the alpine passes, and in 1480 gunpowder was used in the Tyrol to blast rock for the widening of roads. Slowly the pack animal gave way to the wagon, the track to the road. The increasingly sedentary character of large governments made capital towns and cities the hubs of new communications networks, from papal Avignon in the fourteenth century to Vienna and Madrid in the sixteenth.

As the means of sending information and goods improved in this period, so did the means of preserving information. New techniques in writing materials and the invention of movable type illustrate Europe's considerable capacity for importing and adapting techniques from other cultures. Papermaking technique had come to Islamic Spain from China, and with the Christian conquest of Valencia in 1258, paper entered the world of European communications, becoming both cheaper and more durable in the fourteenth and fifteenth centuries. By then the price of paper was one-sixth the price of parchment. Considering that a single bible required between two and three hundred animal skins, the saving was considerable. China had also invented the technique of block-printing: cutting script onto the surface of blocks of wood or other substances and impressing these on paper. Fifteenth-century Europeans adapted this technique in the manufacture of playing cards, and then went on to invent movable metal type, first at Mainz in the 1455 forty-two-line Bible. Type and paper also required ink, and European printers appeared to have developed an oil-based ink, which flows smoothly, perhaps from the contemporary use of new, oil-based paints. The new technology also required capital, and the increased investment in printing, and the growth of a literate public propelled the book trade into a prominent place in fifteenth and sixteenth-century life. Not only books, of course, but laws, newsletters, and official and unofficial printed matter of all kinds helped accelerate the dissemination of information.

The fifteenth century also saw a number of frequent large-scale public assemblies, from regional gatherings to the great international congresses and councils, like the Council of Constance, drew people together from remote corners of Europe and then returned them to their places of origin, their heads full of what they had seen, read, and heard.

By 1360, after more than a century of development, fully operative mechanical clocks had come into being. Once developed, they were widely incorporated in public buildings, first at the church of St. Eustorgio in Milan in 1309 (just three years after Giordano da Pisa's sermon in praise of eyeglasses) and by 1370 in the palace of King Charles V of France. As in other aspects of social and cultural relations, notably weights, measures, and coinage on the one hand and practical and speculative mathematics on the other, towns and lay authorities in general transformed the measuring and proclamation of time.

Besides affecting productivity, measurement, good order, and peace, European technology transformed the face of war. In the fourteenth century, the face of battle was transformed. Cavalry was still important for the prestige of the mounted warrior, but it also still possessed shock value, and in need cavalrymen could fight dismounted. The use of infantry, however, increased, and the assembly, training, arming, and paying an army of professional or mercenary infantry contributed to the increasing costs of war.

With the higher proportion of infantry and the appearance of more highly developed missiles, the armor of the horseman also changed. Required to deflect missiles, pikes, swords, lances, and maces, armor now became full iron and steel plate, replacing the older chain mail. Armor was also strengthened by improved metallurgy, so that by 1400, a good set of plate armor could stop the arrow from a longbow, although it probably could not stop a bolt from the improved fifteenth-century crossbow.

But it could be designed to increase the deflecting character of its surface, a practice that became essential with the introduction of gunpowder. Gunpowder was brought to Europe from China at the end of the thirteenth century, and by the fourteenth it was being used on a very small scale in warfare. The development of heavy metal casting in the manufacture of bells soon provided a means of containing gunpowder and projectile in a single cannon. The use of the cannon—at first as a kind of superior catapult and then quickly adding the capacity of field-artillery—increased during the 1400s, and by the end of that century the mobility and destructiveness of field cannon was causing great consternation among those who depended on thick castle walls to protect them from the enemy. The guns burst the walls, and the inhabitants had to find ways to redesign them. By making the walls thinner but building out from them angle bastions that would deflect cannon fire and cover the breaches in the walls by means of enfilading fire, military architects transformed the thick-walled medieval castle into the geometrically calculated star-fort of early-modern Europe. They did so by mathematical calculations that were just as careful as the calculations necessary in making large guns and projectiles.

From the heavy plow to the cannon, from the water mill to the angle bastion, from the water clock to the mechanical clock, European technology knew little of the conventional divisions of medieval, renaissance, and early-modern history. As the "moderns" knew well, the technical achievements and the technology-mindedness of Europeans were very different from those of the ancient Greeks and Romans. In this one area at least, the moderns surpassed the Greeks and Romans and held their own in debates about which period of history was preferable. Petrarca had said that he would have chosen to live in the period of Cicero if he had had the choice. By the end of the fifteenth century, in spite of their fondness for the revival of antique culture, many other Europeans knew exactly which advantages their own time held over that of Cicero. Research into the history of technology has shown just how much those advantages owed to the farmers, craftspeople, and artists of medieval Europe, not only on land but on the sea as well.

"HERE THERE BEE TYGRES"

In 1298 Rustichello of Pisa, a writer of knightly romances, shared a Genoese prison cell with a Venetian captive named Marco Polo, who told the writer of his eighteen years in China in the service of the Great Khan. Rustichello wrote the stories down in a book that came quickly to be called *Il Milione,* "The Million," because of its tales of the fabulous wealth of Asia and possibly also because Marco Polo was alleged to have brought back great wealth. Thirty years earlier, regular Geonese and Venetian fleets had sailed out of the Mediterranean Sea and into the Atlantic to make commercial connections with the trade networks of northern Europe. In 1291 two brothers of Genoa, the Vivaldi, had outfitted several ships and sailed west out of the Mediterranean to seek new trade routes. The travels to Asia, the establishment of regular maritime contact between the Mediterranean and the Atlantic, and the mystery and interest generated by such adventures as those of the Vivaldi, who disappeared, and Marco Polo, whose story quickly became widely known, suggest a new interest by some Europeans not only in the wonders of the unknown parts of the world but also in the possible material value of the unknown world. The time between the papal missions to the Mongols of John del Pian Carpini in 1245–1247 and William of Rubrouck in 1253–1255 and the establishment of regular sailing routes to the west was very brief. By the 1270s others had begun to travel to Asia.

The traditional geographical knowledge of Europeans before the thirteenth century was most accurate close to home and progressively more imaginative the further from Europe it strayed. In the thirteenth century, however, Europeans learned much about the rest of the world, and their commercial ambitions, systems of communications, and travel reports accumulated more and more geographical knowledge. This knowledge was not, of course, immediately and universally absorbed, but it represented an enormous increment that began to chip away at the tradition of geographical thought received from eleventh- and twelfth-century Europe. That knowledge was a learned and nonexperimental amalgam of several distinct traditions. The knowledge handed down by Roman literature, from Pliny through Isidore of Seville, constituted one such tradition. A second comprised the speculations on such problems as the size and shape of the earth, its habitable and nonhabitable areas, and their climate-problems that had emerged in centuries of commentary on the description of the creation of the world in the Book of Genesis. Third, the efforts of twelfth-century thinkers to describe natural phenomena in terms of Platonic cosmology led to other speculations concerning the nature of the world and its inhabitants. Fourth, there grew up in the twelfth century a large body of literature, ranging from travel accounts to stories of the legendary journeys of Alexander the Great and others, that made much of each of these traditions available to a wider circle of readers.

The only truly impressive body of geographical knowledge developed between the ninth and the thirteenth centuries, that of the Muslim geographers, was virtually ignored in the West, and the legendary travel stories, including even Marco Polo's book, tended to be ignored by the learned. These individuals, for many of whom geography was a branch of theology, tended to regard geographical knowledge as useful insofar as it was consistent with the data from other branches of learning and insofar as it was morally edifying. Most of the traditions that comprised post-Roman geographical knowledge agreed that Jerusalem was at the center of the world, that Europe occupied precisely one quarter of the world, Africa another quarter or less (Europeans had as yet little knowledge of sub-Saharan Africa), and Asia a half, and that the Mediterranean Sea and the Nile valley neatly divided the sections of the world in such a way as to make the land areas resemble a "T" within a large circle. The resulting O-T maps constituted the basis of formal geographical knowledge, and the history of their slow transformation during the fourteenth and fifteenth centuries is one reflection of the new impact of naturalistic geography upon the traditional learning of the twelfth and thirteenth centuries.

The stream of legates, missionaries, adventurers, and merchants who followed John del Pian Carpini into Asia after 1247 swelled quickly. As early as 1260 two Venetian brothers, Maffeo and Nicolo Polo, left the Venetian settlements in the Crimea and traveled with merchandise to the Mongol court at Sarai on the Volga. They then made their way to Bokhara and, in the company of one of Kublai Khan's envoys, to Shangtu in China. By 1269 they had returned to the west with messages and gifts from Kublai Khan to the pope. Their son and nephew Marco (b. ca. 1254) departed with them on another trip to China, which they reached in 1275. The Polo brothers had begun as merchants and traders, but the success of their first journey to China, the Khan's welcome, and their return journey with Marco transformed them from traders into gentlemen ambassadors.

The Polos returned to Italy in 1295, a year after the Franciscan John of Monte Corvino arrived in Beijing, of which he became the first Christian

Europe encounters the world: voyages from 1487 to 1610.

archbishop in 1307. Marco Polo settled in Venice as a moderately wealthy nobleman, spent several years in a Genoese jail as a war prisoner, was released in 1299, and died in Venice in 1324, his mission as papal emissary to the court of the Great Khan unfulfilled. The book about him, *Il Milione,* was widely known, and when Christopher Columbus began to record his plans to reach China two centuries later, he knew the book and regarded himself as following in Marco's footsteps.

Although the "Mongol peace" permitted Europeans both land and sea access to eastern Asia, opportunities did not always provide the rewards that had been expected. The Venetian role in oriental trade declined after the fall of the Latin Empire at Constantinople in 1261, and although Genoa stepped in to assume Venice's former role, Venetian and Geonese rivalry in the eastern Mediterranean and the Black Sea remained marked through the fourteenth century. At its most promising, the route to the East attracted merchants, missionaries, and adventurers. In 1340 Francesco Balduccio Pegolotti wrote a treatise commonly called *La Practica della Mercatura,* in which he described very soberly all the things a merchant would need to know in order to do business among the Mongols.

The work included a remarkable description of the overland route to China (Pegolotti found it much more secure than it has ever been since.)

From the middle of the fourteenth century on, however, the increasingly unstable conditions in eastern Asia associated with the decline of the Mongol Empire, and in western Asia with the rise of Ottoman Turkish power, reduced the opportunities of reaching Asia through lands and seas no longer controlled by friendly, or at least neutral rulers. In turning to the western Mediterranean, and then to the Atlantic, Genoa assumed a predominant role.

During the thirteenth century, as Venice and Genoa were making their economic and political triumphs in the East, the rulers of the kingdom of Aragon were establishing their power not only southward in the eastern Iberian Peninsula into Valencia, but also eastward across the Mediterranean. During the thirteenth century the rulers of Aragon and their subjects, often in loose alliance, captured the Balearic Islands, Sardinia, and acquired the island of Sicily in 1282. In these lands they developed a colonial economy, in which the Genoese participated. In the Iberian Peninsula itself the rulers of both Aragon and Castile extended their conquests southward, to the southern edge of the peninsula, capturing Cadiz in 1268 and Seville in 1291, acquiring the largest populations of non-Christians of any European state in the process, and gaining access to both the Mediterranean Sea and the Atlantic Ocean.

Unlike the Venetians, the Genoese worked most successfully within territories largely ruled by others, and they moved into the Aragonese and Castilian kingdoms easily and smoothly. The deep-water ports of southern Spain were necessary for their large commercial ships and served as useful stopping points on the Genoese route northward through the Atlantic and the English Channel, established since 1277. Along the Mediterranean-Atlantic route, the Genoese shipped alum (necessary for the cloth-finishing processes of the northern textile industry), sugar, and the sweet wines for which northern Europeans were eager.

By the late fourteenth century, the Mediterranean-Atlantic routes had raised Castilian and especially Portuguese interests in yet another area, North Africa. Ever since the tenth century, the Maghreb, the western coast of North Africa, had been the northern destination of the gold caravans that originated in Ghana and crossed the western edge of the Sahara to Ceuta, Oran, Algiers, and Tunis. Copper and salt also came up this route. These products, along with North African wheat, enriched the North African cities and made them attractive—for trade, conquest, or both—to other Mediterranean powers from Norman Sicily in the twelfth century, to the Italian maritime cities in the thirteenth and fourteenth, to the Crusading army of Louis IX of France in 1270, and finally to the Castilian and Portuguese rulers in the fourteenth and fifteenth centuries. In the fourteenth century the gold of the Sudan became a particularly important prize among Christian and North African Muslim powers, and Christians began to obtain clearer information about its sources. A Majorcan portolan map of 1339 noted, "Below the Sahara, on the banks of a river that is the Niger, there is a king whose riches are counted in gold; it is the king of Mali." One chronicler's account of Jaume Ferrer's voyage to West Africa in 1346 stated that his purpose was "to go to the river of gold." By the midfourteenth century, Europeans knew that the source of the gold traded in the cities of the Maghreb was in the West African part of the Sudan and that it was extracted from rivers by black men, about whom a number of legends had circulated among Muslim traders. Europeans also knew that there were powerful, advanced black kingdoms in West Africa whose strength rested on their rulers' control of the gold trade. The great kings of Ghana and Mali controlled access to the gold-mining natives and permitted only their own subjects to trade salt for gold, which they then carried north and traded to the North African caravan merchants.

The greatest of all black Muslim rulers of this period was, as the Majorcan map of 1339 had observed, the king of Mali. By 1375, when Abraham Cresques drew his great Catalan atlas, the brief reference of 1339 had been expanded to a large picture of the black king seated on a throne, holding a globe and (somewhat improbably) the royal scepter of France with a fleur-de-lis at its end. The new legend read, "This black lord is called Musa Melly, lord of the blacks of Guinea. This king is the richest and most noble lord by reason of the abundance of gold that is found in his country." The black king of the 1339 and 1375 Catalan maps was Mansa Musa, who had made a pilgrimage in 1321 to Mecca. There his display of wealth and piety astonished his Muslim coreligionists.

The financial crisis of the late fourteenth century had drastically increased Europeans' need for gold, and the new knowledge of the sources of West African gold raised the possibility of circumventing the Saharan-Maghreb trade routes by sailing directly to the source of the gold. The new maritime importance of Castile and Portugal on the Mediterranean-Atlantic trade routes, the new security of Christian Iberia, and the production of sugar-cane in the eastern Atlantic islands had greatly increased Iberian maritime experience and skill and had also brought the enterprising genius and technological skills of Genoa to bear on the peninsula.

The central, but still obscure, figure in the first Portuguese voyages to the west coast of Africa was Prince Henry the Navigator (1394–1460), the son of King John I of Portugal. Little different in world view or character from other fifteenth-century princely knights, Henry appears to have been particularly interested in the legends of mysterious lands in Africa, especially the reports that Prester John, the legendary Christian king, was to be found in Africa, perhaps in Ethiopia. Interested in measuring the extent of Muslim power and imbued with the Crusade mentality that had driven the earliest stages of the *reconquista,* Henry also thought that his own dynasty and kingdom might be the first to tap African gold at its source. With this mixture of motives—none of which was particularly "scientific" or "modern"—Henry spent vast sums of his own wealth in assembling at Sagres a group of cartographers, scholars, and sailors of all faiths and many languages. Henry was driven by an important youthful experience. In

1415, when he was twenty-one, a military expedition under his father had captured Ceuta on the North African coast, the first Christian landfall in Muslim Africa. For the rest of his life Henry considered that event the beginning of Portuguese expansion, as much for the injury to Islam as for any particular increases in scientific knowledge that it might promote. By 1431 Portuguese fleets had discovered and settled in the Azores and Henry, armed with royal and papal privileges to carry on the *reconquista* in Africa, had begun his annual dispatches of fleets to the west coast of Africa. Shortly after midcentury Portuguese sailors landed in Guinea and began to exploit the gold reserves and the large numbers of slaves, a right that had once belonged exclusively to the Muslim Sahara caravans. By the time Henry died he had fulfilled many of his ambitions. Gold had begun to flow into Portugal, and just before his death Portugal had issued its first gold coin, appropriately called the *crusado*.

The beginning of Portuguese exploitation of the Gold Coast of Africa had two remarkable consequences; the direct acquisition by the Portuguese of large amounts of gold and the beginning of the trade in black slaves that was to remain a source of income first in Mediterranean Europe and later, and to a much greater degree, in the ranching, agricultural, and mining settlements in the New World.

Africa offered not only gold, copper, salt, and slaves, but also the islands of the eastern Atlantic, which became essential bases for Mediterranean and Atlantic sailors who wished to sail down the western coast. By the middle of the fourteenth century, the Canaries, Madeira, and most of the Azores had become known to Europeans, and their conquest, too, had begun. The evidence of maps and sailing charts is reliable from the late fourteenth century, and the European conquest of these islands was complete by the late fifteenth century. The eastern Atlantic islands were important, not only as stopping points on the route to western Africa but also because of their position in relation to the Atlantic Ocean's wind systems. These islands are located at the eastern end of the most climatically favorable route for sailing west—between 35 and 42 degrees north latitude. From them the winds and ocean currents flow westward for nine months of the year. Thus, although the Vivaldi brothers had been lost trying to circumnavigate Africa in 1291, as was the Catalan Jaume Ferrer in 1346, from the middle of the fourteenth century on, the northwest edge of Africa increasingly became the central point, not only for further African exploration but also for the crossing of the Atlantic.

During this period, marine engineering had developed as rapidly, and in as complex a manner, as had conquest and trade, and it stood out in sharp contrast to the lack of development of land transportation. As long as it was forced to remain within the upward limits of animal and human power, land transportation remained generally unchanged between the thirteenth and the nineteenth centuries. On the sea, however, technological and economic influences quickly expanded Europeans' capacities for long-distance travel. Early

European ships were of two types, neither very satisfactory. The round-bottomed cog with a square sail was roomy but slow, and the long, narrow, oar-powered galley was fast but had too large a crew for effective cargo transportation. In the fourteenth century the great hulk was developed in the Baltic. It had a greater carrying capacity but no more speed. At the beginning of the fifteenth century, however, the caravel appeared. The stern rudder, the increased proportion of beam to length, the use of two masts, one of which carried a triangular lateen-rigged Mediterranean sail, the superior hull construction, the reduced crew, and the enormous cargo capacity of around four hundred tons produced the most efficient ship the West had ever known and the most profitable ship afloat. It was also the fastest. The caravel's speed under full sail was exceeded only slightly by the clipper ships of the nineteenth century. By the end of the fifteenth century not only had sail gone far to replace oar but the upward limits of commercial sailing speed had very nearly been reached.

Marine technology and practical navigation quickly outreached geography and cartography. Celestial navigation and the geographical and cartographical knowledge that characterizes more recent marine technology and theory did not come for a century. But the compass, the minutely accurate local sailors' charts called *portolans,* and practical trigonometry for course correction—all of which developed by the end of the thirteenth century—gave European mariners impressive tools. Baltic, North Sea, and Atlantic sailing routes had all been developed by the end of the thirteenth century. During the Spanish *reconquista* sugar-cane-producing settlements on the Atlantic islands of the Canaries and Madeira developed in imitation of the Venetian and Geonese colonies in the eastern Mediterranean. In spite of these practical achievements, however, knowledge of geography and anthropology was still restricted to the descriptions of Marco Polo and the fabulous accounts of Sir John Mandeville's alleged travels in the Near East between 1332 and 1366, which featured semihuman creatures and the catchall warning "*hic sunt leones*"—"here there bee tygres," as the Elizabethans later translated it. Not until Poggio Bracciolini's *Dialogue on Geography,* written in 1447/48, was there an attempt to link informal, learned geography with the actual experience of travelers and sailors. Indeed, there was no word for "explorer" in any European language.

The short-range and immediate interests of Genoa and the Iberian kingdoms had established not only an Atlantic linkage between southern Europe and the Mediterranean and the northern worlds, but they also had begun to open up the long-closed world of northwestern and Western Africa and the even larger world beyond the eastern Atlantic islands. The first of these achievements transformed the economic and political history of Europe; the second presented problems on a scale too vast and complex for any satisfactory solution. From the appearance of the Mongols on, Europeans were brought face-to-face with new kinds of human beings and a world immensely larger—although increasingly more accessible—than they had ever imagined. Asians, Black Africans, and Canarians posed problems of anthropology that Europeans had only a crude means of perceiving, and the discussions of the "human nature" of these new peoples created categories of thought that were later transferred to the still newer worlds of North and South America, and policies of behavior toward them whose consequences are still felt in the late twentieth century. Finally, although Europeans gained a surprising knowledge of the size of the world, they also discovered that they could reach new parts of it in periods of time that were not unthinkable. Columbus's first voyage, from Gomera in the Canary Islands to Santo Domingo in the Caribbean, took 32 days, about twice as long as it had taken Columbus to sail from Palos in Spain to Gomera itself. Not only was the western edge of the Atlantic bounded by promising islands—whether these lands were more Canary Islands, China, or an unknown land mass took some time to discover—but these lands could be reached by existing marine technology, on familiar ships, sailed by routinely trained men. These lands could be mapped, and people far from the voyages or settlements could learn from the maps. Europeans encountered the wider world of the fifteenth and sixteenth centuries provincially prepared, but infinitely ambitious, and much of the rest of later history is the result of that encounter, and the differences in scale of the mental and physical worlds of the later Middle Ages.

THE AMBASSADORS

In 1533, the Augsburg painter Hans Holbein the Younger painted the portrait of two young French ambassadors in London, the noble Jean de Dinteville (1504–1555) and the bishop-elect of Lavaur, Georges de Selve (1509–1541). The painting, titled *The Ambassadors,* serves as a convenient object around which to draw many of the themes in this book.

Jean de Dinteville, on the left in the painting, was Francis I's ambassador to England. He came from an old noble family near the city of Troyes in Champagne, was the local lord of the town of Polisy, and held the ancient office of *bailli* of Troyes. The prominence of French nobility in royal service was apparent in the early sixteenth century, and the lay noble, rather than the cleric alone, participated in those royal affairs that touched other parts of the world besides the kingdom itself. Georges de Selve, son of the president of the Parlement of Paris, was one of six brothers, five of whom were ambassadors in the service of the king of France.

The portrait itself had come of age in the fifteenth century, as the vast surviving number of portraits of individuals remind us, and from that period on it is possible to see the figures of history in ways that were virtually impossible earlier. In general, medieval artists, like medieval biographers, tended to portray an ideal type rather than a particular individual. But the artistic triumphs of the Romanesque and Gothic movements allowed greater artistic freedom and a greater degree of naturalism. By the end of the thirteenth century, first in tomb

Hans Holbein; The Ambassadors (1533). (National Gallery, London).

sculptures and later in portraits of the donors of churches, there is a clear attempt to record the actual physical appearance of individual subjects. The Dukes of Burgundy and their Chancellor, Nicholas Rolin, have themselves left us many portraits, as well as portraits of their female relatives and children. Holbein's portrait catches an important aspect of late medieval artistic technique.

The office of Holbein's subjects had emerged out of the earlier offices of papal legate, personal messenger, and herald. The status and functions of these individuals had become more regularized and more recognized in the early fifteenth century. In 1436 Bernard du Rosier, later bishop of Toulouse, completed the first analysis and description of diplomacy in European history, *The Short Treatise About Ambassadors.* It is difficult for a modern reader to imagine a world of strong and thoroughly governed states touching each other's borders and necessarily having business with each other but not possessing a regular network of formal and informal communications. Such a practice, though, was the invention first of the papacy and in the fourteenth and fifteenth centuries of the western European states. Among the earliest and best-known records of this new institution are the reports of Venetian ambassadors, for Venice, like the papacy, had business everywhere and demanded information as much as any larger power—more strongly, indeed, than many. Not only the circumstances of late medieval states, however, but their unique capacity to borrow from tradition— from Roman law, canon law, chivalric practice, political expediency, and public relations—combined to form the idea, the status, and the office of the late-medieval ambassador. Holbein's painting shows us an institution that grew out of many different sources and that by the early sixteenth century was a recognized but not always welcome figure in the political and diplomatic world of western Europe.

On the two levels of the table that occupies the center of Holbein's painting is a collection of objects that illustrate, literally and symbolically, the ambassadors' world. Each of the astronomical and navigational instruments in the picture can be identified, either with objects whose maker is known and that are presently in the world's museums, or with common types known to have been made around the time of the portrait. Holbein was fascinated with measuring devices, and their presence here both reflects our earlier notice of the tool-mindedness of late-medieval Europeans and suggests just how wide the world of the ambassadors had become. The late fifteenth-century voyages of Vasco da Gama and Columbus had immensely widened that world, and Europeans in turn began to produce instruments and maps to measure and describe it. The celestial globe by Dinteville's left hand matches the terrestrial globe by his left leg. The book in front of the terrestrial globe has also been identified: It is Peter Apian's *Well-Grounded Instruction in All Merchant's Arithmetic.* Apian was a professor of mathematics and astronomy in Bavaria, and he made the celestial globe that can be seen on the higher level of the table.

The open book in front of the lute shows on one page the German words and music of Martin Luther's translation of the hymn "Veni Creator Spiritus," a popular hymn in both reformed Protestant and Roman Catholic churches. It was a hymn particularly associated with Church councils, and by extension with universal harmony under the guidance of the Holy Spirit. The lute, too, was a symbol of musical and hence universal political harmony, and its broken string, meticulously depicted by Holbein, suggests the discord of states in Europe. When William Shakespeare, in writing *Troilus and Cressida,* wished to describe the chaos that comes upon human society when the hierarchical order is dissolved, he also used the familiar musical metaphor:

> The heavens themselves, the planets, and this center
> Observe degree, priority, and place,
> Insisture, course, proportion, season, form,
> Office and custom, all in line of order. . . .
> How could communities,
> Degrees in schools, and brotherhoods in cities,
> Peaceful commerce from dividable shores,
> The primogenitive and due of birth,
> Prerogative of age, crowns, scepters, laurels,
> But by degree, stand in authentic place?
> Take but degree away, untune that string,
> And, Hark! What discord follows.

Harmony in music and harmony in the affairs of men and women was a medieval commonplace that later centuries preserved and used themselves, in spiritual as well as human affairs. The fifteenth-century Dutch music theorist Johannes Tinctoris once wrote that Jesus Christ was the greatest of all musicians, because he had brought into harmony the great discord between God and humankind. Holbein's portrait is thus capable of being "read" as well as looked at. It preserves many of the themes and characteristic features of the culture that took form in the preceding centuries.

This book began with some predecessors of Dinteville and de Selve—the Phoenician and Greek sailors and migrants who set out westward across the Mediterranean Sea to found colonies, spread their way of life and thought among other peoples, and gain wealth and land for themselves. By the beginning of the sixteenth century, Europeans were ready to step out across a far wider sea, regardless of whether or not the people who lived beyond it were ready for them. The peoples who encountered the European explorers, colonists, soldiers, and ambassadors have been dealing ever since, in one way or another, with the consequences of their visits. Parts of the land laws hammered out in twelfth- and thirteenth-century Castile still survive in the laws of Latin America, Texas, and California. The institutional descendants of Henry II's grand jury still assemble in Canada, Australia, Hong Kong, and the United States. The medieval university still has not been replaced as the most efficient means of organizing and disseminating knowledge. States and ambassadors still wrangle about the means of restoring concord to a discordant world. The difference between the world into which the Phoenicians and Greeks stepped and that of the sixteenth-century explorers and ambassadors is one measure of the achievement of medieval civilization. It is a powerful and impressive measure. For Dinteville and de Selve and others like them stepped not only into a far wider world, but into time itself. And the culture they brought with them was the foundation of the modern world.

FURTHER READING

On Byzantium, see Donald M. Nicol, *The Last Centuries of Byzantium, 1261–1453* (London: Hart-Davis, 1972), and *The End of the Byzantine Empire* (New York: Holmes & Meier, 1981). See also the well-told story of Steven Runciman, *The Fall of Constantinople, 1453* (Cambridge: Cambridge University Press, 1965). The best survey of early Ottoman Turkish history is Halil Inalcik, *The Ottoman Empire: The Classical Age, 1300–1600* (London: Weidenfeld & Nicholson, 1973).

On the Mongols and the rise of Muscovy, see Charles J. Halperin, *Russia and the Golden Horde* (Bloomington: Indiana University Press, 1985), and his *The Tatar Yoke* (Columbus, Ohio: Slavica Press, 1985), as well as J. A. Boyle, *The Mongol World Empire 1206–1370* (London: Variorum, 1977).

For Muscovy, see J. L. Fennell, *The Crisis of Medieval Russia 1200–1304* (London-New York: Longman, 1983), and Fennell, *The Emergence of Moscow, 1304–1359* (Berkeley and Los Angeles: University of California Press, 1968); Nancy Shields Kollman, *Kinship and Politics: The Making of the Muscovite Political System, 1345–1547* (Stanford, CA: Stanford University Press, 1987); Gustav Alef, *Rulers and Nobles in Fifteenth-Century Muscovy* (London: Variorum, 1983), and Janet Martin, *Medieval Russia, 980–1584* (Cambridge: Cambridge University Press, 1995).

On Eastern and East-Central Europe, see Jean W. Sedlar, *East-Central Europe in the Middle Ages, 1000–1500* (Seattle: University of Washington Press, 199), *A History of Hungary*, Peter F. Sugar, ed. (Bloomington: Indiana University Press 1990) and on the Balkans, John V. A. Fine, Jr., *The Late Medieval Balkans* (Ann Arbor: University of Michigan Press, 1987).

On the city of Rome after the Avignon papacy, see J. A. F. Thomson, *Popes and Princes, 1417–1517* (Boston: George Allen & Unwin, 1980).

On the changing face of the first Rome, see Charles T. Davis, *Dante and the Idea of Rome* (Oxford: Clarendon Press, 1957), and *Dante's Italy* (Philadelphia: University of Pennsylvania Press). There is a large literature on humanism. See in particular Erwin Panofsky, *Renaissance and Renascences in Western Art* (reprint ed.: New York: Harper & Row, 1972), and Albert Rabil, ed., *Renaissance Humanism Foundations, Forms, and Legacy*, 3 vols. (Philadelphia: University of Pennsylvania Press, 1988).

On technology, see the General Bibliography.

On the growing interest in travel and its literature, see Scott D. Westrem, ed., *Discovering New Worlds: Essays on Medieval Exploration and Imagination* (New York-London: Garland, 1991), and Mary B. Campbell, *The Witness and the Other World: Exotic European Travel Writing, 400–1600* (Ithaca-London: Cornell University Press, 1988). The best account of the development of Mediterranean-Atlantic expansion is now that of Felipe Fernandez-Armesto, *Before Columbus: Exploration and Colonization from the Mediterranean to the Atlantic, 1229–1492* (Philadelphia: University of Pennsylvania Press, 1987), with extensive references.

On Columbus, see William D. Phillips, Jr. and Carla Rahn Phillips, *The Worlds of Christopher Columbus* (Cambridge: Cambridge University Press, 1992), and Felipe Fernandez-Armesto, *Columbus* (Oxford-New York: Oxford University Press, 1991). For the European response to the discoveries, see Fredi Chiappelli, ed., with Michael J. B. Allen and Robert L. Benson, *First Images of America* (Berkeley and Los Angeles: University of California Press, 1976). For the impact on conceptions of humanity, see Anthony R. Pagden, *The Fall of Natural Man* (Cambridge: Cambridge University Press, 1982).

A. G. Dickens, ed., *The Courts of Europe* (New York: McGraw-Hill, 1977), portrays the ambassadors' world, as does Donald Queller, *The Office of Ambassador in the Middle Ages* (Princeton, NJ: Princeton University Press, 1967).

On the idea of the Middle Ages, see Bryce Lyon, *The Origins of the Middle Ages* (New York: Norton, 1972); Wallace K. Fergusson, *The Renaissance in Historical Thought* (Boston: Houghton MiMin, 1948).

On the phenomenon of colonialism, see Robert I. Burns, S.J., *Medieval Colonialism: The Postcrusade Exploitation of Islamic Valencia* (Princeton, NJ: Princeton University Press, 1975), and Robert Bartlett, *The Making of Europe* (cited above).

GENERAL BIBLIOGRAPHY

NOTE

The following general bibliography covers large areas, but it is far from exhaustive, even of the materials in English-language scholarship. The sections entitled Further Reading at the end of each chapter also contain essential material. I have tried to provide suggestions for basic reading in English-language scholarship. Much crucial scholarship is not in English, although that is not listed here. Most of the works cited contain up-to-date bibliographies and should be consulted. Finally, it should be remembered that the divisions within this bibliography are for the sake of convenience, and many of the works listed under a single heading could as easily fit into other sections. I have tried to separate sections for convenience, but the diligent reader should look widely, rather than narrowly, at all of these references.

GUIDES TO MEDIEVAL STUDIES AND BIBLIOGRAPHY

Two excellent introductions to the general character of medieval studies and the types of sources and methodology for dealing with them are R. C. Van Caenegem and F. L. Ganshof, *Guide to the Sources of Medieval History* (Amsterdam: North Holland Publishing Co., 1978), and J. M. Powell, ed., *An Introduction to Medieval Studies* (Syracuse, NY: Syracuse University Press, 1976, revised ed. 1993). Among other important general reference sources are J. R. Strayer, ed., *The Dictionary of the Middle Ages*, 13 vols. (New York: Scribner's, 1982); L. J. Paetow, *A Guide to the Study of Medieval History*, rev. ed. (Cambridge, MA: Medieval Academy of America, 1931); and Gray C. Boyce, *Literature of Medieval History, 1930–1975: A Supplement to Louis John Paetow's 'A Guide to the Study of Medieval History,'* 5 vols. (Millwood, NY: Krause, 1981). For current bibliography, see *International Medieval Bibliography* (Leeds: Leeds University Press, 1967), and R. Rouse, *Annotated Guide to Serial Bibliography* (Berkeley and Los Angeles: University of California Press, 1969).

  Other encyclopedias and dictionaries include Aryeh Grabois, ed., *The Illustrated Encyclopedia of Medieval Civilization* (New York: Mayflower, 1980); Donald Matthew, *Atlas of Medieval Europe* (New York: Facts on File, 1983). A number of religious encyclopedias in their most recent editions contain useful information for the historian: *The New Catholic Encyclopedia* (New York: McGraw-Hill, 1967), and the currently appearing *Jewish Encyclopedia* and the *Encyclopedia of Islam.*

SOURCE MATERIALS IN ENGLISH TRANSLATION

C. P. Farrar and Austin P. Evans, *Bibliography of English Translations From Medieval Sources* (New York: Columbia University Press, 1946), has been continued by M. A. Ferguson, *Bibliography of English Translations From Medieval Sources, 1944–1968* (New York: Columbia University Press, 1973). There are many fine collections of source materials in anthologies. Some of these have been noted in the previously mentioned individual bibliographies, but mention must be made of Brian Pullan, *Sources for the History of Medieval Europe* (New York: Barnes & Noble, 1966), the best single collection of annotated documents in English translation.

  A running bibliography of medieval editions and translations in progress and in print, edited by Louis Gioia, may be found in the various issues of the scholarly journal *Speculum.*

ATLASES

The most readily available atlas is Colin McEvedy, *The Penguin Atlas of Medieval History* (Baltimore: Penguin, 1961). More sophisticated is Geoffrey Barraclough, ed., *The Times Atlas of World History* (Maplewood, NJ: Hammond, 1978). Specialized atlases are also very useful. See, for example, F. Van Der Meer and Christine Mohrmann, *Atlas of the Early Christian World* (London: Nelson, 1958).

COMPUTERS

See Anne Gilmour-Bryson, ed., *Computer Applications to Medieval Studies* (Kalamazoo, MI: Medieval Institute, 1984); R. C. Van Caenegem, *Guide to the Sources of Medieval History*, Part V, Chapter 8 (Amsterdam: North Holland Publishing Co., 1978); James M. Powell, *An Introduction to Medieval Studies*, Chapter 5, by David Herlihy.

INTERNET RESOURCES

The best starting point on the internet is **Labyrinth** (http://www.georgetown.edu/labyrinth/labyrinth-home.html), which offers access to more than a million files throughout the world. The homepage for the Medieval Academy of America is http://www.georgetown.edu/Medieval Academy. Basic introductory services are available at http://www.georgetown.edu/labyrinth/general.html. For medieval history, see http://history.cc.ukans.edu/history/subtree/medieval.html. Once into the Internet, the user will discover dozens of other locations, including a wealth of pictorial material.

FILM AND VIDEOTAPE

The Media Centre, University of Toronto, has produced a number of excellent videotapes dealing with many different aspects of medieval culture.

CHRONOLOGY

A good extensive chronology is that of R. L. Storey, *Chronology of the Medieval World, 400–1491* (New York: D. McKay, 1973). For England there are fine guides by F. M. Powicke and E. B. Fryde, *Handbook of British Chronology*, 2nd. ed. (London: Royal Historical Society, 1961), and C. R. Cheny, *Handbook of Dates for Students of English History* (London: Royal Historical Society, 1945). There is much useful information in Elias J. Bickerman, *Chronology of the Ancient World*, 2nd ed. (Ithaca, NY: Cornell University Press, 1980).

THE PHYSICAL ENVIRONMENT

For climate, see E. LeRoy Ladurie, *Times of Feast, Times of Famine* (New York: Doubleday, 1971), and H. H. Lamb, *The Changing Climate* (London: Methuen, 1966). For human geography, see Emrys Jones, *Human Geography: An Introduction to Man and His World*, rev. ed. (New York: Praeger, 1965), and Derwent Whittlesy, *Environmental Foundations of European History* (New York: Appleton-Century-Crofts, 1949). A brilliant example of working these kinds of data into historical knowledge is Fernand Braudel, *The Mediterranean and the Mediterranean World in the Age of Philip II*, 2 vols. (New York: Harper & Row, 1972). On medieval Europe specifically, see the essays collected in Lester J. Bilsky, ed., *Historical Ecology: Essays on Environment and Social Change*, Part III (Port Washington, NJ: Kennikat Press, 1980).

Two recent works deal with medieval material: Alfred W. Crosby, *Ecological Imperialism: The Biological Expansion of Europe, 900–1900* (Cambridge-New York: Cambridge University Press, 1986); and T. M. L. Wigley, M. J. Ingram, and G. Farmer, eds., *Climate and History* (Cambridge: Cambridge University Press, 1985).

HISTORICAL GEOGRAPHY

See C. T. Smith, *A Historical Geography of Western Europe Before 1800* (London: Longman, 1967); Norman J. G. Pounds, *An Historical Geography of Europe, 450 B.C.–A.D. 1330* (Cambridge: Cambridge University Press, 1976). For an important region see H. C. Darby et al., A *New Historical Geography of England Before 1800* (Cambridge: Cambridge University Press, 1973). and R. A. Dodgson and R. A. Butlin, eds., *An Historical Geography of England and Wales* (New York: Academic Press, 1978).

ARCHAEOLOGY

See Rainer Berger, ed., *Scientific Methods in Medieval Archaeology* (Berkeley and Los Angeles: University of California Press, 1970), and the ongoing research published in the journal *Medieval Archaeology*. A good example of specialized work is M. W. Barley, ed., *European Towns: Their Archeology and Early History* (New York: Academic Press, 1977). See also Kathleen Biddick, ed., *Archaeological Approaches to Medieval Europe* (Kalamazoo, MI: Medieval Institute, 1984).

MEDIEVAL HISTORY: NARRATIVE SURVEYS

The most complete history of the Middle Ages is J. B. Bury et al., eds., *The Cambridge Medieval History*, 8 vols. (Cambridge: Cambridge University Press, 1911–1936); Vol. IV of this history, *The Byzantine Empire*, ed. Joan Hussey appeared in 1966. Vol. II of *The New Cambridge Medieval History*, Rosamund McKitterick, ed., appeared in a new edition in 1995. Other volumes are presently being revised. The most comprehensive recent survey is the series edited by Denys Hay, *A General History of Europe* (New York: Longmans, 1966), which includes volumes by A. H. M. Jones, Christopher Brooke, John Mundy, and Hay dealing with the period 300–1500. Two superbly illustrated collaborative histories are David Talbot Rice, ed., *The Dark Ages* (London: Thames & Hudson, 1965), and Joan Evans, ed., *The Flowering of the Middle Ages* (London: Thames and Hudson, 1966). The first great individual history of medieval Europe—and in the opinion of many still the greatest—is Edward Gibbon, *The Decline and Fall of the Roman Empire,* the most complete edition of which is that of J. B. Bury (London: Methuen, 1909–1914).

The most recent major European work of this kind to be translated is that of Jacques Le Goff, *Medieval Civilization* (Oxford-New York: Basil Blackwell, 1988). See also George Holmes, ed., *The Oxford Illustrated History of Medieval Europe* (Oxford-New York, Oxford University Press, 1988).

DEMOGRAPHY

See J. C. Russell, *Late Ancient and Medieval Population* (Philadelphia: Transactions of the American Philosophical Society, 1958); idem, "Recent Advances in Medieval Demography," *Speculum* 40 (1965), 84–101; and idem, "Population in Europe," in *The Fontana Economic History of Europe,* Vol. 1, *The Middle Ages,* ed. Carlo M. Cipolla (London: Collins/Fontana, 1972), pp. 25–70. See also E. A. Wrigley, *Population and History* (New York: McGraw-Hill, 1969); Josiah Cox Russell, *The Control of Late Ancient and Medieval Population* (Philadelphia: American Philosophical Society, 1985).

ECONOMIC HISTORY

The most comprehensive study is the older collaborative work by J. Clapham and others, eds., *The Cambridge Economic History of Europe,* Vols. I–III (Cambridge: Cambridge University Press, 1941–1961). This work is being revised under the new joint editorship of M. M. Postan and J. Habbakuk; Vol. II, *Trade and Industry in the Middle Ages,* eds. M. M. Postan and Edward Miller, appeared in 1987.

For the early period, see Georges Duby, *The Early Growth of the European Economy: Warriors and Peasants from the Seventh to the Twelfth Centuries* (Ithaca, NY: Cornell University Press, 1974), and Renee Doehaerd, *The Early Middle Ages in the West: Economy and Society* (New York: North Holland, 1978). The famous thesis of Henri Pirenne concerning the nature of the early medieval economy is discussed in A. F. Havighurst, ed., *The Pirenne Thesis,* 3rd ed. (Lexington, MA: D. C. Heath, 1976). The most recent contribution is that of Richard Hodges and David Whitehouse, *Mohammed, Charlemagne, and the Origins of Europe: Archaeology and the Pirenne Thesis* (Ithaca, NY: Cornell University Press, 1983).

For the economic take-off of the tenth and eleventh centuries, see Robert S. Lopez, *The Commercial Revolution of the Middle Ages, 950–1350* (Cambridge: Cambridge University Press, 1976), and Robert S. Lopez and Irving Raymond, *Medieval Trade in the Mediterranean World*) (New York: Columbia University Press, 1955). For the later Middle Ages, see Harry A. Miskimin, *The Economy of Early Renaissance Europe* (New York: Cambridge University Press, 1975). In general, see also Carlo M. Cipolla, ed., *The Middle Ages,* Vol. I of *The Fontana Economic*

History of Europe (London: Collins/Fontana, 1972), and Carlo M. Cipolla, *Before the Industrial Revolution* (New York: Norton, 1976).

On money, see two books by Peter Spufford, *Money and Its Uses in Medieval Europe* (Cambridge: Cambridge University Press, 1987), and *Handbook of Medieval Exchange* (London: Royal Historical Society, 1986).

SOCIAL HISTORY

Perhaps the classic work in medieval social history is Marc Bloch, *Feudal Society* (Chicago: University of Chicago Press, 1961). It should be compared now with Georges Duby, *The Chivalrous Society* (Berkeley and Los Angeles: University of California Press, 1977), and *The Three Orders: Feudal Society Imagined* (Chicago: University of Chicago Press, 1980). Excellent samplings of different kinds of social history may be found in Sylvia Thrupp, ed., *Early Medieval Society* (New York: Appleton-Century-Crofts, 1967), and *Change in Medieval Society* (reprint ed. Toronto: University of Toronto Press, 1988). A splendid specialized study is Georges Duby, *Rural Economy and Country Life in the Medieval West* (Columbia: University of South Carolina Press, 1968). Examples of modern approaches may be found in David Herlihy, *The Social History of Italy and Western Europe, 700–1500* (London: Variorum, 1978); John W. Baldwin, *Masters, Princes, and Merchants: The Social Views of Peter the Chanter and His Circle*, 2 vols. (Princeton, NJ: Princeton University Press, 1970); Hans-Werner Goetz, *Life in the Middle Ages* (Notre Dame: Notre Dame University Press, 1993). On the complex question of wealth and poverty, see Michel Mollat, *The Poor in the Middle Ages: An Essay in Social History* (New Haven, CT: Yale University Press, 1986). Giles Constable, *Three Studies in Medieval Religious and Social Thought* (Cambridge: Cambridge University Press, 1995).

Peasant life is now treated extensively in Robert Fossier, *Peasant Life in the Medieval West* (Oxford-New York: Basil Blackwell, 1988); Leopold Genicot, *Rural Communities in the Medieval West* (Baltimore: Johns Hopkins University Press, 1990); Barbara A. Hanawalt, *The Ties That Bound: Peasant Families in Medieval England* (New York: Oxford: Oxford University Press, 1986).

The best general introduction to medieval slavery is Ruth Mazo Karras, *Slavery and Society in Medieval Scandinavia* (New Haven, CT: Yale University Press, 1988).

On private life, see now the ambitious and important work edited by Philippe Ariès and Georges Duby, *A History of Private Life:* Vol. 1, *From Pagan Rome to Byzantium,* ed., Paul Veyne (Cambridge, MA: Harvard University Press, 1987); Vol. II, *Revelations of the Medieval World,* ed., Georges Duby (Cambridge, MA: Harvard University Press, 1988).

On the shape of the individual human life, see J. A. Burrow, *The Ages of Man* (New York: Clarendon Press, Oxford University Press, 1986), and Elizabeth Sears, *The Ages of Man: Medieval Interpretations of the Life Cycle* (Princeton: Princeton University Press, 1986).

WOMEN AND HISTORY

On women in antiquity and late antiquity, see the references in Chapters 1 and 2.

On the early medieval period, see Suzanne F. Wemple, *Women in Frankish Society: Marriage and the Cloister, 500–900* (Philadelphia: University of Pennsylvania Press, 1981); Karl Leyser, *Rule and Conflict in Early Medieval Society: Ottonian Saxony* (Bloomington: Indiana University Press, 1979); Pauline Stafford, *Queens, Concubines, and Dowagers: The King's Wife in the Early Middle Ages* (Athens: University of Georgia Press, 1984).

An excellent guide to historiography is Susan Mosher Stuard, ed., *Women in Medieval History and Historiography* (Philadelphia: University of Pennsylvania Press, 1987), with an extensive and up-to-date bibliography. Individual collections of studies are in Susan Mosher Stuard, ed., *Women in Medieval Society* (Philadelphia: University of Pennsylvania Press, 1976), and in Derek Baker, ed., *Medieval Women, Studies in Church History: Subsidia,* Vol. I (Oxford: Basil Blackwell, 1978).

On women writers, see Peter Dronke, *Women Writers of the Middle Ages* (New York: Cambridge University Press, 1984); Katharina M. Wilson, *Medieval Women Writers* (Athens: University of Georgia Press, 1984); Marcelle Thiebaux, ed. and trans., *The Writings of Medieval Women* (New York: Garland, 1987); Elizabeth A. Petroff, ed., *Medieval Women's Visionary Literature* (New York: Oxford University Press, 1986); Karen Cherewatuk and Ulrike Wiethaus, *Dear Sister: Medieval Women and the Epistolary Genre* (Philadelphia: University of Pennsylvania Press, 1993).

Research on medieval women has focused on particular places and circumstances. For general surveys, see Shulamith Shahar, *The Fourth Estate: A History of Women in the Middle Ages* (London: Methuen, 1983), and the essays collected in Rosemary Thee Morewedge, ed., *The Role of Women in the Middle Ages* (Albany: State University of New York Press, 1975). Detailed studies are those of Heath Dillard, *Women of the Reconquest: Women in Castilian Town Society, 1000–1300* (Cambridge: Cambridge University Press, 1984); Georges Duby, *The Knight, the Lady and the Priest* (New York: Pantheon, 1983); Penelope D. Johnson, *Equal in Monastic Profession: Religious Women in Medieval France* (Chicago-London: University of Chicago Press, 1991); Clarissa W. Atkinson, *The Oldest Vocation: Christian Motherhood in the Middle Ages* (Ithaca: Cornell University Press, 1991).

Important studies of feminine consciousness and its devotional forms are those by Caroline Bynum, *Jesus as Mother: Studies in the Spirituality in the Late Middle Ages* (Berkeley and Los Angeles: University of California Press, 1982); Bynum, *Holy Feast and Holy Fast: The Religious Significance of Food to Medieval Women* (Berkeley and Los Angeles: University of California Press, 1987).

On various kinds of female authority, see Mary Erler and Maryanne Kowaleski, eds., *Women and Power in the Middle Ages* (Athens: University of Georgia Press, 1987); Carol Adams, Paula Bartley, Hilary Bourdillon, and Cathy

Loxton, eds., *From Workshop to Warfare: The Lives of Medieval Women* (Cambridge: Cambridge University Press, 1984). The extensive study by Martha Howell, *Women, Production, and Patriarchy in Late Medieval Cities* (Chicago: University of Chicago Press, 1986) is a model of its kind.

On queenship, see John Carmi Parsons, *Medieval Queenship* (New York: St. Martin's, 1993).

THE BODY, GENDER, AND SEXUALITY

On the body, see Sarah Kay and Miri Rubin, *Framing Medieval Bodies* (New York: St. Martin's: 1994), and Caroline Walker Bynum, *Fragmentation and Redemption: Essays on Gender and the Human Body in Medieval Religion* (New York: Zone Books, 1992).

On gender and sexuality, see Joan Cadden, *The Meanings of Sex Differences in the Middle Ages: Medicine, Science, and Culture* (Cambridge: Cambridge University Press, 1993); Pierre J. Payer, *Sex and the Penitentials* (Toronto: University of Toronto Press, 1984); Payer, *The Bridling of Desire: Views of Sex in the Later Middle Ages* (Toronto: University of Toronto Press, 1993); James A. Brundage, *Law, Sex, and Christian Society in Medieval Europe* (Chicago-London: University of Chicago Press, 1987); Joyce E. Salisbury, *Sex in the Middle Ages* (New York: Garland, 1991); Dyan Elliott, *Spiritual Marriage: Sexual Abstinence in Medieval Wedlock* (Princeton: Princeton University Press, 1993); Vern L. Bullough and James A. Brundage, *Sexual Practices and the Medieval Church* (Buffalo: Prometheus Books, 1982); Mary F. Wack, *Lovesickness in the Middle Ages* (Philadelphia: University of Pennsylvania Press, 1990). On marriage, see Christopher Brooke, *The Medieval Idea of Marriage* (Oxford: Oxford University Press, 1989) and Philip Lyndon Reynolds, *Marriage in the Western Church: The Christianization of Marriage during the Patristic and Early Medieval Periods* (Leiden-New York-Cologne: E. J. Brill, 1994).

On prostitution, see Leah Lydia Otis, *Prostitution in Medieval Society* (Chicago: University of Chicago Press, 1985), and Jacques Rossiaud, *Medieval Prostitution* (Oxford: Basil Blackwell, 1988). Ruth Mazo Karras, *Common Women: Prostitution and Sexuality in Medieval England* (New York-Oxford: Oxford University Press, 1996).

On homosexuality, see John Boswell, *Christianity, Social Tolerance, and Homosexuality: Gay People in Western Europe from the Beginning of the Christian Era to the Fourteenth Century* (Chicago: University of Chicago Press, 1980).

TRANSPORTATION AND TECHNOLOGY

A. P. Newton, *Travel and Travellers of the Middle Ages* (New York: K. Paul, Trench, Trubner, 1930), is a good general introduction. More recent works are G. Hindley, *A History of Roads* (Secaucus, NJ: P. Davies, 1972), and Albert C. Leighton,

Transport and Communication in Early Medieval Europe A.D. *500–1100* (Newton Abbot: David & Charles, 1972).

There are a number of good general histories of technology, a subject long neglected but extremely important in early European history. Two particularly lively studies are Lynn White, Jr., *Medieval Technology and Social Change* (Oxford: Oxford University Press, 1962), and *Machina ex Deo* (Cambridge, MA: M.I.T. Press, 1969). White's scholarly essays are now collected: *Medieval Religion and Technology* (Berkeley and Los Angeles: University of California Press, 1978). Two recent studies also offer considerable information: Edward J. Kealey, *Harvesting the Air: Windmill Pioneers in Twelfth-Century England* (Berkeley and Los Angeles: University of California Press, 1987), and George Ovitt, Jr., *The Restoration of Perfection: Labor and Technology in Medieval Culture* (New Brunswick, NJ: Rutgers University Press, 1987).

MARITIME HISTORY

The best general account, with an excellent bibliography, is now that of Archibald R. Lewis and Timothy Runyon, *European Naval and Maritime History, 300–1500* (Bloomington: Indiana University Press, 1985). Several earlier works of Archibald R. Lewis remain indispensable: *Naval Power and Trade in the Mediterranean*, A.D. *500–1100* (Princeton, NJ: Princeton University Press, 1951), and *The Northern Seas*, A.D. *300–1100* (Princeton, NJ: Princeton University Press, 1958). There is a readable account in Vincent Cassidy, *The Sea Around Them* (Baton Rouge: Louisiana State University Press, 1968), and a good survey in Pierre Chaunu, *European Expansion in the Later Middle Ages* (New York: North Holland, 1978). See also G. J. Marcus, *The Conquest of the North Atlantic* (London: Boydell and Brewer, 1988).

Specialized studies are collected in Arne Bang-Andersen, Basil Greenhill and Egil Harald Grude, eds., *The North Sea: A Highway of Cultural Exchange, Character, History* (Oslo: Norwegian University Press, 1985), and John H. Pryor, *Geography, Technology and War* (Cambridge: Cambridge University Press, 1988).

On marine technology, see Richard W. Unger, *The Art of Medieval Technology: Images of Noah the Shipbuilder* (New Brunswick: Rutgers University Press, 1991), and on the economic role of the ship, Unger, *The Ship in the Medieval Economy 600–1600* (London-Montreal: Croom Helm-McGill-Queen's University Press, 1980).

The finest survey of the preparation for the Atlantic crossing, dealing with many other related topics as well, is Felipe Fernandez-Armesto, *Before Columbus* (Philadelphia: University of Pennsylvania Press, 1987), the best account of the events leading to Columbus's first voyage.

POLITICAL HISTORY: GENERAL

Medieval political units did not always coincide with modern political societies. For the general character of political life and thought in general, see H. Mitteis, *The State in the Middle Ages* (Amsterdam: North Holland Publishing Co., 1975);

Fredric L. Cheyette, ed., *Lordship and Community in Medieval Europe: Selected Readings* (reprint ed., Huntington, NY: Krieger, 1975); Ewart Lewis, *Medieval Political Ideas,* 2 vols. (New York: Knopf, 1954); and Beryl Smalley, ed., *Trends in Medieval Thought* (New York: Barnes & Noble, 1965); Brian Tierney, *The Crisis of Church and State 1050–1300* (1964; reprint ed. Toronto: University of Toronto Press, 1988).

For the early Middle Ages, see J. M. Wallace-Hadrill, *Early Germanic Kingship in England and on the Continent* (Oxford: Clarendon Press, 1971); P. H. Sawyer and I. N. Wood, eds., *Early Medieval Kingship* (Leeds: School of History, University of Leeds, 1977); Walter Ullmann, *The Carolingian Renaissance and the Idea of Kingship* (London: Methuen, 1969); and Robert Folz, *The Concept of Empire in Western Europe From the Fifth to the Fifteenth Century* (London: Edward Arnold, 1969).

Susan Reynolds, *Kingdoms and Communities in Western Europe, 900–1300* (Oxford: Clarendon Press, 1984) reassesses the experience of collective political participation and mentalities on all levels of medieval society.

For the later period, see Timothy Reuter, ed. and trans., *The Medieval Nobility: Selected Essays* (Amsterdam: North Holland Publishing Co., 1978); Ernst Kantorowicz, *The King's Two Bodies* (Princeton, NJ: Princeton University Press, 1957); See also Antonio Marongiu, *Medieval Parliaments: A Comparative Study* (London: Eyre & Spottiswoode, 1968); Gaines Post, *Studies in Medieval Legal Thought: Public Law and State, 1100–1322* (Princeton, NJ: Princeton University Press, 1964); Michael Wilks, *The Problem of Sovereignty in the Later Middle Ages* (Cambridge: Cambridge University Press, 1963). Antony Black, *Guilds and Civil Society* (Ithaca, NY: Cornell University Press, 1984), contrasts two different and powerful views of political systems.

See also the works cited in the Further Reading sections of Chapter 19, of this text, especially Guenée, *States and Rulers,* and Tierney, *Religion, Law, and Constitutional Thought, 1150–1650.* An extensive new survey is *The Cambridge History of Medieval Political Thought c. 3501–50,* ed. J. H. Burns (Cambridge: Cambridge University Press, 1988).

POLITICAL HISTORY: REGIONAL

The Balkans: John V. A. Fine, Jr., *The Early Medieval Balkans* (Ann Arbor: University of Michigan Press, 1983); Fine, *The Late Medieval Balkans* (Ann Arbor: University of Michigan Press, 1987).

Crusader States and the Mediterranean: See the bibliography in Jonathan Riley-Smith, *The Crusades: A Short History* (New Haven, CT: Yale University Press, 1987). For the Latin kingdom of Jerusalem, see Jean Richard, *The Latin Kingdom of Jerusalem,* 2 vols. (New York: North Holland, 1979). On the Islamic states, see Robert Irwin, *The Middle East in the Middle Ages: The Early Mamluk Sultanate, 1250–1382* (Carbondale, IL: Southern Illinois University Press, 1986), and for several key locations, Anthony T. Luttrell, ed., *Medieval Malta: Studies on Malta before the Knights* (London: The British School at Rome, 1975); Peter W. Edbury, *The Kingdom of Cyprus and the Crusades 1191–1374* (Cambridge-New York: Cambridge University Press, 1991); David Abulafia, *A Mediterranean Emporium* (Cambridge, New York: Cambridge University Press, 1994).

England: Standard and exhaustive, although out of date in some places, is Sir George Clark, ed., *The Oxford History of England,* vols. I–VI (Oxford: Oxford University Press, 1937–1962). The series edited by David C. Douglas, *English Historical Documents* (New York: Eyre & Spottiswoode, 1955—), complements the Oxford series with extensively annotated source materials in translation. Current work is listed in the Cambridge University Press series Bibliographical Handbooks. Especially useful are the volumes edited by Michael Altschul (1969), Bertie Wilkinson (1977), and DeLloyd J. Guth (1978). A standard work is Edgar B. Graves, *Bibliography of English History to 1485* (Oxford: Oxford University Press, 1975). The best short survey is C. Warren Hollister, *The Making of England 55* B.C. *to 1399* (Lexington-Toronto: D. C. Heath, 1992)

France: For all aspects of medieval France, see *Medieval France: An Encyclopedia,* ed. William W. Kibler and Grover A. Zinn (New York-London: Garland, 1995). There is no comprehensive history of medieval France in English. On specific periods, see Jean Dunbabin, *France in the Making, 843–1180* (Oxford-New York: Oxford University Press, 1985); Robert Fawtier, *The Capetian Kings of France* (New York: Barnes & Noble, 1962); Elizabeth H. Hallam, *Capetian France, 987–1328* (New York: Longman, 1980) and P. S. Lewis, *Later Medieval France: The Polity* (New York: St. Martin's Press, 1968). For the countryside, see Marc Bloch, *French Rural History* (Berkeley and Los Angeles: University of California Press, 1970).

Germany: For the early period, see now Timothy Reuter, *Germany in the Early Middle Ages c. 800–1056* (London-New York: Longman, 1991). Three volumes in a recent German series have now been translated into English. Together, they offer the most recent synthesis of medieval German History: Josef Fleckenstein, *Early Medieval Germany* (New York: North Holland, 1978); Horst Fuhrmann, *Germany in the High Middle Ages, c. 1050–1200* (Cambridge: Cambridge University Press, 1986); and Joachim Leuschner, *Germany in the Late Middle Ages* (New York: North Holland, 1980).

Essential for the period before the ninth century is Patrick J. Geary, *Before France and Germany: The Creation and Transformation of the Merovingian World* (New York: Oxford University Press, 1988). For the tenth and eleventh centuries, see Karl Leyser, *Rule and Conflict in an Early Medieval Society: Ottonian Saxony* (Bloomington: Indiana University Press, 1980), and Leyser, *Medieval Germany and Its Neighbours* (London: Hambledon, 1982). On the German ministerials, see Benjamin Arnold, *German Knighthood, 1050–1300* (Oxford: Clarendon Press, 1985). For the Hansa, see Philippe Dollinger, *The German Hansa* (London: Macmillan, 1970). The most recent study of the great opponent of Barbarossa is that of Karl Jordan, *Henry the Lion* (New York: Oxford University Press, 1986). In addition, on the later period, see F. R. H. Du Boulay, *Germany in the Later Middle Ages* (New York: St. Martin's Press, 1983), and two works edited by Gerald Strauss, *Manifestations of Discontent in Germany on the Eve of the Reformation* (Bloomington: Indiana University Press, 1971), and *Pre-Reformation Germany* (New York: Harper & Row, 1972).

Hungary: C. A. Macartney, *Hungary: A Short History* (Oxford: Oxford University Press, 1962), and Ervin Pamlenyi, ed., *A History of Hungary* (London: Collet's, 1975). Specialized studies offer much more recent scholarship: Erik Fugedi, *Kings, Bishops, Nobles and Burghers in Medieval Hungary*, ed. J. M. Bak (London: Variorium, 1986), and Erik Fugedi, *Castle and Society in Medieval Hungary (1000–1437)* (Budapest: Akadémiai Kiadó, 1986).

Ireland: In general, see R. F. Foster, ed., *The Oxford History of Ireland* (Oxford-New York: Oxford University Press, 1989); Michael J. O'Kelly, *Early Ireland: An Introduction to Irish Prehistory* (Cambridge: Cambridge University Press, 1988); Kathleen Hughes, *The Church in Early Irish Society* (Ithaca, NY: Cornell University Press, 1968); Donncha O'Corrain, *Ireland Before the Vikings* (Dublin: Gill and Macmillan, 1972); Francis John Byrne, *Irish Kings and High-Kings* (London: Batsford, 1973); Art Cosgrove, ed., *A New History of Ireland*, Vol. 2, *Medieval Ireland, 1169–1534* (Oxford: Clarendon Press, 1987; 2nd ed. 1993); a volume in the ongoing series edited by T. W. Moody, F. X. Martin, and F. J. Byrne, *A New History of Ireland* (Oxford and New York: Oxford University Press, 1976—). See also James Lydon, *Ireland in the Later Middle Ages* (Dublin: Gill and Macmillan, 1973); and J. F. Lydon, *The Lordship of Ireland in the Middle Ages* (Dublin: University Press of Ireland, 1972).

Italy: J. K. Hyde, *Society and Politics in Medieval Italy, 1000–1300* (New York: St. Martin's Press, 1969); Gino Luzzato, *An Economic History of Italy* (New York: Barnes & Noble, 1961); Daniel Waley, *The Italian City-Republics* (New York: McGraw-Hill, 1969); John Larner, *Italy in the Age of Dante and Petrarch, 1216–1380* (New York: Longman, 1980); Chris John Wickham, *Early Medieval Italy* (Totowa, NJ: Barnes & Noble, 1982); Marvin Becker, *Medieval Italy* (Bloomington: Indiana University Press, 1980).

Poland and Slavic Europe: A. P. Vlasto, *The Entry of the Slavs into Christendom* (Cambridge: Cambridge University Press, 1970); Geoffrey Barraclough, ed., *Eastern and Western Europe in the Middle Ages* (New York: Harcourt Brace Jovanovich, 1970). For Poland, see Alexander Gieysztor and others, eds., *History of Poland*, 2nd ed. (Warsaw: Polish Scientific Publishers, 1979); Tadeusz Manteuffel, *The Formation of the Polish State: The Period of Ducal Rule, 963–1194* (Detroit: Wayne

State University Press, 1982). For the later period, see Paul W. Knoll, *The Rise of the Polish Monarchy: Piast Poland in East Central Europe, 1320–1370* (Chicago: University of Chicago Press, 1972); Richard C. Hoffmann, *Land, Liberties, and Lordship in a Late Medieval Countryside* (Philadelphia: University of Pennsylvania Press, 1990), and Piotr Gorecki, *Economy, Society, and Lordship in Medieval Poland, 1100–1250* (New York: Holmes and Meier, 1992).

Scandinavia: *Medieval Scandinavia: An Encyclopedia,* Philip Pulsianio and Kirsten Wolf, et al., eds. (New York-London: Garland, 1994); Birgit and Peter Sawyer, *Medieval Scandinavia: From Conversion to Reformation, circa 800–1500* (Minneapolis-London: University of Minnesota Press, 1993); David M. Wilson, *The Northern World: The History and Heritage of Northern Europe,* A.D. *400–1100* (New York: Harry N. Abrams, Inc., 1980); P. H. Sawyer, *Kings and Vikings: Scandinavia and Europe* A.D. *700–1100* (London: Methuen, 1982). There is little recent literature on individual Scandinavian states. See Palle Lauring, *A History of the Kingdom of Denmark,* 4th ed., (Copenhagen: Host, 1973). An important source is available in Peter Fisher, trans., *Saxo Grammaticus. The History of the Danes* (Totowa, NJ: Rowman and Littlefield, 1979).

Other important studies include Jesse L. Byock, *Medieval Iceland: Society, Sagas, and Power* (Berkeley and Los Angeles: University of California Press, 1988); Ruth Mazo Karras, *Slavery and Society in Medieval Scandinavia* (New Haven, CT: Yale University Press, 1988); William Ian Miller, *Blooktaking and Peacemaking: Feud, Law, and Society in Saga Iceland* (Chicago-London: University of Chicago Press, 1990); Kirsten Hastrup, *Culture and History in Medieval Iceland* (Oxford: Clarendon Press, 1985).

Scotland: William C. Dickinson, *Scotland From the Earliest Times to 1603,* 3rd ed., rev. and ed. by A. A. Duncan (New York: Oxford University Press, 1977). On rule, see Marjorie O. Anderson, *Kings and Kingship in Early Scotland* (Edinburgh and London: Scottish Academic Press, 1980); G. W. S. Barrow, *Kingship and Unity: Scotland, 1000–1306* (London: Edward Arnold, 1981). On society, see K. J. Stringer, ed., *Essays on the Nobility of Medieval Scotland* (Edinburgh: John Donald, 1985). On one example of Scotland in the world, see Alan MacQuarrie, *Scotland and the Crusades, 1095–1560* (Edinburgh: John Donald, 1985).

Sicily and South Italy: Barbara Kreutz, *Before the Normans: Southern Italy in the Ninth and Tenth Centuries* (Philadelphia: University of Pennsylvania Press, 1991); Donald Matthew, *The Norman Kingdom of Sicily* (Cambridge-New York: Cambridge University Press, 1992) Good readable histories are those of John J. Norwich, *The Normans in the South* and *The Kingdom in the Sun* (London: Longman, 1968, 1970). Steven Runciman, *The Sicilian Vespers* (Cambridge: Cambridge University Press, 1958), addresses the late thirteenth century. For the period of Frederick II, see Ernst Kantorowicz, *Frederick II* (New York: Ungar, 1957).

Spain: See J. Vicens Vives, *Approaches to the History of Spain* (Berkeley and Los Angeles: University of California Press, 1970); J. F. O'Callaghan, *A History of Medieval Spain* (Ithaca, NY: Cornell University Press, 1975); Bernard Reilly, *The Medieval Spains* (Cambridge-New York: Cambridge University Press, 1993); D. W. Lomax, *The Reconquest of Spain* (New York: Longman, 1978); Bernard F. Reilly, *The Contest of Christian and Muslim Spain, 1031–1157* (Cambridge, MA-Oxford: Blackwell, 1992); J. N. Hillgarth, *The Spanish Kingdoms, 1250–1516,* Vol I, *The Precarious Balance, 1250–1410,* and Vol. II, *The Castilian Hegemony, 1410–1516* (New York: Oxford University Press, 1976, 1978) J. R. L. Highfield, *Spain in the Fifteenth Century* (New York: Harper & Row, 1972); Thomas F. Glick, *Islamic and Christian Spain in the Early Middle Ages* (Princeton, NJ: Princeton University Press, 1978); A. Chejne, *Muslim Spain* (Minneapolis: University of Minnesota Press, 1974); L. P. Harvey, *Islamic Spain 1250 to 1500* (Chicago-London: University of Chicago Press, 1990), and R. I. Burns, *The Crusader Kingdom of Valencia,* 2 vols. (Cambridge, MA: Harvard University Press, 1967).

Specialized studies mark much of the best work on medieval Spain. For the early period, see Roger Collins, *Early Medieval Spain: Unity in Diversity, 400–1000* (New York: St. Martin's Press, 1983). On the twelfth century, see R. A. Fletcher, *Saint James's Catapult* (Oxford: Clarendon, 1984). On one important aspect of the Conquest, see the work of R. I. Burns, S. J., *Muslims, Christians, and Jews in the Crusader Kingdom of Valencia: Societies in Symbiosis* (Cambridge, MA: Harvard University Press, 1984). James William Brodman, *Ransoming Captives in Crusader Spain* (Philadelphia: University of Pennsylvania Press, 1986) is an excellent study of a complex topic. For later medieval Spain there is an extensive bibliography in Edward Peters, *Inquisition* (New York: Free Press, 1988), pp. 320–325. See also Peter Linehan, *Spain, 1157–1300* (Cambridge, MA-Oxford: Blackwell, 1990).

On Aragon and Catalonia, see Thomas N. Bisson, *The Medieval Crown of Aragon: A Short History* (New York: Oxford University Press, 1987), and Archibald R. Lewis, *The Development of Southern French and Catalan Society, 718–1050* (Austin: University of Texas Press, 1965).

Switzerland: See E. Bonjour, H. S. Offler, and G. R. Potter, *A Short History of Switzerland* (Oxford: Clarendon Press, 1952); and Thomas A. Brady, Jr., *Turning Swiss: Cities and Empire, 1450–1550* (Cambridge: Cambridge University Press, 1985).

Wales: See Wendy Davies, *Wales in the Early Middle Ages* (Leicester: Leicester University Press, 1982), David Walker, *Medieval Wales* (Cambridge: Cambridge University Press, 1990), and R. R. Davies, *Conquest, Coexistence, and Change: Wales, 1063–1415* (Oxford: Clarendon Press, 1987).

JEWS IN LATE ANTIQUITY AND MEDIEVAL EUROPE

The great study of the Jews in the Roman world is that of Emil Schurer, *The History of the Jewish People in the Age of Jesus Christ*, 3 vols. (rev. ed. Edinburgh: T. and T. Clark, 1973–1987). The new edition, edited by Geza Vermes and others, is not yet complete. Several studies of rabbinic Judaism that are stimulating and learned are by Jacob Neusner, *Early Rabbinic Judaism* (Leiden: Brill, 1975), a volume in the important series Studies in Judaism in Late Antiquity.

See also Alan F. Segal, *Rebecca's Children: Judaism and Christianity in the Roman World* (Cambridge, MA: Harvard University Press, 1986). A classic work on Judaism and Hellenism is that of Martin Hengel, *Judaism and Hellenism* (Philadelphia: Fortress Press, 1981).

Other important works by Neusner include: *Judaism and Christianity in the Age of Constantine the Great* (Chicago: University of Chicago Press, 1987); *From Politics to Piety: The Emergence of Pharisaic Judaism* (Englewood Cliffs, NJ: Prentice-Hall, 1973), and *Judaism in the Beginning of Christianity* (Philadelphia: Fortress Press, 1984).

The place of Jews in Roman imperial law is illuminated in Amnon Linder, *The Jews in Roman Imperial Legislation* (Detroit: Wayne State University Press, 1988).

Volumes III–VIII of Salo W. Baron's *A Social and Religious History of the Jews*, 2nd ed. (New York: Columbia University Press, 1957), deal with most of the Middle Ages and represent the work of one of the greatest modern historians. The range of Baron's concerns is also reflected in his collected essays, *Ancient and Medieval Jewish History* (New Brunswick, NJ: Rutgers University Press, 1972).

The most exhaustive work on the early period is Cecil Roth and I. H. Levine, eds., *The Dark Age: Jews in Christian Europe 711–1096*, Vol. II of Cecil Roth, gen. ed., *The World History of the Jewish People, Second Series: The Medieval Period* (New Brunswick, NJ: Rutgers University Press, 1966). Among particularly useful detailed studies are Joshua Starr, *The Jews in the Byzantine Empire, 641–1204* (reprint ed., New York: Burt Franklin, 1970), and Bernard S. Bachrach, *Early Medieval Jewish Policy in Western Europe* (Minneapolis: University of Minnesota Press, 1977).

A new general history is Mark R. Cohen, *Under Crescent and Cross: The Jews in the Middle Ages* (Princeton: Princeton University Press, 1994). A good collection of documentary evidence is assembled and expertly commented on in Jacob Marcus, *The Jew in the Medieval World* (reprint ed., New York: Harper & Row, 1965). Another collection of documents in translation excellently illuminates the social, political, and legal status of Jews in medieval Europe: Robert Chazan, *Church, State, and Jew in the Middle Ages* (New York: Behrman House, 1980). Chazan has also considered the important outbreak of anti-Judaic violence in connection with the First Crusade: Robert Chazan, *European Jewry and the First Crusade* (Berkeley and Los Angeles: University of California Press, 1987). A fine study of the roots of anti-Semitism is Joshua Trachtenberg, *The Devil and the Jews: The Medieval Conception of the Jew and Its Relation to Modern Antisemitism* (New Haven, CT: Yale University Press, 1943).

Two works by Gavin Langmuir are very important. *History, Religion, and Antisemitism,* and *Toward a Definition of Antisemitism* (Berkeley, Low Angeles: University of California Press, both 1990). Most of the works cited above, and particularly that of Langmuir, contain useful bibliographies. An extensive bibliography of recent studies on the changing Christian perceptions of Jews and Judaism, and on the role of Jews and *conversos* in the early years of the Spanish Inquisition, is found in Edward Peters, *Inquisition* (New York: Free Press, 1988). Particularly important are the studies of David Berger, *The Christian-Jewish Debate in the High Middle Ages* (Philadelphia: Jewish Publication Society, 1979); Jeremy Cohen, *The Friars and the Jews* (Ithaca: Cornell University Press, 1982); Robert Chazan, *Daggers of Faith: Thirteenth-Century Christian Missionizing and Jewish Response* (Berkeley-Los Angeles: University of California Press, 1988).

The most thorough study of a single Jewish community in the Middle ages is S. D. Goitein, *A Mediterranean Society: The Jewish Communities of the World as Portrayed in the Documents of the Cairo Geniza,* Vol. I, *Economic Foundations;* Vol. II, *The Community* (Berkeley and Los Angeles: University of California Press, 1968, 1971). Equally important in studying the impact of Judaism on a very different kind of society is D. M. Dunlop, *History of the Jewish Khazars* (Princeton, NJ: Princeton University Press, 1954). On one powerful force within the Jewish community, see Ivan Marcus, *Piety and Society: The Jewish Pietists of Medieval Germany* (Leiden: Brill, 1981).

THE LATIN CHURCH

The best general history is that edited by Hubert Jedin and John Dolan, *Handbook of Church History,* Vols. I–IV (Freiburg-London-New York: Herder; Burns & Oates; Seabury, 1965–1980). Vol. I is Karl Baus, *From the Apostolic Community to Constantine* (1965); Vol. II is Karl Baus, Hans-Georg Beck, Eugen Ewig, and Hermann Vogt, eds., *The Imperial Church from Constantine to the Early Middle Ages* (1980); Vol. III is Friedrich Kempf, Hans-Georg Beck, Eugen Ewig, and J. A. Jungmann, eds., *The Church in the Age of Feudalism* (1969); Vol. IV is Hans-George Beck, Karl A. Fink, Josef Glazik, Erwin Iserloh, and Hans Wolter, eds., *From the High Middle Ages to the Eve of the Reformation* (1980). The translator is Anselm Biggs. The most recent short account is Joseph H. Lynch, *The Medieval Church: A Brief History* (London-New York: Longman, 1992).

On doctrine, see the vast work of Jaroslav Pelikan, *The Christian Tradition: A History of the Development of Doctrine,* Vols. I–IV (Chicago: University of Chicago Press, 1971–1986: Vol. I, *The Emergence of the Catholic Tradition* (1971); Vol. II, *The Spirit of Eastern Christendom* (1974); Vol. III, *The Growth of Medieval Theology* (1978); Vol. IV, *Reformation of Church and Dogma* (1984).

On liturgy, see Theodor Klauser, *A Short History of the Western Liturgy* (New York: Oxford University Press, 1969), and Cyrille Vogel, *Medieval Liturgy: An Introduction to the Sources* (Washington, DC: The Pastoral Press, 1986).

Among shorter studies of particular periods are, Henry Chadwick, *The Early Church* (Baltimore: Penguin, 1967); R. W. Southern, *Western Society and the Church in the Middle Ages* (Baltimore: Penguin, 1970). Both are superbly readable and reliable, although selective in their approach. See also J. M. Wallace-Hadrill, *The Frankish Church* (Oxford: Clarendon, 1983); Gerd Tellenbach, *The Church in Western Europe from the Tenth to the Early Twelfth Century*, trans. Timothy Reuter (Cambridge: Cambridge University Press, 1993); Colin Morris, *The Papal Monarchy: The Western Church from 1050 to 1250* (Oxford: Clarendon, 1989).

A handy reference is F. L. Cross, ed., *The Oxford Dictionary of the Christian Church*, 2nd ed. (London: Oxford University Press, 1972). A comprehensive bibliography is Henry Chadwick, *The History of the Church: A Select Bibliography*, 3rd ed. (London: The Historical Association, 1973). The best atlases are F. Van Der Meer and Christine Mohrmann, eds., *An Atlas of the Early Christian World* (London: Nelson, 1958), and H. Jedin, K. S. Latourette, and J. Marten, eds., *Atlas zur Kirchengeschichte* (Freiburg: Herder and Herder, 1970).

See also Dom Jean Leclercq, Dom Francois Vandenbroucke, and Louis Bouyer, *The Spirituality of the Middle Ages* (London: Burns & Oates, 1968), Vol. 2 of *A History of Christian Spirituality*. For the later Middle Ages, see the excellent studies by Steven Ozment, *The Age of Reform, 1250–1550* (New Haven, CT: Yale University Press, 1980), and Francis Oakley, *The Western Church in the Later Middle Ages* (Ithaca, NY: Cornell University Press, 1979).

BYZANTIUM AND GREEK CHRISTIANITY

The best introductions are those of Alexander Kazhdan and Giles Constable, *People and Power in Byzantium: An Introduction to Modern Byzantine Studies* (Washington, DC: Dumbarton Oaks, 1982), and Alexander P. Kazhdan, ed., *The Oxford Dictionary of Byzantium*, 3 vols. (Oxford: Clarendon, 1991). In general, see the listings for Further Reading at the end of Chapters 3, 4, and 20 in this text.

There are excellent studies of the governing groups of the East Roman Empire by Michael Angold, *The Byzantine Empire, 1025–1204* (New York: Longman, 1984), and Michael Angold, ed., *The Byzantine Aristocray, IX–XIII Centuries* (Oxford: British Archeological Reports, 1984). On the end of the Empire, see Donald Nicol, *The Immortal Emperor: The Life and Legend of Constantine Palaiologos, Last Emperor of the Romans* (Cambridge: Cambridge University Press, 1994).

Norman Baynes and H. St. L. B. Moss, eds., *Byzantium: An Introduction to East Roman Civilization* (reprint ed., Oxford: Oxford University Press, 1961), consists of essays by experts on various aspects of Byzantine civilization. An excellent survey of Byzantine civilization is H. W. Haussig, *A History of Byzantine Civilization* (New York: Praeger, 1971). Joan M. Hussey, *The Byzantine World* (New York: Harper

& Row, 1961), is a fine brief introduction, as is Robert Browning, *The Byzantine Empire* (Washington, DC: Catholic University of America Press, 1992).

On Constantinople, see David Talbot Rice, *Constantinople: From Byzantium to Istanbul* (New York: Stein & Day, 1965). On Byzantine art, see David Talbot Rice, *Byzantine Art* (Harmondsworth: Penguin, 1968). On religion, see the chapters by Hans-Georg Beck in Friedrich Kempf et al., eds., *The Church in the Age of Feudalism* (New York: Herder & Herder, 1969), and George Every, *The Byzantine Patriarchate, 451–1204* (London: Society for the Promotion of Christian Knowledge, 1947).

Byzantium's impact on neighboring societies is outlined in the important study by Dimitri Obolensky, *The Byzantine Commonwealth* (New York: Weidenfeld and Nicolson, 1971).

Various important elements of Byzantine civilization are explored in Steven Runciman, *The Byzantine Theocracy* (Cambridge: Cambridge University Press, 1977); D. J. Geanakoplos, *Interaction of the Sibling Byzantine and Western Cultures in the Middle Ages and Italian Renaissance (300–1600)* (New Haven, CT: Yale University Press, 1976); and Louis Brehier, *The Life and Death of Byzantium* (Amsterdam: North Holland Publishing Co., 1977).

On culture and ideas, see Alexander Kazhdan and Ann Wharton Epstein, *Change in Byzantine Culture in the Eleventh and Twelfth Centuries* (Berkeley and Los Angeles: University of California Press, 1985).

ISLAMIC HISTORY

See the suggested readings for Chapter 5. A good brief introduction to Muhammad and the rise of Islam is the work of Francesco Gabrieli, *Muhammad and the Conquests of Islam* (New York: McGraw-Hill, 1968). Good biographies of the Prophet are Tor Andrae, *Mohammed: The Man and His Faith* (reprint ed., New York: Harper & Row, 1960), and W. Montgomery Watt, *Muhammad: Prophet and Statesman* (Oxford: Oxford University Press, 1961). Two excellent short introductions are Bernard Lewis, *The Arabs in History* (reprint ed., New York: Harper & Row, 1960), and G. E. von Grunebaum, *Medieval Islam* (reprint ed., Chicago: University of Chicago Press, 1961).

For the *Qur'an*, see R. Bell, *Introduction to the Qur'an* (Edinburgh: Edinburgh University Press, 1970). For general information on Islam, see *Encyclopedia of Islam*, latest ed. (Leiden: Brill, 1960—).

Two distinctive and very different approaches to various aspects of Islamic thought are F. I. J. Rosenthal, *Political Thought in Medieval Islam* (Cambridge: Cambridge University Press, 1962), and E. W. Lane, *Arabian Society in the Middle Ages* (reprint ed., New York: Barnes & Noble, 1971). A. H. Hourani and S. M. Stern, eds., *The Islamic City* (Philadelphia: University of Pennsylvania Press, 1970), collects much important recent scholarship, as does D. S. Richards, ed., *Islam and the Trade of Asia* (Philadelphia: University of Pennsylvania Press, 1971).

A good recent study of Islamic culture is D. M. Dunlop, *Arab Civilization to 1500* (London: Longman, 1971), as is Majid al-Fakhry, *A History of Islamic Philosophy* (New York: Columbia University Press, 1983). There is much related material in several essays included in K. M. Setton, gen. ed., *A History of the Crusades*, Vols. I and II, 2nd ed. (Madison: University of Wisconsin Press, 1969). On the Muslim perspective, see Amin Maalouf, *The Crusades Through Arab Eyes* (New York: Schocken, 1985). Norman Daniel, *The Arabs and Medieval Europe* (London: Longman, 1974), is a good introduction to Islamic-Christian relations. See also Maurice Lombard, *The Golden Age of Islam* (Amsterdam: North Holland Publishing Co., 1975).

LANGUAGE AND LITERACY

See W. B. Lockwood, *A Panorama of Indo-European Languages* (London: Hutchinson, 1972), and Philippe Wolff, *Western Languages A.D. 100–1500* (New York: McGraw-Hill, 1971).

On various periods, see Rosamond McKitterick, *The Uses of Literacy in Early Medieval Europe* (Cambridge-New York: Cambridge University Press, 1990), and Rosamond McKitterick, *The Carolingians and the Written Word* (Cambridge-New York: Cambridge University Press, 1989). On literacy and its problems, see the brilliant work of Brian Stock, *The Implications of Literacy* (Princeton, NJ: Princeton University Press, 1983), and, for literacy and law, Michael Clanchy, *From Memory to Written Record: England, 1066–1307* (Cambridge, MA: Harvard University Press, 1979, 2nd ed. 1993). See also Walter J. Ong, *Orality and Literacy: The Technologizing of the World* (New York: Methuen, 1982).

THOUGHT AND LEARNING

Good general introductions to the early period is M. L. W. Laistner, *Thought and Letters in Western Europe, A.D. 500–900,* 2nd ed. (Ithaca, NY: Cornell University Press, 1957), and Pierre Riché, *Education and Culture in the Barbarian West,* trans. John Contreni (Columbia, SC: University of South Carolina Press, 1976); Philippe Wolff, *The Awakening of Europe* (Baltimore: Penguin, 1968), deals well with the period 800–1142. David Knowles, *The Evolution of Medieval Thought* (New York: Random House, Vintage Books, 1962), is an extensive history of philosophy. M.-D. Chenu, *Nature, Man and Society in the Twelfth Century* (Chicago: University of Chicago Press, 1968), is a classic collection of studies revealing thought in action, as is, in a different way, Alexander Murray, *Reason and Society in the Middle Ages* (Oxford: Clarendon Press, 1978).

On the universities, see the classic work by Hastings Rashdall, *The Universities of Europe in the Middle Ages,* 3 vols., eds., R. M. Powicke and A. B. Emden (Oxford: Oxford University Press, 1936); Anders Piltz, *The World of Medieval Learning* (Totowa, NJ: Barnes & Noble, 1981); Lynn Thorndike, *University Records and Life in the Middle Ages* (reprint ed., New York: Norton, 1975); Gordon Leff, *Paris and Oxford Universities in the Thirteenth and Fourteenth Centuries* (New York: John Wiley, 1968), and most recently, *A History of the University in Europe*, Vol. I, *Universities in the Middle Ages*, Hilde DeRidder-Symoens, ed. (Cambridge: Cambridge University Press. 1989).

MATHEMATICS, SCIENCE, AND MEDICINE

Loren C. MacKinney, *Early Medieval Medicine with Special ·Reference to France and Chartres* (Baltimore: Johns Hopkins, 1937), and *Medical Illustrations in Medieval Manuscripts* (Berkeley and Los Angeles: University of California Press, 1965) constitute a good introduction to the history of medieval medicine; each includes bibliographic guides. B. Lawn, *The Salernitan Questions* (Oxford: Oxford University Press, 1963), is a good introduction to the conceptualization of medical and scientific problems in the Middle Ages. C. H. Talbot, *Medicine in Medieval England* (London: Oldbourne, 1967), is extremely wide-ranging and informative. The work of Nancy Siraisi is essential: *Medieval and Early Renaissance Medicine: An Introduction to Knowledge and Practice* (Chicago-London: University of Chicago Press, 1990), and for a particular place, Michael McVaugh, *Medicine Before the Plague* (Cambridge: Cambridge University Press, 1995).

An extensive bibliography may be found in Edward Grant, *A Sourcebook in Medieval Science* (Cambridge, MA: Harvard University Press, 1974).

Standard histories of medieval science are A. C. Crombie, *Medieval and Early Modern Science*, 2 vols., rev. ed., (New York: Doubleday, 1959), and George Sarton, *Introduction to the History of Science,* 3 vols. (Baltimore: Johns Hopkins, 1947–1958). Edward Grant, *Physical Science in the Middle Ages* (New York: John Wiley, 1971), contains an excellent bibliography. Richard Dales, *The Scientific Achievement of the Middle Ages* (Philadelphia: University of Pennsylvania Press, 1973), offers a fine selection of documents in translation and includes an introduction and bibliography. For all of these fields, see David Lindberg, ed., *Science in the Middle Ages* (Chicago: University of Chicago Press, 1978), and Lindberg, *The Beginnings of Western Science* (Chicago-London: The University of Chicago Press, 1992).

Some of the important work of Anneliese Maier is now available in English in Steven Sargent, ed. and trans., *On the Threshold of Exact Science* (Philadelphia: University of Pennsylvania Press, 1982).

There is a fine introduction to mathematical theory and practice generally in Michael S. Mahoney's essay "Mathematics," in *Science in the Middle Ages,* ed. David C. Lindberg (Chicago: University of Chicago Press, 1980). For a good recent survey of the Muslim contribution, see Ali Abdullah Al-Daffa', *The Muslim Contribution to Mathematics* (London: Kazi Publications, 1977). The relation of mathematics to other sciences is considered in Edward Grant and John E. Murdoch, eds., *Mathematics and Its Applications to Science and Natural Philosophy in the Middle Ages* (Cambridge: Cambridge University Press, 1988).

POPULAR CULTURE

Two recent studies have begun to lay out the dimensions of popular culture in medieval Europe; both are by the Russian historian Aron Gurevich: *Categories of Medieval Culture* (Boston: Routledge & Kegan Paul, 1985), and *Problems of Medieval Popular Culture* (Cambridge: Cambridge University Press, 1988). From the perspective of religion, see Rosalind and Christopher Brooke, *Popular Religion in the Middle Ages: Western Europe, 1000–1300* (London: Thames and Hudson, 1984). For an instance of popular beliefs in action, see Jacques Le Goff, *The Birth of Purgatory* (Chicago: University of Chicago Press, 1981), and Miri Rubin, *Corpus Christi* (Cambridge: Cambridge University Press, 1991).

ON THE MARGINS OF SOCIETY

Marginality is a concept that fascinates historians, particularly when they wish to examine either the image or the reality of established, structured societies. The study of the people excluded not only reveals something hitherto unknown about a society but also serves as a test of the solidarity and coherence of society. Marginality may be investigated in many areas; one of the best introductions to the subject is the work of the Polish historian Bronislaw Geremek, *The Margins of Society in Late Medieval Paris* (Cambridge: Cambridge University Press, 1987), which discusses social perceptions of criminality, prostitution, actors, and beggars. In some respects, the history of women may also be considered in terms of marginality, and not always in the case of begging or prostitution alone. See Leah Lydia Otis, *Prostitution in Medieval Society* (Chicago: University of Chicago Press, 1985), and Anne Barstow, *Married Priests and the Reforming Papacy* (Lewiston, ME: Edwin Mellen Press, 1982). Marginality may include those separated from society by disease, as in the case of leprosy; see Saul N. Brody, *Disease of the Soul: Leprosy in Medieval Literature* (Ithaca, NY: Cornell University Press, 1974); or in the case of homosexuality, for which see John Boswell, *Christianity, Social Tolerance, and Homosexuality: Gay People in Western Europe from the Beginning of the Christian Era to the Fourteenth Century* (Chicago: University of Chicago Press, 1980). From the perspective of society, the definition of marginalization is one element in R. I. Moore, *The Formation of a Persecuting Society: Power and Deviance in Western Europe, 950–1250* (Oxford: Basil Blackwell, 1987), and, as Moore observes, may be equally well traced in the history of religious dissent, anti-Judaism, and other phenomena defined as marginal by social and political action, ranging from popular beliefs and culture to insanity and criminality. For a broad panorama, see the studies of Jacques Le Goff, *Time, Work, and Culture in the Middle Ages* (Chicago: University of Chicago Press, 1980), and for a particularly well-dissected case, Jean-Claude Schmitt, *The Holy Greyhound* (Cambridge: Cambridge University Press, 1983). Marginality might sometimes, but not always, include poverty; see Michel Mollat, *The Poor in the Middle Ages* (Chicago: University of Chicago Press, 1986).

There is a large literature on popular resentment and uprisings during the later Middle Ages, much of it focusing on the English uprising of 1381. Two studies offer general typologies: Michel Mollat and Philippe Wolff, *The Popular Revolutions of the Late Middle Ages* (reprint ed., Winchester, MA: Allen & Unwin, 1973), and Guy Fourquin, *The Anatomy of Popular Rebellion in the Middle Ages* (New York: North Holland, 1978). A number of different disciplines are represented in the collection edited by Francis X. Newman, *Social Unrest in the Late Middle Ages* (Binghamton, NY: Medieval & Renaissance Texts and Studies, 1986). Two able detailed studies and texts are R. B. Dobson, *The Peasants' Revolt of 1381* (New York: St. Martin's Press, 1970; reprint ed. London: Macmillan, 1983), and R. H. Hilton and T. H. Aston, *The English Rising of 1381* (Cambridge: Cambridge University Press, 1984). On the link between popular culture and social protest, see Michael Mullett, *Popular Culture and Popular Protest in Late Medieval and Early Modern Europe* (London: Croom Helm, 1987).

INDEX

This Index is keyed to the main entries in the *Dictionary of the Middle Ages,* ed., Joseph R. Strayer, 12 vols. (New York: Charles Scribner's Sons, 1982–1989).

Numbers in parentheses following main entry indicate volume and page numbers of the corresponding entry in the *Dictionary of the Middle Ages.*

Capitalized entries indicate major articles in the *Dictionary of the Middle Ages,* treating subjects not covered in this book. They indicate a supplement of important topics not treated in any detail, but important for further inquiry.

The particulars of alphabetization in the Index are usually accommodated to the system of the *Dictionary of the Middle Ages.* Cross–references have been made where essential.

Aachen, (1:1) 147, 155
Abbaald Caliphate, (1:6) 97, 101–2, 175–77, 226
Abbo of Fleury, (1:12) 196
Abbet (*see* Monasticism)
Abd-al Rahman I, 101
Abd-al-Rahman II, 200–207
Abelard, Peter, (1:16) 236–39, 229, 243, 244, 245, 247, 248, 256–57, 317
Abu Bakr, (1:24) 97, 98, 99
Abu 'l-Abbas, 97, 101
Acts of the Apostles, 35
ADELARD OF BATH (1:53)
Adhemar of Le Puy, 226
ADOPTIONISM (1:57)
AELFRICH (1:61)
Aethelwold, 166
Afonso Henriques, 210

Africans, 396–97, 398
Ailred of Riveaulz, 317
Ain Jalut, 347
Aistulf, 152
Al-Andalus, 207, 208, 210
Albertus Magnus, (1:126) 306–7, 324, 349
Albigensians / Albigensian Crusade, (1:130) 262
ALCHEMY (1:134)
Alcuin, (1:142) 150, 155
Aldhelm, (1:144) 137
Alexander III, Pope, (1:146) 251, 297
Alexius I Comnenos, (1:157) 225, 226, 228
Alfonso I of Aragon-Navarre, (1:160) 288
Alfonso II of Asturias, 151
Alfonso VI of Leon-Castile, 209, 210, 215, 264
Alfonso X of Castile, (1:161) 289

Alfred the Great, (1:165) 166
Algebra (*see also* Mathematics) (1:167)
Alhazen, 302
Ali, 97, 99
Al-Kwarizmi, 302
Al-Mamun, (8:29) 101, 102
Al-Mansur, (8:89) 207
Almoravides, (1:198) 210
Al-Mustasim, (8:651) 102
Alp Arlsan, (1:203) 226
ALPHABETIZATION (1:204)
ALTAR (1:221)
Ambrose of Milan, (1:230) 43, 46–47, 49, 50,
    108, 265
ANATOLIA (1:239)
ANCHORITES (1:242)
ANDALUSIA (1:243) (*see also al-Andalus*)
ANGEL (1:247)
Anglo-Saxon Chronicle, 131
ANIMALS, DRAFT (1:293)
ANNA COMNENA (1:303)
ANOINTING (1:308)
Anselm of Canterbury, (1:311) 236, 243,
    256, 283
Anselm of Laon, (1:315) 237
Anthony of Egypt, 43–45
ANTICHRIST (1:321)
ANTIFEMINISM (1:322)
ANTISEMITISM (1:338)
Appanage, (1:351) 373
Aquinas, Thomas, (1:353) 67, 307–8, 350–51
AQUITAINE (1:366)
Arabia, (1:369) 93
Arabic, 96, 102, 103, 176–77, 348–49
Arabs, 93–104
Aragon, (1:403)
ARCHAEOLOGY (1:425) 12–14
ARCHITECT (1:440)
Aristotle, (1:456), 67, 102, 103, 177, 238, 303–8,
    324, 349, 351
ARMENIA (1:470)
ARMS / ARMOR (1:521)
Arnald of Villanova, (1:537) 348–49
ARNOLD OF BRESCIA (1:539)
Arthur, (1:564) 318
ARTIST (1:578)
Assisi, Francis of, (1:593) 260–61, 319, 348, 356
Assize of Clarendon (*see* Clarendon)
ASTROLABE (1:602)
ASTRONOMY (1:610)
Athanasius of Alexandria, (1:633) 44–45
Atlantic Ocean, 4, 97–98, 313, 315, 316–18
Attila, 61, 319
ASYLUM (SANCTUARY) (1:631)
Augustine of Canterbury, (1:644) 115, 116, 117
Augustine of Hippo, (1:646) 40, 47–49, 218,
    225, 308, 351, 385–86
Augustus Caesar, 4, 14, 108
Ausculta fili, (2:3) 299
Austria, (2:4) 363

Authenticum Habita, 363
Avars, (2:12) 88, 147
Averroes, (10:571) 103, 208, 302
Avicenna, (11:302) 103, 302
Avignon, (2:15) 349, 352, 385–86

BABENBERG DYNASTY (2:33)
Bacon, Roger, (2:35) 349
Baghdad, (2:44) 97, 101, 103
BAILIFF (2:51)
Baldwin I of Jerusalem, (2:58) 227
BALTIC SEA (2:61)
BARI (2:108)
BARON (2:111)
Bartolus, (2:114) 192
Basil I, Emperor, (2:117) 172
Basil II, Emperor, (2:118) 173
Basil of Caesarea, (2:119) 45, 48
BASILICA (2:123)
BASQUES (2:125)
BAY (2:139)
BEAUTY (2:45)
Becket, Thomas, (2:151) 247, 248, 286, 319
Bede, (2:153) 137, 141, 263
Beguines, (2:157) 325
Benedict Biscop, 136–37
Benedict of Nursia, (2:168) 111, 149, 222, 309
BEOWULF (2:182)
Bernard of Clairvaux, (2:190) 223–24, 227, 229,
    243, 251–52, 256, 258, 267, 274, 275, 319
Bernardino of Siena, (2:195) 356
BETROTHAL (2:207)
BIBLE (2:210)
BIEL, GABRIEL (2:233)
BISHOP (2:252)
Black Death (*see also* Plague), (2:257) 269, 367
Blanche of Castile, (2:270) 294
BLASPHEMY (2:271)
BOCCACIO (2:277)
Boethius, (2:291) 66–70, 196, 235, 238, 303, 371
BOHEMIA (2:297)
Bonaventure, (2:313) 307–8
Boniface, (2:321) 142
Boniface VIII, Pope, (2:323) 297–300, 323,
    337, 351
BOOKS OF HOURS (2:325)
BOROUGH (2:329)
Bouvines, 279, 287, 295
BOTANY, (2:344)
BOW (2:350)
Bradwardine, Thomas, (2:357) 351
BRIDGES (10:409)
BRITTANY (2:377)
BRUGES (2:386), 191, 364, 374
Bulgars / Bulgaria, (2:399) 90, 161, 172, 259
BULL, PAPAL (2:418)
Burgundians / Burgundy, (2:424) 363, 367,
    372–77
BUTLER (2:434)

BYZANTINE CIVILIZATION (2:437)

Caesar, Gaius Julius, **3, 14, 56, 264**
CAESARIUS OF ARLES (3:9), 112
Cairo, (3:13) 99, 103
CALENDARS (3:17)
Caliph / Caliphate, (3:32) 76–81, 119, 138–39, 163–64
Calixtus II, Pope, 220, 251, 267
Canon Law (*see* Law, Canon)
CANONIZATION (3:67)
Canons, Regular, 224–25
Canossa, (3:69) 220
Cantar de mio Cid, (3:70) 209, 319
CAPITULARIES (3:91)
Carta Caritatis, 222
CARTHUSIANS (3:118)
Cassian, John, (3:122) 111, 112
Cassiodorus, (3:123) 66–70
CASTLES (3:143)
CATALONIA (3:174)
Cathars / Catharism, (3:181) 259
CATHEDRAL (3:191)
Catherine of Siena, (3:168) 353, 356
Caucasia / Caucasus, (3:193) 4, 37, 62, 80, 270
Celestine V, Pope, (3:214) 298–99
CELIBACY (3:215), 216
CHAMBERLAIN (3:242)
Champagne, (3:243) 193–94, 202, 203
CHANCERY (3:251)
Chanson de Roland, (3:257) 146
Chansons de geste, (3:257) 318–319
Charlemagne, (3:106; 3:268) 136, 144, 145–59, 160, 189, 207, 272, 274, 345
Charles II of West Francia, the Bald, (3:112) 143, 151, 160
Charles III the Simple, of West Francia, (3:114) 163
Charles IV, Emperor, 363, 375
Charles V of France, (3:269) 367, 373, 391
Charles VI of France, 367–68, 373, 374
Charles VII of France, (3:270) 369–71, 374, 376
Charles VIII of France, 370
Charles of Anjou, King of Sicily, 282, 298
Charles Martel, (3:272; 3:345) 100, 141, 142, 147, 207
CHARTRES (3:276)
Chaucer, Geoffrey, (3:279) 319, 355
China/Chinese, (4:556) 334
Chivalry, (3:301) 314–20
Chretien de Troyes, (3:308) 318, 385
Christina of Markyate, 255
Christine de Pizan, 371–72
CHRISTMAS (3:317)
CHRONICLES (3:325)
CHURCH (3:337)
Cicero, (3:430) 5, 66, 385–86
Cid, (3:383) 209, 264
Cistercians / Citeaux, (3:403) 221–24

Clarendon, Assize of, (3:408) 285
Clement V, Pope, (3:438) 299, 351
CLERGY (3:440)
Clocks, (3:457) 390–91
Clovis, 65–66, 139–40
Cluny, (3:468) 214–15
Cnut, (3:471) 166–67, 204
Cola di Rienzo, (3:478) 387
Columba, (3:485) 114
Columbanus, (3:485) 114
Columbus, Christopher, 399
COMPURGATION (3:508)
Concordat of Worms, (3:525) 220, 273
Conrad I, King of East *Francia,* 161, 168, 202
Conrad II, Emperor, 199, 200, 201
Conrad III, Emperor, 223, 224, 227, 276
Conrad IV, 281
Constance of Sicily, 277
Constance, 198
Constantine the Great, (3:545) 21–23, 40, 46, 54, 66, 108
Constantine V, Emperor, 68, 69, 70
Constantine VII, Emperor, 173
Constantine XI, Emperor, (3:548) 381
Constantinople, (3:549) 55–56, 75–92, 147, 174
CONSTRUCTION (3:558)
CURSES (3:610)
COSTUME (3:614)
Councils, Church, (3:631) 41, 42–43, 76–77, 154–55, 225, 254–55, 264, 267, 273, 306, 349, 351, 352–54, 369, 383, 390
CREEDS (3:675)
CRUCIFIXION (4:12)
Crusades, (4:14) 225–29, 346–49
CYRIL, SAINT, (4:73)

Damasus, Pope, **47, 51**
Dante Alighieri, (4:94) 280, 321–24, 327, 361, 371
DECRETALS (4:122)
Decretum, (4:128) 195, 201
DEVOTIO MODERNA (4:166), 350, 353
Dialectic (*see* Logic)
Dictatus Papae, (4:177) 219
Diet (*see* Food)
DIOCESE (4:191)
Diocletian, Emperor, 20–21, 22, 23, 40, 54
Dionysius Exiguus, (4:192)
Divine Comedy, 323–24
DOMESDAY BOOK (4:237)
Dominic de Guzman, (4:239) 250–51
Donatism, (4:259) 42
DRAMA (4:263)
DUNGEON (4:308)
Durham, (4:315) 310–11

Easter, (4:364) **93**
Ebroin, 141
Education (*see* Schools)

Edward the Confessor, (4:394) 167, 204
Edward I of England, (4:395) 287, 288, 297, 364
Edward II of England, (4:397) 366
Edward III of England, (4:398) 366–67, 387
Edward IV of England, (4:478) 299, 301
Edward the Black Prince (*see* Black Prince)
Egypt, (4:403)
Einhard, (4:412) 150
Electors, German, (5:491) 281, 362–363
Elizabeth of Schönau, 240, 255
Environment, 122–25
Erik, (4:554) 164
Estates-General (*see* Representative Assemblies)
Ethelbert of Kent, 116, 138
Eucharist, (*see* Mass)
Eugenius III, Pope, 224, 274

**Family and Marriage, (4:593) 6–7, 35, 37,
125–28, 129–31**
Famine, (5:1) 329–30
Francis of Assisi (*see* Assisi)
Franks, 64–66
Frederick I Barbarossa, Emperor (5:212) 245,
248, 277, 297
Frederick II, Emperor, 279–82, 322, 362
FRIULI (2:132)

Galla Placidia, (2:91) 59–61
Gelasius I, Pope, (5:374) 77
Gender, 6–8, 35–36, 36–37, 45, 129–31, 305–6,
324–27, 370
Genghis Khan, (5:382) 347
Geography, (5:391) 1, 8–9, 13–15, 119–22
Ghana, 396
Godfrey of Bouillon, 226–27
Golden Bull, 362–63
Gottfried von Strassburg, (5:634) 318
GRAIN CROPS (5:645)
Gratian, Canonist (5:656) 243, 244, 250
Gregory I the Great, Pope, (5:668) 107–110,
115, 136, 137, 138, 219, 265
Gregory IV, Pope, 159
Gregory VII, Pope, (5:669) 211, 218–21
Gregory IX, Pope, (5:671) 246, 261, 269,
279, 281
Gregory of Tours,
Guillaume de Lorris, (6:23) 320
Gunpowder, 391
GYPSIES (6:40)

Hadrian, Abbot, 136
Hadrian, Emperor, 8–11, 15, 16, 54, 81, 108
Hadrian I, Pope, 149, 154
Hadrian IV, Pope, (1:58) 247
Hagia Sophia, (6:55) 80
HAGIOGRAPHY (6:57)
Hansa / Hanseatic League, (6:90) 281

Hartmann von Aue, (6:102) 318
Harun al-Rashid, (6:107) 101, 152
Hattin, (6:265) 229
HEBREW (6:128)
Heloise (*see* Abelard), 255
Henry I, King of East *Francia,* 168, 202
Henry II, Emperor, 168, 199, 200
Henry III, Emperor, (6:162) 198, 217, 219
Henry IV, Emperor, (6:163) 201, 211,
219–20, 225
Henry V, Emperor, 162, 206, 220, 273, 274, 276
Henry VI, Emperor, (6:164) 277, 279
Henry VII, Emperor, 324, 373
Henry I of England, (6:154) 190, 205, 206
Henry II of England, (6:156) 206, 242, 247,
282–86, 290
Henry III of England, (6:158) 283, 288,
362, 364
Henry IV of England, (6:159) 368
Henry V of England, (6:160) 368, 374
Henry VI of England, (6:161) 372
Henry VII of England, 372
Henry I of France, 202
Henry the Lion of Saxony, (6:167) 276, 277
Henry the Navigator, 396–97
Heraclius, Emperor, (6:171) 87–89
HERALDRY (6:172)
Heresy, (6:187) 224
HERMITS (6:212)
Hilda, 136
Hildegard of Bingen, (6:228) 240, 255, 325
HISTORIOGRAPHY (6:238)
HOLY WEEK (6:276)
Honestiores, 19
HOSPITALS (6:287)
HOUSEHOLD (6:299)
Hugh Capet, 161, 202, 203
Huguccio of Pisa, (6:327) 245
Humbert, Cardinal, (6:329) 218
Humiliores, 19
Huns (6:352) 58–59, 61
HUNTING (6:354)
Hus, John, (6:364) 353, 357
HYMNS (6:378)

INDULGENCES (6:446)
Innocent I, Pope, 47
Innocent III, Pope, (6:464) 252, 261, 279,
286, 346
Innocent IV, Pope, (6:465) 210, 262, 281
INNS AND TAVERNS (6:468)
Inquest and Inquisitors, (6:478) 261
Ireland, (6:514) 112–15
Irene, Empress, 153, 154–55, 172
Irnerius, (6:554) 240
Isidore of Seville, (6:563) 116, 393
ITALIAN / ITALY (6:621; 7:2)
Ivan III of Muscovy, (7:20) 383–84

JACQUERIE (7:35)
Jacques Coeur, (7:37) 369–70
James I of Aragon, 288
Jarrow, 137
Jean de Meun, (7:53) 320
Jerome, Saint, (7:57) 51, 385
Jerusalem, (7:58) 19, 20, 21, 54, 56, 66–67, 134, 179–82, 225, 280
Jesus Christ, 22, 23, 26, 40, 55, 74, 75, 195, 207, 212, 228, 321
Jews (*see* Judaism)
JOACHIM OF FLORA (7:113)
Joan of Arc, (7:114) 369–72
John VIII, Pope, 345
John XII, Pope, 169
John XXII, Pope, (7:125) 352, 364
John, King of England, (7:129) 282, 283, 286–87, 292, 356
John, King of Bohemia, 373
John Cassian, (*see* Cassian)
John Duns Scotus, 350
John of Freiburg, 355
John of Gaunt, (7:134) 368
John Hus (*see* Hus)
John of Plano Carpini, (7:137) 392–93
John of Salisbury, (7:139) 247, 248
John the Scot, (7:141) 151
Joseph Bekhor Shor, 266
JUSTICES (7:183)
Justin I, Emperor, 78
Justinian, Emperor, (7:201) 78–87, 91, 105, 248

Khadija, 94
Khalifa (*see* Caliph)
Khazars, (7:240) 100

LANCE (7:323)
Langton, Stephen, (7:337) 286
Las Navas de Tolosa, 289
LATERAN (7:344)
Law (7:388):
  canon, 149, 251, 299
  in England, 240, 284–86
  Islamic (*see Shari 'a*)
  Roman, 4, 6–8, 20, 80–82, 240–41
  study of, 192–96
Lechfeld, Battle of, 169
Leo I, Pope, (7:541) 47, 61, 62, 77, 108
Leo III, Pope, (7:542) 155–56, 159
Leo IX, Pope, (7:543) 211, 217
Leo III, Emperor, (7:544) 89
Leo VI, Emperor, (7:545) 173
Leo the Mathematician, (7:547) 134
Leonardo Fibonacci, 280
LEPROSY (7:549)
LIBRARIES (7:557)

LITERACY (7:594)
Liutprand, (7:634) 152
Logic,
Lombard League, (7:652) 277
Lombards, (7:649) 106, 115–16, 135, 139, 152–53, 211
London, (7:658) 190–91
Lordship (*see also* Nobility)
Lorris, Guillaume de (*see* Guillaume)
Lothar I, 160
Lothar III, 276
Louis VI of France, (7:673) 203, 291, 311
Louis VII of France, 160, 203, 223, 227, 286, 290–91, 311
Louis VIII of France, 294
Louis IX of France, (7:674) 282, 294–95, 297, 316, 395
Louis XI of France, (7:676) 370, 376
Louis of Bavaria, 352, 364
Louis the German, 160
Louis the Pious (3:111) 145–46, 159–60
Lucius III, Pope, 251, 261

Magna Carta, (8:41) 287
Magyars, (8:46) 161, 163, 165, 172–73
Maimonides, (8:49) 266
Mali, 396
Malory, Sir Thomas, (8:60) 318
Marcel, Etienne, 367
Marcian, Emperor, 42
Marco Polo (*see* Polo)
Marcus Aurelius, Emperor, 16, 18, 57, 332
MARKETS (8:143)
Marriage (*see* Family)
Marsiglio of Padua, (8:154) 361
Martin of Tours, Saint, 111–12
Martin V, Pope, 353–54
MASONS (8:172)
MASS (8:181)
Mathematics, (8:205) 103
Matilda of England, 206, 283
Maximilian I, Emperor, (8:230) 363
Mecca, (8:239) 94–95
Medina, (8:262) 95
Mehmet II, (8:264) 380
Mendicant Orders, (8:273)
Merovingian Dynasty, (8:277) 135–36, 139–43
Merton College, 246, 351
Mesta, (8:279) 337
METAL AND METALLURGY (8:283)
Michael VIII Palaeologos, Emperor, (8:302) 347, 380
Michael Scot, (8:305) 280
Milan, (8:376) 219–20
MINING (8:397)
MINTS AND MONEY (8:417)
MISSIONS (8:439)
Mithraism, 29

Mongols, (8:463) 102, 263, 354, 383–84, 392
MOSQUE (8:498)
Muawiyah, 97, 99
Muhammad, (8:522) 94–99, 305
MYSTICISM (9:5)

Nicholas I, Pope, (9:120) 172, 345
Nicholas II, Pope, 211, 218
Nibelungenlied, (9:112) 319–20
NOBILITY / NOBLES (9:147)
Nur-ad-Din, 228

OATH (9:207)
Occam, William, (9:209) 350–51
Odo of Deuil, 291
Odovacar, (9:220) 43, 54
Origen, (9:277) 38
Ostrogoths, (9:289) 59–60, 62–64, 105
Oswald of Northumbria, 137–38, 141
Oswy of Northumbria, 117
Otloh of St. Emmeram, (9:298) 235, 238
Otto I, Emperor, (9:300) 161, 168, 169
Otto II, Emperor, 169, 199
Otto III, Emperor, (9:301) 169, 199, 217
Otto IV, Emperor, 279, 362
Otto of Freising, (9:302) 248
Ottoman Turks (*see* Turks) (9:305), 56, 83, 347,
   357, 380–81

PALAEOGRAPHY (9:332) (*see also* **Writing**)
Papal States, (9:380) 152–53
Paper, (9:388) 175
Paris, (9:401) 291, 296, 303
Parliament, (9:422) (*see* Representative
   Assemblies)
Patrick, (9:462) 113
Paul, 36, 37
Paul the Deacon, (9:467) 150
Peace (9:473):
   of God, 198
PEASANTS' REVOLT (9:477)
Pechenegs, 161, 172–73
Pepin II of Heristal, (9:499) 141
Pepin III the Short, (9:500) 142, 143, 144–48
Perpetua, 36
Peter Damian, (9:508) 218
Peter the Chanter, 260
Peter the Hermit, (9:523) 226
Peter Lombard, (9:516) 244, 307
Petrarca, Francesco, (9:527) 385–88
Philip I of France, 703
Philip II Augustus of France, (9:552) 246, 279,
   283, 291–94
Philip III of France, 295
Philip IV the Fair of France, (9:554) 294–300,
   337, 361, 364
Philip VI of France, (9:555) 293

Philo Judaeus, 31
PHILOSOPHY (9:559)
Photios, (9:619) 172
PICTS (9:641)
PISA (9:663)
Pius II, Pope, 357, 381
Plague, (9:672) 332–35
Plato / Platonism, (9:694) 40, 91, 103, 308
Plow, 184–85
Polo, Marco, 391–94
PREACHING AND SERMONS (10:70)
Prester John, (10:118) 348
PRISON (10:129)
PROSTITUTION (10:154)
PROVENCAL / PROVENCE (10:155)
Pseudo-Dionysius, (10:203) 151
Pseudo-Isidore, 151, 219
PURGATORY (10:215)

Qur 'an, 94–97, 103–4, 175, 176, 302

Rainald of Dassel, (10:25) 248
Rashi of Troyes, (10:259) 266
Ratchis, 152
Representative Assemblies, (10:316) 287–88,
   289, 297
Richard I of England, (10:383) 282, 286
Richard II of England, (10:384) 368
Richard of Bury, (10:386) 387
Robert of France, 202, 203
Robert Grosseteste, 256, 259, 303, 349
Robert Guiscard, (10:433) 211
Robert Pullen, 247
Roger Borsa, 211
Roger the Great Count, (10:440) 211
Romance of the Rose, (10:449) 320, 371, 372
Romanesque, (10:475)
Rome (10:517):
   early, 1–6
   imperial, 4–6, 8–9, 16–20, 26, 28, 54–5
   medieval, 106–7, 273
ROUEN (10:537)
Rudolf of Habsburg, 298, 362–63
Rufinus, (10:545) 245
RUNES (10:557)

SACRAMENTARY (10:605), 149
St. Denis, 146, 238, 310
St. Gall, 146
Saladdin, (10:624) 228
SALT (10:629)
Sancho I of Navarre, 209
Santiago Matamoros, 209, 233–34
Santiago de Compostela, (10:650)
SCHISM (11:44)
SCHOLARSHIP (11:48)
SCHOLASTICISM (11:55)
SCIENCE (11:81)

Seljuk Turks, (*see* Turks)
Shakespeare, William, 263, 401–2
Shari 'a, 96–97, 103–4, 176
Sic et non, 239, 243
Sicily,
Sigismund, Emperor, 353
SILK (11:257)
Simon of Montfort, (11:296) 232
Simon Magus, 217
Simony, 217
Slavery and Slaves (11:330) 188–89
Slavs, 88, 90, 144, 147
Song of Igor's Campaign, 318
Song of the Nibelungs (*see* Nibelungenlied)
Song of Roland (*see* Chanson de Roland)
Stephen II, Pope, (11:481) 152
Stephen of Blois, King of England, 206,
    283, 284
Stephen Langton (*see* Langton)
Suger of St. Denis, (11:502) 291, 310, 312
SWITZERLAND (11:536)
SYLVESTER II, POPE (11:552)

Tacitus, 14–15, 56
Tempier, Etienne, 303, 349
Templars, 299–300, 346, 366
TENURE OF LAND (11:667)
Tertullian, 38
Teutonic Knights, 276
TEXTILES (11:693)
Theobald of Canterbury, 247, 286
Theoderic the Ostrogoth, (12:19) 62–64,
    66–70, 319
Theodora, (12:11) 78–80
Theodora of Tarsus, 136
Theodulf of Orleans, (12:20) 150, 154
Theology (12:20) 194–96 (*see also* Philosophy)
Theophilus, (12:24) 309
Thomas à Kempis, (12:33) 355–56
Thomas Aquinas, (*see* Aquinas)
TITHES (12:62)
TOOLS (12:72)
Towns (*see* Urbanism)
Trajan, Emperor, 8–9, 14

Trotula, 306
TROUBADOR (12:24)

Umar, (12:257) 98–99
Universities, (12:282) 245–48, 302–8, 349–51
Urban II, Pope, (12:302) 220, 225–26, 250, 346
Urban V, Pope, 352
Urban VI, Pope, 352–53
USURY (12:335)

Vandals, (12:354) 59, 62, 66
Vassal, 169–70
VEHICLES (12:367)
Venice, (12:382) 189–91, 194
Verdun, Treaty of, 160
Vikings, 162–65, 232
VIRGIN MARY (12:459)
Visigoths, (12:465) 58–59, 66, 132, 139, 156
Vivaldi brothers, 393, 397

Waldensianism, (12:508) 259
WALACHIA AND MOLDAVIA (12:497)
WALES (12:513)
Whitby, (12:626) 117, 136
Wilfrid of Ripon, 136
William I of England, (12:633) 190, 203, 204–5,
    218, 232
William II of England, 205
William of Occam
William of Pagula, 355
William of Rubrouck, 392
WILLIAM MARSHAL, (12:635)
WINE (12:682)
WITCHCRAFT, (12:638)
WYCLIF, (12:706)

Zacharias, Pope, 143
Zangi, 227, 228
Zealots, 31, 32
Zeno, Emperor, 62, 75, 78
Zenobia, 18
Zoroaster, (12:746) 18, 28, 49, 98